"Character" has become a front-and-center topic in contemporary discourse, but this term does not have a fixed meaning. Character may be simply defined by what someone does not do, but a more active and thorough definition is necessary, one that addresses certain vital questions. Is character a singular characteristic of an individual, or is it composed of different aspects? Does character —however we define it—exist in degrees, or is it simply something one happens to have? How can character be developed? Can it be learned? Relatedly, can it be taught, and who might be the most effective teacher? What roles are played by family, schools, the media, religion, and the larger culture?

This groundbreaking handbook of character strengths and virtues is the first progress report from a prestigious group of researchers who have undertaken the systematic classification and measurement of widely valued positive traits. They approach good character in terms of separate strengths—authenticity, persistence, kindness, gratitude, hope, humor, and so on—each of which exists in degrees.

Character Strengths and Virtues classifies twenty-four specific strengths under six broad virtues that consistently emerge across history and culture: wisdom, courage, humanity, justice, temperance, and transcendence. Each strength is thoroughly examined in its own chapter, with special attention given to its meaning, explanation, measurement, causes, correlates, consequences, and development across the life span, as well as to strategies for its deliberate cultivation. This book demands the attention of anyone interested in psychology and what it can teach about the good life.

CHARACTER
STRENGTHS
AND VIRTUES

The work contained herein is that of the Values in Action Institute,

a nonprofit initiative of the Manuel D. and Rhoda Mayerson Foundation,

directed by Dr. Neal H. Mayerson.

CHARACTER STRENGTHS
AND VIRTUES

A HANDBOOK AND CLASSIFICATION

CHRISTOPHER PETERSON & MARTIN E. P. SELIGMAN

AMERICAN
PSYCHOLOGICAL
ASSOCIATION

OXFORD
UNIVERSITY PRESS

2004

OXFORD
UNIVERSITY PRESS

Oxford New York
Auckland Bangkok Buenos Aires Cape Town Chennai
Dar es Salaam Delhi Hong Kong Istanbul Karachi Kolkata
Kuala Lumpur Madrid Melbourne Mexico City Mumbai Nairobi
São Paulo Shanghai Taipei Tokyo Toronto

Copyright © 2004 by Values in Action Institute

Published by American Psychological Association
750 First Street, NE, Washington, DC 20002-4242
www.apa.org
and
Oxford University Press, Inc.
198 Madison Avenue, New York, New York 10016
www.oup.com

Oxford is a registered trademark of Oxford University Press

Library of Congress Cataloging-in-Publication Data

Peterson, Christopher, 1950 Feb. 18–
Character strengths and virtues : a handbook and classification / Christopher Peterson,
Martin E. P. Seligman
    p. cm.
Includes bibliographical references (p.).
ISBN 0-19-516701-5
1. Character—Handbooks, manuals, etc. 2. Virtues—Handbooks, manuals, etc. I. Seligman,
Martin E. P. II. Title.
BF818 .P38 2004
155.2'32—dc22   2003024320

9 8 7 6 5 4 3 2

Printed in the United States of America
on acid-free paper

PREFACE

C an we hold hope that positive psychology will be able to help people evolve toward their highest potential?" The classification described in this book began with this question, posed by Neal Mayerson to Martin Seligman in 1999. The Mayerson Foundation was concerned that inadequate progress was being made from well-worn problem-fixing approaches and that an approach based on recognizing people's strengths and aspirations might prove more effective. Mayerson turned to Seligman to explore the intersection of the emerging field of positive youth development and Seligman's new push to articulate a new positive psychology. It soon became clear that two prior questions needed to be answered: (1) how can one define the concepts of "strength" and "highest potential" and (2) how can one tell that a positive youth development program has succeeded in meeting its goals?

These two concerns framed the classification project from its inception. The Manuel D. and Rhoda Mayerson Foundation created the Values in Action (VIA) Institute, a nonprofit organization dedicated to the development of a scientific knowledge base of human strengths. Seligman was the scientific director of the VIA Institute, and he asked Christopher Peterson to be its project director. In September 2000, Peterson temporarily relocated from the University of Michigan to the University of Pennsylvania. For the next three years, Seligman and Peterson, with the assistance of a prestigious array of scholars and practitioners, devised a classification of character strengths and virtues (addressing the "good" teenager concern) and ways of measuring them (addressing the program evaluation concern). This book describes the results of this collaboration. We remain greatly interested in positive youth development but now believe that the classification and measurement strategies we have created can be applied much more broadly.

We have been helped mightily along the way. Our specal gratitude is of course expressed to the Manuel D. and Rhoda Mayerson Foundation for creating the VIA Institute, which supported this work. Thanks in particular are due to Neal Mayerson for his vision and encouragement.

Thanks are also due more generally to the other benefactors and boosters of positive psychology. Don Clifton of the Gallup Organization, along with Martin Seligman, convened a meeting of scholars to begin a delineation of the strengths. Much of what follows builds on this beginning. The late Robert Nozick as well as Mihalyi Csikszentmihalyi, George Vaillant, Daniel Robinson, Kathleen Hall Jamieson, and Ed Diener were the heavyweights at this meeting. Three subsequent meetings were held as well, and we thank those in attendance for their important contributions to this project: Bonnie Bernard, Alan Blankstein, Robert Blum, Dale Blyth, Jack Burke, Gaye Carlson, Sonia Chessen, Reginald Clark, Joseph Conaty, Katherine Dahlsgaard, Lucy Davidson, Ed Diener, Elizabeth Dunn, Thaddeus Ferber, Raymond Fowler, Carissa Griffing, Daniel Hart, Derek Isaacowitz, Terry Kang, Robert Kendall, Nicole Kurzer, Kenneth Maton, Donna Mayerson, Neal Mayerson, Richard McCarty, Peter Nathan, Heather Johnston Nicholson, Joyce Phelps, Karen Pittman, Jane Quinn, Gordon Raley, Mark Rosenberg, Peter Schulman, David Seligman, Andrew Shatté, Myrna Shure, Susan Spence, Peter Stevens, Philip Stone, Constancia Warren, Alan Williams, Steve Wolin, and Nicole Yohalem.

The Atlantic Philanthropies, the John Marks Templeton Foundation, the Annenberg/Sunnylands Trust Foundation, and the Department of Education all funded aspects of this project and by supporting positive psychology generously created an atmosphere in which our classification project could be seen as a worthy one.

Individual chapters in Section II of this book were drafted by expert social scientists—see the list of contributors (pp. xiii–xiv)—commissioned by us to review what was known about the various character strengths in the classification. We were fortunate that virtually all of our first choices were able to write these drafts. In a few cases, we commissioned two separate drafts for a given character strength, and these drafts were then melded. All the drafts were thoughtful and thorough, and we think that a fine book would have resulted simply from gathering them together, even without our editing. However, we took a further step and rewrote each draft for consistency in organization and tone. Our editing was deliberately heavy-handed, and the contributors should not be held responsible for any resulting errors.

We were also fortunate to have the advice of distinguished senior social scientists—see the Board of Advisors (p. ii)—while we worked on this project. In particular, the wisdom and support of George Vaillant kept us on track.

Very early chapter drafts were reviewed by youth development experts—Bonnie Bernard, Robert Blum, Reginald Clark, Daniel Hart, Heather Johnston Nicholson, and Kenneth Maton—in a process coordinated by Nicole Yohalem and Karen Pittman of the International Youth Foundation. Later chapter drafts were reviewed by Donald K. Freedheim, Jerold R. Gold, William C. Howell,

Thomas E. Joiner, Randy J. Larsen, and Lee B. Sechrest, and we thank them for their thoughtful suggestions.

We want to thank Gary VandenBos of the American Psychological Association and Joan Bossert of Oxford University Press—both organizations are great friends of positive psychology—for working together to publish this book. We also want to thank Marion Osmun of the American Psychological Association for her editorial work and Susan Ecklund for her thorough copyediting.

We are grateful to Peter Schulman, Terry Kang, Linda Newsted, Chris Jenkins, and Patty Newbold for their help behind the scenes. Lisa Christie and Jennifer Yu brought their sharp eyes and good humor to early drafts of the manuscript. Ilona Boniwell, Tiffany Sawyer, Lauren Kachorek, Tracy Steen, Angela Lee Duckworth, Rachel Kellerman, Robert Biswas-Diener, Emily Polak, Adam Cohen, and Derek Isaacowitz helped with some of the research described here. Katherine Dahlsgaard identifed the six core virtues—wisdom, courage, humanity, justice, temperance, and transcendence—used to organize the specific character strengths in the classification. Nansook Park has been a valued collaborator.

We thank Mihalyi Csikszentmihalyi, Ed Diener, Kathleen Hall Jamieson, and George Vaillant for their leadership on the Positive Psychology Steering Committee. We are grateful as well to Don Clifton, Jim Clifton, and Marcus Buckingham of the Gallup Organization for pioneering work on strengths and showing us that a psychology of human strengths was possible.

And we of course want to thank the more than 150,000 individuals who completed versions of our measures during the past 3 years.

Last, but certainly not least, our families and friends deserve special mention for embodying the strengths that constitute the classification. Virtue may be its own reward, but we too reaped the benefits.

CONTENTS

CONTRIBUTORS

Roy F. Baumeister (Humility and Modesty; Self-Regulation)

Marvin W. Berkowitz (Fairness)

Jessey H. Bernstein (Vitality)

W. Keith Campbell (Humility and Modesty)

Katherine Dahlsgaard (Lessons from History)

Lucy Davidson (Integrity)

Robert A. Emmons (Gratitude)

Julie Juola Exline (Humility and Modesty)

Constance A. Flanagan (Citizenship)

Jonathan Haidt (Appreciation of Beauty)

Andrew C. Harter (Persistence)

Pamela S. Hartman (Perspective)

Nick Haslam (Prudence)

Cindy Hazan (Love)

Thomas E. Joiner (Humility and Modesty)

Lauren V. Kachorek (Humility and Modesty)

Todd B. Kashdan (Curiosity)

Dacher Keltner (Appreciation of Beauty)

Joachim I. Krueger (Humility and Modesty)

Jacqueline S. Mattis (Spirituality)

John D. Mayer (Social Intelligence)

Michael E. McCullough (Forgiveness and Mercy; Kindness)

Nansook Park (Assessment and Applications)

Elizabeth Pollard (Integrity)

Stephen G. Post (Kindness)

K. Ann Renninger (Love of Learning)

Willibald Ruch (Humor)

Richard M. Ryan (Vitality)

Peter Salovey (Social Intelligence)

Carol Sansone (Love of Learning)

Kennon M. Sheldon (Integrity)

Stephen A. Sherblom (Fairness)

Dean Keith Simonton (Creativity)

Jessi L. Smith (Love of Learning)

Tracy A. Steen (Bravery)

Dianne M. Tice (Persistence)

Kathleen D. Vohs (Self-Regulation)

Harry M. Wallace (Persistence)

Monica C. Worline (Bravery)

Stephen J. Zaccaro (Leadership)

SECTION I

BACKGROUND

1. INTRODUCTION TO A "MANUAL OF THE SANITIES"

The classification of strengths presented in this book is intended to reclaim the study of character and virtue as legitimate topics of psychological inquiry and informed societal discourse. By providing ways of talking about character strengths and measuring them across the life span, this classification will start to make possible a science of human strengths that goes beyond armchair philosophy and political rhetoric. We believe that good character can be cultivated, but to do so, we need conceptual and empirical tools to craft and evaluate interventions.

In recent years, strides have been made in understanding, treating, and preventing psychological disorders. Reflecting this progress and critically helping to bring it about are widely accepted classification manuals—the *Diagnostic and Statistical Manual of Mental Disorders* (*DSM*) sponsored by the American Psychiatric Association (1994) and the *International Classification of Diseases* (*ICD*) sponsored by the World Health Organization (1990)—which have generated a family of reliable assessment strategies and have led to demonstrably effective treatments for more than a dozen disorders that only a few decades ago were intractable (Nathan & Gorman, 1998, 2002; Seligman, 1994). Lagging behind but still promising in their early success are ongoing efforts to devise interventions that prevent various disorders from occurring in the first place (e.g., M. T. Greenberg, Domitrovich, & Bumbarger, 1999).

Consensual classifications and associated approaches to assessment provide a common vocabulary for basic researchers and clinicians, allowing communication within and across these groups of professionals as well as with the general public. Previous generations of psychiatrists and psychologists had no certainty, for example, that patients in London who were diagnosed with schizophrenia had much in common with patients in Topeka receiving the same diagnosis. They had no reason to believe that an effective psychological or pharmaceutical treatment of ostensible depressives in Johannesburg would be useful for supposed depressives in Kyoto.

With recent incarnations of the *DSM* and *ICD*, matters have begun to change, but only for half of the landscape of the human condition. We can now describe and measure much of what is wrong with people, but what about those things that are right? Nothing comparable to the *DSM* or *ICD* exists for the good life. When psychiatrists and psychologists talk about mental health, wellness, or well-being, they mean little more than the absence of disease, distress, and disorder. It is as if falling short of diagnostic criteria should be the goal for which we all should strive. Insurance companies and health maintenance organizations (HMOs) reimburse the treatment of disorders but certainly not the promotion of happiness and fulfillment. The National Institute of Mental Health (NIMH) should really be called the National Institute of Mental Illness because it devotes but a fraction of its research budget to mental health.

This handbook focuses on what is right about people and specifically about the strengths of character that make the good life possible. We follow the example of the *DSM* and *ICD* and their collateral creations by proposing a classification scheme and by devising assessment strategies for each of its entries. The crucial difference is that the domain of concern for us is not psychological illness but psychological health. In short, our goal is "a manual of the sanities" (Easterbrook, 2001, p. 23).

We write from the perspective of positive psychology, which means that we are as focused on strength as on weakness, as interested in building the best things in life as in repairing the worst, and as concerned with fulfilling the lives of normal people as with healing the wounds of the distressed (Seligman, 2002). The past concern of psychology with human problems is of course understandable and will not be abandoned anytime in the foreseeable future. Problems always will exist that demand psychological solutions, but psychologists interested in promoting human potential need to pose different questions from their predecessors who assumed a disease model of human nature. We disavow the disease model as we approach character, and we are adamant that human strengths are not secondary, derivative, illusory, epiphenomenal, parasitic upon the negative, or otherwise suspect. Said in a positive way, we believe that character strengths are the bedrock of the human condition and that strength-congruent activity represents an important route to the psychological good life.

What distinguishes positive psychology from the humanistic psychology of the 1960s and 1970s and from the positive thinking movement is its reliance on empirical research to understand people and the lives they lead. Humanists were often skeptical about the scientific method and what it could yield yet were unable to offer an alternative other than the insight that people were good. In contrast, positive psychologists see both strength and weakness as authentic and as amenable to scientific understanding.

There are many good examples of ongoing psychological research that fit under the positive psychology umbrella (see collections by Aspinwall & Staudinger, 2003; Cameron, Dutton, & Quinn, 2003; Chang, 2001; Gillham, 2000; Keyes & Haidt, 2003; R. M. Lerner, Jacobs, & Wertlieb, 2003; Snyder, 2000b; Snyder & Lopez, 2002), but this new field lacks a common vocabulary that agrees on the positive traits and allows psychologists to move among instances of them. We imagine that positive psychology as a whole would be benefited—indeed, shaped and transformed—by agreed-upon ways for speaking about the positive, just as the *DSM* and *ICD* have shaped psychiatry, clinical psychology, and social work by providing a way to speak about the negative. We believe that the classification of character presented here is an important step toward a common vocabulary of measurable positive traits.

Our project coincides with heightened societal concern about good character (Hunter, 2000). After a detour through the hedonism of the 1960s, the narcissism of the 1970s, the materialism of the 1980s, and the apathy of the 1990s, most everyone today seems to believe that character is important after all and that the United States is facing a character crisis on many fronts, from the playground to the classroom to the sports arena to the Hollywood screen to business corporations to politics. According to a 1999 survey by Public Agenda, adults in the United States cited "not learning values" as the most important problem facing today's youth. Notably, in the public's view, drugs and violence trailed the absence of character as pressing problems.

But what is character? So long as we fail to identify the specifics, different groups in our society—despite their common concern for human goodness—will simply talk past one another when attempting to address the issue. For instance, is character defined by what someone does *not* do, or is there a more active meaning? Is character a singular characteristic of an individual, or is it composed of different aspects? Does character—however we define it—exist in degrees, or is character just something that one happens, like pregnancy, to have or not? How does character develop? Can it be learned? Can it be taught, and who might be the most effective teacher? What roles are played by families, schools, peers, youth development programs, the media, religious institutions, and the larger culture? Is character socially constructed and laden with idiosyncratic values, or are there universals suggesting a more enduring basis?

The emerging field of positive psychology is positioned to answer these sorts of questions. Positive psychology focuses on three related topics: the study of positive subjective experiences, the study of positive individual traits, and the study of institutions that enable positive experiences and positive traits (Seligman & Csikszentmihalyi, 2000). Our classification project addresses the second of these topics and in so doing hopes to shed light on the first. One eventual benefit of the classification we propose may be the identification or even the deliberate creation of institutions that enable good character.

■ Thinking About Classification: Lessons From Systematics

Like everyday people, social scientists are fond of making lists: for example, enumerating defense mechanisms, emotional disorders, personality traits, job types, psychosexual stages, parenting practices, attachment styles, and so on. Unlike everyday people, social scientists often go on to reify their lists by giving them "scientific" labels like classifications or taxonomies. Scientific credibility is not gained by assertion but by making sure that the label fits. We call our endeavor an aspirational classification. What does this mean?

A *scientific classification* parses some part of the universe first by demarcating its domain and second by specifying mutually exclusive and exhaustive subcategories within that domain. Both sorts of parsing rules need to be explicit and demonstrably reliable. The validity of a classification is judged by its utility vis-à-vis one or more stated purposes. Are classifiers more interested in marking the perimeter of a scientific territory or in detailing an already agreed-upon domain? Is the classification intended to catalog already known instances or to accommodate new ones as they are encountered? Is it intended to inspire research or to guide intervention?

A classification should not be confused with a *taxonomy*, which is based on a deep theory that explains the domain of concern (K. D. Bailey, 1994). Why these entries but not others? What is the underlying structure? That is, how do the entries relate to one another? When melded with evolutionary theory, for example, the Linnaean classification of species becomes a profound theory of life and the course that it has taken over the millennia. A good taxonomy has the benefits of a good theory: It organizes and guides the activity of an entire discipline.

But there is an important caution here. Along with their added value, taxonomies have a cost not incurred by classifications. Suppose the theory that girds a taxonomy is wrong, contradictory, or inarticulate? Then the activity that is organized and guided becomes self-defeating. Furthermore, it proves highly difficult to change the entries of a taxonomy, even in minor ways, because so much else linked together by the deep theory needs to be altered as a consequence.

Our classification is concerned with human strengths and virtues. From the perspective of positive psychology, itself a new endeavor, the domain of human excellence is largely unexplored. At the beginning of this project, we created a tentative "taxonomy," but it proved beyond our ability to specify a reasonable theory (as a taxonomy requires). However, our efforts did convince us that it was possible to approach closely the classification goals of staking out territory (i.e., defining virtues valued in most cultures) and subdividing it (i.e., specifying instances of these virtues). Our measurement intent of necessity led us to articulate explicit rules for what counts as a strength or not (inclusion and exclusion criteria) and for distinguishing various strengths from one another. These rules further provide the basis for adding new instances of character strengths to the classification.

We already knew our constituencies—psychology researchers and practitioners—and their needs kept us on task as we devised assessment strategies. We disavow all intents to propose a taxonomy in the technical sense, even though previous drafts of our work used that term. A modest description of our endeavor—an aspirational classification of strengths and virtues—preserves the flexibility necessary to proceed. A thoughtful classification, even if tentative, will serve the goals of psychology more productively than a flawed taxonomy, even if the surface entries look exactly the same. We trust to the emerging field of positive psychology as a whole to create one or more theories that will conceptually unify our classification.

■ Thinking About Classification Part Two: Lessons From the *DSM*

As noted, an older cousin of our classification of strengths and virtues is the *Diagnostic and Statistical Manual of Mental Disorders* (*DSM*) sponsored by the American Psychiatric Association (1952, 1968, 1980, 1987, 1994). A catalog of problematic ways of behaving, the *DSM* for several reasons has been a runaway success. First, it has made research into psychological disorders possible by providing a common vocabulary that lends itself to scientific operationalization (measurement). More subtly, the *DSM* has guided research programs by legitimizing investigations of some disorders rather than others. Finally, important societal institutions have endorsed the *DSM*, explicitly or implicitly: the American Psychiatric Association with its imprimatur, NIMH with its funding, insurance companies and HMOs with their reimbursement codes, the pharmaceutical industry, psychiatry and clinical psychology journals, and textbook publishers. Whatever one might think of the *DSM*, one must be conversant with its details in order to function as a mental "health" professional.

The *DSM* is far from perfect, and its weaknesses as well as it strengths have guided us. What are the positive and negative lessons that can be learned from the various incarnations of the *DSM* over its 50-year history? On the positive side, the *DSM* has moved toward behaviorally based criteria and proposed explicit rules for recognizing disorders of interest; it has spawned a family of structured clinical interviews and self-report questionnaires that allow these disorders to be reliably assessed; and, at least in principle, it has moved toward multidimensional (multiaxial) description, doing justice to the complexity of the subject matter it tries to organize. Thus, a full *DSM* diagnosis notes not only clinical disorders (Axis I) but also personality and developmental disorders (Axis II), medical conditions (Axis III), prevailing stressors (Axis IV), and global level of functioning (Axis V).

Following the *DSM* example, our classification includes explicit criteria for character strengths, and it has led us to develop a family of assessment devices (chapter 28). Finally, the present classification is multiaxial in the sense that it directs the attention of positive psychology not only to character strengths but also to talents and abilities, to conditions that enable or disable the strengths, to fulfillments that are associated with the strengths, and to outcomes that may ensue from them.

There are also negative lessons of the *DSM*, especially from the viewpoint of psychology (Schacht & Nathan, 1977). This taxonomy is focused too much on transient symptoms; it is reductionistic and at the same time overly complex, shaped by temporary trends within psychiatry (Vaillant, 1984). Even the current version of the *DSM* lacks an overall scheme, fails to be exhaustive, and—given its medical roots—does not attend much to the individual's setting and culture. It uses categories rather than dimensions, and mixed or not otherwise specified (NOS) diagnoses are among the most frequently used. Many diagnostic entities are so heterogeneous that two individuals warranting the same diagnosis could have no symptoms in common. *DSM* disorders are not well located in their developmental trajectory. Some critics have argued that considerations of reliability have crowded out considerations of validity, and in any event that there are too many disorders (more than 300), perhaps by an order of magnitude or more (Goodwin & Guze, 1996).

What are the implications for our classification of these negative lessons? We hope to do for the domain of moral excellence (character strengths and virtues) what the *DSM* does well for disorders while avoiding what it does poorly. Thus, our classification is based on an overall structure of moral virtues suggested by our historical and cross-cultural reviews. It includes a manageable number of character strengths (24) and is open to the possibility of consolidating those that prove empirically indistinguishable, as well as adding new strengths that are distinct. It approaches character strengths as individual differences—as continua and not categories—and is sensitive to the developmental differences in which character strengths are displayed and deployed. Finally, our creation of assessment instruments never subordinated validity issues to those of reliability.

It is ironic that many of the shortcomings of the *DSM* have resulted from its very success. *DSM-III* and its subsequent versions grew out of a modest attempt some thirty years ago by researchers to standardize the operational definitions of a handful of psychiatric disorders like schizophrenia and manic depression (Feighner et al., 1972). Reliability was the chief goal, and the psychiatric research community was the intended audience. The research diagnostic criteria (RDC) that were the seeds of the modern *DSM* were intended only to be a starting point for research, a common vocabulary to facilitate communication among different research groups investigating ostensibly the same disorder. No one envisioned that the RDC would grow into the dominant taxonomy of psychopathology worldwide, carrying along all that the term taxonomy conveys: for example, implication of a theoretical deep structure, exhaustiveness, reification, and accountability to multiple (and quarreling) constituencies.

We have no way of forecasting the eventual success of the present classification, but we will be satisfied if it provides to psychologists ways of thinking about strengths, naming them, and measuring them. Its proof will be in the science that develops around it, including thoughtful interventions that nurture character strengths in the first place or get them back on track if they have gone astray.

We express two related worries about the science of good character that we envision. First, this science will not thrive if it generates only ho-hum findings that every Sunday school teacher or grandparent already knew. It would be important to show, for example, that prudent individuals avoid unwanted pregnancies or that loving people have good marriages, but these results are not all that interesting. They would not attract to positive psychology the most curious and imaginative scientists from future generations. More intriguing are findings such as:

- the diminishing returns of material wealth for increasing subjective well-being (D. G. Myers & Diener, 1995)
- the lack of realism associated with optimism (Alloy & Abramson, 1979)
- the forecasting of presidential elections from the positive traits of candidates (Zullow, Oettingen, Peterson, & Seligman, 1988)
- the increased life expectancy of Academy Award winners relative to runners-up (Redelmeier & Singh, 2001)
- the increased life expectancy of those who hold a positive view of aging (B. R. Levy, Slade, Kunkel, & Kasl, 2002)
- the prediction of marital satisfaction from smiles in college yearbooks (Harker & Keltner, 2001)
- the foretelling of longevity from expressions of happiness in essays by young adults (Danner, Snowdon, & Friesen, 2001)

Second, we hope that the new science of character addresses explicitly what is invigorating about the good life. As we have written parts of this book, we sometimes found ourselves sounding like bad evangelists, going on and on about virtue but convincing no one, even ourselves, that virtue is worth pursuing. We do not want a grim-faced Cotton Mather as the poster child of positive psychology.

The solution to these potential pitfalls is not at hand. If it were, we would have made it an integral part of our proposed classification. We suspect that the solution lies in yet-to-be-articulated good theory that makes sense of the classification entries, individually and collectively. To hark back to a distinction already made, positive psychology will thrive when classifications like the one here evolve into taxonomies—when there become available one or more deep theories of the good life.

We also suspect that it will be useful for psychologists to keep in mind that our classification is grounded in a long philosophical tradition concerned with morality explained in terms of virtues. The very first Greek philosophers asked, "What is the good of a person?" This framing of morality led them to examine character and in particular virtues. Socrates, Plato, Aristotle, Augustine, Aquinas, and others enumerated such virtues, regarding them as the traits of character that make someone a good person.

Moral philosophy changed with the growing influence of Christianity, which saw God as the giver of laws by which one should live. Righteous conduct no longer stemmed from inner virtues but rather from obedience to the commandments of God. The guiding question therefore changed from inquiries about the traits of a good person to "What are the right things to do?" As Christianity waned in importance, divine law eventually gave way to a secular equivalent dubbed moral law, but the focus remained on specifying the rules of right conduct as opposed to strengths of character. Such well-known ethical systems as ethical egoism, utilitarianism, and social contract theory fall under the umbrella of moral law.

In recent decades, there have been calls within philosophy for a return to the ethics of virtue, starting with Anscombe's (1958) influential criticism that modern moral philosophy was incomplete because it rested on the notion of a law without a lawgiver. Virtue ethics is the contemporary approach within philosophy to strengths of character, and we believe that virtues are much more interesting than laws, at least to psychologists, because virtues pertain to people and the lives they lead. Said another way, psychology needs to downplay prescriptions for the good life (moral laws) and instead emphasize the why and how of good character.

■ Unpacking Character

There are various ways to approach character. A *DSM*-like approach would talk about it as unitary and categorical—one either has character or not. Or one could think about character in terms of underlying processes such as autonomy or reality orientation. One might wed it to an a priori theory. One could view character as only a social construction, revealing of the observer's values but not of who or what is observed. But in all these respects we have taken a different approach.

The stance we take toward character is in the spirit of personality psychology, and specifically that of trait theory, but not the caricature of trait theory held up as a straw man and then criticized by social learning theorists in the 1970s. We instead rely on the new psychology of traits that recognizes individual differences that are stable and general but also shaped by the individual's setting and thus capable of change. The initial step in our project is therefore to unpack the notion of character—to start with the assumption that character is plural—and we do so by specifying the separate strengths and virtues, then devising ways to assess these as individual differences. What we learn can be used to answer other questions about character: its dimensionality, its stability, its enabling conditions and consequences, and so on.

Some of our colleagues who are just as concerned with the good life prefer to look exclusively outside the individual to identify and create the conditions that enable health. They either distrust the notion of character because of its inadvertent political connotations or believe that psychological factors pale in comparison to the impact of situations. We also believe that positive traits need to be placed in context; it is obvious that they do not operate in isolation from the settings, proximal and distal, in which people are to be found. A sophisticated psychology locates psychological characteristics within people and people within their settings broadly construed. Some settings and situations lend themselves to the development and/or display of strengths, whereas other settings and situations preclude them. Settings cannot be allowed to recede into the distant background when we focus on strengths.

Enabling conditions as we envision them are often the province of disciplines other than psychology, but we hope for a productive partnership with these other fields in understanding the settings that allow the strengths to develop. Our common sense tells us that enabling conditions include educational and vocational opportunity, a supportive and consistent family, safe neighborhoods and schools, political stability, and (perhaps) democracy. The existence of mentors, role models, and supportive peers—inside or outside the immediate family—are probably also enabling conditions. There is no reason to think that these conditions equally predispose each of the strengths of interest to us or conversely that all the strengths are equally enabled by a given condition.

We can only do so much at present, but a future goal would be to characterize the properties of settings that enable strengths and virtues (Park & Peterson, 2003b). This characterization would point to features of the physical environment (e.g., naturalness, beauty, and feng shui as studied by environmental psychologists); the social environment (e.g., empowerment as studied by social workers and community psychologists); and both (e.g., predictability and controllability as studied by learning psychologists, novelty and variety as studied by organizational psychologists).

With this said, it is just as obvious that individuals and their traits need to be accorded a central role in understanding the good life. It is individual people, after all, who lead these lives. Despite the importance of the situation in shaping the characteristics of people, everyone brings something to the situation, and everyone takes something away from it. Among the most important of these "somethings" is character, construed as positive traits. The hazards of a personless environmentalism are well known within psychology, and we do not intend to blunder into them.

Another reason to avoid radical environmentalism is that it is spectacularly unwieldy to talk about the good life as being imposed on a person, in the way that psychological troubles can be imposed by trauma and stress. Situations of course make it more or less difficult to live well, but the good life reflects choice and will. Quality life does not simply happen because the Ten Commandments hang on a classroom wall or because children are taught a mantra about just saying no. Again, character construed as positive traits allows us to acknowledge and explain these features of the good life. What makes life worth living is not ephemeral. It does not result from the momentary tickling of our sensory receptors by chocolate, alcohol, or Caribbean vacations. The good life is lived over time and across situations, and an examination of the good life in terms of positive traits is demanded. Strengths of character provide the needed explanation for the stability and generality of a life well lived.

In focusing on strengths of character, we expect them to be numerous but not overwhelmingly so. We treat them as individual differences, in principle and often in practice distinct from one another. We treat them as stable, by definition, but also as malleable, again by definition.

In this first chapter, we lay the foundation of our classification: (a) the overall scheme we devised, which rests on distinctions among virtues, character strengths, and situational themes; (b) the process by which we generated and decided upon entries; and (c) the criteria for a character strength we used to decide which candidate strengths to include and which to exclude. In the course of describing the foundation, we also mention:

- the differences between strengths of character on the one hand and talents and abilities on the other hand
- the situational conditions that enable or disable strengths
- the fulfillments that are inherent aspects of the exercise of character strengths
- the outcomes that may follow from strengths

The focus of the present classification is on strengths, just as the focus of the *DSM* is on clinical disorders. Also like the *DSM*, our classification recognizes that its domain must eventually be described in multiaxial terms. Thus, the identification of someone's signature character strengths would be noted on an Axis I, whereas talents and abilities, enabling and disabling conditions, fulfillments, and outcomes would be noted on additional axes.

■ Distinguishing Virtues, Character Strengths, and Situational Themes

We have found it useful to recognize the components of good character as existing at different levels of abstraction. Thus, our classification scheme is not only horizontal but also vertical (specifying different conceptual levels in a hierarchy). Philosophical approaches to character also propose hierarchies among virtues, but for a different purpose. Because enumerated virtues are numerous and potentially in conflict, philosophers introduce a hierarchy to explain when one or another virtue should be manifested. Indeed, a great deal of discussion has tried to enumerate master virtues (e.g., wisdom, courage, love) that take precedence over all the others. None has won universal acceptance, and we suspect that the master varies across cultures and individuals.

Regardless, our hierarchy is one of abstraction. As psychologists, we are less daunted than philosophers about adjudicating conflicts among character strengths because the relationship of traits to action and the melding of disparate traits into a singular self are after all the concerns of modern personality psychology. The present classification lists character strengths, as have philosophers for centuries, but our categories bring with them rich psychological content and strategies of measurement and hence explanatory power out of the realm and reach of philosophy.

Our hierarchical classification of positive characteristics was modeled deliberately on the Linnaean classification of species, which also ranges from the concrete and specific (the individual organism) through increasingly abstract and general categories (population, subspecies, species, genus, family, order, class, phylum, kingdom, and domain). We distinguish three conceptual levels:

Virtues are the core characteristics valued by moral philosophers and religious thinkers: wisdom, courage, humanity, justice, temperance, and transcendence. These six broad categories of virtue emerge consistently from historical surveys, as detailed in chapter 2. We argue that these are universal, perhaps grounded in biology through an evolutionary process that selected for these aspects of excellence as means of solving the important tasks necessary for survival of the species. We speculate that all these virtues must be present at above-threshold values for an individual to be deemed of good character.

Character strengths are the psychological ingredients—processes or mechanisms—that define the virtues. Said another way, they are distinguishable routes to displaying one or another of the virtues. For example, the virtue of wisdom can be achieved through such strengths as creativity, curiosity, love of learning, open-mindedness, and what we call perspective—having a "big picture" on life. These strengths are similar in that they all involve the acquisition and use of knowledge, but they are also distinct. Again, we regard these strengths as ubiquitously recognized and valued, although a given individual will rarely, if ever, display all of them. We are comfortable saying that someone is of good character if he or she displays but 1 or 2 strengths within a virtue group. Our classification includes 24 strengths, positive traits like bravery, kindness, and hope. At this juncture, we intend these strengths as neither exclusive nor exhaustive, but we expect that subsequent research will help us achieve a nearly exclusive and exhaustive list. This sort of goal has eluded the *DSM*, perhaps because its entries have become too entrenched and attracted too many constituencies, but we intend differently for our classification.

Situational themes are the specific habits that lead people to manifest given character strengths in given situations. The enumeration of themes must take place setting by setting, and it is only for the workplace that this inquiry has begun in earnest. The Gallup Organization has identified hundreds of themes relevant to excellence in the workplace, of which 34 are especially common in the contemporary United States (Buckingham & Clifton, 2001). Among the Gallup Organization's situational work themes are empathy (anticipating and meeting the needs of others), inclusiveness (making others feel part of the group), and positivity (seeing what is good in situations and people).

Remember that these themes are meant to describe how one relates to others in the workplace, but if we look at them a bit more abstractly, empathy, inclusiveness, and positivity all reflect the same character strength of kindness. And if we look at kindness even more abstractly, this character strength—along with the strengths we call love and social intelligence—falls into the broad virtue class of humanity.

On a conceptual level, themes differ from character strengths in several crucial ways. First, they are thoroughly located in specific situations. Work themes are different from family themes, for example, although there may be some overlap in labels. Someone may be competitive at work and at home, but these themes manifest themselves differently. In other cases, a theme may make sense only for describing conduct in a given setting. Even within a domain like work or family, themes may differ across cultures, cohorts, gender, and other important social contrasts. Including themes in our scheme buffers us against the legitimate criticism that there is huge sociocultural variation in how people conceive of goodness. The variation exists at the level of themes, less so at the level of character strengths, and not at all—we assert—at the level of virtues.

Finally, themes per se are neither good nor bad; they can be used to achieve strengths and hence contribute to virtues, but they can also be harnessed to silly or wrong purposes. A sprinter does well (as an athletic competitor) if she tries to run her races as quickly as possible, but a spouse probably does not do well (as a marital partner) if speed is the paramount consideration. A related point about themes is that people can achieve the same result by using different configurations of them. There are different ways to be a good clerk, a good teacher, or—for our purposes—a good person. What is critical is that someone finds a venue in which his or her themes are productive for the desired end.

■ Generating Entries for the Classification

We generated the entries for the classification by work on different fronts. Initial brainstorming involved a core group of scholars (Donald Clifton, Mihalyi Csikszentmihalyi, Ed Diener, Kathleen Hall Jamieson, Robert Nozick, Daniel Robinson, Martin Seligman, and George Vaillant), who created a tentative list of human strengths. Christopher Peterson later joined this group and helped elaborate the initial list, which was presented at several positive psychology conferences and further refined after discussions with conference participants too numerous to mention. Between conferences, Peterson and Seligman devised the framework for defining and conceptualizing strengths that structures this book. Especially helpful were several conversations among Peterson, Seligman, and Marcus Buckingham of the Gallup Organization about the relationship between the present classification and Gallup's work on workplace themes. Also critical were surveys by Peterson of pertinent literatures that addressed good character, from psychiatry, youth development, philosophy, and of course psychology (see chapter 3 for summaries of these literature reviews).

We also collected dozens of inventories of virtues and strengths, from historical luminaries like Charlemagne (S. E. Turner, 1880) and Benjamin Franklin (1790/1961) to contemporary figures like William Bennett (1993) and Sir John Templeton (1995). We consulted statements by the Boy Scouts of America and the Girl Guides of Canada as well as those attributed, with tongue in cheek, to the Klingon Empire. We looked at the goals specified by advocates of character education programs (e.g., M. W. Berkowitz, 2000) and social work from the strengths perspective (e.g., Saleebey, 1992). We identified virtue-relevant messages in Hallmark greeting cards, bumper stickers, *Saturday Evening Post* covers by Norman Rockwell, personal ads, popular song lyrics, graffiti, Tarot cards, the profiles of Pokémon characters, and the residence halls of Hogworts.

Our intent was to leave no stone unturned in identifying candidate strengths for the classification. We combined redundancies and used the criteria described in the next section to winnow the list further. Had we neglected any character strengths deemed important by others, no matter how vaguely defined these might be? And if we had left out someone's enumerated strength, did we have a good reason? For example, we excluded from our classification talents and abilities (e.g., intelligence) and characteristics not valued across all cultures (e.g., cleanliness, frugality, silence). We were not bothered if we had included a virtue or strength not specified in a particular catalog, because the purpose of each catalog dictates its emphases. For example, Charlemagne's code of chivalry for knights of the Holy Roman Empire did not urge them to appreciate beauty, but why should it have? Nor did it urge upon them bravery, because that virtue was a given.

Our initial brainstorming about positive characteristics spontaneously took place at the level of character strengths, which in retrospect suggests that they constitute what Rosch and colleagues (1976) labeled a "natural" level of categorization. Strengths are akin to cats and dogs, tables and chairs: categories that people readily use to make sense of the world in which they live (in this case the moral character of themselves and others). Rosch et al. proposed that natural categories emerge as a way for people to categorize the world at a level that maximizes the perceptual similarity among objects within a category and the perceptual dissimilarity between these objects and those in other categories. Consider this hierarchy:

- kitchen table
- table
- furniture

Their argument is that table represents the basic—that is, natural—level at which people most easily categorize objects. Kitchen table is too concrete, whereas furniture is too abstract. Empirical studies support this idea, showing that cognitive processes such as recognition proceed most efficiently when content is at the basic level. Also, when children start to name objects, they first use terms from the basic level. "Perception" in this analysis should not be taken too literally because it is clear that natural categories exist not just in the realm of things that can literally be seen but also in less tangible realms, such as abnormality or, in the present case, character.

There is an important implication of viewing character strengths as natural categories: Each category encompasses a group of related traits. Together, this group of traits captures the "family resemblance" of the strength, although given traits within the same category are *not* exact replicas of one another (Wittgenstein, 1953). We emphasize this point because we introduce the character strengths in most cases by listing related traits. Thus, the character strength of hope is rendered fully as hope, optimism, future-mindedness, and future orientation (chapter 25). But the reader should not expect to find detailed distinctions within these lists. We instead emphasize the family resemblance.

We call this strategy one of *piling on synonyms,* and besides being faithful to the actual semantic texture of natural categories, it pays the benefit of minimizing subtle connotations, political and otherwise, associated with any given synonym. Thus, "hope" has Christian connotations, which we do not wish to emphasize, whereas "future orientation" has socioeconomic connotations, which we likewise do not wish to emphasize. The only downside is that our shorthand identification of a strength (e.g., "hope") may not convey the acknowledged heterogeneity of the strength.

■ Criteria for a Strength of Character

In this book, we focus on character strengths, the intermediate level of our classification, because they represent a good balance between the concrete (themes) and the abstract (moral virtues). To be included as a character strength, a positive characteristic must satisfy most of the following 10 criteria. These criteria were articulated after we had identified many dozens of candidate strengths and needed a way to consolidate them. We came up with these 10 criteria by scrutinizing the candidate strengths and looking for common features. About half of the strengths included in our classification meet all 10 criteria, but the other half of them do not. Thus, these criteria are neither necessary nor sufficient conditions for character strengths but rather pertinent features that, taken together, capture a "family resemblance" (cf. Wittgenstein, 1953).

CRITERION 1 *A strength contributes to various fulfillments that constitute the good life, for oneself and for others. Although strengths and virtues determine how an individual copes with adversity, our focus is on how they fulfill an individual.*

In keeping with the broad premise of positive psychology, strengths allow the individual to achieve more than the absence of distress and disorder. They "break through the zero point" of psychology's traditional concern with disease, disorder, and failure to address quality of life (Peterson, 2000).

There is a long tradition within philosophy that discusses the meaning of fulfillment. Hedonists and epicurians notwithstanding, most other philosophers agree that fulfillment should not be confused with momentary pleasure or happiness per se, if happiness is construed only as the presence of positive affect and absence of negative affect (Seligman, 2002). Rather, what counts as a fulfillment must pass the *deathbed test*. How might people, if able to collect their thoughts in the face of death, complete the sentence: "I wish I had spent more time _____"? It is doubtful that anyone would say "visiting Disneyland" or "eating butter pecan ice cream." These activities are fun but not fulfilling. At least in our society, the deathbed test is instead met by activities that pertain to work and love broadly construed, as in "I wish I had spent more time making a mark on the world" and "I wish I had spent more time getting to know my children and being kind to my friends." In a less secular society, people might wish that they had spent more time praising God and giving thanks.

It seems that fulfillments must reflect effort, the willful choice and pursuit over time of morally praiseworthy activities. This is why we chose our language carefully to say that character strengths "contribute" to fulfillments rather than "cause" them in the automatic way that Jägermeister causes intoxication. There are no shortcuts to fulfillment.

We hope this analysis does not smack too strongly of Puritanism. We are not opposed to pleasure, and we are certainly not opposed to shortcuts. Self-adhering postage stamps, cruise control, panty hose, plastic garbage bags with drawstrings, microwave popcorn, air-conditioning, canned foods, and automatic redial are among the most noteworthy inventions of the modern world precisely because they are shortcuts. But the value of these and other shortcuts is that they save time and effort that would otherwise be spent on unfulfilling pursuits. The moral significance of a shortcut is only indirect, judged by what one does with the time and effort that have been saved.

What, then, is this contributory relationship of character strengths to fulfillments? Our thinking here has been by the Aristotelian notion of *eudaimonia,* which holds that well-being is not a consequence of virtuous action but rather an inherent aspect of such action. We want to allow for the possibility that some of the ostensible outcomes of the strengths (fulfillments) do not show up at some later point in time, caused as it were by the strength, but instead are part and parcel of the actions that manifest the strength. For example, when you do a favor for someone, your act does not cause you to be satisfied with yourself at some later point in time; being satisfied is an inherent aspect of being helpful.

At present, we have little data on this point, but we believe that given people possess *signature strengths* akin to what Allport (1961) identified decades ago as personal traits. These are strengths of character that a person owns, celebrates, and frequently exercises. In interviews with adults, we find that everyone can readily identify a handful of strengths as very much their own, typically between three and seven (just as Allport proposed). Here are possible criteria for a signature strength:

- a sense of ownership and authenticity ("this is the real me") vis-à-vis the strength
- a feeling of excitement while displaying it, particularly at first
- a rapid learning curve as themes are attached to the strength and practiced
- continuous learning of new ways to enact the strength
- a sense of yearning to act in accordance with the strength
- a feeling of inevitability in using the strength, as if one cannot be stopped or dissuaded from its display
- the discovery of the strength as owned in an epiphany
- invigoration rather than exhaustion when using the strength
- the creation and pursuit of fundamental projects that revolve around the strength
- intrinsic motivation to use the strength

Our hypothesis is that the exercise of signature strengths is fulfilling, and these criteria convey the motivational and emotional features of fulfillment with terms like *excitement, yearning, inevitability, discovery,* and *invigoration.*

The positing of signature strengths linked to the individual's sense of self and identity helps us avoid the trap of equating a strength with a given behavior taken out of context (e.g., operationally defining honesty as "saying whatever one thinks or feels at the moment the impulse flits through consciousness regardless of the circumstances") and then discovering that by this definition, honesty often produces interpersonal disaster. This behavior is *not* in accord with the spirit of honesty. Assessment of strengths is made more difficult by these considerations, but they are imperative. Again, attention to the setting is demanded.

CRITERION 2 *Although strengths can and do produce desirable outcomes, each strength is morally valued in its own right, even in the absence of obvious beneficial outcomes.*

A pragmatic larger society will want to be convinced that character strengths produce more than their own reward, that their exercise reduces the likelihood of distress and dysfunction while encouraging tangible outcomes like:

- subjective well-being (happiness)
- acceptance of oneself
- reverence for life
- competence, efficacy, and mastery
- mental and physical health
- rich and supportive social networks
- respect by and for others
- satisfying work
- material sufficiency
- healthy communities and families

If there were not at least some statistical link between strengths and such outcomes, they would not have appeared across cultures and lasted throughout time. Strengths allow problems of survival to be solved.

However, these outcomes are not part of the definition of a character strength. If a strength is recognized only when it produces a payoff, we do not need the notion of good character to account for human conduct. We can return to a radical behaviorism and speak only of prevailing rewards and punishments. But as Aristotle and other philosophers concerned with virtue persuasively argue, actions undertaken solely for external reasons cannot be considered virtuous, precisely because they are coaxed or coerced, carroted or sticked.

To say that a strength is *morally* valued is an important qualification, because there exist individual differences that are widely valued, contribute to fulfillment, and qualify as signature characteristics (meeting many, if not all, of the hypothesized criteria just enumerated) but still fall outside our classification. Consider intelligence, facial symmetry, immunocompetence, or athletic prowess. These talents and abilities are cut from a different cloth than character strengths like valor or kindness, but what is the difference?

We have devoted considerable thought to the distinction between strengths and virtues on the one hand versus talents and abilities on the other.[1] Talents

---

[1] Hampering this distinction are Western intellectual trends to which we are heir. For example, the Greeks used the term *virtue* to include both moral character and talent, and the word *virtuoso* has survived in the talent domain (although, interestingly, not in the character domain). In Renaissance Florence, physical beauty and moral goodness were regarded as part and parcel of the same individual difference, at least for upper-class women (O'Neill, 2001), and we still may labor under the assumption that what is beautiful is good (cf. Dion, Berscheid, & Walster, 1972).

and abilities on the face of it seem more innate, more immutable, and less voluntary than strengths and virtues. These of course are matters of degree. So, the talent of perfect pitch is always discussed as if it were more innate than the strengths of kindness or modesty, but the ability to read train schedules certainly is not. And suppose it turns out that the character strengths in the present classification prove to be heritable? All other investigated individual differences seem to have some basis in genetic variation, so why not curiosity, for example, or even spirituality and leadership?

To be sure, no one will ever discover single genes that code for specific moral virtues, and any biogenetic account of character will ultimately be phrased in terms of heritable raw ingredients interacting with specific environments and experiences. But the same account already exists for many talents and abilities, so where is the distinction?

We are left, somewhat reluctantly, with the conclusion that character strengths differ from talents and abilities at least because they fall in the moral domain. This is a less-than-satisfactory conclusion because we must cede the designation of a character strength to the larger society and culture. Our early efforts in creating this classification were done with the worry that we would create a list of characteristics that reflected only our own take on the good life. We think we have avoided this problem because we did not include characteristics valued only at the turn of the new century by upper-middle-class agnostic European American academic males (e.g., diversified investment portfolios, wireless Internet access, and reduced teaching loads). As emphasized, the virtues and strengths we include here are ubiquitously recognized as moral across cultures.

There are two further answers that clarify the distinction between character strengths and other dimensions of virtuosity. First is the role played by effort and will in the exercise of these characteristics. Basketball player Michael Jordan was revered for his athletic ability but also for his refusal to lose. In both cases, the talent/strength was practiced and nurtured, but those of us who are not delusional recognize that we can never soar through the air like Michael, with or without the shoes he endorsed. We can imagine, however, that we might arise from our sickbed to do our job as best we can, as Jordan did in a 1997 playoff game against the Utah Jazz, in which only his temperature (103°) exceeded his point total (38). This storied performance represented the melding of a talent with a character strength, yet it is the latter that we value morally.

This chapter is not the right forum for a discussion of free will and determinism, so we will just note in passing our strong suspicion that positive psychology, as the field evolves, will necessarily lead social scientists to grapple anew with the crucial role in human activity played by choice. A morally praiseworthy action is chosen in a way that a merely skilled action is not. All people can aspire to have strong character in a way that they cannot aspire to be good-looking or physically resilient.

A second distinction between character strengths and talents is that the latter seem valued more for their tangible consequences (acclaim, wealth) than are the former. Someone who "does nothing" with a talent like a high IQ or musical skill courts eventual disdain. Witness the ridicule directed at Michael Jordan when he abandoned basketball to pursue a baseball career or the dismay we experience when extremely talented individuals like Judy Garland, Lenny Bruce, Andy Gibb, or Darryl Strawberry are overwhelmed by drug problems. In contrast, we never hear the criticism that a person did nothing with his or her wisdom or kindness. Said another way, talents and abilities can be squandered, but strengths and virtues cannot.

CRITERION 3   *The display of a strength by one person does not diminish other people in the vicinity.*

In many if not most cases, onlookers are elevated by their observation of virtuous action. Admiration is created more than jealousy because character strengths are the sorts of characteristics to which most can—and do—aspire. The more people surrounding us who are kind, or curious, or full of hope, the greater our own likelihood of acting in these ways. Said another way, strengths accompany non-zero-sum games (Wright, 1999). All are winners when someone acts in accordance with his or her strengths and virtues.

One can be skeptical of this criterion, and three reasons are cited to support this skepticism. First, morally praiseworthy acts by others may create shame among those of us who are less brave or less kind. The likelihood of such a reaction is unknown but an interesting empirical issue, as is how people react to such shame. We speculate that many may rise to the next available occasion, which means that they indeed have been elevated by what they have observed.

The second reason for skepticism is that people with ostensibly good character are phony—their virtuous deeds mask insecurity or even deeper psychopathology. A common theme in literature as well as contemporary shock journalism is the moral undressing of a supposedly good person. We are intrigued by these sorts of stories, even as they leave us feeling empty, but are they the rule? And even if true, do the strengths somehow arise only as defenses against the vices? The answer from positive psychology is that we want to see the evidence before dismissing all instances of human goodness as mere displays, disguises, or displacements. And there is no such evidence. Indeed, what runs through the examples of clay-footed celebrities other than the obvious transgressions is some sort of false righteousness on the part of the transgressor. The real sin may not be the obvious one but the failure of authenticity on the part of the sinner.

Another point here is that we see character as plural, and that the existence of nonvirtuous activity (with respect to one strength) does not mean that the individual cannot display other strengths. That baseball manager Pete Rose may have bet on baseball games does not diminish the enthusiasm he displayed for decades as a player.

A third reason that goodness is viewed with skepticism is that virtuous people are thought to be boring. Remember Billy Joel's song lyric that he would rather laugh with the sinners than cry with the saints, because the sinners are much more fun? In a more serious venue, Wolf (1982) phrased the argument this way:

> If the moral saint is devoting all his time to feeding the hungry or healing the sick or raising money for Oxfam then necessarily he is not reading Victorian novels, playing the oboe, or improving his backhand. Although no one of the interests or tastes in the category containing these latter activities could be claimed to be a necessary element in a life well lived, a life in which *none* of these possible aspects of character are developed may seem to be a life strangely barren. (p. 421)

This point would have merit if it were empirically the case that good deeds preclude the development of nonmoral interests, but how could this be true? Character strengths pervade many activities, including reading, music, and sports, and they are associated with popularity (chapter 28). Wolf further said, "I don't know whether there are any moral saints" (p. 419), to which we respond that she looked in the wrong places and at the wrong sorts of activity.

CRITERION 4   *Being able to phrase the "opposite" of a putative strength in a felicitous way counts against regarding it as a character strength.*

Consider flexibility. One can render its opposite in an undesirable way (as inflexibility) but just as easily in a desirable way (as steadfastness). For almost all character strengths and virtues, anyone with a thesaurus can find approximate antonyms with desirable connotations, but the issue is the ease with which this can be done and the excess baggage that gets dragged along in so doing. One can weigh the baggage by a process of *back-and-forth antonym creation*. How quickly does the process fall apart? For example, one possible opposite of honesty is tact, but the obvious opposite of tact is not honesty but rudeness. Honesty, therefore, meets this linguistic test.

This criterion should not be confused with the fact that some strengths and virtues are *bipolar,* that is, there is a negative anchor to the continuum that defines the characteristic (e.g., "kindness" ranges across degrees of mean-spiritedness through a zero point to its increasingly positive instances). Other characteristics are better seen as *unipolar* (e.g., "sense of humor" has a zero point but no meaningful negative range). Our focus in all cases is on the positive end of the strength continuum, but the bipolarity versus unipolarity of given characteristics is an intriguing contrast to keep in mind when we address assessment strategies. We also need to remember the premise of positive psychology that the absence of a weakness is not in and of itself a strength and further that the determinants of strengths versus weaknesses are not simple obverses (Peterson,

2000; Peterson & Chang, 2003; Peterson & Steen, 2002). Bipolarity needs to be established on empirical grounds.

CRITERION 5   *A strength needs to be manifest in the range of an individual's behavior—thoughts, feelings, and/or actions—in such a way that it can be assessed. It should be traitlike in the sense of having a degree of generality across situations and stability across time.*

Strengths differ in terms of being *tonic* (constant) versus *phasic* (waxing and waning depending on their "use"). This distinction has important measurement implications. A tonic characteristic (e.g., kindness or humor) shows itself steadily in a variety of settings, which means that it can be assessed by deliberately general questions posed to an individual and/or informant ("Do you like to tease others?"). A phasic characteristic comes and goes because it is relevant only in settings that afford it. Bravery, for example, does not—indeed, cannot— show itself as one is standing in the checkout line of a grocery store. But if the store is being robbed, then a person can manifest varying degrees of valor.

Philosophers often refer to virtues as corrective, meaning that they counteract some difficulty thought to be inherent in the human condition, some temptation that needs to be resisted, or some motivation that needs to be re-channeled into something good (Yearley, 1990, p. 16). We would not need to posit the virtue of generosity if people were not (sometimes) selfish, the virtue of persistence if people were not (sometimes) idle, or the virtue of bravery if people were not (sometimes) swayed from doing the right thing by fear. What is difficult or challenging need not be front and center when the virtue is displayed. In some cases (e.g., selfishness) what needs to be corrected is a general human tendency. But in other cases (e.g., bravery) what demands correction is an immediately pressing psychological state. Identifying what it is that a character strength corrects should help us identify it as tonic versus phasic.

One or more of our character strengths may prove to be so thoroughly phasic that it will not prove plausible to speak of it as a trait. We worry in particular about what the data will eventually show about the "traitedness" of the strength we include here as open-mindedness (aka judgment, critical thinking). Early on in our project, we identified this characteristic as rationality but then jettisoned this label. First, rationality has earned itself bad connotations; many everyday people juxtapose it with compassion and see it as a stereotypically "male" defense against feeling. Second, there is good reason to doubt that people show across-the-board good versus bad reasoning, at least insofar as this hypothesis has been studied in terms of effective problem solving across disparate domains (Lehman & Nisbett, 1990). There really are Ph.D. mathematicians who cannot balance their checkbooks. "Thinking" may be made possible by a host of rather independent cognitive modules, each devoted to its own sort of content. What this means is that "open-mindedness" would be useful only as an umbrella term for these modules, not as the label for a personality trait. Perhaps the assessment of individual differences in open-mindedness can take place only at the level of themes.

CRITERION 6   *The strength is distinct from other positive traits in the classification and cannot be decomposed into them.*

For example, the character strength of "tolerance" meets most of the other criteria enumerated but is a complex blend of open-mindedness and fairness. The character strength of "patience" melds self-regulation, persistence, and open-mindedness. The reaction of people to the 24 strengths in our classification has never involved the criticism that we have included unimportant aspects of character. Rather, the reaction has been "What about _____?" In all cases to date, the suggested candidate strikes us as a blend of strengths that are included.

The corollary of this criterion is that as assessment proceeds and the relevant data are obtained, we may decide to combine several strengths in the classification because of empirical redundancy and theoretical overlap. For example, curiosity and love of learning appear difficult to distinguish; that is, the same people are usually high, middling, or low on both (see chapter 28). At present, we distinguish these on theoretical grounds because curiosity need not entail the *systematic* acquisition of information as does love of learning, but it may be possible to regard love of learning as a special case of curiosity.

CRITERION 7   *A character strength is embodied in consensual paragons.*

One important way in which the larger culture highlights strengths of character is by providing stories, parables, creeds, mottoes, pledges, songs, and poems that feature people who compellingly demonstrate a given positive trait (e.g., Burrell, 1997; W. Kilpatrick, Wolfe, & Wolfe, 1994). Models may be real (Cal Ripken and persistence), apocryphal (George Washington and honesty), or mythic (Luke Skywalker and authenticity). Regardless, children grow up surrounded by a bevy of potential role models, and a question of critical importance is when and why good lessons are learned from the media versus bad lessons. What leads some folks to fix on Madonna, Eminem, Donald Trump, or professional wrestlers as role models?

We have been reading children's books and the moral role models that figure in them. In some cases, we find strengths glorified, as in Watty Piper's *The Little Engine That Could*. But in other cases, we are a bit dismayed. Curiosity is an obvious human strength, but Hans Rey's *Curious George* is disaster incarnate. Hope is also an unambiguous virtue, but Eleanor Porter's *Pollyanna* is a ninny, and Kate Wiggins's *Rebecca of Sunnybrook Farm* strikes some as simply sugar-coated. As this endeavor continues, we may gain some insight into the character crisis that supposedly threatens our youth (cf. Bennett, 1997). Perhaps Hollywood is not the only culprit.

Strengths are also encouraged by the recognition of actual people in our immediate vicinity who embody to a remarkable extent a given positive trait. These paragons of virtue display what Allport (1961) called a cardinal trait, and the ease with which we can think of paragons in our own social circles gives the lie to the claim that all virtuous people are phony. Certainly, the virtuous people we each know are not phony. They really are kind, or fair, or playful, and so on for all the entries in our classification. In one of our ways of evaluating assessment strategies, we have asked our research assistants to nominate people of their acquaintance who are paragons of virtue and prevail upon them—without full disclosure of why—to complete our measures (chapter 28). No one has had any difficulty thinking of appropriate respondents.

We do not know how many people are paragons of one or another strength, and some intriguing questions can be asked about the relative frequency or infrequency of cardinal strengths. In given cultures or subcultures, are certain paragons more common than others? Are there gender differences? How about developmental differences?

CRITERION 8   *We do not believe this feature can be applied to all strengths, but an additional criterion where sensible is the existence of prodigies with respect to the strength.*

In his theory of multiple intelligences, H. Gardner (1983) directed our attention to children who evidence at a particularly early age exceptional talents in such domains as music, mathematics, and athletics. Prodigies appear only in some fields of endeavor, and Gardner argued that these fields tap biologically based abilities inherent in the human species. Aside from their particular skill, prodigies are otherwise unremarkable children (Feldman, 1993). Popular stereotypes of child prodigies as miniature adults are incorrect.

Suppose these arguments apply as well to the moral domain. Are there kindness prodigies? Are there children who display precocious fairness or bravery? These sorts of questions are completely unexplored, and all we have at present is anecdotal evidence to answer them.

One of our college students told us a story about herself when she was about 9 years of age and worried that her parents might divorce. Without telling her parents, she went to the local library and read books on couples therapy, which is remarkable enough, but what really made us marvel was the rest of her story: She turned dinner conversations with the family into deliberate interventions, encouraging her parents to solve problems jointly, to argue fairly, to express their likes and dislikes about one another in behavioral terms, and so on. She was a prodigy, specifically with respect to the character strength of social intelligence. (And yes, her parents are still married to one another.)

If character prodigies exist, we can make some predictions about them from what is known about other sorts of prodigies. First, their prodigious achievements will not be spontaneous. Rather, they will develop through steps or stages, although more rapidly than do other individuals. Second, prodigies will not achieve their advanced levels without some instruction. We do not know much more about our child couples therapist than what we just conveyed, but we suspect that there were adults in her life—perhaps her parents or perhaps not— who cultivated her social intelligence. Third, and sadly, character prodigies may not grow up to be paragons of virtue because it is rare for a musical or mathematical prodigy to be hailed as a genius when an adult. Perhaps the domain of character is different. We simply do not know.

CRITERION 9   *Conversely, another criterion for a character strength is the existence of people who show—selectively—the total absence of a given strength.*

We again borrowed this criterion from H. Gardner's (1983) discussion of multiple intelligences. He focused on the cases where the selective absence of a skill could be attributed to neurological damage, but the more general point is that certain skills or their absence may segregate themselves from other aspects of the person. They can therefore be regarded as natural groupings able to be approached profitably in biosocial terms.

How might we describe such people? We have sometimes used the phrase "character imbecile" in a deliberate attempt to be jarring. Some of our colleagues do not like this label—and we understand why—but if there is something offensive here, it is not the label but to what it applies: people completely devoid of one or another character strength. Imagine a person with no curiosity about the world, or one who is incapable of loving or being loved. We know these people exist, but we do not know whether their deficiency is specific to a given character strength or general. Our assumption about the plurality of character would be supported by selectivity.

Consider the well-known Darwin Awards, given to individuals—invariably young males—who remove themselves from the gene pool by acting in "really stupid ways" (Northcutt, 2000). Playing Russian roulette with an automatic pistol or tying helium balloons to a lawn chair and floating gently upward (and then falling rapidly downward when the balloons burst) represent colossal failures of common sense—that is, prudence. Perhaps these actions are predisposed as well by massively misguided curiosity.

In contrast to moral prodigies, individuals completely devoid of one or another strength of character have been extensively studied under the rubric of personality disorders, the *DSM*'s Axis II. As a scientific topic, Axis II disorders are problematic—most cannot be diagnosed reliably, and most cannot be treated effectively. But perhaps this state of affairs results from ongoing attempts by psychiatry to medicalize these problematic styles of behaving. If personality disorders were recast as failures of character, more productive insights into them might result.

CRITERION 10   *As suggested by Erikson's (1963) discussion of psychosocial stages and the virtues that result from their satisfactory resolutions, the larger society provides institutions and associated rituals for cultivating strengths and virtues and then for sustaining their practice.*

The rituals that cultivate strengths can be thought of as simulations: trial runs that allow children and adolescents to display and develop a valued characteristic in a safe (as-if) context in which guidance is explicit (cf. Unell & Wyckoff, 1995). High school student councils presumably foster leadership; Little League baseball teams are thought to contribute to the development of teamwork; catechism classes attempt to lay the foundation for spirituality. To be sure, institutions may backfire (think of win-at-all-cost youth hockey coaches or beauty contests for 6-year-olds), but these failures are readily apparent and widely decried.

We have encountered some difference of opinion regarding whether individual parents and teachers try to encourage specific strengths and virtues. Some of us may try to inculcate praiseworthy characteristics, but others of us may regard their development as beyond our control, trusting to the genetic roulette wheel, local schools, youth development programs, or a vaguely defined "society" to bring about strong and virtuous children. We hasten to add that we believe that strengths and virtues can be cultivated, but any interventions to nurture strengths need to be informed by what people in general believe about their origins.

In the United States alone, millions of young people participate in school programs and after-school programs intended to cultivate good character. The almost total absence of program evaluation vis-à-vis this stated goal is remarkable. We can conclude, based on appropriate empirical evidence, that youth who participate in a variety of programs are less likely to show problems like school failure, drug use, violence, unwanted pregnancy, and the like, but the problem-centered focus of evaluation efforts leaves the issue of deliberately cultivated strengths largely unexplored. The programs exist, and their character-relevant goals are explicit. One of the benefits of our classification project may be the provision of research instruments to undertake the needed empirical investigations.

Just as important as creating strengths in the first place are the rules, roles, and norms that sustain them. Although we regard character strengths as traits, they are not evident in any and all circumstances. Prevailing rewards and punishments in a given situation work for or against the display of a particular strength. If one is involved in an automobile accident, kindness is not the trait that should come to the fore, at least insofar as it would give the other participants leverage for an unwarranted insurance claim. Humor is a terrible trait to display when walking through a metal detector at an airport. Conversely, certain occupational roles demand specific strengths of character—for example, family court judges need to be fair, inventors need to be creative, therapists need to have social intelligence, telemarketers need to be hopeful—and we expect that individuals in these roles will either develop the requisite strengths or soon seek other jobs.

Remember our distinction between tonic and phasic strengths. Tonic strengths are those that can be displayed on an ongoing and steady basis, except when there is good reason not to do so, traits like curiosity, modesty, and zest. Phasic strengths are those that rise and fall according to the demands of specifiable situations. One can be brave only when in a situation that produces fear. One can display teamwork only as a member of a group with a common task. One can exercise open-mindedness only in the face of a complex decision. We therefore speculate that tonic strengths are less contextualized than phasic strengths. Regardless, society needs to recognize that both sorts of strengths matter but may require different means of encouragement. In the case of tonic strengths, it may be sufficient *not* to punish those who display them. In the case of phasic strengths, the appropriate way to display a strength needs to be articulated, trained as needed, and of course rewarded. We have interviewed firefighters, for instance, and found that valorous individuals report that the requisite skills for doing their job despite fear have been so overlearned that they are automatized.

■ The Strengths

When we applied these criteria to the many dozens of candidate strengths we identified through brainstorming and literature searches, what resulted was the list of positive traits shown in Table 1.1, categorized under the six core moral virtues that emerge consensually across cultures and throughout time (chapter 2). Remember that this vertical dimension is one of abstractness, and it would be a category mistake to ask if curiosity causes wisdom. Instead, curiosity is an instance of a virtue category that revolves around knowledge and its use. We believe that the positive traits in this classification themselves are ubiquitously if not universally recognized, an assumption we are in the process of checking with cross-national and cross-cultural studies.[2]

In some cases, the classification of a given strength under a core virtue can be debated. Humor, for example, might be considered a strength of humanity

---

[2]With Ilona Boniwell and Nansook Park, we have been asking bilingual/bicultural social scientists to complete a questionnaire (in English); it lists the 24 strengths and asks in each case if there is a comparable concept in the respondent's home culture and whether that concept satisfies our criteria for a character strength. The project is ongoing, but data from more than 30 nations so far support the ubiquity of these strengths. In a related project, Robert Biswas-Diener and Ed Diener conducted focus groups with the Maasai in Africa and the Inuit in Greenland, finding that all 24 strengths in the classification were readily recognized by participants.

TABLE 1.1   *Classification of Character Strengths*

---

1. *Wisdom and knowledge*—cognitive strengths that entail the acquisition and use of knowledge

   Creativity [*originality, ingenuity*]: Thinking of novel and productive ways to conceptualize and do things; includes artistic achievement but is not limited to it

   Curiosity [*interest, novelty-seeking, openness to experience*]: Taking an interest in ongoing experience for its own sake; finding subjects and topics fascinating; exploring and discovering

   Open-mindedness [*judgment, critical thinking*]: Thinking things through and examining them from all sides; *not* jumping to conclusions; being able to change one's mind in light of evidence; weighing all evidence fairly

   Love of learning: Mastering new skills, topics, and bodies of knowledge, whether on one's own or formally; obviously related to the strength of curiosity but goes beyond it to describe the tendency to add *systematically* to what one knows

   Perspective [*wisdom*]: Being able to provide wise counsel to others; having ways of looking at the world that make sense to oneself and to other people

2. *Courage*—emotional strengths that involve the exercise of will to accomplish goals in the face of opposition, external or internal

   Bravery [*valor*]: *Not* shrinking from threat, challenge, difficulty, or pain; speaking up for what is right even if there is opposition; acting on convictions even if unpopular; includes physical bravery but is not limited to it

   Persistence [*perseverance, industriousness*]: Finishing what one starts; persisting in a course of action in spite of obstacles; "getting it out the door"; taking pleasure in completing tasks

   Integrity [*authenticity, honesty*]: Speaking the truth but more broadly presenting oneself in a genuine way and acting in a sincere way; being without pretense; taking responsibility for one's feelings and actions

   Vitality [*zest, enthusiasm, vigor, energy*]: Approaching life with excitement and energy; *not* doing things halfway or halfheartedly; living life as an adventure; feeling alive and activated

3. *Humanity*—interpersonal strengths that involve tending and befriending others

   Love: Valuing close relations with others, in particular those in which sharing and caring are reciprocated; being close to people

   Kindness [*generosity, nurturance, care, compassion, altruistic love, "niceness"*]: Doing favors and good deeds for others; helping them; taking care of them

   Social intelligence [*emotional intelligence, personal intelligence*]: Being aware of the motives and feelings of other people and oneself; knowing what to do to fit into different social situations; knowing what makes other people tick

(continued)

TABLE 1.1   *Classification of Character Strengths* (continued)

4. *Justice*—civic strengths that underlie healthy community life

   Citizenship [*social responsibility, loyalty, teamwork*]: Working well as a member of a group or team; being loyal to the group; doing one's share

   Fairness: Treating all people the same according to notions of fairness and justice; *not* letting personal feelings bias decisions about others; giving everyone a fair chance

   Leadership: Encouraging a group of which one is a member to get things done and at the same maintain time good relations within the group; organizing group activities and seeing that they happen

5. *Temperance*—strengths that protect against excess

   Forgiveness and mercy: Forgiving those who have done wrong; accepting the shortcomings of others; giving people a second chance; *not* being vengeful

   Humility / Modesty: Letting one's accomplishments speak for themselves; *not* seeking the spotlight; *not* regarding oneself as more special than one is

   Prudence: Being careful about one's choices; *not* taking undue risks; *not* saying or doing things that might later be regretted

   Self-regulation [*self-control*]: Regulating what one feels and does; being disciplined; controlling one's appetites and emotions

6. *Transcendence*—strengths that forge connections to the larger universe and provide meaning

   Appreciation of beauty and excellence [*awe, wonder, elevation*]: Noticing and appreciating beauty, excellence, and/or skilled performance in various domains of life, from nature to art to mathematics to science to everyday experience

   Gratitude: Being aware of and thankful for the good things that happen; taking time to express thanks

   Hope [*optimism, future-mindedness, future orientation*]: Expecting the best in the future and working to achieve it; believing that a good future is something that can be brought about

   Humor [*playfulness*]: Liking to laugh and tease; bringing smiles to other people; seeing the light side; making (not necessarily telling) jokes

   Spirituality [*religiousness, faith, purpose*]: Having coherent beliefs about the higher purpose and meaning of the universe; knowing where one fits within the larger scheme; having beliefs about the meaning of life that shape conduct and provide comfort

because playfulness and whimsy can create social bonds. It might also be classified as a strength of wisdom, inasmuch as wit helps us acquire, perfect, and use knowledge. But we had a reason for dubbing humor a strength of transcendence: Like hope and spirituality, it connects us to something larger in the universe, specifically the irony of the human condition, the incongruent congruencies to which playful people call our attention, for our education, amusement, and comfort.

We urge the reader not to be too concerned about the details of how we classified the 24 strengths under the six virtues. We have not measured the virtues per se; they are too abstract and general. We measured only the strengths, and if the data suggest—for example—that playfulness belongs elsewhere because of its co-occurrence with other strengths, we will gladly move it.

The classification we present here is not a finished product, and we expect it to change in the years to come, as theory and research concerning character strengths proceed. After all, the *DSM* has taken more than 50 years to attain its current form. We anticipate that our classification of strengths will similarly evolve, by adding or deleting specific strengths of character, by combining those that prove redundant, by reformulating their organization under core virtues, and by more systematically evaluating them vis-à-vis our 10 criteria. The measurement tools we sketch in chapter 28 should prove useful in crafting future versions of the classification, and we also believe that positive psychology applications—interventions aimed at increasing specific strengths of character and general well-being—will provide empirical grist for the conceptual mill. But let us not get too far ahead of ourselves.

■ Organization of the Volume

This book has three sections. The first section provides background, explains the rationale for the classification scheme and its basis in previous classification efforts, and defines terms.

The second section contains chapters describing the current state of knowledge with respect to each of the 24 character strengths in the classification. Each chapter in the second section uses the following format:

- the consensual definition of the strength (as an individual difference), phrased in terms of behavioral criteria
- the theoretical/research traditions that have studied it
- existing individual difference measures (self-report or informant questionnaires, interviews, assessments from laboratory simulations, in vivo observations, content analyses, and so on)
- known correlates and consequences (outcomes) of the strength
- how the strength develops and is manifest across the life span

- factors that encourage or thwart the development and display of this strength
- if available, information about gender differences and cross-national and cross-cultural aspects of this strength
- if available, information about deliberate interventions that foster it
- what is not known?
- a bibliography of "must-read" articles and books

The third section briefly addresses issues of assessment of strengths and sketches how the classification and assessment package might be used in different practical domains. The most obvious domain of application is the science of positive psychology, but the classification might prove useful as well to youth development, gerontology, family relations (including marriage and child rearing), education, business, the military, leisure and recreation, and even clinical/counseling psychology.

2. UNIVERSAL VIRTUES?— LESSONS FROM HISTORY

In the various enumerations of the moral virtues I had met with in my reading, I found the catalog more or less numerous, as different writers included more or fewer ideas under the same name.
—BENJAMIN FRANKLIN, *The Autobiography*

It is not possible, many argue, to insist on respecting both difference and sameness when it comes to moral values: on honoring individual and cultural diversity while also holding that certain moral values go to the heart of what it means to be human and always have, since the beginning of time, and always must if we are not to lose touch with our humanity.
—SISSELA BOK, *Common Values*

In creating a classification of character strengths, we need to distinguish "character" from related notions, and we need to subdivide character into its components. This latter task is remarkably easy. Indeed, it is so easy that it has been done hundreds if not thousands of times throughout history. Moral philosophers, theologians, educators, legislators, sports writers, and parents all have ideas about what character means, and few have resisted the temptation to articulate a definitive list of the virtues that constitute the well-lived life.

When we undertook our project, we started by creating our own list. With little modesty, we asserted that our list included strengths and virtues valued in all contemporary cultures around the world. But when we showed our list to colleagues, we encountered the frequent objection that there are no strengths and virtues valued across all cultures. Indeed, we were told that the subcultural variations along regional, socioeconomic, religious, and ethnic lines in just the contemporary United States preclude a universal list even for the here and now. We took these criticisms seriously and worried about reifying characteristics valued only at the turn of the new century by upper-middle-class European American academics.

We could have quit, but we are empirically minded. Is it really the case that there is no consensus about the strengths and virtues that are most valued? We undertook a thought experiment and tried to imagine a culture or subculture that did not stress the cultivation of courage, honesty, perseverance, hope, or kindness. Done another way, this experiment requires that we envision parents looking at their newborn infant and being indifferent to the possibility that the child would grow up to be cowardly, dishonest, easily discouraged, pessimistic, and cruel.

Perhaps there are after all some ubiquitous, if not universal, virtues. Perhaps some virtues exist that are so widely recognized that an anthropological veto ("The tribe I study does not have that one!") would be more interesting than damning. But other than nonsystematic brainstorming, how might these be specified?

In describing one prerequisite for wisdom, Kramer (2000) observed that "exposure to alternative knowledge contexts, or perspectives, would facilitate the ability to accept multiple perspectives and critically evaluate human truths" (p. 84). If we 21st-century psychologists were searching for the enduring truths of virtue, we suspected that we might find them in the collected wisdom of the ages (cf. Comte-Sponville, 2001; Templeton, 1995). Hence, we decided to undertake a survey not of the random digit-dial variety but of what early thinkers from far-flung traditions have said about the components of character.

Thus, the purposes of the exercise we describe in this chapter were dual and complementary. The first was a literature search and review of previous influential attempts to list virtues crucial to human thriving. Because the historical inquiry into what strengths make for the most exemplary person or lived life involves the realms of philosophy, religion, politics, and education, the focus was necessarily interdisciplinary and cross-cultural. The second aim was empirical: Would the virtue catalogs of early thinkers within these disciplines converge? Would certain virtues, regardless of tradition or culture, be widely valued?

But which cultures, which texts, and which authors would we consider? The following inclusion and exclusion criteria were employed. We limited the search to ancient cultures recognized for their influential and enduring impact on human civilization and then further restricted our examinations to written texts from these large-scale societies. We meant no snub by excluding from this exercise other intellectually fertile cultures from which written texts are not at present readily available in translation, although we note in passing our future interest in an ethnographic survey of character strengths among nonliterate cultures.

In his broad survey *World Philosophies* (1999), Smart nominated China, South Asia (India, mostly), and the West as the "Great Three"—the most widely influential traditions of thought in human history. We followed Smart's lead and concentrated on these traditions, focusing more specifically on the dominant spiritual and philosophical traditions originating in each: Confucianism and Taoism in China, Buddhism and Hinduism in South Asia, and ancient Greece, Judeo-Christianity, and Islam in the West.

Then, within these traditions, we looked for expository discussions of virtue consensually recognized as the earliest, the most influential, or preferably both. We were particularly attracted to those authors who had deliberately developed a catalog, and were even more pleased when these had clear beginnings and ends in the form of explicitly numbered virtues (e.g., the Ten Commandments, the Holy Eightfold Path). If there was more than one possible entrant, we chose that which reflected the most crucial aspects of the tradition under study. Thus, for example, we did not include Pantanjali's ideas on virtue as outlined in the *Yoga-sutra* (trans. 1979); although this text is the basic one of the sixth orthodox school (yoga) of Hindu philosophy, the virtues as outlined in the *Bhagavadgita* (trans. 1990) are both more inclusive and well known. Occasionally no single text emerged as most representative, in which case we included more than one text per tradition. If we could not find a deliberate or concise exposition on virtue within a tradition, we opted to study its most well known text, as well as respected secondary sources, and extrapolate. For instance, nowhere in the *Analects* (trans. 1992) does Confucius reel off a discrete list of crucial virtues; rather, they are referred to throughout, and the text is so unanimously the one most associated with the tradition that we focused our inquiries there.

■ Core Virtues

Texts and their virtue catalogs were gathered in more or less chronological order. Nominated virtues could be vaguely defined, in which case secondary sources and expert colleagues were consulted to determine the meaning of each entry within its cultural context.

When data collection was complete, analysis involved condensing each list by locating thematically similar virtues and classifying them under an obviously emerging core virtue. By that term, we mean an abstract ideal encompassing a number of other, more specific virtues that reliably converge to the recognizable higher-order category. For instance, the core virtue justice is an abstract term representative of the ideals of more minimalist virtues such as injunctions, laws, and procedural rules for fairness (see Bok, 1995, for further discussion on minimalist values and virtues). To say that particular virtues—*within a tradition*—converge into a core virtue is not to argue that all their features line up perfectly, but rather that they have a coherent resemblance to one another, sharing more features than not. Individual virtues that could not, without pushing and squeezing, be classified within a core virtue category were considered distinct.

Furthermore, to say that certain virtues—*across traditions*—converge onto a core virtue likewise does not mean that we argue for a one-to-one mapping of a virtue across cultures. Certainly an abstraction such as justice will mean slightly different things—and will be valued for different reasons—from one culture to another. Again what we suggest is coherent resemblance: The higher-order meaning behind a particular core virtue will line up better with its cross-cultural counterpart than it will with any other core virtue (e.g., examples of Confucian justice will have more to do with those of Platonic justice than they will with Platonic wisdom). What we sought were instances in which the similarities across cultures outweighed the differences; again, when the core virtue of a particular tradition did not have an obvious cross-cultural counterpart, it was considered as a separate entity in the final analysis.

The literature review in the next section reveals a surprising amount of similarity across cultures and strongly indicates a historical and cross-cultural convergence of six core virtues: courage, justice, humanity, temperance, transcendence, and wisdom. We dub these the High Six. First, however, we characterize each of these six categories.

Courage

French philosopher Comte-Sponville (2001), arguing for the universality of courage, reminded us that while fears and the acts to defeat them vary from society to society, the capacity to overcome fear "is always more valued than cowardice or faintheartedness" (p. 44). D. Putnam (1997) offered an inclusive account of courage by delineating three types: physical, moral, and psychological. Physical courage is the type involved in overcoming the fear of physical injury or death in order to save others or oneself. Moral courage entails maintaining ethical integrity or authenticity at the risk of losing friends, employment, privacy, or prestige. Psychological courage includes that sort required to confront a debilitating illness or destructive habit or situation; it is the bravery inherent in facing one's inner demons.

We follow Putnam's lead and include all three characterizations in the core virtue of courage. We also do not limit our definition to single astonishing acts—chronic courageousness counts, too (see Finfgeld, 1999). This brings us to a perhaps obvious but necessary remark on courage: It has an inner life as well as an outer one. That is, courage is composed of not just observable acts but also the cognitions, emotions, motivations, and decisions that bring them about. Thus, as we examine the ubiquity of courage, although most of the examples that follow are of the physical or soldier-in-battle variety, what we mean abstractly is closer to Cicero's (1949) definition: Courage is "the deliberate facing of dangers and bearing of toils" (*De inventione*, II.LIV.163). We mean courage to include physical valor, yes, but also integrity and perseverance—any act of willfully overcoming into what it is so easy to slip: security, comfort, complacency. We mean doing what is right, even when one has much to lose. Or, to return to Comte-Sponville (2001), "Without courage, we cannot hold out against the worst in ourselves or others" (p. 50).

Justice

The core virtue justice, as already stated, refers generally to that which makes life fair. Intuitively, perhaps, that means the equality of everyone. But we are all well aware that life is not fair, and that "some animals are more equal than others," which is why we need the more pragmatic rendition of justice, that of the laws that give fairness a fair shot (see Rawls, 2001).

In Western industrialized nations, justice generally translates to the notion of equity—the belief that rewards should be apportioned according to contributions or merit (Walster, Walster, & Bersheid, 1978) and that people ultimately get what they deserve (M. J. Lerner, 1980). This particular concept of justice is not universal—collectivist cultures tend to prefer the notion of equality or need when making fairness-based decisions (Murphy-Berman & Berman, 2002; Murphy-Berman, Berman, Singh, Pachauri, & Kumar, 1984; Sampson, 1975). However, whether a culture views justice as equity ("everyone agrees that justice in distribution must be in accordance with some kind of merit"; Aristotle, *Nicomachean Ethics*, 2000, 1131a) or equality/need ("from each according to his abilities, to each according to his needs"; K. Marx, "Critique of the Gotha Program," 1875/1977, p. 569), the shared notion is that some standard should be in practice to protect intuitive notions of what is fair (see N. J. Finkel, 1995, 2000). Hence, the exemplars of justice are those that are civic in nature—fairness, leadership, citizenship, and teamwork.

Humanity

Though both may involve improving another's welfare, we separate the core virtues of justice and humanity. By humanity we are referring to the virtues involved in relating to another—the interpersonal strengths. Certainly justice involves the interpersonal (how could it not?), but it is usually virtuous only when impersonally so ("for fairness' sake"). Put another way, whereas the virtue of justice lies in impartiality, the virtue of humanity relies on doing more than what is only fair—showing generosity even when an equitable exchange would suffice, kindness even if it cannot (or will not) be returned, and understanding even when punishment is due.

Virtues of humanity are rendered within psychology as altruistic or prosocial behavior. Many species, not just primates, appear to behave in ways that reflect altruism (de Waal, 2000; Krebs & Davies, 1993). While there is argument that all altruism is the result of kin protection (Dawkins, 1976; S. E. Taylor, Klein, Lewis, Gruenewald, Gurung, & Updegraff, 2000), social exchange (Foa & Foa, 1975), capitulation to social norms (L. Berkowitz, 1972), or garden-variety egoism (Cialdini, 1991), other theorists have noted that humans sometimes display altruism where the possibility of any advantageous outcome is quite remote, and suggest that empathy and sympathy underlie such admirable behaviors (Batson, 2001; Knight, Johnson, Carlo, & Eisenberg, 1994; Zahn-Waxler, Radke-Yarrow, & King, 1983). Moreover, sympathy can sometimes lead us to violate the principles of fairness, supporting the notion that altruism and justice are independent prosocial motivations (Batson, Klein, Highberger, & Shaw, 1995). Regardless of the real reasons for altruism and prosocial behaviors among humans, the fact remains that we are quite capable of and often

willing to engage in acts of generosity, kindness, or benevolence that are consensually recognized and valued and that elevate those who witness them (Haidt,
2000; see also Fredrickson, 2001).

Temperance

"Everything in moderation," or so the saying goes. Temperance is the virtue of
control over excess. Usually the term is used as a signifier for abstinence, particularly from several of the more pleasant appetites—eating, drinking, smoking, sex.
We mean the term more generally to include any form of auspicious self-restraint.

For instance, temperance translated into psychological terminology becomes self-efficacy or self-regulation, that practiced ability to monitor and
manage one's emotions, motivation, and behavior in the absence of outside help
(Bandura, 1997; Kopp & Wyer, 1994), the failure of which leads rather impressively to all sorts of personal and social problems (Baumeister, Heatherton, &
Tice, 1994; Block, Gjerde, & Block, 1991; Eisenberg, Fabes, Guthrie, & Reiser,
2000). All this shows, however, is that intemperance is unhealthy, not that temperance is all that great. On the plus side, Baumeister and Exline (2000) stated,
"Having strength of character means having the capacity to do what is right and
avoid what is wrong. Self-control, when applied to adaptive or virtuous goals,
is essentially that capacity" (p. 33). Indeed, children, adolescents, and adults who
consistently exercise the muscle of self-control are happier, more productive,
and more successful individuals (Eisenberg et al., 2000; Mischel, Shoda, & Peake,
1988; Pintrich, 2000; Tsui & Ashford, 1994; Zimmerman, 2002). Moreover, because the individual benefits of temperance tend to prompt social ones,
Heatherton and Vohs (1998) argued for the natural selection of self-control,
pointing out that "inhibitions are important for harmonious social interactions,
and evolution has undoubtedly favored those who could control undesirable
impulses" (p. 212). Thus, temperance is a form of self-denial that is ultimately
generous to the self or others—prudence and humility are prime examples.

Transcendence

The transcendent, according to Kant (1781/1998), is that which is beyond human knowledge. We define it here in the broad sense as the connection to something higher—the belief that there is meaning or purpose larger than ourselves.
Transcendence, in other words, is the opposite of nihilism, the contention that
life has no meaning.

In *Man's Search for Meaning*, Frankl (1946/1984) described what he termed
the self-transcendence of human existence:

> Being human always points, and is directed, to something, or someone,
> other than oneself—be it a meaning to fulfill or another human being to

encounter. The more one forgets himself—by giving himself to a cause to serve or another person to love—the more human he is and the more he actualizes himself. (p. 133)

We follow this lead and separate transcendence from religiosity or even spirituality, although both of the latter concepts are examples of what transcendence means. Whereas religiosity implies connection to formal institutions and spirituality does not, both refer to beliefs and practices regarding the sacred, defined as a divine being, higher power, or ultimate reality (L. K. George, Larson, Koenig, & McCullough, 2000; see also Gallup & Jones, 2000). We believe that what is transcendent does need to be sacred but does not need to be divine. Thus, transcendence can be something or someone earthly that inspires awe, hope, or even gratitude—anything that makes our everyday concerns seem trifling and the self seem small. Transcendence, in other words, is that which reminds us of how tiny we are but that simultaneously lifts us out of a sense of complete insignificance.

Wisdom

What distinguishes wisdom? It is a type of intelligence but not one synonymous with IQ, *g* (general intelligence), or academic honors. It is knowledge, yes, but not reducible to the mere sum of books read, or lectures attended, or facts acquired. Perhaps it has something to do with living through hardship, emerging a better person able to share what has been learned with others.

"Wisdom," wrote Kramer (2000), "involves exceptional breadth and depth of knowledge about the conditions of life and human affairs and reflective judgment about the application of this knowledge" (p. 84). According to the researchers at the Berlin Max Planck Institute, wisdom is "good judgment and advice about important but uncertain matters of life" (Baltes & Smith, 1990, p. 87). Erikson (1963) believed wisdom to be the lasting outcome of a favorable resolution of the last psychosocial stage of adult life—ego integrity (acceptance of the triumphs and disappointments of one's life) versus despair (the ultimate belief that one's life has been wasted). And Sternberg (1998) argued that wisdom:

is involved when practical intelligence is applied to maximizing not just one's own or someone else's self-interest, but rather a balance of various self-interests (intrapersonal) with the interests of others (interpersonal) and of other aspects of the context in which one lives (extrapersonal), such as one's city or country or environment or even God. (p. 354)

Hence we define this core virtue as knowledge hard fought for, and then used for good. Wisdom is a form of noble intelligence—in the presence of which no one is resentful and everyone appreciative. The strengths that wisdom encompasses are those entailing the acquisition and use of knowledge into human affairs, such as creativity, curiosity, judgment, and perspective.

■ The High Six Across History and Culture

We now show in detail how each of these six core virtues is evident in the traditions of China, followed by those of South Asia and then those of the West.

China

The two indigenous traditions of China arose contemporaneously in the sixth century B.C.E., and there is argument as to whether they best represent a philosophical, social, or religious system of beliefs. Confucianism, with its emphasis on social criticism and education of the young, became the official state religion by the second century B.C.E. Likewise, early Taoism, though more mystical and esoteric, was a religious-philosophical tradition with its own political exhortations.

Confucian Virtues.   The teachings of Confucius (551–479 B.C.E.) are the most influential in the history of Chinese thought and civilization. His moral and political philosophy, with its prescriptive focus on education and leadership, became the official religion of China by the second century B.C.E. and compulsory study for 2,000 years beyond that (Smart, 1999).

His teachings were recorded mainly in the form of aphorisms, most reliably collected in the *Analects* (Confucius, trans. 1992). His comments on virtue are scattered across the *Analects*, not presented as a formal catalog. There is, however, a general agreement among scholars that there are four or five central virtues espoused in the tenets of Confucianism: *jen* (translated variously as humanity or human-heartedness or benevolence), *yi* (duty or justice or equity), *li* (etiquette or observance of the rites of ceremonious behavior), *zhi* (wisdom or perspicacity), and, possibly, *xin* (truthfulness or sincerity or good faith) (see Cleary, 1992; Do-Dinh, 1969; Haberman, 1998a).

When asked to define humanity (*jen*), Confucius answered, "Love people" (12:22); when asked to operationalize it, he said "If you want to make a stand, help others make a stand, and if you want to reach your goal, help others reach their goal. Consider yourself and treat others accordingly: this is the method of humanity" (6:29). Scholars have described Confucian humanity as the ideal manifestation of human nature or the attitude of sympathetic concern when dealing with others, but not the selfless love exalted in, say, Christianity; acting with humanity is instrumental in that it brings similar treatment from others (Dawson, 1982; Ivanhoe, 2002).

Humanity is considered the virtue most exalted by Confucius, as throughout the *Analects* the core sentiment that constitutes humanity permeates and infuses all others. For instance, the Confucian ideal of duty (*yi*) is not one prescribing humble acquiescence of the many to the undeserving and powerful few; rather, it denotes the mutual respect persons should have in relation to one another, beginning with the familial relationship and extending outward to the state and citizen (Huang, 1997). Put another way, the Confucian notion of justice or duty is not permission for tyranny, as it has often been misinterpreted, but that one is obliged to act honorably and with self-control in all personal affairs rather than with a motive for personal gain: Confucius said, "The noble-minded are clear about duty; little people are clear about profit" (4:16). Dawson (1982), noting the significance in Confucius's contrast of duty and profit, states, "[Duty's] original sense seems to have been natural justice, what seemed just to the natural man before concepts like law and ritual were evolved. . . . it is clearly regarded as the ultimate yardstick against which matters of law and ritual must be judged" (p. 52).

The Confucian precept of good etiquette (*li*) is also best understood as a directive to treat others sensitively: Confucius said, "To master oneself and return to courtesy is humaneness" (12:1). Thus the cultivation of courteousness and deference in one's everyday behavior is the equivalent of the cultivation of humanity, as manners and deference are concerned more with consideration for another's feelings than they are with strict adherence to rules and empty ceremonial custom. Confucian wisdom (*zhi*) is best understood as the functional application of an informed intellect to humanity, justice, and etiquette, while truthfulness (*xin*) is that which is exemplified by fidelity to the ideals of the four preceding virtues (Cleary, 1992).

Confucius does not explicitly mention temperance, but its importance to the humane life is strongly implied. The importance placed on rites presumably involves a respect for propriety and self-control as much as for humanity. Indeed, in both his personal affairs and the *Analects*, Confucius advocated modesty and self-control. Though he could have lived quite comfortably in the employ of many a noble, Confucius instead chose the relatively modest life of a teacher; though known as sage Master Kong to his students, Confucius still argued that true humanity was an impossible ideal for most mortals to attain, including himself (7:33–34). In the *Analects*, he commends as virtuous those who choose to live simply (6:10), refrain from self-aggrandizing boasts (6:14) or extravagance (3:4), and place hard work before reward (6:22).

Another core virtue not explicitly named as of central importance is transcendence. The Chinese did not believe in a divine lawgiver, and Confucius's philosophical focus was clearly on the secular and rational aspects of human functioning, not the cosmic or spiritual (5:13; 11:12). This is not to say Confucius completely ignored the transcendent or that he relegated it to a nonsignificant role (D. L. Hall & Ames, 1987). For instance, excellence in moral conduct is afforded the status of the transcendent: Confucius invoked heaven when discussing the origin of virtue (7:23) and his reverence for sages whose perfect virtue was modeled after the divine (6.17; 16.8; see also Haberman, 1998a).

Taoist Virtues.   The Taoist tradition is the second indigenous one of China. Its creator, Lao-tzu (ca. 570 B.C.E.–?), is said to be a contemporary of Confucius, although there is some debate regarding whether he is one sage or many, and whether the primary work attributed to him, the *Tao Te Ching* (or *The Classic of Tao and Its Virtue*; trans. 1963), came much later than he may have lived (A. C. Graham, 1998; Kohn, 1998; Lynn, 1999).

The central tenet is one of transcendence: The Tao, or Way, that governs the heavens and earth is indescribable, unknowable, and even unnameable (*Tao Te Ching*, trans. 1963, chap. 1). And untranslatable—the Way (its Chinese character depicts a head in motion) refers simultaneously to direction, movement, method, and thought, and so no single word can depict the profundity of its total meaning. Moreover, it is the creator of all things, including virtue (*Te*), but does not act—the Way is spontaneous and without effort (Cheng, 2000; Wong, 1997).

The text of the *Tao Te Ching*, however, can be cryptic and mysterious, and thus attempts, particularly Western ones, to interpret its verses can never be definitive (see Clarke, 2000; LaFargue, 1998). Like Confucius, Lao-tzu attempted to use his philosophy to reform rulers and improve society, but the emphasis was not on virtue as social interaction (Cheng, 2000). For instance, in a particularly famous passage, Lao-tzu seems to advise *against* wisdom, justice, and humanity—the very virtues that Confucius esteemed (as well as what we are arguing are core virtues found even in this tradition):

> Reject sageness and abandon knowledge,
> The people will benefit a hundredfold.
> Reject humanity and abandon justice,
> The people will return to filial piety and parental love. (chap. 19)

Of course, no Taoist scholar argues that Lao-tzu was advocating anarchy, or even a society lacking in these things. Rather, it appears that what Lao-tzu believed in most was the virtue of "naturalness" or "spontaneity" (*tzu-jan*), or that quality of being without effort. Indeed, scholars tend to agree that naturalness is the cardinal virtue of Taoism, with nonaction (*wu-wei*) as the essential method to realize naturalness in social life (Cheng, 2000; Xiaogan, 1998).

Hence, it is not that Lao-tzu argued that rulers should be unjust but that the most justice comes from reigning without ruling (Xiaogan, 1998) or ruling with naturalness:

> The best ruler, the people only know of his existence. . . .
> The best ruler is so relaxed, he hardly talks.
> when he successfully completes his work,
> People all say that for us, it is only natural. (chap. 17, see also chap. 57)

The point is that Lao-tzu esteemed other virtues, but only if they arise from the higher one of spontaneity; later in the *Tao Te Ching* he explicitly cites as important the virtues of humanity, justice, and propriety, but only after (or in the presence of) this higher one (chap. 38, see also Cheng, 2000).

Likewise, wisdom is espoused in both rulers and commoners, but only if that knowledge is the true sort of the Way, not the superficial sort used for cunning: A sage ruler is "a man of subtlety [but] with deep insight," (chap. 15); he does not "insist on his own views, thus he has a clear view," nor does he "justify himself, thus he sees the truth" (chap. 22; see also chaps. 3, 19, 33, 49; and Schwartz, 1994). And temperance, in terms of both humility and restraint from pursuing the false gods of material wealth and privilege, is advocated again and again: "He who becomes arrogant with wealth and power . . . sows the seeds of his own misfortune [chap. 9] . . . he who boasts of his own achievements harms his credibility . . . he who is arrogant experiences no growth in wisdom [chap. 24] . . . he who knows glory, but keeps to humility . . . is sufficient in the eternal virtue [chap. 28]."

South Asia

As with China, there are two main branches of indigenous South Asian religious-philosophical thought. Though its importance has faded there, Buddhism had its origins in South Asia and only later went on to join Confucianism and Taoism as one of the three great traditions of China. Hinduism evolved over thousands of years through the integration of the many religions native to the Indian subcontinent and today remains the region's predominant religion.

Buddhist Virtues.   Buddhism is a philosophical-religious tradition of great variety and far reach—its tenets and practices extend from its birthplace in South Asia to China, Tibet, Korea, Japan, Thailand, Indonesia, and beyond. The origin of all teachings, however, may be traced to the Buddha (563?–483? B.C.E.), or "Enlightened One," who lived at the same time as Confucius and six centuries before Christ. Canonical texts describe his renunciation of his traditional and comfortable life in favor of a search for the end to the chronic suffering of life, death, and rebirth (*samsara*). After years of travel, asceticism, and yogic meditation, the Buddha came upon the path to enlightenment, to *nirvana*— the ultimate destiny of existence, the state of bliss brought on by an effacement of the self and its desires (Bhatt, 2001). The Buddha believed that anyone, with the right sort of practice, could reach nirvana, and he spent the rest of his life teaching people the way to it (Dutt, 1983).

If there can be said to be a fundamental virtue catalog in classical Buddhism, it is the Holy Eightfold Path, a subset of the more inclusive doctrine of the Four Noble Truths *(arya satyani)*, which the Buddha preached at his very first sermon. The Noble Truths are that life is suffering; the cause of this suffering is the "birth sin" of craving or desire; suffering ceases only upon nirvana, the extinction of desire; and nirvana may be achieved only by following the Holy Path (or Middle Way), an eight-pronged strategy to counteract the innate tendency to desire. In turn, the Holy Eightfold Path invokes the notion of perfection or right in one's understanding, thinking, speech, action, livelihood, effort, mindfulness, and concentration (see M. Fowler, 1999; also *Dhammapada*, trans. 2000).

The components of the Eightfold Path have been divided still further into a three-step plan of action consisting of virtue (*sila*), meditation (*samadhi*), and wisdom (*prajña*). The third (right speech), fourth (right action), and fifth steps (right livelihood) involve virtue; six (right effort), seven (right mindfulness), and eight (right concentration) involve meditation; and one (right understanding) and two (right thinking) involve wisdom. The strategy of the Path and the philosophy behind it invoke the core virtues of humanity, justice, temperance, transcendence, and wisdom. Examples, for instance, of virtue as described by various canonical texts include avoiding lies and gossip; abstaining from stealing, killing, or other bad deeds; and earning one's living in a way that does not violate the Path—a Buddhist could not work as a hunter or butcher (Klostermaier, 1999).

A later Buddhist virtue catalog is suggested by what is known as the Five Virtues or Precepts (*pañca-sila*). These are ritually chanted abstentions from harming living things; taking what is not given (theft or fraud); misconduct concerning sense pleasures; false speech (lying); and unmindful states caused by alcoholic drinks or drugs (see P. Harvey, 1990). One can see notions of humanity and justice in the first, second, and fourth precepts, and strong directives toward temperance or self-restraint in the third and fifth precepts.

Finally, there are the four Universal Virtues (*apramana*; also known as "immeasurables") of Buddhism. These are also mentioned in various canonical texts, concern the practical (as opposed to theoretical) aspects of Buddhism, and clearly advocate humanity. They are benevolence (*maitri*), compassion (*karuna*), joy (*mudita*), and equanimity (*upeksa*; see Nagao, 2000).

Buddhism, with its emphasis on nonduality and enlightenment, is a forthrightly transcendent tradition. It is also—due to its fundamental tenet of the impermanence of all things, including the self—one most likely to frustrate Western hermeneutic endeavors. Armstrong (2001) warned against interpreting the *action* section of the Eightfold Path as some sort of collection of moral directives—to do so would be to blur Buddhist teaching (i.e., that voluntary adherence to these precepts helps remove hindrances to clarity and enlightenment) with Western notions of obeisance to a higher power. It is also important to note that Buddhist "virtues" are not metaphysically stable entities (because there are no stable entities in Buddhism) such as they are in many traditions; rather, they are thought or behavior tendencies designed to ultimately end the frustration of desire and craving.

Hindu Virtues.   The collection of sacred texts known as the *Upanishads* deal with spiritual and metaphysical aspects of Hinduism; the earliest of these texts appear to date to the sixth or seventh century B.C.E., marking their existence slightly before the rise of Buddhism. The oldest, the *Brihad Aranyaka Upanishad,* elucidates some of the central theological tenets of early and modern-day Hinduism: the unifying principle of brahman, the sacred absolute power and the creator of the universe; the related notion of the interconnectedness of all things, as all ultimately extends back to brahman; and the cycle of rebirth, which comes from the blending of the self and brahman (Haberman, 1998b; Leaman, 1999). Hinduism and Buddhism diverge in the notion of the self: In the former tradition, the self is eternal, universal, indistinguishable from brahman; in the latter there is no permanent self and no ultimate creator (P. Harvey, 1990).

The emphasis in Hinduism is on personal virtues, such as self-denial and renunciation; these promote self-improvement in the current life and a potential for salvation or the attainment of a higher caste in the next. Hence, one catalog of Hindu virtues, as narrated in the sacred text of the *Bhagavadgita* (trans. 1990), is unsurprisingly intertwined with the notion of caste. This text describes a stratified caste society consisting of the Brahmins (educated aristocrats), Kshatriyas (soldiers), Vaisyas (agricultural and lower-trade laborers), and Sudras (menial laborers). Each of the four castes is distinguished by the characteristic virtues exhibited by its members: The spirituality of the Brahmin shows itself in penance, self-control, forbearance, purity, rectitude, knowledge, experience, and faith; the qualities ascribed to the soldier caste include those of valor (or courage in battle), skill, glory, fortitude, and charity (generosity); the lower castes are assigned the virtues of dutiful performance of labor—little is expected in the way of spiritual and intellectual achievement for these people in their current life (XVIII, 40–45).

Hinduism, with its emphasis on personal improvement, echoes Buddhism but contrasts sharply with the Confucian (and later Athenian) belief in virtue as citizenship. And though their meanings have some cultural specificity, the core virtues are present thematically within the Hindu tradition. Consider wisdom: Although the Hindu (and Buddhist) ideal of attainment of transcendental knowledge of the self does not directly compare with the Confucian notion of the importance of wisdom gained through education and experience, the theme of coming to a higher knowledge is central to all traditions. Transcendence, as invoked by the concept of brahman, is diffused throughout the *Bhagavadgita;* and examples of justice (rectitude), courage (valor), temperance (self-restraint), and humanity (charity) all make their appearance as virtues attributed to specific castes. Notice also that the concept of justice is interwoven with the Hindu belief that actions in one life help to determine caste status in the next. That the text ascribes different virtues for different castes does not argue for nonubiquity within the culture—indeed, it is difficult to imagine that Hindu culture advocates bravery for soldiers and cowardice for everyone else.

The West

In the West, the very first Greek philosophers asked, "What is the good of a person?" This framing of character led thinkers like Plato, Socrates, and Aristotle to examine and enumerate virtues as traits of character. As mentioned in chapter 3, moral philosophy changed with the growing influence of Judeo-Christianity (and later Islam), which saw God as the giver of laws by which one should live and virtue as obeisance to his edicts—shifting the focus of Western discourse on morality from that of inner character to observable actions.

Athenian Virtues.   The first major virtue catalog of the West was articulated by Plato (427–347 B.C.E.) in the *Republic*, his magnum opus on the ideal human society. Here Plato, using Socrates as his mouthpiece, proposes wisdom (*sophia*), courage (*andreia*), self-restraint (*sôphrosune*), and justice (*dikaisunê*) as the four core virtues of the ideal city (trans. 1968; IV, 427e ff.). He argues that these constitute a class-based hierarchy of civic virtues that has its anchor in the makeup of the individual soul (IV, 441c ff.). That is, the desirable division of civic virtues—wisdom belongs to the ruling class, courage to that of the soldier class—is mirrored in an individual's healthily functioning psychology. The soul has its divisions, and to each belongs a virtue—wisdom is exercised by reason, courage by the "spirited" part, self-restraint is imposed on the appetite. In both the civic and individual cases, justice (moral action) will occur when each division is properly carrying out its assigned task (IV, 443d–e; see Johansen, 1998). This Platonic vision of virtue is particularly comparable to the Hindu notion outlined earlier in this chapter: Virtues are categorized along professional and class lines, with the rulers complementary to the Brahmins in their position as virtue specialists.

In the *Nicomachean Ethics*, Aristotle (384–322 B.C.E.), Plato's most accomplished student, picks up the argument that virtuous behavior is a social practice exercised by a citizen of an ideal city (trans. 2000, V.I, 1129a ff.). For Aristotle, virtue is an acquired skill learned through trial and error. Related to this is his characterization of virtue known as the *doctrine of the mean:* One encounters a situation and, basing the decision on reason, experience, and context, picks a course of action from between two extremes of disposition, those of deficiency or excess. The mean between these two *is* virtue (1107a). Generosity, for instance, is the mean between wastefulness and stinginess (1120a); courageousness is the mean between cowardliness or rashness (1116a).

Aristotle's list of the virtues includes the original Platonic four (courage, justice, temperance, wisdom), but to these he adds quite a number of others, such as generosity, wit, friendliness, truthfulness, magnificence, and greatness of soul (Aristotle, trans. 2000, IV). The latter two might sound strange to the modern reader: Magnificence has to do with spending lavishly, though in a tasteful way, on honorable items such as sacrifices or warships (IV.II); greatness of soul refers to thinking oneself worthy of great things, particularly honor (IV.III).

In neither Plato's nor Aristotle's account is transcendence given the official status of virtue. But, as was also the case with Confucius, the notion of transcendence as a crucial good suffuses the works. In the *Republic,* Plato described how the ideal city would be governed; philosophers, whose inner constitution of virtue is such that they are above selfish interests, should rule. But he admits that this state is yet to be realized on Earth, and mortal man must look to the heavens to find its model (IX, 592 a–b). Aristotle invoked the transcendent when he discussed the relationship of virtue and happiness (*eudaimonia*). For Aristotle, happiness is "activity in accordance with virtue" (X.VII. 1177a). He told us in the last book of the *Nicomachean Ethics* that, of all the virtues, wisdom is the most perfect, and the exercise of it—contemplation—constitutes perfect happiness (X.VII, 1177a). A life of contemplation, of perfect eudaimonia, is transcendent because it indicates a "divine element" within the individual and so is an ideal for which to strive. He stated, "If intellect, then, is something divine compared with the human being, the life in accordance with it will also be divine compared with human life" (X.VII, 1177b).

Likewise, humanity (kindness, love) is never specifically named as a virtue in either Athenian account, but notions of shared humanity, of the importance of friendship, of generosity and charitable acts, of giving others pleasure and not pain, are scattered across both works (e.g., Plato, trans. 1968, II, 372b, II, 376b–c, V, 471a–b; Aristotle, trans. 2000, IV.I, IV.VI, VIII.I).

Judeo-Christian Virtues.   The account of the Seven Heavenly Virtues, the classic Christian enumeration of human strengths, is described in Aquinas's (1224–1274) doctrinal work *Summa Theologiae* (trans. 1989). Because the work is celebrated as a successful interpretation of Aristotelian (pagan) philosophy with Christian theology, we will present this text prior to Jewish ones, and hence out of chronological order.

In his virtue catalog, Aquinas deleted all of Aristotle's additions to Plato. He constructed his list by retaining the cardinal virtues of temperance, courage, justice, and wisdom and then adding the three theological virtues proposed by Saint Paul: faith, hope, and charity (or love). Aquinas argues for a hierarchical organization of the virtues—of the cardinal virtues, wisdom is the most important, but the transcendent virtues of faith and hope are more important than that, and of all the seven, charity (love) reigns supreme:

> Having faith and hope in something beyond our human power exceeds all human virtue. As activities faith precedes hope and hope charity; though as dispositions they are all instilled together. . . . but charity is more perfect than faith and hope which, without charity, are not perfect. So charity is the mother and root of all virtue. (II-8, Q. 62, arts. 3–4)

Note that within the Seven Heavenly Virtues, Aquinas enumerated what we believe are the six core virtues: He presents the four cardinal virtues by name, invokes transcendence with the virtues of faith and hope, and humanity with the virtue of charity.

Within the Old Testament, two sections are particularly illustrative of virtues esteemed by Jewish culture: the account of the Ten Commandments received by Moses in Exodus and two books of Proverbs that specifically instruct on the consequences of virtues and vices. The Ten Commandments is a list of "thou shalt's" and "thou shalt not's" from which conclusions regarding the virtues advocated in this tradition may be drawn. The Commandments forbid polytheism, idolatry, taking God's name in vain, murder, adultery, theft, lying, and covetousness, while commanding that the Sabbath be kept holy, and parents honored (Exodus 20:1–17, Revised Standard Version). Justice is implied in prohibitions against murder, theft, and lying; temperance in those against adultery and covetousness; and transcendence generally within the divine origin of the commands.

Sage instructions to Jewish youth on moral and religious behavior are the main concerns of Proverbs. The opening lines of the first book of Proverbs are a call to edification and are quite clear in distinguishing those virtues that Judaism esteems:

> That men may know wisdom and instruction,
> understand the words of insight,
> receive instruction in wise dealing, righteousness, justice, and equity;
> that prudence may be given to the simple,
> knowledge and discretion to the youth.
> The wise man also may hear and increase in learning,
> and the man of understanding acquire skill,
> to understand a proverb and a figure,
> the words of the wise and their riddles. (1:2–6)

Books II (10:1–22:16) and IV (25:1–29:27) of Proverbs are attributed to Solomon and deal specifically with recommendations for virtuous behavior (as well as admonitions against vice). Many of the maxims given here are particularly well known ("A soft answer turns away wrath, but a harsh word stirs up anger," "Hearken to your father who begot you, and despise not your mother when she is old," and "A man without self-control is like a city broken into and left without walls") and are contained within verses 15, 23, and 26, respectively. The verses of Proverbs are plentiful, and many virtues are advocated, often repeatedly. They include integrity (courage); righteousness, just leadership, trustworthiness (justice); love, graciousness, and kindness (humanity); diligence, prudence, humility, and restraint (temperance); hope and fear/love of God (transcendence); and understanding, knowledge, and respect for instruction and teaching (wisdom).

Islamic Virtues.   Islam's core beliefs and practices were formed during and shortly after the life of Muhammad (570–632 C.E.). Revelations communicated to him by the angel Gabriel, recorded in 114 chapters of scripture known as the Koran ("recitation"), founded Muhammad's claim to being Jesus' successor and the last of the prophets. The revelations also established the foundation for his further teaching, which quickly developed into the organized Islamic faith (Leaman, 2002).

Though differing from Judaism and Christianity in crucial ways, Islam nonetheless was influenced by and includes some of these religions' values (Mahdi, 2001). The ideas presented in the Koran are thought to have germinated the tendency to philosophic thought; in turn, the main influence on the development of Islamic philosophy is thought to be the Greeks, though with some Indian strains (Dunlop, 1971).

Islamic philosophy is distinguished from much of the rest of the West by the central inclusion and importance of God (Leaman, 2002). Mahdi (2001) wrote that the "single attitude" that has historically characterized the Islamic community is "gratitude for the revelation and divine law" (p. 17), and so not surprisingly the transcendent plays a central and powerful role in most of the early philosophical texts.

Alfarabi (870–950 C.E.) is distinguished as the "first outstanding logician and metaphysician of Islam" (Fakhry, 1983, p. 107). He is also known for his numerous interpretive works of Platonic and Aristotelian philosophy, and his most concise virtue catalog, given in *Fusul al-Madani* (*Aphorisms of the Statesman;* trans. 1961; also known simply as *Selected Aphorisms*, trans. 2001), is highly reminiscent of theirs. Alfarabi's discussion of virtue, though rare in its relative omission of the divine, is presented here because he is generally regarded as the founder of Islamic philosophy.

Fusul al-Madani is composed of 96 aphorisms that deal with, broadly, the health of the soul. Specifically, Alfarabi describes the government that best nourishes the individual soul in its quest for perfection. Again, this is a forthrightly political work: Alfarabi does not specifically invoke the Prophet, and he mentions the revelation and philosophy only rarely; rather, his focus is on the city-state, and he constantly mentions and describes the activities of the ideal citizen and ruler (Butterworth, 2001).

Much of Alfarabi's catalog will be familiar: Justice in the city-state is of central concern, and virtue is said to be the middle way between two extremes; this echoes Aristotle's earlier doctrine of the mean (trans. 2000, aphs. 61–67). He borrows again from the Athenians when he presents the notion of the divided soul: The soul is split into the Rational and the Appetitive, and the exercise of each part comprises the corresponding Rational and Moral virtues (aphs. 8–9).

It appears that the virtues of the former category are the personal virtues of contemplation; those in the second are the social virtues invoked in dealings with others. Those included in the Rational category are "wisdom, intellect, cleverness, quick-wittedness, and excellent understanding"; those of the Ethical category are "moderation, courage, liberality (generosity), and justice" (aph. 8). Hence, we see a repetition of the Platonic virtues, with a humanity virtue (generosity) added and afforded equal standing. Despite his specific omission of the Prophet, transcendence is present in Alfarabi's account, for he contends that religion and philosophy can be harmonized, and that the exercise of virtue is in itself a spiritual act (e.g., aphs. 68, 81, 86–87, 94).

■ Convergence, Caveats, and Conclusions

The impetus for this exercise was our attempt to create a consensual classification of human strengths while avoiding the criticism that any specific list we proposed would be culturally and historically idiosyncratic. The primary lesson we learn from the historical exercise described in this chapter is that there is a strong convergence across time, place, and intellectual tradition about certain core virtues. As one tradition bled into another, as one catalog infused and then gave way to the next, particular virtues recurred with pleasant tenacity. Although others may appear on some lists and then be lost again, certain virtues, either explicitly or thematically, had real staying power.

Caveats are in order. First, it makes good sense to ask whether all of the High Six are equally ubiquitous. Probably not. Justice and humanity show up the most reliably in that they make every tradition's list; they tend to be named explicitly; and we suspect, given their crucial importance to the survival of even the smallest society, that they are truly universal (Bok, 1995; de Waal, 2000; Ridley, 1996). Temperance and wisdom finish a close second: At least in our survey of the "Great Three" cultures with their long literary traditions, they appear reliably and usually explicitly. Transcendence seems the next most ubiquitous, finishing fifth only because it is the most "implicit" of the core six: Transcendence is rarely nominated explicitly, but the notion that there is a higher meaning or purpose to life, be it religiously underpinned or not, infuses each tradition to the extent that in some decidedly nonreligious entries (such as Plato or Confucius), the notion of virtue serving heaven or the gods seems taken for granted. Finally, courage is very explicitly nominated (usually as physical valor) on most lists but is missing even thematically from others, such as those from the Buddhist, Taoist, and Confucian traditions. We doubt this means bravery is not valued in these traditions, and the more modern definitions of courage discussed earlier can be detected in their classic literatures (cf. Yearley, 1990). We preferred not to do that here, but we do discuss Chinese conceptions of bravery in chapter 9.

Second, we find enormous variability across cultures in terms of what the culture esteems. Whereas each tradition nominated some number of virtues as proper or necessary for the well-lived life, no two lists were identical, and, not surprisingly, many virtues we encountered fell by the wayside because they failed the test of ubiquity, even by expanded and fuzzy criteria. Among culture-bound (nonubiquitous) virtues, a number are very familiar to those of us in the here and now, for example, glory. Other culture-bound virtues seem very exotic from our vantage point, for example, magnificence and naturalness. One virtue—perhaps best termed "duty"—was even a contender for core virtue status. Highly stratified cultures, specifically those described in the Confucian, Hindu, and Platonic traditions, tended to champion role-related duty or class-defined virtues, but these concepts were not present among the other traditions (plus there is good evidence that at least some part of Confucian duty relates to ubiquitous notions of justice). All these examples of nonubiquitous virtues are of course important and deserve serious attention by psychologists, but they were not the main concern of this exercise. We hope that as our classification project evolves, we can turn to these less ubiquitous, culture-bound virtues.

Third, all the traditions we surveyed come from literate, large, and long-lived societies with cities, money, law, and division of labor. None of these cultures existed in total isolation from the others (e.g., the Jewish scholars of the Middle Ages read Aristotle). We do not pretend to know if the High Six characterizes small or short-lived or nonliterate or hunter-gatherer societies.

To summarize, our survey of influential religious and philosophical traditions reveals six broad virtue classes to be ubiquitous. This conclusion has important implications for our attempt to classify positive traits. Most significantly, we have a nonarbitrary basis for focusing on certain virtues rather than others. Much of the ongoing societal discourse on "character" is tilted in one direction or another by less than universal political and personal values. Although our classification is decidedly about such values, it is descriptive of what is ubiquitous, rather than prescriptive or idiosyncratic.

As explained in chapter 1, we use these core virtues to organize our longer list of more specific character strengths. We opt for this strategy for several reasons, including the aforementioned complexity of the general virtues. In each case, we can think of several ways to achieve the general virtue, and our eventual measurement goal led us to focus on these more specific routes (what we term strengths) to the High Six. Thus, the virtue of "humanity" is achieved by the strengths of kindness and generosity on the one hand versus loving and being loved on the other. The virtue of temperance similarly has several routes: modesty and humility, self-control and self-regulation, and prudence and caution. The practical implication of this classification is that it suggests which character strengths are similar and which are not.

The ubiquity of these core virtues suggests the possibility of universality and eventually a deep theory about moral excellence phrased in evolutionary terms (Wright, 1994). One possibility is that these are purely cultural: acquired characteristics that long-lived, moneyed, literate, citified societies with massive division of labor select for. Another possibility is that the High Six are purely biological, that they define the "moral animal." And a third possibility, the one we lean to, is that they are evolutionarily predisposed. These particular styles of behaving may have emerged, been selected for, and been sustained because each allows a crucial survival problem to be solved. Without biologically predisposed mechanisms that allowed our ancestors to generate, recognize, and celebrate corrective virtues, their social groups would have died out quickly. The ubiquitous virtues, we believe, are what allow the human animal to struggle against and to triumph over what is darkest within us.

3. PREVIOUS CLASSIFICATIONS OF CHARACTER STRENGTHS

So far, we have overviewed the classification, focusing on the criteria we used for identifying character strengths (chapter 1), and we have described our historical survey leading to the conclusion that six core virtues—wisdom, courage, humanity, justice, temperance, and transcendence—recur across time and place (chapter 2). In the present chapter, we present more background by describing previous classifications of character strengths and the lessons we learned from them while devising the classification. We focus on the contributions of psychologists but touch as well on how other fields have unpacked the notion of good character. In discussing these previous classifications of character strengths, we compare and contrast them with the present classification. Seeing how other thinkers have classified character in particular helped us to articulate the critera for designating positive traits as character strengths.

■ Lessons From Virtue Catalogs

As mentioned in chapter 1, we collected many dozens of inventories of virtues and strengths, from historical and contemporary sources. We ended up calling these statements virtue catalogs because they occupy a place somewhere between mere lists and more formal classifications.

A catalog intends to be exhaustive and to have mutually exclusive categories. It aspires to stability because it needs to be useful not just now but in the future. Think of a college catalog: It should list all the courses that might be offered to students in the next several semesters. Or think of an L. L. Bean catalog: It should list all the products the company is offering for sale to yuppies that season. These properties of a catalog—exhaustiveness and stability—are together termed its *coverage*. Coverage cannot be judged out of context. One must keep in mind the purpose of the catalog. Who will use it, and why? The *DSM*, for example, has good coverage for the purpose of inpatient psychiatrists, who need to describe to third-party payers the sorts of psychological problems that result in hospitalization, but it has poor coverage for vocational counselors who need to describe the issues and problems of people in the workplace (cf. Schacht & Nathan, 1977).

The typical purpose of virtue catalogs is to provide a language for moral evaluation and discourse, to state the important goals for which individuals and organizations should strive. What these catalogs all leave unsaid is how to recognize progress toward these goals or even what the goals might mean in concrete (measurable) terms. Witness the flap encountered several years ago by the Boy Scouts of America when they tried to interpret their very general value statements in terms of specific sexual orientations.[1] This shortcoming of catalogs illustrates why they do not qualify as scientific classifications. As a parsing strategy, a classification introduces explicit rules for deciding where entries go based on their features. Its rules allow the accommodation of new and potentially ambiguous entries.

Despite their limitations with respect to measurement, the virtue catalogs nonetheless helped us as we brainstormed potential entries for our classification. Had we left out any virtues or strengths deemed important by others, no matter how vaguely defined these might be? If we had left out a listed virtue or strength, did we have a good reason? Table 3.1 illustrates how our classification compares with well-known virtue catalogs by William Bennett (1993), the Boy Scouts of America (1998), Benjamin Franklin (1790/1961), Charlemagne (Turner, 1880), and Merlin (2001). Space does not permit a table with dozens of columns, but the exercise proved to work rather well for every catalog we collected. Across catalogs, all core virtue classes were represented and virtually all character strengths, with the exception of those phrased in modern psychological jargon (e.g., social intelligence). In any given catalog, some of the virtues and strengths we include in our classification were absent because they did not fit the purpose of the catalog in question. For example, humor and appreciation of beauty were not mentioned in the catalogs summarized in Table 3.1, but we have no problem including these in our classification even though some of our esteemed predecessors and contemporaries did not

In other cases, catalogs included strengths that did not fit our classification. Thus, in Table 3.1, the reader can see that cleanliness was explicitly men-

---

[1]We do not intend to criticize everything about the Boy Scouts of America. As is well known, the Boy Scouts award merit badges for proficiency in various areas of conduct, although none relates directly to moral virtues per se. Specific rules exist for deciding that a scout has the competency of concern, whether tying knots or studying amphibians and reptiles. Social scientists trying to devise behaviorally based measures could probably not improve upon these for face validity, clarity, and reliability. The problem the Boy Scouts encountered was in a non-merit-badge domain.

tioned by Benjamin Franklin and the Boy Scouts. Why did we not include it in our final list? We have nothing against hygiene, but in many sectors of the modern world in which running water and antibiotics are taken for granted, cleanliness is what we call a conspicuous-in-its-absence-only strength—not celebrated when present although certainly lamented when absent. Cleanliness therefore fails to satisfy a number of the criteria presented in chapter 1. In any event, a historical view of cleanliness reveals considerable religious significance (cf. the various taboos surrounding food and menstruation in Leviticus and elsehere), so perhaps these aspects of cleanliness indeed show up in the present classification under the rubric of spirituality.

■ Lessons From Psychology

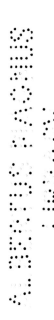

Once upon a time, psychologists were greatly interested in "character"—what it meant and how it could be cultivated (McCullough & Snyder, 2000). But for many reasons the topic fell out of favor. First, a growing sophistication among psychologists about how personal values could unintentionally pervade "objective" research and theory made researchers gun-shy about pronouncements concerning the psychological components of the good life. Gordon Allport, the main personality trait theorist in 20th-century United States psychology, explicitly banished the term *character* from academic discourse concerning personality (Nicholson, 1998). He argued that character was the subject matter of philosophy and not psychology (Allport, 1921, 1927; Allport & Vernon, 1930). The traits he urged psychologists to study were presumably objective entities (Allport dubbed them *neuropsychic structures*) stripped of moral significance and linked to "adjustment" but not imbued with inherent value.

Allport's argument reflected the positivism sweeping social science at this time and its rigid distinction between fact and value. Fact was the province of science, and value was the province of philosophy. Traits were therefore part of psychology, whereas character was not. Although Allport's argument won the day, not all his contemporaries agreed. John Dewey (1922/1998), for example, thought that character and virtue should be included in the subject matter of psychology and indeed that psychology's empirical methods could profitably inform discussions of value by philosophers. The present classification falls squarely within the Dewey vision.

Second, pressing social problems like violence, poverty, and racism as well as psychology's entry into the business of treating psychological disorders further shifted the attention of psychologists away from good character. Human ills of course demand attention. We are not critical of psychology's decision to study problems and devise remedies. We ourselves have spent the bulk of our careers studying psychological disorders. However, an exclusive focus on what is wrong with people can lead us to overlook what is right and precludes the

TABLE 3.1   *Selected Catalogs of Virtues and Strengths*

Character strength	William Bennett	Boy Scouts
Wisdom and knowledge		
Creativity	—	—
Curiosity/love of learning	—	—
Open-mindedness	—	—
Perspective	—	—
Courage		
Bravery	Courage	Brave
Persistence	Work; perseverance	—
Integrity	Honesty; responsibility	Trustworthy
Vitality	—	Cheerful
Humanity		
Love	Friendship	—
Kindness	Compassion	Helpful; friendly; kind
Social intelligence	—	—
Justice		
Citizenship	Loyalty	Loyalty; obedient
Fairness	—	—
Leadership	—	—
Temperance		
Forgiveness and mercy	—	—
Humility and modesty	—	—
Prudence	—	Thrifty; courteous
Moderation	—	—
Self-regulation	Self-discipline	—
Transcendence		
Appreciation of beauty	—	—
Gratitude	—	—
Hope	—	—
Humor	—	Cheerful
Spirituality	Faith	Reverent
Missing		
Cleanliness	—	Clean

Benjamin Franklin	Charlemagne	Merlin
—	—	—
—	—	Acquire knowledge
—	Render righteous judgment	—
Order	—	—
—	—	—
Resolution; industry	—	—
Sincerity	Do not consent to wrong; do not steal; do not perjure yourself	Love virtue; abhor evil
—	—	—
—	—	Love your neighbor
—	Be kind; do good to the weak	Be beloved by allmen
—	—	—
—	Serve the liege lord faithfully; defend the Church	Obedience
Justice	Be merciful to prisoners	—
—	—	When in authority, decide reasonably
—	Forgive as you hope to be forgiven	—
Humility	Be humble	—
Temperance; frugality	Shun excess in eating and drinking	—
—	—	—
Silence; tranquility; chastity	Persevere not in wrath	Fortitude
—	—	—
—	—	—
—	—	—
—	—	—
—	Love God almighty	—
Cleanliness	—	—

possibility that one of the best ways to undo someone's weakness is by encouraging his or her strengths.

Third, another concern of early psychology—the study of genius—became mired down in controversies surrounding intelligence tests, tarnishing by implication the study of character (Gould, 1981). Two babies were thrown out along with the bathwater of just one. As we began work on our classification, we constantly looked over our shoulders, fearing that we would be criticized as politically incorrect or insensitive. We have since discovered—happily—that a concern with good character resides in no single place along the political spectrum. The virtues and strengths on which we focus in this book are close to universally valued. We expect and invite criticism of our attempt to define and measure character strengths, but we do not anticipate this criticism to be on political grounds.

Fourth, the growing popularity of psychoanalytic theory led many psychologists to regard anything positive about people as suspect, the result of unconscious defenses that disguised our real motives—sex and aggression.[2] Even psychologists who would not have considered themselves Freudians participated in this debunking of the good life. Hope and optimism were dismissed as wishful thinking if not outright delusions. Ostensible altruism was viewed as just another strategy for personal gain. Courage was reinterpreted as deficiencies in those parts of the nervous system responsible for fear. And so on. We of course disagree, endorsing the position of positive psychology that human strengths are as authentic as human weaknesses.

Finally, before character fell off the radar screen of psychology, there were some apparent failures by researchers attempting to demonstrate the reality of positive traits. In 1928, Hartshorne and May undertook an ambitious study of moral conduct among school children. These investigators wanted to know if children had a general trait of honesty or dishonesty. Concretely, when given different opportunities to transgress, did the same children always step over the line? Hartshorne and May thought of many situations in which a young person might lie or cheat or steal. Settings included the home, the classroom, and the playground. Findings implied that moral conduct was not particularly consistent. Although correlations across situations were usually positive, they were not of great magnitude, suggesting that honesty was not a general trait.

Decades later, this study and others like it figured prominently in an influential argument by psychologist Walter Mischel (1968) challenging the assumption of consistency with respect to any personality trait. He surveyed studies dealing with consistency—like the Hartshorne and May investigation—and

---

[2]Psychoanalytic theory is not completely negative in its portrayal of human motivation. As is well known, Freud pointed to the abilities to work and to love as hallmarks of well-being, and neo-Freudians like Horney, Sullivan, and Fromm took seriously the ethical underpinnings of the good life.

concluded that there was little evidence to support the widespread assumption of personality consistency. He then suggested that personality theories were across-the-board wrong and should be replaced with a version of learning theory that located "personality" only in particular situations (Mischel, 1973). Behavior was of course sensible and orderly, but its coherence did not stem from psychological traits but rather from the concrete environment and how people think about it. The most radical interpretation of Mischel's conclusion is that there was no such thing as personality. And if there were no personality, then how could one entertain the possibility of character?

Mischel's apparent dismissal of personality is regarded by many psychologists as a wakeup call, and in recent decades personality psychology has been reborn in a much more sophisticated form (Peterson, 1992). No one talks seriously about types of people anymore—personality characteristics are now described along more-versus-less dimensions. No one discusses behavior without reference to the setting, both proximal and distal. No one assesses a personality characteristic with a one-shot measure—this would be akin to limiting the SAT to one question or basing a college grade point average on performance in one course only. And no one believes that people are completely inconsistent across situations.

Indeed, a reexamination of the original Hartshorne and May (1928) data shows a notable degree of cross-situational consistency in honesty versus dishonesty (Burton, 1963). In his critique, Mischel acknowledged positive correlations across situations but went on to dismiss the actual figures as too low to take seriously. But he was mistaken. Without getting into the numerical details, suffice it to say that the correlations of honesty scores across situations are higher than the correlations between cigarette smoking and lung cancer, between antihistamine use and reduced sniffling, or between adherence to an AZT regimen and the progression of AIDS (cf. G. J. Meyer et al., 2001; R. Rosenthal & Rubin, 1982). When expressed in the same metric, these correlations are as robust as the effects of the situation in such well-known social psychology experiments as Milgram's (1963) investigation of obedience or Darley and Latané's (1968) study of unresponsive bystanders (Funder & Ozer, 1983). If we take all these findings seriously—and of course we do—then we should take just as seriously the evidence in favor of personality traits. A psychology of character traits is not a fool's errand. The overarching goal of the present classification is to reclaim psychology's early concern with character by drawing on a century's worth of hard-learned lessons about how to conduct good psychological science.

Even though character has not been of major concern to psychologists for many years, many traditions within the discipline have had something to say about the topic, even if the implications have been indirect. We cannot survey all the relevant traditions, but we offer thumbnail sketches here of some that shaped our thinking.

Thorndike

Perhaps the most influential psychologist in the discipline's early United States history was Edward L. Thorndike. Remembered today chiefly for his pioneering studies of instrumental conditioning and his "law of effect" (the forerunner of Skinner's principles of operant conditioning), Thorndike (1911, 1939, 1940) also wrote extensively on character and how it could be cultivated. In keeping with a behaviorist emphasis on the environment, Thorndike pointed to the setting as crucial in shaping character. He even quantified the goodness of cities in terms of such indices as (a) low death rate; (b) per capita expenditure for teachers' salaries; (c) per capita acreage of public parks; (d) excess of physicians and teachers over domestic servants; and (e) number of automobiles, telephones, and radios. Thorndike phrased most of these indices as positive outcomes—not simply the absence of negatives. Long before positive psychology took form and called for researchers to look beyond the zero points of deficiency, deficit, disease, and disorder, Thorndike proposed that quality of life entailed more than the elimination of problems.

Although he did not follow through to create a concrete measure, Thorndike (1940) also proposed that a person's morality (character) could be measured in quantitative terms, just as intelligence was measured. We would like to believe that he would approve of our decision here to disaggregate character into separate components, just as contemporary psychologists have disaggregated intelligence (cf. H. Gardner, 1983; Sternberg, 1985).

Erikson

Erik Erikson (1963, 1968, 1982) both built upon and modified Freud's stage theory of development by proposing that individuals across the life span must confront and resolve a series of specific social challenges. Different psychosocial virtues develop in each case (Table 3.2). Erikson's theory was useful to us in several ways. First, it is one of the first examples of a psychologically informed classification of character strengths. All of Erikson's virtues have a counterpart in our classification, although not vice versa, perhaps because only some strengths arguably result from the resolution of a social conflict. Consider open-mindedness or appreciation of beauty—their typical developmental precursors are unlikely to involve conflict. Second, Erikson's approach is an explicit reminder that strengths have a developmental trajectory and that certain strengths can lay the foundation for others. Third, it points to the fact that cultures recognize the social nature of people's conflicts and provide their members with help to accomplish the tasks that confront them at different periods of life. Consider the dating rituals institutionalized within our own society. They help young people achieve love by bringing them together precisely when intimacy is their prevailing concern. Here is a useful way of thinking about youth development. Rather than adopting

TABLE 3.2   *Erikson's Psychosocial Stages*

According to Erikson, all people pass through the following stages. Satisfactory resolution of a stage results in a character strength and allows the next stage to be entered. Erikson's term for the resulting character strength is shown in the table along with (in parentheses) the approximately corresponding strength(s) from our classification.

Approximate ages	Characterization	Resulting character strength
Birth to age 1	Infants must learn to achieve a sense of safety, trusting caretakers to provide for their well-being	Trust (hope, gratitude)
Age 1 to age 3	Children must learn to make things happen, to choose, to exercise will	Autonomy (persistence)
Age 3 to age 6	Children must learn to initiate their own activities, thereby gaining confidence in oneself	Initiative (curiosity)
Age 6 to puberty	Children must learn to explore systematically their skills and abilities	Competence (love of learning; creativity)
Puberty to age 18	Adolescents must create a set of personal values and goals by which to live, represented as a coherent identity	Identity (social intelligence; spirituality)
Age 18 to age 25	Young adults must learn to merge their identity with that of another person	Intimacy (love)
Age 25 to age 50	Middle-aged adults must learn to concern themselves with the world and the next generation	Generativity (kindness)
Age 50 to death	Later adults must come to terms with how they have resolved previous issues	Ego integrity (integrity; perspective)

a "more is better" approach to the activities we program for our children, we should stop and ask what we want an activity to accomplish (e.g., to forge curiosity, kindness, or citizenship), whether a child is developmentally ready for this activity and purpose, and whether the details of this activity indeed accomplish its stated goal vis-à-vis a targeted character strength.

We also learned some negative lessons by attending to criticisms of Erikson's work. So, there is little evidence to support his strict stage approach to development, which reaffirms our decision not to wed our classification to a single theoretical framework. For example, it does not seem plausible that generativity appears only in adulthood. Our scheme renders this strength as kindness, and this character trait can show itself very early in life. Even the most literal interpretation of Eriksonian generativity allows it to be seen among children who participate in the March of Dimes, Earth Day celebrations, and the like.

Erikson's theory is probably a better description of men than women, and it is probably a better description of individuals in societies with formal institutions than individuals in other sorts of societies. We need to remain vigilant in our classification efforts not to preclude large segments of the population by inadvertent theoretical assumptions.

Finally, Erikson's theory can also be criticized for proposing a right way to pass through life. A more flexible—and indeed more accurate—position is that there are various routes through life. We do not back off from endorsing good character as a goal for all, but we must allow it to develop in different ways and to manifest itself in different forms.

Maslow

Also influential in our thinking were the writings of Abraham Maslow (1970), who suggested that humans' motives are arranged according to a hierarchy of needs. At the bottom are biologically based needs, such as hunger and thirst. We cannot leave these needs unsatisfied for too long because our lives are at stake. Only when these needs are met does the need to be free from threatened danger arise. Maslow called this need one of safety—both physical and psychological. We need to believe that the world is stable and coherent.

Next in the hierarchy is attachment, which leads us to seek out other people, to love and to be loved. If we successfully satisfy this need for attachment, then we need to feel esteemed, by ourselves and by others. Maslow grouped our needs for knowledge, understanding, and novelty together as cognitive needs and proposed that they are next in his hierarchy. Then we find aesthetic needs: the desire for order and beauty.

Near the top of his hierarchy is self-actualization: "the full use and exploitation of talents, capacities, potentialities" (Maslow, 1970, p. 150). Maslow argued that we must satisfy lower needs before we seek satisfaction of higher needs. The need for self-actualization is difficult to achieve because it becomes relevant only when the needs that fall below it have been successfully addressed. Maslow was particularly interested in the self-actualized individual, to whom he attributed such characteristics as spontaneity, autonomy, sense of humor, and a capacity for deep interpersonal relations. Finally, at the very top of the hierarchy is the need for transcendence, which refers to spiritual and religious needs.

Like Erikson's scheme, the one proposed by Maslow can be recast as a catalog of virtues and strengths. This reformulation can be done with respect to the needs themselves, many of which map rather neatly into what we have identified as core virtues, or with respect to the characteristics of self-actualized individuals, which largely correspond to our more specific character strengths (Table 3.3). Not all the features of self-actualization correspond to particular character strengths, in part because Maslow included several culture-bound traits (e.g., focus on ends rather than means; need for privacy; spontaneity; autonomy), which we did not place in our classification, and in part because he conflated character strengths with what we consider possible

---

TABLE 3.3　*Maslow's Characteristics of Self-Actualized Individuals*

In some cases (~), we suggest a very rough correspondence between dimension of psychosocial maturity and a character strength, but we do not claim it to be a good match.

Characteristic	Approximately corresponding character strength(s)
1. Accurate perception of reality	Open-mindedness
2. Acceptance of oneself	Social intelligence; ~spirituality
3. Spontaneity	None
4. Problem centered	None
5. Need for privacy	None
6. Autonomous	None
7. Freshness of appreciation	Appreciation of beauty and excellence
8. Peak experiences	~Vitality
9. Human kinship	Citizenship
10. Humility and respect for others	Humility and modesty; fairness
11. Deep interpersonal relationships with a select few people	Love
12. Strong but not necessarily conventional ethical standards	Fairness
13. Focuses on ends rather than means	None
14. Nonhostile sense of humor	Humor
15. Creative	Creativity
16. Resistance to enculturation	Integrity; open-mindedness

(but not inevitable) outcomes or fulfillments of these strengths (e.g., problem-centered focus; peak experiences).

Regardless, there is decent overlap between what Maslow regarded as human excellence and the strengths enumerated in the present classification. We also are persuaded by the general idea of a hierarchy of needs, if not Maslow's details, because it underscores the notion that strengths cannot easily develop or be displayed in adverse environments—when basic needs for sustenance or safety go unmet.

We disagree, however, with the specific hierarchy hypothesized by Maslow. We see no reason to place cognitive needs below aesthetic needs, for example, or transcendence needs above attachment needs. Indeed, the particular order in which Maslow arranged different needs has been frequently criticized (Neher, 1991). A parent might run into a burning building to save a stranded child or forgo all manner of personal satisfactions to pay for the child's music lessons. Along these lines, a study comparing homeless individuals and college students in terms of their need for self-actualization found no differences (Sumerlin & Norman, 1992). Strengths do not belong just to the have's of the world; they are also found among the have-not's. As we have already concluded, our classification is well served by not aligning it with a particular theory.

Greenberger et al.

In the 1970s, psychologist Ellen Greenberger and her colleagues began a research program that foreshadowed some of the goals of our classification project (Greenberger, 1984; Greenberger, Josselson, Knerr, & Knerr, 1975; Greenberger & Sørenson, 1974). Drawing upon theoretical discussions by Allport, Freud, Erikson, Maslow, and Robert White, they proposed a multidimensional model of psychosocial maturity for adolescents that went beyond extant discussions of cognitive and intellectual development. A number of their dimensions of maturity correspond to what we describe as character strengths (Table 3.4). Most of our strengths of wisdom are missing from Greenberger et al.'s scheme, which makes sense given the purpose of their classification. And some of Greenberger et al.'s dimensions are missing from our classification because they strike us as culture bound and perhaps historically limited (e.g., tolerance of individual differences and openness to sociopolitical change, respectively). Nonetheless, the fit is good, which is encouraging to us because the focus of Greenberger et al. was on youth, a population of particular interest to us.

Also notable about this research program is that the investigators developed a self-report instrument—the Psychosocial Maturity Inventory—suitable for use with teenagers. The questionnaire was administered to a variety of samples, allowing the researchers to specify through factor analysis the basic structure of their construct. Good support was found for two distinct factors,

TABLE 3.4 *Greenberger et al.'s Model of Psychosocial Maturity*

In some cases (~), we suggest a very rough correspondence between a dimension of psychosocial maturity and a character strength in our classification, but we do not claim it to be a good match.

Dimension (and components)	Approximately corresponding character strength(s)
Individual adequacy	
Reliance on oneself	Creativity
Identity	Spirituality
Work orientation	Persistence
Interpersonal adequacy	
Communication skills	Social intelligence
Enlightened trust	Love
Knowledge of major roles	~Love of learning; ~social intelligence
Social adequacy	
Social commitment	Citizenship
Openness to sociopolitical change	None
Tolerance of individual differences	~Open-mindedness; ~fairness

individual adequacy and social adequacy. The third factor hypothesized on theoretical grounds, interpersonal adequacy, did not clearly emerge; its supposed components loaded on the other factors. In retrospect, this finding does not strike us as surprising, because the interpersonal domain represents the intersection of the individual and the social.

Scores on the Psychosocial Maturity Inventory indeed increase over the teen years, and they are distinct from measures of academic achievement. Furthermore, Greenberger (1984) explored some of the correlates of psychosocial maturity. Good family relations and school involvement are associated with individual adequacy but not—interestingly—with social adequacy.

Jahoda

In 1958, Marie Jahoda wrote a provocative book—*Current Concepts of Positive Mental Health*—that made the case for understanding psychological well-being in its own right, not simply as the absence of disorder or distress. Her argument is of course the premise of contemporary positive psychology, and one wonders why it has taken more than four decades for other psychologists to take up her challenge. Jahoda surveyed what previous thinkers—mainly clinicians—had to say about mental health and integrated their views by proposing half a dozen underlying processes presumably producing the states and traits we dub psychologically healthy. Jahoda labeled them criteria, but they seem to be more processes rather than easily observable contents.

Her analysis of positive mental health in terms of these underlying processes is persuasive, and we have little to add to it in these terms. We considered seriously basing our explication of good character on Jahoda's synthesis but were eventually dissuaded by our measurement goal and by our decision to avoid deep theory. That is, we wanted to start with positive traits and then to develop measures and only as a final step to look deeper within the individual at basic causes. We suspect that such inquiry might confirm much of what Jahoda hypothesized, but that will be an empirical issue. Table 3.5 describes Jahoda's processes and the character strengths that reflect them. The only qualification we offer is that her processes and criteria seem to reflect a Western bias on the person as autonomous rather than interdependent; what we call strengths of humanity and justice—which have an explicit social reference—are not included.

At the same time that Jahoda (1958) published her book, psychologist William Scott (1958a, 1958b) surveyed the existing research literature on mental health, focusing on research definitions (measures) of well-being and empirically established correlates of these measures. Then as now, the majority of studies ostensibly looking at health were really studies of disorder. Scott could draw firm conclusions from this research only about the factors that characterized lack of pathology—good social relationships were the most common correlate. Scott cited a personal communication from Jahoda in which she described her attempts to develop measures of several of her criteria for mental health (i.e., accurate perception of reality and environmental mastery) as less than satisfactory, which is probably why they were never widely used.

TABLE 3.5   *Jahoda's Processes Producing Positive Mental Health*

Process	Approximately corresponding character strength(s)
Acceptance of oneself	Social intelligence
Growth; development; becoming	Curiosity; love of learning
Integration of personality	Integrity; perspective
Autonomy (freedom from social pressures)	Integrity
Accurate perception of reality	Open-mindedness
Environmental mastery	Creativity

Ryff et al.

In the spirit of Jahoda's review and synthesis of (then) prevailing views of mental health, psychologist Carol Ryff and colleagues (1989, 1995; Ryff & Keyes, 1995; Ryff & Singer, 1996, 1998) more recently integrated what different theorists, again mostly clinicians, have said about the psychological components of being and doing well—striving and thriving, as it were. They identified what they called six points of convergence, which agree substantially with those enumerated by Jahoda decades earlier. Most of Ryff et al.'s points of convergence coincide with strengths included in our classification (Table 3.6). Their notion of "personal growth" is somewhat of an exception. By this they mean a person's sense of continued development and ongoing realization of potential, what an earlier generation of humanistic psychologists called self-actualization. Curiosity and love of learning are aspects of this dimension, but they do not fully capture its emphasis on oneself as the major topic about which the individual is curious and loves learning. We think that personal growth as Ryff and her colleagues defined it is culture bound, a concern to the disaffected upper-middle class in the contemporary United States. People in other times, places, and circumstances, with a different notion of who they are and the place they occupy in the world, do not concern themselves with growth of this sort. One might even suspect that it would be dismissed as a frivolous concern—hardly a strength. Along these lines, Ryff et al. did not include what we call the justice virtues, again reflecting a cultural bias.

On the positive side, Ryff and her colleagues developed a self-report measure of their six points of convergence. We intend eventually to check our strengths measures against this instrument. Inspection of the items suggests that their virtues and strengths may be more heterogeneous than the ones we emphasize, but that is an empirical issue.

TABLE 3.6 *Ryff et al.'s Dimensions of Well-Being*

In some cases (~), we suggest a very rough correspondence between a dimension of well-being and a character strength, but we do not claim it to be a good match.

Dimension	Approximately corresponding character strength(s)
Acceptance of oneself	Social intelligence
Positive relations with others	Love; kindness
Autonomy	~Integrity
Environmental mastery	~Creativity
Purpose in life	Spirituality
Personal growth	~Curiosity; ~love of learning

The Big Five Tradition

As early as the Greek philosopher Theophrastus, thinkers have made lists of personality types and traits with the goal of discerning the most basic. The present project can be seen as a special case of this venerable activity, and our work has been influenced by what has come to be known as the *lexical approach* to personality (L. R. Goldberg, 1993).

In 1936, Gordon Allport and Henry Odbert read through an unabridged dictionary and identified the thousands of English-language words that refer to traits. Their list has usually been the starting point for lexical researchers trying to identify basic individual differences. Allport and Odbert roughly classified their list, and their largest category—social evaluation—approaches the sorts of characteristics in which we were interested for the present classification of strengths. However, this category was not preserved in its own right during the decades that followed, probably because of Allport's exclusion of character from the province of personality psychology. Nonetheless, many character terms remained in this list.

Modern lexical researchers have been guided by the synthesis of Warren Norman (1963), who proposed that there are five basic personality traits under which all others can be subsumed. His scheme has come to be known as the Big Five. It has been fine-tuned, confirmed by various measurement strategies (e.g., self-report, observer report), and tested cross-culturally. Apparently, our primate cousins can also be sensibly described along the Big Five dimensions, and so too can inanimate products like automobiles! Some researchers have added one or two other basic traits, but few seriously disagree with the five that Norman highlighted. Other classifications of personality traits, like those proposed by Eysenck, Cattell, and the creators of the MMPI, relate sensibly to the Big Five.

When we look at the Big Five in terms of character strengths, we find that four of the five basic traits have clear counterparts in the virtue domain (Table 3.7), an unsurprising finding given the large number of trait terms in the language that apply to morally valued characteristics. We could probably force other character strengths into the Big Five scheme, but we would be relying on what is known about their nomological nets—for example, we know that hopeful individuals score low on measures of neuroticism; we know that leaders often score high on extroversion; and so on—rather than on the substantive meanings of the strengths.

The Big Five tradition strikes us as largely atheoretical (not a problem in our view of things) and largely nonpsychological (a big problem to us) in that classification per se seems to be the goal, not an understanding of the causes or consequences of the classification's entries. When a new measure of individual differences is reported in the literature, one or another lexical research group invariably conducts a study linking the new measure to existing Big Five inventories. There is invariably convergence, but rarely is it so striking that one

---

TABLE 3.7 *The Big Five*

Trait (and representative examples)	Approximately corresponding character strength(s)
Neuroticism (worried, nervous, emotional)	None
Extroversion (sociable, fun-loving, active)	Vitality; humor; playfulness
Openness (imaginative, creative, artistic)	Curiosity; creativity; appreciation of beauty
Agreeableness (good-natured, softhearted, sympathetic)	Kindness; gratitude
Conscientiousness (reliable, hardworking, punctual)	Self-regulation; persistence

---

would conclude that the new measure is superfluous, probably because the Big Five traits are very broad and unlikely to capture the meaning of a more nuanced individual difference. Perhaps the point is that when new individual differences are proposed and studied, part of making sense of them is showing that they are consistent with the Big Five tradition, and we expect this will prove to be the case for the strengths in the present classification.

Cawley, Martin, and Johnson

More immediately instructive to us was the lexical approach of Michael Cawley, James Martin, and John Johnson (2000). Like Allport and Odbert decades earlier, Cawley et al. read through a dictionary and used linguistic criteria to winnow entries to virtue terms. Among their criteria was the question: Can the appropriate form of a word be used sensibly in the sentences:

- "I ought to be _____"
- "I ought to show _____"

If so, the word refers to a human virtue. In other words, the term should have an adjective form as well as a noun form. Note how *patience* meets these criteria ("I ought to be patient," and "I ought to show patience"), whereas other social evaluations (beauty, fame, wealth) do so awkwardly or not at all. A virtue or strength describes a person as well as what the person does.

Redundancies were eliminated, leaving a total of 140 unique virtue terms. Items for a self-report questionnaire were written, asking respondents to endorse the degree to which these terms described them and their actions in concrete situations. Several hundred university students completed the resulting Virtues Scale, along with a typical measure of the Big Five.

Factor analysis of the Virtues Scale revealed four factors that were sensibly related to Big Five scores (Table 3.8). Again, we can find substantial overlap between Cawley's virtue factors and entries in our classification, although missing are what we term strengths of wisdom and strengths of justice, as well as strengths subsumed by the Big Five openness to experience factor, probably because Cawley et al. excluded the relevant words from their initial list. One more comment: Notice that "meekness" as identified by Cawley et al. was negatively associated with the Big Five neuroticism factor, not positively as one might think if this were reflecting anxiety-driven reticence (cf. humility and modesty; chapter 20).

Cawley et al.'s approach was valuable to us because it alerted us to how linguistic criteria could be used to designate some traits as character strengths, to the viability of asking people about their own strengths in a face-valid self-report questionnaire, and to one possible way in which various character strengths might cluster into virtue factors. We intend eventually to check our measures of strengths against the Virtues Scale introduced by Cawley and his colleagues. Because our list is arguably more inclusive, we expect not only the obvious convergence but also evidence for divergent validity, especially with respect to wisdom and justice strengths.

Kohlberg

We have explained how moral character largely fell off the research agenda of most psychologists in the 20th century. The best known exception to this generalization is research into moral development, which began with Piaget's (1932/1965) pioneering investigations of how children at different stages of cognitive development reasoned about the morality of everyday acts and was

TABLE 3.8   *Cawley et al.'s Virtue Factors*

Factor (and representative examples)	Big Five correlate(s)	Approximately corresponding character strength(s)
Empathy (concern; sympathy; friendliness)	Agreeableness	Kindness
Order (discipline; scrupulousness; caution)	Conscientiousness	Self-regulation; prudence
Resourcefulness (purpose; perseverance)	Conscientiousness; neuroticism (-)	Spirituality; persistence
Serenity (meekness; forgiveness; patience)	Agreeableness; neuroticism (-)	Humility; forgiveness; gratitude

carried through by psychologist Lawrence Kohlberg (1981, 1984). His work is well known, so much so that his theory of moral reasoning is the only instance most can think of as a psychological approach to morality. Obviously, we too were aware of his work, although close scrutiny led to the conclusion that it followed a very different direction than what we intended for the present classification.

Kohlberg was interested in moral reasoning and not moral behavior per se. He certainly was not interested in character strengths associated with moral behavior and explicitly dismissed "virtues" as a concern. Kohlberg's was a thoroughly cognitive approach to moral reasoning about the actions of other people, and he proposed that children passed through stages of reasoning constrained by their general cognitive abilities. Specifically, moral development according to Kohlberg increasingly transcends the particular and moves to the use of general standards of justice, equality, and respect.

As is well known to students of psychology, Kohlberg studied moral reasoning by posing moral dilemmas to research participants. Respondents are asked to decide what would be right or wrong and then to justify this decision. To Kohlberg, how one justifies the course of moral action is more important than the actual decision. As noted, Kohlberg's theory of moral development embodies a stage approach. A particular individual either is at a given level of reasoning or is not. People pass through these levels in the proposed sequence only. These stages are regarded as a universal aspect of human nature. Kohlberg proposed three general levels of development.

According to Kohlberg, *preconventional reasoning* takes into account only rewards and punishments. Morality is placed outside the individual. A child at the level of preconventional morality would say that people should not steal because they would be punished if caught. Those exhibiting *conventional reasoning* justify moral action in terms of society's rules and conventions. Most adolescents and adults think in these terms. Their concern is with conforming to social standards, rules, or laws. Someone at the level of conventional morality would say that people should not steal because it is against the law to do so. *Postconventional reasoning,* apparently shown by only 20% of the adult population, involves the application of one's own abstract standards. Those at this level recognize that laws and rules are useful but sometimes in conflict. In resolving moral conflicts, people at this stage try to judge the relative importance and intentions of different laws. Someone at this level might explain that stealing is justified if it is done to save the life of another person, because respect for another's property must give way to respect for human life.

We could have shoehorned some of the character strengths we enumerate into this scheme but did not do so because the fit would be awkward. Instead, we have relied on Kohlberg's work in our discussion of one character strength in particular, fairness (chapter 17).

Although we took from Kohlberg's work the insight that morality in general shows a developmental trajectory and that so too—by implication—does character, we disagreed with his particular trajectory and rank ordering. In part, we were echoing the familiar criticism of Kohlberg's approach that it overemphasizes abstract rules and principles (what we call justice strengths) while downplaying caring and compassion (what we call humanity strengths). And in part, we were criticizing the cultural bias inherent in Kohlberg's scheme. For example, Americans phrase their moral judgments in terms of individual considerations, whereas Indians speak in terms of interpersonal ones, apparently relegating themselves to the conventional level (J. G. Miller, 1994).

Finally, the relationship between moral reasoning and moral behavior is not clear. Research in the Kohlberg tradition often assumes that the former leads to the latter without explicitly showing that it does. Some studies find that people at the level of postconventional reasoning are less likely than others to lie or cheat, but other investigations do not find the expected link (Clarke-Stewart, Friedman, & Koch, 1985). Researchers interested in moral development have tended to neglect the emotional and motivational aspects of morality, which doubtlessly influence whether thought is translated into action (Blasi, 1990; Nunn & Hazler, 1990). Thus, believing that someone faced with a given dilemma should proceed with a specific course of action is not the same thing as doing so if the situation were actually to present itself.

Vaillant

Another influence on our thinking was George Vaillant's (1971, 1977, 1993, 2000) theorizing about psychodynamic defense mechanisms. Vaillant hypothesized that the various defenses can be ranked from relatively immature defenses such as denial to relatively mature defenses such as sublimation, depending on the degree to which the individual using the defense distorts reality. The mature defenses identified by Vaillant have been linked to both psychological and physical well-being, and when habitual, they can be construed as character strengths (Table 3.9).

Some of the character strengths are akin to these defenses, although the fit is at best approximate because the defenses are styles of coping more than contents of behavior. We also disavow the connotation of defense as solely a reaction to threat and regard as an empirical question whether defenses qua character strengths play themselves out on an unconscious level, as most psychodynamic theories assume. Vaillant's theorizing demonstrates that good character can be construed, even from a Freudian perspective, in such a way that does not reduce strength to something negative. Indeed, Vaillant's empirical documentation of the benefits of mature defense mechanisms was one of the important triggers of the positive psychology movement.

TABLE 3.9   *Vaillant's Mature Defense Mechanisms*

Defense	Approximately corresponding character strength(s)
Altruism	Kindness
Anticipation	Curiosity; hope
Humor	Humor
Sublimation	Love of learning; persistence
Suppression	Self-regulation

Gardner

Ever since its beginnings in the work of Galton, Binet, Terman, and Spearman, intelligence has usually been regarded as a singular characteristic that people showed across a variety of domains. Not all intelligence theorists have made this assumption (e.g., Thurstone, Guilford, and Cattell), instead preferring to look at intelligence as plural or multiple—a set of distinct and specific abilities. Harvard psychologist Howard Gardner (1983, 1993b, 1993c) is the best known advocate of the view of intelligence as plural, and we have borrowed from his ideas in conceptualizing character as plural.

In particular, he proposed explicit criteria for identifying a distinct intelligence, and we deliberately borrowed this strategy—not the criteria themselves—in our own work (chapter 1). For example, is a particular set of skills selectively isolated by brain damage? If damage to nervous tissue selectively attacks or spares a given competence, then one can argue that it has a biological basis, which Gardner felt to be important in designating a specific competence as a basic intelligence. Additional criteria include a distinctive developmental history for a set of skills, an associated set of symbols that people use in exercising these particular skills, and the existence of prodigies who excel at them. When all these criteria point to the same ability, it became an "intelligence" in Gardner's scheme.

Gardner thus identified six types of intelligence, several of which have long been the concern of traditional intelligence researchers:

- linguistic intelligence—sensitivity to the meanings and functions of language
- logical-mathematical intelligence—competence at organizing ideas in abstract ways

- spatial intelligence—capacity for visual or spatial imagery, including the ability to transform images

His other categories are more unique as types of intelligence:

- musical intelligence—ability to produce and organize sounds according to prescribed pitch and rhythm
- bodily intelligence—kinesthetic mastery over body movements
- personal intelligence—ability to access one's own feelings and those of others

We do not regard intelligence per se as a strength or virtue—we place it in the talents and abilities group—and we can say the same thing about Gardner's specific intelligences, with one exception: personal intelligence. Gardner himself acknowledged that personal intelligence stands apart from the other abilities of concern to him, and although he did not say so, we think that the chief differences are the virtue-laden context in which personal intelligence operates and its mutability. Thus, it makes sense to include some version of personal intelligence in our classification of character strengths (cf. chapter 15).

Schwartz et al.

Drawing upon earlier work by Rokeach (1973) in values, Shalom Schwartz and his colleagues proposed that there are 10 distinct and universally recognized values (S. H. Schwartz, 1994; S. H. Schwartz & Bilsky, 1987, 1990; S. H. Schwartz & Sagiv, 1995). Although values are not identical to virtues, there should be a relationship given Schwartz's working definition of a value as "conceptions of the desirable that influence the way people select action and evaluate events" (S. H. Schwartz & Bilsky, 1987, p. 550). Virtues embody values when the behavior they organize and direct becomes habitual. Schwartz et al. arrived at their particular 10 by considering "universal" requirements of survival, for individuals and societies:[3] satisfaction of biological needs; coordination of social interaction; and facilitation of societal functioning. From these requirements, they

---

[3]A similar conclusion was offered by philosopher Sissela Bok (1995), who also grappled with the task of identifying universal values. Her insight was that the level of abstraction matters in deeming values universal or not. In very general terms, people in all times and places endorse three sets of values: (a) positive duties of mutual care and reciprocity; (b) negative injunctions against violence, deceit, and betrayal; and (c) norms for rudimentary fairness and procedural justice in cases of conflict regarding positive duties and/or negative injunctions. Bok called these moral values "minimalist" because they are the minimal requirements for a viable society. But there are also "maximalist" values—more numerous, extensive, elaborated, and culturally situated: for example, teachings of the Roman Catholic Church with respect to contraception and abortion. Any given cultural group of course endorses both minimalist and maximalist values and usually has no reason to distinguish between them. But if one wishes to speak across groups— as when members of the United Nations make pronouncements to the entire world about human rights—it behooves one to keep them straight.

specified 44 individual values, which cross-cultural research suggests can be grouped into 10 classes distinguished by people around the world. The 10 values themselves can be grouped into four higher order groups of values.

Table 3.10 presents the 10 universal values and their corresponding strengths in our classification. The fit is very good. We do not have a category that broadly captures hedonism—pleasure per se. The inclusion of hedonism as a universal value stems from Schwartz et al.'s biological emphasis, not part of our vision of character strengths.

Schwartz et al.'s values—the 44, the 10, and the 4—could presumably be represented in a hierarchy akin to what we suggest for the present classification of strengths and virtues. These theorists instead opted for a circumplex model, in keeping with their goal not only of understanding what the universal values might be but also of understanding their structure—that is, their interrelationships. Their circumplex has two dimensions referring to the interests served by the value—individual versus collective; and by the goal type—instrumental (modes of behavior; e.g., obedience) versus terminal (end states; e.g., wisdom). We find the second dimension especially useful because it addresses a matter we have glossed over in our classification. Our strengths are a mixed lot, like psychological traits in general. Some of the strengths we include refer to psychological processes and

---

TABLE 3.10   *Schwartz et al.'s Universal Values*

In some cases (~), we suggest a very rough correspondence between a universal value and a character strength, but we do not claim it to be a good match.

Value	Approximately corresponding character strength(s)
Achievement	Persistence
Benevolence	Kindness
Conformity	Citizenship; self-regulation
Hedonism	~Appreciation of beauty and excellence
Power	Leadership
Security	Gratitude
Self-direction	~Creativity
Stimulation	Curiosity; love of learning
Tradition	Humility; spirituality; prudence
Universalism	Perspective; fairness

others to psychological content. Perhaps this sort of dimension will help us make sense of the structure of the proposed classification.

Schwartz et al. developed a questionnaire for measuring the degree to which people in different cultures emphasize different values. As noted, research supports their contention that the ability to distinguish among these is near universal and that the two-dimensional circumplex captures the structure. There are also some culturally specific emphases and exceptions to the generalizations. For example, among Japanese students, friendship falls into what Schwartz calls security, rather than into benevolence, where it fits for most other cultures (S. H. Schwartz & Sagiv, 1995). This makes sense if one assumes that the Japanese regard friendship as a way of achieving security rather than expressing care.

The Values Questionnaire of Schwartz et al. is not identical with the measures of strengths we have developed. It measures what people value, not their traits or habitual actions. But insofar as the definition of a strength includes being sensitive to it in others and celebrating it when present, one expects convergence. We intend eventually to compare responses to our character strength measures with those to Schwartz et al.'s measure.

Evolutionary Psychology

Of concern to evolutionary psychologists are the characteristics found attractive in a mate (Buss, 1989, 1994, 1998; Buss et al., 1990; Feingold, 1992). We need not delve into ongoing debates about whether these characteristics have been selected in the course of human evolution, whether there exist male–female differences in the most valued of these, or whether short-term preferences differ markedly from long-term preferences. Rather, we simply observe that extensive cross-national and cross-historical studies—based on surveys and content analyses of personal ads—reveal much the same list of valued characteristics. Many of these are strengths of character (Table 3.11). The individual differences that do not have a counterpart in our classification fall into the talents and abilities domain, which we think of as more immutable and less voluntary than character strengths.

We need to take very seriously the list of desired character strengths that emerges from evolutionary psychology because one of our issues entails the universality of strengths and virtues (chapter 2). Evolutionary psychologists are interested in what is generally true of people—in human nature, as it were—so if a strength is on their list, it needs to belong on our list. We are therefore pleased that the character strengths we identify almost all have counterparts. Indeed, the strengths identified by evolutionary psychologists as desirable in mates agree well with the strengths that people most seek in close friends, the most valued of which are character strengths like honesty and responsibility (e.g., General Social Survey, 2001).

TABLE 3.11 *Desirable Characteristics in a Mate*

In a survey of 9,474 men and women in 37 nations, Buss et al. (1990) asked about the most desirable characteristics in a mate. Although there were gender differences and national differences, which these researchers tended to emphasize, the characteristics in this table were the most widely valued across all samples.

Characteristic	Approximately corresponding character strength(s)
Ambition and industriousness	Persistence
Dependable character	Integrity; citizenship; prudence
Desire for home and children	Love
Education and intelligence	Creativity; love of learning; perspective
Emotional stability	Self-regulation
Good cook and housekeeper	None
Good financial prospect	None
Good health	Vitality
Good looks	None
Mutual attraction—love	Love
Pleasing disposition	Kindness; gratitude; humility; humor
Refinement; neatness	Appreciation of beauty and excellence
Sociability	Citizenship; social intelligence

Resilience

Although it is a truism that stress and adversity take a toll, the question arises, "Why do some children exposed to terrible events show good or even exceptional outcomes in their wake?" This question has guided several decades of research into what was initially termed *invulnerability* (Anthony & Cohler, 1987) and now is labeled *resilience* (Masten, 2001; Rutter, 1999). According to the prevailing assumption in this research, the resilient child must be benefiting from protective factors, and researchers have therefore tried to articulate what these might be and how they function. Some of the identified factors are the sorts of character strengths with which our classification is concerned, although resilience researchers have usually looked beyond the individual child for protective factors, finding them within the family, peer group, or community. Here, then, is an important caution for us in our classification project: Do not examine character strengths in isolation from the social contexts in which they develop (or not) and in which they result (or not) in desirable outcomes.

Studies of resilience, by definition, also focus on risk factors. Risk factors and protective factors are cumulative and interactive. Indeed, a protective factor can affect problems in a variety of ways (Coie et al., 1993):

- by directly decreasing the problem
- by interacting with the risk factor to buffer its effects
- by disrupting the process leading from the risk factor to the problem
- by undoing the risk factor

Thus, another caution from research into resilient children is that strengths must sometimes be studied in relation to adversity. There is a temptation to regard positive psychology as focusing on the stress-free individual, but this is a mistake. Character may not even be relevant unless someone is called on to develop it and/or show it, a point to which we return when discussing lessons we have learned from philosophy's study of virtues.

Research in this tradition often identifies resilience by the absence of negative outcomes, not the presence of positive outcomes, and there is some sleight of hand in going from the statement that a child is not depressed or not using drugs to saying that he is doing well (cf. Peterson, 2000). We wish that resilience research were more true to its original premise of trying to understand good outcomes in the wake of adversity, not simply the diminution of bad outcomes.

Still another caution from this research is that resilience is not a unitary trait or characteristic. A child may display resilience with respect to some stresses and vis-à-vis some outcomes but not with respect to other stresses and other outcomes (Pianta & Walsh, 1998). Perhaps resilience is better regarded as an umbrella term, just as we regard character.

Can we therefore unpack resilience? A number of theorists have attempted to do so, dividing protective factors into environmental ones (e.g., good parent–child relationship; strong extended family) and internal ones, which include some of the character strengths from our classification. A representative list of these internal factors is shown in Table 3.12 (from Kumpfer, 1999). They strike us as a very mixed set of characteristics, drawn from different domains and across different conceptual levels. Some are what we call talents, including physically based ones (e.g., attractiveness, good health) and abilities (e.g., intelligence). Some are very specific instances of procedural knowledge (e.g., homework skills). Still others are what we regard as outcomes of strengths (e.g., happiness). Finally, others strike us as character strengths but culturally specific ones (e.g., peer resistance, multicultural competence). In any event, if we exclude these sorts of protective factors—without dismissing their importance—we are still left with a number of good matches to the character strengths in our classification.

Missing in the resilience literature is any discussion about which protective factors are relevant for whom, under what stressful circumstances, and with

TABLE 3.12 *Internal Resilience Factors (Kumpfer, 1999)*

In some cases (~), we suggest a very rough correspondence between an identified resilience factor and a character strength, but we do not claim it to be a good match.

Protective factor	Approximately corresponding character strength(s)
Spiritual/motivational factors	
Dreams and goals	Hope
Purpose/meaning in life	Spirituality
Spirituality	Spirituality
Belief in uniqueness of oneself	None
Independence (autonomy)	~Integrity
Hope and optimism	Hope
Determination and perseverance	Persistence
Cognitive competencies	
Intelligence	None
Academic achievement and homework skills	None
Ability to delay gratification	Self-regulation; prudence; hope
Reading skills	None
Moral reasoning	Fairness
Insight	Perspective
Interpersonal awareness	Social intelligence
Self-esteem	None
Planning ability	Open-mindedness
Creativity	Creativity
Behavioral/social competencies	
Social skills and street smarts	Creativity; social intelligence
Problem-solving skills	Creativity; open-mindedness
Multicultural and bi-gender competencies	~Social intelligence
Empathy	Social intelligence
Emotional stability and emotional management	Prudence; self-regulation
Happiness	~Vitality
Recognition of feelings	Social intelligence
Emotional management skills	Self-regulation
Ability to restore self-esteem	Self-regulation
Humor	Humor
Physical well-being and physical competencies	
Good health	~Vitality
Health maintenance skills	None
Physical talent development	~Persistence
Physical attractiveness	None

respect to what desirable outcomes. However, one can glean from the literature the working hypothesis that highly specific links do not exist, in part because of bidirectional effects among virtually all the variables in the potential equations. We hope that the present classification, because it is highly attentive to the definition of character strength, can be useful in future resilience research concerned with this particular class of protective factors.

Conclusions

Throughout this survey of a century of psychological inquiry into people's positive characteristics, we have commented on the lessons we learned. Let us now gather these together. First, when psychologists speak of positive characteristics, almost all phrase them in terms of personality traits: relatively stable and general individual differences. There are other types of human strengths—talents and abilities, for example, or instances of procedural knowledge—but these are readily distinguishable from the traits we identify as character strengths.

Second, almost all psychologists propose a variety of character strengths. The exact number differs, from a mere handful to several dozen, but the difference is largely one of the abstractness with which the strengths are described. Taking this into account, there is good agreement across past classification efforts about the appropriate entries. At the same time, we found that many previous classifications can be faulted for inadvertent bias—cultural and/or theoretical—that led theorists to include some strengths we regard as bounded while excluding others that we regard as ubiquitous. The present classification needs sufficient breadth and generality to be useful beyond the here and now.

Third, most previous classification efforts address strengths as they exist among adults. There are some exceptions that look at positive traits among young people. Missing in most cases is a link between these two approaches. Most would agree that character strengths develop across the life span, but we do not know much about how this happens. One of the long-term goals of our classification project is to begin in earnest such developmental inquiry. Crucial to this work will be serious attention to the individual's setting, proximal (e.g., the family of origin) and distal (e.g., the culture). In calling for psychology to study positive traits, we do *not* mean personality predispositions taken out of context.

Fourth, there is no consensus about how to represent the relation among entries in a classification. Some theorists grounded their classification in an a priori theory and generated a structure on theoretical grounds. As explained, we find this strategy premature. Other theorists used factor analysis or similar descriptive techniques to identify underlying dimensions or clusters of strengths. We followed a somewhat different strategy, relying on the history of moral and religious theorizing to identify broad classes of virtues (chapter 2), filling in the details with psychological investigations of positive traits falling into these classes (chapters 4–27), and then only as the final step relying on statistical methods to structure our classification (chapter 28).

Fifth, when psychologists devise measures of character strengths, they rely on face-valid self-report questionnaires. Many psychologists are skeptical of what people say about themselves, but we conclude that the yield of research using various virtue inventories has been rich enough to justify their continued use. Perhaps the distrust of self-reports about what is good stems from business-as-usual psychology, which has trouble recognizing anything inherently positive about people. We return to this point in chapter 28 on assessment.

■ Lessons From Youth Development

Youth development is an interdisciplinary field that draws broadly on different social sciences to understand children and adolescents (Larson, 2000). It embraces an explicit developmental stance: Children and adolescents are not miniature adults, and they need to be understood on their own terms. Youth development also emphasizes the multiple contexts in which development occurs. Particularly influential as an organizing framework has been Bronfenbrenner's (1977, 1979, 1986) ecological approach, which articulates different contexts in terms of their immediacy to the behaving individual. So, the *microsystem* refers to ecologies with which the individual directly interacts: family, peers, school, and neighborhood. The *mesosystem* is Bronfenbrenner's term for relationships between and among various microsystems. The *exosystem* is made up of larger ecologies that indirectly affect development and behavior, like the legal system, the social welfare system, and mass media. Finally, the *macrosystem* consists of broad ideological and institutional patterns that collectively define a culture. There is the risk of losing the individual amid all these systems, but the developmental perspective reminds us that different children are not interchangeable puppets. Each young person brings his or her own characteristics to life, and these interact with the different ecologies to produce behavior.

Youth development has always had a strong interest in application (Catalano, Berglund, Ryan, Lonczak, & Hawkins, 1999). Throughout much of the 20th century, these applications were directed at youth problems such as school dropout, juvenile crime, alcohol and drug use, and unwanted pregnancy. The earliest interventions targeted young people in crisis (i.e., they helped youth with problems), and the more recent interventions have been preventive (i.e., they supported youth before problems developed). The earliest applications were very much seat-of-the-pants endeavors, uninformed by research. This state of affairs changed in light of information from longitudinal studies about the predictors of specific problems (e.g., Jessor & Jessor, 1977). This information provided explicit targets for interventions, and theory began to guide practice.

Another change that has occurred as the field of youth development matured is that prevention efforts that target but a single problem came under criticism. Many problems co-occur and have the same risk factors. Broad-based interventions can therefore have broad effects. Part of the broadening of youth development and its applications was a call for studying and eventually cultivating what has come to be known as *positive youth development*—desirable outcomes such as school achievement, vocational aspirations, community involvement, good interpersonal relations, and the like. As Pittman (1991, 2000) phrased this change, "Problem-free is not fully prepared." Here is where youth development converges with positive psychology and its premise that the best in life is not simply the absence of disorder and dysfunction.

Youth development proponents seem to have an ambivalent relation with the notion of character, perhaps because of its objectionable implication that the kids would be okay if they only learned to say no. Needless to say, a concern with character—virtues and strengths in the case of the classification— does not preclude acknowledgment of the role played by Bronfenbrenner's multiple systems in shaping the person, for better or for worse. Indeed, if youth are to be developed, we need to say just what it is about them that develops. We suggest that one answer is their character, unpacked in the way that we have done so.

As an applied field, youth development marches to the drummer of societal priorities. At least as far as the nation's youth are concerned, the reduction of their problems has been the priority, for good reasons. "Positive" outcomes can be a difficult sell when juxtaposed with tax cuts, pothole repair, and defense spending. But there is good reason to believe that attention to positive outcomes has the additional effect of reducing negative outcomes. Researchers at the Search Institute in Minneapolis have studied what they call *developmental assets*, which include external factors like family support and adult role models, and internal factors like commitment to learning, positive values, and sense of purpose (Benson, Leffert, Scales, & Blyth, 1998; Leffert et al., 1998; Scales, Benson, Leffert, & Blyth, 2000). Youth with more of these assets not only show fewer problems but also display more evidence of thriving (e.g., school success, leadership, helping others, and physical health). The internal assets of interest to these researchers correspond to many of the character strengths we have identified (Table 3.13).

Two qualifications are in order about this correspondence. First, the developmental assets are contextualized—defined with respect to behavior in the school, the peer group, or the community—whereas character strengths are deliberately broad personality traits. Second, the handful of developmental assets that do not match up with character strengths (i.e., cultural competence and self-esteem) are culture-bound. They are valued in the contemporary United States but not part of our vision of ubiquitous character strengths. Regardless, the correspondence on the whole is excellent and supports the entries ther justification. To be sure, there are many demonstrable benefits of education vis-à-vis the reduction of problems, but these need not be part of the argument in favor of supporting schools and school programs. Perhaps the day will come as well when kindness and curiosity are also regarded as traits worth cultivating because they are good. In the meantime, we can point to research like that by the Search Institute.

One way in which youth development advocates address character is by speaking about competencies. Like the components of resilience discussed earlier, the various faces of competence include traits, talents, abilities, skills, and particular instances of procedural knowledge. We think it would be profitable to distinguish among these. Being able to use a condom and knowing how to take public transportation are important competencies for many young people, but these practical skills exist at different conceptual levels than traits of prudence or practical intelligence.

There is also a tendency in the youth development field to regard competencies (including character) as outcomes of intervention programs, coequal with the reduction of problems, rather than mediators: that is, factors cultivated by the program, which in turn produce the outcomes of interest. To some degree, this issue is one of semantics and how one wishes to represent patterns in longitudinal data. But it also speaks to an important conceptual distinction. We think character matters in part because behavior follows from it. As psychologists, we think person-level variables are as important as system-level variables. They do not compete, and one need not choose one over the other. Indeed, system-level factors can influence an individual's behavior only by affecting something about the individual.

In closing this section, we note briefly the conclusions of two recent literature reviews of intervention programs for youths, the first focusing on "negative" psychological outcomes (symptoms and disorders) and the other on "positive" psychological outcomes (striving and thriving). Despite the millions of young people involved in such programs, scientifically respectable outcome studies with pre–post designs, comparison groups, and objective measures are apparently very scarce: 34 in the case of negative outcomes (M. T. Greenberg, Domitrovich, & Bumbarger, 2001) and 42 in the case of positive outcomes (Catalano et al., 1999). Interestingly, though, there was convergence of conclusions about effective programs, even though the type of outcome measure varied dramatically within and across the reviews:

- *More is better.* Weekend workshops or one-shot lectures are not effective interventions; however, programs in which youth spend many hours over extended periods of time are effective in reducing negative outcomes and encouraging positive outcomes.
- *Earlier is better.* The most effective programs do not wait for their participants to enter adolescence but instead start with younger children.

TABLE 3.13 *"Internal" Developmental Assets (from Leffert et al., 1998, Table 1)*

In some cases (~), we suggest a very rough correspondence between a developmental asset and a character strength, but we do not claim it to be a good match.

Asset	Approximately corresponding character strength(s)
Commitment to learning	
Achievement motivation	~Love of learning; ~curiosity
School engagement	Love of learning
Homework	Persistence
Bonding to school	Citizenship
Reading for pleasure	Curiosity; love of learning
Positive values	
Caring	Kindness
Equality and social justice	Fairness
Integrity	Integrity
Responsibility	~Integrity
Restraint	Self-regulation; prudence
Social competencies	
Planning and decision making	Hope; open-mindedness
Interpersonal competence	Love; social intelligence
Cultural competence	~Social intelligence
Resistance skills	Self-regulation; prudence
Peaceful conflict resolution	Perspective; ~social intelligence; ~leadership
Positive identity	
Personal power	~Creativity
Self-esteem	None
Sense of purpose	Spirituality
Positive view of personal future	Hope

in both lists, which were generated by very different processes. When the focus is on strengths among youth, society can have it both ways: Reduction of negative outcomes, and encouragement of positive outcomes.

At least as an intellectual point, we observe that virtues and strengths are worth cultivating in their own right, with or without a payoff. Whether the larger society is ready to accept what seems to us (and to thinkers across the centuries) to be obvious is not clear, but we are encouraged by the fact that society has long "bought" higher education as an unalloyed good that needs no fur-

- *Broad is better.* The most effective programs target several systems simultaneously: for example, home *and* school. In Bronfenbrenner's terms, the action is in the mesosystem.
- *Sophisticated is better.* Programs that work best take a "person-in-environment" approach. They do not address just internal factors like character strengths, and they do not address just external factors like school safety. Instead, they address both.

The lessons from youth development for the present classification are several, and they correspond to the conclusions we drew from previous attempts by psychologists to classify positive traits. First, we are encouraged by the demonstration that strengths among young people can be specified, measured, and shown to have tangible consequences. Second, although our project is of course concerned with character strengths, these cannot be taken out of context in understanding when and how young people thrive. Strengths are embedded in Bronfenbrenner's multiple ecologies. So far, we have tersely lumped these ecologies together under the rubric of enabling conditions, but these conditions need to be unpacked as fully as character itself. Third, along these lines, a developmental perspective is useful in understanding strengths. Fourth, we are reminded that not everything positive about young people is captured by the notion of character strengths. The other components of competence—internal assets other than personality traits—also deserve the attention of anyone interested in promoting the best in people.

■ Lessons From Philosophy

Long before there was positive psychology, or even psychology, philosophers grappled with issues of morality and ethics. In our endeavor to describe good character, we have learned much from these efforts. As it has taken form over thousands of years, the philosophy of ethics has three related realms (Yearley, 1990):

- the study of *injunctions*: commands and prohibitions, for example, the "thou shalt nots" and the occasional "thou shalts" in the Ten Commandments
- the listing and organizing—usually hierarchically—of *virtues*: predispositions to act in ways leading to a recognizable human excellence or instance of flourishing
- the analysis of *ways of life* protected by the injunctions and picked out by the virtues

The second and third realms are obviously most relevant to our classification project, although they are vaguer than the first realm, which is often approached by philosophers who strip away psychological considerations.

Rachels (1999) provided a useful summary of how Western philosophers throughout history have approached morality. The initial question posed by philosophers dictates the direction their inquiries take. As noted in chapter 1, the very first Greek philosophers asked, "What is the good of a person?" This framing of morality led them to examine character and in particular virtues. Socrates, Plato, Aristotle, and others enumerated such virtues, regarding them as the traits of character that make someone a good person.

Let us amplify a point we made in chapter 1: This framing changed with the growing influence of Christianity, which saw God as the giver of laws by which one should live. Righteous conduct no longer stemmed from inner virtues but rather from obedience to the commandments of God. Whereas the early Greeks regarded reason as chief among the virtues, Christian thinkers like Saint Augustine distrusted reason. One must subordinate oneself to God, whether or not it seemed "reasonable" to do so (cf. the dilemma of Job). The guiding question of moral philosophy therefore changed from inquiries about the traits of a good person to "What are the right things to do?" As Christianity waned in importance, divine law eventually gave way to a secular equivalent dubbed moral law. Human reason was reintroduced to the philosophy of morality, but the focus remained on specifying the rules of right conduct.

But virtues would not go away. In recent decades, there have been calls within philosophy for a return to the ethics of virtue (Anscombe, 1958). "Virtue ethics" is the contemporary approach within philosophy to strengths of character. As described by Rachels (1999), virtue ethics must do the following:

- explain what a virtue is
- list the character traits that are virtues
- explain what these traits mean
- explain why these specific traits are desirable
- address whether virtues are the same for everyone or differ from person to person or culture to culture

With respect to the last matter, Rachels (1999) argued in favor of at least some universal virtues:

> Even in the most disparate societies, people face the same basic problems and have the same basic needs. . . . it may be true that in different societies the virtues are given somewhat different interpretations, and different sorts of actions are counted as satisfying them; and it may be true that some people, because they lead particular sorts of lives in particular sorts of circumstances, will have need of some virtues more than others. But it cannot be right to say simply that whether any particular character trait is a virtue is never anything more than a matter of social convention. The major virtues are mandated not by social convention but by basic facts about our common human condition. (pp. 186–187)

Consistent with this argument, one of the goals of our classification is to specify ubiquitous if not universal strengths of character. However, unlike Rachels, we did not deduce this goal as a plausible one but rather observed that much the same virtues indeed are valued throughout history and across cultures (chapter 2).

Yearley (1990) summarized the modern field of virtue ethics. First, the typical definition of a virtue in effect identifies it as a personality trait, that is, "a disposition to act, desire, and feel that involves the exercise of judgment and leads to a recognizable human excellence or instance of human flourishing" (p. 13). Moreover, virtues are not segregated mechanisms with automatic effects on behavior. Most philosophers emphasize that virtuous activity involves choosing virtue for itself and in light of a justifiable life plan. In more psychological language, a virtue is a property of the whole person and the life that person leads. People can reflect on their own virtues and talk about them to others. They may of course be mistaken, but virtues are *not* the sort of entities that are in principle outside of awareness or the realm of self-commentary (cf. Nisbett & Wilson, 1977). This conclusion is an important one when we turn to the matter of assessing virtues (chapter 28).

Second, listed virtues are typically numerous, drawn from different levels of abstractness, and potentially in conflict. A hierarchy of virtues is therefore introduced by most philosophers to help determine when one or another virtue should be manifested. Indeed, a great deal of discussion has tried to enumerate master virtues (e.g., wisdom, courage, kindness) that take precedence over the others. None has won universal acceptance. Regardless, the exercise of a virtue is invariably discussed as reflecting choice, so in this sense rationality is always an overarching theme, as it was to the early Greek philosophers.

Third, in the act of displaying a virtue, someone does not think of the virtue per se or the way of life to which it is related. "I do not act benevolently in order to be benevolent or to be seen as benevolent by myself or others. . . . I act benevolently because the situation I face fits a description of a situation that elicits my benevolence" (Yearley, 1990, p. 14). Virtue, like the devil, is in the details.

Fourth, enumerated virtues and their hierarchical organization depend on the way of life—the cultural ethos—in which they are embedded. Indeed, the way of life can dictate the content of a virtue. "Whether we can call courageous Robert E. Lee's decision to lead the Confederate Army . . . often will rest on the respondent's actual or assumed social location" (Yearley, 1990, pp. 12–13). This conclusion also has important assessment implications. Concrete questions about virtuous action must be tailored to the cultural reality of the potential respondents. We can measure curiosity or kindness in all corners of the world and across all stages of life, but we need to ask different questions in so doing.

Fifth, virtues are often referred to as corrective, meaning that most if not all counteract some problem thought to be inherent in the human condition, some temptation that needs to be resisted, or some motivation that needs to be rechanneled into something good. Note the potential tension with the stated goals of positive psychology. In accentuating the positive, we cannot ignore the negative. If virtues are usually corrective, they can only be discussed in this context. Conditions of adversity, whether external or internal, must be part of what we address in discussing character strengths. Trauma may or may not build character, but it probably is one of the best ways to reveal it.

In contrast to the different versions of moral law, virtue ethics pays benefits, chiefly its ability to explain moral motivation. Virtue ethics can also accommodate the fact of partiality (Rachels, 1999). Let us explain. Essentially all ethical systems are based on the premise that people are moral equals. But the principle of moral impartiality does not square with the way that people actually live and render moral judgments. Often we are partial to friends and family members, and no one takes us to task for acting this way. The resolution from virtue ethics is that the issue of when to be partial versus impartial depends on the virtue in question. We should love our friends and family members (partiality) and be benevolent to people in general (impartiality). The conflict disappears.

At the same time, virtue ethics strikes many philosophers as incomplete. It does not explain what we should do.

> Why shouldn't a person lie, especially when there is some advantage to be gained from it? Plainly we need an answer that goes beyond the simple observation that doing so would be incompatible with having a particular character trait; we need an explanation of why it is better to have this trait than its opposite. (Rachels, 1999, p. 191)

A related problem is that virtue ethics does not explain how we should adjudicate moral conflict. What happens when two virtues are in conflict, pushing us in altogether different directions?

The philosophical answer to these shortcomings of virtue ethics is to combine this approach with one or another theory of moral conduct (i.e., versions of the moral law tradition; Holmes, 1998; Rachels, 1999). The psychological answer is probably simpler because the relationship of traits to action and the melding of disparate traits into a singular self are precisely the concerns of modern personality psychology. The present classification lists character strengths, just as do the proponents of virtue ethics, but our rendering of strengths brings with them richer psychological content and greater explanatory power.

Let us mention the specific substantive work of Yearley (1990) to make one final point about virtue ethics. Yearley was especially interested in the comparative study of virtue. How can one compare (and contrast) specific virtues across different philosophical and cultural traditions? Yearley suggested two strategies, both of which were followed by our inquiry across culture and history as described in chapter 2. The first is to expand a virtue by extending its range and thus its meaning. So, bravery historically was seen as a virtue of the warrior. But current conceptions see it also as a virtue of how people face psychological or physical difficulties. Indeed, in the modern era, the paradigm case of bravery is not the soldier with his smart bombs but instead the medical patient facing with equanimity long odds against survival.

The second strategy is to introduce the notion of semblances of virtue. One identifies distinctions among types of roughly similar virtuous activities. One then turns around and asks of all the possible distinctions, how many are shared by two conceptions of virtue? Comparison is thus not either-or but a matter of degree.

In creating the present classification, we also used several other ideas from virtue ethics. We heeded the demand of virtue ethics philosophers to be clear about the meaning of character in general and character strengths in particular. We assumed that the important virtues are numerous, that they are related to one another, and that they are linked to a way of life in turn embedded in a cultural and historical setting. Although we arranged our character strengths in a hierarchy, it is not one of importance and motivational precedence but rather one of abstractness. We leave the issue of "master" virtues to empirical study. In sum, we can describe our classification as the social science equivalent of virtue ethics, using the scientific method to inform philosophical pronouncements about the traits of a good person.

SECTION II

STRENGTHS
OF CHARACTER

INTRODUCTION: STRENGTHS OF WISDOM AND KNOWLEDGE

CRITERIA FOR *Strengths of Wisdom and Knowledge*

	Fulfilling	Morally valued	Does not diminish others	Nonfelicitous opposite	Traitlike	Distinctiveness	Paragons	Prodigies	Selective absence	Institutions and rituals	
	1	2	3	4	5	6	7	8	9	10	TALLY
Creativity	X	X	X	X	~X	X	X	X	X	X	10/10
Curiosity	X	X	X	X	X	X	X	X	X	X	10/10
Open-mindedness	X	X	X	X	~X	X	X		X	X	9/10
Love of learning	X	X	X	X	X		X	X		X	8/10
Perspective	X	X	X	X	X	X	X		X	X	9/10

~ Somewhat satisfies criterion.

Strengths of wisdom and knowledge include positive traits related to the acquisition and use of information in the service of the good life. In psychological language, these are cognitive strengths. Many of the strengths in our classification have cognitive aspects—for example, social intelligence, fairness, hope, humor, and spirituality—which is why many philosophers concerned with virtue consider wisdom or reason as the chief virtue making all others possible. However, there are five character strengths studied by psychologists in which cognition is especially salient. As an introduction to this section, we comment briefly on each of these, focusing on how they satisfy the 10 criteria for a character strength described in chapter 1 (see Criteria Table).

■ Creativity [Originality, Ingenuity]

As an individual difference, creativity entails two essential components. First, a creative person must produce ideas or behaviors that are recognizably original—novel, surprising, or unusual. However, originality per se does not define creativity. The relevant behaviors or ideas must also be adaptive. The individual's originality must make a positive contribution to that person's life or to the life of others. It must entail speaking to an audience, not solipsism. Appreciate that a behavior or idea might be adaptive without being at all original. Indeed, most of our daily activities are initially learned from modeling and then become habitual and automatized, untouched at any point by originality. Creativity so defined meets our criteria for a character strength.

CRITERION 1 *Fulfilling* By definition, creativity of all stripes is fulfilling. Wealth and acclaim may follow in the wake of certain creative acts, but these consequences are probably not why people pursue them in the first place or even why they continue to pursue them. Creation feels good. Said another way, creative pastimes, like art or music, are intrinsically motivated. Even a duct-tape Einstein, who has solved an immediate practical problem, takes pride in what he has done, above and beyond devising a solution to the problem at hand.

CRITERION 2 *Morally Valued*   Creativity is morally valued. As we noted in chapter 1, there is an indeterminate perimeter around what is morally valued and what is not, but we think it fair to say that a creative product and by implication its creator have brought beauty, elegance, or function into the world. The creation of something beautiful is a moral good because it elevates others. In the case of everyday creativity, the lives of others may be improved as the invention is disseminated. Consider the mundane yet wonderful example of Post-Its.

The importance of creativity as a human capacity cannot be overemphasized. Our homes and offices are filled with furniture, appliances, and other conveniences that are the products of human inventiveness. We amuse ourselves with the comics in the daily paper, take novels with us to while away the hours on the plane or at the beach, go to movie theaters to see the latest blockbuster, watch television shows and commercials, play games on the computer, attend concerts from classical and jazz to rock and soul, visit museums that display the artistic artifacts of cultures and civilizations—again all implicitly bearing ample testimony to the consequences of the creative mind. The buildings we enter, the cars we drive, the clothes we wear—even the music we hear in the elevators—are all exemplars of some form of creativity. Not surprisingly, creativity is often seen as a good attribute for people to possess. Teachers expect their students to display some creativity in their science projects and term papers. Executives at high-tech firms expect their research and development units to devise new products and their marketing units to conceive novel strategies to promote those products. At a more personal level, creativity is often seen as a sign of mental health and emotional well-being. In fact, various art and music therapies have emerged that promote psychological adjustment and growth through creative expression.

CRITERION 3 *Does Not Diminish Others*   Along these lines, creativity does not diminish other people. By requiring that creativity be adaptive, we guarantee that many benefit when one is creative. Indeed, one creative person may inspire others to creative acts. Consider the onetime renegade art movement of Impressionism, begun by a few disenfranchised artists who could not persuade the academy to hang their paintings. But Impressionism eventually became an influential movement in its own right.

CRITERION 4 *Nonfelicitous Opposite*   The obvious antonyms of *creative* are undesirable: *dull, boring, insipid, monotonous, unimaginative, uninspired,* and so on. The character strength of creativity therefore satisfies our antonym test.

CRITERION 5 *Traitlike*   Creativity is traitlike: People can be arranged along a continuum of originality, and they more or less stay there. One qualification is in order. As chapter 4 details, psychologists studying creativity often distinguish between Big Creativity—as shown by famous artists and scientists—and Everyday Creativity, what we might call ingenuity or cleverness. Examples of Everyday Creativity are easy to generate. Consider our friends and neighbors who find uses for objects we might put in the trash, or who arrange the furniture in their offices or apartments to be both aesthetic and functional. Consider people—not us—who find uses for word-processing programs not envisioned by their creators. What is the link between Big Creativity and Everyday Creativity? It is unknown, and so we cannot conclude at present that across-the-board creativity per se is a trait. Future researchers need to look at the associations between these two types of creativity. Do they reflect common psychological processes? Do they have similar origins? Most important, do they co-occur in the same individuals?

CRITERION 6 *Distinctiveness*   Creativity is not decomposable into any of the other classified strengths, although we hasten to point out that it can be blended with many, if not all, of them. So, a person high in creativity and gratitude might devise novel yet appropriate ways of expressing thanks. A person high in creativity and humor is the one who invents a joke rather than just passing it on.

CRITERION 7 *Paragons*   There are acknowledged paragons of creativity, some so well known as to be almost clichéd: Albert Einstein, Madame Curie, Michelangelo, Dom Perignon, Bill Gates, Ludwig Wittgenstein, George Washington Carver, Pablo Picasso, Thomas Edison, Walt Disney, Neil Simon, and Florence Nightingale.

CRITERION 8 *Prodigies*   There are also well-recognized prodigies—Wolfgang Amadeus Mozart, Anne Frank, Ron Howard, and Bobby Fischer come to mind—although we must be careful not to confuse the prodigious display of technical expertise in some domain with prodigious creativity.

CRITERION 9 *Selective Absence*   The absence of originality, virtually by definition, is common. Let us simply label it as conformity and refer the reader to the decades of thoughtful discussion by social psychologists regarding its pros and cons (e.g., Asch, 1956). But what about those strikingly devoid of creativity? We suggest that attention to triteness might help us to identify such unfortunate folks. Think of all the interviews you have heard with professional athletes, most of whom give the most scripted answers imaginable. There of course is triteness in all venues of life, and we suspect that in some societies—like the contemporary United States—it creates a cultural contradiction. We the people value originality yet love to follow fads, whether watching clones of last year's popular television shows or buying this season's hot Christmas present for our kids or getting tattooed and pierced.

CRITERION 10 *Institutions and Rituals*   For Big Creativity, there are a myriad of ways in which society tries to encourage and cultivate its various forms: art classes, music lessons, creative writing workshops, and the like. The encouragement of Everyday Creativity is less obvious, but if one looks, there are many examples. Heloise's household tips, for example, are not only a catalog of creative solutions to problems around the house but also an example of how things like this might get created in the first place. The how-to genre is a thriving one, and books include countless examples of Everyday Creativity. Or consider what we think is a neglected form of creativity: entrepreneurial genius as shown by amazon.com's Jeff Bezos, McDonald's Ray Kroc, and the Border brothers of bookshop fame.

■ Curiosity [Interest, Novelty-Seeking, Openness to Experience]

Chapter 5 defines curiosity as one's intrinsic interest in ongoing experience. Curious people pursue experiential novelty, variety, and challenge. Like creativity, curiosity satisfies our criteria for a character strength.

CRITERION 1 *Fulfilling*   As an intrinsically motivated trait, curiosity is fulfilling. Finding out an answer, having a new experience, learning a new fact—all satisfy the curious individual. Someone who is not curious evidences no such fulfillment and may even be disquieted by novel experiences. Because curiosity can never be satisfied in the same way twice, it may fuel the expansion of oneself, inasmuch as new experiences and new information are integrated once obtained.

CRITERION 2 *Morally Valued*   Curiosity is usually valued. We thrill when our children discover activities that engage them. We are flattered when someone is curious about our opinions and experiences. We find attractive someone with "lots of interests," even if they do not coincide with our own. In personal ads, for example, a common gambit is the listing of one's interests, for example, NPR, *New York Times* crossword puzzles, piña coladas, travel, and music. In some cases, the advertiser may be fishing for a partner in these particular pastimes, but in other cases, we suspect that the intended point is the more generic message "I am interested and therefore interesting." Nonetheless, curiosity can have a downside. An overly curious person may strike others as intrusive. One of the hallmark behaviors of curiosity is the constant asking of questions, but not all questions are appropriate in all situations. "Have you always been this fat?" "Why aren't you married?" "How much money do you make?" An overly curious person may stick his or her nose into danger, by ignoring "no trespassing" signs, literally or metaphorically.

CRITERION 3 *Does Not Diminish Others*   The social costs of excessive curiosity notwithstanding, curiosity does not usually diminish other people. It is fun to interact with someone who is intrigued by everything. Although we are aware of no research on the point, we suspect that curiosity can be contagious.

CRITERION 4 *Nonfelicitous Opposite*   The obvious antonyms of curiosity are undesirable: *boredom, ennui, disinterest, world-weariness,* and so on. These are terrible psychological states and underscore the social value accorded to the presence of curiosity, even in the extreme.

CRITERION 5 *Traitlike*   Curiosity is an individual difference that emerges in infancy and perhaps has a biological basis. Research suggests that curiosity is stable across the life span: Curious children grow into curious adolescents who become curious adults.

CRITERION 6 *Distinctiveness*   Curiosity is not readily decomposable into other classified strengths. As noted in chapter 1, we suspect that love of learning, a strength we discuss shortly, might be a special case of curiosity. Many of the examples just cited, when they entail the systematic accumulation and application of new information and skills, do double duty as examples of love of learning (chapter 6). Also, it was difficult for us to describe curiosity in the concrete without lapsing into language that sounded like another character strength: vitality and zest (chapter 12). We think the difference lies in the cognitive flavor of curiosity. Curious people want to know things. Zestful people may or may not display their strength of enthusiasm in cognitive ways.

CRITERION 7 *Paragons*   Acknowledged paragons of curiosity include explorers and adventurers. We were taught that Columbus and Magellan were motivated by economic concerns, a search for more efficient trade routes, but surely curiosity was also behind their voyages. We can be sure that mountain climbers like Edmund Hillary were not looking for trade routes. Timothy Leary did not embark on his LSD experiments to secure his job at Harvard University. Whatever their other motives, these people were strikingly curious.

CRITERION 8 *Prodigies*   There are also curiosity prodigies, children who go beyond the typical why?-ing of the young to display uncanny interest in the world about them. For example, Helen Keller was obviously curious about the world that lay beyond her damaged senses.

CRITERION 9 *Selective Absence*   The absence of curiosity might be identified with smug complacency, but the research reviewed in chapter 5 links it instead to boredom, an aversive state associated with anxiety and depression. Regardless, people with no curiosity exist, and some come to our attention in the wake of terrible crimes—the next-door neighbors of murderers and kidnappers who were exposed to clues galore yet never were curious enough to note these as unusual.

CRITERION 10 *Institutions and Rituals*   Society tries to cultivate curiosity, although we think the typical strategies miss the point. Societal emphasis is usually on identifying experiences that a child might find interesting. Children are exposed to a smorgasbord of academic, artistic, and athletic activities and then are encouraged to sample them until they find one that they like. Adolescents in the United States are encouraged to play the field when they begin dating. Colleges allow students to have undeclared majors. This smorgasbord approach assumes that the activity drives curiosity, and the emphasis accordingly is on finding the right experience. From the viewpoint of a psychology of character strengths, we suggest that this approach is incomplete. Of course, some activities are more interesting to some people than to others, but curiosity is an individual difference of demonstrable generality. If curiosity per se can be cultivated, no one need ever search for interesting experiences—one will simply have them.

■ Open-Mindedness [Judgment, Critical Thinking]

A strength included in virtually all virtue catalogs, ancient and modern, is one that refers to a way of thinking variously referred to as judgment, critical thinking, rationality, or open-mindedness. Although we have never doubted that a strength of this ilk belongs in our classification, we have struggled from the very beginning of our project with the right way to label it so that its connotations did not swamp its denotations. We learned early on from focus groups that at least some people (i.e., young adults in the United States) reacted negatively to the first label we chose—rationality—because they juxtaposed it with emotion and intuition and saw it both as the province of stereotypical males (who disagree with others by branding their thinking irrational) and as a strategy for denying authentic feelings. Consider Mr. Spock of *Star Trek* fame. Our informants did not own rationality, and our early attempts to create self-report questionnaire items tapping this strength did not fare well when it was framed this way.

Even more troubling about the term *rationality* is research showing that good thinking can be very topic specific. People who can do calculus or formal logic effortlessly may not be able to make change or embark on the best career path.

The defeatist solution to these problems in conceptualizing this strength would be to jettison it altogether from our classification, but another strategy is to try to approach rationality not in terms of the content of beliefs but in terms of the judgment processes that produce them. Here we start to use different words: *flexible, broad-minded, complex,* and *open*. These terms describe good thinking in terms of its style rather than its end products. The benefit of this view is that it does not require us to judge the quality of people's thinking by the veracity of their conclusions (which we can do in mathematics but in precious few other domains). And we do not have to agree with people's beliefs to recognize that in some cases they were arrived at thoughtfully whereas in other cases they were not.

For this reason, we have rendered this character strength specifically as open-mindedness and more generally as judgment. We wish to emphasize that the open-minded person works at this style of thinking. He or she is not indecisive, wishy-washy, nihilistic, or permissive. Neither does the open-minded thinker bring this style to bear on all matters. Red traffic lights mean stop, and viewing this signal from all possible angles is simply stupid. The open-minded thinker engages this style when confronted with an appropriately complex judgment in which evidence for and against a belief must be examined and weighed. Let us take a look at how well judgment in these terms satisfies our criteria for a character strength.

CRITERION 1 *Fulfilling*   Good judgment is fulfilling, in part because it leads to good decisions and in part because it contributes to a coherent view of the world. Most of us feel satisfied when we have made a thoughtful decision, when we know the reasons for our beliefs. Open-mindedness makes the examined life possible.

CRITERION 2 *Morally Valued*   Good judgment is valued, and open-mindedness especially so. Parents and teachers alike want children to look at both sides of complex issues. Open-mindedness shows up in perspective taking and is an important cognitive ingredient of empathy. Conversely, we all have acquaintances and colleagues—and sometimes employers—who embrace the "my way or the highway" approach to life, and we fault their style of thinking even when we happen to agree with their conclusions.

CRITERION 3 *Does Not Diminish Others*   Assuming that observers themselves are sufficiently open-minded, the observation of open-mindedness on the part of others can be elevating. It certainly can defuse emotional issues under discussion. Like the other strengths so far discussed, good judgment is probably contagious (e.g., town meetings), although the evidence is stronger for the contagion of closed-mindedness (e.g., mob violence, lynching). Chapter 6 describes well-known examples of contagious bad judgment under the rubric of groupthink (Janis, 1982). At the individual level, the negative consequences of functional fixedness—being unable to break one's mental set in solving problems—have been familiar for decades (Luchins, 1942).

CRITERION 4 *Nonfelicitous Opposite*   Consider inflexibility, rigidity, intolerance, prejudice, ethnocentrism, authoritarianism, dogmatism, prejudice, and stereotyping—all entail the opposite of open-mindedness and have generated large research literatures within social psychology demonstrating that these antonyms of good judgment are remarkably undesirable (e.g., Adorno, Frenkel-Brunswik, Levinson, & Sanford, 1950). There is likewise a long tradition with clinical psychology that describes various disorders in terms of inflexible cognitive styles (Kendall, 1992). From this viewpoint, psychological disorder is produced by irrational or illogical ways of thinking, and the common solution suggested is the cultivation of open-mindedness about personally relevant beliefs.

CRITERION 5 *Traitlike*   What about the traitedness of this individual difference? As chapter 6 describes, people vary with respect to open-mindedness, and it shows a degree of cross-situational generality, so long as each situation involves a complex decision.

CRITERION 6 *Distinctiveness*   Judgment is not decomposable into other classified strengths, although the converse may not be true. That is, open-minded thinking is probably an ingredient in character strengths like love of learning, leadership, social intelligence, and prudence, all of which entail the broad examination of relevant evidence.

CRITERION 7 *Paragons*   There exist consensually recognized paragons of open-mindedness. For example, we think of psychologist William James, who vigorously recruited to his Harvard department one of his ideological opponents. A friend was surprised and asked why James had done this, given that he disagreed so strongly with the man's ideas. James replied, "Because now all points of view are represented."

CRITERION 8 *Prodigies*   Judgment prodigies probably cannot exist until children achieve the Piagetian cognitive stage of formal operations, allowing abstract and hypothetical thinking.

CRITERION 9 *Selective Absence*   People devoid of judgment are so rampant as to require little documentation. Indeed, chapter 6 describes open-mindedness as a corrective against the deeply rooted human tendency to accord one's own beliefs special status as unassailable and to seek out information consistent with them (cf. Greenwald, 1980).

CRITERION 10 *Institutions and Rituals*   Societal institutions for cultivating open-mindedness include high school debate, op-ed pieces, political debates, education generally, and the clichéd advice to list pros and cons of difficult decisions. One of the rationales for a liberal arts education or international travel is that it encourages open-mindedness. Cognitive therapy as developed by Albert

Ellis (1962) and Aaron Beck (1976) involves a host of strategies for remedial training in good judgment. One might hope that television shows of the *Crossfire* genre, featuring hosts on opposite sides of the political spectrum, might encourage good judgment by viewers, but we doubt it. None of the individual hosts remotely displays open-mindedness, although they do a spectacular job interrupting one another.

■ Love of Learning

Love of learning[1] can be conceptualized in different ways. One view sees it as an inherent part of all human nature, especially evident in the very young, who are driven to learn about the world they have entered, but also apparent across the life span in so-called effectance motivation: the drive to interact competently with the world, which necessarily entails learning how to do so (R. W. White, 1959). Another view sees it as a contextualized individual difference, apparent with respect to given subject matters (e.g., flowers or dinosaurs). When this individual difference is general across topics, we can speak of love of learning as a strength of character. People who possess the general trait of love of learning are positively motivated to acquire new skills or knowledge or to build on existing skills and knowledge. As pointed out in chapter 7, love of learning has not been studied as a general character strength, so our conclusion that it satisfies our criteria is tentative. It nevertheless seems to fare well vis-à-vis these criteria.

CRITERION 1 *Fulfilling* Love of learning is inherently fulfilling—that is why it is called love. The person high in this character strength experiences positive feelings when acquiring new skills and knowledge, even when frustrations intrude. Learning viewed in this way is a challenge, not the automatic acquisition of microscopic habits. We offer the qualification that the positive feelings may not always be front and center in awareness while learning occurs. Instead, the person may be in a state of flow and not especially mindful of anything other than the task at hand of learning something new (Csikszentmihalyi, 1990). Adults may take classes in photography or origami, at community colleges or local YMCAs, not as career preparation but because it is satisfying to learn something new whether or not professional expertise is obtained. The flip side of these examples is the continuing education required of physicians, with classes often held in holiday resorts to make learning palatable.

---

[1]In English, we apparently have no single word that captures love of learning. In Chinese, there is a single phrase—*hao-xue-xin*—that translates into English as the "heart and mind for wanting to learn" and nicely captures this strength of character (Li, 2002).

CRITERION 2 *Morally Valued*   Love of learning is valued in its own right. This strength is one of the most treasured by teachers when they see it in their students. Rare are the parents who do not want their child to stay in school and learn as much as possible, with or without a payoff. Indeed, love of learning is valued in virtually all roles, and to describe someone as intellectually alive is a compliment of the highest order.

As we have developed our classification, we have frequently been called upon to provide a so-what answer with respect to why various character strengths deserve attention. As argued in chapter 1, we do not think kindness, honesty, and playfulness require any justification; they simply are desirable. But not everyone is convinced in such cases, and we have therefore felt obliged to sketch the adaptive consequences of these styles. The notable exception is love of learning, because at least in our society, learning has become an unalloyed good requiring no justification. When politicians or citizen groups call for better schools, no one ever asks why. We hope the day will arrive when all character strengths need no extrinsic justification, but for the time being, we point mainly to love of learning as inherently valued.

CRITERION 3 *Does Not Diminish Others*   Someone's love of learning can elevate other people in the vicinity. We thrill when our children throw themselves into learning about a new topic or when they finally find a college major they love. As we suggested in the cases of creativity and curiosity, love of learning may also be contagious, and whereas our own classroom experiences have not been as mythic as those depicted in *Dead Poets Society*, we have seen the love of learning steal from one student to another until all are engaged.

CRITERION 4 *Nonfelicitous Opposite*   The obvious antonyms of love of learning are negative—*intellectual resistance* and *inertia*. We also remind the reader of the antonyms of curiosity, which when attached to learning can be used to describe the opposite of this character strength—all are negative.

CRITERION 5 *Traitlike*   Love of learning is a trait that for some is stable across life. The phrase *lifelong learner* has entered our everyday lexicon to refer to an individual continually driven to acquire new information. As university teachers, we have learned never to refer to our older students as anything other than students because that is exactly what they are.

CRITERION 6 *Distinctiveness*   As already discussed, we suspect that love of learning is a decomposable strength, and pending our further research, we will conclude that this criterion for a character strength is *not* met.

CRITERION 7 *Paragons*   Paragons of learning encompass both well-known scholars and everyday people. A famous example that is neither is the young

Abraham Lincoln, who walked back and forth 20 miles to a library to borrow a grammar book. Or remember the varied accomplishments of Benjamin Franklin and Thomas Jefferson, which included the founding of great universities.

We recently heard a talk by psychologist Laura King, who described her experiences as a tutor in an adult literacy program. Her student had an epiphany about literacy when he realized that reading was not something that one turned on and off. Street signs, for example, were always there to be read, and he reveled in his ability to read them. As Professor King tells the story, her student then said, "The world is filled with signs to be read." We all loved learning about this individual.

CRITERION 8 *Prodigies*   Prodigies of learning also exist, and indeed are among the most frequently documented prodigies; for example Jean-Jacques Rousseau, John Stuart Mill, Johannes Kepler, René Descartes, William Pitt, and Samuel Taylor Coleridge all showed prodigious learning accomplishments (C. M. Cox, 1926). Closer to psychology, we have the example of Jean Piaget, who published his first paper at age 11. In the here and now, we have the example of Basie Gitlin, a Connecticut eighth grader who has collected antiquarian books since the age of 9. We recently heard him interviewed on *Book TV,* and what is most striking is not his collection of 2,500 titles but the intelligence and humor with which he can discuss them and their place in history.

CRITERION 9 *Selective Absence*   Is there anyone who does not love learning in at least one domain? As noted, one can be skeptical about the existence of an across-the-board absence of this strength, except as a symptom of profound depression or catatonia. We can think of no other examples, so we tentatively suggest that this strength criterion is *not* satisfied by love of learning.

CRITERION 10 *Institutions and Rituals*   Perhaps more so than for any other character strength in our classification, practices have long been institutionalized in all societies to cultivate and sustain love of learning: schools of all types, training programs, apprenticeships, internships, mentoring relationships, and so on. To be sure, the content of the information or skill to be imparted varies drastically across institutions, but each institution tries to convey a love for the process that goes beyond specific content.

■ Perspective [Wisdom]

The final cognitive strength is most commonly described by psychologists as wisdom, but because we use this term to label this entire virtue class, we have opted instead to call the specific strength *perspective*. We alert the reader to the possible source of confusion. Perspective (wisdom) refers to the ability to take stock of life in large terms, in ways that make sense to oneself and others. Perspective is the product of knowledge and experience, but it is more than the accumulation of information. It is the coordination of this information and its deliberate use to improve well-being. In a social context, perspective allows the individual to listen to others, to evaluate what they say, and then to offer good (sage) advice. Directions back to the interstate do not qualify as wisdom, unless the highway is the metaphoric route to the life well lived. The investigation of perspective so defined is flourishing today. This character strength well satisfies our criteria for a character strength.

CRITERION 1 *Fulfilling*   Perspective is fulfilling for the individual and society. It makes the less tangible forms of social support possible, and we know that social support is beneficial, obviously for the recipient, but more interestingly for the provider as well.

CRITERION 2 *Morally Valued*   Virtually by definition, perspective is morally valued. Our own society has not institutionalized the role of the sage as have other cultural traditions with identified village elders, but we nonetheless know and celebrate the wise men and wise women in our vicinity. We turn to them when we are troubled or confused about the larger issues of life. Perhaps psychotherapists function as sages for the upper middle class (cf. J. Smith, Staudinger, & Baltes, 1994).

CRITERION 3 *Does Not Diminish Others*   Again by definition, perspective is elevating. We may not always follow wise advice, but we are impressed when we hear it. Wisdom imparted can trigger an aha experience. The major religious leaders of history—for example, Jesus, Lao-tzu, the Buddha, the Prophet—provided perspectives that galvanized entire cultures. When wrongdoing is carried out in the name of religion, it is not the imparted big-picture perspective that is misused but rather individual tenets taken out of context by disciples who themselves are anything but wise.

CRITERION 4 *Nonfelicitous Opposite*   The antonyms of wisdom—*foolishness, thoughtlessness,* and *idiocy*—are obviously negative.

CRITERION 5 *Traitlike*   Perspective is an individual difference both stable and general. Empirical studies of wisdom often solicit community nominations of wise individuals, and these are readily forthcoming.

CRITERION 6 *Distinctiveness*   Perspective is not decomposable into other strengths in our classification, although it may allow some of these other strengths—for example, social intelligence, leadership, self-regulation—to be displayed in the most optimal fashion.

CRITERION 7 *Paragons* Perspective is consensually embodied in various paragons, including the religious leaders already mentioned and in more secular forms in elder statesmen and stateswomen like Winston Churchill, Jimmy Carter, and Eleanor Roosevelt and revered musicians like Itzhak Perlman, B. B. King, and Carlos Santana. In his theorizing, Carl Jung even elevated the paragon of wisdom to archetypal status, arguing that the image of the sage is a human universal.

CRITERION 8 *Prodigies* We doubt that perspective prodigies are common because a child's level of cognitive development must allow sufficiently abstract thinking to afford a perspective worth imparting. Nonetheless, in light of research suggesting that wisdom need not be accompanied by gray hair and wrinkles, we conclude that the lower age limit for the manifestation of perspective has yet to be established. It is much lower than senior citizenship.

CRITERION 9 *Selective Absence* Foolish people also exist, even among the elderly, and we refer the reader to Erikson's (1963) discussion of sapientism, the pretense and perversion of wisdom seen among those who have failed to live well and who begin every sentence with "When I was your age _____." We remind the reader of Shakespeare's Polonius and every pompous blowhard, on the left or the right, who interrupts and shouts down other pompous blowhards on political talk shows.

CRITERION 10 *Institutions and Rituals* Our last criterion for a character strength is the existence of societal institutions that cultivate and nurture the strength. Perspective—wisdom—has long been viewed as the province of the elderly, so this criterion is often met only in an indirect way by allowing people to age and then according those who have aged well special status as advice givers. Interestingly, as we describe in chapter 8, there are apparently few differences in wisdom across the adult years, which means that this passive intervention is based on an incorrect assumption.

Less indirect are apprenticeships in which a younger individual learns from an older individual, not only the technical aspects of some craft or skill but also the larger perspective in which techniques can be wisely deployed. The contemporary United States, as a youth-oriented culture, may not even cultivate perspective in these indirect ways. We want our leaders and even our network news commentators to be young and fresh, uncontaminated as it were by the experiences that we know produce wisdom. We even value youthfulness in our teachers, confusing enthusiasm and the ability to relate with perspective. The good news here is ongoing research, described in chapter 8, showing that perspective can be cultivated even among the relatively young. We can only hope that the fruits of this research will lead to the creation of explicit rituals for encouraging this valued strength.

4. CREATIVITY

[Originality, Ingenuity]

The following case illustrates the transformational power of creativity. It also provides an instructive middle case between the extraordinary creativity of the world-renowned genius and the more mundane creativity shown in everyday problem solving.

■ *At age 68, Elizabeth Layton was a retired homemaker and aging grandmother, living out her final years in a small prairie town in Kansas (Layton, 1984). There was really nothing outstanding about her except for one fact: She frequently suffered profound depression. Indeed, for more than three decades she had undergone all kinds of therapy, including drugs and electroshock. Nothing really helped, but she managed to persevere. And then disaster struck. Her youngest son died after a prolonged illness, plunging her into the darkest despair ever. On several occasions she contemplated suicide as the only exit from her seemingly insurmountable depression. Yet following up her sister's wise suggestion, she enrolled in a drawing class. Elizabeth's art teacher recognized her elderly student's talent even before the course was completed. Elizabeth just loved to draw and draw and draw, creating one sketch after another with great facility and expressiveness. Besides allowing her to release pent-up feelings and beliefs—about death, sadness, AIDS, racism, nuclear war, American commercialism, and other personal and social issues—painting gave Elizabeth something to look forward to each day. She found her mission in life. Her works began to be displayed in art museums and galleries, first locally and then in a traveling exhibit that toured the nation. By the time she died in 1993, she had produced nearly a thousand drawings that made a deep impression on admirers all over the United States. To be sure, Elizabeth will not go down in history as a Michelangelo or a*

Picasso. Yet that was never her intention, nor do her artistic accomplishments matter most from the standpoint of a positive psychology of character. The significant fact is that creativity allowed her to live out her final 15 years with a joy and a sense of purpose that she had been denied all the previous decades of her life. Moreover, while pursuing her vision, she managed to bring happiness and meaning to others. Elizabeth Layton's long life and brief career thus amply illustrate creativity's potential as a constructive human capacity. ■

■ Consensual Definition

As an individual difference, creativity entails two essential components. First, a creative person must produce ideas or behaviors that are recognizably original. The individual must be capable of generating ideas or behaviors that are novel, surprising, or unusual. However, originality alone does not signify that a person possesses creative ability. Individuals suffering from severe mental disorders, such as schizophrenia, often exhibit behaviors and express ideas that appear highly original. Even within the range of normal psychological functioning, some persons may appear more eccentric than creative in their activities or interests. Hence arises the necessity of the second component. The behaviors or ideas must be not only original but also adaptive. To be adaptive the individual's originality must make a positive contribution to that person's life or to the lives of others. Bizarre hallucinations and delusions like those that characterize schizophrenia lack this feature. Instead of solving life's problems, these symptoms make life all the more problematic. At the same time, a behavior or idea might be adaptive without being at all original. Most of our daily activities that we carry out habitually are highly adaptive without containing an ounce of originality.

Neither originality nor adaptiveness constitutes a discrete, all-or-none criterion. Both admit to degrees. This means that creativity itself varies across individuals. At one extreme are those individuals who rarely if ever come up with an original idea, and when they do, that idea seldom works. At the other extreme are those persons who become highly recognized for their exceptional creativity, such as great scientists, poets, composers, and painters (Gardner, 1993a). Such extreme originality is sometimes referred to as Big C creativity (Simonton, 2000). Somewhere between these two extremes are those who manifest what might be considered little c or everyday creativity—what we refer to as ingenuity. Such persons are able to generate creative solutions to the various problems they encounter at both home and work, but their creativity does not result in products that make a substantial impression on others beyond their immediate circle of family, friends, or coworkers.

■ Theoretical Traditions

Initially, creativity was associated with the divine rather than the human. Many of the world's religions have a concept of a god or gods who act as creators or makers. In the Judeo-Christian-Islamic tradition, for instance, the Supreme Being is commonly identified as the Creator of the universe, the world, and all that inhabit it, including human beings. Even when individual humans exhibited creativity, the performance was attributed to divine inspiration of some kind. An example is the ancient Greek belief in the Muses. There was a Muse for all major creative activities of classical times, including heroic and epic poetry, lyric and love poetry, sacred poetry, tragedy, comedy, music, dance, and even astronomy and history. The corresponding Muse was thought to provide a guiding spirit or source of inspiration for the mortal creator. This usage underlies several commonplace expressions, such as to say that one has lost one's Muse when one has run out of creative ideas.

Genius is another concept closely identified with creativity throughout history. This concept harks back to the ancient Romans. According to Roman mythology, each individual was born with a guardian spirit who watched out for the person's fate and distinctive individuality. With time, the term was taken to indicate the person's special talents or aptitudes. Although in the beginning everybody could be said to have a genius, at least in the sense of possessing a unique capacity, the term eventually was confined to those whose gifts set them well apart from the average. The expression *creative genius* thus unites two concepts with Greek and Roman roots pertaining to how the spiritual world permeates human affairs. Outstanding creativity was the gift of the gods or spirits, not a human act. Even during the Italian Renaissance, when European civilization was becoming secularized by the advent of humanism, rudiments of this ascription remained. For instance, Michelangelo's contemporaries often ascribed his creative genius to divine powers.

With the increased secularization of Western thought, the locus of creativity gradually moved from the spiritual to the human world. Once this cultural shift took place, the phenomenon became the subject of psychological inquiry. Several of the great figures in the discipline's history took an interest in creativity, including Francis Galton, William James, Sigmund Freud, Wolfgang Köhler, Max Wertheimer, and B. F. Skinner.

Nonetheless, the psychologist who probably deserves the most credit for establishing creativity as a critical research topic is the psychometrician J. P. Guilford, whose 1950 presidential address before the American Psychological Association is often considered a call to arms on behalf of this heretofore overlooked subject. More important, Guilford (1967) made many direct contributions to the research literature, most notably by devising widely used instruments for assessing individual differences in creativity. In the latter half of the 20th century, the interest in creativity steadily grew and diversified such that researchers were covering a fairly wide range of subtopics.

Following a minor lull in activity in the 1970s, creativity research attained new heights in the 1980s and 1990s. This growth is demonstrated by (a) the advent of several creativity handbooks (e.g., J. A. Glover, Ronning, & Reynolds, 1989; Sternberg, 1999a); (b) the appearance in 1988 of the *Creativity Research Journal*, which complemented the *Journal of Creative Behavior* founded in 1967; and (c) the 1999 publication of the two-volume *Encyclopedia of Creativity* (Runco & Pritzker, 1999). Creativity now can be considered as a legitimate topic for scientific inquiry in mainstream psychological research.

The study of creativity has attracted a great variety of psychologists representing a diversity of subdisciplines. Cognitive psychologists tend to focus on the thought processes that underlie the phenomenon, sometimes implementing their theories as computer programs that attempt to simulate creativity. Social psychologists are more likely to concentrate on the interpersonal relationships and social influences that are most prone to enhance or inhibit individual creativity. Some developmental psychologists scrutinize the early childhood and adolescent experiences that best contribute to the growth of creative potential, and other developmental psychologists examine the realization of that acquired potential during the life course. Personality psychologists investigate the motives, values, interests, traits, and styles most strongly associated with personal creativity. Clinical psychologists, finally, may show more fascination with creativity as a treatment technique, as in the case of art therapy.

As a consequence of this range, certain topics in creativity research cut across the various subdisciplines of the field. An example is the large literature on the creative product, especially in the arts. Whereas cognitive psychologists examine the mental processes involved in the perception of a painting, poem, or musical composition, personality psychologists look at how certain stable personal dispositions affect the judgment of artistic creations. Developmental psychologists investigate how artistic expression changes over the life span, whereas clinical psychologists study artistic expression as a diagnostic tool. All the while, social psychologists document the settings and expectations that encourage the output of effective artistic products.

Coupled with this disciplinary diversity is the impressive variety of theoretical perspectives that have been brought to bear upon the subject. Indeed, it is difficult to conceive a single major theoretical orientation that has not tried to make a contribution to our understanding of human creativity. In particular, the list includes psychoanalytic, behaviorist, Gestalt, information-processing, and humanistic theories—virtually every great school of psychology. Nevertheless, it is also true that a large proportion of the studies devoted to creativity have been more empirically than theoretically oriented. Of special importance here is the considerable body of work dedicated to devising means to assess individual differences in creativity, the topic to which we now turn.

■ Measures

Psychologists wishing to assess individual differences in creativity have a tremendous range of instruments from which to choose. Before investigators can settle on any single test or battery of tests, they must address four major questions. First, what is the age of the target population? Some measures are specifically designed for school-age populations, whether children or adolescents, whereas other measures are targeted at adult populations. Second, which domain of creativity is to be assessed? Not only may creativity in the arts differ substantially from creativity in the sciences, but there also may be significant contrasts within specific arts (e.g., music versus literature) or sciences (e.g., mathematics versus invention). Third, what is the magnitude of creativity to be evaluated—everyday problem-solving ability or eminent creativity that earns awards and honors? Fourth, which manifestation of creativity is to be targeted? That is, the investigator must decide whether creativity manifests itself primarily as a product, a process, or a person. Some instruments postulate that creativity takes the form of a concrete product, others assume that creativity involves a particular type of cognitive process, while still others posit that it entails a personal disposition of some kind.

Of these four questions, it is the last that is perhaps the most crucial. Assessment strategies differ dramatically depending on whether creativity is best manifested as a product, process, or person (Table 4.1). The significance of this point should become apparent in what follows.

Product Measures

Ultimately, a creative idea should take some concrete form, such as a poem, story, painting, or design. Hence, one obvious approach to creativity assessment is to measure the quantity or quality of productive output. A case in point is the Consensual Assessment Technique devised by Amabile (1982). Here a research participant is asked to make some product, such as a collage or a poem, which is then assessed by an independent set of experts. This technique has proved especially useful in laboratory experiments on the social circumstances that are most likely to favor creative behavior. However, this approach has at least two disadvantages. First, the creativity of an individual is decided according to performance on a single task. Second, the assessment is based on a task that may not be representative of the domain in which the individual is most creative. For instance, a creative writer will not necessarily do well on a task in the visual arts, such as making collages.

An alternative is to assess individual differences in creativity according to products that the person has spontaneously generated. For example, the Lifetime Creativity Scales assess creative behavior by asking participants to self-identify examples of their own creative achievements (R. Richards, Kinney,

TABLE 4.1   *Approaches to Creativity Measurement*

The creative product

Assumption	Creativity generates creative products; the products may have either personal or social importance
Benefits	Based on objective, verifiable behaviors
Drawbacks	May not be applicable to all forms of creativity; problem of weighting products (poems versus novels)
Examples	Consensual Assessment Technique; Lifetime Creativity Scales

The creative process

Assumption	Specific mental processes underlie the creative act
Benefits	Strong foundation in theories of the creative process
Drawbacks	Validity depends on theory's validity; creativity may not entail distinct cognitive processes
Examples	Remote Associates Test; Unusual Uses Test

The creative person

Assumption	The capacity for creativity requires a specific profile of traits and/or developmental experiences
Benefits	Can use already established personality measures; biographical inventories have more general applicability (e.g., deceased individuals can be studied)
Drawbacks	Frequently low validity coefficients; profiles may vary according to field (e.g., science vs. art)
Examples	Creative Personality Scale; How Do You Think Scale

Lunde, Benet, & Merzel, 1988). According to this approach, creativity assessment is based on multiple products in the domain that the individual finds most germane to personal creative expression. Although this instrument has proven validity and utility, it can be objected that a product's creativity requires an external assessment, such as that provided in the Consensual Assessment Technique. Furthermore, this instrument is clearly aimed at everyday creativity rather than creative output that is highly valued professionally or socially.

One way to assess Big C creativity is to use a productivity measure. Thus, the creativity of scientists may be gauged by counting journal articles and that of inventors by counting patents. Often such measures of pure quantity of output are supplemented by evaluations of quality. For example, the quality of a scientist's productivity may be assessed by the number of citations to his or her work. Another approach is to assess creative impact in terms of awards and honors received or the evaluations of experts in the field—a tactic that dates back to Francis Galton (1869). One especially innovative strategy is Ludwig's (1992) Creative Achievement Scale, which provides an objective approach to evaluating a creator's lifework. This scale has proved useful in addressing the classic question of whether exceptional creativity is associated with some degree of psychopathology (the mad-genius debate).

Process Measures

One major drawback of product measures is that they are barren of truly psychological content. These measures stress outward behavior and its impact rather than internal mental states. Yet presumably some special thought processes underlie these creative products; accordingly, psychologists can instead devise instruments that tap into these crucial processes. For example, Mednick (1962) theorized that creativity requires the capacity to generate remote associations that can connect hitherto disparate ideas. He implemented this theory by devising the Remote Association Test (RAT), which has seen considerable use in subsequent research. A person taking the RAT must identify a word that has an associative linkage with three separate stimulus words—for example, associating the word *chair* with the given words *wheel, electric, high.*

An even more popular set of measures was devised by Guilford (1967) in the context of his multidimensional theory of intelligence. These measures assess various kinds of divergent thinking, which is supposed to provide the basis for creativity. Divergent thinking is the capacity to generate a great variety of responses to a given set of stimuli. Unlike convergent thinking, which aims at the single most correct response, ideational productivity is emphasized. A specific instance is the Unusual Uses Test, which asks research participants to come up with as many uses as possible for ordinary objects, such as a toothpick or paperclip. The participants' responses can then be scored for fluency (number of responses), flexibility (number of distinct categories to which the responses belong), and originality (how rare the response is relative to others taking the test).

Although the foregoing measures were initially conceived for assessing creativity in adults, comparable measures have been devised for use with children and adolescents. Indeed, such measures have become especially commonplace in educational settings. Probably the most well known instruments for this purpose are the Torrance Tests of Creative Thinking (Crammond, 1994). Although designed to assess creativity in the early developmental years, these tests have been shown to have long-term predictive validity well into adulthood.

Person Measures

Process measures of creativity operate under the assumption that creativity requires the capacity to engage in somewhat distinctive cognitive processes. Not all psychologists agree with this position. In the first place, performance on process instruments often can be enhanced by relatively straightforward training procedures, and sometimes performance enhancements can occur by changing the instructional set when administering the test (i.e., the command to "be creative!"). In addition, creative individuals appear to have distinctive noncognitive characteristics that set them apart from persons who fail to display creativity. This has led some psychologists to propose that creativity be assessed by person-based measures.

The most frequently used instruments assess creativity via the personality characteristics that are strongly correlated with creative behavior. These personality assessments are of three kinds. The assessment may simply depend on already established scales of standard tests, such as the Minnesota Multiphasic Personality Inventory or Eysenck's Personality Questionnaire. These measures will tend to yield the lowest validity coefficients. This should not be surprising given how few of the items on these scales relate directly to the creative personality.

The assessment may be based on the construction of a specialized subscale of an already established personality test. For instance, Gough (1979) devised a Creative Personality Scale from his more general Adjective Check List. Highly creative individuals tend to check adjectives such as *capable, clever, confident, humorous, individualistic, informal, insightful, intelligent, interests wide, inventive, original, reflective, resourceful, self-confident,* and *unconventional,* but not to check adjectives like *affective, commonplace, conservative, conventional, dissatisfied, submissive,* and *suspicious.* The validity coefficients are a little bit better than in the previous type of instrument.

The assessment may rely on a measure that is specially constructed to gauge individual differences in creative personality. These tend to have the highest validity coefficients of all. An example is the How Do You Think Scale that gauges whether a person has the interests, values, energy, self-confidence, humor, flexibility, playfulness, unconventionality, and openness associated with creativity (G. A. Davis, 1975). Highly creative people consider as self-descriptive such items as "I am very curious," "I often reflect on my personal values," "I enjoy some amount of ambiguity in my life," "I am very independent," "I am very likely to do things on impulse," and "I am a risk-taker." Indicative of low creativity, in contrast, is endorsement of such items as "I worried about being considered foolish," "I am neat and well-ordered," and "I avoid activities which are a little frightening."

An alternative person-based approach is predicated on the assumption that creative potential emerges by means of a particular set of developmental experiences. These experiences may reflect either genetic predilections (nature) or acquired inclinations (nurture). For example, Schaefer and Anastasi (1968) designed a biographical inventory that identifies creativity in adolescent boys. The items tap such factors as family background, school activities, and extracurricular interests. Moreover, the inventory discriminates not only creative from noncreative adolescents but also between scientific and artistic creativity. Similar biographical inventories have been devised for both children and adults.

■ Correlates and Consequences

Two primary conclusions can be drawn about the attributes of highly creative individuals (Cassandro & Simonton, 2003; Simonton, 1999a, 2000, 2002). First of all, creative people are not necessarily intellectually brilliant, at least not as measured by standard intelligence tests. One certainly does not have to have a genius-level IQ to exhibit creative thought and behavior. Indeed, persons can be extremely high in psychometric intelligence yet score low on any accepted measure of creativity. However, the reverse is not true. That is, highly creative individuals are not unintelligent. All are at least above average in intellectual ability. A figure that is often put forward in the literature is that persons with an IQ of 120 or above are perfectly capable of exhibiting the highest levels of creativity. Because this is close to the average IQ of a college graduate, this number does not impose a highly restrictive requirement. In addition, even persons with lower intelligence scores can display significant amounts of everyday creativity. Intellectual ability places a severe restriction on creativity only when that ability falls below the population mean.

The second conclusion complements the first: What really distinguishes creative individuals is not their intelligence but their disposition (Feist, 1998). Such people are characterized by what may be styled a creative personality defined by a distinctive set of traits. Specifically, highly creative persons tend to be independent, nonconformist, unconventional, even bohemian, and they are likely to have wide interests, greater openness to new experiences, and a more conspicuous behavioral and cognitive flexibility and risk-taking boldness. However, it must be recognized that the particular nature of the expected personality profile depends appreciably on the same factors that determine the choice of the optimal assessment instrument. In other words, the profile varies according to the age of the target population, the domain of creativity to be assessed, the magnitude of creativity to be evaluated, and the manifestation of creativity that is to be targeted. This dependency may be illustrated by the following examples.

Scientific creators are distinguishable from artistic creators at several points in the profile. For instance, the former tend to be less independent, more conventional, less open to new experiences, and more intelligent. The latter, in contrast, tend to be more emotionally sensitive. In many respects, scientific creators tend to have profiles that fall midway between artistic creators and those more typical of the general population.

Whatever the domain, the expected profile varies according to the magnitude of creativity displayed. Individuals who display more everyday forms of creativity have personalities that fall closer to the general norm, whereas those who exhibit award-winning forms of creativity tend to have personality profiles that are more distinctive. Indeed, highly creative scientists are often more similar to artistic creators than to their less creative colleagues.

Moderating factors like these must be taken into consideration when discussing an issue that dates all the way back to Plato and Aristotle—the mad-genius issue. Creativity and psychopathology are often viewed as going hand in hand. Furthermore, some empirical evidence suggests that this image has some basis in fact. Highly creative individuals are often inclined to exhibit above-normal levels of symptoms that are often associated with clinical diagnosis. Examples include introversion verging on withdrawal, depression, manic episodes, and seemingly antisocial behaviors. In addition, epidemiological studies show that creativity tends to be higher in those persons who come from family lines in which psychopathology is more common than the norm.

Despite these findings, there are several reasons for believing that creativity does not bear an essential connection with mental disorder. First, the incidence rates for various psychopathologies vary considerably across creative domains. For instance, although artistic creators, and especially poets, are highly susceptible to mental disorders, particularly depression, scientific creators are far more emotionally stable. Second, it is not always clear that creativity invariably depends on psychopathology. Not only do the vast majority of creators fail to exhibit any symptoms, but what symptoms that do appear are often the consequence of their creativity rather than the other way around. For example, creators must frequently overcome obstacles and face criticisms that seldom plague more average lives. Third, highly creative individuals possess certain traits, such as ego-strength, that provide compensatory mechanisms. Creators appear to exploit their symptoms (e.g., bizarre ideas, manic behavior) to increase their effectiveness. Indeed, humanistic psychologists, such as Abraham Maslow and Carl Rogers, have argued that creativity is strongly associated with healthy traits, most notably the capacity for self-actualization. Creativity might even be interpreted as a highly successful adaptation to pathological tendencies—a lifelong coping behavior that converts a potential liability into a major personal asset.

■ Development

Developmental psychologists have devoted a considerable amount of research to two questions. First, what early experiences best contribute to the growth of creative potential? In general, creativity is best nurtured in homes that provide many opportunities for intellectual, cultural, and aesthetic stimulation. For instance, the homes are more likely to contain many books and magazines, and family recreation will often include concerts, exhibits, museums, and travel. The parents tend to be more highly educated than average and to favor child-rearing strategies that encourage the development of independent interests. The school environment is also important. Creative growth is most favored by teachers who are flexible and who support free exploration.

For creativity to advance beyond its everyday forms, however, the individual must acquire considerable expertise within the chosen domain of creative activity. This need for expertise acquisition is often expressed as the 10-year rule (Hayes, 1989). According to this rule, no person can make creative contributions to a particular domain without first devoting a full decade to the mastery of the necessary knowledge and skills. In many areas of creativity, role models and mentors have a large part to play in the acquisition of this domain-specific mastery.

Second, once a person attains adulthood, how is that potential realized? One of the oldest empirical topics in the study of creativity is the relation between age and creative achievement. Indeed, the first quantitative inquiry on that subject was published in 1835. Typically, this research has found that creative productivity first increases to reach a maximum output rate somewhere in the late 30s or early 40s and thereafter gradually declines. Nonetheless, the post–peak age decrement is moderated by many variables. These moderators include the magnitude of creativity displayed, the domain of creative achievement, and the age at which a person launched his or her career. Also significant is the fact that the ratio of outstanding products to run-of-the-mill works does not vary over the life span (the equal-odds rule; Simonton, 1997).

Studies of longitudinal changes in everyday creativity are far more rare. The few studies that have been conducted appear to show an age decrement similar to that just noted. At the same time, the empirical research also shows that more practical forms of creativity—problem solving devoted to issues arising in life and work—peak much later in life. In fact, such pragmatic creativity often evolves into the wisdom of old age (chapter 8). Regardless, more studies need to be conducted of how everyday creativity functions in the last years of life. As life expectancies increase, it is becoming obvious that ever more of a person's life will fall in the so-called retirement years. Yet relatively little research has focused on how to make those years more creative. Such investigations can help older persons use creativity as a compensation for the various losses that tend to accompany the aging process.

■ Enabling and Inhibiting Factors

Although individual differences in creativity tend to be fairly stable over time, there are a number of ways in which creativity can be enhanced or discouraged. On the positive side, creativity is facilitated by environments that are supportive, reinforcing, open, and informal. Indeed, performance on creativity tests can often be increased simply by instructing individuals to "be creative!" Furthermore, highly creative individuals tend to work on several problems or projects simultaneously, frequently incubating ideas about one while working on another, and thereby permitting internal cross talk or cross-fertilization. On the negative side, the expression of creativity can be prevented when persons are put under time pressure, when their work is closely supervised or constantly subjected to critical examination, or when severe constraints are imposed on the range of solutions. Research suggests that it is actually easier to inhibit creativity than it is to facilitate it.

A great deal of creativity takes place in group settings, such as scientific laboratories or research and development teams in industry. As a result, some investigators have examined the factors that encourage or discourage creativity in problem-solving groups. A prime example is the extensive work on group brainstorming. Although the findings are too complex to review here, they do suggest that creativity often requires a delicate balance among several influential variables. In the absence of this balance, groups are usually less creative than if the group members worked alone.

■ Gender, Cross-National, and Cross-Cultural Aspects

Far too much of the research has concentrated on North American majority-culture, middle-class males. Although some of the research findings might be applied directly to women and ethnic minorities, such extrapolations are dangerous in the absence of scientific data. Indeed, there is already ample evidence that certain developmental processes operate differently for men and women, or for blacks and whites. Moreover, cross-cultural studies are needed to determine the convergence and divergence of various results across national boundaries. For instance, creativity in more traditional cultures may not operate in the same fashion as it does in modern industrialized nations.

More progress has been made in understanding the larger social, cultural, political, and economic factors that influence individual creativity. It is evident that sometimes creativity blossoms in a civilization or nation to produce a golden age, whereas other times a sociocultural system may descend into a dark age. Even within a relatively short period, creativity may exhibit substantial fluctuations. Downward shifts in creative activity, for instance, can often be attributed to war or economic depression. On the other hand, upward shifts can frequently be ascribed to a society's openness to new ideas and values imported from other cultures.

■ Deliberate Interventions

The belief that creativity can be deliberately nurtured is widely held yet poorly supported by appropriate research (Nickerson, 1999). Certainly, we know how to set the stage for creativity—impart the domain-relevant skills to people, provide them with one or more supportive mentors, and preclude the inhibiting situational factors already discussed. But then what? Several further interventions have been suggested.

Perhaps the best known approach is brainstorming, designed to enhance creativity within a group. People throw out ideas in a context that is explicitly uncritical, with the hope that other ideas will be stimulated, presumably good ones. There is some evidence that brainstorming encourages the generation of good ideas, but less evidence that the process sustains the actual translation of these ideas into creative products (cf. Parnes & Meadow, 1963). In any event, the research findings on the effects of brainstorming are complex and do not allow simple conclusions about a best practice intervention embodying this strategy (Amabile, 1996; P. B. Paulus, 1999; P. B. Paulus & Nijstad, 2003; Rickards, 1999).

An individual-level analogue of brainstorming entails deferring judgment about the quality of one's work at its initial stages (Parnes, 1963). In the domain of writing, for example, this is called the spew method for obvious reasons—a writer spews out sentences without editing (or spell checking) and only later goes back to polish and refine (H. S. Becker, 1986). It has even been suggested that writers who use word processors turn off the monitor on their desktop computer while writing initial drafts. We suspect this strategy works better in some creative domains than in others—for example, writing and other verbal domains versus studio art and other nonverbal domains—and we further suspect that it might be more applicable to small c creativity than to Big C creativity.

Another individual-level strategy entails the teaching of heuristics abstracted from the observation of creative people approaching their work. Sometimes these are conveyed as acronyms, like SCAMPER: substitution, combination, adaptation, modification, putting to other uses, elimination, and rearrangement (Eberle, 1977). Another heuristic entails simply setting one's work aside for a time, presumably while ideas incubate. Anecdotal support exists for the effectiveness of such heuristics, but again, none appears a guaranteed route to creativity.

Nickerson (1999) surveyed several formal intervention programs, all designed for use with schoolchildren to enhance their creative problem solving—for example, the Productive Thinking Program (Covington, Crutchfield, Davies, & Olton, 1974), the Cognitive Research Trust Program (de Bono, 1973), and Project Intelligence (Adams, 1986), among others. These programs consist of units delivered over time as part of a classroom curriculum. Targeted are the various components of creative thought and problem solution. These interventions appear somewhat successful in the short run, although the skeptic can worry that the interventions seem to teach to the test used to measure their success. In any event, long-term follow-up is lacking, as is fine-grained investigation of which units impart critical ingredients and which do not.

Nickerson (1999) summed up his review of these formal programs by reminding those of us interested in enhancing creativity that the imparting of formal rules for creative problem solving is less likely to result in truly creative products or people than is an emphasis on less tangible dispositions like curiosity, intrinsic motivation, risk taking, and self-management. He also recommended that students be taught what he called supportable beliefs about creativity, chiefly that it usually takes years of training and effort to produce a work of genius.

■ What Is Not Known?

Although a considerable body of research has accumulated over the years, many unresolved empirical questions remain. These must be addressed before psychologists can have a complete understanding of creativity as a positive personal attribute. The following questions are probably the most urgent.

First, more needs to be learned about the genetic basis of creativity. Francis Galton (1869) had argued that the capacity for creative achievement was almost entirely inherited. Although this view was clearly too extreme, it is also evident that there exists some genetic foundation of this trait. After all, many of the individual-difference variables that correlate with creativity, such as intelligence and introversion, are known to have fairly large heritability coefficients. At the same time, it is becoming increasingly apparent that the genetic basis for creativity is far more complex than originally supposed. Instead of the simple additive inheritance of a mere handful of traits, creativity may entail complex multiplicative inheritance of dozens of traits (Simonton, 1999c). In addition, it is very likely that this genetic foundation interacts in intricate ways with various environmental circumstances. These complicated genetic-environmental interactions probably place constraints on interventions intended to enhance creativity. These interactions may also determine the connection, if any, between creativity and mental disorder.

Second, psychologists still know very little about the precise relation between little c and Big C creativity. On the one hand, some researchers have simply assumed that a single continuous dimension connects everyday creative acts and those that result in creative products that have a substantial impact on others. This dimension might consist of some composite of intellectual abilities and personality traits that individually vary along some differential continuum. On the other hand, some investigators have argued that Big C creativity is qualitatively distinct from little c creativity. In particular, there might exist certain thresholds for specific requisite traits, such as a minimum level of intelligence or domain-specific expertise. If so, some discontinuity or quantum jump would separate those who are creative in everyday life from those whose creativity has a broad influence on other lives.

Third and last, more research needs to be done on how creativity relates to other human virtues. For example, how does creativity relate to courage, integrity, fairness, optimism, generosity, leadership, or spirituality? Although creative genius is often associated with sickness and egotism, it is frequently linked with exceptional mental health as well. This latter association is apparent in Maslow's (1959) profile of the self-actualizing person. Besides creativity, this profile includes such positive attributes as spontaneity; an efficient perception of reality; an appreciation of the beautiful and the sublime; autonomy and independence; an acceptance of self, others, and nature; a focus on social and universal problems rather than the personal; an identification with and sympathy for humanity; a democratic character structure with corresponding freedom from prejudice; and even mystic experiences or oceanic feelings. This profile applies not just to everyday self-actualizers but also to creative geniuses of the magnitude of Einstein and Goethe. Yet we know very little about which virtues are necessarily found with creativity, and which enjoy only a very tenuous relationship at best. On the one hand, creativity may function like intelligence in the sense that it is unrelated to many other human assets. On the other hand, it is possible that certain virtues bear an antagonistic relation with creativity, so that creativity entails a certain cost with respect to otherwise being a good person. Yet the existence of such trade-offs cannot be fully established without a better understanding of the full scope of the assets that are the focus of research in positive psychology.

■ Must-Read Articles and Books

Cassandro, V. J., & Simonton, D. K. (2003). Creativity and genius. In C. L. M. Keyes & J. Haidt (Eds.), *Flourishing: Positive psychology and the life well-lived* (pp. 163–183). Washington, DC: American Psychological Association.

Feist, G. J. (1998). A meta-analysis of personality in scientific and artistic creativity. *Personality and Social Psychology Review, 2,* 290–309.

Runco, M. A., & Pritzker, S. (Eds.). (1999). *Encyclopedia of creativity.* San Diego, CA: Academic Press.

Simonton, D. K. (2000). Creativity: Cognitive, developmental, personal, and social aspects. *American Psychologist, 55,* 151–158.

Simonton, D. K. (2002). Creativity. In C. R. Snyder & S. J. Lopez (Eds.), *The handbook of positive psychology* (pp. 189–201). New York: Oxford University Press.

Sternberg, R. J. (Ed.). (1999). *Handbook of creativity.* New York: Cambridge University Press.

5. CURIOSITY

[Interest, Novelty-Seeking, Openness to Experience]

■ *Maverick scientist John Lilly was a pioneer in electronics, biophysics, neurophysiology, psychology, and cybernetics. He was the world's leading authority on the effects of sensory deprivation and isolation on the human mind as well as intraspecies communication between humans and dolphins. What galvanizes someone to pursue expertise in such a wide range of disciplines? Although we can certainly point to Dr. Lilly's need for mastery, one of many traits differentiating him from his peers was his insatiable thirst for knowledge—his curiosity and interest in the world. Based on his own empirical research, cross-fertilized readings in Western science and Eastern religion, and personal explorations into altered states of consciousness via sensory deprivation tanks, psychotropic drugs, and Eastern mind–body practices, Dr. Lilly focused his life and career on exploring the seemingly limitless boundaries of consciousness. Lilly believed all human experiments must be initially conducted on oneself. The precarious nature of his self-experimentation, frequently entailing the use of LSD, ketamine, and the absence of personnel to monitor his physical safety, continued despite risks and losses to his professional career and personal life. Lilly believed the growth in knowledge outweighed the costs. Both intrepid and reckless, Lilly personified the character strength of curiosity (for details, see Jeffrey & Lilly, 1990; Lilly, 1972a, 1972b).* ■

■ Consensual Definition

Curiosity, interest, novelty-seeking, and openness to experience represent one's intrinsic desire for experience and knowledge. Curiosity involves the active recognition, pursuit, and regulation of one's experience in response to challenging opportunities. Although not all of us are as curious as John Lilly, curiosity is ubiquitous, manifest in the mundane activities that make our daily lives more fulfilling:

- being absorbed in the plot of a movie
- completing a crossword puzzle without awareness of time passing
- opening and reading with eagerness a handwritten letter
- watching the flight of a seagull
- conversing with an intriguing stranger
- examining a picture of Siamese twins conjoined at the head
- pondering the aftermath of a date
- listening carefully to a new song on the radio

All individuals experience curiosity, but they differ in its depth and breadth, and in their threshold and willingness to experience it.

Despite overlap among curiosity, interest, novelty-seeking, and openness to experience, they can be hierarchically arranged. Curiosity and interest are sometimes used interchangeably. When individuals experience these positive emotional-motivational states, they initiate and sustain goal-directed behaviors in response to incentive cues. For example, someone at the beach notices a black suitcase floating in the ocean and decides to swim after it to determine its contents. Upon discovering it to be empty, her curiosity may dissipate. However, her curiosity may also increase in light of why the suitcase was in the ocean, what was in it, and whether its contents have washed ashore. Or perhaps not. The point is that individual differences in curiosity abound in terms of frequency, intensity, and duration of exploration.

Novelty-seeking reflects an individual's propensity for seeking novel and exciting experiences to elevate stimulation to an optimal level; this includes a willingness to endure high levels of risk (e.g., pain and injuries when rock climbing, rejection when meeting new people) to obtain the benefits of novelty. Although curiosity and novelty-seeking are both goal-oriented systems with a positive emotional core, curiosity seems broader in scope, encompassing both novelty-seeking (so-called diversive curiosity) and specific curiosity (increasing one's knowledge). In principle, novelty-seeking should have stronger associations with courage and sociability, and negative relationships with boredom and anxiety. In contrast, specific curiosity should have stronger links to openness to new values and ideas, a future orientation, and the frequency and enjoyment of problem solving.

Finally, openness to experience is a higher order personality dimension involving receptivity to novel fantasies, feelings, ideas, and values. Curiosity is a fundamental motivational component of all openness facets. Yet high openness also entails imaginative, artistic, and unconventional sensibilities neither necessary nor sufficient for curiosity per se. Similarly, individuals can be high in openness, expressing a willingness to understand themselves and be open-minded, yet reluctant to challenge and expand themselves. The experience of curiosity is more of a mechanism of action (cognitively, emotionally, and/or behaviorally), whereas openness is more of a psychological predisposition. Although curiosity, novelty-seeking, and openness are all associated with a myriad of positive outcomes, novelty-seeking may also lead to negative outcomes if it results in illegal substance use, risky sexual behavior, and the like.

■ Theoretical Traditions

Throughout history, curiosity has been both lauded as a virtue and a source of creativity and denounced as hubris and vanity (Saint Augustine, 1943). Curiosity can certainly be dichotomized into unfavorable or favorable, given that peeping at bedroom windows is distinct from exploring exotic plants in a nature preserve. The present focus will be on the virtuous forms of curiosity.

William James (1890) called attention to "moral, intellectual, and aesthetic feelings" (p. 458) that are automatic pleasures in response to novel stimuli. James differentiated between two types of curiosity. The first entailed an emotional blend of excitement and anxiety with respect to exploring and enjoying novelty. The second was scientific curiosity or metaphysical wonder, evoked by "an inconsistency or a gap in . . . knowledge" (p. 429). This two-dimensional model, novelty-seeking and specific curiosity, recurs in the contemporary literature.

Influenced by Darwin, James observed that attention is a limited resource and that individuals tend to focus on stimuli fostering excitement or personal meaning. In evolutionary terms, attraction to novel stimuli is adaptive because it increases knowledge, but the fear of novelty is also adaptive because the unknown may be dangerous. Thus, curiosity is inextricably bound to anxiety and approach–avoidance conflicts. Individuals with a strong endowment of curiosity proffer a specific advantage in life because attention is more fluid, and novel ideas, objects, and relationships can be found, enjoyed, explored, and integrated into an expanding self. In principle, these aspects of curiosity aid survival—for example, finding plants with medicinal properties, increasing social resources, discovering new habitats.

A proliferation of drive theories appeared in the mid-20th century to explain what makes people curious. Early experimental psychologists found rats that would explore unfamiliar wings of mazes and engage in play in the absence of drive satiation (Krechevsky, 1937). These findings led them to define curiosity itself as a homeostatic drive in the same vein as hunger, thirst, and sex. However, proposing that curiosity is an instinctual drive remains nonfalsifiable because other motivational or cognitive processes responsible for exploration are always present.

The demise of the homeostatic drive model led to a lengthy theoretical debate on whether curiosity and exploration were (a) internally driven by the desire to avoid boredom and monotony (H. Fowler, 1965) or (b) externally driven by the lure of novel, complex, or ambiguous stimuli (Berlyne, 1967). Numerous studies and interpretations support these ostensibly opposed positions (Voss & Keller, 1983). More important, the theoretical conflict between these models created an impasse that blocked further study. Both positions have merit, as long as we posit multiple pathways to the evocation and satiation of curiosity. However, attributing curiosity solely to internally or externally generated sources does little to explain its properties, how it is elicited, why the same activity can generate intense curiosity in some but not others, and how it develops.

Also absent from these drive theories is the notion that one's curiosity and exploratory behaviors partly depend on outcome expectancies like risk appraisal and the depth of one's knowledge. Unadulterated novelty is exceedingly rare, with individuals relating most novel stimuli to what they know, expect, and can categorize. Curiosity cannot be divorced from what is remembered, and so cognitive theories of curiosity began to be proposed.

These cognitive models focus on how one's curiosity involves a desire to make sense of the world and to feel competent in recognizing violations of mental representations (Deci, 1975; Kagan, 1972). Consider the interest most of us would experience when meeting a nuclear physicist with a penchant for heavy metal rock music. These models propose that individuals are motivated to resolve incongruity by the search for an optimal "correspondence between expectancy and perception" (Hebb, 1949, p. 149). The cognitive process theory posits that curiosity is a function of assimilating and accommodating novel stimuli into one's schematic framework of the self and the world (Beswick, 1971). Greater curiosity emerges from difficulties integrating information into one's schematic framework, sensitivities to discrepancies in the environment, and comfort with the anxiety-provoking nature of conceptual conflicts. This model leads to a rich avenue of untested and falsifiable hypotheses, although cognitive models have yet to account for the fact that knowledge fuels rather than quells curiosity. They also fail to account for the relationships between intelligence and curiosity. Finally, most cognitive models posit that individuals want to resolve curiosity, implying that curiosity is somehow aversive, an assumption at odds with the everyday experience of any engrossed reader, moviegoer, scientist, or parent of an infant—all can readily attest that curiosity is a positive, rewarding state.

More recent theories depict curiosity as a multifaceted system evoking a wide range of human emotions, cognitions, and behaviors that can be satiated by a variety of sensory and cognitive channels (Boyle, 1989; Langevin, 1971). Spearheaded by the work of Daniel Berlyne (1962), curiosity and exploratory tendencies have been segmented into novelty-seeking (diversive curiosity) and specific curiosity, thereby influencing large bodies of disparate research.

Novelty-seeking is best described as an emotional-motivational state facilitating the search for stimulation occasioned by novelty, complexity, uncertainty, or conflict, irrespective of specific questions or problems. According to work led by Zuckerman (1994) and his colleagues, individuals appear to differ in their desire for experience seeking, thrill and adventure seeking, boredom suscepti- bility, and willingness to take risks to obtain novelty.

Specific curiosity is best described as an orientation toward investigating specific objects, events, and problems to understand them better and be chal- lenged by them. An extensive body of research has been devoted to individual differences in specific curiosity (Cacioppo, Petty, Feinstein, & Jarvis, 1996). These two curiosity dimensions appear to be complementary in that novelty- seeking readily leads to stimulus encounters resulting in specific problems fueling specific curiosity behaviors. Individuals differ as to whether they pur- sue and enjoy complex cognitive activities or are relieved to avoid cognitively taxing curiosity experiences. Those who enjoy complex cognitive activities ex- perience a wide range of positive subjective experiences and demonstrate virtuous attributes (Cacioppo et al., 1996).

Echoing early evolutionary models, Spielberger and Starr's (1994) optimal stimulation/dual process theory posits that the pursuit of optimal subjective experiences entails curiosity and anxiety. When curiosity is stronger than anxi- ety, individuals explore their environment (diversive curiosity). When anxiety is stronger than curiosity, individuals tend to disengage from goals to reduce stimulation to a more manageable level. Optimal stimulation purportedly con- sists of subjective pleasantness and challenge, accentuated with mild anxiety. Information-seeking behaviors (specific curiosity) are activated to reduce some of the initial uncertainty arising from novel activities, sustaining more moder- ate, optimal levels of stimulation. State curiosity is a function of individual dif- ferences in stimulation thresholds. Although Spielberger developed an assessment battery to measure anxiety and curiosity, researchers tend to focus exclusively on curiosity or anxiety, not both. Surprisingly, the basic tenets of this model have undergone few empirical tests (Kashdan, 2002; Peters, 1978). However, the re- sults of these studies support this framework as a link between fundamental appetitive and aversive processes.

Despite the longevity of the two-factor diversive-specific model of curios- ity, aside from factor analyses of self-report instruments, there is a general ab- sence of substantiating evidence. Contemporary researchers tend to focus on either diversive, specific, or general curiosity, leading to three ostensibly iso- lated bodies of research. Additionally, the most extensive work in the field is on openness to experience, one of the Big Five core personality traits (McCrae & Costa, 1997a). Openness has been conceptualized as the receptivity to and need for experience, as well as related values, imagination, and artistic sensi- bilities. In light of all the work on different facets of curiosity, it is surprising that the majority of work is minimally represented, if not ignored, in literature reviews (Loewenstein, 1994; Spielberger & Starr, 1994). Future work must ex- plore the differential correlates and predictive utility of these curiosity con- structs, thereby testing the viability of multidimensional models.

Based on early work on cognitive development, the personal growth facilitation model of curiosity posits that recognizing and pursuing novelty, uncertainty, and challenge is the foundation for enhancing personal and interpersonal capital (Kashdan, Rose, & Fincham, 2002). The reciprocally driven process includes (a) greater allocation of attention and energy to recognizing and pursuing cues of novelty and challenge, (b) cognitive evaluation and behavioral exploration of challenging activities, (c) deep absorption in these activities, and (d) integration of curiosity experiences by assimilation or accommodation. The process of generating, sustaining, and integrating curiosity experiences is tantamount to expanding personal resources. The two essential components of curiosity posited by this model, appetitive exploration and flowlike task absorption, served as the basis for the trait and state Curiosity and Exploration Inventories. Despite preliminary support for appetitive motivational processes linking curiosity to an expansion in interpersonal resources, the basic mechanisms need further empirical study.

Experiencing curiosity evokes positive affect, motivating individuals to seek new experiences and reinforcing their exploration (Ainley, 1998; Kashdan & Roberts, 2002, in press). Feelings of competence and control resulting from integrating novel experiences engender further positive affect (R. M. Ryan & Frederick, 1997). Thus, curiosity begets further curiosity. This relationship is even more pronounced as one becomes cognizant of information that can reduce meaningful gaps in knowledge. A profitable direction for future research includes understanding the causal directions of these positive feedback loops.

Individuals have idiosyncratic hierarchies wherein certain activities and stimulation sources are more appealing than others—music, movies, celebrity gossip, scientific breakthroughs. Besides perceived desirability, one's level of curiosity is likely to be a function of the fit between thinking styles and novelty sources; for example, introverts are less likely than extroverts to ask questions in school. Although early educational research provides some evidence for this thesis (Beswick & Tallmadge, 1971), much remains to be learned about individual differences and contextual factors that moderate curiosity and its desirable consequences. Why might one identical twin be drawn to the study of economics and the other to clinical psychology?

One psychological context with a profound effect on curiosity is the state of boredom. When bored, highly curious individuals are oriented to finding novelty and are sensitive to environmental nuances that can increase arousal. Boredom foreshadows impulsive and delinquent behaviors (Zuckerman, 1999). However, the right temperamental combinations can alternatively lead to blocks in productivity and creativity. When activities are perceived as boring but meaningful, individuals deploy strategies to enhance interest and sustain effort toward goals (Sansone, Weir, Harpster, & Morgan, 1992). High-curious individuals are probably more likely than low-curious individuals to be able to generate interest in activities that are meaningful or unavoidable.

■ Measures

Coincidental with the proliferation of theoretical models, a number of self-report questionnaires have been developed to measure individual differences in curiosity. There also exist indices of novel behavior that can be used to assess state curiosity. These assessment strategies show a range of construct validity. Most measures address isolated lower order factors of curiosity such as general curiosity, novelty-seeking, specific curiosity, academic curiosity, scientific curiosity, and, to measure perceptual curiosity, the duration of focused attention to common versus irregular and ambiguous figures. The most widely used measures are described in Table 5.1.

Many self-report measures lack adequate psychometric properties (alphas less than .60; Langevin, 1971). In contrast, the widely used State–Trait Curiosity Inventory (STCI; Spielberger, 1979) and nearly identical Melbourne Curiosity Inventory (MCI; Naylor, 1981) are composed of transparent items—for example, "I am curious"—with high item homogeneity resulting from redundancy. Indeed, the original items for the STCI and MCI tapping antagonistic states of boredom and anxiety were dropped due to their orthogonal relationships with curiosity items. Naylor (1981) defended these actions by stating, "It was decided to concentrate on the development of a curiosity scale without the concern for balance since this seemed to create more problems than it was intended to solve" (p. 174). Given the existence of multidimensional models of curiosity, and strong empirical relations between cognitive ability and curiosity, one wonders what exactly these scales are measuring. Sometimes they are simply labeled as information-seeking or specific curiosity scales (Spielberger & Starr, 1994).

A major limitation of many self-report measures is that they rely on items pertaining to specific objects and events such as interest in schoolwork, museums, computers, drug use, or surfing (H. I. Day, 1971; Kreitler, Kreitler, & Zigler, 1974; Litman & Spielberger, 2003; Zuckerman, Eysenck, & Eysenck, 1978). Clearly, nonrandom error accounts for some of the explanatory power of these measures. Greater curiosity will be ascribed to individuals with the best match between personal preferences and domain-specific items (Loewenstein, 1994). For example, cultural differences would be artificially inflated if Americans were interested in different activities than Europeans and these various activities were represented by scale items. Despite this limitation, the Sensation-Seeking Scale—Form V (SSS-V; Zuckerman et al., 1978) is the most widely used measure of novelty-seeking. Factor analyses have found that novelty-seeking and information-seeking/specific curiosity fall out separate dimensions (Langevin, 1971; Spielberger & Starr, 1994). The four subscales of the SSS-V appear to measure diversive curiosity. However, the construct of diversive curiosity is broader than a "willingness to take physical, social, legal, and financial risks for the sake of such experiences" (Zuckerman, 1994, p. 27). Some individuals prefer novel

TABLE 5.1   *Measures of Curiosity and Related Constructs*

State-Trait Curiosity Inventory (STCI)

Spielberger (1979)

Self-report questionnaire composed of 10 face-valid items reflecting global interest and wonder

- Internal reliability (alpha coefficients): ~.95 for trait scale; ~.94 for state scale
- Test–retest reliability: not available
- Construct validity: correlates –.08 –.35 with SSS-V subscales; ~.40 with openness to experience, locus of control, optimism, and self-esteem; and ~–.40 with negative affect

Sensation-Seeking Scale–Form V (SSS-V)

Zuckerman et al. (1978)

Self-report questionnaire composed of 40 items addressing thrill and adventure seeking, experience seeking, disinhibition, and boredom susceptibility

- Internal reliability (alpha coefficients): .56 –.82 for separate scales; ~.85 for total score
- Test–retest reliability: .89 for 3 weeks; .75 for 6–8 months
- Construct validity: correlates ~–.45 with anhedonia scales; –.54 with arousal avoidance; ~.30 with divergent thinking tests; and .25 with Need for Cognition Scale

Need for Cognition Scale (NCS)

Cacioppo & Petty (1982)

Self-report questionnaire composed of 34 items addressing the degree to which individuals enjoy and engage in thinking and solving complex problems

- Internal reliability (alpha coefficients): ~.90
- Test–retest reliability: .88 for 7 weeks; .66 for 8 months
- Construct validity: correlates ~.60 with curiosity scales; ~–.30 with measures of dogmatism and discomfort with ambiguity; and ~.40 with achievement tests

Openness to Experience Scale of the NEO-PI-R

Costa & McCrae (1992)

Self-report questionnaire composed of 48 items reflecting a broad orientation to being high in imagination, aesthetic appreciation, intellectual curiosity, and open-mindedness

- Internal reliability (alpha coefficients): .81
- Test–retest reliability: .68 –.79 for different facets over 6-year interval
- Construct validity: correlates ~.40 with indices of curiosity, novelty-seeking, cognitive flexibility, divergent thinking, and creativity

Curiosity and Exploration Inventory—Trait and State Versions (CEI)

Kashdan & Roberts (in press)

Self-report questionnaire composed of 7 items addressing appetitive strivings for novel and challenging activities and the propensity to be deeply absorbed in activities

- Internal reliability (alpha coefficients): .63–.74 for separate scales; ~.76 for total score
- Test–retest reliability: ~.80 for separate dimensions and total score for 1 month
- Construct validity: correlates ~.40 with indices of curiosity, novelty-seeking, positive affect, and appetitive motivation; ~–.40 with boredom proneness and social anxiety

and challenging experiences that are absent of danger, like viewing stars through a telescope. In creating the Impulsive Sensation-Seeking Scale, Zuckerman, Kuhlman, Joireman, Teta, and Kraft (1993) eliminated all domain-specific items, acknowledging this potential confound in prior incarnations of the SSS.

Two other well-established curiosity-relevant measures are the Need for Cognition Scale (NCS; Cacioppo & Petty, 1982) and the Openness to Experience Scale (Costa & McCrae, 1992). Each of these measures has been refined and well validated. The NCS, which is best conceptualized as a lower order factor of curiosity, appears to assess individual differences in specific curiosity or the tolerance and enjoyment of effortful thinking. The construct of openness is a broad dimension of personality, subsuming "vivid fantasy, artistic sensitivity, depth of feeling, behavioral flexibility, intellectual curiosity, and unconventional attitudes" (McCrae, 1996, p. 323), demonstrating positive influences on social attitudes (e.g., prejudice), relationships, and creativity. However, as a means of further understanding the role of curiosity in generating growth, openness may be less valuable than other facets of curiosity (i.e., sensation-seeking, need for cognition, state curiosity). The specific role of curiosity as an emotional-motivational component of openness will need to be further validated.

Shorter versions of novelty-seeking, curiosity, and openness scales have been created and validated. Child versions of novelty-seeking and openness scales have also been created, and the simple wording of the STCI makes it appropriate for younger populations.

More recently, we have the Curiosity and Exploration Inventory (CEI), a brief seven-item measure comprising exploration (appetitive strivings for novelty and challenge) and flow (deep absorption in activities); initial analyses found no evidence for differential diversive and specific curiosity factors (Kashdan & Roberts, in press). The CEI has good psychometric properties and construct validity. Upon controlling for the overlapping construct of trait-positive affect, the CEI demonstrates unique relationships with appetitive motivational constructs.

There is a long history of experimental and naturalistic studies on the contextual and individual difference factors influencing state and trait curiosity (for a review of visual paradigm studies, see Voss & Keller, 1983). To assess child curiosity, studies have had teachers, peers, and independent observers rate curiosity using Likert scales with behavioral referents (for innovative tasks and reliable indices, see Alberti & Witryol, 1994; Coie, 1974). For instance, teachers were asked to rank-order children in curiosity using the following definition: (a) reacts positively to new or strange stimuli in the environment by exploring/manipulating them, (b) indicates a desire to better understand themselves and/or the environment, (c) visually searches for novelty, and (d) long-standing engagement with stimuli to increase understanding (Coie, 1974).

To assess specific curiosity, Loewenstein, Adler, Behrens, and Gillis (1992) used a set of innovative perceptual and epistemic tasks testing the following predictions: (a) The more information obtained in an area that closes a gap in knowledge, the greater one's curiosity will be to understand the rest, and (b) the more meaningful the domain of information, the greater one's curiosity. In one experiment, participants were seated with a series of upside-down body part photographs constituting a person. Participants were randomly shown a specific number of body parts. After successively turning over the appropriate photographs, participants were asked to guess the age of the person. As outcome measures, they were asked three curiosity-related questions: How curious are you in knowing the person's actual age, how curious are you in seeing all the photographs, and is it worth 50 cents to see all the photographs?

Interpersonal curiosity has been assessed with a reciprocal self-disclosure task wherein individuals take turns asking and answering questions that escalate in personal and emotional intensity, mimicking the process of intimacy development (Kashdan & Roberts, in press). Cognitive and behavioral indices of curiosity can include the direction and intensity of attentional resources, facial expressions of interest, and responsiveness during the interaction.

For these and other curiosity paradigms, construct validity will need to be demonstrated. Because these studies assess short-term curiosity, future work needs to assess idiosyncratic interest in the novel topics, objects, or activities under study. Similarly, anxiety levels (e.g., children differ in their perception of teacher threat) and individual thinking styles (e.g., introvert vs. extrovert) may influence the manifestation of curiosity. To improve the reliability of findings, multimethod approaches are necessary. Most important, baseline measures of curiosity and anxiety are not uniformly reported, raising the question of whether curiosity is evoked by experimental stimuli. Because curiosity is a transient state and participants may be curious about curiosity studies, baseline data should be obtained as a context for understanding within-person curiosity changes.

■ Correlates and Consequences

Curiosity, novelty-seeking, and openness to experience are all associated with desirable psychosocial outcomes. This includes general positive affect, willingness to challenge stereotypes, creativity, preference for challenge in work and play, perceived control, and negative relationships with perceived stress and boredom (Cacioppo et al., 1996; McCrae & Costa, 1997a; Zuckerman, 1994). The emotional-motivational state of curiosity appears to fuel positive emotions such as excitement, enjoyment, and attentiveness (Ainley, 1998; Kashdan & Roberts, 2002, in press), facilitating complex decision making (Kreitler et al., 1974) and goal perseverance (Sansone & Smith, 2000). In a longitudinal study of 7th- to 11th-grade students, "students designated as being interested in the broad domain of learning reported their school experience as more satisfying (positive affect), as being important to their future (opportunity), having good relationships with teachers, and having a sense that they would succeed (achievement)" (Ainley, 1998, p. 264). When the school environment was perceived as unthreatening, college students with high trait curiosity asked nearly five times as many questions as students with low trait curiosity (Peters, 1978).

Meta-analyses show that curiosity accounts for approximately 10% of the variance in academic learning and performance (Schiefele, Krapp, & Winteler, 1992) and 36% of the variance in self-selected career choices (Lent, Brown, & Hackett, 1994). Greater curiosity-related behaviors and cognitions are consistently associated with greater learning, engagement, and performance in academic settings (e.g., Harackiewicz, Barron, Tauer, & Elliot, 2002) and work organizations (e.g., Reio & Wiswell, 2000). For clients being treated for physical and psychological conditions, greater intrinsic motivation for treatment goals predicted greater adherence and better outcomes (e.g., R. M. Ryan, Plant, & O'Malley, 1995; G. C. Williams, Gagne, Ryan, & Deci, 2002).

As for interpersonal relationships, both trait and state curiosity predict positive subjective experiences and interpersonal closeness as rated by self and interaction partners, above and beyond other affect and motivational variables (Kashdan & Roberts, 2002, in press; Kashdan et al., 2002). Highly curious individuals experience greater intimacy with novel interaction partners as a function of directing attention and capitalizing on positive qualities of partners and conversations and self-generating interest and fun during interactions (Kashdan et al., 2002). Based on these findings, it seems reasonable to conclude that curiosity facilitates appetitive behaviors leading to positive development. Future work might continue to explore the operating mechanisms linking curiosity to desirable outcomes in various life domains.

In a provocative 5-year follow-up study of a geriatric sample, after controlling for age, education, and health variables, initial levels of state and trait curiosity were significantly greater in survivors than in those who died (Swan & Carmelli, 1996). Despite the need for replication, the data advocate research to better understand pathways by which curiosity may influence subjective well-being and mortality rates.

As for unique associations, trait openness, general curiosity, and specific curiosity are positively associated with intelligence, problem-solving ability, autonomy, self-esteem, and subjective well-being (Cacioppo et al., 1996; Kashdan et al., 2002; Marshall, Wortman, Vickers, Kusulas, & Hervig, 1994; McCrae, 1993–1994). Novelty-seeking has been shown to be associated with some less than desirable outcomes such as impulsivity, fascination with violent and sexual events, and antagonism/anger expressiveness (Aluja-Fabregat, 2000; Zuckerman, 1994). High novelty-seeking, in conjunction with low conscientiousness, may lead to the pursuit of short-term gratification at the expense of future negative consequences. High novelty-seeking children overly exposed to mass media violence may be more susceptible to increases in their own violent behavior. High novelty-seeking individuals who engage in impulsive delinquent activities (i.e., drugs, promiscuous sex, stealing) and associate with like-minded peers may be more susceptible to adjudicated criminal lifestyles. Whether high novelty-seeking is satiated by illicit or licit means is likely to be a function of parent–child relations, self-esteem, and opportunities to engage in challenging activities that satisfy one's needs for competence, mastery, and personal meaning. However, research in this important area is sorely lacking.

■ Development

Although different cultural rules are likely to influence its manifestation, signs of curiosity emerge in infancy (Izard, 1977). Interest–excitement is an innate, transcultural emotional phenomenon (Silvia, in press). Upon being elicited by the appearance of new or salient stimuli, corresponding responses include physiological arousal, subjective pleasure, and behavioral exploration of the environment (choreographing vocalization, motor action, thinking). In infants, curiosity manifests as visual searching for novelty and engagement with desired stimuli. Essentially, curiosity is activated by person–environment interactions. Infant temperament and the curiosity and fear evoked by the environment begin to set the stage for whether novel stimuli are categorized as dangerous or reinforcing (M. Schulman, 2002). Characteristics of trait behavioral inhibition, a predisposition to fear and withdraw from novel settings, people, and objects, begin to manifest and solidify as early as 21 months of age (Kagan, 1989). Social situations, being inherently ambiguous and complex, provide an important context for eliciting curiosity. Behaviorally inhibited children may experience not only greater distress and impairment than their more approach-oriented peers but also less positive affect and self-expansion opportunities that stem from exploring, understanding, and strengthening bonds with unfamiliar people and objects (Garcia-Coll, Kagan, & Reznick, 1984; Reznick et al., 1986).

Individual differences in curiosity are likely to dovetail with the development of internalized templates in the first years of life about caregivers as a source of security and reliability and the self as being worthy and lovable (Bowlby, 1988). Those children who deem caregivers as more nurturing and autonomy granting are better equipped to regulate the inherent anxiety of novelty, thereby leading them to be more open to new experiences and mastery over developmental tasks (McCrae & Costa, 1988). Contemporary models of attachment have found that adults develop attachment styles and that the level of perceived security in close relationships is associated with greater curiosity behaviors (Mikulincer, 1997). This research bodes well for curiosity interventions, as future studies can test whether young children deprived of positive parent–child relationships can rekindle the curiosity, exploration, and growth opportunities missing during formative years. As for working models of the self, research needs to account for the roles of self-esteem, hope, and other positive traits as potential determinants of the human motive to maximize pleasure and experience curiosity.

Although longitudinal studies comparing children and adults are lacking, it appears that diversive, specific, and epistemic curiosity all appear to remain quite stable across the life span (Cacioppo et al., 1996; Spielberger, 1979). As for novelty-seeking, it can be confidently stated that thrill and adventure seeking, disinhibition, and a susceptibility to boredom all tend to decline with advancing age (Giambra, Camp, & Grodsky, 1992; Zuckerman et al., 1978). This is not surprising, as the willingness to take personal risks for novelty can be expected to decline as a result of new reasons for longevity (e.g., grandchildren).

There is no neurobiological work on curiosity per se, but there is extensive work on the related positive biobehavioral approach system (BAS; Depue, 1996). The BAS is characterized by a strong sensitivity to incentive cues in the environment that facilitate positive emotional experiences (Carver & White, 1994). In modeling the structural framework of the BAS, curiosity is included as one of the processes mediating relations between initial reward cues and goal-directed approach behaviors (Depue, 1996). On the neurological level, evidence finds greater dopamine activity to coincide with positive affective responses (i.e., interest, curiosity) to rewarding stimuli (see review in Depue & Collins, 1999). Second, individual differences in trait measures of the BAS and positive affect are more strongly related to resting left prefrontal cortex asymmetry than other stable brain wave patterns (Sutton & Davidson, 1997). These provocative findings imply that the BAS (and trait curiosity) may be partially hardwired. Neurological (e.g., dopamine release), emotional-motivational, and behavioral BAS components are proposed to work in synchrony to meet the goals of maximizing pleasure. One limitation of this model is the proposed directionality of these components. Complex reciprocal relationships can be expected, including the interactive role of other relevant traits like anxiety sensitivity, which are unlikely to be as simple as the hierarchical structures being espoused. Exploring the interplay of various BAS components has vast potential for enhancing our understanding of the biopsychosocial underpinnings of curiosity.

Gene-linkage studies have shown that novelty-seeking is associated with the D4 dopamine receptor gene in animals (D4DR; Dulawa, Grandy, Low, Paulus, & Mark, 1999) and humans (Benjamin, Ebstein, & Belmaker, 1997). Despite some replication failures, at least four studies have confirmed this relationship (Ebstein & Belmaker, 1997). Additional support stems from work finding the D4DR to be a genetic marker for attention-deficit/hyperactivity disorder (ADHD; Sunohara et al., 2000). On a continuum ranging from behavioral inhibition to impulsivity problems, ADHD is an extreme manifestation of novelty-seeking. Nonetheless, single genetic markers for broad personality constructs are rare. There is merit in exploring genes that interact with D4DR to influence novelty-seeking. Knowledge of the genetic loci of novelty-seeking can improve our understanding of its developmental trajectory and how genetic predispositions interact with environmental choices, like the selection of peers and careers.

Twin studies have estimated the genetic and environmental influences on openness to experience (Bergeman et al., 1993). According to Loehlin (1992), 43% of the variance is explained by genetic influences (a conservative estimate that assumes multiple gene interactions). This figure is greater than the genetic influences for other Big Five personality traits. For openness, there was negligible evidence for the influence of shared rearing environments (6%), with the remaining variation likely to be proportioned among unshared environments, gene–environment interactions, and method error. The strong genetic component of openness may be due to the evolutionary survival value of curiosity/ openness, the neurological underpinnings of the BAS, or the strong association between openness and intelligence (itself a highly heritable characteristic; McCrae & Costa, 1997a). Regardless, high heritability coefficients do not imply that traits are immutable. The 51% of unexplained variance in openness suggests that curiosity may be amenable to intervention. It remains to be seen whether biological and genetic influences differ among curiosity dimensions.

■ Enabling and Inhibiting Factors

In his seminal work, Berlyne (1960) argued that an individual's interest in something is a function of inherent novelty, complexity, uncertainty, and conflict. There appears to be a point of diminishing returns wherein stimuli can become too confusing or ambiguous to be rewarding. Experimental studies have found that acquiring specific knowledge evokes curiosity, the desire for further information, and upward spirals among these constructs (Loewenstein et al., 1992). The experience of competence- or mastery-based rewards also encourages future curiosity.

Consider individuals who begin to take tennis lessons and upon learning how to swing the racket, shift their feet across the court and use torque motion to hit with more speed and precision; they become more interested in playing again, more cognizant of advanced techniques to be learned (e.g., hitting with topspin), and more interested in expanding their competence. Levels of curiosity are a function of the perceived probability that specific knowledge is attainable (probability) and the perceived probability that one's personal resources can be expanded upon integrating new knowledge (desirability). Factors that affect probability and desirability can be expected to encourage or thwart curiosity. Curiosity can be thwarted by a failure to appreciate what one does not know (Loewenstein et al., 1992). Impediments may include overconfidence, dogmatism, low cognitive resources to process stimuli, and pathological conditions such as narcissism, psychopathy, and schizophrenia.

As for other factors interfering with curiosity and exploration, experimental studies have found anxiety to inhibit curiosity and exploration in interpersonal interactions (Kashdan & Roberts, in press), classroom settings (Peters, 1978), and voluntary interest in playing with puzzles (Plant & Ryan, 1985). Social interaction anxiety (e.g., fear of meeting new people, initiating conversations) has also demonstrated unique, negative relationships with curiosity (Kashdan, 2002). Furthermore, states of excessive self-focused attention appear to interfere with curiosity (Rodrigue, Olson, & Markley, 1987) and exploration of the environment (Plant & Ryan, 1985). This work fits with attentional capacity models positing that individuals have limited resources at any one time, and that excessive self-absorption interferes with the ability to recognize and attend to rewarding features of the environment.

Beliefs that one can act volitionally in a situation (autonomy) robustly facilitate curiosity in various tasks, settings, and domains (Deci & Ryan, 2000). A large body of research shows that internal pressures such as guilt and fear, external pressures such as threats and punishment, and tangible external rewards diminish curiosity for specific tasks. There is also evidence of dynamic, reciprocal relationships between high levels of curiosity and greater competence-related beliefs (e.g., Tracey, 2002) and feelings of belongingness and closeness to others (Mikulincer, 1997).

■ Gender, Cross-National, and Cross-Cultural Aspects

Gender differences are notably absent in general and specific curiosity as well as openness. Men do tend to report greater novelty-seeking than women on the Thrill and Adventure Seeking (TAS) and Disinhibition (DIS) subscales of the SSS-V (Zuckerman et al., 1978). The TAS assesses preferences for specific dangerous activities such as surfing and rock climbing, and the DIS assesses lack of social and sexual constraints. Gender differences may be a function of gender role orientations rather than biological differences.

A critical deficiency in the curiosity literature is its failure to investigate ethnic differences. European Americans tend to report greater novelty-seeking than African Americans on the TAS subscale (Zuckerman, 1994). However, cross-national differences in novelty-seeking may be an artifact of the domain-specific items of the SSS-V. The specific activities targeted in the TAS such as skiing and surfing are unlikely to be equally accessible or reinforcing in different ethnic and socioeconomic samples. This problem can be resolved by using measures of curiosity that assess more than the willingness to engage in dangerous and risky activities. Cross-cultural differences would be best studied by measures that are not tied to domain-specific European American activities.

Evidence for cross-cultural convergence has been demonstrated for general curiosity (Ben-Zur & Zeidner, 1988), novelty-seeking (Zuckerman et al., 1978), epistemic curiosity (Verplanken, 1991), openness to experience (McCrae, 1996), and their correlates (e.g., political values, education level). However, most of these studies have compared the United States with Canada, England, the Netherlands, Israel, Spain, Australia, and New Zealand, which have comparable political infrastructures and societal values. More work is needed on comparisons between individualistic and collectivist societies.

■ Deliberate Interventions

Studies have shown that specific facets of environments (e.g., perceived threat, autonomy supportive) and activities (e.g., competitiveness, meaningfulness) influence state curiosity (Silvia, in press). Yet how malleable is enduring curiosity? What are the roles of cognitive abilities and intelligences? With the advent of measurement advances, the next step is to design and test interventions to cultivate curiosity in meaningful contexts (academic, social, work, leisure). Optimal psychological states arise from experiences where one's skills are perfectly balanced with immediate challenges, entailing intrinsic motivation and absorption (i.e., curiosity) and feelings of perceived control (Csikszentmihalyi, 1990). Curiosity interventions will need to address age differences and moderators of outcomes (i.e., identifiers of subgroups with particularly good or poor responses) and to assess immediate gains as well as the more distal consequences.

Curiosity is fueled by both increased knowledge and awareness of knowledge gaps in areas that are personally meaningful and engaging. Despite the absence of research on interventions, it can be interesting to speculate on ideas. Candidates for intervention modules include increasing mindfulness of what is known and unknown, facilitating autonomy and competence experiences, and setting up mentor relationships in personally meaningful domains. It can be hypothesized that more open-ended learning experiences such as creating ice cream to learn physics or taking a yoga class to learn the anatomy of different muscle groups may not only increase momentary curiosity but create enduring curiosity. The pursuit of activities that foster curiosity and learning may be an adaptive coping mechanism to deal with emotional and social distress (e.g., midnight basketball leagues for poverty-stricken inner-city youth, teaching chess or checkers to psychiatric inpatients with high cognitive functioning) and a means to perpetuate opportunities for positive experiences (e.g., writing journals as an avocation and potential career). The potential resilience afforded by cultivating curiosity-enriching experiences, and the promotion of virtuous cycles, is an open forum for future basic and applied research.

■ What Is Not Known?

There are a number of potentially fruitful areas for future research:

- What are the causal pathways leading from curiosity to personal growth?
- What pathways lead to the development of licit versus illicit means of satiating curiosity?
- Does the exploratory behavior of children and adolescents create more enriched environments amplifying cognitive, interpersonal, and intrapersonal development?
- What are the familial and developmental antecedents to curiosity (e.g., parental child-rearing characteristics, crystallizing experiences, cognitive ability, other traits, peer relations)? What is their association with curiosity and exploration across the life span?
- What are the outcomes of individuals with differential curiosity profiles, such as strong curiosity in one versus many domains?
- Can dispositional curiosity be cultivated? What are the best strategies, and what are the most suitable contexts for intervention?

■ Must-Read Articles and Books

Cacioppo, J. T., Petty, R. E., Feinstein, J. A., & Jarvis, W. B. G. (1996). Dispositional differences in cognitive motivation: The life and times of individuals varying in need for cognition. *Psychological Bulletin, 119*, 197–253.

Csikszentmihalyi, M. (1990). *Flow: The psychology of optimal experience.* New York: HarperCollins.

Loewenstein, G. (1994). The psychology of curiosity: A review and reinterpretation. *Psychological Bulletin, 116*, 75–98.

McCrae, R. R., & Costa, P. T. (1997). Conceptions and correlates of openness to experience. In R. Hogan, J. Johnson, & S. Briggs (Eds.), *Handbook of personality psychology* (pp. 825–847). San Diego, CA: Academic Press.

Sansone, C., & Smith, J. L. (2000). Interest and self-regulation: The relation between having to and wanting to. In C. Sansone & J. M. Harackiewicz (Eds.), *Intrinsic and extrinsic motivation: The search for optimal motivation and performance* (pp. 341–372). San Diego, CA: Academic Press.

Silvia, P. J. (in press). *The psychology of interest.* New York: Oxford University Press.

Spielberger, C. D., & Starr, L. M. (1994). Curiosity and exploratory behavior. In H. F. O'Neil & M. Drillings (Eds.), *Motivation: Theory and research* (pp. 221–243). Hillsdale, NJ: Erlbaum.

Voss, H., & Keller, H. (1983). *Curiosity and exploration: Theories and results.* New York: Academic Press.

6. OPEN-MINDEDNESS

[Judgment, Critical Thinking]

■ One person well described as an open-minded thinker was the Harvard psychologist Richard Herrnstein. As a teacher, he was thoughtful and open to all ideas. His work was similarly careful, scholarly, and responsive to other points of view without necessarily accepting them. Herrnstein made major contributions to behavior theory and to the psychology of decision making, but it is easiest to illustrate his openness in another area. In his writing about the IQ controversy, he took the controversial "hard line" in favor of the view that IQ mattered in life and was highly heritable, with both factors together resulting in a hereditary meritocracy. In this writing, he criticized the evidence that IQ was easily malleable by education. In 1979, a new government came into power in Venezuela. Luis Alberto Machado, a lawyer and friend of the new president, had written about the malleability of human intelligence in an amateur pop-psychology sort of way. Machado wanted to try an experiment to uplift the intelligence of Venezuela's people through education. He enlisted the help of several outside consultants (with advice from Herrnstein, in fact) to develop pilot programs. He wanted to convince a skeptic, so he wanted to have Herrnstein as a member of a team that would evaluate the main program. (Parenthetically, we note that Machado was evidencing certain strengths here as well.) Herrnstein was reluctant at first, but he gave in. The way he told the story later was that Machado and others invited him for cocktails and served what Herrnstein described as "a very nice wine." Herrnstein ended up drinking most of the bottle, while his hosts looked on, smiling. When he found out that the bottle was very old and worth several hundred dollars, he felt guilty. He said that this was what made him agree. Really, we think, he wanted to be open. In the end, he was the first author of the article describing the positive results of the program (Herrnstein, Nickerson, de Sanchez, & Swets, 1986). ■

■ Consensual Definition

Open-mindedness is the willingness to search actively for evidence against one's favored beliefs, plans, or goals, and to weigh such evidence fairly when it is available. Its opposite has been called the *myside bias*, which refers to the pervasive tendency to think in ways that favor one's current views (cf. Greenwald, 1980). Individuals with the strength of open-mindedness would probably endorse statements such as the following:

- Abandoning a previous belief is a sign of strong character.
- People should always take into consideration evidence that goes against their beliefs.
- Beliefs should always be revised in response to new evidence.

Such individuals would probably disagree with statements such as these:

- Changing your mind is a sign of weakness.
- Intuition is the best guide in making decisions.
- It is important to persevere in your beliefs even when evidence is brought to bear against them.
- One should disregard evidence that conflicts with one's established beliefs.

It is of course a legitimate question whether people can report accurately that these indeed are the ways that they go about forming and holding beliefs, but this is nonetheless a promising direction. As we describe in this chapter, there are assessment strategies that tap more directly open-mindedness, and at least some of these strategies converge with self-reports.

It is difficult for us to recognize open-mindedness as a general and persistent strength without knowing a person's thinking in detail (Stanovich, 1999). The most public of thinkers are intellectuals (writers, scholars), political leaders, and social commentators. Some of these people seem to blow a horn through their entire careers that plays but one note. Such people might still engage in a lot of open-minded thinking, concluding over and over that they are right, after considering the counterevidence—consider political pundit Bill O'Reilly and his self-labeled no-spin zone. Conversely, major changes in thinking—like David Stockman, who metamorphosed from an antiwar activist to a loyal follower of Ronald Reagan—might result from external factors (such as the end of the Vietnam War) as opposed to an active consideration of relevant evidence.

The importance of open-mindedness arises from the massive evidence that people are biased in favor of ideas that are already strong in their minds. The term *bias* means that people's thoughts and judgments are compared to an ideal standard, a normative model. For most of the research in this field, the normative standard is one of fairness to ideas, regardless of one's initial views. Often this normative standard is difficult to define. For example, many of our beliefs are more likely to be true than false, so we have good reason—on this basis alone—to think that any given belief is likely to be true. Open-mindedness does not require us to believe in extrasensory perception on the basis of one statistically significant demonstration; nor does it require us to spend time examining the details of this demonstration.

Despite these sorts of difficulties, a great deal of research supports the existence of biases, in cases where a normative model can be clearly specified. Other research supports the existence of general and stable individual and developmental differences in the magnitude of bias and conversely its absence. The claim that open-mindedness is a strength of character is thus based on evidence that it counteracts a pervasive weakness in thinking, the tendency to favor ideas that are strong (Perkins, Bushey, & Faraday, 1986). Active open-minded thinking is an example of what virtue ethicists call a *corrective virtue*, and what it specifically corrects is the widespread myside bias.[1]

■ Theoretical Traditions

The human understanding when it has once adopted an opinion draws all things else to support and agree with it. And though there be a greater number and weight of instances to be found on the other side, yet these it either neglects and despises, or else by some distinction sets aside and rejects, in order that by this great and pernicious predetermination the authority of its former conclusion may remain inviolate.
—FRANCIS BACON

In the case of any person whose judgment is really deserving of confidence, how has it become so? Because he has kept his mind open to criticism of his opinions and conduct. Because it has been his practice to listen to all that could be said against him; to profit by as much of it as was just, and expound to himself . . . the fallacy of what was fallacious.
—JOHN STUART MILL

Bacon and Mill were just two of many scholars over the centuries who emphasized the need for open-minded thinking. Socrates and Confucius made similar arguments, although the Bible did not. Arguably, the Bible has been resilient as doctrine in part because it never encouraged its followers to question anything, including the Bible itself. In 20th-century psychology, some of the early

---

[1]We should be clear that some biases in thinking are so widespread that even the best thinkers display them if they have not received formal and specific education concerning the relevant normative models (J. Baron, 2000). Examples include Bayes's theorem and statistical regression to the mean. In these cases, it is unreasonable to expect that open-mindedness will automatically correct them.

proponents of open-mindedness were John Dewey (1933) and Otto Selz (1935). Dewey's ideas on open-minded thinking influenced many others in American psychology, both directly and indirectly (e.g., Brim, Glass, Lavin, & Goodman, 1962; D'Zurilla & Goldfried, 1971).

Perhaps the most influential of the second generation of open-mindedness scholars was Irving Janis (1982), who argued that the myside bias (which he labeled *groupthink*) was responsible for foreign policy fiascos such as the U.S. invasion of the Bay of Pigs in Cuba. Janis emphasized the thought process of groups, such as the U.S. president and his advisers, rather than that of individuals, but the same arguments apply at the individual level. Janis recommended that groups improve their decision making by assigning group members to function as devil's advocates (an interesting phrase, to be sure) to make certain that the other side was heard and considered.

Herek, Janis, and Huth (1987) examined the thinking of U.S. presidents (and their advisers) about how the United States should respond to 19 international crises from the Greek civil war in 1947 to the Yom Kippur war in 1973. Historical records of decisions were evaluated for several symptoms of defective decision making, including the following:

- gross omissions in surveying objectives (inadequate search for goals)
- failure to examine major costs and risks of the preferred choice (inadequate search for evidence)
- gross omissions in surveying alternatives (inadequate search for possibilities)
- selective bias in processing information at hand (biased interpretation)

Outcomes were assessed by experts in international affairs, from the point of view of taking into account the best interests of the United States and (separately) the best interests of the world. The symptoms of poor decision making correlated with poor outcomes from either point of view. It is possible that the judgments of symptoms were influenced by the judges' knowledge of the outcome, but the correlations were high, and some of the crises were quite obscure, so the effect is probably a real one.

■ Measures

At least three general strategies of assessing open-minded thinking exist in the research literature (Table 6.1). The first uses a self-report survey to ask people about their beliefs. In some cases, an inference is made that respondents are open-minded or not based on the content of the beliefs they endorse. Early and well-known examples include the F-Scale of Adorno, Frenkel-Brunswick, Levenson, and Sanford (1950), which measures the degree to which one agrees with authoritarian (fascist) notions, and the Dogmatism Scale of Rokeach

TABLE 6.1   *Measures of Open-Mindedness*

1. Self-report surveys
  F-Scale (Adorno et al., 1950)
    30 items
    Internal consistency: alpha = ~.80

  Dogmatism Scale (Rokeach, 1960)
    40 items
    Internal consistency: alpha = ~.80

  Beliefs About Good Thinking (Stanovich & West, 1997, 1998, 2000)
    10 items
    Internal consistency: alpha = .50

2. Content analysis of verbal statements
  Paragraph Completion Test (Schroder, Driver, & Streufert, 1967)
    5 items
    Interrater reliability = ~.90

  "This I Believe" Test (Harvey, 1964)
    Varying number of items
    Interrater reliability = ~.90

  Integrative Complexity (Suedfeld & Tetlock, 1977; Suedfeld, Tetlock, & Streufert, 1992)
    Interrater reliability = ~.85

3. Expert analysis of arguments
  Argument Evaluation Test (Stanovich & West, 1998, 2000)
    23 scenarios
    Interrater reliability = ~.75

(1960), which measures agreement with absolutist notions of all stripes. On the face of it, those who score low on these measures are more open-minded than those who score high, but these surveys are obviously problematic for the purpose of measuring this character strength as we have defined it. Not only do they conflate a style of thinking with the content of one's beliefs, but they also fail to tap—even indirectly—the process by which these beliefs are established or sustained.

A more useful self-report strategy is therefore one that asks respondents specifically about their thinking styles. Stanovich and West (1997, 1998) devised a self-report survey using items like the ones cited earlier in this chapter. These items measure beliefs about good thinking and assume that the person who is open-minded is more likely to endorse such a thinking style than is someone who is not open-minded. Along similar lines, we have designed our own self-report survey about open-mindedness, which converges with nominations by other people (chapter 28).

The second assessment strategy uses content analysis of verbal statements about various issues to judge the complexity of the thinking that presumably gave rise to them. Are alternative perspectives acknowledged? Is reference made to evidence, pro and con? Early examples of this strategy include the Paragraph Completion Test of Schroder, Driver, and Streufert (1967) and the "This I Believe" Test of O. J. Harvey (1964). In each case, respondents are provided with a stem item like "This I believe about gun control. . . ." What they write (or say) in response is then coded for complexity. Like the self-report surveys just mentioned, these are not ideal measures of open-mindedness because they drag in potential confounds, in this case individual differences in verbosity, verbal fluency, and perhaps general intelligence. But the researchers who developed these content analysis approaches were aware of the hazards posed by such third variables and tried to control for them. The resulting evidence for construct validity is good (K. M. Goldstein & Blackman, 1978).

The best-known contemporary example of content analysis to measure this strength of character is Suedfeld and Tetlock's measure of integrative complexity, derived from the measures just described (Suedfeld & Tetlock, 1977; Suedfeld, Tetlock, & Streufert, 1992). Integrative complexity encompasses two aspects of how people think about matters: *Differentiation* refers to an individual's ability to apply different perspectives to a particular issue, and *integration* refers to an individual's ability to see connections between and among these divergent perspectives. Low levels of integrative complexity are characterized by a rigid and simplistic view of events, where a single point of view is considered correct, and all other perspectives are seen as illegitimate, flawed, or ridiculous. This content analytic strategy has been applied to all sorts of verbal material, such as public speeches, letters, and diary entries, and not just to statements produced in response to a researcher's request (F. Lee & Peterson, 1997). Integrative complexity is scored on a scale of 1 to 7 and takes into account both differentiation and integration as just defined. A score of 1 is given to a statement that expresses only a one-sided view, neglecting obvious arguments on the other side, thus failing to differentiate the two (or more) sides of an issue. For example:

> *Abortion is a basic right that should be available to all women. To limit a woman's access to an abortion is an intolerable infringement on her civil liberties. Such an infringement must not be tolerated. To do so would be to threaten the separation of church and state so fundamental to the American way of life.*

A score of 3 is given when the statement is differentiated—that is, when it includes arguments (evidence or goals) for both sides:

> *Many see abortion as a basic civil liberty that should be available to any woman who chooses to exercise this right. Others, however, see abortion as infanticide.*

A score of 5 or higher is given when the person making the argument succeeds in integrating opposing arguments, presenting a reflective statement about the criteria by which arguments should be evaluated:

> *Some view abortion as a civil liberties issue—that of the woman's right to choose; others view abortion as no more justifiable than murder. Which perspective one takes depends on when one views the organism developing within the mother as a human being.*

The integration part of the scoring system does not fit well with the concept of open-mindedness as we have characterized it here. But in many of the published studies, differentiation accounts for most of the correlations with external variables (J. Baron, 2000).

The third strategy most directly assesses actual thinking but is also the most time-consuming; it leads a research participant through an argument and then asks experts to judge the open-mindedness displayed. Stanovich and West's (1998) Argument Evaluation Test is a representative example:

- The respondent begins with Dale (for example) stating an opinion about some social issue—*The welfare system should be drastically cut back in size.*
- The respondent indicates his or her own agreement or disagreement.
- Dale then gives a justification—*Because welfare recipients take advantage of the system and buy expensive foods with their food stamps.*
- A critic then presents a counterargument—*Ninety-five percent of welfare recipients use their food stamps to obtain the bare essentials for their families.*
- Dale rebuts the counterargument—*Many people who are on welfare are lazy and don't want to work for a living.*
- The respondent then evaluates the strength of the rebuttal using a 4-point scale.
- The respondent's answer is compared with those given by experts— philosophy professors and Stanovich and West themselves.

To estimate myside bias, the researchers attempt to predict the respondent's ratings from both the expert ratings and the respondent's own opinion about the issue. Myside bias is defined as a demonstrable positive effect of the individual's own beliefs. That is, people showing myside bias are those who deviate from the expert ratings in the direction of their own opinions, rating arguments as better when they agree with that opinion. Most people show some myside bias, but some are more biased than others. So, what we have here is a content-valid measure of open-minded thinking. The more such items are used—the Stanovich and West test employs 23 different arguments—the more confidence we have that an actual trait is being measured.

Scores on the Argument Evaluation Test converge with Stanovich and West's (1997, 1998) self-report scale measuring open-mindedness, each supporting the validity of the other. This correlation between beliefs and conduct is also encouraging if we want to increase this way of thinking. It implies that we can change conduct by convincing people that open-mindedness is desirable, that is, by teaching them about the psychological research showing its benefits.

J. Baron (1991) found similar results. Research participants were asked how they thought people ought to respond to challenges to their beliefs. How, for example, should college students respond when they meet new ideas about religion or politics? Respondents were classified according to whether or not they thought people ought to think further, with a view to revising their beliefs if warranted. They were also asked to give grades (A through F) to hypothetical thinking protocols for the quality of thinking. Some protocols considered arguments on only one side of an issue. For example, on the question of whether automobile insurance rates should be higher for city dwellers than for suburbanites: *My first thought is that each group of people should pay for its own accidents. City dwellers surely have more accidents, and their cars get broken into and stolen a lot more.* Other arguments presented evidence on the opposite side as well: *On the other hand, it doesn't seem fair to make people pay for things they can't help, and a lot of people can't help where they live.* Respondents' thinking itself was also measured by looking at whether they themselves produced two-sided or one-sided arguments when asked to consider some question concerning public policy. Those people who gave higher grades to two-sided protocols, and who thought that people should be open-minded when beliefs are challenged, were more likely than others to show two-sided thinking themselves.

In another study, J. Baron (1995) asked college students to grade lists of thoughts made about abortion, supposedly in preparation for a class discussion. A majority gave higher grades to lists with arguments all on one side than to lists with arguments on both sides, even when the one-sided arguments opposed their own positions. Those who gave higher grades to one-sided lists were the same ones who tended to give arguments all on one side when making their own lists, whereas those who approved of two-sided lists were themselves more likely to create these.

■ Correlates and Consequences

In reviewing the correlates and consequences of open-mindedness, we decided not to address except in passing the vast literature that measures this trait with self-report questionnaires like the F-Scale. As emphasized previously, these are problematic operationalizations given our interest in open-mindedness as a style of thinking. Furthermore, the relevant studies have an unwavering uniformity in their conclusions: Endorsement of authoritarian, dogmatic, and ethnocentric ideas is invariably associated with undesirable correlates and consequences—hardly surprising given that these studies were largely undertaken by American investigators with American research participants in the years following World War II.

Of greater interest to us are studies that assessed open-mindedness in more direct ways. Much of this work has been done by cognitive psychologists as opposed to personality psychologists, which means that we know more about the relationship of open-mindedness to other styles of thinking than to the usual suspects included in personality batteries—like the Big Five traits, mood and well-being, coping styles, and so forth.

Consider Kuhn's (1991) study of reasoning about social issues. Research participants of different ages and educational backgrounds were given a structured interview about such topics as "What causes prisoners to return to crime after they're released?" The interview was designed to determine whether people could imagine alternatives to their own favored theory, what they considered as evidence for and against their theory, what a critic would say of their views, and how they would answer the critic. Respondents who were either young or lacked formal education often failed to provide alternatives. Sometimes the answers to interview questions about alternative theories were simply restatements of their own theories in different words. Such respondents also confused questions about evidence with questions about the theory itself.

These findings converge with earlier findings of Kuhn, Amsel, and O'Loughlin (1988) that people asked to interpret scientific evidence gave much the same answer to the question "What do the findings show?" as to "What do you think is true?" even when the findings were at odds with their own theories. Part of the interview concerned attitudes toward truth. Respondents were asked about their confidence in their own theory, about whether experts could know the truth, whether people could hold different views, and whether different views could all be correct. Kuhn et al. classified the responses as reflecting three kinds of implicit theories of knowledge.

Absolutist theories held that experts could be certain of the truth and that the respondent was certain of the truth, too. Most of those supporting absolutist theories, paradoxically, also agreed that other theories could be true. The paradox was sometimes resolved by the assertion that the respondent was correct because people are entitled to their own theories, so that his or her theory is personally true. The majority of research participants were absolutist, even among college students.

Multiplist theories of knowledge hold that experts are not certain and that conflicting theories can be simultaneously correct. Responses in this category often referred to personal experience or emotion as the grounds for belief. Those classified here owned their beliefs, as indicated by the following responses to the question "Would you be able to prove this person wrong?" "No, I would just be able to say I disagree with you and this is why and you can't tell me that my experience is wrong because this is what my experience was" (Kuhn et al. 1988, p. 182); "You can't prove an opinion to be wrong, I don't think . . . an opinion is something which somebody holds for themselves. You can't change their opinion or alter it. They have their own opinion" (p. 182).

Evaluative theorists held themselves to be less certain than experts. They held that "viewpoints can be compared with one another and evaluated with respect to their relative adequacy or merit" (p. 188), even if certain knowledge is impossible. Only 14% of those who had attended college fell into this category, as did 5% of the noncollege group. People in this category were less likely than others to be sure or very sure that their theory was correct; absolutist individuals were the most likely.

Kuhn et al. argued that opinions held unreflectively are as good as useless. Reflection involves considering at least one alternative and finding evidence that favors one's own view more than it favors the alternative(s), or evidence that impugns the alternatives more than one's view. These are the same moves that are required when people defend their views in dialogic arguments with others. In order to engage in such reflection, "Individuals must also hold the implicit epistemological theory that treats argument as worthwhile, as a fundamental path to knowing. In other words, people must see the point of argument, if they are to engage in it" (p. 201). People who hold that everyone's opinion is equally valid have no incentive to learn the standards of argumentation and belief formation. Of course, merely knowing these standards is not sufficient, if one does not adopt them as one's own, but one must know them to adopt them, and teaching them may encourage adoption.

The usual interpretation of these measures is that more open-mindedness is better. This does not necessarily need to be true. Many good qualities—indeed, virtually all of those discussed in this book—are Aristotelian virtues, best practiced in moderation. But the myside bias seems to be pervasive. Everyone suffers from it to some degree, but of course each of us thinks that others suffer more, and some of us are correct.

Good thinking—specifically active open-mindedness—does seem to correlate with good outcomes. Stanovich and West (1997, 1998) found correlations between open-mindedness, as measured by the Argument Evaluation Test, and several other tasks. Students with less myside bias did better on a test of logical syllogisms and the Wason four-card problem, a test involving attention to statistical evidence rather than anecdotes, a measure of efficient hypothesis testing, and a measure of the perception of correlations. Other tasks did not show such correlations, such as a measure of inappropriate extreme confidence or correct use of Bayes's theorem in probability judgment. Stanovich and West suggested that these effects are so widespread that there is little variation from person to person, regardless of the level of open-mindedness. Those low in myside bias also had better scores on tests of general cognitive ability, such as the Scholastic Achievement Test and the Ravens Progressive Matrices. These results suggest that open-minded thinking leads to better results in many tasks.

Other evidence for the benefits of critical thinking comes from experiments in which research participants are instructed to think of arguments on their side, the other side, or both sides, or they are given no instructions. The typical result is that instructions to consider one's own side have no effect, relative to the control condition (no instructions), because most people are doing this anyway. Instructions to consider both sides, or just the other side, reduce some bias of interest. C. A. Anderson (1982), for example, found that asking people to think of arguments on the other side increased the person's sensitivity to total discrediting (in the type of study described earlier), thus reducing the bias.

If we look at integrative complexity as measured by content analysis, we find similar correlates with effective performance in a variety of domains, presumably because complex thinkers attend to more information, in particular contradictory notions (Winter, 1996). Complex thinkers are less swayed by singular events and are more resistant to suggestion and manipulation than are simple thinkers. The cognitively complex are better able to predict how others will behave and are less prone to projection (Bieri, 1955). Indeed, the cognitively complex may be better able to accommodate stress (Suedfeld & Piedrahita, 1984).

■ Enabling and Inhibiting Factors

There is ample evidence that open-mindedness can be enabled or inhibited by the way that ideas are framed to people. Some studies ask people simply to list arguments on both sides of a question. A typical finding is that people find it easier to list arguments on their own side. More to the point, when they are prodded to come up with arguments on both sides, they can produce more arguments on the other side (Perkins et al., 1986). Presumably, they have these arguments in their memories but do not try to produce them when first asked. What remains to be determined is whether sustained experience with these frames produces the open-mindedness trait of interest to us.

Janis and Mann (1977) argued that good thinking is likely to happen when a decision is important, when the decision maker has time to make it, and when it is possible that some outcome is acceptable. Severe time pressure, or the perception of hopelessness, leads to the most extreme forms of myside bias, or to total disorganization (panic).

Further support for the situational determinants of open-minded thinking comes from more recent research by Tetlock (1986). People think in a more actively open-minded way when they must make a judgment or decision involving values (goals) that are both strong and conflicting. Tetlock showed this effect by asking college students to write down their thoughts about questions that involved conflicting values, such as "Should the [Central Intelligence Agency] have the authority to open the mail of American citizens as part of its efforts against foreign spies?"—a question that pits national security against individual freedom. Each research participant was asked to rank all the values that were pitted against each other by the various questions. Tetlock measured differentiation of the response, which was, in essence, the tendency to consider both sides. The differentiation of one's thinking was higher when the values underlying the question were ranked close together (and when they were both highly ranked). People thus tended to give a differentiated answer to the question about opening mail if they valued both national security and individual freedom. People who ranked only one of these values highly found the question easy to answer and were less prone to consider evidence on both sides.

Hindsight bias is the effect of knowledge on our judgment of what we presumably would say without that knowledge. For example, when people are told the outcome of a historical event, a case study, or a psychology experiment, and are then asked what probability they would have assigned to that outcome if they did not know it, they often give higher probabilities than individuals who did not know the outcome (Fischhoff, 1975). This effect is reduced by asking people before they make their judgments to think of reasons why the outcome might not have occurred, or simply to think of the other side (Arkes, Faust, Guilmette, & Hart, 1988; Slovic & Fischhoff, 1977).

Another bias that is reduced by such instructions is inappropriate extreme confidence. When people are asked to answer a difficult question (one that they might answer incorrectly), and then asked for a probability that they gave the correct answer, high probabilities are typically much too high. For items such as those on the Graduate Record Examination, probabilities of 100% are associated with accuracies of around 75%. This is a very robust phenomenon (Fischhoff, Slovic, & Lichtenstein, 1977). This effect has several independent causes, but one of them is the tendency to think of reasons why one's answer is correct and ignore reasons why it might be incorrect. When asked to think of reasons on the other side, or both sides, research participants give fewer 100% responses, and their accuracy on these responses increases—although never to 100% (Koriat, Lichtenstein, & Fischhoff, 1980).

It may be easier to inhibit open-mindedness than to enable it. Consider these lines of research documenting pervasive cognitive tendencies that work against open-minded thinking.

Selective Exposure

People maintain their beliefs by exposing themselves to information that they already know is likely to support what they want to believe. Liberals tend to read liberal newspapers, and conservatives tend to read conservative newspapers. In an experiment conducted during the 1964 election campaign, individuals were given an opportunity to order free brochures either supporting the candidate they favored or supporting his opponent (Lowin, 1967). All received samples of the contents of each brochure. When the arguments in the sample were strong and difficult to refute, people ordered more brochures supporting their own side than brochures supporting the other side. When the arguments in the sample were weak and easy to refute, however, individuals tended to order more brochures on the other side. People can strengthen their own beliefs by convincing themselves that the arguments on the other side are weak or that their opponents are foolish, as well as by listening to their own side. Many other studies have found this sort of bias toward information that can strengthen desired beliefs (Frey, 1986).

Primacy Effects

Often we can create a belief in the laboratory, and the belief then becomes resistant to counterevidence. Thus, the evidence that comes first matters more. When research participants have no reason to think that the order matters, this is a clear bias. When the order of evidence does not matter in fact, the order should not affect their final beliefs.

A vivid example is the so-called total discrediting effect (C. A. Anderson, Lepper, & Ross, 1980). In one study, research participants were given questionnaire responses of two different firefighters, one rated as better than the other at the job. Some participants were given evidence indicating that risk taking is positively associated with fire-fighting performance; others were given the reverse. The evidence was then discredited by telling the individual that the evidence was totally fabricated (showing someone the evidence that other individuals received), and the belief was then assessed. The direction of the initial belief manipulation continued to influence the belief, even after discrediting.

Polarization

Another normative principle is that mixed evidence—equally strong on both sides—should not strengthen belief. Yet in some situations, people discount the evidence against their belief and then proceed to count the evidence on their side, forgetting that it seems better only because they did not subject it to critical scrutiny. In a classic example, C. G. Lord, Ross, and Lepper (1979) selected research participants who had indicated that they either favored or opposed capital punishment. Each individual was then presented with mixed evidence on the effectiveness of capital punishment in deterring crime. Each person read two reports, one purporting to show effectiveness and the other purporting to show ineffectiveness. The procedure was manipulated so that only the first document reported deterrence (for half of the research participants) and only the second document reported deterrence (for the other half).

The effect of each report on the individual's belief was stronger when the report agreed with that belief than when it did not. Research participants rated the report that agreed with their initial opinion as more convincing and found flaws more easily in the reports that went against their initial opinion. In the end, research participants polarized; that is, they became stronger in their initial beliefs, regardless of its direction. If anything, mixed evidence should have made them less sure of their beliefs.

■ Development

From diverse studies, we can conclude that open-mindedness increases with age (throughout childhood and early adulthood) and education (e.g., Kokis, Macpherson, Toplak, West, & Stanovich, 2002), as long as we understand that this is not an inevitable developmental or pedagogical journey. The data are inconsistent on whether there is a decrease in open-mindedness among the elderly; the effect—if it exists—may be forestalled by social support, education, and/or good physical health (e.g., Pratt, Diessner, Pratt, Hunsberger, & Pancer, 1996; Pratt, Pancer, Hunsberger, & Manchester, 1990). The data are also inconsistent about the role of significant life events in increasing or decreasing open-minded thinking in their immediate wake (cf. Suedfeld & Bluck, 1993).

O. J. Harvey, Hunt, and Schroder (1961) speculated that integrative complexity (their cognate of judgment) is facilitated by child-rearing practices that emphasize interaction with the environment and the child's induction of beliefs from this interaction as opposed to what they call unilateral training, in which parents impose on their child abstract rules for living. They reported retrospective data in support of this theory, but these data are far from conclusive.

■ Gender, Cross-National, and Cross-Cultural Aspects

Regardless of how open-mindedness is measured, there is little evidence of gender differences except insofar as specific thinking tasks entail mathematical reasoning, in which case males perform better than females (West & Stanovich, 2003).

We know almost nothing about cultural variations in open-mindedness, although West and Stanovich are undertaking the relevant studies with their various measures of critical thinking (Caroline Ho, personal communication, December 11, 2002). Other psychologists have looked at cultural differences in cognitive styles related to open-mindedness, finding that members of collectivist cultures think more holistically than those of individualistic cultures. One manifestation of this difference is that Asians can accommodate contradictions more readily than Westerners (Nisbett, Peng, Choi, & Norenzayan, 2001). Does this mean that Asians are more open-minded than Westerners? We do not yet know, and in the meantime, we can only speculate that cultures which differ in their endorsement of open-mindedness as a desirable way to think might also differ in the actual critical thinking shown by the culture's members.

■ Deliberate Interventions

Can judgment itself be taught? Some studies suggest that it can be. More generally, the values that promote open-mindedness might be acquired like other values, partly from school, partly from home, and partly from other media of acculturation.

A number of training studies have been directed at behavior that resembles open-mindedness. Selz (1935) reviews a few interesting early studies. One of the most revealing of these studies was a thesis written by Jakob Andrae under Selz's supervision. In this study, an experimental and control group of students, aged 11 to 13, were given an intelligence test consisting of completion tests (stories with words left out), word ordering, verbal analogies, and number-series completions. The experimental groups was given training on only the completion test for 1 hour on two successive days. The training was designed to make students take into account the requirements of the task, checking each possible answer to see if these requirements were met. They were taught both to explain why answers did not meet the requirements and to justify answers when they seemed to fit. The training was done in the form of what seemed to be a lively competitive exercise in which students were called upon to defend their answers at the blackboard while other students in the group chimed in with criticisms and explanations. After the training, a second intelligence test was given. The experimental group showed substantial improvement not only on the completion test but also on all the others, to roughly the same extent. For example, on one of the completion tests, the experimental research participants improved from 60% to 78% correct, and the control participants improved from 60% to 63%; on the analogy test, the experimental research participants went from 28% to 69%, and the controls went from 33% to 41%. Of great interest, we think, is the finding that the experimental group was more than twice as likely as the control group to scratch out an answer and correct it in the posttest (244 times vs. 103), although the experimental research participants were less likely to do this in the pretest (22 times vs. 41). Again, this finding held to a roughly equal extent over all tasks. Although these results were from a short-term study with an immediate posttest, there is no reason to think that they would change qualitatively with more extensive training and a more delayed posttest.

In more recent studies, Perkins (1985) documented some effect of graduate training on a measure of myside bias but no significant effect of college or high school. Perkins et al. (1986) observed only small effects of various courses that emphasized thinking, but a 16-session course for high school students that they designed nearly doubled the number of other-side arguments concerning issues not discussed in the course (with a slight increase in quality as well, and no effect on the number of myside arguments). Students were taught that the arguments they consider should be true (to the best of the thinker's knowledge), relevant to the issue, and complete—that is, all important arguments should be considered. Controversial issues were discussed in class, and students were encouraged to generate and evaluate (for truth and relevance) arguments on both sides, especially the other side.

Kuhn et al. (1988) and Kuhn (1991) found results that could also be interpreted this way: Philosophy graduate students were less subject to a type of myside bias in scientific thinking than were other students, and, in general, education encouraged the belief that truth emerges from a process of critical inquiry in which both sides must be considered. In sum, the results together indicate that education can reduce myside bias and change standards but, in many cases, does not do so. A more intentional effort may be needed.

■ What Is Not Known?

Despite the importance of open-mindedness, much remains to be learned about this positive trait. The following are some areas that need further exploration:

- As mentioned throughout the chapter, the link between belief and conduct (i.e., the endorsement of critical thinking vs. its actual display) needs to be explored more fully, with an eye to identifying the conditions of congruence.
- Much more research needs to be done to establish the nomological net of open-mindedness as a personality trait. We know a fair amount about open-mindedness as a cognitive style but very little about the people who do or do not display this style. Provocative results have been reported by Tetlock, Peterson, and Berry (1993), who found that cognitively complex business managers were higher in initiative, more creative, and more open than their cognitively simple peers, but they were also less conscientious, more narcissistic, and somewhat more antagonistic in their dealings with others. Similar findings were reported by Feist (1994), who found that cognitively complex scientists were more eminent than cognitively simple scientists yet also more likely to be seen as hostile and exploitative. Theoretical discussions of open-mindedness, including our own, imply a highly flattering view of those who have this

trait, but these data suggest a more complex (and interesting) reality (cf. Tetlock, Armor, & Peterson, 1994).

- We need more fine-grained studies of the development of this strength, and we also need to know more about deliberate interventions that nurture and sustain it (J. Baron, Badgio, & Gaskins, 1986).

- Largely unexplored is the role played by positive emotions in facilitating or inhibiting open-mindedness. Strong negative emotions make a person less open-minded (e.g., Cook & Peterson, 1986; Orbach, Mikulincer, Stein, & Cohen, 1998), but what about strong positive emotions? Fredrickson's (1998) theory of positive emotions proposes that states like joy broaden one's cognitive repertoire, but this may or may not mean that the person becomes more open-minded. Indeed, extreme positive feelings may be just as incompatible with rationality as extreme negative feelings (Shafir & LeBoeuf, 2002), which is a sobering thought for positive psychologists. In bolstering people's happiness, do we inadvertently undercut their critical thinking?

- Why is open-mindedness apparently so rare, and why does it seem so vulnerable? Perhaps the answer is simply that many psychologists who have investigated this cognitive style have been interested in showing limits and exceptions to rational models of thought, and they have been highly successful in their efforts (e.g., Kahneman & Tversky, 1973). But perhaps there is a more intriguing answer, namely, that the inherent architecture of the human mind works against open-mindedness, in which case our general statements about the readiness of people to embrace virtue (chapter 1) have a striking exception in this particular strength. As Katharine Hepburn's character said in *The African Queen,* "Nature . . . is what we are put in this world to rise above."

■ Must-Read Articles and Books

Baron, J. (2000). *Thinking and deciding* (3rd ed.). New York: Cambridge University Press.

Kuhn, D. (1991). *The skills of argument.* New York: Cambridge University Press.

Stanovich, K. E. (1999). *Who is rational? Studies of individual differences in reasoning.* Mahwah, NJ: Erlbaum.

Stanovich, K. E., & West, R. F. (1998). Individual differences in rational thought. *Journal of Experimental Psychology: General, 127,* 161–188.

7. LOVE OF LEARNING

What does love of learning look like? Consider Linnea, a 10th grader in a blue-collar, primarily white, public school on the outskirts of a large U.S. city. At the school Linnea attends, teachers typically assume that assigned work will not get done for their class because their students have jobs outside of school and little family support for academics.

███ *Linnea signed up to take Latin initially because she liked mythology.*
During Language Month at her school, she showed up in class dressed as a
goddess. Her teacher described her behavior as wonderful, in character, and a
bit eccentric. "Linnea likes the idea of doing Latin," her teacher reports. "She
speaks Latin with me. Who does that?"

Interestingly, the other students in Linnea's class took in stride the fact that
she showed up dressed as a goddess. In fact, each day when students in the Latin
class recount the Latin moments *that they have had since the last class*
meeting—references to a Latin word, the history and/or mythology of Rome
and ancient Greece, and so on—Linnea typically recounts about 17 of them,
almost always connected to movies she has just watched. Her teacher notes that
the other students in the class jokingly roll their eyes as Linnea goes down her
list, but because they like and respect her, they listen with good humor.

Linnea is in the second year of Latin. She and a number of others in her
class typically stop in to visit her Latin teacher in the morning before school.
Unlike most of her peers, however, Linnea also shows up for class having
completed all the assignments each day and always has additional contributions
like the Latin moments to make. The teacher does not think that Linnea has to
work very hard to do these assignments. Her teacher observed, "When we are
doing translation of English to Latin, she just pays attention to endings and gets
them. This is hard for most of her peers." Asked to describe what she does when

she does run into a difficulty in Latin, Linnea replies, "If there's a sentence I don't know how to translate, I'll look at the other sentences around it and see how they are set up and try to set it up the same way; or, I'll just keep working until it makes sense. Whenever we learn something new, I like pick it up right away."

Linnea has positive feelings about learning new things in Latin and confidence that she can keep working until she can make sense of what she is learning. She has made different kinds of connections to the content and has developed strategies for figuring out what she does not immediately know (Renninger & Hidi, 2002; Schoenfeld, 1992). Linnea also feels supported in her efforts to learn, despite a school culture in which doing homework and pursuing the study of Latin are uncommon (A. M. Ryan, Pintrich, & Midgley, 2001). She has a sense of possibility (Markus & Nurius, 1986) and is autonomous in her decision to dress like a goddess, recall Latin moments, and speak Latin with her teacher (Deci, 1992).

About her history class, on the other hand, Linnea commented, "I wish I knew why I have to learn history. . . . When it comes to history my mind becomes a sieve. It will hold the information long enough to pass the test, but then afterward, I'll only remember the highlights." Despite Linnea's sense that she is not really learning history in her history class, her grades are high. In fact, she is considered a strong student in all her classes. Reflecting on the history class, in particular, she comments that she never knows what to expect in that class. She also notes, though, that the history class is like Latin in that "I do well in both classes, and the teachers love me."

Even though Linnea earns good grades in her history class, she says she is not able to retain what she has learned in that class. The similarities between history and Latin, from her perspective, appear to be the personalities of the teacher and their relationship to her, not the structure or the focus of the class. Thus, even though she feels loved, the open question is whether Linnea is receiving the kind of support she needs to stretch herself so that she can engage the content of history and possibly develop a love of learning for it.

Importantly, Linnea has positive feelings for Latin and knows a great deal about it. She feels confident that she can do the tasks of the Latin class. She generates her own ways of interacting with the subject matter, and she is able to identify and make use of additional resources to pursue her interest for Latin. In contrast, she does not appear to have a way to connect to the history content, even though she feels valued by the teacher. It appears that she has a need to have both positive feelings and an ability to begin working and asking curiosity questions of the content if she is to develop a love of learning for it.

It is an open question whether Linnea has a love of learning as a general strength, or whether she instead has a love of learning Latin or a well-developed interest for Latin. It is also an open question whether she has the potential to develop the more general strength if she learns to regulate her own learning and to generate connections for herself to her other classes, including the history class. ■

■ Consensual Definition

Love of learning is a strength that teachers would like to see in their students, that parents want to encourage in their children, that therapists support in their clients, and that employers try to foster in their employees. In fact, love of learning is a strength to which researchers and the lay public seem able to point with ease, even though it has not been the specific focus of a research literature. Instead, love of learning has been discussed in relation to major conceptual dimensions of a number of constructs, including motivational orientation, competence, value, and well-developed interest.

Love of learning is characterized here as referring both to a general individual difference and to a universal but individually varying predisposition to engage particular content (e.g., Latin, videogames, music) or well-developed individual interest (Renninger, 1990, 2000). Love of learning describes the way in which a person engages new information and skills generally and/or the well-developed individual interest with which he or she engages particular content. When people have love of learning as a strength, they are cognitively engaged. They typically experience positive feelings in the process of acquiring skills, satisfying curiosity, building on existing knowledge, and/or learning something completely new (Krapp & Fink, 1992). This strength has important motivational consequences in that it helps people to persist in the face of setbacks, challenges, and negative feedback—when positive feelings may be temporarily infused with negative feelings associated with frustration until a path or resolution for their problem is identified (Krapp & Fink, 1992; Neumann, 1999; Renninger, 2000). Love of learning describes the process of engaging content that may or may not result in immediate achievement or any immediate benefit to achievement as defined by some external standard like academic tests (Harackiewicz, Barron, & Elliot, 1998). Instead, over time a person may develop a deeper or wider knowledge of contents to be learned and be positioned to make substantial and creative contributions to others' understanding of them.

It is likely that people with love of learning as a general strength would strongly endorse statements such as the following:

- I can't do this task now, but I think I will be able to do it in the future.
- I like to learn new things.
- I will do whatever it takes in order to do a task correctly.
- Learning is a positive experience.
- I care more about doing a thorough job than whether I receive a good grade.

Furthermore, it is likely that people who have a well-developed individual interest, or love of learning, for a particular content area would endorse statements such as these:

- Relative to the other things that I know, I know a lot about (the content area).
- Relative to the other things that I like, I like (the content area).
- I spend as much of my time doing (the content area) as possible.
- Working on (the content area) is hard work, but it never really feels like hard work.
- I know that if I put my mind to it, I can figure out how to do (the content area) really well.

■ Theoretical Traditions and Measures

Love of learning has been included as a partial descriptor of many constructs but rarely discussed as a strength in its own right. For this reason, measures that tap into love of learning tend to be subscales of other measures (e.g., when measuring how much someone says they enjoy thinking about complex things as part of Cacioppo and Petty's, 1982, Need for Cognition Scale). Rather than list all measures that may include some items that reflect love of learning, some examples of measures are identified here in terms of the theoretical traditions in which they have emerged: motivational orientation, competence, value, and well-developed individual interest (Table 7.1).

Motivational Orientation

Several researchers have developed measures of general motivational orientation that distinguish between intrinsic and extrinsic motivation. These measures focus on why someone engages in activities, with items that reflect autotelic reasons (e.g., because they provide challenge, satisfy curiosity, and create interest and enjoyment) used to identify an intrinsic motivational orientation. Many of these items are considered to directly address love of learning because people who endorse them to describe their own learning suggest that they learn for the sake of learning. Items used to identify an extrinsic motivational orientation, in contrast, suggest that learning activities are a means to an end (e.g., to get good grades, to win a promotion, to please someone else).

The presumed relationship between intrinsic and extrinsic motivational orientations differs as a function of theoretical perspective (Ames, 1992; Covington, 1984; Deci & Ryan, 1985a; Harter, 1981; Lepper & Henderlong, 2000; see discussion in Sansone & Harackiewicz, 2000). These differences are reflected in the measures of motivational orientation that have been developed. One of the more widely used measures of motivational orientation is the Work Preference Inventory (WPI; Amabile, Hill, Hennessey, & Tighe, 1994). In the WPI (consisting of 30 items), the intrinsic and extrinsic motivation scales are potentially independent. Individuals can endorse both intrinsic motivation ori-

---

TABLE 7.1   *Measures of Love of Learning*

Motivational orientation

Work Preference Inventory (WPI)
    Amabile, Hill, Hennessey, & Tighe (1994)

Academic Motivation Scale (AMS)
    P. Vallerand et al. (1992)

Children's Academic Intrinsic Motivation Inventory (CAMI)
    Gottfried (1986)

Competence

Achievement Motivation Scale
    Elliot and Church (1997)

Patterns of Adaptive Learning Survey (PALS)
    Midgley et al. (1998)

Orientation Scale
    Skaalvik (1997)

Value

Task Value Scale
    Eccles (1984)

Well-developed individual interest
Various content-specific scales, e.g., Green-Demers,
    Pelletier, Stewart, & Gushue (1998)

---

entation items (e.g., "I enjoy tackling problems that are completely new to me") and extrinsic motivation orientation items (e.g., "I am strongly motivated by the recognition I can earn from other people"). The intrinsic motivation scale includes two subscales, enjoyment and challenge, and the extrinsic motivation scale includes two subscales, outward and compensation. The more people endorse intrinsic motivation items on this scale, the more likely they are considered to possess the strength of love of learning (even if they also find extrinsically motivated reasons to engage in learning).

The Academic Motivation Scale (AMS; Vallerand et al., 1992), on the other hand, builds on Deci and Ryan's (1985b) self-determination theory. The AMS scale (consisting of 28 items) is subdivided into seven subscales that assess three types of intrinsic motivation (intrinsic motivation to know, to accomplish things, and to experience stimulation), which are typically collapsed into one index of intrinsic motivation and three types of extrinsic motivation (external, introjected, and identified regulation), which are presumed to vary from less to more self-determined, respectively. All items represent reasons that one attends college. Following completion of the scale, an overall index is computed to determine the likelihood that a person's college attendance can be attributed to an intrinsically motivated love of learning rather than more extrinsic factors.

The WPI and AMS are used primarily with college-age and older populations. Intrinsic motivation of elementary school and high school age students is typically assessed using Gottfried's (1986) Children's Academic Intrinsic Motivation Inventory (CAMI). CAMI, which is designed to evaluate students' self-reported enjoyment of learning and mastery, includes subscales to assess an overall level of academic intrinsic motivation, as well as intrinsic motivation levels within particular subject areas (e.g., reading, math, social studies, and science). Versions have been developed for both elementary school and high school age students.

Competence

Measures of competence acquisition or maintenance have also included items that reflect love of learning. These measures tend to reflect several kinds of competence-related dimensions, including perceptions of one's capacities and abilities (Bandura, 1986; Marsh, Craven, & Debus, 1991); achievement motivation, or the importance a person attaches to achieving competence in general or specific to a domain (Helmreich & Spence, 1978; Jackson, 1974); the meaning of achieving (or failing to achieve) competence for self-worth (Harter 1998); and the kind of achievement goals a person adopts in a particular learning context (Butler, 1987; Dweck, 1986; Harackiewicz, Barron, Carter, Tauer, & Elliot, 2000; Midgley et al., 1998; Nicholls, 1984). To experience love of learning, researchers studying competence suggest, people must feel (or expect to feel) some sense of competence and efficacy in the learning process; that is, they must feel that they *are* mastering a skill, filling in the gaps in their knowledge, and so on.

The paradox, however, is that learning, by definition, also includes trials in which one fails, feedback that one's hypothesis was wrong, realizations that the current path will not work, and so on (Sansone & Morgan, 1992). To explain this paradox, researchers have distinguished between different kinds of achievement orientations, based on achievement goals people adopt. They hypothesize that these different achievement orientations result in different responses to negative feedback. Some goal orientations are considered to be more conducive to a love of learning than others.

A student with a mastery (or task or learning) orientation, for example, is considered to strive for achievement defined in terms of individual mastery, with his or her progress measured in terms of improvement and effort. In contrast, a student with a performance (or ability or ego) orientation is considered to strive for achievement with progress measured in terms of performance relative to others or some externally defined standard (e.g., grades). Many researchers suggest that the pursuit of mastery goals is most likely to be associated with a love of learning, because this orientation allows one to maintain a sense of efficacy while learning (Dweck & Leggett, 1988). Different achievement orientations are also expected to inform the kinds of strategies adopted in pursuit of these goals and the emotions one experiences as a person meets (or fails to meet) them. The kinds of strategies and emotional reactions that help to define and foster a love of learning are also linked to a mastery orientation. For example, students with a mastery orientation are more likely to report using elaboration strategies (e.g., "When reading, I try to connect the things I am reading about with what I already know") and report greater interest in and enjoyment of the topic being studied (Harackiewicz et al., 2000).

According to a number of researchers, the strategic and emotional differences between mastery and performance goals are even greater if a finer distinction is made between approach and avoidance goals (Elliot & Church, 1997; Linnenbrink & Pintrich, 2000; Midgley et al., 1998; Skaalvik, 1997). *Approach goals* are those that lead a person to move toward a positive outcome (i.e., moving toward mastery or demonstrating competence), whereas *avoidance goals* are goals framed in terms of avoiding a negative outcome (i.e., avoiding the failure to master a task or demonstrating incompetence). People with approach mastery goals might be more likely to have love of learning as a strength than would people with avoidance goals. (When learning is examined outside of the classroom, however, performance approach goals may also be conducive to engagement in and enjoyment of learning, particularly for individuals higher in achievement motivation; see Barron & Harackiewicz, 2000.)

There are a number of measures of a mastery orientation (and, more recently, approach mastery orientations). The scale reported by Elliot and Church (1997) has three subscales: mastery orientation (6 items), approach performance goals (6 items), and avoidance performance goals (6 items) (a recent revision of the scale also includes a mastery avoidance subscale; see Elliot & Sheldon, 1998). Individuals who highly endorse the mastery orientation items (e.g., "I prefer course material that really challenges me so I can learn new things") might be expected to be those with a greater love of learning. Similarly, as part of the Patterns of Adaptive Learning Survey (PALS), Midgley and colleagues (1998) assess three kinds of orientations: task orientation (5 items), performance approach goal (5 items), and performance avoidance goal (6 items). Individuals who highly endorse the task orientation items (e.g., "An important reason I do my academic work is because I like learning new things") might be expected to show greater love of learning. Finally, Skaalvik (1997) proposes four subscales: task orientation (6 items), self-enhancing ego orientation (5 items), self-defeating ego orientation (7 items), and avoidance orientation (4 items). Students who score highly on the task orientation subscale (e.g., "What I learn in my university classes makes me want to learn more") might be expected to reflect greater love of learning (see M. Smith, Duda, Allen, & Hall, 2002, and Jagacinski &

Duda, 2001, for a comparison of the psychometric properties of these and other achievement goal scales, e.g., Nicholls's, 1984, Success in School scale).

Value

In addition to the value attached to achieving competence, people who exhibit a love of learning might also be expected to place greater value on the content of what they learn (or expect to learn). For example, the Task Value Scale developed by Eccles and her colleagues (1984; see Eccles & Jacobs, 2000; Wigfield & Eccles, 2000, 2002) measures four dimensions (tapped by 2 items each) that contribute to the overall level of task value. The four subscales include utility (e.g., "In general, how useful is what you learn in [class topic]?"); importance (e.g., "Is the amount of effort it will take to do well in [class topic] this year worthwhile to you?"); interest (e.g., "How much do you like doing [class topic]?"); and perceived cost (e.g., "How much does the time you spend [working on class topic] keep you from doing other things you would like to do?").

Findings from work with the Task Value Scale suggest that values can predict intentions and decisions about activity more strongly than expectancies for success (Wigfield & Eccles, 2002). Thus, people with a greater love of learning could be expected to report greater value for a learning task. In this sense, value might also be expected to contribute to a person's motivation to persist in learning, even when this persistence comes at a cost to the other activities to which the person might be attracted. Wigfield and Eccles (2002) also noted, however, that there may be developmental differences that need to be explored. As they point out, children tend to be optimistic about their competence and performance. Thus, children's abilities to successfully self-regulate and make informed decisions about their own activity might require a match between children's values and their performance. For children, it may be that value can be said to support motivation for task engagement but is not necessarily sufficient for predicting the quality of this engagement.

Well-Developed Individual Interest

Well-developed individual interest is characterized by a person's ongoing and ever deepening cognitive and affective relation with particular content; as such it mirrors the more general strength, love of learning. As the most developed phase of interest development, well-developed individual interest is reliably associated with full engagement for particular content(s) (e.g., Renninger & Wozniak, 1985). A person working with a content of well-developed individual interest is typically able to persevere in his or her efforts despite the types of frustration that challenging work with content can represent (Krapp & Fink, 1992; Prenzel, 1992; Renninger & Hidi, 2002; Renninger & Leckrone, 1991).

Measures of well-developed individual interest assess individual engagement with particular content(s) or the content focus of knowledgeable groups of individuals, such as figure skaters in training, where knowledge and value for the activity can be assumed (Green-Demers, Pelletier, Stewart, & Gushue, 1998). Among young children, well-developed individual interest has been identified using naturalistic observation over extended periods, where knowledge and value are operationalized in terms of repeated, independent, sustained, and complex behavior across different content (Renninger, 1989, 1990; Renninger & Hidi, 2002; Renninger & Leckrone, 1991; Renninger & Wozniak, 1985). Similarly, among older elementary and high school age students, individual interest has been assessed using self-reported levels of stored knowledge and positive feelings for particular content relative to the other content with which the student is involved and, in some cases, independent assessment of student activity as confirmation of self-report (Ainley, Hidi, & Berndorff, 2002; Benton, Corkill, Sharp, Downey, & Khramsova, 1995; Gräber, 1998; Haussler, 1987; Haussler & Hoffmann, 1998; Renninger, Ewen, & Lasher, 2002).

Assessment of older student and adult interest has tended to focus more specifically on identification of the quality of affective engagement at least in part because it is presumed that participants have some knowledge of the content with which they work (Alexander & Murphy, 1998; Koeller, Baumert, & Schnabel, 2001; Krapp & Lewalter, 2001; P. K. Murphy & Alexander, 1998).

■ Correlates and Consequences

Despite the fact that love of learning has not been studied as a strength in its own right, data nonetheless suggest that love of learning supports positive experiences (Csikszentmihalyi, 1978), which, in turn, may predispose psychological and physical well-being. Certainly, people who experience a love of learning appear more likely than others to appreciate what they learn (Covington, 1999). Compared with others who do not have love of learning as a strength, they are more likely to do the following:

- have positive feelings about learning new things
- have the ability to self-regulate efforts to persevere, despite challenge and frustration
- find connections to the content to be learned, generate strategies for approaching this content, and then take the time to rethink their understanding and strategy selection
- feel autonomous
- feel challenged
- have a sense of possibility
- be resourceful (e.g., find models for themselves)

- be self-efficacious
- feel supported by others in their efforts to learn

Taken together, these correlates may predict positive mental and physical health patterns. Some researchers have suggested that greater engagement in education early in life can protect against cognitive impairment in later life (Katzman, 1973), although this point is still debated (e.g., Gilleard, 1997). The ability to sustain interest and develop new interests has been associated with engagement in learning and healthy, productive aging (Krapp & Lewalter, 2001; Renninger & Shumar, 2002; Snowdon, 2001). In addition, the fields of business and technology have increasingly emphasized the need to reconceptualize education as one of lifelong learning, as job demands and requirements continue to change rapidly. Individuals in the workforce with greater love of learning might be expected to be more likely to seek out and meet these challenges (McCombs, 1991).

More generally, the degree to which individuals experience interest and enjoyment as they learn should translate into decreased stress (Sansone, Wiebe, & Morgan, 1999), which over the long term should result in greater physical and emotional well-being (Elliot & McGregor, 2001; Helson & Srivastava, 2001). Similar to what has been identified with other positive subjective experiences (Seligman & Csikszentmihalyi, 2000), therefore, a positive relation between love of learning and happiness, well-being, and physical health might be expected.

■ Development

Love of learning describes a process of engaging with new information and skills that is generally positive and that can withstand the frustrations of challenge and negative feedback. On one hand, this strength distinguishes between individuals in terms of their motivational orientations and goals for learning. On the other hand, it appears that almost all individuals may have some of this strength, in the sense that they can be identified as having well-developed individual interest for at least a few contents. In fact, Travers (1978) suggested that if some interest cannot be identified for a person, this itself is a sign of pathology.

Based on findings from studies of well-developed interest (Krapp & Fink, 1992; Renninger et al., 2002; Renninger & Hidi, 2002), related findings from studies of talent (Csikszentmihalyi, Rathunde, & Whalen, 1993), and discussions of passion (Fried, 1996, 2001), it appears that this strength needs to be nurtured if it is to be sustained over time. Well-developed individual interest cannot develop without challenges (Renninger, 2000). As Fried (2001) notes, the learning environment needs to be appreciated as a web of relations: the learner and the materials; the teacher (parent, therapist, employer) to the materials; the learner to the teacher; the teacher to the learner's academic work (chore, problem, or job); the learner to peers regarding academic work; and the relation among the learner, parents, and teacher regarding academic work. In order for love of learning to be sustained, the individual needs to learn in a context in which each of these relations supports engagement and collaboration.

Interestingly, there appear to be developmental differences in the amount of support students may ideally need and the likelihood that they will struggle to understand and ask their own questions of the content with which they work. Young children usually immerse themselves in the process of engaging the world around them (Piaget, 1966). They also typically do not have many constraints placed upon them about what normative behavior necessitates. Over time, interested engagement appears to either be sustained or abate in relation to the support received from the environment (including others such as parents, teachers, peers, as well as challenges provided by texts, tasks, and schools).

Some research suggests that interest declines with age, especially for academic content as students enter middle and high school (P. L. Gardner, 1985; Krapp, 2000; Sansone & Morgan, 1992; Wigfield, Eccles, MacIver, Reuman, & Midgley, 1991). However, it also appears that the constraints of the school setting (e.g., limited course options, grades, pedagogical practices) may limit opportunities for interest development (Foellings-Albers & Hartinger, 1998; L. Hoffmann, 2002; Renninger & Hidi, 2002). Moreover, studies on which discussions of interest development are often based have tended to focus on student interest for a discrete set of academic subjects rather than accounting more broadly for the range of possible contents for which students at these ages might have a love of learning or well-developed interest (e.g., videogames, professional soccer). Usefully, the study of the impact of individual interest on adult development does suggest that regardless of what the specific content of interest is, the presence of and the ability to sustain interest benefit the person and his or her place of employment and/or family relations (Krapp & Lewalter, 2001; Renninger & Shumar, 2002; Snowdon, 2001).

■ Enabling and Inhibiting Factors

Even if people do not experience love of learning as a general strength, most people do experience a love of learning for content areas of well-developed individual interest (Travers, 1978). A person does not need to be an expert to have a well-developed individual interest for a content area. Rather, a well-developed interest emerges in relation to a person's developing knowledge (and opportunities to develop this knowledge with which the person can connect) *and* the stored value that accrues from the feelings of competence and sense of possibility that a development of knowledge represents (Renninger, 2000).

Conditions for supporting the development of individual interest, and presumably a love of learning more generally, may need to be set up as direct interventions. A number of situational factors have been identified that support learning to learn (Hidi, 1990; Schraw & Lehman, 2001). These include strategies that teachers (parents, therapists, or employers) can use to adjust instruction; tasks that are designed to meet the strengths, interests, and needs of students (children, patients, or employees); and methods people can use to self-regulate their own learning (Sansone et al., 1992).

Antecedents and conditions that influence a person's abilities to find connections to content to be learned, generate and revise strategies, feel support, and self-regulate activity to engage particular content areas include the following:

- positive feelings for the particular content area
- knowledge about the content area relative to the other involvements they have
- belief that a task is doable
- curiosity about a task that manifests itself in the asking of curiosity questions
- the ability to identify and make use of resources in order to work on a task

■ Gender, Cross-National, and Cross-Cultural Aspects

References to love of learning are often invoked in conjunction with discussions of the motivation to effectively master and manipulate the environment (Berlyne, 1949; Dewey, 1913; White, 1959). For this reason, the potential to develop a love of learning has often been discussed as universal. Recent research suggests that even if the seeds for love of learning are universal, the form it takes and the conditions that foster it may differ as a function of the cross-nation or within-nation culture in which the person lives (Banks, McQuater, & Hubbard 1977; Jacobs, Finken, Griffin, & Wright, 1998). For example, Iyengar and colleagues (e.g., M. Hernandez & Iyengar, 2001; Iyengar & Lepper, 1999; see related discussion in Greenfield, 1994) have suggested that engagement in and enjoyment of learning may be supported by fostering individual agency in cultures that emphasize independence (e.g., many Western cultures), and by fostering community agency in cultures that emphasize interdependence (e.g., many Asian cultures). Similarly, Li (2002) suggested that the love of learning concept within the Chinese culture "stresses seeking knowledge and cultivating a passion for lifelong learning, fostering diligence, enduring hardship, persistence, concentration, 'studying hard' regardless of obstacles, and feeling 'shame-guilt' for lack of desire to learn" (p. 248). Thus, instead of individuals feeling shame or guilt as the result of failing to achieve, as is hypothesized within Western cultures, the Chinese model suggests that shame or guilt results from failing to *want to* learn.

Similarly, there is no reason to expect gender differences in the predisposition to experience love of learning or well-developed individual interest, although there may be differences as a function of the contexts or domains in which love of learning surfaces, the form it takes, and the kinds of within-domain contextual and interpersonal factors that support it. For example, there tend to be no gender differences in the degree of achievement motivation reported by males and females, although females tend to score slightly lower on the competition subscale of the Work and Family Orientation scale (Spence & Helmreich, 1983), and males tend to score slightly higher on the "goof off" or work avoidance subscale of the Success in School Scale (Nicholls, 1984). In addition, males and females may have different initial levels of interest for particular topics as a function of sex-typed experiences (Hoffmann, 2002; Renninger, 1992). Males and females may also have different expectations for success in different domains, which can influence the degree of interest and value of that domain (Eccles, 1984, 1994; Wigfield & Eccles, 2000). Finally, women tend to experience a greater interpersonal focus in achievement domains (e.g., Strough, Berg, & Sansone, 1996), and this focus can translate into different goals while students engage in learning, the use of varying strategies to regulate interest and motivation, and diverging sensitivity to feedback (e.g., J. L. Smith, Morgan, & Sansone, 2001). Differences of domain and interpersonal focus may also lead males and females to develop different contents of interest because they influence the process of making connections to past experiences and valued aspects of the self, as well as the degree of support for using relevant strategies (Renninger, 2000; Renninger & Hidi, 2002).

Findings such as these suggest that there may be other important moderating factors of the development and maintenance of love of learning that differ as a function of the cultural and social background of the person that have yet to be identified.

■ Deliberate Interventions

Cultivation of the general strength (love of learning) or its more content-specific form (well-developed interest) may need to be recognized as a process that requires a person to first overcome existing feelings, prior experiences, misconceptions, stereotypes, and so forth. As Dewey (1913) observed, any deliberate intervention needs to focus on providing conditions that allow a person to develop his or her understanding; this, in turn, will result in valuing and sustained efforts to really understand content.

The case of Linnea and her Latin classmates is an example of a teacher's deliberate intervention to establish conditions that will support students' abilities to learn, and perhaps eventually develop the strength of love of learning. Although only 2 other students beside Linnea were identified as having a well-developed interest for Latin, the other 38 students could all be said to have a maintained situational interest for Latin—these numbers are notable for this population of students, although this level of engagement would be remarkable in any classroom, in any school. A maintained situational interest is an earlier phase in the development of interested engagement that can, with support over time, emerge as an individual interest (Hidi & Renninger, 2003).

That these students, in this population, are willing to assume the challenge of learning Latin and complete most of the assigned work may be attributed to the fact that the class is hard and that the teacher has structured it so that they can learn (see related discussion in J. C. Turner et al., 2002). The Latin class is active, and the curriculum builds on the students' everyday experience. In particular, the teacher's use of Latin moments, current events, and project work enables the students to make meaningful and authentic connections to the Latin they are learning (Bransford, Brown, & Cocking, 1999)

Furthermore, the students know that the teacher likes them, and she communicates her understanding of their efforts to organize themselves to learn (Noddings, 1992; A. M. Ryan et al., 2001). The teacher also has a clear plan for the class that builds on what the students know, focuses on the students as learners, and conveys an expectation that they can and will learn (Barth 2001; Palmer, 1998). Interestingly, the content of what the students are asked to learn is not in itself engaging material for adolescents—Latin phrases, verbs, and a book about a senator who is called back to Rome. Rather, it appears to be the connection that the students have developed to the teacher, and the way in which she has structured their learning in the class over time, that support the students' situational interest for and information about ways to engage and make sense of Latin.

As the experience of Linnea and her peers suggests, the teacher (parent, therapist, employer) plays a pivotal role in whether interventions to support learning generally and a love of learning more specifically are to be successful. A teacher is in a position to adjust instruction through the particular methods that are employed, which is what this Latin teacher does for her students. The teacher can also work to adjust the content of what is taught, which this teacher does to a more limited extent. Finally, the teacher can work to support the students' abilities to self-regulate their learning, which this teacher does not do in any developed way, although she notes that this is something she has as a goal. Interestingly, the emphasis placed on the teacher as needed facilitator is echoed by Csiksentmihalyi, Rathunde, and Whalen's (1993) assertions that without family support it is unlikely that a child's talent will be developed. In fact, they comment that it is a myth that a child's talent will either surface or survive without support from others.

The person who does not have love of learning as a strength, or a well-developed individual interest for content to be learned, needs support to find ways to connect to learning. Moreover, even if people love learning, they need support to sustain the frustration that is inherent in challenging assumptions, the identification and learning of new skills, and so forth (Csiksentmihayli, Rathunde, & Whalen, 1993; Fried, 2001; Renninger, 2000; Renninger & Hidi, 2002; Steele, 1997). Steele's (1997) wise schooling intervention, for example, is aimed at creating and helping minority college freshmen maintain a love of learning so that they will be less likely to drop out of college. Building on the work of Treisman (1992), the intervention includes several methods that may be applied to smaller groups of students (minority and nonminority). First, the intervention provides students with knowledge and challenge by framing the intervention itself as a select opportunity offered to students with a high learning potential. Framing the experience in this way curtails any feelings of being singled out for remedial or lower level learning expectations. In addition, students meet for challenging content-based workshops (e.g., math, writing) that teach skills and learning strategies at a high, fast-paced level. Second, the intervention serves to foster a social network and help students fulfill interpersonal needs through offering a focus for connecting to each other through content that is of interest. This is accomplished by having students live near each other in the same wing of a dormitory for the first semester, as well as having students meet weekly in small discussion groups to talk about an informal (personally relevant) reading assignment. Although highly intensive and expensive, this program has shown promising results.

Another type of intervention is derived from laboratory and classroom studies of environments that facilitate mastery-approach orientations to learning and task performance (Harackiewicz, Barron, Carter, Lehto, & Elliot, 1997; Roney, Higgins, & Shah, 1995; Turner et al., 2002). A mastery-approach intervention emphasizes self-improvement, understanding, and the value of learning for its own sake. Turner et al. (2002) describe mastery-approach classroom environments as characterized by teachers who transfer responsibility to the students for learning, promote question asking, and encourage students to seek help for further understanding. In mastery-approach classrooms, student answers to questions are typically negotiated with the teacher and other students, and errors are viewed as constructive. Importantly, the organization of these classrooms is also intended to facilitate collaborations between students to meet their social goals and foster joint responsibility for learning. This is important because individuals can have interpersonal goals that they see as part of the achievement activity. For these individuals, greater interest is fostered when the activity is structured to allow both achievement and interpersonal goals to be met (Isaac, Sansone, & Smith, 1999; J. L. Smith et al., 2001).

Interestingly, one complication of mastery-approach classrooms is that short-term measures of student achievement may at first suggest lack of achievement because students are focused on learning and understanding rather than demonstrating the ability to perform. The mastery-approach intervention is most effective if implemented by a teacher, or a familiar other, who can relate to the learner in terms of more than his or her academic abilities (A. M. Ryan et al., 2001). It provides support for learning both through the familiar other and in terms of the students' knowledge of the task or classroom. It is also important that the student perceives the structure of the classroom or the task as having a mastery approach. This can be accomplished by emphasizing goals. In fact, Harackiewicz and Elliot (1993) reported that low achievement-oriented students are likely to spend more of their free time with and enjoy tasks more when they are told that they will be evaluated based on how skills develop and improve, whereas the same students are less likely to spend free time with and enjoy tasks when performance and skill demonstration is emphasized as an outcome (see related findings in Assor, Kapland, & Roth, 2002).

Interventions such as these address individual needs for experiencing belongingness, competence, positive feelings, and utility (Bergin, 1999). They have multiple components and provide a number of ways for students to anchor what they do know in the task or materials to be learned (Cognition and Technology Group at Vanderbilt, 1990, 1991).

In addition to providing opportunities for students to think together and revise their initial understanding of tasks, students also need to be involved in tasks that are (a) complex enough to require collaboration and encourage sharing of differing perspectives, and (b) authentic and meaningful (S. R. Goldman et al., 1998). Linnea's ability to know that she was learning in her Latin class, but not in her history class, appears to be linked to the way in which she was able to anchor her learning in the two classrooms. Whereas the content of each class is largely factual, the structure of the Latin class includes participation that is meaningful and focused (Wade, 2001). Participation in this class includes sharing what is understood and revising this understanding based on new information. In the history class, on the other hand, as one of Linnea's peers commented, "We screw around for 3 days, take 20 minutes of notes, and then take a test." In fact, the history teacher prioritizes getting to know the students over history content, and like the Latin teacher includes project work and discussions as methods. Thus, successful intervention does not appear to be simply a function of a caring teacher and/or the use of interactive tasks but requires that students have an understanding of the goals for their work in the class.

The overall organization of the history class is much less structured than the Latin class, and from the students' perspectives feels sort of "hit-or-miss." Linnea, like her peers, does not appear to have a clear sense of what she is expected to learn in history, or why. As a result, it is not surprising that Linnea feels there is more that she might be learning from the history class. The complication for her seems to be that the class does not have an analogue to "history moments" or opportunities to make connections between her everyday experience and the history she is learning.

The Latin moments exercise taken by itself is emblematic of interventions that involve adjusting the features of texts and tasks to capture students' attention (see reviews by Hidi, 2001; Hidi & Berndorff, 1998). Lepper and Cordova (1992), for example, designed external intervention programs to increase children's interest in topics such as graphing and computer programming. Their approach includes embellishing components of the task (e.g., graphing a point in space) with personally engaging factors (e.g., calling the point to be graphed "cheese" for a "mouse" to find in the space). Enhancing the motivational appeal of the task was found to significantly increase the children's reported desire to work on similar problems in class (without the embellishments) as well as their learning of the material. Similarly successful studies include interventions that use interest to enhance students' attention to text (McDaniel, Waddill, Finstad, & Bourg, 2000); reading of text (e.g., Hidi & Baird, 1986; Sadoski & Quast, 1990; Schraw, Bruning, & Svoboda, 1995; Wade, Buxton, & Kelly, 1999); and comprehension of text (Schiefele, 1996, 1999; Schiefele & Krapp, 1996).

Garner and colleagues, however, have reported deleterious effects when interesting but unimportant information (termed *seductive details*) is added to text (Garner, Alexander, Gillingham, Kulikowich, & Brown, 1991; Garner, Brown, Sanders, & Menke, 1992; Wade, 1992). Findings from these studies underscore the importance of matching interventions to enhance task interest to the behaviors required to learn the material. In other words, interventions to enhance interest should not interfere with the learning demands (see Lepper & Henderlong, 2000; Sansone & Smith, 2000). It is difficult, however, to always know a priori when an intervention to increase task interest will support learning, especially if the intervention itself is also assumed to be of interest to the student.

An alternative approach is suggested by the research of Sansone and colleagues (Sansone & Morgan, 1992; Sansone & Smith, 2000; Sansone et al., 1992). In addition to a person's interest and engagement in learning being regulated by external interventions (such as by embellishments or teacher support), this research suggests that older students and adults can actively regulate their own interest and enjoyment. In particular, external interventions that enable the individual to see the activity as something to value can result in the person actively engaging in strategies that make the activity more interesting for himself or herself. For individuals working with a task or in a domain they do not find interesting, the presence of (a) a good reason to do the task and (b) options to make the task more interesting can lead the individual to self-regulate his or her experience of interest and subsequently redefine the task so that it becomes more interesting. This type of intervention is particularly effective over time because it involves the student in learning how to assume responsibility for his or her own learning.

When students are in a position to self-regulate interest for learning, this type of intervention has the advantage of being readily available when and where an individual chooses to use it. Given that interest has been shown to be a powerful influence on sustained attention and comprehension, it appears likely that promoting self-regulation of interest for learning may result in positive motivational and performance outcomes in the long term—especially if the intervention to enhance interest complements the behaviors needed for learning.

■ What Is Not Known?

As discussed here, love of learning refers both to a general strength and individual difference, and to an individually varying but universal predisposition to reengage particular content or well-developed interest. Love of learning has been discussed in relation to the conceptual dimensions of different constructs; however, a number of open questions remain about love of learning and how it develops:

- When and how are real-life connections to materials to be learned made for the person who has a love of learning?
- What effect does the opportunity for different learning task alternatives and strategies have on the experience of love of learning?
- How well do people learn who do not have love of learning as a strength?
- Do people with love of learning as a strength differ from others in the number of well-developed individual interests that they can be identified as having?
- What is the role of other individual difference and contextual factors on love of learning (e.g. global self-esteem, fear of failure, socioeconomic status, and race and gender based on stereotypes)?
- What are the long-term personal and societal benefits and consequences of the love of learning? Do these extend beyond academic outcomes such as health-related issues and family and other interpersonal relationships?
- What types of conditions are needed to enable children to learn to self-regulate their interest for learning?
- Is the ability to self-regulate innate? At what age is a child able to learn to self-regulate his or her interest for learning? How do the skills of self-regulation of motivation change over the life span?
- Is a person more likely to self-regulate his or her engagement with a content of well-developed individual interest than a content of less-developed individual interest? Is it possible to use well-developed individual interest as a scaffold for helping a student to develop the strength love of learning?
- What are the long-term outcomes of self-regulating interest for learning?

■ Must-Read Articles and Books

Covington, M. V. (1999). Caring about learning: The nature and nurturing of subject matter appreciation. *Educational Psychologist, 34*, 127–136.

Csikszentmihalyi, M., Rathunde, K., & Whalen, S. (1993). *Talented teenagers: The roots of success and failure.* New York: Cambridge University Press.

Fried, R. L. (2001). *The passionate learner: How teachers and parents can help children reclaim the joy of discovery.* Boston, MA: Beacon Press.

Harackiewicz, J. M., Barron, K. E., Carter, S. M., Lehto, A. T., & Elliot, A. J. (1997). Predictors and consequences of achievement goals in the college classroom: Maintaining interest and making the grade. *Journal of Personality and Social Psychology, 73*, 1284–1295.

Hidi, S., & Berndorff, D. (1998). Situational interest and learning. In L. Hoffmann, A. Krapp, K. A. Renninger, & J. Baumert (Eds.), *Interest and learning: Proceedings of the Seeon Conference on Interest and Gender* (pp. 74–90). Kiel, Germany: IPN.

Hoffmann, L. (2002). Promoting girls' learning and achievement in physics classes for beginners. *Learning and Instruction, 12*, 447–465.

Krapp, A., & Lewalter, D. (2001). Development of interests and interest-based motivational orientations: A longitudual study in vocational school and work settings. In S. Volet & S. Järvela (Eds.), *Motivation in learning contexts: Theoretical and methodological implication* (pp. 201–232). London: Elsevier.

Renninger, K. A. (2000). Individual interest and its implications for understanding intrinsic motivation. In C. Sansone & J. M. Harackiewicz (Eds.), *Intrinsic and extrinsic motivation: The search for optimal motivation and performance* (pp. 375–407). New York: Academic Press.

Sansone, C., Weir, C., Harpster, L., & Morgan, C. (1992). Once a boring task always a boring task? Interest as a self-regulatory mechanism. *Journal of Personality and Social Psychology, 63*, 379–390.

Steele, C. M. (1997). A threat in the air: How stereotypes shape intellectual identity and performance. *American Psychologist, 52*, 613–629.

8. PERSPECTIVE

[Wisdom]

▨ *Popular images of a sage person coalesce around elderly men with long white beards: for example, Gandolf from* Lord of the Rings, *Albus Dumbledore from* Harry Potter, *or Charles Darwin in his later years. However, if we define sagacity as the ability to offer useful advice to others about the pragmatics of everyday life, we very quickly identify Esther Pauline Friedman Lederer as a more appropriate—and certainly more popular—icon of the character strength of perspective. Who? Known as Eppie to her friends and family, and as Ann Landers to the readers of her advice column for almost half a century, Esther Lederer at the time of her death in 2002 had a readership of 90 million people, making her the most widely read newspaper columnist in history.*

Her columns were crisp and clear, witty and sometimes sarcastic. But they also touched on the real issues that matter to real people: from the serious (heartbreak and divorce, ungrateful children and meddlesome in-laws, illness and death) to the whimsical (whether toilet paper should run over the top or down the wall). She did not shy away from taking strong positions on anti-Semitism, racism, the Vietnam War, abortion, handguns, and federal funding for cancer research. Her readers ranged from teenagers to the elderly, and she continued to grow and change as an advice giver to the perplexed as the world itself changed. One did not have to agree with her opinions to recognize that she "had her thumb on everything," tolerating neither nonsense nor sugar coating. Although she had a staff that sorted through the 2,000 letters she received every day, she wrote all the columns herself.

Esther Lederer had many of the characteristics that research has linked to perspective. She read widely and was passionately interested in the world. She worked behind the scenes for political causes. She had deep and sustained friendships. She enjoyed going out in the evening as well as the simple pleasures of life, often writing her column in the bathtub. Unlike previous advice columnists, she frequently turned to experts for advice, using their wisdom to shape her own. She was an optimist and a humanist, even believing that people's handwriting had improved throughout the 20th century.

Her life was not without trouble. She was the victim of anti-Semitism as a teenager in Sioux City, Iowa. Her long-standing feud with her twin sister ("Dear Abby") was well known; their reconciliation was less publicized. She and her husband (the founder of Budget Rent-a-Car) divorced after 36 years of marriage. When diagnosed with bone marrow cancer, she refused what would have been debilitating treatment and worked to the very end. She wanted no funeral—considering it "folderol"—but was accorded the ultimate honor by the Chicago Tribune *syndicate, which owned her column: Despite a cash value estimated at $1 million, the name "Ann Landers" was retired.* ■

■ Consensual Definition

Due to differing theoretical and methodological approaches, psychology lacks a single definition of wisdom and perspective. Most psychologists have conceptualized wisdom in one of three ways: in terms of wise processes, wise products, or wise people. The good news is that the resulting characterizations of wisdom overlap, especially with respect to the one of most interest to us: perspective as a positive trait possessed by wise people (Assmann, 1994; Baltes, 1993; Kekes, 1995; Lehrer, Lum, Slichta, & Smith, 1996). We see agreement that this character strength:

- is distinct from intelligence
- represents a superior level of knowledge, judgment, and capacity to give advice
- allows the individual to address important and difficult questions about the conduct and meaning of life
- is used for the good or well-being of oneself and that of others

If modesty did not intrude, individuals with the character strength of perspective would strongly endorse such statements as the following:

- I have self-knowledge.
- I bring both feeling and rationality into decisions.
- I realize larger patterns of meaning or relationship.
- I have a wider perspective.
- I have a strong need to contribute to others and society.
- I take into consideration the needs of others.
- I understand the limits of what I can know and do.
- I am able to see to the heart of important problems.
- I have an accurate view of my strengths and weaknesses.

- I am turned to for advice.
- I behave in a manner consistent with my own personal standards.

■ Theoretical Traditions

At one time, the topic of wisdom occupied the attention of virtually all philosophers and theologians concerned with the good life and how to lead it (chapter 2). Wisdom was variously defined as erudition, especially in regard to philosophy or science; as the ability to judge correctly in matters relating to life and conduct; and as understanding what was true, meaningful, or lasting. An emphasis on scholarly learning is found in writings by the pre-Socratic philosophers (e.g., Heraclitus) and the classical Greek philosophers (e.g., Socrates, Plato, and Aristotle). An emphasis on good judgment in the service of effective living is found in writings from the ancient Near East (Greeks, Hebrews, and Egyptians) and ancient Middle Eastern civilizations (Sumerians, Babylonians, Canaanites, and Phoenicians). And an emphasis on one's insight into transcendent ends rather than practical means is found in the works of early Christian theologians like Saint Augustine.

Some thinkers combined these definitions. For example, the notion that wisdom involved religiously based transcendental knowledge predominated in Western thought until the reemergence of the Greek traditions of Stoicism and skepticism, resulting in a reformulation of what was considered wise (E. F. Rice, 1958). This reformulation blended Christian and classical ideas, allowing for the possibility of a worldly based, practical wisdom as well as a divinely inspired, transcendent wisdom. Thus, wisdom oriented the individual toward living in the world in such a way as to transcend it, a way of being in the world but not of it. In this case, practical wisdom served as a stepping-stone to transcendent wisdom—worldly perfection led to divine enlightenment. The Cartesian conceptualization of wisdom was similarly complex (J. D. Collins, 1962). Descartes viewed wisdom as the counterpoint to scientific knowledge: Knowledge involved the accumulation of facts, whereas wisdom involved the organization and interpretation of those facts. Wisdom ranged from the earthly to the divine, with one achieving wisdom in a hierarchical, linear fashion from good sense to inspired judgment and understanding.

These definitions subsume large chunks of the character domain that we have stretched over this entire volume and even include what we regard as talents and abilities (see chapter 1). Although we acknowledge these early "wisdom" traditions as important, we offer the qualification that they embraced so much of virtue that they foreshadowed current thinking on many character strengths and not simply the work described in this chapter. Indeed, current psychological work on wisdom is much more circumscribed, which is one reason we prefer the term *perspective* as a synonym for modern conceptions of wisdom that stress the useful and impartable worldview of the wise person.

Another point to emphasize about modern psychology's approach to wisdom is that until rather recently there simply was no approach. To explain this conspicuous neglect of wisdom, Holliday and Chandler (1986) identified four primary culprits, namely, psychology's:

- aversion to mentalistic explanations
- allegiance to logical positivism, which restricted inquiry into externally valid concepts
- mechanistic metaphor that human competence decreases with age due to wear and tear, rendering wisdom—the presumed accomplishment of the elderly—mythic at best
- tendency to equate knowledge with technical-analytic expertise, while ignoring or dismissing the practical and emancipatory knowledge that wisdom entails

This latter trend has led some researchers to define wisdom to fit the concept within other, better understood, constructs and more acceptable forms of knowledge:

> Contemporary psychological accounts of what it might mean to be wise are seen to generally suffer from a kind of assimilation bias which threatens to reduce wisdom to an extreme version of some other already better understood psychological construct. By such lights wisdom is seen as nothing but hyperbolic and age-encrusted intelligence, or a 5th or 6th stage in cognitive or moral maturation, or even as an exaggerated technical expertise. (Holliday & Chandler, 1986, pp. vii–viii)

To caricature this approach, it would approach the wisdom of Gandhi in terms of his technical expertise at weaving under stressful circumstances and of course miss the point of his strength. Describing poorly understood concepts in familiar terms may make science simpler, but it obscures those aspects of wisdom that make it unique and important. The potential role of perspective as an indicator of competency in the latter half of life is precisely what has led to its reemergence in modern psychological inquiry. However, despite more than a decade of contemporary research on wisdom, current definitions are still largely cognitive.

Two contemporary research groups are highly involved in the study of wisdom: Paul Baltes and colleagues at the Max Planck Institute for Human Development in Berlin and Robert Sternberg and colleagues at Yale University (e.g., Baltes & Staudinger, 2000; Sternberg, 1998). The former researchers approach wisdom from the perspective of life span developmental psychology and specifically gerontology, whereas the second group's starting point was cognitive psychology and specifically so-called practical intelligence. Comparisons and contrasts between these approaches are instructive.

Both research groups trace their work to the philosophical wisdom traditions just mentioned, and both distinguish between implicit theories of wisdom (the so-called folk psychology of wisdom that tells us how the people in general describe and recognize wise people) and explicit theories of wisdom (psychological accounts of the processes that give rise to wise behavior). It is with respect to explicit theories that the two research groups most differ.

Baltes and Staudinger (2000) defined wisdom as expertise in the conduct and meaning of life. Thus, the wise person is someone who has expert knowledge about the meaning of life (what really matters) and how to plan and manage a meaningful life. Like any domain of expertise, the relevant knowledge can be divided into factual knowledge and procedural knowledge.

Sternberg's (1990a) original theorizing about wisdom also emphasized tacit (procedural) knowledge, but his more recent ideas stress as well feelings and values and especially the notion of balance among these psychological characteristics and the settings in which people find themselves (Sternberg, 1998). What is a wise response in one situation may be less so in another, or even foolish. Indeed, Sternberg proposed that wisdom may to some degree be domain specific, although it can exist at a more general level if only by taking the form of individuals being wise enough to know when they have reached the limits of their sagacity.

The distinctions between the explicit theories girding these approaches are abstract and are contained in proposed research agendas, as opposed to empirical studies testing these theories or pitting them against one another. These investigations have now begun, however, and there is convergence in that both groups approach the assessment of wisdom in terms of the paradigm case of giving advice with respect to ill-defined yet important social dilemmas or conflicts.

■ Measures

Given the complexity of wisdom per se and even of perspective more specifically, it is not surprising that researchers have approached the assessment of this character strength in different ways, depending on their theoretical perspective. Among those who emphasize "wise" processes, we see wisdom captured by attending to postformal, dialectical, and dialogical modes of thought (Assman, 1994; Hartman, 2000; Kramer, 1990; Kramer & Bacelar, 1994; Labouvie-Vief, 1990; Sinnott, 1998; Sternberg, 1990b, 1998, 1999b; Valera, 1999).

Among those who choose to focus on "wise" products, we see an approach that provides concrete tasks that allow individual differences in perspective to be manifest (Hartman, 2000; Staudinger, Lopez, & Baltes, 1997; Staudinger, Maciel, Smith, & Baltes, 1998; Staudinger, Smith, & Baltes, 1992; Wink & Helson, 1997). For example, research participants are confronted with broad and ill-defined life dilemmas involving hypothetical characters and asked to think aloud about what might be done in such a situation. Their responses are then evaluated by expert judges according to explicit criteria.

A representative approach is the one used by the Max Planck group. Individuals are presented with a social dilemma like "Someone receives a telephone call from a good friend who says that he or she cannot go on like this and has decided to commit suicide" (Baltes & Staudinger, 2000, p. 126). The respondent is asked to talk aloud in response to the query "What might the individual receiving this phone call take into consideration and then do?" Responses are tape-recorded, transcribed, and then coded on 7–point scales using explicit rules for judging the degree to which each of five criteria for wisdom are met in the response:

- rich factual information (e.g., social norms)
- rich procedural information (e.g., how to offer advice, how to adjudicate life goals)
- life span contextualism, meaning knowledge about such contexts of life as family, friends, and work and how they figure into life at its various stages
- relativism of values and life priorities; not an "anything goes" relativism but instead the appreciation that individuals and groups hold different values that variously structure their priorities
- recognition and management of uncertainty

Trained judges agree substantially in their scoring of protocols, and different respondents achieve comparable scores across dilemmas as well as across time. Consistent with our conceptualization of character strengths as personality dimensions, Baltes and Staudinger (2000) regard the resulting wisdom scores as "more-versus-less" continua. The "wisest" products are of course those that receive the highest scores on the different dimensions, but wisdom so assessed is a matter of degree.

Sternberg (1998) described a similar approach to the assessment of wisdom and perspective that emphasizes tacit knowledge used in real-world pursuits. Individuals are interviewed and asked to describe how they have handled critical situations on their jobs. This information is used to create scenarios about job-related problems. Research participants are given these scenarios and options to be rated on scales of goodness. These options vary in the degree to which they embody Sternberg's notion of wisdom as using tacit knowledge to balance personal and interpersonal interests and achieve a common good. The profile is scored according to its similarity to that provided by experts.

Finally, among those who are most interested in wise persons, we see wisdom regarded as a personality characteristic or personality structure (e.g., Erikson, 1963; Hartman, 2000; Wink & Helson, 1997). These operationalizations are based in either implicit theories of wisdom or explicit theories, or some combination. Accordingly, people may be asked to nominate "wise" individuals of their acquaintance, who are then studied with an eye to characterizing their personality. Or people may be asked to articulate in abstract terms their own notion of wisdom, and then personality scales tapping this notion are identified or created and used to measure individual differences in perspective (e.g., Clayton & Birren, 1980; Sternberg, 1986a, 1990a). Examples of these scales are described in Table 8.1.

A version of this latter strategy was undertaken by Hartman (2000), who used a Q-sort procedure to establish the personality prototype of wisdom held by expert psychologists and then to rate research participants in terms of how well they fit this prototype. The experts arrayed statements from Block's (1978) California Q-Sort in accord with how closely they captured "wisdom." There was substantial agreement across the experts. The most prototypical items included the following:

- is able to see to the heart of important problems
- has insight into own motives and behavior
- appears straight-forward, forthright, candid in dealing with others
- is turned to for advice and reassurance
- behaves in an ethically consistent manner[1]

The next step in this assessment strategy is to use the full Q-sort to rate other information (e.g., interviews, personality test scores, life events) about research participants and then to assign "wisdom" scores according to the degree to which the wisdom items were sorted as highly characteristic. Reliability is satisfactory across expert raters as well as for individual research participants; that is, the placement of given "wisdom" items is correlated with the placement of other such items.

These three approaches to the measurement of wisdom converge. For example, Hartman (2000) showed that measures reflecting each of the preceding approaches correlated with one another: Wise products are generated by wise persons using wise processes. Baltes, Staudinger, Maercker, and Smith (1995) found similar results.

---

[1]Other items were identified as highly uncharacteristic of wise people, but these were (wisely) not used in subsequent research because they were also indicative of maladjustment and would guarantee correlations with well-being rather than allow them to emerge.

TABLE 8.1   *Measures of Wisdom and Perspective*

ACL Practical Wisdom Scale

Wink & Helson (1997)

Self-report questionnaire composed of 14 indicative and 4 contraindicative items from the Adjective Check List (Gough & Heilbrun, 1983)

- Internal consistency: alpha = .74–.81
- Test–retest reliability: r = .40–.41

Transcendent Wisdom Scale

Wink & Helson (1997)

Open-ended question from which responses are content coded for themes related to transcendent wisdom; responses received a score of 1 to 4 for the degree to which they reflect self-transcendence or self-development

- Internal consistency: alpha = .81–.86
- Test–retest reliability: r = .50

CAQ Wisdom Scale

Hartman (2000)

Observer-based measure derived from the California Q-Sort (Block, 1978) and consisting of the 12 most characteristic personality descriptors of the 100 descriptors available; items are sorted on a 1 to 9 scale, ranging from extremely uncharacteristic or negatively salient to extremely characteristic or positively salient

- Internal consistency: alpha = .66–.94
- Test–retest reliability: r = .36–.57

Acquired Wisdom Scale

Hartman (2000)

Open-ended question from which responses are content coded for themes related to acquired wisdom; responses are coded as present or absent by two expert coders; these individual codes are then combined to create three levels of acquired wisdom (intrapersonal, interpersonal, and transpersonal) based on the notion that the process of moving from one level to the next involves the differentiation and disidentification of the lower level (e.g., from personal experience to abstract principle), which is then replaced by an integration of the lower with the higher (e.g., personal experience of an abstract principle)

- Internal consistency: alpha = .87

CPI Wisdom Scale

Hartman (2000)

Non-face-valid, self-report-based measure of wisdom composed of 70 items from the California Psychological Inventory (Gough, 1987)

- Internal consistency: alpha = .73–.83
- Test–retest reliability: r = .35–.67

■ Correlates and Consequences

Although empirical investigations of wisdom and perspective are relatively new, it is clear that this individual difference is associated with a variety of indices of successful aging, including psychological and physical well-being, satisfaction in multiple life domains, psychosocial development, and psychological resources. Most studies have been cross-sectional, finding that wisdom is more robustly linked to the well-being of older people than are objective life conditions such as physical health, socioeconomic status, financial situation, and features of the physical and social environments (Ardelt, 1997; Baltes, Smith, & Staudinger, 1992; Bianchi, 1994; Clayton, 1982; Hartman, 2000; Thomas, 1991). Research has also shown that wisdom is distinct from intelligence as measured by IQ tests, although some overlap exists (Sternberg, 2000). Finally, there are hints that wisdom is associated with such personality traits as maturity, open-mindedness, even-temperedness, sociability, social intelligence, and the absence of neuroticism (e.g., Staudinger et al., 1997). Little longitudinal work has yet been done on the consequences of wisdom, although Hartman (2000) found that wisdom evident among women at age 43 predicted their well-being at age 53. In particular, wisdom foreshadowed the successful management of the midlife menopausal transition.

Most studies of the correlates of wisdom have looked at samples of older adults. However, one of the most interesting empirical facts about perspective—to be described shortly—is that this character strength is not the sole province of the elderly. Accordingly, the correlates and consequences of wisdom among younger adults are largely unknown yet in need of investigation.

■ Development

Wisdom is usually thought to be not only a positive predictor of successful aging but also a product of it (Assmann, 1994; Birren & Fisher, 1990; Labouvie-Vief, 1990; Sternberg, 1990b; Taranto, 1989). Ordinary people associate wisdom with experience (Sternberg, 1986a), and those who are young attribute it to those who are old (Heckhausen, Dixon, & Baltes, 1989; Orwoll & Perlmutter, 1990). However, studies have largely failed to find age-related differences in self-ratings of wisdom among individuals ranging from their 20s to their 90s or in wisdom-related performance (Orwoll & Perlmutter, 1990; J. Smith, Staudinger, & Baltes, 1994; Staudinger et al., 1992, 1998).[2] This is an intriguing and important finding that exemplifies a premise of our project that measures of character strengths can lead to discoveries unanticipated by mere theorizing. This finding has the

---

[2]The work of Wink and Helson (1997) is an exception. These researchers found that in both men and women, self-ratings of practical wisdom increased from the late 20s to the early 50s.

more specific implication that interventions to nurture wisdom and perspective can take place at a relatively early age. Indeed, recent work with adolescents has suggested that the primary period of development in wisdom-related knowledge before early adulthood may be the age from about 15 to 25 years (Pasupathi, Staudinger, & Baltes, 2001).

In the absence of deliberate interventions, how does wisdom develop? Contemporary views of adult development emphasize the potential for personality change across the life span (Erikson, 1963) but further stress that attention must be paid to structured life transitions and how they are negotiated by the individual (Whitbourne, Zuschlag, Elliot, & Waterman, 1992). Other than wrinkles, there may be few inherent changes with age. Instead, personality changes in adulthood—including the development of perspective—is a function not of the passage of time but of life experiences and how people respond to them. Allport (1961) phrased this point well:

> Maturity of personality does not have any necessary relation to chronological age. A well-balanced lad of eleven, "wise beyond his years," may have more signs of maturity than many self-centered and neurotic adults. A sound college student may have greater maturity than his own parent, or even grandparent. Often, of course, riper experience and the continual meeting and mastering of obstacles and of suffering, do confer greater maturity with advancing age. But the parallel is far from perfect. (p. 277)

Research on the role of life experience in the development of wisdom has been limited, but there are some inklings about the particular experiences associated with increases in perspective-related knowledge. For example, contexts such as mentoring or being mentored may facilitate the development of wisdom (Baltes & Staudinger, 1993; J. Smith et al., 1994). Similarly, Staudinger and colleagues proposed that certain occupational settings or social positions may provide "structured training and continued, varied and possibly graded experience in thinking about difficult personal and life problems and [thus] should facilitate access to and acquisition of this knowledge system, both by selection into these professions and by training" (J. Smith et al., 1994, p. 991). Wisdom-related performance may be related to selection into as well as experience in different experiential contexts such as the profession of clinical psychology. However, without relevant longitudinal data, the relationship between experiential contexts and wisdom remains tentative. Along these lines, Wink and Helson (1997) explored the role of occupation (again, clinical psychology) on age-related changes in self-reported wisdom. They found a steeper rate of increase in practical wisdom among psychologists from the late 20s to the early 50s than the rest of the sample.

In her longitudinal study of women at midlife, Hartman (2000) explored the possibility that changes on the sample level, or the lack thereof, may mask underlying individual differences in change. Because individual differences in change are not likely to be random, she examined the role of inner- and outer-directed life experiences as factors that might explain who shows increases in wisdom with age and who does not. She found no mean differences in wisdom from the 40s to the 50s; however, using standardized residual change scores, she found that multiple measures of both inner- and outer-directed life experiences predicted increases in perspective from the 40s to the 50s. The inner-directed predictors of this change in wisdom from the 40s to the 50s included ego resilience, generativity motivation, creative potential, personality integration, and coming to terms with life choices. Outer-directed predictors of this change included self-tasks, relationship changes, recent total stressful life events, and recent total negative life events.

Hartman (2000) also found support for the idea that certain individuals are able to attain higher levels of wisdom earlier in the life course than is traditionally recognized (the 40s), providing evidence for the existence of what she called precocious wisdom. The specific factors responsible for the development of precocious wisdom by the 40s included total career tasks and total relationship changes from the 30s to the 40s, recent total stressful life events, and, in particular, total career events. Furthermore, a measure of ongoing personality integration from the 30s to the 50s predicted the development of wisdom on time, by age 53.

■ Enabling and Inhibiting Factors

Hartman's (2000) longitudinal study of women at midlife identified several factors that enable or inhibit the development of wisdom and perspective. In her investigation, path analyses revealed that personality plays a significant role as an antecedent predictor of the development of wisdom at midlife, with creative potential and creative productivity serving as independent paths to wisdom, and generativity motivation significantly predicting the development of wisdom at midlife. Furthermore, Hartman (2000) found that the accumulation of a wide range of adult experiences precedes the development of wisdom.

Life Tasks

First, ongoing and active participation in life in the form of self-generated life tasks foreshadowed the development of wisdom by midlife. Second, overall involvement in life tasks in the late 30s and early 40s played the largest role in forecasting wisdom by the early 50s. Third, engaging in certain life tasks at times consistent with normative societal expectations facilitated the development of wisdom by the 50s. Finally, engaging in more career tasks in the late 30s and early 40s led to the development of precocious wisdom by age 43. These findings suggest that engaging in the right tasks at the right time can have important long-term effects on adult personality development and that to the extent that individuals are afforded opportunities to engage in particular life tasks (e.g., career tasks for this cohort of women), certain life tasks may hold more importance for personality development for different groups of individuals.

Adjustment

In terms of objective indicators of conventional adjustment, the results suggest that while a certain degree of conventionality is related to the development of wisdom, perspective does not depend simply on one's adjustment to societal expectations. Specifically, the findings for career adjustment are consistent with the results for life tasks, indicating that career development plays a significant role for the development of wisdom in these women. The results for psychological adjustment suggest that wisdom is not wholly dependent on never having any psychological problems or concerns, for example, for which one sought counseling. Likewise, having physical illnesses or hospitalizations alone does not preclude one from developing wisdom. Clearly, how one responds to psychological and physical challenges plays an important part in whether or not one develops wisdom. The measure of conventional adjustment used in this study, however, is dependent only on objective evidence and therefore cannot capture one's response to these challenges. Finally, mirroring the results for psychological and physical adjustment, objective indicators of social adjustment, such as length of marriage or having children, in and of themselves say nothing about whether or not one will develop wisdom.

Coming to Terms With Life Choices

The importance for wisdom of "coming to terms" with life choices was captured by Birren and Fisher (1990) in the following way:

> Wisdom seems to emerge as a dialectic that, on one pole, is bounded by the transcendence of limitations and, on the other, by their acceptance. Wisdom is tested by circumstances in which we have to decide what is changeable and what is not. (p. 324)

Hartman (2000) found that those who had regrets but had come to terms with them by age 53 were wiser at age 53 than those who had no regrets or those who had regrets but did not resolve them.

Life Changes

When Freud was asked, "What should a normal person be able to do?" he replied, "He should be able to love and work" (Allport, 1937, p. 275). Accordingly, there is evidence that those who have made more major life changes in the domains of love and work were higher in the development of wisdom by midlife (Hartman, 2000). Furthermore, making more major life changes, particularly during the 30s, appears to have a positive effect on the development of wisdom.

Stressful Life Experiences

Stress is not always bad—it can play a facilitative and transformative function by prompting one to accommodate challenge. Ardelt (1998) found that those classified as relatively wise in old age were just as likely to have experienced economic hardship during the Great Depression as those considered low on wisdom. However, those scoring higher on wisdom who experienced hardship during the Depression years became on average more psychologically healthy in the 10 years following the Great Depression, whereas their less wise counterparts tended to show psychological declines during the same period. Those who were spared economic hardship did not change significantly during this period, although those who were wiser among them tended to be psychologically healthier at each point in time. Ardelt (1998) argued that since wisdom and psychological health are empirically and theoretically related, these results support the notion that wisdom may be acquired through the successful resolution of crises and hardship.

Finally, Hartman (2000) found that experiencing more stressful life events across time can facilitate the development of wisdom. However, as the ratio of negative stressful life events across adulthood increased in relation to total stressful life events across adulthood, the results changed. A high rate of negative stressors appeared to play an inhibitory role in the development of wisdom, in general, and particularly among those low in ego resilience. Ego resilience— the capacity to integrate and find meaning and purpose in stressful life events— appeared to play a significant role in the development of wisdom regardless of the number or ratio of negative events one has experienced. These results suggest that ego resilience is a generalized capacity for flexible and resourceful adaptation to external and internal stressors that serves as an important personality resource and prerequisite for the development of perspective.

■ Gender, Cross-National, and Cross-Cultural Aspects

Demographic variations in wisdom have not been systematically explored. Given the strong evidence that particular life experiences shape wisdom, we can speculate that demographic variations in wisdom exist to the degree that critical life experiences occur along these lines. That is, because the opportunity to participate in transformative life tasks may vary as a result of gender, race, and class, the extent to which one is afforded these opportunities may directly affect the development of wisdom.

Empirical research into the cultural aspects of wisdom is also lacking, although work is emerging in this area (Takahashi & Bordia, 2000). It is important to know to what extent our current conceptualizations and operationalizations of wisdom reflect the cultural context in which they were developed. This would require both etic and emic approaches to the cross-cultural study of wisdom.

■ Deliberate Interventions

Staudinger and Baltes (1996) showed experimentally that social collaboration—whether internal via a virtual inner dialogue or external via discussion—facilitated wisdom-related performance if persons had time afterward to reflect on the discourse. Moreover, older adults benefited more from the actual dialogue than did young adults, providing some of the first evidence for an intervention that specifically helps older adults more than younger ones. These findings can be interpreted as evidence for the importance of a collective (interpersonal) approach to the cultivation of wisdom. To return to the previously described findings that clinical psychologists tend to score high on measures of perspective, perhaps ongoing supervision is a critical ingredient.

Another deliberate intervention for cultivating perspective is the Teaching for Wisdom Program currently under way at Yale University (Sternberg, 1999b, 2001). The premise of this program is that many students (and indeed many adults) are intelligent but not wise. They may have admirable records in school and even on the job yet make poor judgments about their own lives and for the lives of others. This intervention embodies Sternberg's (1998) balance theory of wisdom by applying it to instruction at the middle school level. In particular, the question addressed is whether students who are taught their regular subject matter knowledge with infusion of the balance theory of wisdom show increased wisdom-related skills relative to students who are taught in conventional ways. The intervention entails the following:

- classic works of literature and philosophy exposing students to the "wisdom of the ages"
- discussions, projects, and essays to draw out the lessons learned from reading
- encouragement of students to reflect on truth and value as they have meaning for one's self
- emphasis on what Sternberg calls practical intelligence—wisdom deployed for social ends
- a Socratic method on the part of teachers to model perspective for students

Sternberg (1999b) also described more specific ways to infuse perspective into a school curriculum: for example, learning about American history not just from the point of view of the Europeans who "discovered" the New World but from the point of view of the original American inhabitants who did not know they needed to be discovered; learning about science as the tentative endeavor it is; interpreting novels and plays in the context in which they were written; learning "foreign" language as part of cultural studies; and so on. Most generally, Sternberg (1999b) recommended integration of an entire curriculum, a good idea in any event but especially if the goal is to produce "wise" students.

■ What Is Not Known?

Given the recent development of various measures of wisdom, the field would benefit from an understanding of the unique and overlapping contribution of each. The "gold standard" approach to assessment is arguably wisdom-relevant performance at social dilemmas, but this procedure is time-consuming and requires expert judges to evaluate performance. Efficient self-report measures need to be explored more fully. Results to date suggest their utility, but questions remain. To what degree do self-reports of wisdom reflect social desirability or—worse—narcissism? The wise person has been described as one who "knows that one does not know" (Meacham, 1983, 1990; Sternberg, 1990a), and we fear, along with Erikson (1964), that no one who is truly wise would ever claim to be so. Perhaps the most valid attribution of wisdom must come from others (cf. Hoare, 2000). But perhaps not. Maybe a nontransparent self-report measure can avoid potential biases.

It is currently unknown whether there are any biological or neuropsychological bases of wisdom. Do people who score higher in wisdom have greater hemispheric symmetry or communication between the hemispheres suggestive of increased integration of cognitive functions? The emergence of measures of wisdom should allow for these types of investigations.

As noted, the cultural context of wisdom must be explicitly studied, especially in light of Sternberg's (1998) notion that wisdom can only be judged relative to the settings in which one finds oneself.

Finally, the long-term consequences of wisdom, as well as the effects of deliberate interventions for both individuals and society, deserve greater attention.

■ Must-Read Articles and Books

Baltes, P. B., & Staudinger, U. M. (2000). Wisdom: A metaheuristic (pragmatic) to orchestrate mind and virtue toward excellence. *American Psychologist, 55,* 122–136.

Holliday, S. G., & Chandler, M. J. (1986). *Wisdom: Explorations in adult compe-tence.* Basel, Switzerland: Karger.

Staudinger, U. M., Lopez, D. F., & Baltes, P. B. (1997). The psychometric location of wisdom-related performance: Intelligence, personality, and more? *Personality and Social Psychological Bulletin, 23,* 1200–1214.

Staudinger, U. M., Maciel, A. G., Smith, J., & Baltes, P. B. (1998). What predicts wisdom-related performance? A first look at personality, intelligence, and facilitative experiential contexts. *European Journal of Personality, 12,* 1–17.

Sternberg, R. J. (Ed.). (1990). *Wisdom: Its nature, origins, and development.* Cambridge, UK: Cambridge University Press.

Sternberg, R. J. (1998). A balance theory of wisdom. *Review of General Psychology, 2,* 347–365.

Wink, P., & Helson, R. (1997). Practical and transcendent wisdom: Their nature and some longitudinal findings. *Journal of Adult Development, 4,* 1–15.

INTRODUCTION:
STRENGTHS OF COURAGE

CRITERIA FOR *Strengths of Courage*

	Fulfilling	Morally valued	Does not diminish others	Nonfelicitous opposite	Traitlike	Distinctiveness	Paragons	Prodigies	Selective absence	Institutions and rituals	
	1	2	3	4	5	6	7	8	9	10	TALLY
Bravery	X	X	X	X		~X	X	X	X	~X	9/10
Persistence	X	~X	X	X	X		X	X	X	X	9/10
Integrity	X	X	X	X	~X	~X	X	X	X	X	10/10
Vitality	X		X	X	X		X	X	X	X	8/10

~ Somewhat satisfies criterion.

Strengths of courage entail the exercise of will to accomplish goals in the face of opposition, either external or internal. We mentioned in chapter 3 how philosophers have regarded virtues as corrective because they counteract some difficulty inherent in the human condition, some temptation that needs to be resisted, or some motivation that needs to be checked or rechanneled. It is debatable whether all character strengths are corrective in one or more of these senses, but the following four strengths in our classification clearly are, and we discuss them here in terms of how they satisfy our criteria for a character strength (see Criteria Table).

■ Bravery [Valor]

The historical prototype of the character strength of bravery, and indeed this entire virtue class, is the physical valor shown by warriors on the battlefield. Bravery in the face of imminent death is not the equivalent of fearlessness because fear is certainly experienced. Rather, bravery is the ability to do what needs to be done despite fear. This view of bravery allows the strength to be applied beyond the domain of battle to saying or doing the unpopular but correct thing, to facing a terminal illness with equanimity, and to resisting peer pressure regarding a morally questionable shortcut.

CRITERION 1 *Fulfilling* Bravery is fulfilling. We feel good when we do the right thing, whether standing up for justice in the face of an angry group or giving a toast at a wedding despite knocking knees. The world is filled with things that produce fear, and virtually all of us with intact nervous systems experience it. But when we can act regardless of our fear, segregating our physiology from the rest of us, we are fulfilled.

CRITERION 2 *Morally Valued*   Bravery is morally valued and so widely celebrated as to need little documentation that this criterion is satisfied. Let us merely observe that *heroic* is a synonym for *brave* and that all cultures have heroes. Some come to our attention on the battlefield but also from other venues. The former Soviet Union and China, for example, quite deliberately made exceptional farmers, factory workers, party members, and mothers into heroic cultural icons.

CRITERION 3 *Does Not Diminish Others*   Along these lines, elevation is invariably produced when we observe bravery or even just hear about it. The aftermath of the 9/11 attacks gave us many stories of valor, and we all have a favorite. Some have been retold many times, like the presumed events on Flight 43. Other stories are not so well known, and one that thrills us involves a young physician who on that fateful day went to the rubble of the World Trade Center to help. As she later told a television reporter, she became so shaken that she actually fled the scene shortly after arriving. Several blocks away, she took stock of her fear and proceeded to write her social security number on her arm with lipstick. Having conquered what she feared most—an anonymous death as opposed to death per se—she was able to return to the scene and help those in need.

CRITERION 4 *Nonfelicitous Opposite*   The opposite of valor is *cowardice* or *spinelessness*. The paralyzing anxieties and neuroses that may plague us can also be seen as the absence of bravery, and countless studies by clinical psychologists and psychiatrists document the negative aspects of these states.

CRITERION 5 *Traitlike*   Is bravery a trait? We have encountered a difference of opinion here. Some of our colleagues argue persuasively that bravery however construed is an attribute of an act rather than a person. Of course, the act is performed by an individual, but how many brave acts must be done for us to say that someone is brave? Soldiers do not win multiple Congressional Medals of Honor. Whistle-blowers do not reveal wrongdoing at every occupational stop on their résumés. Rosa Parks did not stay in her seat on every Alabama bus she happened to take. All these people are remarkably brave, but is their exceptional bravery a trait sustained across time and situation or a single instance of rising mightily to a unique occasion? Research has not addressed this question, but the counterargument in favor of bravery as traitlike is that it does not adhere just to exceptional acts any more than creativity marks only timeless works of art. If the latter were true, perhaps only Michelangelo or Leonardo da Vinci should be called creative, although we of course have no problem using the label more generally. If valor is a trait, we need to look for evidence in its more mundane manifestations over time (cf. Finfgeld, 1999). Whether someone who shows an ongoing version of valor also shows bursts of extreme bravery then becomes an interesting empirical question.

CRITERION 6 *Distinctiveness*   Valor is distinct from most of the other strengths in the our classification, although it perhaps can be seen as a contextualized form of persistence or integrity.

CRITERION 7 *Paragons*   Some paragons of valor are so well known that we need merely mention their names or groups: Joan of Arc, the signers of the Declaration of Independence, Patrick Henry, Audie Murphy, the Tuskegee airmen, the Japanese-American soldiers of the 442nd Regimental Combat Team, and Bernadette Soubirous of Lourdes. Equally celebrated someday may be Cynthia Cooper of WorldCom, Coleen Rowley of the FBI, and Sherron Watkins of Enron, who were named the 2002 Persons of the Year by *Time* magazine for their courage in revealing wrongdoing at their respective places of emplyment (Lacayo & Ripley, 2002).

You may not recognize the names of George Fox, Alexander Goode, Clark Poling, and John Washington, but you probably know what they did—these World War II army chaplains willingly gave up their life jackets to soldiers as the USS *Dorchester* sank. And you probably do not recognize the names of Daniel Brethel, Andrew Desperito, Martin McWilliams, and Raymond York, but they were among the firefighters who died just doing their jobs when the towers of the World Trade Center collapsed. Yet another famous paragon has no name known to history: the young Chinese man who stood his ground against an army tank in Tiananmen Square.

Consider the police and military specialists who defuse bombs (Rachman, 1990). Think of the Ugandan nurses and doctors like Matthew Lukwiya who contracted Ebola hemorrhagic fever while tending to other victims of this lethal virus, or the Soviet firefighters who knowingly gave their lives controlling the Chernobyl disaster. Or just remember your boss who stood up and took the heat at work when something went wrong, whether or not it was of her doing—like Attorney General Janet Reno did with respect to the Waco fiasco. Most of us know someone who was diagnosed with a fatal illness and ended up comforting us when we could not bear the news.

CRITERION 8 *Prodigies*   Prodigies of bravery exist. Medal of Honor winners include teenagers like Marine PFC Melvin Earl Newlin, who despite mortal injuries, single-handedly held off two Viet Cong assaults by drawing fire to himself until his comrades could regroup and repel the attack. Or consider the African American children who helped desegregate schools in the southern United States (Coles, 1964).

CRITERION 9 *Selective Absence*   Those who lack bravery—that is to say, cowards—also exist. History tells of heroes but also of traitors and deserters. And perhaps like bravery, cowardice adheres to acts as well as to people, and we all regret our Pontius Pilate moments. Social psychologists have discussed the failure to intervene in an emergency as pluralistic ignorance, relying on the inaction of others to encode a circumstance as not requiring action (Darley & Latané, 1968), but this perspective works only when matters truly are ambiguous. When we know what needs to be done but refrain out of fear, we are not ignorant but cowardly.

CRITERION 10 *Institutions and Rituals* Because bravery is often seen as an extraordinary act, there seem to be few deliberate attempts to cultivate this strength besides the Boy Scout injunction to its members to be brave. However, seeing valor as an everyday trait allows us to identify societal practices that have the effect of "en-couraging" appropriate action in the face of fear. Fear of speaking in public is one of the most common fears in the modern world, and it is best overcome by just doing it. Thus, parents and teachers encourage tongue-tied children to say their piece. Along these lines, friends and family members encourage the fearful among us to get on an airplane, to jump into the deep end of the swimming pool, to call someone on the phone for a date, or to go out on the dance floor. One can look at these strategies as in vivo desensitization—that is, the counterconditioning (eradication) of fear—but at least in our own experience with such activities, fear has not been banished, just its debilitating consequences. We both have given thousands of lectures over the decades but remain nervous in the moments before we begin. What has changed with experience is our knowledge that we can do what we need to do. Thus, we prefer a cognitive interpretation of our bravery. We have interviewed firefighters given awards for their valor, and no one reported to us being unafraid when rescuing people from burning buildings. Instead, all reported that they knew their jobs so well that they were able to perform them automatically, despite fear. Here we think is a general formula for cultivating bravery: Teach what needs to be done when fear occurs, and it will be done.

■ Persistence [Perseverance, Industriousness]

Finishing what one has started, keeping on despite obstacles, taking care of business, achieving closure, staying on task, getting it off one's desk and out the door—all refer to the strength of character we identify as persistence, perseverance, and industriousness. Not as flashy a strength as bravery, persistence nonetheless shares with it the mustering of will to perform in the face of contrary impulses. Here it is not fear that threatens action but boredom, tedium, frustration, and difficulty, on the one hand, and the temptation to do something easier and perhaps more pleasurable, on the other. Persistence, perseverance, and industriousness satisfy our criteria for a character strength.

CRITERION 1 *Fulfilling* Persistence is fulfilling. We have elsewhere argued that strength-congruent activity can produce a state of flow for all the entries in our classification (Seligman, 2002), but the argument is especially easy to make in the case of this particular strength. When sustained activity results from an internal strength, as opposed to threats or deadlines, it is highly engaging. When the activity is complete, it produces satisfaction.

CRITERION 2 *Morally Valued*   Persistence is morally valued. We admire the busy bee, the tortoise but not the hare, the little engine that could, and Rocky Balboa answering the bell again and again (in movie after movie). Whether these mythic figures actually achieve their goals is not what we admire; rather, it is their perseverance that draws our attention and acclaim. At the same time, we acknowledge a downside to diligence when it takes the form of perseveration. Aristotle's doctrine of the mean reminds us that too much diligence can be as much a vice as too little, and Kenny Rogers's song "The Gambler" similarly reminds us that we need to "know when to hold them" but also "when to fold them."

CRITERION 3 *Does Not Diminish Others*   Persistence can elevate others in the vicinity. If you have ever watched a long-distance race, you know that onlookers cheer the stragglers as much as the winners, so long as the slow-footed runners actually cross the finish line. Likewise, we enjoy watching Special Olympians, not just those who win a competition but all those who show up and ultimately finish. And we are baseball fans who thrilled when we watched Cal Ripken play in his 2,131st straight game.

CRITERION 4 *Nonfelicitous Opposite*   The obvious antonyms of persistence are all negative: *laziness, sloth, giving up, not trying, losing heart, losing interest, taking shortcuts, cutting corners, going for the quick fix,* and *vacillation.* We have spent most of our careers studying helplessness, which can be recast as an antonym of this strength of character. The helpless individual does not persevere at difficult tasks, even when effort would be rewarded (Peterson, Maier, & Seligman, 1993).

CRITERION 5 *Traitlike*   This strength is a trait. Among the most extensively studied individual differences are achievement motivation and explanatory style, and both reflect persistence (or its absence). The evidence is clear that these and allied individual differences are stable across time and setting (see chapter 10).

CRITERION 6 *Distinctiveness*   Persistence is distinct from most of the other strengths in the present classification, although there does appear to be substantial overlap with self-control and regulation of oneself. This latter strength, which we discuss in chapter 22, may be the more inclusive one, with industry and perseverance being the special case of regulating one's motivation to complete a task. At present, though, we maintain a distinction because the strength of diligence is explicitly shown across time, whereas control and regulation of oneself have a more here-and-now flavor.

CRITERION 7 *Paragons*   Paragons of persistence include the figures from fable and fiction already mentioned but also real people like Bill Porter, the record-setting traveling salesman with cerebral palsy featured in the movie *Door to Door*; the indefatigable publisher Helen Gurley Brown; and network correspondent Connie Chung, who began her work in television as a typist but persisted until she was finally allowed to write stories, then to obtain stories, and finally to present stories on the air, first locally and then nationally. The dogged determination of Thomas Edison is itself mythic—consider that he tried more than 6,000 substances before hitting on carbonized cotton thread as a useful filament for the electric lightbulb. Edison reportedly said that "genius is 99% perspiration and 1% inspiration." Mac Anderson, the founder of Successories, the inspirational poster series that decorate so many office cubicles, listed Abraham Lincoln as one of his heroes (Ahrens, 2001). He called Lincoln "the essence of persistence" because Lincoln lost six elections and failed in two businesses but persisted to become perhaps our greatest president. Finally, we have watched enough television biographies of entertainers to know that there is no such thing as an overnight success. Most of those who burst on the scene should really be celebrated for their persistence at a very difficult career.

CRITERION 8 *Prodigies*   Persistence prodigies include children who item by item collect stamps, coins, baseball cards, or autographs as opposed to those who buy them in lots. They include the paper boy or girl who rises at dawn to deliver the local *Herald* or *Tribune*. They include youngsters from a pre-Velcro era who worked for hours to learn how to tie their shoes.

CRITERION 9 *Selective Absence*   What about people who display absolutely no persistence? They certainly exist. "You're not trying" is harsh criticism all too frequently delivered to those around us. "Close enough for government work" is another way of saying that the informal norm for civil service does not entail diligence. And what about the by now familiar but still shocking stories of airport security guards who do not detect weapons being brought through their scanners? We do not mean to tar all civil servants and security guards with the same moral brush, particularly those who are poorly paid and inadequately trained, but we do know that the sufficiently industrious person can rise above the most frustrating restraints to do a good job. Not to be diligent under difficult circumstances may be understandable, but that does not make it a virtue.

CRITERION 10 *Institutions and Rituals*   Society has established many rituals for cultivating and sustaining this strength of character. Cleaning one's plate before having dessert and finishing one's chores before watching television are familiar routines for most American children. So, too, used to be playing out the game to the final out, and we wonder what inadvertent lessons are taught by the mercy rule in Little League baseball. Life does not come with a reset button, and we do not believe that games should have this option either. Regardless, we urge our children, students, employees, and ourselves to keep trying and believe (perhaps correctly) that it is the sustained effort that we reward and not the final accomplishment. We make lists of things, propose 5-year plans, and declare New Year's resolutions—all attempts to index our progress at difficult tasks and chunk thankless activity into manageable segments; perseverance is thereby served. As we explain in chapter 10, psychologists have developed effective strategies for persistence training.

■ Integrity [Authenticity, Honesty]

The person who speaks the truth is honest, but we regard this character strength in broader terms. It includes truthfulness but also taking responsibility for how one feels and what one does. It includes the genuine presentation of oneself to others (what we might term *authenticity* or *sincerity*), as well as the internal sense that one is a morally coherent being (what we might term *integrity* or *unity*). As chapter 11 explains, empirical research into this character strength has seldom done justice to its richness, on the one hand investigating specific behaviors like cheating among schoolchildren or workplace theft among employees and on the other using self-report measures to assess acceptance of oneself and the like. Moral transgressions like lying and cheating are of course relevant to honesty, but if they are trivial or taken out of context, they miss the depth and breadth of the strength and, in any event, provide insight only into its absence. Self-report measures that do not make contact with the social context in which integrity is deployed run the risk of solipsism.

Most agree that integrity, authenticity, and honesty are basic human strengths, but the psychological database is spotty, in large part because they are such complex characteristics. The procedurally simplest thing for a researcher would be to define this strength in objective terms (e.g., saying things that are unambiguously accurate) and proceeding to measure it accordingly. This works only insofar as there is a correct answer against which to check what a person says or does. "I called you on the phone last night at 9:30, but no one answered" is either true or false. But our interest in this character strength goes far beyond the veracity of such statements and those who make them.

When our focus is on the authenticity facet of this character strength, a further complication is introduced by consideration of social roles. If we greet our waiter with the polite "How are you?" and are regaled with a story about his gastrointestinal complaints, what do we have? He is honest in a technical sense and probably genuine in his suffering. But is he authentic as a waiter? Probably not, because he is violating the expected norms of the role. There is a tendency, at least among Americans, to dismiss roles as mere disguises or masks—somehow phony and insincere. We want to know the real person behind the role. We do not take this route, recognizing that role enactment is part of human nature and in most, if not all, cultures highly lauded when done well. There is no deception involved when everyone shares the same expectations about how waiters should behave; we judge genuineness in the context of these expectations.

Classifying this strength as a virtue of courage—hence an unambiguously corrective virtue—highlights the need to look for integrity in situations and circumstances in which the easy thing to do is not the right thing to do. One does not draw on character to follow the rules when there is a referee or test proctor nearby or a highway patrol car on one's bumper. And it is easy to be sincere when there is no cost to telling someone the truth.

CRITERION 1 *Fulfilling*   We have no hesitation in saying that this character strength is fulfilling, and the point is especially easy to make when the strength is at odds with prevailing rewards and punishments. There is no discernible motive other than internal satisfaction (fulfillment) for calling a cashier's attention to an error in our favor or reminding a train conductor that he did not take our ticket or setting the record straight after undeserved praise. Such clichés as "Be true to yourself" or "Virtue is its own reward" could conceivably apply to any of the strengths in our classification, but they seem to refer best to integrity and authenticity. One of our grandfathers used to say, "Tell the truth so you don't have to remember what you said," and the wryness of this adage disguises the more fundamental point that honesty is fulfilling.

CRITERION 2 *Morally Valued*   Integrity, authenticity, and honesty are highly valued, especially in close relationships. We can forgive our friends and lovers for treating us poorly, but misrepresenting themselves or deceiving us takes matters to a different plane of transgression. Studies of the most valued traits among friends and spouses always identify honesty and dependability as paramount. We also want our leaders to be honest and dependendable, at least in their dealings with us as followers, and we are sickened when politicians or CEOs obscure their bad deeds with excuses and legalistic mumbo jumbo. How different might recent history have been had Bill Clinton simply said, "I cheated on my wife"?

CRITERION 3 *Does Not Diminish Others*   The display of this character strength never diminishes onlookers. When what we see in people is what we get from them and, further, who they actually are, we are satisfied even if we are displeased. "I am not attracted to you," "Your grant proposal does not merit funding," or "That looks terrible on you" may be difficult to hear and just as difficult to say, but they keep the record straight and make the world coherent. And sometimes, the down-to-earth person can raise us to the heavens. We have occasionally encountered home repairmen who show up when they promise or who keep to their estimate or even tell us that it would be cheaper to buy a new appliance.

CRITERION 4 *Nonfelicitous Opposite*   The antonyms for this strength are negative: *deceitfulness, lying, insincerity, phoniness, pretentiousness*, and *falseness*. When we describe a person or an act as spurious or counterfeit, we are decrying the absence of authenticity.

CRITERION 5 *Traitlike*   Integrity, authenticity, and honesty—separately measured—show a degree of stability and generality. As described in chapter 3, social learning theorists in the 1970s made much of the supposed finding by Hartshorne and May (1928) that honesty (or, more accurately, dishonesty) was not consistently shown across situations. However, more recent examination of these and other data show as much cross-situational generality as we find for almost any personal trait (Bem & Allen, 1974; Burton, 1963). Missing are studies linking integrity as acceptance of oneself and authenticity as interpersonal sincerity with honesty as shown (or not) in specific acts.

CRITERION 6 *Distinctiveness*   This character strength does not collapse into other character strengths in our classification, although depending on the situation in which it is required, it may overlap with bravery or perseverance. Social intelligence may help set the stage for integrity—if one is to be true to oneself, one must have a knowledge base to do so—but integrity involves the exercise of will in a much more explicit way than does social intelligence.

CRITERION 7 *Paragons*   Paragons of integrity include Honest Abe Lincoln and those well-known individuals cited by Maslow (1970) as self-actualized: for example, Thomas Jefferson, Benjamin Franklin, George Washington, Albert Einstein, Aldous Huxley, William James, Spinoza, Goethe, Pablo Casals, Pierre Renoir, Robert Browning, Walt Whitman, Henry Wadsworth Longfellow, Eleanor Roosevelt, Jane Addams, Albert Schweitzer, and Ralph Waldo Emerson. We all know individuals whose word truly is their bond, or who are without pretense, or who tell it like it is. Journalists with integrity do not slant a story to fit their biases. And the CEOs who hire amoral accounting firms to cook the books have their counterparts in those like Lee Iacocca, who accurately appraised the corporate well-being of Chrysler (poor) and set about improving it (approaching the U.S. Congress for loan guarantees).

CRITERION 8 *Prodigies*   A list of integrity prodigies might include the young George Washington, at least if the cherry tree event actually took place. We are on firmer ground when we point to our childhood friends who 'fessed up to breaking a window or carrying a Halloween prank too far. Indeed, children may have a difficult time sustaining a lie, and we often regard the utterances of children as pure in their authenticity: "The emperor has no clothes." The interesting psychological question is what happens along the way to adulthood: Why do some people maintain a style of spontaneous honesty, whereas others do not?

CRITERION 9 *Selective Absence*   Some of these latter individuals become dissemblers, phonies, and posers, folks that a previous generation called plastic people or game players. Adjectives like *ingratiating, unctuous, sycophantic, creepy,* and *brownnosing* are applied to them. There is no shortage of celebrities whose public lives unraveled when they were caught in a lie: the rapper Vanilla Ice, the lip-synchers Rob Pilatus and Fabrice Morvan of Milli Vanilli, the Notre Dame football coach-for-a day George O'Leary, the presidential hopeful and plagiarist Joe Biden, the straying husband Frank Gifford, and so on. We of course have no idea if these individuals are pervasively dishonest—they probably are not—but the public has seized upon their acts as epitomizing the absence of this character strength.

CRITERION 10 *Institutions and Rituals*   The larger society attempts to cultivate this strength from the very beginning of one's life with such admonitions as tell the truth, follow the rules, and be true to yourself. The Roman Catholic sacrament of confession can be seen as an honesty and authenticity ritual. Childhood games and sports make rules explicit and the virtue of following them clear. At the same time, other lessons may be conveyed that undercut this strength, as when victory is elevated above sportsmanship—then we see steroid use (in football), the falsification of birth certificates (in Little League baseball), rolling starts (in sprinting), and flopping (in basketball). Indeed, sports in general and major league baseball in particular have a curious stance toward cheating. The hidden-ball trick, spitters, stealing signs, corked bats, brushbacks, and the phantom tag are considered part of the national game and may even be celebrated when players and coaches get away with them. But even in this nebulous region, a higher order authenticity prevails in the form of not whining if one is caught and punished. And there are even informal rules for throwing at a batter—the pitcher can intimidate but not injure (i.e., avoid high heat) and should do so only when there has been a provocation.

We think that sports are popular not just because they allow us to thrill in vicarious victory and agonize in vicarious defeat but also because they allow an ultimately innocuous forum for public discussion of honesty. More serious examples of the attempt to inculcate honesty include the ethics courses routinely taught in medical schools, law schools, clinical psychology programs, and business schools. We wonder about their actual success in creating honest professionals. From the viewpoint of positive psychology, we suggest that the more effective courses would be those that pay more attention to what one should do to be an ethical practitioner as opposed to what one should not do to avoid being an unethical one (cf. Handelsman, Knapp, & Gottlieb, 2002). The psychotherapeutic realm, especially the humanistic-existential genre, gives us strategies for nurturing integrity and authenticity.

■ Vitality [Zest, Enthusiasm, Vigor, Energy]

The final member of this virtue category is a different sort of strength because it is as much a property of the body as it is the mind. Vitality refers to feeling alive, being full of zest, and displaying enthusiasm for any and all activities. We describe people with this strength as vigorous and energetic, bright-eyed and bushy-tailed, bouncy and perky, peppy and high on life. They have joie de vivre. We hasten to point out that vitality as we conceive it is not the same thing as hyperactivity, nervous energy, tension, or mania. Rather, vitality is zest that is experienced as volitional and fulfilling as it is brought to bear on life's worthy activities. It is enthusiasm *about* and zest *for*. We classify it as a strength of courage because vitality is most noteworthy (and therefore most praiseworthy) when displayed in circumstances that are difficult and potentially draining.

Vitality was a late addition to our classification because it is rarely named in classical sources as an explicit virtue (see chapter 2). However, vitality belongs on the list because it is implied in earlier classification efforts—Eastern and Western—and no less contributory to the good life for its historical implicitness. Indeed, if the good life entails nothing more than the joyless performance of good deeds, then it is not a life that is lived but merely one that is ploddingly enacted. How can we urge good character upon individuals and devise strategies for encouraging character if there is not an experiential payoff? Zest and enthusiasm are the proof of the character pudding. Vitality directly reflects eudaimonia—the inherent fulfillment produced by virtue-congruent activity—and reminds us that fulfillment is not an abstract judgment but an experienced psychological state. Vitality is how self-actualization feels (Maslow, 1970). Vitality is a way to describe the engagement and absorption of flow (Csikszentmihalyi, 1990).

We may eventually decide that vitality is best described as a style that characterizes the display of other strengths, especially those that are owned by someone. If so, then vitality is a strength without a specific content. But it is still a strength, just as curiosity and love of learning are strengths even though they need not be attached to any particular domain of knowledge. For the time being, we believe that zest can be shown even in the absence of other notable strengths. Otherwise unremarkable people who are enthusiastic become remarkable because of their energy. With this context provided, let us turn to how well vitality as a distinct strength satisfies our criteria.

CRITERION 1 *Fulfilling*   The experience of vitality is fulfilling; subjective feelings of satisfaction and engagement are part of its very definition.

CRITERION 2 *Morally Valued*   Enthusiasm is highly valued and admired. We want to see it in our children, our mates, our friends, our students, and our employees. When we describe people as fun, we may or may not mean they are funny, but we certainly mean that they have twinkling eyes and approach ongoing life with gusto and relish. We deliberately cultivate our own vitality, through restorative experiences like nature walks or spa retreats, through physical exercise and other health-promoting activities, and through meditation disciplines that encourage our sensory awareness and thereby our attention to the joy of being alive. We hesitate to conclude that enthusiasm per se is morally valued; this judgment will usually follow only when the activity pursued with enthusiasm is itself moral. However, if life lived well—with vigor and energy—is a good thing, and of course it is, then perhaps enthusiasm in these terms is morally valued.

CRITERION 3 *Does Not Diminish Others*   The observation of vitality can be elevating. Enthusiasm is contagious, and it broadens our own sense of what is possible and what can be done. There is a Philadelphia police officer who directs evening rush hour traffic through the University of Pennsylvania campus. We have often taken a deliberate detour to the corner of 36th and Walnut simply to watch him do his job because he does it with such flourish and flamboyance, as if he were the drum major of a marching band in seat belts. Everyone watching him smiles, even those in the cars he has stopped. We suspect that traffic duty is not the sexiest assignment for a police officer, but the enthusiasm this man brings to bear on his assignment reminds us that we, too, should have zest for the assignments in our lives.

Like the other strengths in our classification, enthusiasm can have an interpersonal downside. Almost all of us have had the experience, when feeling depressed or beleaguered, of being annoyed by someone with boundless energy and cheer. We want to smack them alongside the head and tell them to get serious—life is not all fun and games. But what is it that we are actually trying to curb? Certainly not their sense of being alive—after all, we want them to be sensitive to our own sobriety—but only their way of showing it at that time.

CRITERION 4 *Nonfelicitous Opposite*   The obvious antonyms of this strength are negative: *sluggish, depressed, subdued, dull, jaded, listless, limp, lethargic,* and—notably—*lifeless.*

CRITERION 5 *Traitlike*   Vitality is an individual difference of demonstrable generality. It has a wide array of robust correlates in both the psychological and the physical realm. To summarize the research findings detailed in chapter 12, vitality is associated with well-being of all stripes.

CRITERION 6 *Distinctiveness*   As we have discussed, vitality can be distinguished conceptually from the other entries in our classification, but because this strength often flavors other strengths of character—for example, curiosity, love of learning, kindness, perseverance—it may prove difficult to distinguish it empirically.

CRITERION 7 *Paragons*   Paragons of vitality include exercise gurus like Jack LaLane, Richard Simmons, and Tony Little and inspirational speakers like Tony Robbins. The Dalai Lama exudes enthusiasm, and so too does Bruce Springsteen in concert. No one could be more alive than Robin Williams making ad-lib jokes or James Carville offering ad-lib political commentary— whether or not we find either of them funny or insightful. We invite the readers to think of their favorite teachers, and we bet that they all possessed ample enthusiasm. Indeed, we have surveyed our own undergraduate psychology students about the teachers who most inspired them, learning that the conveyed subject matter was not the source of the inspiration but rather the zest brought to bear by their teachers on the subject matter, be it social psychology or differential equations.

CRITERION 8 *Prodigies*   Prodigies of enthusiasm are easy to find, and the easiest place to find childlike enthusiasm is of course among children. Consider the ebullience of gymnast Mary Lou Retton (and contrast it with the stoicism of Nadia Comaneci or the dysphoria of Svetlana Khorkina).

CRITERION 9 *Selective Absence*   Consider the slugs, black holes, and wet blankets among us, the folks previous generations labeled sticks-in-the mud, bummers, drags, or downers. Perhaps some of these people are sick or depressed (see chapter 28), and we can excuse their lack of enthusiasm as being imposed on them by chance or circumstance. But other people are simply draining and sour, and we avoid them if at all possible.

CRITERION 10 *Institutions and Rituals*   Various institutions and rituals for cultivating and sustaining enthusiasm are discussed in chapter 12. Let us mention here an additional example, the 16th- and 17th-century radical religious tradition of enthusiasm, so named because its adherents "would not, could not, contain their zeal within the organized limits of religious conventions" (Lovejoy, 1985, p. 1). The enthusiasts believed that all people could be directly enlightened by God and saw little need for Scripture or clergy. This movement was exemplified by the well-known Quakers (who trembled and quaked) and the less well-known Ranters (who believed themselves so full of the Holy Spirit that they loudly proclaimed, by word and deed, that there was no sin). In this example, we have the intriguing implication that zest can emerge from a belief system and further that it can be nurtured by group activity.

9. BRAVERY

[Valor]

Our imagination has been captured by the story of Sir Ernest Shackleton. A British polar explorer, Shackleton was on Scott's first unsuccessful voyage to reach the South Pole and made a return voyage that came within 97 miles of its goal. This famous voyage earned him international acclaim and a British knighthood. Shackleton's most well known adventure, however, and the one that made him an icon of bravery, is the voyage of the Endurance, which set out in 1915 to take a crew of explorers across the entire Antarctic continent (Lansing, 1959; Worsley, 1931). This audacious plan was doomed almost from its beginning, when the Endurance was caught in the ice pack in the Weddell Sea. Shackleton and crew were forced to abandon their ship and live on the ice pack, where they survived for more than a year, traveling across 850 arduous miles. Though they had only the provisions they could carry from their sinking ship, not one crew member was lost during the long ordeal. Shackleton's bravery and leadership are credited with the accomplishment of such an impossible survival story.

Shackleton's most prominent characteristic was his purposefulness. After a grueling boat journey that ultimately brought Shackleton to a populated island from which rescue could be attempted, his only thought was the immediate return to the Antarctic to retrieve the rest of the crew. Before they separated for the final boat journey, Shackleton's utmost rule was unity for the party. He would not allow the party to be divided, understanding that the display of valor among the group's members was what sustained their ability to keep going. When Shackleton finally supervised the rescue of the last of the men from their shelter on Elephant Island, he showed more emotion than he ever had before, calling out, "They are all there! Every one of them! They are all saved!"

■ Consensual Definition

The meaning of bravery shifts across contexts. There is an essence, however, that speaks across social settings, cultures, and disciplinary divides. Shelp (1984) came as close to a consensual definition as exists: "the disposition to voluntarily act, perhaps fearfully, in a dangerous circumstance, where the relevant risks are reasonably appraised, in an effort to obtain or preserve some perceived good for one self or others recognizing that the desired perceived good may not be realized" (p. 354). Several elements of the definition warrant emphasis:

- Valorous action must be voluntary, and coerced action cannot qualify.
- Bravery must also involve judgment—an understanding of risk and an acceptance of the consequences of action. Hence, a courageous person must have a disposition to take risks, yet must also overcome a disposition to take unconsidered risks.
- Bravery requires the presence of danger, loss, risk, or potential injury. Without a sense of danger, risk, or vulnerability, there is no bravery in an act. Bravery is valuable because it allows people to dampen their immediate response to danger and evaluate the appropriate course of action. Bravery involves the mastery of fear rather than fearlessness.

Bravery raises the moral and social conscience of a society (May, 1978). Because bravery entails judgment, the ends that a person's action serves are part of the consideration about whether an act reflects bravery. People distinguish between courageous and foolhardy action. Bravery is usually considered doing what is right, including confronting the status quo or opposing an unhealthy idea, and as such, it takes on a moral tone. Even outside of an explicit moral context, Finfgeld (1999) found that people facing terminal illness regard bravery as being of service to others and acting toward a higher purpose. For observers, action toward worthy ends seems more courageous than simply risky action (Szagun, 1992). Hence, we are reluctant to designate a murderer as courageous, even when he takes great risks to accomplish his crime (Shelp, 1984).

■ Theoretical Traditions

Bravery has occupied a significant place in the mythology and folk wisdom of many cultures, as well as holding an abiding concern in Western philosophy at least since the early Greek philosophers and even longer in Eastern religious philosophies (Walton, 1986; Yearley, 1990). Plato provided one of the earliest works on the subject of bravery, taking care to differentiate between valor and rashness. His *Dialogues* were written at a time when warfare was the ultimate proving ground for bravery, and a soldier who did not hesitate to face the dangers of battle was deemed brave. But in Plato's account of a dialogue between

Socrates and the Athenian general Laches, Socrates observed that "thoughtful courage is a quality possessed by very few," whereas "rashness and boldness, and fearlessness which has no forethought, are very common qualities" (Hamilton & Cairns, 1961, p. 140). Forethought, in the view of Socrates and Plato, was the essential element separating bravery from rashness.

Forethought was also advanced as a prerequisite for bravery by Thomas Aquinas (Haitch, 1995). Indeed, Aquinas named prudence as the principle virtue, with bravery subordinate to it. It is prudence that provides the wisdom to assess danger; bravery then allows reason to prevail despite fear. It is interesting to note that the word *courage* is derived from the French word *coeur*, from the Latin *cor*, meaning heart (hence the terms lionhearted and fainthearted); but these words were not in common usage when Aquinas wrote his treatise on bravery. The term used by Aquinas for bravery was the Latin *fortitudo*, a word with a more rational connotation.

More recently, psychoanalytic writers approached this strength as a spirited response to psychological danger (Prince, 1984). Putnam (1997) argued that the concept of psychological bravery has not been properly recognized in ethics and asserted that the psychological bravery involved in facing fears generated by our own habits is essential to well-being. Along these lines, C. Goldberg and Simon (1982) argued that people draw upon bravery to confront the concerns of everyday life. Through courageous action, the self affirms that it matters in the world. In this view, bravery is reflected in acts that postpone or deny benefit to the self yet create a bond with humanity. Studies of people who engage in extreme acts of bravery, such as whistle-blowers or Holocaust resisters, also support a link between valor and a sense of belonging to a greater humanity (Shepela et al., 1999). Accordingly, bravery may have implications for psychological healing because many modern psychological illnesses are distinguished by difficulty making meaningful commitments to others. Psychoanalytic theory holds that bravery is a quality that allows people to conquer their fear of commitment. In this sense, bravery would be essential to psychological healing or to any attempt at psychological change (C. Goldberg & Simon, 1982; Howard, 1976; Prince, 1984).

From a social psychological perspective, most research on bravery has looked at war and its aftermath. Perhaps the most remarkable finding from this body of work is that people are able to carry on in the face of the extraordinary challenges of life during war (Rachman, 1990; Suedfeld, 1997). In fact, researchers find that facing challenge often brings out perseverance, ingenuity, mutual aid, cohesion, and social support in a community. Social psychologists, like psychoanalysts, have concluded that bravery is present as part of people's daily ability to face challenges.

As the concept of bravery evolved over the centuries, it changed gradually from an emphasis on proving oneself in warfare to include an appreciation for the taking of social and economic risks as dictated by conscience. The dichotomous aspect of the concept of bravery may be expressed in contrasts: physical bravery versus moral bravery, offense versus defense, aggression versus endurance. W. I. Miller (2000) observed that "those on the left of the 'versus' tend to be noisier than those on the right" (p. 106). But despite the fanfare and folklore that exalt physical displays of bravery, Aquinas called martyrs rather than warriors the purest examples of courageous individuals. And he declared endurance, a form of moral bravery entailing patient suffering over a long period, to be the primary act of bravery.

Whatever the circumstances testing bravery, fear must be overcome. Physical bravery is characterized by a fear of bodily injury or death. In its most classic form, it is the valor of the battlefield, though variations abound. Anything that elicits a fear of physical harm—even something as mundane as a contact sport—may call forth bravery in the fearful individual. It is also possible for a fear of shame, opprobrium, or similar humiliations to spur physical bravery, producing what is called the courage born of fear.

Moral bravery often relates to fear of others' opinions. Looking foolish before peers, for example, is a common fear. But moral bravery compels or allows an individual to do what he or she believes is right, despite fear of social or economic consequences. The fear that can summon moral bravery takes many forms: fear of job loss, fear of poverty, fear of losing friends, fear of criticism, fear of ostracism, fear of embarrassment, fear of making enemies, or fear of losing status. The consequences of these fears may be of short or long duration. Though physical bravery is often expressed quickly, in fleeting bursts of action, a morally courageous choice to do what is right may extend its impact on the individual over a lifetime, calling forth the bravery of endurance. As there are many kinds of feared consequences, there are many dimensions to moral bravery, ranging from the social bravery represented by Rosa Parks to the political bravery shown, however infrequently, by elected officials. The opportunities to act with moral bravery are numerous, and the fears calling for moral bravery are as varied as individuals themselves.

The distinction between physical and moral bravery seems obvious. Less obvious, at least initially, is a distinction between moral bravery and what may be a third variation in the complex, psychological bravery. According to Putnam (1997), an individual in need of psychological bravery fears loss of psychic stability. Millions of individuals summon psychological bravery every day to face their fears and anxieties, but their courageous behavior can be invisible to others. For example, few would be aware of the emotional distress of an individual with obsessive-compulsive disorder who shakes hands, despite an intense fear of contamination. Admitting a psychological problem and seeking help may have social costs, such as embarrassment or ostracism—does the reader remember Thomas Eagleton?—and a fear of this type of consequence links psychological bravery to moral bravery. Likewise, summoning psychological bravery may result in psychological or physical pain, again linking psychological bravery and moral bravery (and even physical bravery). But a major difference lies beyond the similarities. Whereas an individual may fear a loss of ethical integrity if moral bravery fails, psychological bravery confronts a fear of "loss of the psyche—a destabilizing of the 'self'" (Putnam, 1997, p. 2). Though psychological bravery is sometimes considered a type of moral bravery, it may be prudent to keep their distinctions in mind.

■ Measures

In contrast to the large theoretical literature, little empirical research has focused on bravery (but see Table 9.1). It is difficult to create conditions in psychology laboratories that require meaningful bravery (Deutsch, 1961). Most of the existing research accordingly relies on case studies, interviews, or responses to hypothetical scenarios. In contrast to most of the other character strengths described in this book, valor has inspired virtually no psychological scales attempting to measure it as an individual difference. When courage or valor items are included in self-report measures, they are listed along with many other items asking about values or important qualities; they do not focus specifically on factors presumably involved in courageous action.

■ Correlates and Consequences

The lack of reliable and valid measures translates into few well-documented correlates of dispositions toward bravery. However, existing research suggests some potential correlates:

- prosocial orientation (Shepela et al., 1999)
- internal locus of control (Shepela et al., 1999)
- self-efficacy or self-confidence (Finfgeld, 1999)
- valuing independence or freedom (Larsen & Giles, 1976)
- valuing socially important achievements (Larsen & Giles, 1976)
- ability to delay gratification (Goldberg & Simon, 1982)
- ability to experience multiple emotion states at once (Szagun & Schauble, 1997)
- age (Rothschild & Miethe, 1999; Szagun & Schauble, 1997)
- risk taking (Shelp, 1984; Spreitzer, McCall, & Mahoney, 1997)
- action orientation (McCall, 1994)
- knowledge of a context (Rachman, 1990; Spreitzer et al., 1997)
- low levels of arousal under stress (Cox, Hallam, O'Connor, & Rachman, 1983; O'Connor, Hallam, & Rachman, 1985)
- experienced oneness with others or with humanity (Goldberg & Simon, 1982; Shepela et al., 1999)

TABLE 9.1   *Measures of Courage*

Method	Exemplary Study	Most Common Approach
Interview	Szagun & Schauble (1997)	Administration of descriptive questions about courage or solicitation of retrospective accounts of courage
Narrative response	Szagun (1992)	Administration of short scenarios followed by a series of questions about the courage of actors in the stories
Video response	Evans & White (1981)	Administration of video containing fear stimulus followed by questions about self-related responses and characters in video scenarios
Case study	C. Goldberg & Simon (1982)	In-depth life studies or retrospective accounts of courageous incidents, drawing mainly on life narratives or therapeutic interviews
Behavioral response	Szagun (1992)	Administration of scales inquiring about typical behavior in response to dangerous or risky situations
Value surveys	Rokeach (1973)	Rank ordering of values that are important in participants' lives
Self-report of social values	Larsen & Giles (1976)	Rating importance of social values concerning achievement vs. freedom to distinguish between social courage and existential courage
Self-report of willingness to take a stand	Spreitzer et al. (1997)	Self-report response to items asking about typical behaviors that involve speaking out or challenging authority
Coping	Furnham & Akande (1997)	Rating courage along with other coping behaviors

Some additional correlates may include tolerance for ambiguity or uncertainty; an ability to assess risk across situations; an inclination toward reflection; and involvement in socially worthy aims. Taken together, this is a provocative list of correlates that makes contact with a number of the other character strengths discussed in this book and that deserves systematic study.

If we look at the correlates of valor in a specific context—like the workplace—we find some additional correlates of bravery that may be generalizable. Whistle-blowing is a frequently studied paradigm case of workplace bravery. A nationwide study found few demographic or attitudinal differences between people who speak up and those who remain silent (Rothschild & Miethe, 1999). Neither gender, marital status, religiosity, nor supervisory position influenced the likelihood of whistle-blowing. There was a slight effect of age, with older people being somewhat more likely to report wrongdoing. An attitude correlated with whistle-blowing was the belief that decisions should be made according to general rules rather than on a case-by-case basis—the character strength we describe as fairness (see chapter 17).

Bravery can be as dangerous as it can be valuable. Consider again whistle-blowing. Common consequences include depression and anxiety, feelings of isolation and powerlessness, increased distrust in others, declining physical health, financial decline, and familial problems (Rothschild & Miethe, 1999). Telling the truth may set one free, but it does not necessarily make one happy. Nonetheless, 90% of the whistle-blowers in Rothschild and Miethe's (1999) survey would, if they had it to do over again, pursue the same course of action and endure the same consequences.

Entering and sustaining high-quality connections with others can be a consequence of bravery (Worline, Wrzesniewski, & Rafaeli, 2002). In a medical context, Shelp (1984) suggested that a true physician–patient relationship involves bravery because doctor and patient must together negotiate disease, pain, and suffering to promote healing. In a family context, Fowers (1998) suggested that bravery is required to surrender to vulnerability within marriage. Because self-disclosure and honesty go hand in hand with the potential to be hurt and rejected, bravery may help to sustain close relationships (Fowers, 1998; Prince, 1984). Way (1995, 1998) linked the daily practice of bravery with the development of authenticity in relation to others and youths' ability to enter into rewarding relationships.

Valorous action has consequences within important social units as well. People in small groups or social units who witness another person's valorous action may experience a feeling of elevation and may be inspired to act courageously themselves (Haidt, 2000). For example, Rachman (1990) found that among groups of particularly brave soldiers, each was motivated to act primarily by the others. The reputation of an especially valorous group of soldiers—for example, the highly decorated 442nd Regimental Combat Team —may help to knit the unit together, and the cohesive unit further supports bravery.

■ Development

Much more is known about developmental trends in how people think about bravery than in how they act bravely. People come to conceptualize bravery differently as they mature. Very young children perceive physical acts rather than psychological ones as courageous (Evans & White, 1981; Szagun, 1992; Szagun & Schauble, 1997). Adolescents have a more developed sense of psychological complexity and hence understand social risks as involving bravery (Evans & White, 1981; Szagun, 1992). Adults are better able to acknowledge fear as part of the experience of bravery, in part because they are able to conceptualize and discuss experiences in which multiple emotions compete (Szagun & Schauble, 1997).

Though the literature suggests a developmental trend toward an increasingly sophisticated appreciation of what it means to be courageous, it provides few clues as to whether an individual's likelihood of acting with valor changes across the life span. Looking at age differences, Cavanagh and Moberg (1999) pointed toward the literature on thrill-seeking behavior and noted that younger people are more prone to such behaviors than older people. They added, however, that although people with a proclivity toward thrill-seeking may find it easier to perform in the face of fear than people who are not so inclined, there is not a clear-cut relationship between thrill seeking and bravery. In fact, it could be argued that someone who finds high-risk activities to be particularly aversive yet acts anyway is braver than a thrill seeker who might look forward to the rush that comes from taking risks.

Looking for the earliest expressions of bravery, it would seem appropriate to describe a child's behavior as brave once he or she is old enough to appreciate the riskiness of an act, experience consequent fear, and choose to act despite the fear. But beyond an individual's initial experience with bravery, many questions arise regarding the effect of maturity on brave behavior. Are younger people more likely than older people to engage in acts of physical bravery? Are older people more likely than younger people to engage in acts of moral bravery? Does psychological bravery increase or diminish with age? These questions have no clear answers but provide invitations to further research into the development of bravery.

Finfgeld (1999) suggested that the ability to act with bravery takes shape in youth and is influenced by important life events. This perspective is echoed in Way's (1998) portrait of urban teens—*Everyday Courage.* As Heath (1999) pointed out, the negative characteristics of urban teens from impoverished neighborhoods have been massively overgeneralized by social scientists, but Way's work provides an important contrast. Way has emphasized that bravery is especially important for teens engaged with risk (cf. U. Beck, 1992; Lightfoot, 1997; McAdams, 1993). In the context of a future that is marked by unpredictability and risk, bravery is an everyday requirement. In such settings, the development of everyday bravery is marked by building ties with others, developing moral bonds, exchanging information with peers, and taking responsibility for one's own life story.

■ Enabling and Inhibiting Factors

Existing research suggests several factors that may enable valor (Chaleff, 1996; M. Gross, 1994; A. Rogers, 1993; Shelp, 1984; Shepela et al., 1999; Way, 1998; Wilkes, 1981):

- contextual messages supporting courage
- contextual support of prosocial values and an emphasis on truth telling
- strong leadership
- trust
- clear expectations for behavior
- community ties

Those who respond to challenge with a mastery orientation toward their own experience may be able to sustain brave activity more easily than people without such a mastery orientation (cf. Dweck, 1986; Dweck & Leggett, 1988). Shepela and her colleagues (1999) asserted that a prosocial orientation is a necessary part of the development of bravery and may provide one moderating variable. Secure attachment and prosocial role models may also facilitate the development and display of bravery (C. Goldberg & Simon, 1982; Shepela et al., 1999; Way, 1998).

Others have suggested that the amount of power others have to punish an act is negatively correlated with acting bravely (Deutsch, 1961; Van Eynde, 1998). This might mean that people who are lower in an organizational hierarchy are less likely to exhibit brave action because they have less freedom to act, and that courageous followership involves confronting those in power (Chaleff, 1996). Because leaders and those in power are under less threat of punishment by others, their freedom to act may be correlated with bravery.

Bravery can be promoted by practice (moral habit), by example (modeling), and by developing certain attributes of the individual (self-confidence) or group (cohesion). But in addition to these factors promoting bravery, there appear to be personality dispositions that make individuals more or less likely to act bravely. Most of the research identifying these personality traits has focused on the military, an organization that offers a ready subject pool and engages specifically in the business of bravery, albeit primarily physical bravery. Studies with military personnel suggest that social traits (e.g., sociability and a sense of belonging) contribute to brave behavior (Gal, 1995). Although social traits may seem unrelated to physical bravery, their role is obvious when one recalls the previously discussed importance of group cohesion, mutual responsibility, and modeling in fostering brave acts. It appears that by encouraging group interaction, social qualities in turn contribute to the individual's brave behavior.

Additional personality characteristics associated with bravery were identified in a study comparing two groups of combatants during the Korean War. Those decorated for bravery or evaluated by peers as good fighters were more socially mature, more intelligent, and more emotionally stable (Gal, 1995).

In his study of military bomb disposal operators, Rachman (1990) found similar results: Those engaged in the dangerous task of bomb disposal were "an unusually well-adjusted group of people" (p. 304), scoring above the mean on psychometric tests measuring psychological well-being. And among bomb disposal operators singled out from the others for commendation for particular valor, tests revealed a slight but significant superiority in overall psychological health and physical fitness. In addition, most of them scored zero on hypochondriasis—that is, they had no physical or mental complaints. The combined findings of these various studies suggest that personality characteristics may influence an individual's behavior when a need or opportunity for brave behavior arises. However, it seems clear that the influence of personality traits will be enhanced or tempered by other determinants, previously discussed, that promote or thwart bravery.

■ Gender, Cross-National, and Cross-Cultural Aspects

Few empirical studies have examined the role of sex differences in relation to bravery, though W. I. Miller (2000) suggested that the concept of bravery is more available to men than to women because of its long connections with military service (cf. Lieblich, 1997). It was primarily men who wrote the history over the centuries, so it is not surprising that men's interpretations prevailed, and the stereotypes attached to bravery remain strongly ingrained. This is true even as the physical demands of warfare have lessened in much of the world, creating an arena in which women are as capable as men of displaying physical bravery. Will women be acknowledged as equal to men in bravery if and when their behavior in war earns a Medal of Honor or Silver Star? W. I. Miller (2000) asked the question and was doubtful, noting that such awards would elicit suspicions of political correctness (cf. the popular movie *Courage Under Fire*); he predicted that women will have made it only when they, like men, are court-martialed for cowardice.

Bravery and the ideal of the heroic have been celebrated across history and culture. We find hero myths and bravery tales across virtually all cultures (cf. chapter 2). Lash (1995) surveyed many of these tales—from the Polynesian story of Wonderworker to the Hindu story of Vishnu to the Celtic account of clan hero Fergus mac Roich to the biblical story of Ezra—and hypothesized that the hero myth originated deep in human prehistory and the survival dramas of the species. Malinowski (1926) asserted that there is an intimate connection between myth and ritual acts, moral deeds, and social organization. The discovery of myths of the courageous around the globe is not simply a discovery of similar stories; it reveals a similar attention to bravery in different kinds of rituals, different conceptions of morality, and the organization of different societies. Joseph Campbell (1949) echoed the insight of Malinowski in showing that the journey of the hero, across many different cultures, is the journey of ordinary people through the difficulties of life.

Some particular ideas about bravery are worth mentioning in that they reveal similarities in ideas about bravery across culture, time, and space. For instance, ancient Greek society celebrated bravery as an ideal of the soldier—the golden mean between reason and action (Pears, 1978). This notion of bravery has traveled across Western cultures and still informs Western philosophy (Walton, 1986). Aquinas, one of the Western philosophers most concerned with bravery, was deeply indebted to Aristotle's ideas about bravery.

Long before the development of Aristotelian thought, however, ancient Chinese philosophy was concerned with the notion of valor. Mencius, writing in the fourth century B.C.E., developed a philosophy of bravery (Yearley, 1990). Mencius, like later Western philosophers, dismissed the military ideal of bravery and moved his thinking into the realms of self-knowledge and religion, developing an ideal of bravery as steadfastness that fuels people's attempts to live a virtuous life (Yearley, 1990). By reading Mencius, we see the evolution of the idea of bravery that is involved not only in physical deeds but also in the development of true self-respect—a kind of self-respect that mirrors higher values and allows one to approach a meaningful life. True self-respect, according to Mencius, is based on the vales of benevolence, dutifulness, conscientiousness, truthfulness, and delight in what is good. Bravery, in Chinese philosophy, is the quality that allows people to pursue those values, hold steadfast to them in times when they are challenged, and remain true to them when faced with conventional social ideals that conflict with full human excellence.

Later Eastern philosophy and religion reflect this central tenet that brave action is both an internal and an external endeavor. Modern Buddhism teaches this internal and external steadfastness when it talks about warriorship in a spiritual sense: "The essence of warriorship, the essence of human bravery, is refusing to give up on anyone or anything" (Trungpa, 1978, pp. 33–34). In an entirely different cultural context, the Navajo emergence myth emphasizes a similar kind of internal and external steadfastness, introducing people to the experience of darkness and chaos that must be endured on the way to life, growth, and development (Moon, 1970). This ancient emergence myth focuses in part on the role of evil in the development of all life; consequently, personal development requires steadfastness and bravery in the face of evil and difficulty.

In the modern United States, cultural differences in ideas about bravery are contained in differences between ethnic groups. Coles (1964) studied the children who helped to desegregate southern schools. He wrote about the deep differences that children from white and black families faced—differences that changed the very meaning of childhood. In particular, however, he documented the steadfastness with which black (and a few white) children and their families acted in relation to race hatred. In this characterization of bravery, Coles reprised Mencius, Aquinas, and the themes of bravery that arise across disparate cultures.

Way (1998), investigating children from disadvantaged neighborhoods three decades after Coles, found a major difference between these children and the white, middle-class ideal of childhood. Although these disadvantaged children value things such as communication, friendship, keeping a positive yet realistic attitude about life, and balancing school demands with individual energies, they are also consistently engaged in sustaining their devotion to a mother and a vigilant awareness about dealing with discrimination. An emphasis on awareness of discrimination and working for social justice is also part of the bravery that is celebrated in traditional Cinco de Mayo celebrations among Mexican populations (Vargas, 1999). Eisler (1999) similarly identified bravery among Jewish people as based in the challenge of fighting injustice. Sustaining bravery in these cultural groups in the United States operates on a different value system and set of activities than that typically associated with mainstream American society, particularly in its emphasis on challenging racism, injustice, and discrimination.

In Western cultures an act of bravery, particularly physical bravery, is generally considered to be exceptional. It is an action that occurs outside the norm, beyond the routine call of duty. In some cultures, however, bravery is expected of every member of society. Bravery is duty, rather than an act beyond duty's call. And to ensure that bravery is in fact the norm in these cultures, individuals are socialized to perform brave acts. The behavior of the Japanese soldiers and civilians during World War II provides a good example of how successful a policy of socialization can be in the widespread promotion of bravery. In defending Saipan, 41,244 out of 43,683 Japanese soldiers died rather than surrender, and there were mass suicides among the Japanese civilians (W. I. Miller, 2000). These actions, so puzzling to the Western mind, were appropriate and even expected under the Japanese field code that extolled bravery and presented shame as its only alternative. Honor was linked to service to the homeland, even unto death, and surrender meant disgrace.

■ Deliberate Interventions

As noted, the etymological root of the word *courage* is the Latin *cor*, or "heart." Courage is often portrayed in stories and myths as taking heart, symbolically allowing people to act in the face of fear. Aquinas wrote extensively about the problem of teaching bravery, concluding that one cannot foster bravery directly but can only foster a sensitivity to fear along with good judgment (Yearley, 1990). Aquinas must have had a point. No psychological interventions that are described in the academic literature, other than psychoanalysis itself, attempt to directly foster bravery.

Psychoanalysts working in the Jungian tradition attempt to help people cultivate bravery by working with the system of archetypes that Jung proposed. A popular version of this kind of psychological work on developing a heroic system of archetypes is represented in Pearson's (1998) book *The Hero Within*. Pearson described six archetypes and how knowledge of these archetypes, and developing a balance of them, can help aid psychological development and deepen self-knowledge. She provided self-tests and self-development tools at the end of the book. In regard to bravery, the Warrior archetype is specifically relevant. This archetype embodies the ability to confront fear and act in the face of psychological danger. It also emphasizes authenticity, principle, responsibility, and acting on behalf of others.

Related to the root of the word courage is *encouragement*, which refers literally to giving heart to another. Encouragement as a concept in psychology has been most influenced by Adler (1946), who proposed that discouragement was at the root of many mental health problems and the seed of destruction in many interpersonal relationships. Adler and his followers developed a system of interpersonal skills that allow one person to acknowledge another, lead another toward self-reflection, and acknowledge another's effort or contribution. This form of interpersonal skill, referred to as encouragement, is conceived of separately from extrinsic reward and praise because of its focus on accepting people as they are and orienting them toward self-reflection and intrinsic motivational states (Pitsounis & Dixon, 1988). Admittedly, encouragement as envisioned by Adlerian psychologists is removed from the concept of courage itself, but an appreciation of the factors involved in encouragement nonetheless suggests how one might nurture bravery.

For example, among the specific skills of encouragement in the context of therapy are faith and belief in the client; acceptance of the client as he or she is; validating the goal and intention of the client's behavior; and reframing the client's behavior in a positive light (Sherman & Dinkmeyer, 1987). The skill of encouragement seems to be most often reflected through verbal comments that demonstrate acceptance, emphasize effort, or appreciate performance and contributions (Pitsounis & Dixon, 1988). Other writers, focusing on encouragement as a parenting skill, include in the skill of encouragement such things as using words that build self-esteem, planning experiences that create success, spending time with another person, use of humor, recognizing effort, and showing appreciation for cooperating (Kelly & Chick, 1982).

In educational settings, research shows that encouragement is related to the development of

- positive self-concept (J. I. Gilbert, 1989; Kyle, 1991; Riley, 1995)
- higher motivation (Capps, 1984; Van Hecke & Tracy, 1987)

- the ability to learn from mistakes (Hitz & Driscoll, 1989; Huhnke, 1984)
- perseverance (Rathvon, 1990)

However, Abramowitz, O'Leary, and Rosen (1987) cautioned that encouragement may work differently for some children, and they do not find that it is consistently related to better behavior in the classroom. Many interventions that focus on at-risk youth, people in transition from school to work, older students, migrant children, and women in science use some form of encouragement (Carns & Carns, 1998). The findings on the results of encouragement as an intervention strategy suggest potential benefits and demand more rigorous research.

Several popular psychology books attempt to teach bravery. Though not built on a foundation of research, these books walk people through self-awareness exercises and share stories of bravery (e.g., Pearson, 1998; M. Williams & Paisner, 2001). Often these books and exercises involve showing people's triumphs over adversity and building a sense of common humanity through inspiring stories (e.g., Waldman & Dworkis, 2000).

One of the most well known of these popular psychology texts that promises to help people build a braver life is by Robbins and CoVan (1993). This set of ideas is representative of the general popular psychology approach, building on a physiological, habitual, and attitudinal approach to cultivating bravery. Physiologically, people are encouraged to find a sense of courageousness within their body, and to use classical conditioning to associate some movement with the bodily sensation of power. Habitually, people are encouraged to become aware of their language and thought patterns and to break the ones that are especially limiting. Attitudinally, people are encouraged to engage in imagination and visualization exercises that help support a valorous disposition and help them with emotion regulation.

As noted, because of its long association with physical risk and military service, bravery is often more available to men than to women. In keeping with this trend, popular psychology books that focus on the development of mature masculinity often discuss how a man might reclaim his valor (e.g., Bly, 1992; Keen, 1992). Perhaps in response to books such as these, another current genre of popular psychology books focuses on bravery among women. Some relate stories of brave women's lives (e.g., Martin, 2001). Others follow a workbook format, giving women exercises that help them engage in reflection and self-discovery that may build a more positive outlook in general and a more brave attitude toward life (e.g., Walston, 2000).

Various types of Buddhist practice are also designed with much the same vision of cultivating bravery. For instance, Tonglen practice (Chodron, 1991, 2001) is designed to use breathing techniques to help people become aware of their thought patterns, and to breathe in fear and breathe out bravery and kindness. These techniques, which are a kind of active meditation, can be used in any situation in which one feels afraid; they are designed to help people develop physiological awareness, positive habitual thought, and appropriate emotion regulation.

Using qualitative interview data from people with terminal illnesses, Finfgeld (1999) explored factors that foster the development of bravery. She cites having a strong value system, hope, optimism, and self-confidence as the most important psychological factors that support bravery. Finfgeld (1999) also suggested that social modeling, particularly of brave family members or close others, can help a terminally ill person sustain and foster bravery through the course of his or her illness. Research on minority influence in social psychology mirrors the findings related to the importance of social modeling. In their group dynamics experiments, Nemeth and Chiles (1988) have demonstrated that group members who are exposed to dissent in the group reduce their levels of conformity.

Shelp (1984) proposed that a physician's psychological presence can affirm life in a patient and facilitate the patient's ability to be brave in the face of illness. More broadly stated, the assertion that relationships that involve psychological presence can foster bravery is supported by research by A. Rogers (1993) on bravery in the lives of girls and women. Mutual respect, admiration, validation, and acts of kindness from others are aspects of relationship that can foster bravery (Finfgeld, 1999).

This power of social groups to sustain bravery has been found in other contexts as well. A particularly brave tribe of Native Americans, the Mohawks, have been called skywalkers because of their ability to navigate heights (Hill, 1987). Members of the tribe became particularly well known when they assisted with the building of the Empire State Building and other Manhattan skyscrapers. Members of the tribe are reputed to have said that they would not work with anyone who was not afraid—emphasizing the interrelationship of fear and bravery among those who are highly trained in dangerous work (Worline et al., 2002). Natural talent in navigating heights developed from fording streams and rivers on slender logs that were native to their surroundings seems to be related to the Mohawks' ability to work at great heights, though this is a matter of debate (Oswalt & Neely, 1999). However, members of the tribe worked in small, related tribal crews and would rarely work with outsiders. Their membership in these small, tight-knit groups likely promoted bravery among the skywalkers.

■ What Is Not Known?

Because of the problems of establishing an operational definition of bravery and adequately measuring the concept, little empirical work on psychology focuses on this basic virtue, especially as a stable and general individual difference. Many of the findings reported in this chapter are merely suggestive, in the sense that they result from single studies that have not been part of a rigorous stream of replication and debate. Before psychology attempts to create interventions that will foster bravery, the field requires much more research on factors that foreshadow bravery. Cross-cultural and cross-national work on bravery has very rarely been attempted, and rigorous cultural work on bravery is another necessity. Sex differences in the experience and consequences of brave action are likewise unknown.

The social aspects of bravery present an interesting area for further research. Whereas the social importance of bravery is generally accepted, little research examines particular social implications of brave action. Psychologists have discovered very little about the dynamics involved in processes of witnessing bravery. In general, research on bravery remains one of psychology's open frontiers.

■ Must-Read Articles and Books

Deutsch, M. (1961). Courage as a concept in social psychology. *Journal of Social Psychology, 55,* 49–58.

Evans, P. D., & White, D. G. (1981). Towards an empirical definition of courage. *Behaviour Research and Therapy, 19,* 419–424.

May, R. (1978). *The courage to create.* New York: Bantam Books.

Miller, W. I. (2000). *The mystery of courage.* Cambridge, MA: Harvard University Press.

Putnam, D. (1997). Psychological courage. *Philosophy, Psychiatry, and Psychology, 4,* 1–11.

Rachman, S. J. (1990). *Fear and courage* (2nd ed.). New York: W. H. Freeman and Company.

10. PERSISTENCE

[Perseverance, Industriousness]

■ *In the summer of 1855, 16-year-old John D. Rockefeller needed a job. He had just completed a 3-month course in bookkeeping, and he made a list of the companies in his hometown of Cleveland that might need a bookkeeping assistant. Cleveland was booming with businesses, but none was willing to take a chance on someone so young and inexperienced. For weeks, Rockefeller spent 6 days a week walking hot streets in his suit and tie, trying to find work. He was rejected from every business on his list. Rockefeller responded to this potentially crushing setback by simply starting over, requesting interviews from the same firms that had denied him days earlier. Eventually, a produce shipping company executive rewarded Rockefeller's persistence and hired the boy who would become the richest and most powerful businessman in the world (see Chernow, 1998, for an account of Rockefeller's job hunting travails).* ■

Rockefeller's story exemplifies persistence, an important human strength. He refused to quit when faced with disappointment and discouragement. He believed in himself when others did not, and his determination and positive mind-set allowed him to accomplish great things. Of course, perseverance does not guarantee success, but success is often unattainable without it. To achieve meaningful accomplishments, one must withstand setbacks. There are times when quitting is more prudent than persisting, but more often, it is the person who perseveres who is rewarded. In this chapter, we review psychological research on the predictors and consequences of human persistence.

■ Consensual Definition

We define *persistence* as voluntary continuation of a goal-directed action in spite of obstacles, difficulties, or discouragement. Simply measuring how long someone works at a task does not adequately capture the essence of perseverance because continuing to perform something that is fun or rewarding does not require one to endure and overcome setbacks. We use the terms *perseverance* and *persistence* interchangeably, as have most previous researchers, though the connotations of perseverance are more uniformly positive than the connotations of persistence.

We regard perseverance somewhat more narrowly than have some other researchers. For example, attitude researchers sometimes use the terms *belief perseverance* or *attitude perseverance* (usually with the Canadian pronunciation accenting the second syllable) to refer to the maintenance of attitudes or beliefs in the face of contradictory evidence. Because the maintenance of attitudes and beliefs does not involve active behavior, this process does not fit our definition of persistence. Similarly, persistence in merely thinking about a goal (i.e., ruminative persistence) could not be considered perseverance according to our definition. We also note the distinction between perseverance and *perseveration*, two terms that resemble each other in spelling, pronunciation, and meaning. *Perseveration* describes the continual repeating of an action that is essentially a default response. In other words, the action described by perseveration is typically neither active nor voluntary and thus does not require the overcoming of obstacles. We do not address the concepts of perseveration or thought perseverance further in this chapter because they are not directly relevant to perseverance as a strength of character.

■ Theoretical Traditions

This chapter focuses on persistence by humans. Jaynes (1976) suggested that task persistence is a uniquely human strength. With some exceptions, most animals do not persist at any given task longer than 20 minutes before moving on to the next task (although parents may protect the offspring from cold or predators for longer times, they frequently cease actively tending the young and move on to grooming, sleeping, and so on, even while on guard duty). Many human accomplishments require individuals to persist at one task for an extended period—days, weeks, and even lifetimes. In Jaynes's view, persistence is a prerequisite of civilization. As humans persisted at food production tasks such as farming for lengthy periods, food surpluses were produced, which required societal organization for surplus storage and protection. Thus, according to Jaynes (1976), the rise of government and civilization as we know it could not have been accomplished without the task persistence of large numbers of individuals.

Despite Jaynes's assertion, some research suggests at least a precursor of persistence in animals. The theory of learned industriousness suggests that, if effort is rewarded, individuals of various species are likely to show a high degree of effort or persistence at subsequent tasks (Eisenberger, 1992). Studies using rats (Eisenberger, Carlson, & Frank, 1979; Eisenberger, Myers, & Kaplan, 1973; Inglis & Shepherd, 1994) and gerbils (Forkman, 1996) support the theory of learned industriousness and demonstrate persistence in food gathering in rodents. Thus, animals as well as humans can be trained to persist at goal-directed tasks, but we restrict our discussion to human perseverance for the remainder of this chapter.

Relatively little research has been undertaken for the primary purpose of gaining insight into persistence. Often, information about perseverance must be gleaned from studies that measured persistence as an outcome of a different variable in which researchers were more interested. Hence, research on persistence is scattered through many areas, and no single tradition of theoretical and empirical work has become dominant in persistence research.

Although we view perseverance as a human strength, clearly there are circumstances in which persistence is maladaptive, and this fact has not escaped researchers. In fact, the downsides of persistence may have been overstated because researchers are intrigued by the paradoxical nature of costly persistence. Although costly persistence may appear to contradict the spirit of positive psychology, we cannot discuss perseverance as a human strength without distinguishing good and bad persistence. The research we review offers some clues about the personal qualities that help people to make appropriate decisions about when to persist and when to quit. Indeed, the same factors that promote costly persistence may also contribute to effective persistence.

People who persevere generally expect that their persistence will be rewarded with the outcome they seek. This has been shown in several ways, using direct measurement or manipulation of expectancies about the present task, a more general sense of self-efficacy, and self-perceived high ability at the task (which helps people expect to succeed). W. U. Meyer (1987) showed that people who perceived themselves to have high ability persisted longer than others at both easy and difficult tasks. An internal locus of control, which reflects the belief that the self can generally exert successful control over its outcomes, has been associated with more persistence after initial failure (H. Weiss & Sherman, 1973). Janoff-Bulman and Brickman (1982) concluded that people who expect to succeed at a task are generally more persistent than others. Locke (1997) found that self-efficacy enhances persistence. Several studies have found that positive outcome expectancies promote greater persistence, whereas negative outcome expectancies reduce persistence and foster a tendency to withdraw from the task, especially among people who focus attention on themselves (Carver, Blaney, & Scheier, 1979; Duval, Duval, & Mulilis, 1992). Following initial failure, high self-efficacy and favorable expectancies of success produced the biggest increase in persistence (E. Jacobs, Prentice-Dunn, & Rogers, 1984). In gambling, people who have near wins on slot machines persist longer than people who lose more definitively, presumably because the near win fosters positive expectancies that one can succeed (Kassinove & Schare, 2001). A meta-analysis by Multon, Brown, and Lent (1991) found a significant positive relationship between self-efficacy and persistence on academic tasks, and this relationship was replicated across several measures of persistence, including time spent on task, number of items or tasks attempted or completed, and number of academic terms completed.

Perseverance is also related to attributional or explanatory style. The concept of explanatory style emerged from the attributional reformulation of the theory of learned helplessness (Abramson, Seligman, & Teasdale, 1978). Attributional style can account for the fact that a person's habitual manner of explaining events along dimensions of internality, stability, and globality predicts how he or she responded to negative events (Peterson & Seligman, 1984). People whose explanatory style creates feelings of learned helplessness following negative events have more difficulty persisting in their goals than do people who attribute bad events to less stable and global causes (Peterson & Park, 1998). Thinking that bad things are going to happen no matter what you do (the learned helplessness response) is not likely to lead to greater persistence, whereas expecting positive outcomes can increase the motivation to try and persist (Peterson, Maier, & Seligman, 1993; Peterson & Seligman, 1984). Peterson (2000) highlighted the connection between optimism and persistence: Optimistic people are more likely to persevere than pessimistic people.

Self-esteem has also been linked with persistence. In laboratory studies, people with high self-esteem scores have been shown to persist longer than others in the face of failure (e.g., Shrauger & Sorman, 1977; Tafarodi & Vu, 1997). The notion that high self-esteem would foster perseverance is somewhat intuitive, insofar as high self-esteem fosters confidence that one will eventually be able to succeed. However, the relationship between self-esteem and perseverance also depends on other factors. Several researchers have found that individuals with high self-esteem are simply better at making proper decisions about when to persist and when to quit (e.g., Janoff-Bulman & Brickman, 1982; McFarlin, 1985; Sandelands, Brockner, & Glynn, 1988; see McFarlin, Baumeister, & Blascovich, 1984, for an exception). For example, DiPaula and Campbell (2002) found that people with high self-esteem persisted longer than those with low self-esteem only when no alternative goal was available (i.e., when persistence was presumably adaptive).

The effects of self-esteem on persistence indicate that symbolic implications about the self are often involved in how people approach tasks. People are generally reluctant to lose or even risk losing some of their self-esteem, and so whether they persist at a task or give up and withdraw may depend on which course of action holds less threat of esteem loss. A variety of factors contribute to such threats. By definition, difficult tasks carry a high risk of failure, but as long as the difficulty is well recognized, the threat is minimized because it is no disgrace to fail at a very difficult task (in contrast to failing at an easy task, which can be acutely embarrassing or humiliating). Starnes and Zinser (1983) found that people persisted longer at solving problems when they had been told that the problems were difficult as opposed to easy. At first this result may seem paradoxical because easy tasks would in principle offer higher expectancies of greater success. But giving up early on easy tasks is better than continuing to fail, whereas the difficult tasks represent less threat to self-esteem, and so people are more willing to take a chance on continuing to work at the tasks of recognized high difficulty. Along the same lines, Frankel and Snyder (1978) found that people withdrew effort and gave up after initial failure when the task was presented as only moderately difficult because they did not want to risk further humiliation, whereas they were willing to persist much longer (even after initial failure) if the task was presented as extremely difficult. A. Miller and Hom (1990) found that telling people that tasks were very difficult offset the reduction in persistence that otherwise followed initial failure.

The fear of losing esteem (and desire to gain esteem) may involve other people's appraisals rather than just the performer's self-appraisal. Geen (1981) studied whether people would persist longer while the experimenter was watching, as compared with how long people persisted when they believed no one was paying attention to them. He found that the presence of the observer (the experimenter) led to longer persistence if the initial outcomes were successful but not if the initial outcomes involved failure. These results dovetail well with the findings on perceived difficulty of the task. Initial success encourages people to believe that the observer will perceive them favorably, and so they are willing to persist relatively long. In contrast, failure makes them presume that the observer is forming an unflattering impression of them, and so they become reluctant to persist, especially amid the risk of continued failure. The importance of symbolic implications about the self implies that people persist longer when they feel personally responsible for choosing the task, because that personal responsibility makes the task (and its eventual outcome) more relevant to the self. Indeed, Kail (1975) found that people who chose to perform a particular task persisted longer on it than people who were simply assigned to perform it.

A large body of literature indicates that people sometimes self-handicap, or put barriers in the way of their own success, to protect and enhance their self-esteem and the esteem in which others hold them. Self-handicapping is often operationalized as a failure to persist, especially to persist at practice or preparation for a major task (e.g., Ferrari & Tice, 2000; Rhodewalt, Saltzman, & Wittmer, 1984). Self-handicapping by failing to practice serves to protect and enhance esteem by altering the attributions that can be made after success or failure. If one fails to practice enough before a test and then fails, the reason for the failure is somewhat ambiguous. The failure could be due to low ability, or it could also be due to lack of practice. If one fails to practice enough before a test and then succeeds, then one can claim very high ability, because one succeeded despite the handicap of little or no practice. Self-handicapping thus protects esteem in the case of failure and enhances esteem if one should succeed despite the handicap of inadequate practice. Tice (1991) found that people with both high and low self-esteem sometimes self-handicapped by failing to persist at practice for an upcoming test, but that they failed to persist for different motivational and esteem-related reasons. People with low self-esteem were more likely than those with high self-esteem to self-handicap, or fail to persist at practice, to protect themselves from failure, whereas people with high self-esteem were more likely to self-handicap to enhance their successes (should they succeed despite the inadequate practice).

Recent work has also suggested that persistence may depend on self-control and may therefore decline when the energy required for self-control has been depleted. Several studies have found that people are less likely to persist on difficult or unsolvable problems if they have already exerted self-control on a prior task, such as attempting to control their thoughts or emotions (Muraven, Tice, & Baumeister, 1998) or resisting the temptation to eat chocolates and cookies (Baumeister, Bratslavsky, Muraven, & Tice, 1998). Some recent evidence suggests that the capacity for self-control is enhanced by positive emotions (Tice, Dale, & Baumeister, 2003), and there is evidence that people in good moods persist longer (and perform better) at solving tasks (Kavanagh, 1987).

Taken together, these findings suggest that persistence in the face of failure is relatively difficult and that people are often inclined to give up and turn their attention elsewhere. Failure is unpleasant and discouraging, and so persistence requires overcoming the natural tendency to quit. The tendency to quit seems to have two sources, and so some positive force may be required to offset those two. The first is the blow to self-esteem (and public esteem) implicit in failure, which is aversive and makes people wish to withdraw. To overcome this, a resource of high self-esteem is helpful (so that the initial failure does not make the person feel too bad about the self) or favorable expectancies of further success (which helps the person maintain faith that there will eventually be a boost to self-esteem when success is finally achieved). The second source of difficulty is that persistence requires overriding one's natural tendency to quit when the task seems intolerable, and this overriding constitutes a form of self-control or self-regulation, which depends on a form of energy that can easily be depleted by exertion. Positive influences like good moods or a well-tested capacity for self-control should help the person have the resources required for persisting.

■ Measures

Unlike for many of the other strengths included in this book, research on perseverance has not inspired development of related individual difference measures. Still, a variety of personality factors and other individual differences have been linked to persistence. The previous section mentioned one important factor—self-esteem. This section focuses on additional individual differences relevant to persistence.

Ability is one perseverance-relevant individual difference. People with high ability should be more willing than other people to persist on tasks (at least those relevant to their abilities), based on reasons covered in the previous section: People with high ability have high expectancies of eventual success, and they often have favorable self-appraisals that can help overcome the discouraging effects of initial failure. Furthermore, people with high ability presumably make more early-stage progress toward their goals than do less able people, which should help their confidence and motivation. Indeed, more than half a century ago, Ryans (1939) pointed out that it is easy to confuse ability with persistence. Still, the relationship between ability and persistence is probably limited to task-specific abilities. Nygard's (1977) comprehensive review failed to find a clear relationship between global intelligence and persistence on assorted tasks. Thus, the appropriate conclusion may be that people persist on tasks at which they believe they are specifically talented, but high generalized ability does not necessarily produce increased persistence on all tasks.

Motivational differences are also highly relevant to persistence. Expectancy-value theorists have understood for many years that people who believe they can attain a challenging goal generally do not persist in working toward that goal unless they place high value on achieving it (e.g., Feather, 1961). People who have strong motivational orientations toward control and mastery are more likely to persist, presumably because they are driven to master the task by succeeding and hence are willing to put in more time and effort to achieve that success. People high in autonomy persist longer in the face of failure than others (Koestner & Zuckerman, 1994). A high desire for control has been linked with increased persistence on difficult tasks (Burger, 1985). A mastery orientation has been associated with greater persistence on various tasks, ranging from practicing with toys (Hupp & Abbeduto, 1991) to practicing golf putting (Dorsel & Salinsky, 1990). A literature review by Ames (1992) concluded that mastery goals promote perseverance in the face of difficulties and setbacks.

The concept of achievement motivation combines the goal of mastery with the theme (covered earlier) of symbolic implications for self. People with high achievement motivation want to achieve successes and avoid failures (McClelland, Atkinson, Clark, & Lowell, 1953; Trope, 1975). The desire to achieve success has been shown to predict greater persistence (Atkinson & Litwin, 1960), especially for challenging tasks that offer more promise of symbolic and informational benefits to the self (Nygard, 1977). The other half of achievement motivation, namely, the desire to avoid failure, has provided mixed results with respect to persistence (see Nygard's 1977 review), with some findings suggesting that a high desire to avoid failure increases persistence (e.g., Feather, 1961; C. P. Smith, 1964), whereas others suggest that failure avoidance reduces persistence (Atkinson & Litwin, 1960). Very possibly these mixed results reflect the dilemma we described earlier, in which the person confronted with discouraging failure must decide whether giving up or continuing to fail represents the greater risk of esteem loss.

Not surprisingly, people persist longer (even in the face of failure) when they are more intrinsically motivated to perform the task, as is the case when people enjoy the task (aside from the setbacks) or they believe it plays a central role in their own identity. Vallerand and Bissonnette (1992) found that intrinsic motivation made students less likely to drop out of school (although extrinsic motivation had a similarly positive effect on scholastic persistence). Hyland et al. (1988) found that people persisted longer on tasks that they felt were linked to their identities or were intrinsically exciting. People who find ways to make a task more interesting and appealing are also better able to persist (Sansone, Weir, Harpster, & Morgan, 1992; Werner & Makela, 1998).

A smattering of other personality factors has also been related to persistence. People high in emotional control persist longer (Zaleski, 1988). Hardiness, defined as "a constellation of personality characteristics that function as a resistance resource in the encounter with stressful life events" (Kobasa, Maddi, & Kahn, 1982, p. 169), has also been shown to predict persistence (Wiebe, 1991), apparently because individuals who are high in hardiness have a sense of commitment to their lives, a belief that they can control events, and a view of change as a positive challenge. These three beliefs may make hardy individuals less likely to quit when they encounter failures and setbacks (Kobasa, 1979). The Type A coronary-prone personality trait has been linked to persistence, but the nature of the links are complicated (e.g., Strube & Boland, 1986), and the multifaceted nature of the Type A trait makes it difficult to know what aspect of it is most relevant to persistence. People who view themselves as procrastinators report an inability to persist at difficult tasks (Ferrari, 1993). Tice and Baumeister (1997) found that procrastinators not only received lower grades but also got sick more and had more visits to health clinics than nonprocrastinators.

Few personality scales measure persistence directly (but see Table 10.1). One exception is Lufi and Cohen's (1987) 40-item Persistence Scale for Children. Examples from this scale include the following:

- I do many things on the spur of the moment.
- I need lots of encouragement in order to complete many things.
- When I fail in something, I am willing to try again and again forever.
- I won't try to solve a problem again and again if I don't find the solution the first time I try it.
- I usually give up easily when I do not succeed.

A number of questionnaires include a persistence subscale or factor. Persistence is a subscale from an independent factor of the Tridimensional Personality Questionnaire (TPQ; Cloninger, Przybeck, & Svrakic, 1991). Interestingly, high

---

TABLE 10.1 *Measures of Persistence*

Persistence Scale for Children
Lufi & Cohen (1987)

Persistence Subscale of the Tridimensional Personality Questionnaire
Cloninger, Przybeck, & Svrakic (1991)

Persistence Subscale of the Self-Control Scale
Tangney, Baumeister, & Boone (in press)

Persistence Subscale of the State Self-Control Scale
Twenge, Tice, & Harter (2001)

Adult Inventory of Procrastination
McCown & Johnson (1989)

Perseverance Subscale of the Survey of Work Values
Wollack, Goodale, Wijting, & Smith (1971)

---

persistence scores on the TPQ have been linked with a particular pattern of neurological activity (Benjamin et al., 2000), suggesting that certain brain patterns are associated with greater or lesser task persistence.

Persistence is also a component of the Self-Control Scale (Tangney, Baumeister, & Boone, in press; see chapter 22). Items that measure persistence on the Self-Control Scale include the following:

- I am lazy.
- I wish I had more self-discipline.
- I am good at resisting temptation.
- People would say I have iron self-discipline.
- I am not easily discouraged.
- I am able to work effectively toward long-term goals.
- People would describe me as impulsive.
- I get carried away by my feelings.
- I do many things on the spur of the moment.

Twenge, Tice, and Harter (2001) developed the State Self-Control Scale, a state measure of Tangney, Baumeister, and Boone's (in press) Self-Control Scale. The purpose of the State Self-Control Scale is to measure a person's current ability to engage in self-control, including persistence.

Procrastination scales also measure the related concept of persistence. For example, the Adult Inventory of Procrastination (McCown & Johnson, 1989) contains items such as "I am not very good at meeting deadlines" (for a thorough discussion of procrastination scales and the role of perseverance in avoiding procrastination, see Ferrari, Johnson, & McCown, 1995). The Survey of Work

Values measures persistence among workers (Wollack, Goodale, Wijting, & Smith, 1971). Items that assess perseverance include "A worker should feel some responsibility to do a decent job whether or not his supervisor is around."

■ Correlates and Consequences

The benefits of persistence are well and widely recognized. First and foremost, persistence increases one's chances of attaining difficult goals. Relatively few major undertakings are marked by a steady stream of progress and positive feedback. Setbacks and problems are typically encountered, and these can be discouraging, but if the person gives up, he or she will not reach those goals. Persistence is thus often necessary if success is to be achieved.

A second benefit is that persistence may enhance the person's enjoyment of subsequent success. Festinger's (1957) theory of cognitive dissonance emphasized that people's attitudes sometimes reflect the need to justify the effort they have expended, and well-known studies such as that by Aronson and Mills (1959) confirm that people do like things more if they have had to endure suffering or difficulties in order to reach them. In our view, the available research does not justify a sweeping conclusion that enjoyment of all outcomes is enhanced by the degree of suffering or persistence required to reach them in a linear fashion, but there is sufficient basis for concluding that such enhancement can and does occur sometimes.

A third benefit of persistence is that it may improve the person's skills and resourcefulness. People who overcome obstacles to reach their goals must sometimes develop new approaches and techniques or new ways to solve problems, and these newly acquired skills can be beneficial in subsequent undertakings. Military history presents almost endless examples of this pattern, because hardly any general was ever able to enjoy a long career without defeats and setbacks, and the difference between the successful and unsuccessful ones often consisted of which ones could learn from mistakes. The most successful military innovators, such as Frederick the Great of Prussia (Fraser, 2001) or the Zulu emperor Shaka (Morris, 1965), had to contend with well-organized opponents who outnumbered them and sometimes inflicted serious defeats, but these remarkable individuals responded by developing new tactics and methods that brought eventual success and indeed gradually enabled their armies to outclass their rivals and become, for a time, the foremost fighters on their respective continents (eventually, of course, their enemies conceded the superiority of these innovations and copied them, which has been the nearly universal fate of successful military innovations; see McNeill, 1982).

The fourth and final benefit of persistence is that it can enhance the person's sense of self-efficacy, provided that success is ultimately reached. Bandura's (1977) theory of self-efficacy emphasized that experiences of mastery that come with persistence in the face of obstacles give people an increased and generalized sense of being able to accomplish things. Self-efficacy involves the expectation of being able to exert control and perform effectively to bring about desired outcomes, and that sort of confidence may be especially enhanced by hard-won victories.

Although persistence may be beneficial most of the time, there is no disputing that it can backfire. Some undertakings are indeed impossible and doomed, and persistence merely increases the total costs in effort, time, and other resources that are expended fruitlessly. Indeed, the example of military innovation used in the preceding section could be invoked in a different way to demonstrate the costly futility of some forms of persistence. Frederick and Shaka succeeded precisely because they changed and adapted their methods as they encountered setbacks, difficulties, and challenges. Had they persisted with the old-fashioned, tried-and-true methods, they would have been conquered and forgotten. As scholars like McNeill (1982) and Keegan (1993) have observed, the norm has often been for military forces to begin each new war using the tactics that they developed during preceding wars, often failing to appreciate how technological and other advances have rendered them obsolete. Long intervals between major wars can create especially significant gaps between new weapons and old tactics. Europe had only relatively minor, brief wars for most of the 19th century, and so there was relatively little pressure to improve on the tactics. But the massed cavalry charges and stand-and-shoot tactics that were effective in Napoleon's day were poorly suited to the battlefields of World War I, when machine guns could mow down a swath of troops in seconds and rifles could pick off soldiers accurately at considerable distances. Generals who persevered in the use of outmoded tactics cost the lives of countless young men.

Likewise, the Zulu story is a poignant illustration of this principle. It appears that Zulu military innovation started and ended with Shaka, and his successors simply continued to use his tactics and methods. Morris (1965) described how visiting English friends once demonstrated for Shaka the use of firearms, but the great emperor was unimpressed, asserting that the rifle was inferior to the spear as a weapon of battle. Shaka observed, correctly, that the musket could fire only once, was accurate for only a few hundred yards, and then required time-consuming reloading. A charge of spear carriers against muskets would therefore suffer one round of bloody losses but could then overrun the gunners before they could reload. Unfortunately for the Zulus (because it led to their defeat), Shaka's views were not tested in his own time but half a century later, by which time guns had improved drastically in speed and accuracy, and the spear-carrying warriors were massacred. Shaka himself would probably have refined and adapted his tactics to the new realities of battle, but his successors simply persisted with the frontal assault armed with spears, and the Zulu empire was destroyed.

Perseverance is considered by many scholars to be a key personal characteristic required for successful entrepreneurship (McClelland, 1987). However, persistence does not always predict business success, presumably because it is better to persevere only when success is a reasonable possibility (McClelland, 1987). An archival study of the airline and trucking industries showed patterns that paralleled those of military history: Initial success caused companies to persist with their strategies even as these became obsolete, and this persistence led to declines in performance (Audia, Locke, & Smith, 2000).

Persistence tends to produce further persistence, insofar as people will stay with a course of action because they have already invested some time, energy, money, or other resources in it (e.g., Staw, 1976). If people perceive that they are very close to attaining the goal for which they have been persisting, they are more resistant to quitting (J. Z. Rubin & Brockner, 1975). They persist longer if they have made a public commitment to this course of action, and they persist longer to the extent that they feel personally responsible for making the decision (Staw, 1976). In another variation on this same theme of personal involvement, they persist longer when they think other people will regard them unfavorably for quitting (Brockner, Rubin, & Lang, 1981).

Thus, in a nutshell, persistence is only effective when used judiciously. The individual (or group) must make a correct appraisal of whether persistence in the face of failure will produce eventual success or simply more failure. An influential chapter by Janoff-Bulman and Brickman (1982) articulated the dilemma nicely. They were among the first to recognize that persistence was not uniformly beneficial, and indeed they proposed that the consequences of ill-advised persistence are often more negative than the consequences of giving up too soon. When outcomes are uncontrollable or goals are impossible to reach, it is adaptive to give up (Wortman & Brehm, 1975). Thus, the key to success is not persistence as such but the ability to know when to persist and when to quit (Janoff-Bulman & Brickman, 1982), and then to persist when it is advisable.

■ Development

Undoubtedly, persistence becomes easier and more successful with increasing age, at least up to middle adulthood. A stable attention span and tolerance for frustration take time to develop. Infants and toddlers prefer relatively easy (moderate difficulty) tasks and persist longer on them than on highly difficult ones (Redding, Morgan, & Harmon, 1988). Cognitive ability is an important predictor of persistence in infants (Yarrow, Morgan, Jennings, Harmon, & Gaiter, 1983), but the correlation between persistence and cognitive ability decreases as children get older (Redding et al., 1988).

A study of the mediators of persistence among children was undertaken by Masters and Santrock (1976). They found that children persisted longer on motor tasks when they labeled them as fun rather than as not fun, and as easy rather than difficult. They also persisted longer when they expressed pride as opposed to being self-critical. Persistence was also facilitated by reminding oneself of unrelated pleasant events, which can be an important strategy for affect regulation and tolerating frustration.

Research on delay of gratification can also be considered relevant to persistence, although we mention it only briefly here because it is covered elsewhere in this volume. The ability to delay gratification enables the person to overcome immediate impulses in favor of rewards that are in the future, which parallels the challenge of persistence. Children who were better able to delay gratification at age 4 were later found to have better social skills, academic performance, and coping ability when they were retested more than a decade later, during late adolescence (Mischel, Shoda, & Rodriguez, 1989).

■ Enabling and Inhibiting Factors

According to learned industriousness theory, individuals with a history of reward for effortful behavior are more likely to exert greater effort in the future than are individuals with a history of reward for low-effort behavior (Eisenberger, 1992). Effort training in the laboratory has demonstrated that effortful persistence behavior can be increased by rewarding effort. Eisenberger and his colleagues have amassed an impressive research program demonstrating that effort training can increase subsequent persistence, even at tasks not directly related to the training (e.g., Eisenberger & Adornetto, 1986; Eisenberger & Leonard, 1980; Eisenberger, Mitchell, & Masterson, 1985; Eisenberger, Park, & Frank, 1976; Eisenberger & Selbst, 1994). Other researchers have also provided additional support for effort training and the theory of learned industriousness (e.g., Drucker, Drucker, Litto, & Stevens, 1998; Hickman, Stromme, & Lippman, 1998; Quinn, Brandon, & Copeland, 1996).

Social support appears to be a valuable aid for encouraging persistence. Gloria, Kurpius, Hamilton, and Willson (1999) found that social support led to an increase in the academic persistence of African American students. Zaleski (1988) found that people who had close, supportive relationships were better able to persist and exert effort than those without such relationships. A possible explanation of the benefits of social support was provided by Vallerand, Fortier, and Guay (1997), who found that self-determination mediated the link. Social support fostered a sense of self-determination, which in turn predicted better academic persistence (measured by completing school instead of dropping out), whereas a decrease in social support led to a decrease in self-determination and a resultant rise in the likelihood of dropping out of school.

Receiving positive feedback also contributes to greater persistence, and this, too, may be linked by an increase in the sense of self-determination. S. A. Kelley,

Brownell, and Campbell (2000) showed that when mothers gave their 2-year-old children positive and corrective feedback, the children persisted longer at both easy and difficult tasks. In a sample of 10- and 11-year-old girls, Draper (1981) likewise found that positive feedback following initial failure helped increase persistence on a discrimination task. In an adult (college) sample, Deci (1971) found that telling people they had performed well led them to spend more of their own free, discretionary time on the same tasks. This was a sign that positive feedback increases intrinsic motivation as well as a sense of competence and efficacy (Deci & Ryan, 1992).

It must be acknowledged, however, that the benefits of positive feedback have not been uniformly found. P. B. Paulus and Konicki (1973) found that negative evaluations from others led to greater perseverance on a task as compared with positive or no evaluations. Mueller and Dweck (1998) found that children who were praised for intellectual ability after an initial failure were less persistent on a subsequent task and reported less enjoyment of the task, as compared with children who were praised for effort.

Other rewards (other than praise or positive feedback) show the same patterns as praise and positive feedback, which is to say the weight of evidence suggests that persistence can be improved by them, but some contrary findings exist to suggest that the issue is complex. Eisenberger (1992) suggested that there should be a simple linear relationship, such that reinforcement would lead to greater persistence, but Drucker et al. (1998) found a curvilinear relationship. Intermediate levels of reinforcement increased persistence, whereas both high and low levels of reinforcement reduced persistence. Nation, Cooney, and Gartrell (1979) found that persistence on motor tasks was increased by partial reinforcement, whereas continuous reinforcement led to less persistence. In a similar vein, Hantula and Crowell (1994) found that irregular reinforcement made people more likely to recommit resources to a course of action that had produced initial failure, as compared with continuous or intermittent reinforcement. A. Miller and Hom (1990) found that offering (extrinsic) rewards increased persistence on tasks that were highly relevant to people's self-identifications but decreased persistence on tasks seen as irrelevant to the self. Rewards could not override the general tendency to reduce persistence after initial failure on unsolvable problems.

Some extrinsic rewards have been shown to reduce persistence, especially by reducing intrinsic motivation. People who perform tasks for money (Deci, 1971), prizes (Harackiewicz, 1979), or awards (Lepper, Greene, & Nisbett, 1973) lose interest in performing the task for its own sake and hence are less willing to devote their own free time to the task. This overjustification effect is most pronounced when rewards are anticipated in advance (Lepper et al., 1973) and highly salient (Ross, 1975). The implication is that salient, anticipated rewards shape the experience of performing the task, so that the person comes to see the self as performing the task only for the sake of the reward, and persistence may drop off sharply after the reward is no longer available. In contrast, if the reward is presented or structured in a way that conveys positive feedback about competence, thereby enhancing the task's symbolic value for the self, it can increase intrinsic motivation and hence persistence (Harackiewicz, Manderlink, & Sansone, 1984).

Multiple personal problems and pathologies have been associated with decreased persistence on tasks. These patterns suggest that various problems deplete the person's resources, including self-regulatory strength and self-confidence, and so these resources cannot be marshaled to help the person persist in the face of failure. These problems can briefly be listed as follows: Mentally retarded children have been shown to have less persistence than normal children on challenging motor tasks (Kozub, Porretta, & Hodge, 2000). Learning-disabled children are rated by their teachers as less persistent and more prone to give up than normally achieving children (Ayres, Cooley, & Dunn, 1990). In a laboratory study, fourth- and fifth-grade learning-disabled boys showed less task persistence even though they were more likely to make external attributions for failures (D. E. Friedman & Medway, 1987). Numerous studies have found impaired persistence among children diagnosed with attention-deficit/ hyperactivity disorder (ADHD; Hoza, Waschbusch, Owens, Pelham, & Kipp, 2001; Humphries, Swanson, Kinsbourne, & Yiu, 1979; Lufi & Parish-Plass, 1995; Milich & Okazaki, 1991; Wigal et al., 1998). This deficit is hardly surprising in view of the short attention span that is one of the diagnostic and indeed defining criteria of ADHD, but some evidence suggests that it is exacerbated by a tendency to attribute success to luck (Hoza et al., 2001). Depression has been linked to reduced persistence and impaired performance following failure on an unsolvable task (Brightman, 1990). In fact, very young children of depressed mothers have also been shown to be less persistent on a challenging task, as compared with the offspring of nondepressed mothers (Redding, Harmon, & Morgan, 1990).

We suggested previously that good self-control may be an important contributor to persistence. Consistent with this, people with self-control deficits in other areas have been shown to be less persistent on tasks. Smokers persist less than nonsmokers on laboratory tasks (Quinn et al., 1996). Habitual drug use may constitute further training in impulsivity and hence low persistence (Quinn et al., 1996). Alcoholic young men have been shown to persist less than nondrinkers and light drinkers on anagram and diagram tasks (Cynn, 1992). The findings regarding ADHD may also support the role of self-control, insofar as some experts have concluded that deficits in self-control and self-regulation are central to the disorder (Barkley, 1997).

Likewise, we proposed that the relevance of tasks to the self was instrumental in determining persistence. That conclusion is further supported by evidence that self-awareness can moderate the impact of feedback and related factors on persistence. Scheier and Carver (1982) found that success feedback improved persistence, but only among people with a high focus on self. Carver et al. (1979) found that the benefits of favorable expectancies on persistence were enhanced by high attention to self. Likewise, the impact of attributing initial failure to external sources (which improves persistence) has been found mainly among people with high self-awareness (Kernis, Zuckerman, Cohen, & Spadafora, 1982).

■ Gender, Cross-National, and Cross-Cultural Aspects

Gender differences in persistence have been studied, but the results are neither fully clear nor consistent. Nygard (1977) found that girls tended to persist longer than boys on anagram and arithmetic problems. Girls are also less likely than boys to drop out of high school (Summers, 2000). Some studies have found that females possess somewhat greater self-control than males in both normal populations (Bjorklund & Kipp, 1996) and prison populations (Ainslie, 1987). However, boys are more likely to attribute failure to external, modifiable factors such as effort, whereas girls typically attribute failure to lack of ability (Dweck, Goetz, & Strauss, 1980), and the greater emphasis on effort makes boys more likely than girls to persist in the face of prolonged task failure (Dweck & Reppucci, 1973). Males like games of skill more than females and are more persistent at skills tasks than females (Deaux, White, & Farris, 1975). In general, most studies find that gender differences in self-control are small or negligible (Tangney et al., in press).

Only a smattering of findings exist to indicate cross-cultural variations in persistence. It is difficult to know whether the general lack of such findings indicates that researchers have thus far neglected to study the topic or, more profoundly, whether persistence depends on the same factors and principles in different cultures. Blinco (1992) found that Japanese children persisted longer on puzzles than did American children, although the difference was found only under noncompetitive conditions that included performing independently, in isolation from other students, and without teacher assistance.

Research by Iyengar and Lepper (1999) concluded that the links between culture and persistence depended on a number of factors, such as personal choice. American students with independent self-construals (see Markus & Kitayama, 1991) persisted longest if they had high degrees of choice; in contrast, they showed less intrinsic motivation and less persistence if the task was chosen for them. In contrast, Asian American children were more intrinsically motivated and persisted longer if the tasks were chosen for them by an authority figure. Presumably, cultures that foster industriousness may also promote perseverance, but evidence supporting this claim is lacking.

■ Deliberate Interventions

Persistence is one human strength that can certainly be improved. A variety of studies have shown that people who receive training at effort and persistence can exhibit significant improvement in their ability to persevere in the face of failure. Hickman et al. (1998) exposed research subjects to high-effort training in the form of practicing with difficult and demanding tasks, and these people subsequently persisted longer than others at solving maze problems. Eisenberger, Kuhlman, and Cotterell (1992) found various benefits from effort training on persistence, and these benefits depended on individual differences. That is, participants who initially had a high-cooperative orientation showed increased persistence on cooperative tasks in the wake of high-effort training. Individualistic participants responded to the same training with increased persistence on competitive tasks. Meanwhile, participants who were initially classified as competitive responded to the high-effort training with increased persistence on both cooperative and competitive tasks.

Nation and Massad (1978) proposed a model for persistence training as a form of therapy to help counteract pathological patterns of learned helplessness and depression. Craske (1985) exposed participants who had exhibited signs of learned helplessness to a form of training that encouraged them to attribute failure to low effort rather than to low ability, on the assumption that attributions to effort would encourage people to persist (and try harder) in the future. Craske found that this training led to greater persistence on unsolvable puzzles among female but not among male participants. This is consistent with findings that explanatory style is predictive of persistence (Seligman & Schulman, 1986) and findings that females are more prone to suffer from (and to fail to persist because of) attributing failure to lack of ability, as noted earlier (Dweck et al., 1980).

In a similar vein, Dweck (1975) examined several kinds of training on subsequent persistence in the face of failure, using a sample of children who had exhibited learned helplessness in response to failure. The children in her study showed significant improvements in persistence (and in task performance outcome) when they had been trained to take responsibility for failure and attributed failure to insufficient effort. An alternative treatment that simply provided children with success experiences was less effective.

These findings regarding the benefits of training converge well with other evidence highlighting factors that influence persistence. In particular, persistence can be increased by teaching people to regard their initial failures as reflecting their own lack of effort. Although some might be skeptical of such an approach insofar as it leads people to blame themselves for failure, its benefits have been established. Apparently, teaching people to blame failures on their own low effort encourages them to believe that outcomes are under their control and that they should keep going, preferably with an increase in effort.

■ What Is Not Known?

There is undoubtedly much about persistence that remains unknown, but here we highlight what we consider the most compelling unanswered questions for future researchers to address:

- Can people be trained to make appropriate decisions about when to persist and when to give up? Training people to persist seems easy enough, but can people be easily trained to make proper persistence decisions? High self-esteem has been linked with adaptive persistence decisions, but it seems unlikely that high self-esteem per se is driving the effect. What facets of self-esteem are key for perseverance? What factors should people focus on when deciding whether to persist?
- Do laboratory perseverance effects mirror real-world perseverance? Many psychological phenomena are manifested similarly in the lab and the field, but is perseverance? Perseverance tests in the lab generally measure behavior over a duration of perhaps half an hour, and the setbacks involved are relatively benign. Can researchers safely assume that the predictors of lab persistence also predict real-life perseverance?
- Is perseverance a quantity versus quality trade-off with regard to goal achievement? Do people miss out on attaining many meaningful, albeit less grandiose, goals in their dogged pursuit of one or a few truly challenging goals? A related issue is whether people with diverse goals can more easily rebound from failure and continue persevering toward a given goal. Having alternative goals may encourage quitting, but they could also conceivably buffer one's ego from threatening failure or help one to recover from setbacks.
- Do certain cultures promote or hinder perseverance more than others? If so, why? As mentioned earlier, few cross-cultural studies of perseverance have been undertaken. If perseverance does differ across cultures, perseverance probably differs across eras as well: Is perseverance more or less common in modern times than in the past?

■ Must-Read Articles and Books

Abramson, L. Y., Seligman, M. E. P., & Teasdale, J. D. (1978). Learned helplessness in humans: Critique and reformulation. *Journal of Abnormal Psychology, 87,* 49–74.

Bandura, A. (1977). Self-efficacy: Toward a unifying theory of behavioral change. *Psychological Review, 84,* 191–215.

Bjorklund, D. F., & Kipp, K. (1996). Parental investment theory and gender differences in the evolution of inhibition mechanisms. *Psychological Bulletin, 120,* 163–188.

Eisenberger, R. (1992). Learned industriousness. *Psychological Review, 99,* 248–267.

Hickman, K. L., Stromme, C., & Lippman, L. G. (1998). Learned industriousness: Replication in principle. *Journal of General Psychology, 125,* 213–217.

Mischel, W., Shoda, Y., & Rodriguez, M. L. (1989). Delay of gratification in children. *Science, 244,* 933–938.

Nation, J. R., & Massad, P. (1978). Persistence training: A partial reinforcement procedure for reversing learned helplessness and depression. *Journal of Experimental Psychology: General, 107,* 436–451.

11. INTEGRITY

[Authenticity, Honesty]

■ *Sojourner Truth (1797–1883) was born Isabella Baumfree, a slave, in New York in 1797 and was freed by state law in 1827. She changed her name after having a religious vision. She became an itinerant preacher, antislavery activist, and advocate for women's suffrage. She worked tirelessly to assist newly freed Southern slaves and even petitioned Congress to give former slaves land in the West (Women in History, 1991). Although illiterate, Sojourner Truth was a powerful orator and used her chosen name for rhetorical emphasis, as in hoping to sojourn to the ballot box sometime in her life. She spoke from the authority of her convictions, at times under life-threatening conditions, and evidenced the power of the truth: "I carry no weapon; the Lord will preserve me without weapons; I feel safe even in the midst of my enemies; for the truth is powerful and will prevail." In 1851 she spoke at a women's suffrage convention in Akron, Ohio, and delivered the legendary "Ain't I a Woman" speech, linking sexism and racism to denial of the essence of being—integrity—and made explicit the denial by sexism and racism of incontrovertible truth. Sojourner Truth proclaimed, "That man over there says that women need to be helped into carriages, and lifted over ditches, and to have the best place everywhere. Nobody ever helps me into carriages, or over mud puddles, or gives me any best place. And ain't I a woman?"* ■

■ Consensual Definition

Integrity, authenticity, and honesty capture a character trait in which people are true to themselves, accurately representing—privately and publicly—their internal states, intentions, and commitments. Such persons accept and take responsibility for their feelings and behaviors, owning them, as it were, and reaping substantial benefits by so doing. Individuals with the character strength of integrity would strongly endorse such statements as these:

- It is more important to be myself than to be popular.
- When people keep telling the truth, things work out.
- I would never lie just to get something I wanted from someone.
- My life is guided and given meaning by my code of values.
- It is important to me to be open and honest about my feelings.
- I always follow through on my commitments, even when it costs me.
- "To thine own self be true, and thou canst not then be false to any man."
- I dislike phonies who pretend to be what they are not.

The word *integrity* comes from the Latin *integritas*, meaning wholeness, soundness, untouched, whole, and entire. Some researchers contend that the construct remains vague and ill defined after more than 50 years of research (Rieke & Guastello, 1995). We suggest the following definition, phrased in terms of behavioral criteria:

- a regular pattern of behavior that is consistent with espoused values—practicing what one preaches
- public justification of moral convictions, even if those convictions are not popular
- treatment of others with care, as evident by helping those in need; sensitivity to the needs of others

Although they share a common thread of meaning, integrity, authenticity, and honesty, each has somewhat different connotations. Honesty refers to factual truthfulness and interpersonal sincerity. *Authenticity* refers to emotional genuineness and also psychological depth. *Integrity* refers to moral probity and self-unity; in terms of moral character, it seems the most generic of these terms and in any event the one we highlight in this chapter.

■ Theoretical Traditions

The concept of psychological integrity appeared relatively recently on the historical scene, because the concept of the psychological self, on which the concept of integrity rests, seems itself to have emerged in the Western world only within the last 500 years (Baumeister, 1987). The concept of self apparently evolved through several stages since its first appearance, corresponding to advances in technological and cultural evolution. In the early modern period (16th century), traditional class-based role structures began to weaken, leading to an increased awareness of the self as an inner entity potentially separate from its environment. Next came the Puritans, who struggled to overcome their sins and inner weaknesses and were motivated to believe that their own inner self was one of the elect—predestined for heaven. The obvious potential for self-serving biases inherent in this arrangement forced them to face the possibility of self-deception or inauthenticity. In the romantic period (17th and 18th centuries), there arose the concept of the self as a hero on a quest. In this view, the self must overcome social strictures and internal inhibitions in order to find itself and also find personal fulfillment. And in the Victorian period (19th century), the pendulum swung back, as fulfillment was said to occur through self-denial and moral rectitude rather than through self-expression and discovery.

Throughout this time it was always assumed that one's personal self was something real. However, the Victorian self of the late 19th century was ripe for undermining, given the hypocrisy and repression endemic to this era, as satirized in Samuel Butler's *Way of All Flesh*. In addition, breakthroughs in scientific understanding were occurring. Theoretical perspectives converged on the conclusion that the self is a powerless myth and that its quest to find and express itself therefore is a hopeless delusion. The bottom fell out of the self in the early 20th century, an event from which the self and those who study it have still not fully recovered. In this chapter, we consider some of these challenges to the potential for authentic selfhood.

Darwinism legitimized the view of humans as mere animals, no different from any other animal. Freudian theory painted a dark and pessimistic portrait of human beings, as creatures driven by instinctive and antisocial urges of which they were largely unconscious. Operant behaviorism further delegitimized the self, viewing it as the epiphenomenal by-product of linguistic conditioning. Positivism asserted that reality is inherent only in immediate sense data, and of course, self-experience is far from this. Sociologists depicted the self as a set of empty masks, roles, and performances programmed by social norms and role requirements. Even the cognitive revolution within psychology did not restore the self, viewing it as a mere by-product of dissonance reduction processes by which people convince themselves that they chose to be what they have been programmed to be (Deci & Ryan, 1991).

Delegitimization of the phenomenal self continues even today, as postmodernism asserts that "there is no inner self to which our actions should be true" (Gergen, 1991, p. 188); terror management theory views the self as a defense against existential death-terror (J. Greenberg, Pyszczynski, & Solomon, 1995); and cognitive self psychology views the self as a mere set of images to be protected, affirmed, and enhanced (J. D. Brown, 1998). Unfortunately, none of these theoretical perspectives is able to accommodate the concept of integrity, which relies on the assumption that there is something in there to which a person may or may not be true. Nevertheless, there have been many attempts in recent decades to assert, or to find a new basis for, the integrity of the psychological self.

Jung (1939) argued that there is indeed an authentic self beneath the multiple personas, capable of growth and of ever-increasing contact with rich meanings embedded within human nature. This more optimistic perspective was taken up by the ego psychologists, who discussed the concept of free ego energy (Hartmann, 1964); the possibility of contacting one's true (rather than false) self (Winnicott, 1958); and the possibility of psychic unity (versus splitting and fragmentation; Kernberg, 1976). In philosophy, the phenomenologists and existentialists emphasized the struggle of the self to achieve a truly authentic existence. For example, Heidegger (1962) discussed the need to recover one's self from society, at the same time that one recovers one's being-in-the-world. Sartre (1956) focused on the problem of bad faith, arguing that integrity is found only by embracing the inescapable reality of personal choice. Laing (1960) focused on the divided self, in which people divorce their inner self from the self they project to the world, leading to radical confusions. Implicit in all these perspectives is the idea that societal failings and inadequate nurturing push people to adopt false or inauthentic selves.

The concept of psychological integrity was given its most important expression by the humanistic psychologists of the 1960s. C. R. Rogers (1961) made integrity (or congruence) the cornerstone of his theory, defining it as occurring when "the feelings the person is experiencing are available to him, available to his awareness, and he is able to live these feelings, be them, and is able to communicate them if appropriate" (p. 61). Some feelings can be difficult to detect on-line, and Rogers argued that they may be obscured precisely because a person is committed to a self-image inconsistent with these feelings. Thus, ironically, the cognitive self may be the very cause of its own deeper blindness or inauthenticity. Rogers viewed the optimal therapeutic relationship as one in which the therapist is as honest, genuine, and accepting as possible in relations with the client, enabling the client to better contact, express, and accept his or her own emotional experiences. This humanistic model of the optimal helping relationship still predominates within contemporary counseling practice.

Despite its enduring relevance in applied settings, the humanistic perspective has faded from the theoretical mainstream of social psychology, which is now dominated by more cognitive theories. Again, cognitive perspectives sidestep the question of whether the self is real and thus provide little basis for engaging the question of whether or not a person is being authentic. For example, although many of us would agree with the folk wisdom that we should try to be ourselves, social-cognitive theories have no way of making sense of this statement. So, the self is still struggling to recover itself within modern academic psychology. In the following we attempt a brief explication of the importance of being true to oneself, drawing on contemporary evolutionary theory, dynamical systems theory, and life span developmental theory.

Before considering these perspectives, we must first define the self as a special kind of mental representation. Specifically, the self is a mental projection of the underlying organism, an on-line simulation being run within the biocognitive computer (Kuhl & Goschke, 1994). In somewhat different terms, the self is a lived character in an unfolding personal drama (McAdams, 1999), one that is constantly updated (Damasio, 1999). The self is thus a phenomenal fiction, both in that the content of the regnant self-narrative can be somewhat arbitrarily or randomly determined, and in that the self-narrative may be an inaccurate or even inadequate simulation of the underlying organism's actual condition (Sheldon & Elliot, 1999). Rather than being powerless, however, this fiction has several important functions, including supplying high-level goals and standards for the action system, supplying animated personas for effective social interchange, and supplying defenses against anxiety and mortality.

From this perspective, the question of psychological integrity becomes whether the phenomenal self accurately represents and authentically expresses the actual needs, emotions, and interests of the organism in which it is embedded. How closely does the fiction mirror reality? According to C. R. Rogers (1961), the closest approaches occur when a person strongly values discovering the truth of his or her internal experience and is willing and able to accept what he or she finds. Epstein's (1973) definition of the self as a theory is consistent with this view, if one assumes that there is an underlying personal reality to which the self-theory refers, more or less accurately.

From an evolutionary point of view, an accurate or authentic self-function should be highly adaptive (Sedikides & Skowronski, 1997), for at least three reasons. First, people able to correctly bundle their own underlying condition into their self-experience stand to gain self-regulatory benefits, as their ongoing choices and adjustments can be based on accurate and updated readouts of their actual needs and situation. This is precisely C. R. Rogers's (1961) definition of the fully functioning human being—someone well attuned to his or her changing emotional responses, and able to accept this internal information and act appropriately upon it. Second, integrity is also likely to yield social benefits, as authentic persons are well liked (Hodgins, Koestner, & Duncan, 1996; M. D. Robinson, Johnson, & Shields, 1995), presumably enabling them to create more adaptive cooperative alliances (Sober & Wilson, 1998) and receive more social support (Ryan & Solky, 1996). The primary adaptive environment for *Homo sapiens* has long been the social environment (Caporael, 1997), and although at times competitive and Machiavellian, personality styles can yield substantial adaptive benefits; on the whole, cooperators and coalition formers have fared best within human societies (Buss, 1999; Sober & Wilson, 1998). Third, one can argue that authentic experiencing and behaving is highly adaptive simply because it tends to promote more complex and integrated task performances (Deci & Ryan, 1985b), as well as reduced chronic stress and autonomic activation (Pennebaker & Keough, 1999).

Dynamical systems perspectives provide another way of viewing self-authenticity (Nowak & Vallacher, 1998). These perspectives treat life as an entropy-reducing process, coping with disturbances and thereby tending over time toward order and complexity (Maturana, 1999). Human beings, with their unique ability to abstract patterns and make meaning even from traumatic experiences, embody such organizational processes par excellence. Notably, however, increases in order and complexity are dependent upon the efficient processing and utilization of information, including emotional information (Vallacher & Nowak, 1999). The more a person is able to contact and represent his or her underlying condition, the better he or she can actively expand and develop that condition. Consistent with this perspective, C. R. Rogers (1961) argued that only authentic persons are able to engage fully in the process of becoming. In contrast, a person who sacrifices authenticity to preserve a partial or rigid self-image, or to deceive or manipulate others, likely sacrifices much potential for personal growth and positive change.

Life span developmental theory also provides a way of viewing integrity. Such an approach regards personality growth as the unfolding of implicit teleological trends over time (Sanderson & Cantor, 1999). For example, psychobiographical analyses reveal that notable achievers typically pursue their discipline relentlessly across their life spans, following their interests wherever they lead (Gruber & Wallace, 1999). Often these implicit trends originate very early in the creator's childhood. Although acting *in*consistently with one's own implicit interests and developmental trends can sometimes pay off, the data suggest that those who ignore their deeper impulses, curiosities, and values typically experience suboptimal outcomes (Sheldon & Elliot, 1999). For example, the latter types tend not to be the ones who make a mark on history (Simonton, 1999b).

The question of the reality of the self remains an important one in the philosophical literature. Little consensus has been reached, however, because theorists in different camps (i.e., nativist, naturalist, computational, deconstructionist) start from irreconcilable assumptions. In psychology, however, significant empirical progress has been made in understanding both the contextual conditions that foster authenticity in the moment and in characterizing the integrated or self-attuned personality.

Much of this progress has occurred within self-determination theory, which for three decades has been attempting to bring rigor to humanistic theorizing (Deci, 1975; Deci & Ryan, 1985b, 2000). Self-determination theory postulates a universal human need for autonomy, which is satisfied when people feel free to do what is most interesting and personally important (Deci & Ryan, 2001). According to self-determination theory, one hallmark of autonomous or authentic behavior is that it feels internally caused. Thus, one potential indicator of inauthenticity is that a person feels that his or her behavior is externally caused; that is, the person does not acknowledge the fact that he or she selected a particular behavior.

According to self-determination theory, two classes of factors can lead to inauthentic behavior, one situational and one personological. First, controlling social contexts, which do not provide choice and do not take the controllee's perspective into account, can lead people to suppress or ignore their emotional experiences and to feel that their behaviors are not their own. Research implies that authorities should be as autonomy-supportive as possible so that their charges may experience maximal choice and behave most authentically. Second, controlled personality styles can lead people to feel a sense of passivity and dependence. Such persons need to recognize the inevitability of choice, to use Sartre's terminology, so that they can take more responsibility for their actions and become more involved in selecting self-appropriate actions.

Other contemporary researchers also acknowledge the importance of psychological integrity. For example, Sheldon's work on self-concordance (Sheldon, 2002; Sheldon & Elliot, 1999; Sheldon & Houser-Marko, 2001) examines the extent to which self-generated personal goals accurately represent the person's implicit interests and values. In this view, inauthentic goals are goals over which the person does not claim ownership (despite having created them ex nihilo). Waterman's (1993a, 1993b) work on *eudaimonia* applies the Eriksonian identity development paradigm to the issue of psychological integrity, specifically considering whether particular activities allow people to express their deeper commitments and sense of identity. Harter (1999) studied the phenomenon of voice, that is, the ability to express what one really believes, thinks, and feels. Specifically, she asked whether adolescent females lose voice—become inauthentic—during the transition to womanhood. M. D. Robinson et al. (1995) took an experimental approach to examine what kinds of self-presentations lead others to perceive that the presenter is being authentic. They found that people who give balanced self-descriptions, acknowledging both strengths and weaknesses, are perceived by others as most authentic. Finally, Sheldon, Ryan, Rawsthorne, and Ilardi (1997) examined authenticity as a moderator of Big Five trait expression within different social roles, showing that the true self and the trait self are not identical. Specifically, participants reported the greatest amount of enjoyment within particular social roles when they felt authentic in playing those roles, independently of what their personality trait scores suggested they should enjoy.

■ Measures

We divide our discussion of measurement into two parts that reflect the bifurcated nature of research into this positive trait: measures of authenticity, on the one hand, and measures of integrity/honesty, on the other (Table 11.1)

Authenticity

Few measures of authenticity exist. Given the subtlety of the construct, measuring it via direct self-report can be problematic (Mitchell, 1992). First, impression management considerations may limit one's willingness to admit inauthentic behavior. Second, knowledge availability may also play a role be-

---

TABLE 11.1   *Measures of Authenticity, Honesty, and Integrity*

Authenticity

OVERT

Experienced Authenticity Measure
> Sheldon, Ryan, Rawsthorne, & Ilardi (1997)
> Designed to measure experienced authenticity within different social roles

Adolescent Voice
> Harter, Waters, Whitesell, & Kastelic (1998)
> Measures the freedom perceived by adolescents to express what they "really" believe, think, and feel

COVERT

Locus of Causality
> Ryan & Connell (1989)
> Measures whether a particular behavior feels internally caused (authentic) or not (inauthentic)

Leader Authenticity
> Henderson & Hoy (1983)
> Measure of leader authenticity, based on subordinates' perceptions

Honesty

OVERT

Personal Value Scales
> Described in J. Robinson, Shaver, & Wrightsman (1991)
> Designed to assess the extent to which individuals admire specific values (e.g., honesty, kindness, loyalty)

Specific Interpersonal Trust Scale
> Described in J. Robinson, Shaver, & Wrightsman (1991)
> Designed to assess the degree of interpersonal trust held by one individual for a specific other person

Personality Traits Scale
> Rind & Gaudet (1993)
> Designed to assess 18 attributes in young adolescents, including honesty, leadership skills, and trustworthiness

Station Employee Applicant Inventory
> London House, Inc. (1999b)
> Designed to assess honesty, interpersonal cooperation, drug avoidance, temperament, etc.

COVERT

Psychological Screening Inventory—Endorsement of Excessive Virtue

Lanyon (1993)

34-item measure designed to identify persons who portray themselves as very high in personal virtuousness (e.g., total honesty, moral excellence, thorough trustworthiness)

Truthfulness Measure

A. Kelly, Kahn, & Coulter (1996)

Designed to assess how truthful participants report their "self-presentations" to a counselor

Honesty and Kindness Story Tasks

Lamborn, Fischer, & Pipp (1994)

Designed to examine children's and youths' ability to understand and explain stories about honesty and kindness

Integrity

OVERT

Morally Debatable Behaviors Scale

Katz, Santman, & Lonero (1993)

Measures justifiability of behaviors reflecting moral issues such as stealing, abortion, prostitution

Comparative Emphasis Scale

Meglino, Ravlin, & Adkins (1989)

Designed to measure workplace values, such as honesty and integrity

Personnel Selection Inventory

London House, Inc. (1999a)

Designed to assess work values, employee–customer relations, honesty, tenure, etc.

Moral Integrity Survey

Olson (1998)

Designed to assess the degree to which participants morally discern, consistently behave, and publicly justify a single moral conviction

Employee Integrity Index

Described in Alliger, Lilienfeld, & Mitchell (1996)

62-item measure designed to assess dishonesty in the workplace

(continued)

TABLE 11.1   *Measures of Authenticity, Honesty, and Integrity* (*continued*)

Stanton Survey

> Klump, Reed, & Perman (1985)
>
> Designed to explore employee attitudes and behaviors in relation to company morale, stealing and dishonesty, etc.

Phase II Profile Integrity Status Inventory

> Lousig-Nont & Ishmael (1985)
>
> Designed to screen prospective employees' attitudes toward honesty

Academic Integrity Interview

> Stiff, Corman, Krizek, & Snider (1994)
>
> Designed to assess college students' attitudes and practices regarding academic honesty

COVERT

Imaginative Endings

> Sumner (1976)
>
> Designed to assess self-reliance, integrity, self-respect, honesty, determination, etc., in adolescents aged 13 to 18

Search Institute Profiles of Student Life: Attitudes and Behaviors Survey

> Search Institute (1996)
>
> Designed to assess developmental assets such as commitments, positive values, competencies, and positive identity

Giotto Integrity Test

> Rust (1999)
>
> A work-based personality questionnaire designed to assess integrity

ABILITIES Index

> D. Bailey, Simeonsson, Buysse, & Smith (1993)
>
> Measures "integrity of physical health" in children with disabilities

Personnel Reaction Blank

> Described in Alliger, Lilienfeld, & Mitchell (1996)
>
> 70-item measure designed to assess personality traits such as conscientiousness, reliability, and emotional stability

---

cause some people who are behaving inauthentically might be unaware of it. Third, intelligence, education, and personality development likely play a role, inasmuch as it takes a certain minimal level of sophistication to be able to understand the difference between authenticity and inauthenticity. In short, simply asking participants "how authentic are you in your daily life?" may not work.

Reid Report/Reid Survey

    Described in Willis (1985)

    Designed to predict workplace theft

Life Experience Inventory—Revised

    Ash (1988)

    Measures childhood and early family experiences; social, recreational, and educational experiences; and personal feelings, such as "faulty societal values"

Adult Identity Interview

    Whitbourne (1986)

    Examines two dimensions: identity strength and flexibility; semistructured interview during which respondents describe their identities regarding present work and family situations

    Appropriate for adults aged 20–65

Ego Identity Scale

    Tan, Kendis, Fine, & Porac (1977)

    Measures Eriksonian ego identity; self-report, forced choice between two statements for each item as to which best describes the individual; one item in pair indicates ego identity, and the other, identity diffusion

Erikson Psychosocial Stage Inventory

    Rosenthal, Gurney, & Moore (1981)

    Examines two dimensions: identity strength and flexibility; semistructured interview during which respondents describe their identities regarding present work and family situations; appropriate for adults aged 20 to 65

Extended Objective Measure of Ego Identity Status (EOMEIS) and Objective Measure of Ego Identity Status (OMEIS)

    Bennion & Adams (1986); Grotevant & Adams (1984)

    Designed to measure Eriksonian ego-identity formation; assesses ideological and interpersonal identity; self-report questionnaire uses 6-point Likert scales; appropriate for individuals aged 14 to 40; has short form of 24 items, named Objective Measure of Ego Identity Status (OMEIS)

Ryan and Connell's (1989) perceived locus of causality concept provides a less direct but perhaps more valid approach to measurement. People are asked to rate why they perform a particular motivated behavior, in terms of four reasons ranging from internal to external causation. "Because I'm really interested in this" and "because it expresses my values" represent two autonomous reasons for acting, which are indicative of authenticity in that the self is experienced as the cause of the behavior, and the behavior expresses the underlying personality. In contrast, saying that one acts "because the situation is making me" or "to avoid feeling guilty" represents controlled and perhaps inauthentic behavior because the self is not experienced as the cause of the behavior, and the behavior does not express growth-oriented facets of the personality.

Another measurement approach was taken by Sheldon et al. (1997), who used the following five items to ask people about the authenticity of their behavior within each of five social roles:

- I experience this aspect of myself as an authentic part of who I am.
- This aspect of myself is meaningful and valuable to me.
- I have freely chosen this way of being.
- I am only this way because I have to be (reversed).
- I feel tense and pressured in this part of my life (reversed).

Notably, this approach does not require people to endorse items such as "I behave falsely when I play this role" or "I am dishonest in the way I play this role," and thus the impression-management concerns already mentioned may be less salient.

Harter, Waters, Whitesell, and Kastelic (1998) reported data from their measure of voice, that is, the extent to which people feel free to express their actual perceptions, thoughts, and emotions to others. They asked a sample of adolescents to complete a five-item measure of voice, separately with respect to parents, teachers, male classmates, female classmates, and close friends.

An observer-based approach was used by Henderson and Hoy (1983) in their scale to assess (perceived) leader authenticity. This scale, which is given to the leader's subordinates, measures a leader's emphasis on self-expression within the role, nonmanipulation of subordinates, and acceptance of personal and organizational responsibility.

Because of the potential problems posed by impression management or self-deceptive processes, it might be desirable to be able to measure inauthenticity using non-self-report methods. For example, polygraph methodologies use autonomic reactivity to assess whether people are speaking falsely, with considerable success. Unfortunately, guilty criminals know they are lying, whereas individuals who are behaving inauthentically may not know this. Nevertheless, there are promising indications that indirect methodologies, such as response latency analysis, implicit attitudes assessment, and textual content analysis, will be able to quantify inauthenticity (Sheldon, 2002). In addition, fMRI and PET methodologies hold promise for quantifying neural integration (or the lack of it) at the systemic level (Damasio, 1999).

Despite measurement difficulties, it is clear that authenticity can be measured via self-report, especially using measures that focus on inauthenticity (such as feelings of being controlled or feelings of uncertain identity). Furthermore, such items can be administered to relatively young persons, as in the study of adolescents reported by Harter et al. (1998). However, it is unlikely that younger children could respond meaningfully to questions about authenticity, given their relative lack of sophistication (see later discussion).

Honesty and Integrity

In contrast to the murky measurement of authenticity, honesty in the narrow sense of truth-telling has been amply studied with face-valid approaches that ascertain "truth" and compare it with what the respondent says or does. For example, Cassey and Burton (1982) assessed children's honesty with a spelling test. The test uses sets of letters that the child is instructed to unscramble to make words. The child is instructed to grade his or her own paper from a covered answer sheet when 2 minutes are up. The set is timed with an alarm clock. Children are allotted 5 minutes to both take and correct the test. Dishonesty is measured by the children's behavior: looking at the answer key early, changing or adding answers after the time is up, or working past the 2-minute time limit.

Austin et al. (1991) used the following method to assess children's honesty:

> The child was invited to listen to a story about two puppets whose parents had just made cookies. The parents had placed restrictions on how many cookies the puppets could have and when the puppets could have them, but the puppets were anxious to have more cookies anyway. While the parent is out of the room the puppets take a few more cookies. The child was then asked to give feedback five different times on the puppets' actions, what the puppets should do next, and whether or not the puppets should tell their mother what they had done. (p. 190)

Along these lines, measures of workplace honesty and integrity are common in the human resource management arena. The term *honesty test* is often used interchangeability with *integrity test* (Mikulay & Goffin, 1998). Whatever the label, the pen-and-paper integrity testing business is a multimillion-dollar industry (Dwight & Alliger, 1997). These tests are designed to predict on-the-job theft, gross misconduct, and other types of counterproductive work behavior (Association of Test Publishers, 1994). Integrity tests have been categorized into two types: overt and personality-oriented tests. Overt tests typically assess theft attitudes and requests for admissions of theft or other wrongdoing. Personality-oriented tests have a broader focus and attempt to assess constructs such as dependability, conscientiousness, social conformity, thrill seeking, trouble with authority, and hostility (Sackett & Wanek, 1996).

Evidence suggests that some applicants fake integrity tests! Alliger and Dwight (2000) conducted a meta-analysis of the susceptibility of integrity tests to faking and coaching. Their findings suggest that overt integrity tests are particularly susceptible to faking good and coaching, whereas personality-based measures were more resistant to faking good and coaching. Not surprisingly, some researchers conclude that it is unclear what integrity tests measure (Camara & Schnieder, 1995; Rieke & Guastello, 1995). Integrity tests seem to spread an impossibly broad net and may reflect individual differences in conventionality, dependability, depression, drug avoidance, energy level, honesty, hostility, job commitment, moral reasoning, proneness to violence, self-restraint, sociability, thrill seeking, vocational identity, wayward impulses, and work ethic (T. Becker, 1998).

In 1991, a task force of the American Psychological Association (APA) was charged with reviewing currently available commercial preemployment honesty and integrity tests (L. R. Goldberg, Grenier, Guion, Sechrest, & Wing, 1991). The primary conclusions of their report are as follows: (a) The field of honesty testing would benefit from increased openness concerning development and scoring of tests, research reports, and basic psychometric information; (b) evidence supports the tests' criterion-related validity; (c) publishers should conform to the APA Standards for Educational and Psychological Testing; (d) marketing claims for these tests "vary from circumspect to fraudulent" (p. 20); and (e) additional construct validity research is needed. The task force's review was generally supportive of preemployment honesty and integrity tests, although it was critical of publishers' marketing techniques and resistance to sharing information on the tests.

To make integrity testing more useful, T. Becker (1998) suggested the following prima facie valid integrity test items: (a) I value (reason, purpose, and self-esteem); (b) I am (rational, honest, independent, just, productive, and proud); (c) My values, goals, and behavior are congruent; and (d) I am willing to do whatever is necessary to live according to my most cherished values. Becker also suggested including measures of self-deception and impression management along with integrity measures because integrity items may elicit a social desirability response bias. Further, rating by others (e.g., peers), in lieu of self-reporting, would reduce concern about self-serving bias and method variance. Finally, if feasible, researchers should attempt to assess whether actual behavior is consistent with one's morally justifiable principles (T. Becker, 1998). Of the measures considered in this review, the Moral Integrity Survey (MIS) is a particularly promising paper-and-pencil objective measure of moral integrity suitable for administration to adolescents and adults (Olson, 1998). Factor analysis of the MIS suggests two factors: (a) feeling integrity and behaving accordingly and (b) thinking about moral integrity.

■ Correlates and Consequences

Consistent with Deci and Ryan's (2000) claim that humans have a psychological need for autonomy or integrity, measures of integrity typically correlate with measures of psychological well-being broadly defined: for example, positive mood, life satisfaction, openness to experience, empathy, self-actualization, and conscientiousness (see Ryan & Deci, 2000, for a review). Integrity is also associated with positive interpersonal outcomes. For example, Henderson and Hoy (1983) showed that teachers' perceptions of their elementary school principal's authenticity were positively correlated with their ratings of their own social need fulfillment on the job, and negatively correlated with teachers' ratings of their principal's status concern. Also, as noted, M. D. Robinson et al. (1995) showed in an experimental study that authentic persons are better liked.

Consistent with the thrust of these findings, integrity tests have the largest correlation with the Big Five dimension of conscientiousness, although a linear composite of the conscientiousness, agreeableness, and emotional stability described integrity better than any one dimension alone (Ones, Viswesvaran, & Schmidt, 1995; Sackett & Wanek, 1996). Furthermore, integrity tests and measures of social desirability—sometimes called "lie" scales—are substantially correlated (Sackett & Wanek, 1996).

Perhaps the most elaborate chain of correlates associated with psychological integrity is provided by Sheldon's longitudinal path models describing the effects of self-concordance (i.e., authentic goals) upon personal goal pursuit and changes in psychological well-being. One set of studies demonstrated that goal self-concordance predicted enduring effort investment, which leads to greater goal attainment (Sheldon & Elliot, 1999). Attainment in turn predicted daily need satisfaction over the course of the study. There was also an interaction between attainment and self-concordance, such that need satisfaction is greatest when attained goals are self-concordant ones. Finally, aggregate daily need satisfaction during the study predicted increases in global well-being from the beginning to the end of the study. Another study tested a five-wave longitudinal model, showing that initial self-concordance predicted goal attainment, which predicted even greater self-concordant goal selection for a second striving period, which predicted even further gains in goal attainment, which led finally to enhanced ego development (Sheldon & Houser-Marko, 2001). In other words, consistent with Rogers's claims concerning the link between integrity and becoming, self-concordant individuals were best poised to experience an upward spiral of growth and positive change.

An interesting line of work has looked at the social-level correlates of this character strength. For example, educational administrators' integrity—operationalized as nonmanipulation of subordinates, salience of self over role, and accountability—is associated with trust in the organization and teacher trust in the principal (Busman, 1992). In the business world, subordinates may perceive managers who have been trained to follow narrowly prescribed positive relationships with subordinates as manipulative. The manager's authentic behavior, defined as "being what you are," establishes more effective workplace relationships (S. Herman, 1971).

■ Development

Developmental changes in children's conception of honesty, or the objectivity of truth, have long been of interest to scholars (Kalish, 2000). Much of the research on children's honesty is heavily based on Piaget's pioneering research as published in the *Moral Judgment of the Child* (Bussey, 1992). Piaget's focus was on the role of intentionality in children's definitions and evaluations of false statements. Piaget (1932/1965) questioned approximately 100 children aged 6 to 12 on 12 domains of moral reasoning, which included lying. An analysis of their responses across all of the domains led Piaget to identify two distinct styles of moral reasoning. The first style, moral objectivity, was displayed by children until approximately age 8. Younger children focused on the visible, external events and sanctions that led to lies being equated with curses and mistakes, and their wrongness measured in proportion to their consequences. The second subjective style of moral reasoning focused on inner processes such as the liar's intention to deceive. Piaget found age differences for evaluations and definitions of untruths. Specifically, young children were more willing than older children to define swearing, mistaken guesses, and exaggerations as lies. In addition, they gave harsher ratings than did older children to untrue statements that were unintentional as compared to deliberate (Peterson, Peterson, & Seeto, 1983).

Bussey and Grimbeek (2000) investigated young children's conceptions of lying and truth-telling. Children were presented with vignettes that depicted a character either lying or telling the truth about committing a misdeed. Four-year-olds correctly classified 88% of true statements as truths and false statements as lies, while 7- and 10-year-olds were completely correct 100% of the time. Children of all ages rated lies more negatively than truths; however, 4-year-olds were less likely to appreciate the goodness of telling the truth over lying than were the 7- and 10-year-olds, who rated truths more positively than lies.

The trend toward increasing honesty and integrity throughout childhood does not necessarily continue in adolesence. A Gallup Poll of 501 American teenagers aged 13 to 17, conducted in January through April 2000, provides a glimpse of the prevalence of cheating among American teens (Gallup News Service, 2000). In a randomly selected national sample, 44% of American teens admit to having cheated on a test or exam. This rate rises to 53% for older teens. Furthermore, 63% report that cheating goes on "a great deal" or "a fair amount." Equally disturbing, almost half of the teens surveyed do not regard cheating as a very serious matter.

In a study of moral integrity, Olson (1998) failed to find differences between adolescent and adult scores on the Moral Integrity Survey. Adolescents and adults shared similar feelings, behaviors, and thoughts on their moral integrity. Thus, developmental differences between adolescents and adults on moral integrity were not supported by this study.

One of the best models of the development of integrity is provided by identity status theory (Marcia, 1994; Waterman, 1999). According to this theory, in the ideal case, adolescents progress from a foreclosed identity status (in which they mirror the ambitions and values of important others without questioning them); through a moratorium status (in which they question their former sense of identity, exploring the options preparatory to making an informed choice); to an achieved identity status (in which they have consciously committed to an identity). Along the way they may or may not spend time in a diffused identity status, in which they reject or ignore the problem of identity formation. For example, the son of a surgeon may first assume unquestioningly that he, too, will attend medical school (foreclosed status); when he reaches college, he may begin having new experiences that call this assumption into question (moratorium status); and he may finally decide that his talents and interests lie more in music or the arts. If the father is too resistant or unbending, the son may drop out for a time, eschewing achievement concerns altogether (diffused status).

In terms of the self as a more or less accurate theory, those who reach the achieved identity status have likely succeeded in creating a self that correctly represents their implicit goals, talents, and values. In contrast, those who remain in the foreclosed status may cling to a more fictional self that does not correctly represent their actual interests and potentials, and which is thus inauthentic. Rogerian theory provides one way of understanding why someone may remain stuck in a foreclosed identity, namely, because important mentors approve of the adolescent only when he or she conforms to the mentors' own desires and expectations.

Another appealing model, provided by Harter (1999; Harter & Monsour, 1992), draws on cognitive-developmental theory, proposing that the creation of an adequate self requires the ability to recognize conflicting traits in the self and to resolve those conflicts via higher order abstractions. For example, an early adolescent may feel distress over being talkative with friends but shy with the opposite sex. Later, with the arrival of formal operational thinking, her self-theory evolves to include the fact that, although one's behavior may differ in different situations, there are reasons for this, and one is still the same person underneath. From this perspective, intelligence or cognitive ability may be a crucial determinant of integrity. One limitation of this perspective, however, is that many people with little education or intelligence seem to have selves of obvious integrity, authenticity, and honesty. This implies that integrity may be determined by values and life experience as much as by cognitive ability, although little research has examined this question.

■ Enabling and Inhibiting Factors

Parents can encourage honesty in their children. When children commit wrongdoings, the severity of their anticipated punishment will influence whether they will confess or lie about their transgression. Parents can discourage their children from lying about transgressions by emphasizing that the punishment for lying will be harsher than the punishment for the transgression (Quinn, 1988). While parents can encourage their children to be honest, they also directly and indirectly inform them that deception is socially appropriate. For example, parents directly tell children to pretend to like a gift, even if they do not. Children indirectly learn about deception from their parents' behavior. For example, a parent may act happy to see a neighbor, but prior to the neighbor's arrival, expressed a desire not to see him or her (Lewis, Stanger, & Sullivan, 1989).

We seem to know more about how to inhibit this character strength than how to enable it. For example, children respond more dishonestly to an honesty dilemma when they discuss it with peers than when they are asked to respond without peer corroboration. Peer corroboration seems to encourage decisions based on self-interest and ones that are less honest than decisions produced by the child alone (Austin et al., 1991).

Psychosocial stressors, including divorce, abuse, and neglect, may also promote lying in children. Children may lie by commission or omission to please an abusive parent. For these children, skillful lying can be necessary for survival, as detection may prompt further abuse. Family attitudes and actions concerning lying provide children with models for their behavior (Quinn, 1988).

As noted, controlling or insensitive social contexts, which do not take individuals' perspectives and needs into account, may lead to inauthentic behavior. To know oneself properly, one may need to be known by others. Inauthenticity is also promoted when mentors and authorities provide only contingent positive regard, without taking into sufficient account the mentee's own needs and potentials. For example, as mentioned earlier, parents pushing their children too hard to become athletes or doctors may promote the development of false selves in those children. Consumer culture may also give rise to inauthentic behavior, by promoting the message that one is valuable or successful only if one has the right look, job, or possessions. Many people fall prey to these messages, thus failing to find richer sources of meaning in their lives (T. Kasser, 2002). Finally, cultural norms and practices may de-emphasize authentic self-portrayal. Expectations for uncritical social conformity (e.g., "America, love it or leave it") and the imperatives of mass culture (e.g., thinness, consumerism, fashion, or sports idolatry) make it difficult to develop integrity. They either work against self-reflection or create a schism between individual recognition and expression of self and social approbation. At a more deleterious level, stigma, bigotry, and discrimination can circumscribe opportunities for authentic living for entire groups. Accordingly, multiculturalism and diversity awareness may provide social support for development of individual integrity. A pluralistic society contributes to self-acceptance, acceptance of others, and congruence between sense of self and action in the world. At their best. multiculturalism and diversity awareness are part of a safe environment in which individuals can live authentically (Flowers & Richardson, 1996).

■ Gender, Cross-National, and Cross-Cultural Aspects

Little empirical work has been conducted specifically with the construct of authenticity, and thus little is known about gender differences. Harter (1999) evaluated the question of whether women suppress or fail to develop "voice." She found that woman per se are no less likely to have voice, but that participants (male and female) with more feminine gender identities were somewhat less likely to have voice. Research on self-determination theory's construct of psychological autonomy, which is similar to authenticity, has sometimes found gender differences such that women feel more autonomy. This difference is inconsistent, however, perhaps because of canceling forces: Women may be more attentive to their inner emotions and needs, but they also exist in a socio-cultural context in which their autonomy may be less supported, leading to weak effects overall. Again, as suggested by Harter's work, experienced autonomy may depend more on the person's gender identity than on physical sex.

Deci and Ryan (2000) argued that autonomy is a universal psychological need, and some data support this hypothesis. For example, autonomous goal pursuit was associated with well-being in a South Korean as well as in a U.S. sample (Sheldon et al., 2003), and autonomous classroom motivation was linked to academic adjustment in Japan just as in the United States (Hayamizu, 1997; Tanaka & Yamauchi, 2000). Nevertheless, substantial data also suggest that mean levels of psychological authenticity may vary across cultures. In general, Asian cultures give less emphasis to the self as an independent entity, viewing it as more determined by social contexts and relationships (Markus, Kitayama, & Heiman, 1996). Such cultures also give less emphasis to self-consistency. For example, Cross, Kanagawa, Markus, and Kitayama (1995) showed that Japanese participants gave very different self-descriptions in different contexts; Suh (2001) showed that members of a Korean sample suffered less from such self-fragmentation; and Iwao (1997) showed that Japanese participants were much less likely than U.S. participants to voice their real thoughts during a disagreement.

Taken together, these findings may suggest that sincere and honest self-presentation is less important in Asian cultures. However, this does not mean that Asian selves have less integrity or that they betray their deeper values and commitments. Instead, it only indicates that their values and sources of authenticity are different. It is also important to remember that inconsistency is not the same thing as inauthenticity, as one may vary one's behavior from setting to setting and still own that behavior. This would seem to be the case in Asian cultures, which have elaborate vocabularies for describing the person-in-setting. From C. R. Rogers's (1961) perspective, the problems of inauthenticity arise not because a person hides his real emotional reactions from others (as may sometimes be appropriate) but because he hides them from himself. Notably, however, cultural contexts that frown too strictly on self-expression may tend to discourage development of the ability to notice and articulate one's own subtler responses. This may limit artistic achievement and/or creative innovation within such cultures (Lubart, 1999).

■ Deliberate Interventions

There is no shortage of interventions that attempt to cultivate this character strength, although only a few have been empirically evaluated. Cassey and Burton (1982) assessed the effectiveness of verbal self-instructions for training first- and fourth-grade children to be honest. Children were instructed using three levels of generality: do-don't (most specific), cheating (more general), and honesty (most general). Interestingly, results indicated that employing the most general training term, *honesty*, was most effective in promoting generalized honest behavior.

Among youth development programs that intend to encourage integrity and honesty, we have the Boy Scouts of America (see http://www.scouting.org/nav/about.html); the World Association of Girl Guides and Girl Scouts (see http://www.gsusa.org/about/gsprogram.html); the Children's Defense Fund (see http://www.childrensdefense.org/moral-start.htm); and Girls Incorporated (see http://www.girlsinc.org). Systematic evaluations of the effects of these programs on the targeted traits do not yet exist.

Some attention has been paid to the possibility that authenticity is amenable to coaching (Chessick, 1996). Authenticity coaching represents a nonmedicalized, nonstigmatizing form of psychological assistance aimed at self-enhancement for personal effectiveness. It has been popular in the business sector, but convincing outcome research does not exist.

Spiritual practice, particularly Zen, Taoism, and other approaches entailing meditation, reflection, and enlightenment, has also been proposed as contributing to integrity (Rahilly, 1993). Along these lines, "authentic" educational practice attempts to integrate thinking, feeling, and acting (Leahy, 1986) by disrupting the unidirectional flow of information from the teacher to the students and thereby provide opportunities for student expression and exploration that help establish integrity (Harter, Waters, & Whitesell, 1997). Again, convincing outcome research does not exist.

Client-centered psychotherapy, still employed in many counseling settings and practices, is the prototypical example of an intervention designed to enhance integrity (C. R. Rogers, 1971). This approach assumes that clients have lost contact with, or failed to develop contact with, their true feelings and beliefs. Often this occurs because the client is committed to a limited or inaccurate self-concept, which would be threatened by recognizing his or her underlying feelings. In Epstein's (1973) terms, the person may be overly committed to an inaccurate self-theory, just as a scientist may be overcommitted to a pet theory that no longer seems to fit the facts. In such interventions the therapist tries to model honest responding for the client, showing that the truth is preferable even when it is painful. The therapist also attempts to give the client unconditional positive regard, showing the client that he or she can express himself or herself honestly and still maintain the therapist's respect. Over time, the client develops a new view of himself or herself, one more adequate to his or her actual feelings and personality (C. R. Rogers, 1961).

Little intervention work has taken the form of a true experiment. However, Sheldon, Kasser, Smith, and Share (2002) made one such attempt, creating a two-session intervention designed to help typical undergraduates to increase ownership of their personal goals. Although the experimental treatment did not affect measured self-concordance directly, the researchers found a significant interaction such that participants who were already striving for more self-concordant reasons derived substantial goal-attainment benefits from the intervention. This in turn led to even greater self-concordance for these advantaged participants, suggesting that the intervention helped the strong get stronger. Thus, again, it appears that authentic persons are poised for upward spirals. Unfortunately, those striving for *in*authentic reasons within Sheldon et al.'s (2002) study did not benefit from the brief intervention. This suggests that self-selection into the intervention, and/or a longer or more effective intervention, may be necessary for the weak to get stronger.

■ What Is Not Known?

The idea that human beings struggle for greater integrity is one that rings true for most people, even though it is difficult to define. We can all recognize the plight of Holden Caulfield, the protagonist of *Catcher in the Rye*, who deplored the phonies he encountered. Despite its compelling intuitive meaning, the question of what being authentic (or true to oneself) really means remains elusive. The following presents just a sampling of the lingering issues.

The problem of evil is one significant challenge for the concept. Can an evil person be authentic? Perhaps some people must behave manipulatively or aggressively in order to be true to themselves. C. R. Rogers (1971) disagreed, arguing that humans have a naturally positive nature until it is obscured by negative experience. Rogers also pointed out that a criminal who experiences success in therapy does not thereby become a better criminal but instead finds more productive ways of being. From our own perspective, evil people can be authentic; that is, their sense of self can be true to their antisocial motives and personality dispositions. However, these people are unlikely to thrive because their motives and personality dispositions are incongruent with positive human nature and universal psychological needs. Still, developing a self that accurately represents one's personality may be an important first step in changing that personality—evil people who realize who they have become may then be motivated to become something different.

Another issue is the problem of the referent—to what is the authentic person being true? Considerable confusion can arise when people say, "I must be true to myself," because it is not clear if by "self" they mean "my concept of myself and my conscious commitments" or "my underlying personality and needs." The very concept of inauthenticity implies that these two things can be out of alignment, although the person need not be aware of this. Perhaps these two ways of being true to oneself actually represent two somewhat different forms of integrity, as one can imagine a person who in her behavior is true to a false concept of herself, while being false to her true personality (i.e., an extroverted woman fails to express her beliefs because her culture trains her to think that women have nothing to say). Indeed, a double negative may apply, in that in some cases being false to one's false self-concept may be a route to heightened growth and adaptation! Furthermore, if one considers universal positive human nature as a third level underlying both personality dispositions and the self-theory, then the possible combinations of truth and falsehood (or match and mismatch) become complex indeed!

Philosophical conundrums aside, empirically we still need to know much more about the neural and cognitive bases of authentic and inauthentic behavior. As we suggested, it is likely that deeply self-deceived or self-divided persons manifest distinctive patterns of neural activity (such as reduced activation in the left frontal lobe, or multiple distinct and inconsistent functional profiles; Damasio, 1999), which remain to be charted. We also need to know more about the conditions that both promote and prevent authentic self-experience and self-development. For example, some have argued that trauma and loss are actually beneficial for the development of psychological depth (Simonton, 1999b). Thus, it will be important to find out what kinds and amounts of challenge best help young people to develop authentic personal identities, without overwhelming this vital process. Finally, it will be important to link feelings of psychological integrity with behavioral and observer-based measures of honesty and authenticity. Although theory implies that these should be intercorrelated, the data remain to be collected.

■ Must-Read Articles and Books

Baumeister, R. (1987). How the self became a problem: A psychological review of historical research. *Journal of Personality and Social Psychology, 52,* 163–176.

Bussey, K. (1992). Lying and truthfulness: Children's definitions, standards, and evaluative reactions. *Child Development, 63,* 129–137.

Deci, E. L., & Ryan, R. M. (2000). The "what" and "why" of goal pursuits: Human needs and the self-determination of behavior. *Psychological Inquiry, 4,* 227–268.

Epstein, S. (1973). The self-concept revisited: Or a theory of a theory. *American Psychologist, 28,* 404–416.

Harter, S. (1999). *The construction of the self: A developmental perspective.* New York: Guilford Press.

Laing, R. D. (1960). *The divided self.* Harmondsworth, UK: Penguin.

Piaget, J. (1932/1965). *The moral judgment of the child.* New York: Free Press.

Rogers, C. R. (1961). *On becoming a person: A therapist's view of psychotherapy.* Boston, MA: Houghton Mifflin.

Sheldon, K. M. (2002). The self-concordance model of healthy goal-striving: When personal goals correctly represent the person. In E. L. Deci & R. M. Ryan (Eds.), *Handbook of self-determination research* (pp. 65–86). Rochester, NY: University of Rochester Press.

Sheldon, K. M., Ryan, R. M., Rawsthorne, L., & Ilardi, B. (1997). "True" self and "trait" self: Cross-role variation in the Big Five traits and its relations with authenticity and well-being. *Journal of Personality and Social Psychology, 73,* 1380–1393.

Trilling, L. (1972). *Sincerity and authenticity.* Cambridge, MA: Harvard University Press.

Waterman, A. S. (1999). Identity, the identity statuses, and identity status development: A contemporary statement. *Developmental Review, 19,* 591–621.

12. VITALITY

[Zest, Enthusiasm, Vigor, Energy]

A vital person is someone whose aliveness and spirit are expressed not only in personal productivity and activity—such individuals often infectiously energize those with whom they come into contact.

■ *Such a person is Doug Newberg, PhD, founder of Resonance, a group that consults with business, sport, and public organizations to enhance individual and group performance. Both Doug's life and his work reflect vitality and vigor. Doug himself was a top sport performer, playing with one of the winningest basketball teams in NCAA history. Years later he remains an active athlete, not only in basketball but in biking, roller blading, boating, running, snowboarding, and hiking. As he says, it's not about health or fitness but about enriched living. Equally active is his generative work, helping others reach their potential and perform at their optimal levels. His consultations are based not only on his own knowledge but on that gleaned from continuous investigation of top performers in myriad fields of activity, from entrepreneurs to musicians, from scholars to athletes. He loves his work, even on the most challenging of days. Doug reflectively attempts to live authentically, and engender that authenticity and mindfulness in others by connecting deeply with them, their goals, and their concerns. In so doing, he exudes energy and catalyzes it in those around him. Indeed, for Doug, resonance means authentic attunement and engagement with life, and from that process he derives the excitement and integrity that fuel his own vitality, vigor, and performance, as well as that of others.* ■

■ Consensual Definition

Vitality describes a dynamic aspect of well-being marked by the subjective experience of energy and aliveness (R. M. Ryan & Frederick, 1997). As an indicator of organismic wellness, vitality is directly and interactively related to both psychological and somatic factors. At the somatic level, vitality is linked to good physical health and bodily functioning, as well as freedom from fatigue and illness. At the psychological level, vitality reflects experiences of volition, effectance, and integration of the self at both intrapersonal and interpersonal levels. Psychological tensions, conflicts, and stressors detract from experienced vitality.

Individuals with a high level of vitality would strongly endorse such statements as these:

- I feel alive and vital.
- I have energy and spirit.
- I nearly always feel awake and alert.
- I feel energized.
- I feel full of pep.
- I rarely feel worn out.

A person who is vital is energetic and fully functioning. As a description of an organismic state, vitality is a dynamic phenomenon, pertinent to both mental and physical aspects of functioning. This dual nature of vitality is reflected in its definition as "mental and physical vigor" (*New Merriam Webster Dictionary*, 1989). At a deeper level vitality refers to feeling alive. The word is derived from *vita*, or "life," such that one who is vital feels alive, enthusiastic, and spirited. A person feels such aliveness when physically well, when psychologically integrated rather than fragmented, and when he or she experiences meaning and purpose rather than feeling lost, disconnected, or aimless.

Although vitality is related to energy, simply using the word *energy* as a synonym for *vitality* can be a bit misleading because vitality entails only energy experienced as positive and available to the self (Nix, Ryan, Manly, & Deci, 1999). Someone who is tense, angry, or jittery is energized but not necessarily vital. Indeed, some forms of activation are draining rather than vitalizing, such as the arousal and nervousness associated with intrapsychic or interpersonal conflict. Accordingly, the presence of such states has been negatively associated with subjective vitality in empirical studies (R. M. Ryan & Frederick, 1997). Nervous energy due to overarousal or caffeine similarly exemplifies a tense energy state that can and must be distinguished from true vitality (Thayer, 1996).

Although vitality represents a positive emotional state, it is more specific than happiness and has distinct determinants and correlates (Nix et al., 1999). Vitality is an activated positive emotion and thus differs from happiness per se, which can include nonactivated states such as contentment, pleasure, satisfaction, and so on. Those with vitality also exhibit enthusiasm, which they direct toward whatever activities they choose to engage.

Finally, it is clear that the energy associated with vitality is distinct from caloric energy (Selye, 1956); caloric intake, except when extremely low, is largely unrelated to vitality. Ingestion of calories can sometimes decrease vitality

(Thayer, 1996), and at times caloric output (e.g., physical exertion) can actually increase vitality (A. M. Myers et al., 1999).

Vigor is a word with similar meanings, being derived from the idea of liveliness. The *New Merriam Webster Dictionary* (1989) defines *vigor* as "active strength or energy of body or mind," reflecting that it, like vitality, refers to both somatic and psychological wellness. That which invigorates also vitalizes, and thus we treat these terms as equivalent constructs.

■ Theoretical Traditions

Concepts of organismic energy and vitality have been central topics in a variety of Eastern philosophies and healing traditions. Prominent among them is the ancient Chinese concept of *chi*, which represents, in part, a vital force or energy that is the source of life, creativity, right action, and harmony. A similar concept in Japan, *Ki,* refers to the energy and power one has available to draw on and is related to physical, mental, and spiritual health. Balinese healers refer to the concept of *bayu*, a vital spiritual or life force underlying growth and resistance to illness. The notion of vitality is also apparent in the numerous health practices intended to increase the influence of vital energies. Acupuncture, reiki, and yoga exemplify such approaches, and in each, vitality represents an active inner force that facilitates both mental and physical health and performance (Cleary, 1991).

Western scholarship has also addressed vitality. Freud's (1923) well-known economic model links the individual's experience of conflict-free energy to psychological health. According to this psychodynamic model, each individual has a finite amount of libido, or psychic energy, to invest. The more that the individual is free of repression and conflict, in the view of Freud and later ego psychologists, the greater is the individual's access to this energy and, hence, the greater the ego strength, and the vitality and creativity associated with it (Hartmann, 1958). Although Jung, Reich, Winnicott, Perls, and other psychodynamic theorists differed in the details of their energy models, they all converged on the idea that psychological conflict resolution and integration are connected to greater availability of energy to the self—or vitality—whereas repression, stress, and conflict detract from it.

Hans Selye (1956), in his theory of stress, also discussed energy and linked it to health, though he focused his theory at more of a biological than a psychological level. He posited that every individual possesses a limited reservoir of adaptation energy that is critical to the maintenance of health. Distinct from caloric energy, adaptation energy nevertheless is required when an individual is faced with physiological and environmental stressors. If this energy source is depleted, the individual is susceptible to physiological damage.

R. M. Ryan and Deci (2000) reintroduced the concept of vitality as part of their self-determination theory. According to the theory, humans have inherent or intrinsic energies that are either facilitated or hindered in their expression by various factors associated with psychological needs (Deci & Ryan, 2000). Specifically, vitality is conceptualized as a critical index of eudaimonic (as opposed to hedonic) well-being. That is, vitality is seen as reflecting an individual's being fully functioning and self-realized as opposed to merely being happy or pleased (R. M. Ryan & Deci, 2001). In the self-determination theory view, vitality is catalyzed by circumstances in which a person can express all aspects of his or her functioning, which requires that basic physical and psychosocial needs are supported, including the needs for autonomy, competence, and relatedness. Vitality is diminished when social contexts engender feelings of ineffectance, disconnection, or those associated with heteronomy such as alienation or being controlled.

These theoretical perspectives have recently been complemented by empirical approaches to vitality that involve well-validated and reliable self-report questionnaires, and studies have explored the correlates and consequences of the constructs. These approaches commonly assume that vitality is a phenomenologically accessible and salient issue—that people can readily report feelings concerning the energy they possess. These approaches also agree that vitality is affected by both mental and physical factors. This means that one's vitality can be influenced by psychological factors such as feelings of conflict versus volition, or by physical factors such as illness states, fatigue, or diet. Some empirical studies of vitality have, however, focused more on psychological inputs, and others on physical ones.

Research by Thayer (1996, 2001) addressed the topic of energy using an explicitly biopsychological model. He emphasized that it is impossible to disentangle mental and bodily states: A change in one will have an effect on the other, as well as on energy and mood. In his model, Thayer (1989, 1996) described two bipolar arousal continua, one ranging from energy to tiredness, the other from tense to calm. In keeping with the biopsychological model, Thayer considered these two measures of arousal to encompass central bodily states that also have conscious components (Thayer, Newman, & McClain, 1994). In describing moods, he linked these two continua to describe states such as calm–energy or tense–tiredness. The state he labeled calm–energy comes closest to the concept of vitality, as in this state one feels energetic and vigorous yet focused and in control of the energy one possesses. Thayer (1996) described this state as the ideal most of us would like to achieve. Thayer has used this conceptual and measurement model as a foundation for research into the dynamics of mood and arousal. He has especially emphasized the relations of energy-related moods to diurnal rhythms, diet, drugs, exercise, and other aspects of health behaviors.

Drawing on self-determination theory, R. M. Ryan and Frederick (1997) developed a theory and measure of subjective vitality defined as a positive feeling of aliveness and of having energy available to the self. The measure of subjective vitality has been validated in both trait and state forms, and therefore can be used to look both at individual differences between people and at factors over time that affect changes in vitality within the person. Akin to Thayer's biopsychological view of energy, subjective vitality is conceived of as an "organismic" concept, such that physical and psychological factors can interactively affect it. Ryan and Frederick (1997) provided evidence for this standpoint by demonstrating that individual differences in subjective vitality are associated with differences in health, lifestyle (e.g., smoking), and physical and mental illness. Similarly, they showed that people with chronic pain report less vitality than do matched comparisons. However, the extent to which pain saps vitality was also predicted and shown to be moderated by the individual's perception of control over the pain.

In addition, Ryan and Frederick proposed that subjective vitality is directly influenced by fulfillment or deprivation with regard to basic psychological needs for autonomy, competence, and relatedness (R. M. Ryan & Deci, 2000). In a number of studies, their measure of subjective vitality has been associated at both between- and within-person levels of analysis with variations in need fulfillment. For instance, Kasser and Ryan (1999) related individual differences in vitality to issues of volition or autonomy in an elderly nursing home sample. Reis, Sheldon, Gable, Roscoe, and Ryan (2000) showed in diary-based studies how all three psychological needs contribute to the prediction of within-person daily changes in subjective vitality, and Nix et al. (1999) showed in experimental studies that whereas task success can produce happiness, only success at autonomously motivated tasks maintained or enhanced vitality. Finally, in new research, Bernstein and Ryan (2001) argued that subjective vitality can be affected by contact with nature. They demonstrated within-individual changes in subjective vitality as a function of contact with outdoor natural environments as compared with human-made or artificial contexts.

Penninx et al. (2000) focused on some related psychological factors in their construct of emotional vitality, which they defined as (a) having a high sense of personal mastery, (b) being happy, (c) having low depressive symptomatology, and (d) having low anxiety. They considered their measure of emotional vitality to be a comprehensive indicator of emotional vigor and have used it in studies of disabled older women (Penninx et al., 1998). Selecting this combination of emotional variables to represent emotional vitality rests on the assumption that each contributes a separate and distinct component to overall emotional functioning. In both their research and theorizing, the focus of Penninx and colleagues has been on factors associated with emotional vitality in the face of aging and physical disability.

■ Measures

Vitality is clearly a complex construct reflecting positive physical and mental well-being, and measurements of it can emphasize different components. Because the researchers who have designed scales to measure vitality have had different emphases, there exist several different assessments of vitality or vigor, each measuring a slightly different construct. We review six selected measures that have shown both empirical and practical utility (Table 12.1).

All these assessments are based on structured self-reports. Some rely on adjective ratings, whereas others incorporate structured questions concerning energy, enthusiasm, anergia, and related issues. Because vitality is generally defined as phenomenally accessible, the use of self-report seems particularly appropriate in this sphere.

Profile of Mood States (POMS)

One of the first measures of vitality was reported by McNair, Lorr, and Droppleman (1971), who stimulated work on the concept through their development of the 65–item Profile of Mood States, a widely used measure of six mood or affective states that takes about 5 minutes to complete. The POMS contains a subscale of interest here labeled vigor-activity. Eight adjectives make up this subscale (*lively*, *active*, *energetic*, *cheerful*, *alert*, *full of pep*, *carefree*, and *vigorous*). Participants rate each adjective in terms of how strongly they have felt it during the past week, including the current day, on a 5–point scale ranging from 0 (not at all) to 4 (extremely). The POMS is factor analytically derived, and all six factors (subscales) have been reliably identified, measured, and replicated in populations of Veterans Administration male psychiatric outpatients, male college students, and male and female outpatients at a teaching institution. This factor structure holds up even if the rating period is altered to measure feelings "right now," that is, when the POMS is used as a state measure. Based on the validation samples, the original authors recommended that the POMS be used as a measure of mood states and changes in mood states in psychiatric outpatients, as well as for research purposes for normal subjects aged 18 and older who have some high school education (McNair et al., 1971). Since its origin, the POMS has been used in a wide variety of studies.

The internal consistency (alpha coefficient) of the vigor-activity factor is approximately .88; test–retest reliability for 3 weeks is .65, and for 5 weeks, .43. However, these test–retest indices probably correspond to the lower bound of the subscale's reliability, as they were obtained from a sample entering outpatient treatment at a psychiatric center: Mood states, including vitality, hopefully would change in the context of treatment. Indeed, such fluctuations underscore the dynamic nature of a variable such as vitality, rather than any lack of validity.

In terms of construct validity, vigor-activity scores have been shown to be significantly lower during periods of prolonged drinking (Nathan, Zare, Ferneau, & Lowenstein, 1970): A group receiving psychotherapy over a brief 4-week period showed a trend for improvement in vigor (Lorr, McNair, &

TABLE 12.1 *Measures of Vitality and Vigor*

Profile of Mood States (POMS)

    McNair, Lorr, & Droppleman (1971)

    This is a self-report questionnaire composed of 65 adjectives, 8 of which assess the subscale vigor-activity, a mood of vigorousness and high energy; respondents rate each adjective on a 0–4 scale. Ratings are usually done according to how one has felt "during the past week including today," but can also be used to measure feelings "right now."

- Internal reliability (alpha coefficients): ~.88
- Test–retest reliability: ~.65 (3 weeks); ~.43 (6 weeks)
- Construct validity: lower during periods of prolonged drinking; improved in group receiving brief (4-week) therapy; significant and negative correlations with measures of depression, anxiety, and somatization

Activation–Deactivation Adjective Check List (AD ACL)

    Thayer (1967, 1978)

    This self-report questionnaire is composed of 20 items, 10 of which assess the energy–tiredness continuum, and 10 the tension–calmness continuum; respondents rate each adjective on a 4-point scale according to how they feel "at this moment." High scores on both energy and calmness correspond to an arousal state called calm-energy, which is analogous to vitality.

- Internal reliability (alpha coefficients): information unavailable
- Test–retest reliability: ~.79–.93 (when checklist completed twice in immediate sequence)
- Construct validity: factor analytic studies show two bipolar activation dimensions rather than four independent activation factors

Short-Form Health Survey (SF-36)

    Ware & Sherbourne (1992)

    Self-report questionnaire composed of 36 items, 4 of which assess the vitality subscale, a measurement of energy level and fatigue. Respondents rate items on a 6-point scale.

- Internal reliability (alpha coefficients): ~.87
- Test–retest reliability: information unavailable
- Construct validity: the scale has been shown to correlate moderately with both physical and mental health components in a test of construct validity using psychometric criteria; using clinical criteria, scale scores were shown to decrease with decrements in health status, with patients with serious medical and psychiatric conditions scoring significantly lower than those with more minor medical or psychiatric problems; the subscale has been shown to be sensitive to the impact of disease and treatment in patients with hypertension, prostate disease, and AIDS

Emotional Vitality (EV)

    Penninx et al. (1998)

    This is a self-report measure that categorically assesses for emotional vitality in disabled older (65+ years) women; to be emotionally vital, respondents

(continued)

TABLE 12.1   *Measures of Vitality and Vigor* (*continued*)

must endorse (a) feelings of mastery on two items rated on a scale of 1 to 4; (b) score 8 or higher on a 1–10 rating of happiness; (c) score below a predetermined cutoff score of 10 on a 30-item Geriatric Depression Scale; and (d) have indicated no more than one of four rated symptoms of anxiety.

- Internal reliability (alpha coefficients): information unavailable
- Test–retest reliability: information unavailable
- Construct validity: emotionally vital older women have been shown to have the best health status, and older women possessing EV showed reduced risk over a 3-year period for new disability and mortality; EV is more strongly associated with disability level than with age, and in a population of older, disabled women the percentage of emotionally vital individuals decreased as severity of disability increased; EV women shown to more often have the support of a confidant, received adequate emotional support, and had fewer negative life events during the past year

Vitality Plus Scale (VPS)

Myers et al. (1999)

This self-report questionnaire was designed to assess the psychological and physical benefits of exercising in older adults. It is composed of 10 items, which respondents rate on a 1–5 scale according to how they are "currently" feeling.

- Internal reliability (alpha coefficients): ~.82
- Test–retest reliability: ~.87 (1 week over which participants did not change patterns of activity)
- Construct validity: correlates –.45 with total number of self-reported health problems and also inversely correlated with being overweight, using medications, and being limited in type or amount of physical activity; positively correlated with current level of physical activity

Subjective Vitality Scale (SVS)

R. M. Ryan & Frederick (1997)

This is a self-report questionnaire composed of seven items that reflect positive feelings of aliveness and energy available to the self, which respondents rate on a 7-point scale. SV can be measured as either a trait or a state variable.

- Internal consistency: ranges from .80 to .94 in various studies
- Test–retest reliability: .64 (8 weeks)
- Construct validity: when used as a trait measure, correlates negatively with depression, anxiety, general psychopathology, negative affect, and physical symptoms; correlates positively with life satisfaction, self-actualization, positive affect, physical self-efficacy, and body-functioning self-esteem; of all six subscales of the POMS, the SVS correlates most highly with vigor-activity, and negatively with fatigue and depression; when used as a state measure, relates to daily fluctuations of both psychological and physical variables

Weinstein, 1964), and compared with patients treated with placebo, those treated with chlordiazepoxide (Librium) have shown significantly greater increases in vigor (McNair, Goldstein, Lorr, Cibelli, & Roth, 1965). In tests of concurrent validity (McNair et al., 1971), the vigor scale was shown to have significant and negative correlations with measures of depression, anxiety, and somatization. Vigor-activity also is negatively related to the other POMS scales representing depression, tension, anger, fatigue, and confusion. Finally, using the Crowne and Marlowe (1960) test of social desirability, a relatively low correlation with vigor was found (.33).

The Activation–Deactivation Adjective Check List (AD ACL)

At much the same time, Thayer (1967, 1978) developed his own adjective checklist to have a simple, rapid way to assess momentary states of arousal or activation. His self-report questionnaire, the AD ACL, measures arousal using four variables that represent two orthogonal and bipolar arousal dimensions. Participants rate the AD ACL adjectives on a somewhat unique 4-point scale which includes these response alternatives: definitely do not feel; feel slightly; cannot decide; and definitely feel. However, Thayer (1986) demonstrates that other rating scales may be used without harm to the factor structure. The full 20-item scale takes less than 60 seconds to complete.

At the high end of one of these two arousal continua is a variable named *energy*, which consists of five adjectives: *lively, energetic, active, vigorous,* and *full of pep.* At its low end is tiredness, a state of low arousal represented by the adjectives *sleepy, drowsy, tired, wide-awake* (reversed), and *wakeful* (reversed). Representing the high end of the other arousal continuum is a third variable labeled *tension,* characterized by the adjectives *jittery, intense, fearful, clutched-up,* and *tense.* Finally, anchoring the low end of this second arousal continuum is the variable calmness, which comprises the following adjectives: *quiet, placid, still, at-rest,* and *calm.* An individual who scores high on energy and calmness would be considered to be in a state of calm-energy, a state Thayer identified as ideal (Thayer, 1996) and which Nix et al. (1999) argued was closest to that of vitality. The two arousal continua have been replicated repeatedly (Thayer, 1986).

Because test–retest reliability measuring any substantial period of time is of limited use when transient activation states are of concern, Thayer collected test–retest reliabilities for individuals who took the AD ACL twice in immediate sequence, so that their activation states were unlikely to have changed (Thayer, 1978). Using this method, Thayer reports test–retest reliability coefficients that ranged from 0.79 to 0.93, with a coefficient of 0.89 for the energy scale. Additional reliability estimates based on communalities were reported; energy was estimated to have a reliability of .92 using this method.

Short-Form Health Survey (SF-36)

Ware and Sherbourne (1992) developed the 36-item Short-Form Health Survey or SF-36, intended as a broad but brief standardized measure of physical and mental health constructs. It was constructed for use with diverse populations in areas such as health policy evaluations, general population surveys, and clinical research and practice. The SF-36 is composed of eight subscales, one of which is labeled vitality, intended to reflect general physical and mental well-being (McHorney, Ware, & Raczek, 1993). The following four items make up the vitality subscale:

- Did you feel full of pep?
- Did you have a lot of energy?
- Did you feel worn out? [reversed]
- Did you feel tired? [reversed]

Note that the adjectives contained in these four items all appear in at least one of the two previously mentioned scales. Note also that this scale uses fatigue and tiredness as the opposites of having energy.

Ware and Sherbourne (1992), reporting on the development of the SF-36, note that most of the items in the survey were adapted from health status assessment instruments that had been in use for between 20 and 40 years. The major criteria for selecting items for the new measure were corresponding full-length scales from two relevant earlier measures: The items selected for each of the SF-36 scales were intended to reproduce the "parent" scale as closely as possible. However, the criterion measure consisted of only six scales, with vitality being one of the new scales added so that the new measure would be better at capturing differences in subjective well-being. The four items selected for this scale are described as having an "impressive record of empirical validity" (Ware & Sherbourne, 1992, p. 477); were intentionally balanced between favorably and unfavorably worded items to reduce response set effects; and were intended to be heterogeneous for purposes of increased content and empirical validity.

McHorney et al. (1993) reported that the SF-36 vitality subscale "cross-loads" on factors representing both physical and mental health, as had been expected. However, in spite of a good convergent validity for physical and mental health effects, this scale of subjective general well-being converged across separate factors, leading the authors to describe it as having poor discriminant validity. Nonetheless, in tests of item-discriminant validity, each of the four vitality items routinely correlates more highly with its hypothesized scale than with any of the other seven scales (McHorney, Ware, Lu, & Sherbourne, 1994).

The internal consistency reliability coefficient is approximately .87 for the vitality subscale (McHorney et al., 1994). Responses to the vitality scale tend to be negatively skewed, but in an analysis of ceiling or floor response effects, neither appeared to be a problem (McHorney et al., 1994).

Emotional Vitality

Penninx et al. (1998) developed what they call a comprehensive indicator of emotional vitality appropriate to populations of older women. Emotional vitality is assessed by combining indices drawn from previous measures related to (a) personal mastery, (b) happiness, (c) depressive symptoms, and (d) symptoms of anxiety. The measure is categorical: A person is classified as either emotionally vital or not. Those categorized as emotionally vital must endorse feelings of mastery on two item items rated on 1–4 scales; score 8 or higher on a 1–10 rating of happiness; score below a predetermined cutoff score of 10 on a 30-item Geriatric Depression Scale; and have indicated no more than one of four rated symptoms of anxiety. These criteria were chosen for their face validity, as well as based on an "a priori hypothesis that each contributes separately to overall emotional functioning" (p. 809). In descriptive research, Penninx et al. (1998) showed that both age and health status are predictive of emotional vitality, though the latter shows a stronger association. Penninx et al. (2000) further showed over a 3-year period that possessing emotional vitality reduces risk among disabled women for subsequent new disabilities and mortality. Internal consistency and test–retest reliability coefficients for this scale are currently unavailable.

The Vitality Plus Scale

The Vitality Plus Scale was developed specifically to measure the psychological and physical benefits of exercising in older adults (A. M. Myers et al., 1999). To do this, these researchers wished to capture, in a brief instrument, "multiple, interrelated aspects of 'feeling good' relevant to the exercise experience" (p. 457). The 10 items in this scale, some of which parallel the content of items in previously existing measures such as the POMS and SF-36, focus mainly on physiological and somatic aspects of vitality, with participants rating items such as "Sleep poorly" to "Sleep well" and "Often have aches and pains" to "Have no aches and pains" on 5-point scales. There were also several cognitive or psychological items represented on continua such as "Often restless or agitated" to "Feel relaxed," and "Low energy level" to "Full of pep and energy." The scale was constructed to measure somewhat enduring patterns of sleep and energy level rather than moment-specific feelings; therefore, when answering the questions, subjects are instructed to respond in terms of how they usually feel in their current lives.

    The internal consistency of this scale is reported as .82, and item-total scores (the correlation between an item and the total score) range from 0.23 to 0.58; both support the homogeneity of the scale. Test–retest reliability was found to be .87 over a 1-week period in which all participants reported not having changed their normal patterns of activity.

In terms of construct validity, scores on the Vitality Plus Scale were inversely correlated with total number of self-reported health problems ($r = .45$), as well as with being overweight, using medications, and being limited in type or amount of physical activity due to illness, injury, and/or disability. Vitality Plus Scale scores were positively related to current level of physical activity, as well as to placing a high importance on regular physical activity. In a stepwise multiple regression, the three variables that emerged as the best predictors of Vitality Plus scores, together accounting for 30% of variance, were total number of health problems, perceived health status, and age.

The Subjective Vitality Scale

The phenomenon of subjective vitality has been examined both conceptually and empirically by Ryan and Frederick (1997). The theory behind the concept of subjective vitality is described earlier in this chapter; the SV scale was designed to measure this concept, and a series of studies was undertaken to empirically assess whether the scale measured what it was intended to theoretically.

From an initial pool of 19 items, a 7-item scale emerged that was deemed to reflect a phenomenological sense of aliveness and vitality. Participants rated these items on 7-point scales from 1 (not at all) to 7 (extremely) regarding their perceptions of how each item applies. Items are structured statements such as "I feel alive and vital," "I have energy and spirit," and "I nearly always feel awake and alert." The Subjective Vitality Scale was specifically formulated to pertain to energy and to avoid specific emotion adjectives and direct references to physical states, as both emotions and physical conditions are expected to be antecedents and correlates of fluctuations in vitality. Items were also factor analyzed in different studies along with items concerning (a) purposiveness and having goals and (b) happiness, to ensure the discriminant status of the vitality construct.

In the original validation studies, Ryan and Frederick found, in multiple samples, internal reliabilities (alphas) exceeding .80. Test-retest stability over an 8-week period for individuals who entered one of two physical activity programs was found to be .64. Recently, Bostic, Rubio, and Hood (2000) used structural equation modeling to examine further the Subjective Vitality Scale's item structure. They replicated the single-factor structure but also found that removing the one negatively worded item from the initial seven-item Subjective Vitality Scale produced a better fitting model. In addition, when they allowed the error between two of the remaining six items in this slightly more parsimonious scale to covary, their model displayed an even better fit. Notably, these researchers then cross-validated the preceding results with a separate sample. It appears that the retained six items represent the most efficient measure of subjective vitality.

The Subjective Vitality Scale, when used as a trait measure, has been correlated with both physical and mental health variables. Robust relations with mental health indices including depression, anxiety, life satisfaction, self-actu-alization, general psychopathology, positive and negative affect, and others have been established in college-age, adult, and elderly populations (Kasser & Ryan, 1999; R. M. Ryan & Frederick, 1997). In addition, when Ryan and Frederick (1997) related subjective vitality to the POMS subscales, subjective vitality cor-related most highly with vigor-activity, as expected, and was negatively associ-ated with fatigue and depression scales. There was no relation between subjective vitality and POMS anger, tension, and confusion subscales. On the physical side, subjective vitality has been related to physical symptoms in general and on a daily basis; to the experience of pain and its controllability; to physical self-ef-ficacy; and to body functioning self-esteem. In the context of a weight-loss pro-gram, change in vitality was related to change in body mass index (BMI), as well as greater exercise adherence (R. M. Ryan & Frederick, 1997).

As noted, a state version of the Subjective Vitality scale has also been em-ployed and in several published studies has been shown to be reliable and to relate to daily fluctuations of both psychological and physical variables (e.g., Reis et al., 2000; R. M. Ryan & Frederick, 1997; Sheldon, Ryan, & Reis, 1996). The Subjective Vitality scale can be accessed from the following Web site: http://www.selfdeterminationtheory.org.

■ Correlates and Consequences

The results obtained from across the various existing measures and the research programs associated with them bespeak the importance of vitality as a marker of optimal human functioning. It is clear that the experience of vitality is de-pendent on health, broadly defined, and that virtually any factor that affects health influences vitality. Thus, as already described, symptoms of physical ill-ness, disability, and immunological dysfunction have all been associated with lower vitality.

Moreover, even in the absence of manifest disability, health-related lifestyle behaviors can also affect vitality: Smoking, poor diet, and lack of exercise are all associated with lower subjective vitality (R. M. Ryan & Frederick, 1997). Thayer (1986), for example, has shown numerous times that moderate exer-cise—such as a brisk 10-minute walk—tends to increase subjective energy and, to a lesser extent, decrease tension for up to 2 hours after the exercise has been completed. Eating a small sugar snack, on the other hand, is associated with significantly higher tension just 30 minutes after the snack has been eaten. And although energy increases and tiredness decreases initially after the snack, both then reverse directions later so that by 2 hours after the snack, energy has de-creased and tiredness increased beyond what they were to begin with (Thayer, 1987). Such studies demonstrate the sensitivity of the state ratings to biological changes related to lifestyle behaviors.

At a strictly psychological level, vitality is associated with experiences of autonomy, effectance, and relatedness. For example, for individuals who participated in a weight-loss intervention, vitality was significantly positively correlated with autonomous reasons for continuing to participate in the program (R. M. Ryan & Frederick, 1997). Both trait-level (between-person) and day-level (within-person) competence scores have been shown to covary with vitality level (Sheldon et al., 1996). And relatedness to others can also affect vitality levels: Nursing home residents who had a greater number of different social contacts had significantly higher levels of vitality (Kasser & Ryan, 1999). Also in this study, both autonomous self-regulation and perception of staff autonomy support significantly predicted greater levels of vitality.

Nonetheless, vitality is complexly determined, a fact that is exemplified by those individuals who, in spite of physical disability or pain, maintain a sense of vitality. For example, in one sample of very old and severely disabled women, approximately 20% nonetheless possessed emotional vitality (Penninx et al., 1998). Ryan and Frederick (1997) showed that in a population suffering from debilitating pain, pain level per se did not detract from vitality. Instead, pain fright was negatively associated with vitality, as was attending treatment for external as opposed to internal reasons. Some of the factors that may influence one's sense of vitality and contribute to its resilience are one's feelings of personal causation, optimism, and perceptions of social support.

Vitality not only appears to be a correlate of health and well-being but also may actually contribute to it. That is, vitality may be a "protective factor," at least as regards subsequent mental and physical disability in older women.

Finally, vitality appears to be unrelated to gender, as none of the major measurement approaches have identified significant gender differences in validation studies. Although differences in vitality as a function of age have not been studied, vitality appears to be a salient variable in studies of all age groups and thus to be a useful indicator of health across the life span.

■ Enabling and Inhibiting Factors

Research summarized by Ryan and Frederick (1997) points to both physical and social-contextual factors that facilitate versus undermine vitality. On the physical side, illness, pain, and fatigue all inhibit vitality. In addition, smoking, poor diet, and lack of exercise are associated with lower vitality, though few casual studies have been done to examine how this association obtains. Hsiao and Thayer (1998) and Thayer (1987) reviewed several studies showing the influence of diet and exercise on energy.

Social contexts also influence vitality. In several studies, factors that are associated with support for autonomy have been shown to be positively associated with an individual's vitality (R. M. Ryan & Frederick, 1997). Nix et al.

(1999) and Thayer and Moore (1972) both provided experimental evidence showing how controlling contexts can undermine subjective energy or vitality. In addition, several field studies have linked the factors of autonomy and relatedness or intimacy to increased vitality (e.g., Reis et al., 2000).

■ Development

Most studies have examined individual differences within age-constrained samples. To date, no comprehensive life span studies have been accomplished, and longitudinal studies have been few. The developmental course of vitality is simply unknown. However, Thayer (2001) speculated that insofar as there may be age affects on energy, they may be the results of changes in activity levels and changes in metabolic rate, both of which have been empirically related to age.

■ Gender, Cross-National, and Cross-Cultural Aspects

Research to date has not found any consistent gender effects on measures of vitality, vigor, or energy. Regarding cross-cultural research, the Subjective Vitality Scale (R. M. Ryan & Frederick, 1997) has been used cross-culturally, and using structural equation modeling (T. D. Little, 1997) in several multinational samples, it has established construct equivalence against stringent criteria. Translations in German, Korean, Turkish, Bulgarian, French, and other languages exist. It is thus useful in cross-cultural research and comparisons. Translations also exist for Ware and Sherbourne's (1992) Short-Form Health Survey into Swedish, German, and Chinese (Bullinger, 1995; Fuh, Wang, Lu, Juang, & Lee, 2000; M. Sullivan, Karlsson, & Ware, 1995); and psychometric testing appears to support the cross-cultural application of these translations. A U.S.-Spanish version has also been created and evaluated for certain uses with Cuban-American subjects (Arocho & McMillan, 1998). Thayer (1996) reports that the AD ACL has been translated into several languages and has been successfully used cross-nationally. However, despite the international scope of research on energy, cross-cultural comparisons in levels of vitality have not to date been a focus of systematic research.

■ Deliberate Interventions

Vitality is a preferred human state, and people often seek out restorative contexts in which to recover vitality and energy. One example is contact with nature, which appears to have an influence on subjective vitality (Bernstein & Ryan, 2001). Interventions such as Outward Bound, ropes courses, or other outdoor challenges explicitly claim to engender vitality, but so far there has been no specific empirical demonstration of this. Another example is exercise (Myers et al., 1999), which also can yield increased vitality. Some programs that have fostered exercise in people's lives appear to increase energy and decrease depressive symptoms, provided that activities are interesting or fun (R. M. Ryan & Frederick, 1997).

Further investigations of variables that can directly foster vitality are warranted, but one assumes based on the experimental and construct validation literatures reviewed here that engaging people in activities that raise spirit, from music to arts, and sports to social contact, may have promise in this regard. Particularly helpful would be experiencing sampling studies that could investigate within-person changes in vitality and vigor, and thus isolate covariates and the circumstances associated with the strengthening or diminishment of such positive subjective energy. Intervention and/or experimental studies have the promise of helping researchers better grasp what causes vitality, and what can be done practically to foster this optimal state.

■ What Is Not Known?

Because vitality has only recently come into more intensive research focus, there is more unknown than known about this salient aspect of well-being. Indeed, exploration of vitality is still in its early stages. What follows are some of the areas in need of further exploration, each of which builds off of some of the questions raised by the research reviewed in this chapter. Vitality is clearly influenced by exercise and exertion. However, effort and exertion sometimes appear to add to vitality, and sometimes to drain it. Predicting those conditions in which effort drains versus catalyzes vitality is a currently underexplored issue (e.g., Nix et al., 1999). Vitality is theorized, and to some extent has been shown to be a protective factor regarding subsequent health and well-being (e.g., Penninx et al., 2000). However, how vitality plays a role in resilience, either physical or psychological, is not well understood. Examinations of the relations of vitality experiences to immunological status would be helpful in this regard. More generally, the question as to whether subjective vitality is merely a marker or a true mediator of well-being remains underexamined (R. M. Ryan & Frederick, 1997).

Vitality is a state of activation, with clear neurological underpinnings. The specificity of patterns of activation associated with vitality versus other arousal patterns has begun (Thayer, 1996) but still remains somewhat primitive. As noted, little is known about developmental or cultural influences on vitality. Even basic information on changes in vitality across the life span is unavailable, despite the existence of studies in different age groups.

■ Must-Read Articles and Books

McHorney, C. A., Ware, J. E., Lu, J. F. R., & Sherbourne, C. D. (1994). The MOS 36-Item Short-Form Health Survey (SF-36): III. Tests of data quality, scaling assumptions, and reliability across diverse patient groups. *Medical Care, 32,* 40–66.

McHorney, C. A., Ware, J. E., & Raczek, A. E. (1993). The MOS 36-Item Short-Form Health Survey (SF-36): II. Psychometric and clinical tests of validity in measuring physical and mental health constructs. *Medical Care, 31,* 247–263.

Penninx, B. W. J. H., Guralnik, J. M., Bandeen-Roche, K., Kasper, J. D., Simonsick, E. M., Ferrucci, L., et al. (2000). The protective effects of emotional vitality on adverse health outcomes in disabled older women. *Journal of the American Gerontological Society, 48,* 1359–1356.

Penninx, B. W. J. H., Guralnik, J. M., Simonsick, E. M., Kasper, J. D., Ferrucci, L., & Fried, L. P. (1998). Emotional vitality among disabled older women: The women's health and aging study. *Journal of the American Gerontological Society, 46,* 807–815.

Ryan, R. M., & Frederick, C. (1997). On energy, personality, and health: Subjective vitality as a dynamic reflection of well-being. *Journal of Personality, 65,* 529–565.

Thayer, R. E. (1996). *The origin of everyday moods: Managing energy, tension and stress.* New York: Oxford University Press.

Thayer, R. E. (2001). *Calm energy.* New York: Oxford University Press.

Ware, J. E., & Sherbourne, C. D. (1992). The MOS 36-Item Short-Form Health Survey (SF-36): I. Conceptual framework and item selection. *Medical Care, 30,* 473–483.

INTRODUCTION:
STRENGTHS OF HUMANITY

CRITERIA FOR *Strengths of Humanity*

	Fulfilling	Morally valued	Does not diminish others	Nonfelicitous opposite	Traitlike	Distinctiveness	Paragons	Prodigies	Selective absence	Institutions and rituals	
	1	2	3	4	5	6	7	8	9	10	TALLY
Love	X	X	X	X	X	X	X	X	X	X	10/10
Kindness	X	X	X	X	X	~X	X	X	X	X	10/10
Social intelligence	X	X	X	X	X	~X	X	X	X		9/10

~ Somewhat satisfies criterion.

Strengths of humanity include positive traits manifest in caring relationships with others, what S. E. Taylor et al. (2000) referred to as dispositions to tend and befriend. The entries in this virtue class resemble those we identify as justice strengths, with the difference being that strengths of humanity are brought to bear in one-to-one relationships, whereas those of justice are most relevant in one-to-many relationships. The former strengths are interpersonal, the latter broadly social. Three of the strengths in our classification exemplify positive interpersonal traits, and as an introduction to this section, we comment briefly on each in terms of how they satisfy our criteria for a character strength (see Criteria Table).

■ Love

In its most developed form, love occurs within a reciprocated relationship with another person. We therefore exclude unrequited love, crushes of all types, stalking, hero worship, and being a fan. These sorts of relationships may feel on one end like love, but because the feelings run in only one direction, they fall outside the perimeter of this character strength. Accordingly, this strength subsumes romantic love and friendship, the love between parents and children, mentoring relationships, and the emotional bonds between teammates, coworkers, and so on. The extensive social psychological literature on liking and loving is relevant to our understanding of this strength, but we emphasize here the common features that make these relationships possible as opposed to their distinct aspects (Z. Rubin, 1973). As chapter 13 points out, love is marked by the sharing of aid, comfort, and acceptance. It involves strong positive feelings, commitment, and even sacrifice. This strength satisfies our criteria for a character strength.

CRITERION 1 *Fulfilling*   Love is fulfilling. Poets have extolled this strength, and most of us have known the exhilaration of losing ourselves in a relationship as well as the contentment of finding ourselves in one. This crazy little thing called love has been the subject and inspiration of too many songs to list and—with proper framing—is the glue that holds together the relationships deemed critical by Confucius for societal stability. To the Western eye, the Confucian relationships (between leader and follower, husband and wife, parent and child, and so on) seem most marked by status differences, but just as critical are the reciprocated feelings and behaviors of each party in each relationship (chapter 2). Wherever we might find ourselves, we want to fall in love, and we want to stay in love, and, most basically, we want to be fulfilled in love.

CRITERION 2 *Morally Valued*   Love is morally valued, almost by definition. Our close relationships with other people make us human. To be capable of intimacy is to be popular, and to be popular is—usually—to be capable of intimacy. Remember the deathbed test we proposed in chapter 1 as proof of the fulfilling nature of character strengths and their behavioral manifestations. A corollary of this test asks with whom we would want to spend our last moments in life, and the answer of course is friends and family members.

CRITERION 3 *Does Not Diminish Others*   This strength does not diminish others in the vicinity. Obviously, the other in a reciprocated relationship is fulfilled, but mere observers are also elevated when they see two people together who share positive feelings. When we are dining alone in restaurants, our eyes are drawn to couples who are talking and laughing with one another; they make us feel good. Our eyes also are drawn to couples who sit in grim or awkward silence and do nothing but study their respective appetizers; they make us feel sad.

CRITERION 4 *Nonfelicitous Opposite*   The absence of reciprocated love is clearly negative: *alienation, estrangement*, and *loneliness*. The opposite of love is even more so: *hatred, loathing, spite*, and *abhorrence*.

CRITERION 5 *Traitlike*   The ability to love and be loved is traitlike, evident across time and situation. Indeed, patterns of secure attachment established in infancy show up decades later in romantic relationships, as do patterns of insecure attachment. The specific ways in which reciprocal attachment is shown by infants, children, adolescents, and adults differ, but there is nonetheless continuity in the underlying processes and mechanisms, including those at the neurobiological level (Insel, 1997).

CRITERION 6 *Distinctiveness*   Love is not strictly decomposable into the other classified strengths, although some of them—for example, kindness, social intelligence, hope, humor, and vitality—represent value added to this strength and perhaps even contribute to it. Because these other strengths need not involve love, we do not collapse intimacy into them.

CRITERION 7 *Paragons*   Romeo and Juliet, Brian Piccolo and Gayle Sayers, George Burns and Gracie Allen, Paul Newman and Joanne Woodward, Serena Williams and Venus Williams, and Fox Mulder and Dana Scully embody the essence of reciprocated attachment. Other paragons of love can be drawn from the reader's own familiarity with loving sons who call their moms every day on the phone or loving dads who always help their much more worldly daughters plan out a travel itinerary.

CRITERION 8 *Prodigies*   We are not aware of deliberate research into love prodigies, but securely attached infants would be the first place to look. Indeed, perhaps love prodigies are so common as to be overlooked. Given the prolonged helplessness and dependency of children, evolution of necessity unfolded to make them capable of loving and being loved. How does the saying go? Children are financially worthless but emotionally priceless. In the meantime, we have the example from the 2000 United States Olympic trials for tae kwon do, in which teenager Esther Kim gave up her spot on the team so that her best friend, Kay Poe, who was injured, could compete.

CRITERION 9 *Selective Absence*   Those who seem unable to love are also well known. What about the Hollywood celebrities who have been married half a dozen or more times? What about our acquaintances who cannot sustain a friendship? Axis II of the *DSM* describes such maladaptive styles as narcissistic personality disorder ("Enough about me . . . how did you like my last show?"), antisocial personality disorder, and schizoid personality disorder; all are marked by the striking absence of reciprocated attachments. Infantile autism also seems marked by a striking absence of this character strength.

CRITERION 10 *Institutions and Rituals*   The larger society provides rituals and institutions galore that help us establish relationships, such as sleepovers, pen pals, chat rooms, mixers, and personal ads in the contemporary United States, and group dates and arranged marriages in other parts of the world. Less attention seems to be paid to cultivating the strength of interpersonal attachment per se, although there is a thriving self-help and pop psychology genre that advises people how to have better relationships. Whether the advice is useful can be debated, but it is eagerly sought. Many of us join clubs or pursue hobbies not because we want to become expert at swing dancing or stamp collecting but because they provide a way to meet people and to pursue the common interests that make friendship and romance possible.

Criticisms of the love myths extant in the United States are well known. The popular media convey strikingly unrealistic expectations about romantic love, which may contribute to our society's alarmingly high rate of divorce. The point is that rituals for sustaining love are less established than those for sparking it, and we suspect that greater attention to lasting friendships—which seem much more common than lasting romances—might suggest some useful strategies for import.

■ Kindness [Generosity, Nurturance, Care, Compassion, Altruistic Love, "Niceness"]

This character strength describes the pervasive tendency to be nice to other people—to be compassionate and concerned about their welfare, to do favors for them, to perform good deeds, and to take care of them. Kindness can be a fleeting act directed toward strangers, as when we give up our seat on a bus to a young mother holding an infant, or it can entail a profound gift within an established relationship, such as donating bone marrow or a kidney to a close relative. Smiles and pleasantries incur little cost, whereas sheltering the victims of persecution can be potentially lethal—but all fall within the province of this positive trait, which satisfies our various criteria for a strength of character.

CRITERION 1 *Fulfilling*   This strength is fulfilling, sometimes deeply so. One of the psychosocial virtues identified by Erik Erikson (1963) is generativity, a concern with matters outside oneself and specifically the well-being of the next generation. Taking care of one's children or younger colleagues makes us feel complete and content. One of our students told us of a marathon long-distance call in which she tutored her nephew in algebra. Not a mathematics whiz herself, she found the task extremely difficult. She was not even sure that she had been helpful, but regardless, she felt wonderful for having given to him the gift of her time and concern.

CRITERION 2 *Morally Valued*   Kindness is morally valued and—labeled as *caritas*—was elevated by Saint Paul to the status of a cardinal virtue (chapter 2). When we interview youngsters about the characteristics of a good person, they usually respond by enumerating acts of kindness and generosity.

CRITERION 3 *Does Not Diminish Others*   Observation of altruism elevates us. We were recently told a story about a research project directed by Kathleen Hall Jamieson, an ambitious intervention with high school classes aimed at increasing the civic involvement of students. In urban schools across the country, social studies classes are established in which students learn about the issues and candidates in pending mayoral elections. They take what they have learned into the community and raise the consciousness of the electorate in various ways.

In a given year, the class that does the most praiseworthy job is given a rather substantial cash award by a panel of expert judges. There are no strings attached to this prize, and a class could conceivably throw a pizza party, buy CDs, or take a field trip. This is never what they do. Instead, they purchase band uniforms or basketballs for the school and in one case even hired plumbers to repair the school's toilets. But the example that caught our hearts in our throats was the high school class that used its award to build a playground for the elementary school students in their neighborhood. Part of this elevation may result in the contagion of kindness. Merely seeing someone else act in an altruistic way leads others to do the same, at least in the short run (Bryan & Test, 1967). Calling this process modeling makes it seem more automatic and less morally significant than it actually is.

CRITERION 4 *Nonfelicitous Opposite*   The obvious opposites of kindness are *selfishness, stinginess,* and *mean-spiritedness.* When we describe someone as *petty,* we seem to mean that they refrain from acts of generosity and nurturance.

CRITERION 5 *Traitlike*   Kindness is traitlike. Although social psychologists have extensively studied the situational influences on altruistic acts (e.g., Batson et al., 1988), an equally important tradition has approached altruism as a personality trait (chapter 14). People can be arranged along a dimension of altruism, and their placement is linked to their behavior in a variety of domains.

CRITERION 6 *Distinctiveness*   Kindness, generosity, and nurturance are not decomposable into other strengths in our classification, although some qualifications are needed. First, kindness shares a family resemblance with love, and in chapter 14, we use *altruistic love* as a synonym for sustained generosity and compassion. Second, character strengths like social intelligence, fairness, and citizenship may contribute to kindness, although they are neither necessary nor sufficient.

CRITERION 7 *Paragons*   Paragons of kindness are easy to identify. Among the saints honored by the Roman Catholic Church are individuals who performed such incredible acts of generosity that they were seen as inspired by God, for example, Francis of Assisi, whose religious life began in an epiphany when he embraced a leper he met on the road; Zita of Lucca, the patron saint of domestic workers, who was famous for helping the sick, the poor, and the imprisoned; Angela Salawa of Kraków, who tended to World War I soldiers of all nationalities; and Katharine Drexel of Philadelphia, who founded dozens of mission centers and schools for Native Americans. The charitable contributions of international philanthropist George Soros are staggering. Along these lines, Americans are famous for helping out others in the wake of hurricanes, earthquakes, or other disasters. So many people rushed to New York in the aftermath of the 9/11 attacks that public service announcements soon urged others not to make the trek. We mentioned earlier people who donate kidneys to their relatives; they are kind enough, but how about people who donate a kidney to a stranger, simply because medical advances now make this possible? In the fictional realm, we need look no further for paragons of kindness than the protagonists of O. Henry's touching short story "The Gift of the Magi."

CRITERION 8 *Prodigies*   Prodigies of kindness are also easy to identify. We all have at hand examples of precociously generous children who perform small but touching acts of kindness for others—giving their toys and dolls to less fortunate children, collecting pennies for UNICEF, tending to stray cats and dogs, or mowing the lawns of housebound neighbors. And we draw your attention to yet another saint, Elizabeth of Hungary, the patroness of Catholic charities, who as a privileged teenager began a life of prayer, sacrifice, and service to the poor and sick. If we were to search more systematically for kindness prodigies, we would heed the speculation that sibling relationships are the crucible of altruistic acts (Dunn & Munn, 1986)—so, compared with only children, children from larger families may have a head start in developing and showing kindness and generosity. Ice skater Michelle Kwan—not an only child—began early in her storied career the practice of donating to hospitalized children the teddy bears that her fans threw on the ice following her routines.

CRITERION 9 *Selective Absence*   We turn from these elevating examples of kindness to bureaucrats behind the counter at the Department of Motor Vehicles who send us to the back of the line when we have neglected to dot an "i" or cross a "t" on some opaque form, people who tell us that our intended vacation site is an overrated rip-off, or acquaintances who pass on with glee malicious gossip. We have the familiar example of Ebeneezer Scrooge from *A Christmas Carol*. And maybe it is just us, but what is Howard Stern's public persona if not meanness incarnate?

CRITERION 10 *Institutions and Rituals*   Societal rituals for cultivating kindness include the assignment of chores to children and the frequent parental injunctions to share toys and desserts. Community service requirements in high school have many goals, but increasing altruism is one of the most important. Or consider programs like Big Brothers/Big Sisters, which facilitate nurturance. More generally, charities benefit not only the recipients but also those who donate their money and, more important, their time by teaching them about generosity. When the cynical among us dismiss charitable contributions as tax write-offs, we miss the obvious point that the financially optimal strategy is to give nothing.

■ Social Intelligence [Emotional Intelligence,
    Personal Intelligence]

In chapter 15, we use the term *hot intelligence* to refer to a family of individual
differences reflecting the ability to process hot information—signals concerning motives, feelings, and other psychological states directly relevant to the well-
being of oneself and others. In the current literature, this strength is sometimes
discussed under the rubric of emotional intelligence or personal intelligence,
and previous generations of psychologists labeled it as insight, psychological-
mindedness, social inference, interpersonal judgment, or (accurate) impression
formation. We opt for *social intelligence* as the generic label to underscore its
interpersonal relevance and hence its moral flavor. Unlike the other strengths
in our classification, social intelligence lacks obvious linguistic continuity with
the various virtues and strengths cataloged over the centuries by philosophers
and theologians (chapter 2), but we suspect that Aristotle, Confucius, and others would have no difficulty recognizing it even in its modern psychological
phrasing. Indeed, the familiar injunctions to know thyself or to walk a mile in
my shoes seem to urge social intelligence upon us all. In any event, social intelligence satisfies our criteria for a character strength.

CRITERION 1 *Fulfilling*   Social intelligence is fulfilling. Insight into our own
motives or those of others is satisfying, even if we do not like the answer. Freud's
psychoanalysis can be recast in positive psychology terms as a strategy for cultivating this character strength, and so too can other therapeutic approaches
ranging from Gestalt therapy ("get in touch with your feelings") to cognitive
therapy ("identify your automatic thoughts") to couples therapy ("ask your
partner what he/she wants") to remedial social skills training from a cognitive-
behavioral perspective ("think about how that would make other kids feel").

CRITERION 2 *Morally Valued*   Social intelligence is morally valued. When we
were college students, we read Robert Heinlein's science fiction tale *Stranger in
a Strange Land* and added the Martian verb *grok* to our everyday vocabulary.
To *grok* someone is to understand him or her fully as a psychological being, and
grokking was a deliberate goal in all our interactions. Today's college students
may not deliberately *grok* anyone, but our surveys of them suggest that among
the character strengths on which we focus, social intelligence is one of the most
frequently self-nominated and by implication one of the most valued.

  As chapter 15 details, psychology's study of social intelligence has been
mightily influenced by the theories and methods developed to study general
intelligence. This influence has been a mixed blessing, and for our purposes—
to propose this individual difference as a strength of character—the downside
is clear. We regard general intelligence (g or IQ) as a talent or ability that falls
outside the moral realm (chapter 1). To label this strength as any sort of intel-

ligence brings with it implications of strong genetic influence, immutability, cultural bias, socioeconomic elitism, and squanderability, although there is little evidence to support such a characterization. Along these lines, past studies of insight from a psychodynamic perspective explicitly defined insight as an appreciation of one's own inherently conflict-ridden nature. According to this definition, those entertaining the positive psychology premise that goodness and excellence are as authentic—in themselves or others—as defect and deficiency can never achieve insight, and we find this a thoroughly wrong conclusion.

The solution to these issues is to emphasize the social aspects of social intelligence as much as the intelligence aspects, which is why we have classified social intelligence as a strength of humanity and not as a cognitive strength. We need to look at the social actions that show social intelligence, and here we have no difficulty recognizing that these can be learned and enacted by people in any and all walks of life. Furthermore, social intelligence qua social skills can never be squandered.

CRITERION 3 *Does Not Diminish Others*   Especially in these terms, the display of a hot intelligence elevates others. To be understood is as fulfilling as to understand. Social intelligence allows the uniqueness of everyone to be acknowledged. "Being treated as an individual" is a critical feature of excellent schools (N. Park & Peterson, 2003b), and social intelligence on the part of teachers makes this treatment possible. Automated telephone menus, no matter how clever, leave us all feeling empty because there is not even the possibility of social intelligence behind them. Indeed, one of the critical skills of everyday living in the modern world is learning how to shortcut these menus as quickly as possible to get to a human being on the other end—one, we hope, who understands us.

CRITERION 4 *Nonfelicitous Opposite*   The opposite of social intelligence is patently undesirable. We can turn to popular culture and suggest *clueless* as an antonym of social intelligence, or we can turn to various psychology literatures for such negative antonyms as *self-deceived* and *lacking insight*. An aspect of stereotyping—treating people as members of a social category rather than as psychologically rich individuals—suggests yet another undesirable antonym of social intelligence. People may even stereotype themselves and thereby become socially stupid, as shown in the phenomenon of person-role merger, in which a person embraces as his or her complete identity some role that is being played, such as aerobics instructor, football coach, or school librarian (R. H. Turner, 1978). The problem is not having a role, or even enacting it well, but in shearing away one's unique psychological makeup in so doing.

CRITERION 5 *Traitlike*   Social intelligence is an individual difference of stability and generality. Broadly construed, it is a key ingredient in social skills that go beyond mere politeness and probably a contributor to the acceptance of oneself that characterizes serenity (K. T. Roberts & Aspy, 1993).

CRITERION 6 *Distinctiveness*   Social intelligence is conceptually distinct from the other strengths in our classification, although it may prove to overlap considerably with perspective (wisdom) when the focus there is on sage advice about social matters. Social intelligence can certainly set the stage for such character strengths as kindness, intimate attachment, leadership, and playfulness, so we are not surprised at the empirical associations we find among these strengths of character (chapter 28).

CRITERION 7 *Paragons*   However they might have arisen, paragons of social intelligence exist. Among historically well-known individuals, we have such candidates as Gandhi and Eleanor Roosevelt (H. Gardner, 1983). Social intelligence is embodied as well in more contemporary leaders like Robert Kennedy, Ronald Reagan, Mario Cuomo, and Malcolm X. The charismatic leadership shown by such individuals entails many skills and strengths, but social intelligence seems chief among them. In the wake of the events of 9/11, Mayor Rudy Giuliani of New York City showed an uncanny ability to say what people needed to hear in the way they needed to hear it. And even when we disagree with the lay psychology promoted by Tony Robbins and Oprah Winfrey, we marvel at their social presence and their social intelligence. Ditto for master teachers, preachers, psychotherapists, and even football coaches who have found professional roles in which their social intelligence allows them to excel. Today's best known poets did not write sonnets or couplets but popular songs— for example, Smokey Robinson, Bob Dylan, Carole King, John Lennon, Joni Mitchell, James Taylor, Bonnie Raitt, Bruce Springsteen, and Tracy Chapman, to name some of our own favorites—some of which become anthems because they voice the psychological concerns of an entire generation.

CRITERION 8 *Prodigies*   There also exist prodigies of social intelligence, although we have to rely mainly on our personal experiences to identify them. Like perspective (chapter 8), social intelligence reaches its apex with maturity, so prodigies are best spoken of not in absolute terms but relative to their cohort. Social intelligence prodigies do not usually come to the world's attention (teenage songstress Janis Ian is an exception). Chapter 1 related the story of our own student who displayed prodigious social intelligence, and chapter 15 gives another excellent example. More generally, we all know kids—even toddlers— who can apprehend our psychological states and offer what we need at the moment: a hug or a cookie (or both).

CRITERION 9 *Selective Absence*   Individuals who are strikingly deficient in social intelligence lack any understanding of themselves or others. These are people who misread our intentions and inadvertently misrepresent their own. They say the wrong thing at the wrong time. They tell us a joke when we are preoccupied with weighty matters, or they construe our own playfulness in literal terms. At the pathological extreme, we have alexithymia (the inability to identify one's feelings) and infantile autism, often discussed as a cognitive disorder but perhaps more accurately seen as the massive failure of social intelligence to develop.

CRITERION 10 *Institutions and Rituals*   As a modern character strength, social intelligence does not have well-established rituals and institutions for its explicit cultivation. However, some of the components of social intelligence—for example, perspective taking and knowledge of oneself—are targeted by venerable practices like make-believe games, storybooks, turn taking, and recitation of our likes and dislikes. Given the high value placed on social intelligence, perhaps formal practices have not arisen because it is cultivated informally in casual conversation and gossip, which often involves the attempt to decipher what lies behind the actions of others and occasionally ourselves. In the contemporary United States, psychology has been the most popular undergraduate major in college for decades, even though the explicit job market for those with baccalaureates can be meager at best. We suspect the real appeal of this major is that it aids and abets the desire of students to hone their social intelligence. Psychology provides a vocabulary for making sense of oneself and others, and in these terms, psychology is the most relevant major there could be in a psychologically minded culture like our own.

Chapter 15 describes ongoing intervention research with young people that tries to inculcate deliberately the character strength of social intelligence. If and when this work bears fruit and becomes incorporated into school curricula or after-school programs, we can point to the identified procedures as deliberate institutional practices.

13. LOVE

■ *Greg Manning could see from the terrace of his apartment that the jet had struck near the offices of Cantor Fitzgerald, where his wife worked as a senior vice president and partner. For the next half hour he paced frantically, stopping only to pound the wall and cry out her name. He was certain that his vibrant and beautiful Lauren was dead, but he was wrong. That morning she had lingered saying good-bye to their 10-month-old son, Tyler, and as a result arrived at the World Trade Center a few minutes later than usual. She had just entered the lobby of Tower One when a fireball descending through an elevator shaft propelled her back into the street, totally engulfed in flames. A bond salesman who witnessed this raced over, put out the fire that was consuming her, and remained at her side until an ambulance arrived. At the hospital, her face swollen beyond recognition, she told Greg the pain was so excruciating she had been praying to die but then out of love for him and Tyler made the decision to fight for her life. Within a few minutes she slipped into a drug-induced coma that would last for many weeks. Her parents came immediately from their home in Georgia to alternate bedside and babysitting duties with Greg. During his hospital shifts, Greg ignored Lauren's unconscious state, reading poetry to her and playing her favorite CDs, all the while reassuring her that she was loved, that he would take care of her, that everything would be okay. During his home shifts, he took Tyler to birthday parties and play dates, read and sang to him, and documented his development on videotape for Lauren's future viewing. Remarkably, he also found time each day to send e-mail updates on her condition to friends and family. Saving Lauren meant replacing more than 80% of her skin, often multiple times. Some of the grafts used synthetic or donor skin and from the outset were considered temporary, whereas others that were hoped to be permanent simply did not take. To compound the horror, part of her left ear was destroyed, and several fingers of her left hand required partial amputation. Although Greg would sob in the arms of friends, he never wavered in his devotion to Lauren or his confidence that she would pull through. Exactly 3 months after admission to the hospital, Lauren saw her new, scarred face for the first time. The predictable shock and sadness were tempered by the fact that her husband had prepared her through repeated reminders that she always had been and always would be his soul mate, and in his eyes was as beautiful as ever. Six months after that terrifying morning, against the slimmest of odds, Greg Manning took his wife home. Those closest to the case agree that Lauren survived through a combination of grit and love.* ■

■ Consensual Definition

Love represents a cognitive, behavioral, and emotional stance toward others that takes three prototypical forms. One is love for the individuals who are our primary sources of affection, protection, and care. We rely on them to make our welfare a priority and to be available to us when needed. They make us feel safe, and we are distressed by prolonged separations from them. The prototype of this form is a child's love for a parent. Another form is love for the individuals who depend on us to make them feel safe and cared for. We comfort and protect them, assist and support them, make sacrifices for their benefit, put their needs ahead of our own, feel happy when they are happy. The prototype of this form is a parent's love for a child. The third form is love that involves passionate desire for sexual, physical, and emotional closeness with an individual whom we consider special and who makes us feel special. The prototype is romantic love.

Relationships can involve more than one type of love. For example, best friends may love each other in both a child–parent and a parent–child way in the sense that each leans on as well as looks out for the other. Relationships can involve different types of love at different points in time. For example, people may gradually shift from a child–parent to parent–child form of love as they grow up, and their parents get older. Relationships can begin with one type of love and acquire other types over time. For example, dating couples may initially love each other only in a romantic way but eventually begin to love each other in child–parent and parent–child ways as well. Mate relationships are unique in being the only social tie that encompasses all three forms of love.

Individuals with this strength would likely agree with the following:

- There is someone with whom I feel free to be myself.
- There is someone I trust to help and support me.
- There is someone I hate to be away from for very long.
- There is someone for whom I would do almost anything.

- There is someone whose happiness matters as much to me as my own.
- There is someone whose welfare I am committed to.
- There is someone with whom I am physically affectionate.
- There is someone in whose company I feel deep contentment.
- There is someone I am passionate about.

To appreciate just how basic this capacity is, one must consider its evolutionary roots. Our continuation as a species depended on our ability to successfully negotiate at least three adaptive challenges. First, we had to survive what in the animal kingdom is the longest period of immaturity and dependency. Second, we had to find and then retain a mate long enough to reproduce. And third, we had to provide adequate care to our offspring so that they, too, survived to reproduce. The result of these challenges is that we are by nature capable of all the emotions, cognitions, and behaviors that each challenge requires. We think and feel about and behave toward our parents in a way that helps ensure our survival. Likewise, we think and feel about and behave toward our children in a way that helps ensure their survival. And we think and feel about and behave toward partners in a way that helps ensure reproduction. Each challenge is associated with a different (proto)type of love. Humans have theorized about love and relationships for as long as they have theorized about anything. Surprisingly, it has only been in the last 30 years or so that the methods of empirical science have been applied to the task of understanding and explaining love. And for much of this time research proceeded along two separate pathways, with developmental psychologists investigating parent–child bonds and social psychologists studying adult romantic relationships. Recently these two areas of inquiry began to merge, and the integration has thus far proved fruitful. The capacity to love and be loved is now viewed as an innate, species-typical tendency that has powerful effects on psychological and physical health from infancy through old age. It has also been established that this capacity can be affected in deep and lasting ways by early relationship experience.

■ Theoretical Traditions

It has often been suggested that love is a relatively modern and thoroughly Western phenomenon (De Rougement, 1940), but in fact love in all its forms is evident in the lore of ancient civilizations from Egypt to China to Africa (Mellen, 1981). Over the centuries many great thinkers, from Plato to Stendhal, have written extensively about love, although Freud was the first to propose a formal theory (Freud, 1905b). The neo-Freudians who followed made interpersonal relationships or object relations even more central to their theories (Bettelheim, 1988; Horney, 1950). In a separate but simultaneous endeavor, researchers were investigating mother love in nonhuman primates (Harlow, 1958).

It was more than a decade later that social psychologists began to weigh in on the topic of love (Rubin, 1973). In 1975 two of the pioneers, Ellen Berscheid and Elaine Hatfield, received a grant from the National Science Foundation for a series of studies on love and attraction and, in addition, an award from a U.S. Congressman for what, in his view, was the greatest waste of government funding that fiscal year. In a press release Senator William Proxmire of Wisconsin stated:

> I object to this not only because no one—not even the NSF—can argue that love is a science; not only because I'm sure that even if they [the researchers, whose grant was for $84,000] spend $84 million or $84 billion they wouldn't get an answer that anyone would believe. I'm also against it because I don't want the answer. I believe that 200 million other Americans want to leave some things in life a mystery, and right on top of the things we don't want to know is why a man falls in love with a woman and vice versa. (Cited in Hatfield, 2000)

The researchers persevered (Berscheid & Walster, 1978), and empirical work on the topic began to flourish.

In 1983, Harold Kelley and a team of leading social psychologists coauthored a volume that signaled the emergence of a new field of research on interpersonal relationships (H. H. Kelley et al., 1983). They used interdependence theory (Thibaut & Kelley, 1959) as their guiding framework. The field has continued to focus primarily on romantic relationships, including evolved mating strategies (Buss & Schmitt, 1993) and components of romantic love such as intimacy, passion, and commitment (Aron & Westbay, 1996; Fehr & Russell, 1991; Reis & Shaver, 1988; Rusbult, 1983; Sternberg, 1986b).

With the exception of popular evolutionary models of mating, which tend to ignore feelings of affection between mates (Hazan & Diamond, 2000), the capacity to love and be loved could be addressed from any of the preceding perspectives. Attachment theory (Bowlby, 1969, 1973, 1979, 1980) was selected for several reasons. First, it integrates insights and data from an exceptionally broad range of disciplines and domains, including ethology, control systems theory, psychoanalysis, cognitive psychology, and evolutionary theory. Second, it is applicable across ages as well as across genders and cultures and even species. Third, it offers models of both normative and individual-differences phenomena. Fourth, it accounts for the universal human tendency to form bonds of love from infancy through old age. Fifth, it has served as the basis for more empirical research than any other theory of love, including hundreds of studies of infant–parent relationships and hundreds more of adult romantic relationships.

In 1950, British psychiatrist John Bowlby was invited by the World Health Organization (WHO) to report on the mental health of children who had been orphaned by the war. The take-home message of his report was that normal development appears to require a "warm and continuous relationship" with at least one adult caregiver. The conclusion was consistent with the observations of many psychiatrists and social workers around the world: Children reared in orphanages, even where their basic needs were adequately met, nevertheless suffered from the lack of opportunities to form enduring emotional bonds. Most displayed pathological behaviors (e.g., head banging, clinical depression), and many failed to thrive. Indeed, some died simply from a lack of love.

The WHO report (Bowlby, 1951), which stressed the importance of emotional bonds, resulted in major changes in the way children in orphanages and residential nurseries were treated, but it left important questions unanswered. Why should the absence of an emotional attachment have such profound and pervasive effects? And how, exactly, did the effects occur? Bowlby devoted the next 20 years of his life to searching for answers.

The quest led him into literatures far removed from his psychoanalytic training. It was in the field of ethology, and specifically the work of Lorenz (1956) on imprinting among goslings and Harlow (1958) on bonding in rhesus monkeys, that he eventually found the explanation he had been seeking. The young of many altricial species, which are too immature at birth to care for themselves, have an evolved predisposition to become attached to an adult protector or caregiver. Bowlby reasoned that the human infants and children who were not faring well despite adequate routine care were suffering the consequences of a thwarted innate need for attachment.

The explication of and supporting evidence for this new theory ultimately filled three volumes (Bowlby, 1969, 1973, 1980). A core concept is an inborn attachment behavior system that functions to enhance survival by regulating proximity to a caregiver. The dynamics of the attachment system are apparent in the behavior of a typical 1-year-old in relation to his mother: He continuously monitors her whereabouts and plays contentedly as long as she is nearby, but if the distance between them becomes too great, he will be upset and redirect his attention and effort toward reestablishing proximity. Bowlby contended that this system is operative throughout the life span, "from the cradle to the grave" (Bowlby, 1979, p. 129). Other features of attachment theory, including the processes by which attachment bonds are formed, the ways in which the function and nature of attachment change between infancy and adulthood, and the development of parental and sexual love, are discussed in detail later in this chapter.

■ Measures

A variety of attachment measures have been developed. They differ depending on whether the research involves infants, children, adolescents, or adults. They range from behavioral observations to self-reports, including both questionnaires and interviews. They differ additionally in whether the focus is parent–

offspring or peer and romantic relationships. In general they are designed to assess individual differences, but they vary in the number of patterns or styles and whether such differences are conceptualized as continuous dimensions or discrete categories (Table 13.1).

For infants and young toddlers, the standard assessment tool is the Strange Situation Test (Ainsworth, Blehar, Waters, & Wall, 1978), which is composed of eight brief episodes:

1. *Stranger escorts Mother and Baby into the laboratory.* The stranger is always an adult female (because infants perceive unfamiliar women as less threatening than unfamiliar men); the baby is typically 12 months old (because infants of this age are attached, capable of crawling, and at the peak of separation distress); the mother was presumed to be the primary caregiver (but subsequent studies have been conducted with fathers, grandmothers, and other caregivers).

2. *Mother and Baby are left alone* to get comfortable in the unfamiliar setting. Age-appropriate toys are made available to encourage exploration and play.

3. *Stranger enters.* At first, she sits quietly next to Mother. Then she initiates conversation (because it has been found that children are less fearful of a stranger who interacts in a friendly manner with their caregiver). Finally, she engages Baby in play (a chance for the two to become more familiar).

4. *Mother departs,* leaving Baby with Stranger. (In theory, the separation should activate the infant's attachment system and be evident in disrupted play and/or overt expressions of distress.)

5. *Mother returns* as Stranger leaves. (In theory, the infant should be sufficiently comforted by the caregiver's presence and/or contact to eventually resume play.)

6. *Mother departs again,* this time leaving Baby alone.

7. *Stranger returns.* (In theory, because the infant is not attached to the stranger, her presence and/or contact will not be fully soothing.)

8. *Mother returns* as Stranger leaves. (In theory, the infant should be fully soothed by the caregiver's presence and/or contact.)

Trained coders rate the videotaped behavior of infants during the two post-separation "reunion" episodes. A classification is assigned based on the overall pattern of scores on four dimensions—proximity seeking, contact maintenance, resistance, and avoidance.

In Ainsworth et al.'s original study, the majority of infants behaved just as expected. They played contentedly in their mother's (but not the stranger's) presence, were upset by separations from their mother (but not the stranger), and were soothed by contact with their mother (but not the stranger). This pattern was labeled *secure.* Unexpectedly, two other patterns were also observed.

TABLE 13.1   *Measures of Attachment*

Strange Situation (SS)

Ainsworth, Blehar, Waters, & Wall (1978)

This laboratory procedure is used with 12- to 18-month-olds. Behavior during two postseparation "reunion" episodes is rated on four 7-point scales (proximity seeking, contact maintenance, resistance, and avoidance). Ratings are used for classification into one of three basic patterns: secure, ambivalent, or avoidant. Requires intensive training.

- Intercoder agreement: as high as 88% across labs
- Test–retest reliability: as high as 96% for 2- to 6-month intervals
- Continuity of classifications: as high as 82% over a 4-year period
- Construct validity: correlates with relevant behavior in naturalistic settings

(For information on the "disorganized" pattern, and a comprehensive review of attachment measures for preschool and kindergarten-age children, see Solomon & George, 1999.)

Adult Attachment Interview (AAI)

C. George, Kaplan, & Main (1985); Main & Goldwyn (1984)

This semistructured, hour-long protocol consists of 18 questions about childhood relationships with parents, attachment-relevant experiences (e.g., of separation and loss), and meaning attributed to these relationships and experiences. The resulting narrative is transcribed verbatim and then coded according to content, language, and especially coherence. Codes are used for classification into one of four categories: autonomous, preoccupied, dismissing, or unresolved. Requires intensive training.

- Intercoder agreement: as high as 95%
- Test–retest reliability: as high as 90% for a 3-month interval
- Continuity of classifications: as high as 70% for a 4-year period
- Construct validity: correlates with parenting behavior and infant SS

(For a detailed and comprehensive review of the AAI's history, coding, reliability, and validity, see Hesse, 1999.)

Adult Attachment Prototypes (AAP)

Hazan & Shaver (1987, 1990)

This self-report measure consists of paragraph-long descriptions of each of three romantic attachment styles: secure, ambivalent, and avoidant. Subjects choose the one they consider most descriptive of their typical feelings about romantic partners.

- Test–retest reliability: 70% over intervals of 1 week to 4 years
- Construct validity: correlates with relevant romantic experiences and outcomes

(For a detailed review, see Crowell et al., 1999; Feeney, 1999.)

(continued)

TABLE 13.1   *Measures of Attachment* (*continued*)

Relationship Styles Questionnaire (RSQ)
  Griffin & Bartholomew (1994)
  This is a 30-item self-report inventory on which Likert ratings are used to assign individual scores on each of two dimensions (model of self and model of others) and/or each of four attachment styles (secure, preoccupied, fearful, and dismissing).
  ▪ Internal reliability: r's of .65 for scales assessing each style
  ▪ Construct validity: correlates with relevant romantic experiences and outcomes
  (For more on the RSQ, see Bartholomew & Shaver, 1998.)

Experiences in Close Relationships (ECR)
  Brennan, Clark, & Shaver (1998)
  This is a 36-item self-report inventory in which Likert ratings are used to assign individual scores on each of the two dimensions (anxiety and avoidance) that have been found to underlie all self-report measures of adult attachment as well as Ainsworth et al.'s classification scheme for infants.
  ▪ Internal reliability: greater than .90 for both dimensions
  ▪ Construct validity: correlates with relevant romantic experiences and outcomes
  (For the most up-to-date review and analysis of self-report measures of adult attachment, see Fraley, Waller, & Brennan, 2000.)

Inventory of Parent and Peer Attachment (IPPA)
  Armsden & Greenberg (1987)
  This multi-item self-report inventory was designed for use with adolescents and is suitable for subjects as young as 12 years of age. It assesses perceived quality (i.e., security) of relationships with mothers, fathers, and peers.
  (For the most comprehensive overview of adolescent attachment, see Allen & Land, 1999.)

Some infants appeared anxious in the unfamiliar surroundings and did little exploring even when their mother was present. And although they were extremely distressed by the separations and sought contact with their mother when she returned, they tended to resist her attempts to provide comfort (e.g., by pushing her away, stiffening their bodies when held, or indicating a desire to be put down though still upset). As a consequence, they were not fully soothed. This pattern of loudly demanding but angrily resisting comfort was labeled *ambivalent* (sometimes called resistant) attachment.

Other infants appeared to be unusually independent. Their exploratory behavior seemed to be little affected by whether their mother was present, and they showed little if any distress when separated from her. They not only did not seek contact when she returned but actively avoided it (e.g., by averting gaze, turning away, or ignoring her invitations to approach). This pattern was labeled *avoidant* attachment. Ainsworth suspected that these infants were upset but not showing it—a hypothesis that was later confirmed by physiological evidence. Babies who displayed no overt distress during separations nevertheless had significantly elevated heart rates that increased further when they were reunited with their mothers (Sroufe & Waters, 1977).

Although the majority of infants are easily classified using this scheme, there is consistently a small minority whose behavior appears to be a mix of ambivalence and avoidance. Subsequently, a fourth category, labeled *disorganized*, was added (Main & Solomon, 1990).

By 20 months, most youngsters are no longer distressed by brief separations from attachment figures, making the Strange Situation an invalid indicator of attachment patterns. Thus several variations were introduced to accommodate normative developmental change, including longer separations (Stevenson-Hinde & Shouldice, 1995) and the addition of other tasks (DeMulder & Radke-Yarrow, 1991). (For a thorough discussion and analysis of attachment measures from infancy through school age, see J. Solomon & George, 1999.)

One of the tenets of attachment theory is that early attachment experiences form the basis of working models or characteristic ways of thinking about relationships. Thus for theoretical reasons, measures of attachment in adulthood focus more on the mental representations than on overt behavior. There are also practical reasons for this emphasis. Unlike infants, adults do not typically burst into tears when their attachment figure merely leaves the room.

In accordance with this emphasis on mental models, C. George, Kaplan, and Main (1985) created the Adult Attachment Interview (AAI). Interviewees are asked a series of questions regarding childhood relationships with parents and then assigned to one of four categories: autonomous, preoccupied, dismissing, or unresolved. The classification scheme is based on Grice's (1975) maxims regarding discourse, with greater weight given to coherence than content. What matters is not so much what people say but how they say it. Individuals are classified as *autonomous* if their accounts are believable, detailed, relevant, and clear regardless of whether the experiences they report are positive or negative. If their accounts are marked by oscillation between positive and negative portrayals, excessive irrelevant details, and lingering anger toward parents, they are classified as *preoccupied*. The label of *dismissing* is applied to individuals who describe parents in idealized terms but have difficulty providing supportive details or examples, seem generally uncomfortable with the interview topics, and downplay the importance of relationships. Individuals who report attachment-related traumas of loss and/ or abuse and manifest confusion in discussing them are classified as *unresolved*.

A number of studies (summarized in Van Ijzendoorn, 1992) have found high correspondence between adults' AAI classifications and their infants' Strange Situation classifications: autonomous-secure, preoccupied-ambivalent, dismissing-avoidant, unresolved-disorganized, respectively. Such findings suggest that attachment patterns formed in infancy shape the way individuals later relate to offspring. But it is important to note that the AAI was developed on the basis of what parents of infants in the three classification groups had to say about their own early attachment experiences. Thus the AAI relates to the Strange Situation just as it was designed to do.

As developmental psychologists were investigating parent–offspring relationships, social psychologists had constructed a separate field of research on adult relationships. In 1984, an integration of these two lines of research was proposed (Shaver, Hazan, & Bradshaw, 1984). The authors argued that despite the focus on different life phases and the use of different methods, the phenomena being investigated were essentially the same, and much could be gained by merging the two areas of inquiry. Specifically, they proposed that Bowlby's theory on the innate predisposition for emotional bonding and Ainsworth's findings on individual differences in interpersonal functioning could serve as an integrative framework for research on relationships across the life span.

In 1987, Hazan and Shaver published the results of the first test of this new perspective. Both research and anecdotal evidence suggested that adults differ in how they approach and experience romantic relationships. Some enjoy closeness and find it easy to establish, expect partners to be trustworthy and reliable, readily turn to them for comfort and support, and offer the same in return. Others worry excessively about being abandoned, want more closeness than partners are able or willing to give, and often feel anxious or angry. Still others are uncomfortable with closeness, find it difficult to fully trust partners, and prefer to maintain some emotional distance from them. They value independence over closeness, tend to withdraw rather than seek comfort when distressed, and are not particularly interested in or skilled at being supportive. To Hazan and Shaver, these differences sounded very much like the secure, ambivalent, and avoidant attachment patterns that Ainsworth had identified in infants; thus they translated them into terms appropriate for adults and offered research participants three prototypical "attachment styles" from which to choose the most self-descriptive.

As Hazan and Shaver noted in their original article, this forced-choice format had several limitations. Requiring participants to choose only one of three complex alternatives presumed that attachment styles are mutually exclusive when, in reality, some individuals may be best characterized by a combination of styles. In addition, reliance on a single item raised concerns about reliability. Several improvements have since been made in the measurement of adult attachment styles.

One was to allow research participants to rate each of the prototypes on a continuous scale (M. B. Levy & Davis, 1988). This approach acknowledged that not all individuals would find the prototypes equally applicable; for example, some might be more secure, ambivalent, or avoidant than others. It also allowed for consideration of different patterns. For instance, subjects who view themselves as primarily secure may differ in their degree of ambivalence or avoidance, and the differences may have important implications for relationship functioning and outcomes.

A second improvement was to divide the paragraph-length descriptions into sentence-length statements that could be rated on Likert-type scales (N. L. Collins & Read, 1990; Feeney & Noller, 1990; Simpson, 1990). This approach allows respondents to agree with some parts of a particular style while disagreeing with other parts. It provides a clearer and more precise picture of an individual's attachment orientation.

A third improvement was to expand the small set of statements into a larger number of items (e.g., Brennan & Shaver, 1995; Feeney, Noller, & Hanrahan, 1994). This approach made it possible to assess aspects of attachment not covered by the original Hazan and Shaver prototypes. The addition of multiple items to assess each aspect also improved reliability. (For a comprehensive list and review of these measures, see Brennan, Clark, & Shaver, 1998.)

The decomposition and expansion of the Hazan-Shaver prototypes led to the important discovery that the same two dimensions underlie all self-report measures of adult attachment. One dimension is anxiety (an emotional response concerning abandonment fears), and the other is avoidance (a behavioral response of social withdrawal). These are virtually identical to the two dimensions underlying Ainsworth et al.'s (1978) infant attachment patterns.

One of the current debates in the field is whether individual differences in adult attachment are best conceptualized and measured as differences in degree (dimensions) or kind (types). In an innovative approach to the question, Fraley and Waller (1998) conducted a taxometric analysis of self-report measures. They concluded that the data support a dimensional, not a typological, model. They also noted that imposing a categorical model on dimensional data has several drawbacks, including reduction of statistical power and underestimation of the magnitude of relations among variables.

In the midst of efforts to improve the original Hazan-Shaver measure, Bartholomew proposed a somewhat different approach (Bartholomew, 1990; Bartholomew & Horowitz, 1991). She argued that the dimensions underlying self-report measures of adult attachment could alternatively be conceptualized as model of self (positive vs. negative) and model of others (positive vs. negative). She argued further that the two dimensions, which are logically independent, produce four rather than three attachment styles. She labeled them by borrowing names from Main's and Ainsworth's typologies and described them by rewording the Hazan-Shaver prototypes. The four styles are *secure, preoccupied* (ambivalent), *fearful* (avoidant), and *dismissing* (a second type of avoidance, characterized by compulsive self-reliance, not represented in the original Hazan-Shaver taxonomy).

A major challenge has been deciding how best to assess attachment in adolescence given that it is a period of transition between a focus on family relationships to increasing focus on relationships with peers, including the emergence of sexuality. Some researchers have opted to use the AAI, which emphasizes relationships with parents. Others have used the various romantic (peer) attachment measures. One of the more popular approaches for assessing attachment in this age group looks at relationships with both parents and peers (Armsden & Greenberg, 1987). (For a comprehensive overview of adolescent attachment, see Allen & Land, 1999.)

■ Correlates and Consequences

Investigations of the correlates and consequences of various attachment patterns can be divided into two broad categories. One involves longitudinal studies of children assessed in the Strange Situation during infancy; the other concerns relationship functioning and outcomes of adults with different attachment styles.

Children who were securely attached in infancy are later more likely than their insecure counterparts to exhibit what has been termed *assertive relatedness* toward parents (Lyons-Ruth, 1991). They explore more enthusiastically and are more persistent in problem-solving tasks but also more inclined to ask for help and seek contact comfort when needed (e.g., Londerville & Main, 1981; Matas, Arend, & Sroufe, 1978; Waters, Wippman, & Sroufe, 1979). In other words, they show a healthy balance between dependency and autonomy. In relation to teachers, they require relatively less contact, guidance, and discipline and are less likely to show attention-seeking behaviors, impulsivity, frustration, and helplessness (Sroufe, Fox, & Pancake, 1983). Their teachers like them more than children who are not securely attached and expect more of them. In relation to peers, children with secure attachment histories are more skilled at interaction and elicit more positive responses (Pierrehumbert, Iannotti, & Cummings, 1985; Pierrehumbert, Iannotti, Cummings, & Zahn-Waxler, 1989; Vandell, Owen, Wilson, & Henderson, 1988); have more friends and are more popular (Sroufe, 1983); and are less likely to be bullies or victims (Troy & Sroufe, 1987).

Of course, secure attachment in infancy does not guarantee good developmental outcomes, but research has consistently confirmed that it conveys advantages in several domains. Most notably, it is associated with more positive relationships with parents, teachers, and peers. And of all the predictors of overall adjustment, the quality of social functioning is among the strongest. Being securely attached to a caregiver in the first year of life provides a solid foundation for affect regulation and exploration, as well as the expectation of future responsiveness from and the tendency to turn to and rely on others during times of need. (For a comprehensive review of the sequelae of early attachment patterns, see Colin, 1996.)

Secure attachment in adolescence and adulthood also has numerous positive correlates and consequences. The list includes more supportiveness and less rejection toward partners in joint problem-solving tasks (Kobak & Hazan, 1991); safer sex practices (Brennan & Shaver, 1995); fewer psychosomatic symptoms in response to stress (Mikulincer, Florian, & Weller, 1993); greater likelihood of seeking support when distressed (Simpson, Rholes, & Nelligan, 1992); using compromise (Pistole, 1989) rather than destructive strategies (Gaines et al., 1997) of conflict resolution; less deterioration of trust in the initial phases of relationship development (Keelan, Dion, & Dion, 1994); higher self-esteem (Brennan & Bosson, 1998); less depression (Carnelley, Pietromonaco, & Jaffe, 1994); less partner abuse (Dutton, Saunders, Starzomski, & Bartholomew, 1994); and less likelihood of divorce (Hazan & Shaver, 1987).

In sum, securely attached adolescents and adults cope more effectively with the stresses of life and are more skilled at forming social ties that are enduring, satisfying, and characterized by trust and intimacy. Both of these skills predict better psychological adjustment and physical health.

The foregoing findings provide a general sense of the correlates and consequences of secure attachment in adulthood, but they represent only a small subset of the now vast empirical literature. In the decade following Hazan and Shaver's original report, some 800 journal articles and book chapters on adult attachment were published. (For reviews, see Feeney, 1999; Hazan & Shaver, 1994; and Shaver & Hazan, 1993.)

■ Development

Attachments can be distinguished from other types of social relationships in terms of four defining features, which are evident in behavior toward attachment figures: seeking to stay near to or in contact with (*proximity maintenance*), turning to for comfort or reassurance (*safe haven*), being upset by unexpected or prolonged separations (*separation distress*), and using the attachment figure as a base of security from which to explore and operate in the world (*secure base*).

The dynamic balance between attachment and exploration is an integral part of behavior at all ages, but changes as a function of development are to be expected. One predictable change concerns the time and distance from the attachment figure that can be comfortably tolerated. The average 12-month-old will exhibit greater distress (and more disrupted exploration) as a result of even brief separations than will the average 36-month-old. By late childhood or early adolescence, longer separations are usually negotiated without undue upset, and separation distress is rare except in cases where attachment figures are unavailable for an extended period.

Another important developmental change concerns the integration of attachment with other behavior systems. Infant–caregiver relationships involve complementary systems. The attachment system helps ensure that infants will feel and behave toward caregivers and love them in a way that enhances survival; the caregiving system helps ensure that caregivers will feel and behave toward infants and "love" them in a way that enhances survival. Adult romantic relationships tend to be reciprocal, with each partner loving the other in both an attachment and a caregiving kind of way. These relationships additionally involve the sexual system, which helps ensure that partners feel and behave toward and love each other in a way that enhances reproduction. Thus, in the process of normative development the three types of love described at the beginning of this chapter, each of which corresponds to a specific behavior system, become integrated.

Although the attachment system is innate, attachment bonds take time to develop. From 0 to 2 months of age, the coordination of infant reflexes and caregiver instincts virtually guarantees frequent, enduring infant–caregiver contact (proximity maintenance). From 2 to 6 months, infants learn to associate particular caregivers with the alleviation of distress and begin to selectively turn to these individuals for comfort (safe haven). Around 6 to 8 months of age, concurrent with the onset of crawling, infants start showing upset if their preferred caregivers are unavailable (separation distress) but increased confidence and exploration if they are available (secure base). Note that the defining features of attachment emerge not simultaneously but in sequence.

An infant's primary attachment figure is not simply one of several possible protectors but the individual with whom he or she has a special and privileged relationship. Nevertheless, most infants also have secondary and even tertiary attachment figures, including aunts, baby-sitters, day care providers, grandparents, and so forth. Over the course of development, changes occur in the composition and structure of this hierarchy of attachment figures. New people may be added and/or others dropped. Parents tend to be lifelong members, but they eventually assume a position of secondary importance relative to romantic partners (Bowlby, 1979).

Two developmental questions are of particular interest: How do individuals make the transition from parental to peer attachment? And how do peer attachments form? Both questions were addressed in two related studies, one with children and adolescents ranging in age from 6 to 17 and another with adults from 18 to 82 years of age (Hazan & Zeifman, 1994). The results suggest that the processes of attachment formation and transfer involve the sequential addition of attachment features.

In the first study, the majority of children and adolescents were peer oriented in terms of proximity maintenance, preferring to spend time in the company of peers rather than parents. In regard to the safe haven component, there was a shift between the ages of 10 and 14, with peers coming to be preferred over parents as sources of support and reassurance. For the majority, parents continued to serve as bases of security and primary sources of separation distress throughout adolescence. Only among the oldest participants (aged 15–17 years) was there evidence of full-blown peer attachments—that is, peer relationships containing all four defining features—and nearly all were with romantic partners.

In the second study, the majority of adults were peer oriented in both proximity maintenance and safe haven behavior, preferring to spend time with and seek emotional support from peers rather than from parents. But findings for the other two attachment features depended on whether or not participants had a romantic partner and, if so, for how long. Those involved in romantic relationships of at least 2 years' duration overwhelmingly named partners as sources of separation distress and secure base (compared with approximately one third who were in shorter relationships and none whose relationships were shorter than 1 year). Those in relatively new relationships and those without romantic partners tended to name a parent as their base of security and the individual whose extended absence they found most distressing.

It appears that the end point of complementary parental attachment serves as the starting point for reciprocal peer attachment. The establishment of a secure base in early childhood facilitates social exploration. Increased time in the company of peers fosters mutual confiding, comforting, and a reliance on peers as havens of safety, thereby paving the way for attachment formation. It is important to note that very few participants in the studies described here were attached—in the technical sense—to friends. Peer relationships meeting the definitional criteria of attachment were almost exclusively of the romantic variety. It suggests that sex plays a central role in peer attachment. Sexual maturation may serve as a catalyst for redirecting social attention and activity toward mating, as is the case in many other species (Hinde, 1983). Furthermore, sexual exchanges create a social context that is conducive to attachment formation.

Freud (1905b) was among the first to write about the striking similarities in the physical intimacy that typifies lovers and mother-infant pairs, both of whom spend much time engaged in mutual gazing, cuddling, nuzzling, suckling, and kissing in the context of prolonged face-to-face, skin-to-skin, belly-to-belly contact and the touching of body parts otherwise considered "private." Although some forms of intimate contact may occur in isolation within other types of social relationships (e.g., kissing among friends), in virtually every human culture the collective occurrence of these most intimate of interpersonal exchanges is restricted to parent-infant and pair-bond relationships (Eibl-Eibesfeldt, 1975).

There is some evidence that the chemical basis for the effects of close physical contact may be the same for lovers and mother-infant pairs. Oxytocin, a substance released during suckling/nursing and thought to induce infant attachment and maternal caregiving, is also released at sexual climax and has been implicated in the cuddling that often follows sexual intercourse (Carter, 1992).

In sum, pair bonds and infant-caregiver relationships show conspicuous similarities in the nature of physical contact, and these differentiate them from other classes of social relationships. The consequence of repeated interactions of this uniquely intimate sort is the development of a specific and distinctive type of bond—namely, an attachment (Hazan & Zeifman, 1999).

■ Enabling and Inhibiting Factors

Attachment theory is based on the idea that the capacity to love and be loved is an aspect of human nature that evolved because our species would not otherwise have survived. However, the same adaptive forces responsible for our innate capacity to love and be loved resulted in our also being, by nature, malleable and responsive to environmental input. The fact that we are all born with an attachment system motivates us to develop survival-enhancing bonds, but it cannot guarantee the formation of such bonds, nor can it ensure that the bonds will be of optimal quality. Can others be counted on for support and comfort? Is it helpful to turn to them when distressed? The answers to such questions are learned through experience and form the bases of "internal working models." Once formed, these mental representations take on a life of their own and are carried into new relationships, where they can affect thoughts, feelings, and behavior in a self-perpetuating way.

The discovery of two insecure patterns of infant attachment motivated a search for the factors that foster or thwart secure attachment. Infants in the original Ainsworth et al. (1978) study were seen in the lab at 12 months of age and also observed in their home environments for several hours every few weeks throughout the first year of life. The main finding to emerge from this large body of naturalistic observational data was that caregiver sensitivity is key. Infants whose caregivers responded promptly, warmly, and reliably to their bids for contact, especially when the infants were distressed, tended to develop a secure attachment. In Ainsworth's view, the reason these infants behaved as they did in the lab at 1 year of age—that is, explored contentedly in the caregiver's presence, were distressed by separations but quickly soothed by contact—was that they had learned through experience that their caregivers could be counted on. Infants whose caregivers were insensitive (not skilled at reading their signals), intrusive (would interrupt their play to hold them), and inconsistent (sometimes responsive and sometimes unresponsive to their distress) tended to develop an ambivalent attachment. This pattern was reflected in their lab behavior at 12 months. Having learned through experience that they could not count on or predict the reactions of their caregiver, they were clingy, too anxious to explore, and extremely distressed by separations; they sought but then angrily resisted comfort, and consequently were not fully soothed. Infants whose caregivers consistently rejected their bids for comfort, and even expressed an aversion to close physical contact with them, tended to develop an avoidant attachment. Their subsequent behavior in the lab—keeping their distance, not showing distress over separations, actively avoiding contact during reunions—made sense in terms of previous experience. They had adopted a strategy of trying to comfort themselves to avoid the painful rejection they had learned to expect.

Ainsworth et al.'s findings raised the obvious question of just how stable infant patterns of attachment are. Do they affect only the infant's relationship with a single caregiver at a particular point in time, or do they foreshadow the way one will relate to all others throughout life? The answer lies somewhere between these two extremes.

Patterns of attachment are initially relationship-specific, but through the process of internalization and mental representation they eventually become traitlike properties of individuals that are carried into new interpersonal situations. One who has developed a working model of others as warm and responsive behaves differently than one who expects others to be unpredictable or rejecting.

Working models of attachment, like personality traits, are perpetuated by three kinds of person–environment interactions: reactive, evocative, and proactive (Caspi & Bem, 1990). The way individuals react to new people (e.g., whether another's nonacknowledgment is attributed to distraction or rejection), the kinds of reactions they evoke from others (e.g., friendliness or hostility), and the kinds of interpersonal situations they proactively seek out or avoid (e.g., social or solitary activities) tend to confirm preexisting models.

However, between birth and death most individuals have relationships with many different people, and each has the potential to modify attachment working models. Bowlby (1973) stated explicitly that models are gradually constructed out of experiences in infancy, childhood, and adolescence; only then do they become relatively resistant but still not impervious to change.

What fosters the capacity to love and be loved is the experience of sensitivity on the part of significant others. If our signals are read accurately and responded to promptly, warmly, and consistently, we learn to expect the same in the future and also how to provide the same. If, on the other hand, our signals are misread or ignored, it engenders anxiety and anger. This not only undermines confidence in others and the natural inclination to turn to them in times of need but also impairs the ability to respond effectively to their needs for comfort and care.

■ Gender, Cross-National, and Cross-Cultural Aspects

It is common in developmental psychology to test for sex differences, even if none is predicted, and attachment researchers have generally followed this tradition. But after literally hundreds of studies reported no sex differences in attachment classifications or their precursors, it became widely accepted that gender is irrelevant to attachment. However, subsequent work suggested otherwise. In the broader field it has often been found that males are more vulnerable to various psychosocial stressors than are females, and when attachment researchers began to study nonnormative high-risk samples, they found the same. Factors such as very low socioeconomic status, presence of a stepfather, full-time day care, and maltreatment have all been found to increase the probability of insecure attachment more among boys than girls (Colin, 1996). In addition, the results of long-term follow-up studies indicate that the behavioral sequelae of insecure attachment also differ, for example, with boys being more aggressive and girls more dependent (Turner, 1991).

In the domain of adult attachment, whether gender differences are found seems to depend in large part on which measure is used. Studies employing the Adult Attachment Interview (AAI; Main & Goldwyn, 1984) have not reported gender differences. Neither have studies using the Adult Attachment Prototypes (AAP; Hazan & Shaver, 1987, 1990). The absence of male–female differences in AAP classifications is especially surprising in light of superficial similarities between the insecure patterns and sex-role stereotypes. The clingy, dependent, ambivalent style sounds stereotypically female, and the cool, aloof, avoidant style sounds stereotypically male, and yet females are no more likely than males to self-classify as ambivalent and males no more likely than females to self-classify as avoidant. However, the results of one study (Kirkpatrick & Davis, 1994) suggest an interaction between sex roles and attachment styles. Heterosexual couples that included an ambivalent female and an avoidant male were significantly more common and enduring than couples consisting of an avoidant female and an ambivalent male. In contrast to the AAI and AAP, the Relationship Styles Questionnaire (RSQ; Griffin & Bartholomew, 1994) is associated with gender differences that correspond to sex-role stereotypes. Specifically, females are more likely than males to be classified as fearful-avoidant, and males are more likely than females to be classified as dismissing-avoidant (Brennan, Shaver, & Tobey, 1991).

The possibility of cultural differences in attachment has been extensively explored by developmentalists. Not long after the Strange Situation paradigm was introduced, questions arose about its cross-cultural validity. In particular, concerns were raised regarding cultural variation in norms of infant care and infant–caregiver contact. For instance, it seemed likely that infants who had been in near-continuous physical contact with their mothers day and night since birth would be much more stressed by the brief separations of the Strange Situation than infants accustomed to day care and separate bedrooms. As a consequence, infants who were inconsolable not because of problems in their relationships with caregivers but rather due to the terrifyingly unfamiliar situation might be mistakenly classified as insecurely attached.

Such concerns were addressed in meta-analyses of data from Strange Situation studies in six countries (Germany, Israel, Japan, the Netherlands, Sweden, and the United States). Secure attachment was the modal pattern in all (Van Ijzendoorn & Kroonenberg, 1988). In addition, it was found that coders in each of the countries were using Ainsworth et al.'s instructions in the same way and that infants who were from different countries but shared an attachment classification behaved similarly (Van Ijzendoorn & Kroonenberg, 1990). Although secure attachment is the most common pattern across cultures, there have been reports of cross-cultural differences in the distribution of insecure attachment patterns. Specifically, ambivalence is more common than avoidance in Israel and Japan, whereas the reverse is observed in Germany and the Netherlands. Such differences appear to correspond to related variations in parenting practices. Specifically, in cultures where more distal caregiving is the norm, insecure attachment is more likely to take the form of avoidance; where more proximal caregiving is the norm, insecurity is more commonly of the ambivalent type (Colin, 1996). It is worth noting that the initial development of the Strange Situation paradigm was informed by extensive and detailed naturalistic observations of infant–caregiver interaction made by Ainsworth during the time she resided in Uganda. The findings from cross-cultural studies are consistent with attachment theory in that attachment behavior appears to be both universal and adapted to local caregiving environments. To date, there have been no systematic investigations of possible cultural differences in adult attachment.

■ Deliberate Interventions

There is abundant evidence that secure attachment is associated with more desirable outcomes at all ages, which naturally raises the question of whether anything can be done to remedy insecure attachment. Intervention studies have generally focused on either infant–caregiver bonds or adult romantic relationships.

One topic of debate in the attachment field is whether individual differences in the way babies behave in the Strange Situation reflect the way they have been treated by caregivers (Ainsworth's view) or (alternatively) their inborn temperaments. Although infants differ innately in terms of proneness to distress, temperament classifications do not predict attachment classifications, whereas caregiver sensitivity does (Vaughn, Lefever, Seifer, & Barglow, 1989). Nevertheless, infants with irritable temperaments are harder to soothe and require greater than average caregiver sensitivity. As a consequence, such infants are at increased risk for developing insecure attachments.

In one study, a sample of temperamentally irritable infants and their caregivers was randomly assigned to an experimental or control condition (van den Boom, 1994). When the infants were between 6 and 9 months of age, caregivers in the experimental group were trained in sensitive responding. Then at 1 year of age, Strange Situation assessments were done. The effects of the intervention were dramatic. Compared with the control group, infants in the experimental group were almost three times as likely to show a secure pattern of attachment. Follow-up studies found that the effects of the intervention were enduring and were still evident more than 2 years later not only in child–caregiver relationships but also in child–peer interactions (van den Boom, 1995).

The principles of attachment theory have been similarly applied to adult relationships. A good example is emotionally focused couples therapy (EFT; S. Johnson & Greenberg, 1985). A major assumption of EFT is that distressed couples get stuck in negative interaction patterns that preclude the sensitivity necessary for secure bonding. EFT entails nine treatment steps. The first four involve assessment and de-escalation of negative interaction cycles. The next three are designed to create events that change patterns of interaction and foster bonding experiences. The last two steps focus on helping couples to integrate the changes into their daily lives. Seven studies (mostly randomized clinical trials) have examined the effectiveness of EFT as indexed by psychological and dyadic adjustment as well as relationship satisfaction. The effect sizes have been quite large relative to the average for psychotherapy research with couples. Upwards of 70% show significant improvement. Moreover, the effects of the intervention are even stronger in 3-month follow-ups, indicating that dyadic adjustment continues to improve after therapy has ended. (For a more detailed account of EFT and a comprehensive review of study findings, see S. Johnson, Hunsley, Greenberg, & Schindler, 1999.)

In sum, secure attachment at all ages depends on the sensitivity of attachment figures. The results of intervention studies with infants, parents, and couples provide compelling evidence that sensitivity is a skill that can be taught and learned, and that can transform troubled relationships into well-functioning, satisfying ones.

Positive changes in attachment security have also been observed in the absence of deliberate interventions. For example, naturally occurring improvements in caregivers' social support systems or decreases in life stress are associated with increases in infant security (Colin, 1996). In adulthood, insecurity tends to diminish over time if relationships simply endure or if one partner happens to be secure (Crowell, Fraley, & Shaver, 1999). Such findings help elucidate the processes by which secure and insecure patterns are maintained or modified.

Researchers have yet to explore the full range of promising intervention strategies. In theory, positive interpersonal experiences of any sort have the potential to change internal working models of attachment and consequently attachment-related thoughts, feelings, and behaviors. Possible candidates include Big Brothers/Big Sisters, family support interventions, parent education, mentoring programs, and individual therapy.

◼ What Is Not Known?

Here are some areas in need of further study:

- Research conducted within the framework of ethological attachment theory has focused almost exclusively on the child-to-parent form of love. Comparatively little is known about the parental/caregiving or romantic/sexual forms.
- There is abundant evidence that having an attachment figure in one's life conveys significant psychological and physical health benefits. Much remains to be learned about the mechanisms underlying such effects.
- When two people love each other, they are connected at multiple levels. The emotional and behavioral levels have been extensively investigated, but much more work needs to be done in the realm of cognitive and information-processing effects.
- Findings from animal models suggest that bonds of love involve physiological co-regulation, which may help explain the physiological dysregulation that follows separation and bond disruption. The notion that physiological co-regulation is an inherent aspect of human socioemotional bonding has yet to be systematically investigated.
- The degree to which early love experiences shape subsequent interpersonal expectations and orientations has been the focus of countless studies. Nevertheless, considerable work must still be done to achieve precise models of continuity and change.
- Evolutionary models of human mating focus almost exclusively on sex differences in selection criteria and mating strategies. What is needed are evolutionary models that take into account the fact that mates tend to love each other and love their joint offspring.

◼ Must-Read Articles and Books

Ainsworth, M. D. S., Blehar, M. C., Waters, E., & Wall, S. (1978). *Patterns of attachment: Assessed in the strange situation and at home.* Hillsdale, NJ: Erlbaum.

Bowlby, J. (1969). *Attachment and loss: Vol. 1. Attachment.* New York: Basic Books.

Bowlby, J. (1973). *Attachment and loss: Vol. 2. Separation: Anxiety and anger.* New York: Basic Books.

Bowlby, J. (1980). *Attachment and loss: Vol. 3. Loss, sadness, and depression.* New York: Basic Books.

Crowell, J. A., Fraley, R. C., & Shaver, P. R. (1999). Measurement of individual differences in adolescent and adult attachment. In J. Cassidy & P. R. Shaver

(Eds.), *Handbook of attachment: Theory, research, and clinical applications* (pp. 434–468). New York: Guilford Press.

Hazan, C., & Shaver, P. R. (1987). Romantic love conceptualized as an attachment process. *Journal of Personality and Social Psychology, 52,* 511–524.

Hazan, C., & Shaver, P. R. (1994). Attachment as an organizational framework for research on close relationships. *Psychological Inquiry, 5,* 1–22.

Solomon, J., & George, C. (1999). The measurement of attachment security in infancy and childhood. In J. Cassidy & P. R. Shaver (Eds.), *Handbook of attachment: Theory, research, and clinical applications* (pp. 287–316). New York: Guilford Press.

14. KINDNESS

[Generosity, Nurturance, Care, Compassion,

Altruistic Love, "Niceness"]

■ *Dame Cicely Saunders was trained as a nurse, a medical social worker, and finally as a physician. Since 1948 she has been involved with the care of patients with terminal illness. She founded Saint Christopher's Hospice in London as the first research and teaching hospice linked with clinical care in 1967. This has been a pioneer in the field of palliative medicine and has links with those developing such work around the world. She holds the prestigious Order of Merit as well as many honorary degrees. Aged 84 in 1999, Dame Cicely addressed an audience in Cambridge, Massachusetts, indicating that even though she is officially retired, she still goes into Saint Christopher's each day to help out with routine care, joining the hospice teams as they care for patients who are dying and assisting with the tasks of care. Dame Cicely appears to most observers to have a genuinely warm and attentive affective presence, a kind of palpable altruistic love, which has served to inspire the people around her over the years. In addition to this general compassion, she also seems to act from a sense of self-identity, that is, a sense that this is just the kind of caring that people must do for one another. She does not view herself as extraordinary. In addition to being an inspiring presence, Dame Cicely is also a practical woman with a sense of how to create lasting institutions. She is universally revered as the founder of the hospice movement. She selected the word* hospice *because in the medieval period, a hospice was simply the place where travelers could rest. She saw that those on the journey of dying are also travelers, and hence she applied the term in this narrower sense. Dame Cicely has a strong sense of equal regard for all humanity, regardless of race, creed, or other idiosyncrasies (Saunders, 1999).* ■

■ Consensual Definition

Kindness, generosity, nurturance, care, compassion, and *altruistic love* are a network of closely related terms indicating a common orientation of the self toward the other. This orientation can be contrasted with solipsism, in which the self relates to others only insofar as they contribute to his or her agenda and are therefore considered useful. Kindness and altruistic love require the assertion of a common humanity in which others are worthy of attention and affirmation for no utilitarian reasons but for their own sake. The affective or emotional ground of such kindness distinguishes it from a merely dutiful or principle-based respect for other persons. Such affective states are expected to give rise to helping behaviors that are not based on an assurance of reciprocity, reputational gain, or any other benefits to self, although such benefits may emerge and need not be resisted.

Individuals with this strength would strongly endorse statements such as the following:

- Others are just as important as me.
- All human beings are of equal worth.
- Having a warm and generous affect seems to bring reassurance and joy to others.
- Giving is more important than receiving.
- Doing good for others with love and kindness is the best way to live.
- I care for the ungrateful as well the grateful.
- I am not the center of the universe but part of a common humanity.
- People who are suffering need compassion.
- People in need require care.
- It is important to help everyone, not just family and friends.

■ Theoretical Traditions

The practice of other-regarding or altruistic love is the foundation of moral and spiritual life in all the major world religions and in most successful virtue traditions (Batson, 1991). *Agape* is a Greek word that describes an unlimited, unselfish, and accepting form of love. It was appropriated by early Christianity and perhaps best described by Saint Paul as love that was patient, kind, unenvious, humble, generous, and forgiving. This form of love is present in all the major world religions, from the Jewish notion of *chesed* (steadfast love) and the Buddhist ideal of *karuna* (compassion) to rough equivalents in Islam, Hinduism, Taoism, Confucianism, and Native American spirituality. Roman antiquity created the myth of Cura, the goddess of care, and also developed the concept of *philantropia.*

In the Western Enlightenment, Scottish moralists such as David Hume and Adam Smith based their ideas on careful empirical descriptions of sympathy, and later German phenomenologists focused on empathy and care as the foundation of ethical living. Among modern feminists, the ethics of care has been described as an empathic responsiveness to others, in contrast to the contractarian tradition of enlightened self-interest. As is well known to students of psychology, unconditional love was the centerpiece of the work by Carl Rogers.

Altruism is usually contrasted with egoism. An altruist intentionally acts for the other's sake as an end in itself, rather than as a means to public recognition or internal well-being. The altruist no longer perceives of self alone as the center of worth. Altruism, especially when it extends beyond biological relations (kin altruism) and "tit-for-tat" calculations grounded in self-interest (reciprocal altruism), is widely lauded and commonly considered a foundation of spiritual and moral life. In its fullest expression, which may include significant self-sacrifice in the aid of strangers or even enemies, altruism is a source of perennial fascination across cultures.

What is at the very core of altruistic love, which is distinguished from general altruism by its deep emotional features and full affirming presence? We all know what it feels like to be valued in this way. We remember loving persons who conveyed this affirmation through tone of voice, facial expression, or hand on the shoulder at a time of grief. How uniquely human is altruistic love? What are the building blocks that might be found in nonhuman species, and can we apply such knowledge to human enhancement? How do we encourage love by worldview (including principles, symbol, and myth) and imitation to achieve consistency? Altruistic love is the most complex and impressive expression of human altruism.

■ Measures

Kindness and altruism are most commonly studied as discrete behaviors in field and laboratory studies. However, some experimental work has also attempted to measure these constructs as traitlike dispositions (Table 14.1). Most measures of kindness, altruism, and prosocial behavior as a trait have relied on self-report. It is important to recognize that self-reports of one's own altruistic tendencies may be prone to distortions due to the obvious social desirability in most social settings of being seen as generous, helpful, and giving. Therefore, it is important to consider the extent to which such self-reports also converge with other measures, such as informant reports or observations of actual altruistic behavior.

Rushton, Chrisjohn, and Fekken (1981) developed a self-report measure called the Self-Report Altruism (SRA) scale. This scale manifested adequate

---

TABLE 14.1   *Measures of Kindness*

Altruism Facet Scale for the Agreeableness Measure of the NEO-PI-R
   Costa & McCrae (1992)
   This is a self-report questionnaire consisting of 8 items that reflect active
   concern for the welfare of other people; items are rated on a scale from 0
   (strongly disagree) to 4 (strongly agree).
   ▪ Internal consistency reliability: alpha = ~.75 (self-rating form) and .80
     (other-rating form)
   ▪ Test–retest reliability: ~.75 (2 weeks; see Yang et al., 1999)
   ▪ Construct validity: correlates highly with other self-report personality
     measurements, including the adjectives *warm, softhearted, gentle, kind,*
     and *tolerant*; also correlates with measures of nurturance, friendliness,
     and femininity; self-ratings correlate with peer ratings ($r = .33$) and
     spouse ratings ($r = .57$)

Self-Report Altruism (SRA) Scale
   Rushton, Chrisjohn, & Fekken (1981)
   This self-report questionnaire consists of 20 items that ask participants how
   often they have engaged in 20 altruistic behaviors (e.g., "I have given direc-
   tions to a stranger"); respondents endorse items on a 5-point scale (where 1 =
   never and 5 = very often).
   ▪ Internal consistency reliability: alpha = ~.70
   ▪ Test–retest reliability: unknown
   ▪ Construct validity: correlates highly with scores from a peer report
     version of the same instrument, as well as with peer's global ratings of
     participants' altruistic qualities; also correlates positively with likelihood
     of having completed an organ donor card, personality measures of
     sensitivity, empathy, social responsibility, nurturance, and people's
     responses to emergency rescue scenarios

---

correlations with informant reports and is also useful for predicting stated
willingness to engage in particular helping behaviors. In addition to the considerable evidence for its validity, this measure recently has also been translated into other languages, including Chinese (Chou, 1996) and Hindi
(Khanna, Singh, & Rushton, 1993), making it potentially useful in cross-
cultural applications.

   Another self-report measure of altruistic tendencies is the Altruism facet
subscale of Costa and McCrae's (1992) NEO-PI-R. As with the Rushton measure, this subscale (which is a facet of the Agreeableness dimension) has considerable evidence for its reliability and validity. As well, it has been translated
into a wide variety of languages (McCrae & Costa, 1997b).

■ Correlates and Consequences

The consequences of kindness can be quantified in a number of metrics. Insofar as kindness and altruism are viewed as the major motives behind volunteerism (admittedly, a tenuous assumption; Omoto & Snyder, 1995), the number of hours volunteered by persons in the United States attests to the massive social consequences of kindness. In 1998 alone, people in the United States volunteered nearly 20 billion hours of their time, worth nearly $226 billion (Independent Sector, 1999).

In addition to such tangible societal (qua economic) benefits that result from kindness, some evidence suggests that a certain form of helping behavior—namely, volunteerism—is associated with many measures of mental and physical health for benefactors. This may be especially true for older adults (Van Willigen, 2000; Wheeler, Gorey, & Greenblatt, 1998). Relatedly, it also appears that people receive mental health benefits from the intervention of older adult volunteers (Wheeler et al., 1998).

It is conceivable that the psychological and physical benefits of volunteering eventuate in longer life. Two recent studies (Musick, Herzog, & House, 1999; Oman, Thoresen, & McMahon, 1999) found that among community-dwelling older adults, volunteering led to reduced risk of early death. Although these studies are preliminary, and some of their conclusions are contradictory (e.g., whether the apparent protective effects of volunteering are stronger for people with different levels of overall social support), both studies suggest that older adults who engage in service to the community may reap benefits that increase longevity.

Secular and devotional literatures from around the world are replete with stories of individuals who experienced changes in their personality, well-being, and goals after receiving altruistic love from another person. However, we know very little about the transforming power of such acts of altruism. Specifically, it would be helpful to investigate how such love causes changes in the recipient, how long the love must be sustained, and how lasting this change is. It would also be useful to study how receiving such love unleashes the capacity to love, thereby producing a shift from egoism to altruism, and on how hatred, fear, anger, and resentment might be reduced.

■ Development

It is becoming clear that the extent to which adults manifest various aspects of kindness and prosocial behavior can be predicted on the basis of their behavior during childhood and adolescence. Young adults' self-reported prosocial dispositions are related to the degree of empathy, sympathy, and prosocial behavior they manifested years earlier (Eisenberg et al., 2002). Moreover, prosocial moral judgment among young adults can be predicted on the basis of the degree of prosocial behavior that one manifested during the preschool years (Eisenberg et al., 2002).

To some extent, the disposition toward altruism—as operationalized by self-report scales such as that by Rushton et al. (1981)—may have a large heritable component. Rushton, Fulker, Neale, Nias, and Eysenck (1986) reported evidence from twin research which indicated that approximately 50% of the variance in self-reported tendencies toward altruistic behavior was due to additive genetic factors. The lion's share of the remaining variance was attributable to unique aspects of the individual environment, with only a trivial amount due to common environment. A considerable amount of the variance in agreeableness itself—the Big Five trait that may form a basic foundation for the altruistic personality—appears to be heritable (Plomin & Caspi, 1999). Moreover, at least one study suggests that as much as 28% of the variance in empathic concern for others may be attributable to additive genetic factors (M. H. Davis, Luce, & Kraus, 1994).

■ Enabling and Inhibiting Factors

In considering the factors that enable and inhibit altruism and kindness, it is helpful to differentiate between altruism as a trait and altruism as a discrete behavior in response to a particular situation.

Altruism as a Trait

An important question dominating the literature on kindness and altruism has been whether some people possess a reliable disposition toward altruistic behavior. Scholars have long presumed that there are types of people who, by virtue of the traits they possess, are predisposed toward altruism and other types of prosocial behavior. Although a variety of traits have been implicated as features of the altruistic personality, three have been predominant in investigators' attempts to identify these traits empirically: (a) empathy/sympathy, (b) moral reasoning, and (c) social responsibility (e.g., Batson, Bolen, Cross, & Neuringer-Benefiel, 1986; Carlo, Eisenberg, Troyer, Switzer, & Speer, 1991; Eisenberg et al., 1989).

Empathy/Sympathy.   Empathy and sympathy are other-oriented emotions that commonly are defined as either (a) the ability to experience the affective state of another person or (b) a soft, tender emotion of pity and concern that is associated with imagining the plight of another person. Empathic and sympathetic tendencies have been shown to predict not only self-report measures of the disposition toward altruistic behavior (Rushton et al., 1981; Rushton, Fulker, Neale, Nias, & Eysenck, 1989; Unger & Thumuluri, 1997) but also informants' ratings of people's actual tendencies toward altruistic behavior (McNeely & Meglino, 1994) and helping in emergency situations (Bierhoff, Klein, & Kramp, 1991).

The trait of empathy holds a special status in modern understandings of kindness because empathic affect is believed by some to be a reliable facilitator of an altruistic motivation to help (e.g., Batson, 1990). Batson et al. (1986) reported data indicating that scores on self-report measures of empathic tendencies are not reliably related to increased helping of others when people can easily justify their decisions not to help (i.e., in situations in which they might choose not to help if not truly motivated to aid the other person), whereas they are related to helping in situations in which it is more difficult to justify one's choice not to help. This finding led Batson et al. to conclude that personality traits may promote helping generally, but not necessarily helping that is specifically motivated by the desire to improve the well-being of the person in need. Interestingly, Carlo et al. (1991) found the same effect but interpreted it in a theoretical context that allowed them to conclude that this finding was evidence in support of the notion of an "altruistic personality." Regardless of which side one takes in this debate, the important lesson seems to be that the effects of dispositional factors such as empathy on helping seem to be more salient in some situations (viz., when, at a practical level, it is quite difficult not to help) than in others (viz., when it is easy to avoid helping).

Moral Reasoning. People with more sophisticated and developed moral reasoning abilities are more helpful toward others in general. Children with other-oriented moral cognitions reliably tend to be more helpful toward their peers (P. A. Miller, Eisenberg, Shell, & Fabes, 1996). Moreover, students who employ more internalized reasoning and reasoning that focuses on the needs of other people appear to engage in more prosocial behavior (e.g., Carlo, Koller, Eisenberg, Da Silva, & Frohlich, 1996). In contrast, children who make their decisions about whether to help other people based on hedonistic concerns (e.g., consideration of the amount of satisfaction or pleasure they will be forced to forgo if they decide to help) tend to engage in less prosocial behavior.

Social Responsibility. People who are high in social responsibility (L. Berkowitz & Lutterman, 1968) believe that they have a personal ethical responsibility to care for the welfare of other people, including strangers and their neighbors (e.g., they would be likely to endorse the statement "Every person should give some of his time for the good of his town or country"). People high in social responsibility are more likely to render aid at the site of automobile accidents than are people lower in this trait (Bierfhoff et al., 1991), are more willing to accept shocks for a bystander when they are unable to avoid exposure to the other person's plight (Batson et al., 1986), and exhibit greater cooperation in mixed-motives dilemmas

(De Kremer & Van Lange, 2001) than do people with lower levels of social responsibility (see also Midlarsky, Kahana, Corley, Nemeroff, & Schonbar, 1999).

As implied earlier, among the Big Five personality dimensions, agreeableness is likely to be the most important correlate of kindness, prosociality, and altruism. Conversely, people who are high in altruistic tendencies tend to manifest low levels of antisocial and narcissistic traits (S. R. Axelrod, Widiger, Trull, & Corbitt, 1997), suggesting that these personality disorders (or traits associated with them) may inhibit kindness. Agreeableness also appears to stimulate greater concern for the welfare of other people in dilemmas in which people share access to a common pool of resources that can be depleted by overuse (Koole, Jager, van den Berg, Vlek, & Hofstee, 2001).

Altruism as a Discrete Behavior

In addition, there have been efforts to identify the factors that govern people's altruistic responses to particular interpersonal situations in which another person is in need of help.

Positive Mood.   One interesting and well-documented effect is that people who are put into a positive mood are considerably more willing to help others than are people who are in a neutral mood (Carlson, Charlin, & Miller, 1988). This effect has been reproduced across a wide variety of positive mood inductions and a wide variety of measures of helping. The effect of positive mood on helping behavior is considerable, with people in positive moods approximately one half of a standard deviation more helpful than are people in neutral moods. In general, however, the positive mood–helping relationship is strongest when giving help is pleasant and the help does not require sustained effort. Carlson et al. also found evidence that good moods have stronger effects on helping among people over age 30 than among people younger than age 30. The effects of good mood on kindness-related behaviors are mediated in part by heuristic versus effortful decision making. People who are in a good mood feel more secure and, as a result, more willing to rely on consensus and reciprocity heuristics (e.g., imitating the cooperative behavior of others) rather than effortful processing (e.g., adjusting one's personal cooperative effort in response to the perceived cooperativeness of other people) in deciding how much to cooperate (Hertel, Neuhof, Theuer, & Kerr, 2000).

Empathy.   A final highlight of the work on the situational approach is the long-standing debate over whether a true altruistic motivation exists. Batson (1990, 1991) has hypothesized that altruistic motivation to help a person in need is a function of the amount of empathic emotion the individual experiences toward the person in need. In situations in which an individual does not experience empathy toward a person in need, the altruistic motive does not appear to be stimulated, and thus, helping behavior that might arise does not appear to be altruistic per se. Researchers have offered a wide variety of alternative explanations for the empathy–helping link that do not require the concept of altruistic motivation (e.g., Cialdini, Brown, Lewis, Luce, & Neuberg, 1997; Cialdini et al., 1987; K. D. Smith, Keating, & Stotland, 1989), but the evidence does appear to support the idea that true altruistic motivation is a distinct human possibility (see Batson, 1990, 1991, 1997).

■ Gender, Cross-National, and Cross-Cultural Aspects

Of particular concern to researchers over the last several decades is the possibility that gender may differentially influence whether one gives or receives help in real-world dilemmas. Eagly and Crowley (1986) summarized this large literature and reported a very small tendency for men to provide help more readily than do women. Although this effect was statistically significant, it was so small as to be nearly meaningless (i.e., on average, men were .07 standard deviations more helpful than were women). Moreover, it is important to keep in mind that most of these studies focus on chivalrous acts toward strangers—that is, altruistic behavior that is accompanied by a strong gender stereotype—but not acts of kindness and altruism within existing relationships, a form of helping that may be more common among women. Interestingly, women were reliably more likely to be recipients of other people's helping behavior, suggesting that women receive more help from both men and women than do men.

Research by R. C. Johnson et al. (1989) addressed possible cross-cultural differences in giving help. These researchers compared the scores of students from Australia, Egypt, Korea, the Republic of China (Taiwan), the United States, and Yugoslavia on a 56-item scale on which participants indicated the frequency with which they engaged in each of 56 helping behaviors. They found some evidence for cross-national differences in the mean frequencies of self-reported help-giving in these samples, although the differences are difficult to interpret (see also den Ouden & Russell, 1997; Hedge & Yousif, 1992). Jha, Yadav, and Kumari (1997) also reported religio-cultural differences in self-reported altruistic behavior among young adults (ages 20–35), with Christian respondents scoring higher on self-reported altruism than did Hindus or Muslims.

■ Deliberate Interventions

Despite the massive literatures on moral development in education and guidance, surprisingly little seems to be known about how to encourage kindness and altruism directly. This oversight is rather astonishing. Studies that evaluate the effectiveness of interventions for encouraging kindness in the context of parenting, mentoring, and education would be most welcome.

■ What Is Not Known?

Despite a wealth of important findings related to the personality and social factors that influence altruism, many other questions remain regarding the "roots" and "fruits" of altruism. The following questions could be productively studied by psychologists, as well as other scientists from the social, biological, and medical sciences:

- What are the evolutionary origins and neurological substrates of altruism and altruistic love? How might these interface with cultural, religious, and social factors?
- What are the physiological correlates of altruistic love both given and received?
- What role does attachment play in the expression of altruistic love?
- How does the giving or receiving of altruistic, compassionate love affect physical health and mortality?
- How does such love affect persons with mental or physical illnesses, especially in severe cases?
- How does the receiving of such love influence persons with cognitive deficits—for example, persons with retardation or dementia, or persons with serious mental disorders?
- To what extent are health care professionals motivated by altruistic love, and how does this affect them and their patients?
- How do altruism and altruistic love enter into the context of organ donation, in which the donation of organs is viewed as a "gift of life" for the stranger in need?
- What means are available to expand or extend altruism and altruistic love to those thought of as outside one's social group? How do we define the "outsider," and how does this influence our attitudes and actions?
- Are there specific spiritual practices (e.g., types of prayer, meditation, silence, worship) that might help to encourage altruistic love?
- What can economic research tell us about the nature and expression of altruism and altruistic love? How does such love affect our attitudes and behaviors toward money and the use of wealth? What is the basis of philanthropy, and can it be successfully encouraged?

■ Must-Read Articles and Books

Batson, C. D. (1991). *The altruism question: Toward a social-psychological answer.* Hillsdale, NJ: Erlbaum.

Batson, C. D. (1997). Self-other merging and the empathy-altruism hypothesis: Reply to Neuberg et al. (1997). *Journal of Personality and Social Psychology, 73,* 517–522.

Batson, C. D., Bolen, M. H., Cross, J. A., & Neuringer-Benefiel, H. E. (1986). Where is the altruism in the altruistic personality? *Journal of Personality and Social Psychology, 50,* 212–220.

Carlson, M., Charlin, V., & Miller, N. (1988). Positive mood and helping behavior: A test of six hypotheses. *Journal of Personality and Social Psychology, 55,* 211–229.

Cialdini, R. B., Brown, S. L., Lewis, B. P., Luce, C., & Neuberg, S. L. (1997). Reinterpreting the empathy-altruism relationship: When one into one equals oneness. *Journal of Personality and Social Psychology, 73,* 481–494.

Cialdini, R. B., Schaller, M., Houlihan, D., Arps, K., Fultz, J., & Beaman, A. L. (1987). Empathy-based helping: Is it selflessly or selfishly motivated? *Journal of Personality and Social Psychology, 52,* 749–758.

Eagly, A. H., & Crowley, M. (1986). Gender and helping behavior: A meta-analytic review of the social psychological literature. *Psychological Bulletin, 100,* 282–308.

Eisenberg, N., Miller, P. A., Schaller, M., Fabes, R. A., Fultz, J., Shell, R., et al. (1989). The role of sympathy and altruistic personality traits in helping: A reexamination. *Journal of Personality, 57,* 41–67.

Rushton, J. P., Fulker, D. W., Neale, M. C., Nias, D. K. B., & Eysenck, H. J. (1986). Altruism and aggression: The heritability of individual differences. *Journal of Personality and Social Psychology, 50,* 1192–1198.

Smith, K. D., Keating, J. P., & Stotland, E. (1989). Altruism reconsidered: The effect of denying feedback on a victim's status to empathic witness. *Journal of Personality and Social Psychology, 57,* 641–650.

15. SOCIAL INTELLIGENCE

[Emotional Intelligence, Personal Intelligence]

People who are high in emotional intelligence, one of the positive traits discussed in this chapter, exhibit special capacities in regard to experiencing and strategizing about emotion. They are adept at perceiving emotions in relationships, and they display a keen understanding of their emotional relationships with others, as well as of the meanings of emotions in those relationships. Such emotional understanding is exhibited by a 16-year-old young woman whose emotional intelligence was tested as part of a study of teenagers and the conflicts they experience with their peers. She was the highest scorer in the group. Here she describes a conflict she had with some friends. The follow-up questions asked by the interviewer appear in square brackets.

■ *Once my friends wanted to sneak in someone's room and paint them while he slept. It began as joking around ("wouldn't this be funny"; "could you believe it if?"). Then it slowly evolved into dares ("I bet you wouldn't," or "I dare you to"). I felt like it was betraying the trust I had with the other person, I didn't feel right with sneaking up on a sleeping person with no way to defend himself, and I thought doing this would make the person have his feelings hurt. I know how little pranks like this could really hurt someone's feelings, make them feel like everyone is making fun of them, taking away their dignity and disrespecting them. I won't do that to someone because I understand how badly that can hurt. [How did you handle it?] Told them straight out that it was a degrading thing to do and they shouldn't be so cruel. Asked them how they would like it? [Relation to long-term goals?] I'm not sure. One of my everyday goals is to try my hardest not to judge or make fun of someone. [Parents' reaction?] They would have been proud, but it's just one of those things that sort of never gets talked about because they would have also said, I ruined a perfectly harmless joke. [Parents' goals?] My parents want me to be respectful (Mayer, Perkins,*

Caruso, & Salovey, 2001, p. 136; see also Vitello-Cicciu, 2001, for similar cases among nurse managers).   n

■ Consensual Definition

Intelligence refers to the ability to think abstractly—to understand similarities and differences among things, to recognize patterns, and to see other relations. Intelligence can be divided into subtypes that focus on a specific area of reasoning. For example, cognitive intelligence divides into verbal, perceptual-organizational, and spatial intelligences, among others (J. B. Carroll, 1993). There also exists a group of hot intelligences, so called because they process "hot" information: signals concerning motives, feelings, and other domains of direct relevance to an individual's well-being and/or survival. Three such intelligences are reviewed here: personal, social, and emotional intelligence. Collectively, these intelligences are concerned with the ability to carry out abstract reasoning in the domain of hot information. Hot information—and the hot intelligences that interpret that information—concern information of direct personal relevance for survival and well-being (Mayer & Mitchell, 1998).

Intelligences concern the broader capacity of the person to carry out abstract reasoning. This capacity is independent of a person's self-concept. For example, it is possible for a person to think of herself as intelligent and yet to be without the capacity to reason effectively. Empirical studies have repeatedly shown that self-estimated intellectual abilities do not bear a close relation to actual abilities (D. L. Paulus, Lysy, & Yik, 1998). For that reason, intelligences are typically defined in terms of actual performance at problem solving. People who are high in hot intelligence are said to be able to perform certain tasks well, such as the following:

- identify emotional content in faces, voices, and designs (emotional intelligence)
- use emotional information to facilitate cognitive activities (emotional intelligence)
- understand what emotions mean regarding relationships, how they progress over time, and how they blend with one another (emotional intelligence)
- understand and manage emotion (emotional intelligence)
- accurately assess one's own performance at a variety of tasks (personal intelligence)
- accurately assess one's own emotions and feelings (emotional, personal intelligence)
- accurately assess one's own motives (personal, social intelligence)
- use social information to get others to cooperate (social intelligence)

- identify social dominance and sociopolitical relationships among individuals and groups (social intelligence)
- act wisely in relationships (social intelligence)

Emotional intelligence concerns the ability to use emotional information in reasoning. Such emotional information can be of internal or external origin. Personal intelligence involves accurate self-understanding and self-assessment, including the ability to reason about internal motivational, emotional, and, more generally, dynamic processes. Social intelligence concerns one's relationships with other people, including the social relationships involved in intimacy and trust, persuasion, group memberships, and political power. Conceptually, the three intelligences described here overlap, but empirically the degree of overlap is not well understood.

■ Theoretical Traditions

The term *intelligence* has a long history. In the Western world, the cognitive sphere was first split off from other ideas such as aesthetics by the ancient Greeks (Burt, 1955). The advent of intelligence testing in the 1900s lent a more modern shape to the concept of intelligence, and by 1921 a half dozen or more definitions of intelligence were offered up in a symposium recorded in the *Journal of Educational Psychology* ("Intelligence and its measurement," 1921). Therein can be found E. L. Thorndike's definition of intellect as "the power of good responses from the point of view of truth or fact" (p. 124); L. M. Terman's statement that "an individual is intelligent in proportion as he is able to carry on abstract reasoning" (p. 128); and L. L. Thurstone's more complex formulations (p. 204). Others, such as S. L. Pressey, were content simply to measure intelligence and observe what intelligence tests predicted (p. 144). A more recent symposium of intelligence researchers followed along similar lines, highlighting that intelligence involves, above all else, abstract reasoning and, secondarily, adaptation (Sternberg & Detterman, 1986).

Beyond definitions, much effort has been expended to determine whether there is one or more than one intelligence (e.g., N. Brody, 2000; H. Gardner, 1983). This is an issue concerning the degree to which performances on different sorts of tasks are correlated. If all mental performances rose and fell in lockstep, then it would be convenient to describe the aggregate: one intelligence. If, on the other hand, each mental performance was independent of the others, then each one would represent its own individual intelligence, and it would not make sense to speak of a general intelligence. The reality, as it turns out, is midway between these two extremes. It is generally appropriate to model human performance either as a single ability or as multiple abilities. The single ability is roughly the average of such performances. More precisely, it represents a single statistical factor that underlies all mental performance. Multiple intelligences arise, on the other hand, when one chooses to split up mental performance into subsets. It is from such splits that one arises at such concepts as multiple intelligences: "verbal intelligence," "perceptual-organizational intelligence," "spatial intelligence," and the like. Each adjectival term—*verbal, perceptual, spatial*, and so forth—defines the area to which the intelligence applies. For the purposes of this chapter, one important division among intelligences is the broad division between the intelligences that are cognitive, or "cold," on the one hand, and intelligences, that are "hot," or that focus on motivation, emotion, or other personal and social issues, on the other (Mayer & Mitchell, 1998).

Of the hot intelligences, social intelligence has the longest scientific lineage. Social intelligence was first described by Thorndike (1920), who defined it as "the ability to understand and manage men and women, boys and girls—to act wisely in human relations" (p. 228). Fairly soon after its introduction, research on the topic began, and it has been pursued more or less continuously since then (Walker & Foley, 1973). Measures were introduced in the mid-1930s, and those, too, have been pursued to the present, albeit with concerns that they are not distinct from general intelligence (Cronbach, 1960).

The next of the hot intelligences, the personal intelligences, has a more recent lineage. In his influential book *Frames of Mind: The Theory of Multiple Intelligences*, H. Gardner (1983) proposed the existence of personal intelligences and divided them into an "intrapersonal intelligence," which was mostly focused internally, and an "interpersonal intelligence," which resembled the social intelligence discussed by Thorndike and others. We will refer to intrapersonal intelligence here simply as personal intelligence and contrast it with the earlier-proposed social intelligence. Unlike social intelligence, personal intelligence has a very short history.

The third of the hot intelligences, emotional intelligence, was first defined and researched as a measurable concept in the early 1990s (Mayer, DiPaolo, & Salovey, 1990; Mayer & Salovey, 1993; Salovey & Mayer, 1990). The advent of emotional intelligence entailed synthesizing research findings from several loosely related areas in the psychological literature (e.g., intelligence, emotions, personality; Salovey & Mayer, 1990, pp. 189–190). Although the term *emotional intelligence* had been mentioned sporadically beforehand (e.g., Leuner, 1966; Payne, 1986), it could not be defined adequately until those various scientific literatures were connected. Part of the effort involved drawing together ability measures in such areas as nonverbal sensitivity (which includes a mix of emotional and social-relational judgments) and aesthetics and looking at the common emotional thread that ran through them (e.g., R. Rosenthal, Hall, DiMatteo, Rogers, & Archer, 1979). Emotions researchers were encouraged to think further about emotion as information when computer scientists began to ask how computers could understand emotion (Mayer, 1986, 2000). The early

1990s saw the first formal definitions, formal measures, and call for research in the area.

The areas of hot intelligence have been investigated somewhat separately despite their conceptual interrelations. In fact, the ability tests presently under development to measure them have not yet been used in the same studies, and so their intercorrelations are unknown. Research on each of the three approaches to intelligence—social, personal, and emotional—can be divided into two areas: psychometric studies and componential analyses. Roughly speaking, the psychometric approach focuses on abilities and individual differences; the componential approach focuses on the knowledge structures and processes—the mental architecture—underlying the intelligence (Sternberg, 1977).

The field of social intelligence is most highly developed, having had a head start of about 60 to 70 years. At the same time, various setbacks in the study of social intelligence have led to very slow progress in the field. These failures chiefly have to do with the repeated finding that social intelligence is sufficiently similar to general intelligence as to be difficult to measure independently (for reviews of these issues, see Kihlstrom & Cantor, 2000; Walker & Foley, 1973). Enough evidence (or hope) that social intelligence is distinct has been present to ensure the development of several assessment batteries of social intelligence. Guilford's structure of intellect model provided a definition that has shaped many of the ability tasks employed to measure social intelligence today. A technical report by O'Sullivan, Guilford, and deMille (as cited in Kihlstrom & Cantor, 2000, p. 361; O'Sullivan, Guilford, & deMille, 1965) viewed social intelligence primarily as involving six areas:

- cognition of behavioral units: the ability to identify the internal mental states of individuals
- cognition of behavioral classes: the ability to group other people's mental states on the basis of similarity
- cognition of behavioral relations: the ability to interpret meaningful connections among behavioral acts
- cognition of behavioral systems: the ability to interpret sequences of social behavior
- cognition of behavioral transformations: the ability to respond flexibly in interpreting changes in social behavior
- cognition of behavioral implications: the ability to predict what will happen in an interpersonal situation

In addition to expressly psychometric approaches to individual differences in social intelligence, a good deal of research has been focused on the sorts of expert knowledge that go into being socially intelligent. For example, Cantor and Kihlstrom (1987) focus on the development of social knowledge rather than on intelligence per se. They interpret social intelligence to refer to what a person knows and does not know about his or her surrounding world and how such knowledge shapes the individual's activities. Their approach, which has its origins in G. A. Kelly's (1955) personal construct theory, has not yet yielded any scales of general ability.

The central approach to personal intelligence is Gardner's theory of multiple intelligences. Gardner's (1983) original theory stated that there are at least seven kinds of intelligence, each associated with a different brain system and, consequently, potentially unrelated to one another (chapter 3). As noted earlier, Gardner postulates two personal intelligences: one intrapersonal (personal) and the other interpersonal (social). Gardner joins these two intelligences because he views them as forming an integrated whole. Here we attempt to separate out aspects relevant to intrapersonal, or simply personal, intelligence, as we already have covered social intelligence. Personal intelligence is said by Gardner to involve the following five areas:

- access to internal signals, particularly emotions and moods
- knowledge of how well the individual performs at various tasks
- an understanding of one's own mental processes
- an emerging identity that entails a sophisticated delineation of the self
- a sense of self that is differentiated from others (H. Gardner, 1993b, pp. 246–252)

Gardner's list of those with high personal intelligence includes Socrates, Jesus Christ, Mahatma Gandhi, and Eleanor Roosevelt. An alternative contemporary approach takes an evolutionary perspective on personal intelligence, viewing it as an active information-gathering process concerning one's internal processes (Park & Park, 1997).

The ability model of emotional intelligence views it as the capacity to think intelligently about emotions and the capacity of emotion to enhance intellectual activities (Mayer & Salovey, 1997; Mayer, Salovey, & Caruso, 2000; cf. Salovey & Mayer, 1990; Salovey, Mayer, & Caruso, 2002).[1] More specifically, emotional intelligence skills are divided into four parts or branches (often referred to as the four-branch model; Mayer & Salovey, 1997):

- perceiving emotions: the ability to perceive emotions in oneself and others accurately (Branch 1)
- using emotions to facilitate thought: the capacity to integrate emotions in thought and to use emotions in a way that facilitates cognitive processes (Branch 2)

[1]Emotional intelligence has undergone a number of popularizations, for example, in a best-selling trade book (Goleman, 1995). As can be the case, a variety of popular and commercial reinterpretations of emotional intelligence ensued—some heavily marketed. These models mix together various personality characteristics such as reality testing, assertiveness, persistence, and the like that do not pertain specifically to either emotion or intelligence, or their combination. Such models are reviewed and analyzed elsewhere (Matthews, Zeidner, & Roberts, 2002; Mayer, 2001; Mayer, Salovey, & Caruso, 2000).

- understanding emotions: the capacity to understand emotional concepts and meanings, the links between emotions and the relationships they signal, and how emotions blend and progress over time (Branch 3)
- managing emotions: the capacity to monitor and regulate emotions for personal and social growth and well-being (Branch 4)

As will be seen, most studies of the four-branch model have focused on the measurement of individual differences in emotional intelligence. As with social intelligence, however, there is an extensive body of literature on the psychological processes underlying each area of emotional intelligence (see Feldman-Barrett & Salovey, 2002). There also exist alternative, self-report approaches to its measure (e.g., Salovey, Woolery, & Mayer, 2001).

■ Measures

As a matter of definition, intelligence is conceptualized as an ability or capacity. For that reason alone, the preferred method of measuring intelligence is through measures of mental performance. The well-known predictive validity of verbal and perceptual-organizational intelligence tests for school and job performance has been established exclusively on the basis of ability testing techniques. Indeed, such ability measures yield unique variance that is at best poorly approximated by self-reports of intelligence (D. L. Paulus et al., 1998). Ability measures of hot intelligences such as emotional intelligence also yield unique variance and are only poorly approximated by self-report (Brackett & Mayer, 2003; Salovey, Mayer, Caruso, & Lopez, 2003). One place where self-report may be useful is in personal intelligence, which is sometimes operationalized as the discrepancy between self-assessment and actual performance. This review of measures will focus on ability measures of the hot intelligences and proceed according to the chronological introduction of the intelligences: social, personal, and emotional (Table 15.1).

The primary contemporary scale of social intelligence was developed by Jones, Day, and colleagues (Jones & Day, 1997; J. E. Lee, Wong, Day, Maxwell, & Thorpe, 2000). In the scale tasks, participants interpret videos of people's actions or interpret social phraseology (e.g., forms of politeness) according to the context in which it might be used. Factor analysis of the tasks suggests that this scale includes separate performance measures of social knowledge and social inference, and these are said to reflect crystallized and fluid social intelligence, respectively. The performance scales show considerable discriminant validity with cognitive intelligence, with correlations between individual social and cognitive intelligence tests below $r = .20$. The Jones and Day scale draws its lineage from the O'Sullivan and Guilford studies, and two of the four tasks are drawn from that work (O'Sullivan & Guilford, 1976).

TABLE 15.1   *Measures of Social, Personal, and Emotional Intelligence*

Social Intelligence
Factor-Based Social Intelligence Tasks
   Jones & Day (1997)
   ▪ Reliability: internal consistency (alpha coefficient): .52–.86
   ▪ Test–retest reliability: unknown
   ▪ Validity: content valid; discriminant validity vis-à-vis cognitive IQ

Personal Intelligence
Psychological Mindedness Assessment Procedure
   McCallum & Piper (1997)
   ▪ Reliability: interrater reliability: .88–.96
   ▪ Test–retest reliability: unknown
   ▪ Validity: predicts better psychotherapy outcome in settings where psycho-
     dynamic psychotherapy is practiced

Emotional Intelligence
Mayer-Salovey-Caruso Emotional Intelligence Test (MSCEIT)
   Mayer, Salovey, & Caruso (2002)
   ▪ Reliability: internal consistency (split half): overall: .91–.93; area subscales
     = .86–.90; branch subscales = .76–.91
   ▪ Test–retest reliability: .86
   ▪ Validity: content valid in relation to the four branch model of emotional
     intelligence; tests of structural validity indicate one overall factor, two
     area-level subfactors, and four branch-level subfactors that correspond to
     the test's primary scales and subscales; discriminant validity studies
     indicate the test is distinct from cognitive IQ and self-reports of empathy;
     predictive validity indicates that, among other findings, heightened
     emotional intelligence relates to fewer problem or deviant behaviors
     (see text)

The tests available for personal intelligence are the weakest of those measuring the three intelligences. When Gardner proposed his theory of multiple
intelligences (in which intrapersonal and interpersonal intelligences were first
discussed), he discouraged the use of traditional psychometric tests, relying
instead on conceptual and neurological arguments for their existence. Nonetheless, some empirical measures were developed by others. An early empirical
assessment of these measures gave rise to the development of two apparently
similar tests with different names (Plucker, Callahan, & Tomchin, 1996). One
is the Discovering Intellectual Strengths and Capabilities through Observation
while allowing for Varied Ethnic Responses (DISCOVER) test. The other is the
Problem Solving Assessment Technique (PSA; Reid, Udall, Romanoff, & Algozzine, 1999). Although both tests stemmed from batteries originally intended to
measure multiple intelligences, the focus was on interpersonal intelligence (clos-

est to social intelligence). Factor structures of the test indicated that interpersonal intelligence (like early measures of social intelligence) merged into verballinguistic intelligence measures (Plucker et al., 1996). As a consequence, both the DISCOVER and the PSA are now said to measure only linguistic, spatial, and logical-mathematical intelligences. The current test development emphasis (as implied by the DISCOVER test's name) has focused on looking at different responses that might reveal intelligence across ethnic groups. This is a noble goal. Regrettably, however, the tests fall somewhere between inconclusive and irrelevant regarding Gardner's personal intelligences (Sarouphim, 1998, 2000).

A test that may be more promising for personal intelligence is the Psychological Mindedness Assessment Procedure (McCallum & Piper, 1987), a performance test in which the participant watches a series of videotaped vignettes and must answer the question "What seems to be troubling this woman?" The responses are scored according to the sophistication of the viewer's response. One difficulty is that the responses are calibrated according to a psychodynamic viewpoint. Those who employ alternative theoretical perspectives on personality may question the validity of the scoring key. On the other hand, the nature of personal insight involved in personal intelligence is likely to include some psychodynamic formulations. Gardner viewed Freud's development of psychodynamic theory as an instance of personal intelligence in operation. The McCallum and Piper scale is reliable and shows good evidence of validity in predicting therapy outcome (e.g., Piper, McCallum, Joyce, Azim, & Ogrodniczuk, 1999). For these reasons, it may be uniquely promising among currently available measures of personal intelligence.

Finally, in the case of emotional intelligence, the central performance test in the area is now the Mayer-Salovey-Caruso Emotional Intelligence Test, or MSCEIT. This test has grown out of a series of studies on assessing emotional intelligence as an ability. Early performance tasks demonstrated the existence of reliable individual differences in emotional perception and related them to criteria such as empathy and emotional openness (Mayer et al., 1990; Mayer & Geher, 1996). Some were discouraged by the apparently modest reliabilities of the early scales but agreed that they assessed a new source of individual differences (Davies, Stankov, & Roberts, 1998). Those early scales were next incorporated into a more comprehensive measure, called the Multifactor Emotional Intelligence Scale (MEIS). The MEIS contained 12 individual tasks of emotional intelligence keyed to the four-branch model of emotional intelligence (see earlier discussion). This scale met customary psychometric standards for a new instrument, with an overall coefficient alpha reliability of above $r = .96$. Factor analyses indicated that there existed a general factor of emotional intelligence and that subfactors roughly corresponding to the four-branch model also were justified. Emotional intelligence was related to but different from both cognitive intelligence and self-reported empathy (Mayer, Caruso, & Salovey, 1999). The MEIS test was, however, quite lengthy. A revised version of the test—the

MSCEIT V2.0—achieved a reliability of above $r = .90$ and now has been standardized on a sample of 5,000. It is a more convenient length for research, involving a 30- to 45-minute administration, and it offers expert scoring based on a sample of 20 PhD-level emotion specialists (Mayer, Salovey, Caruso, & Sitarenios, 2003). The test possesses content and factorial validity (Mayer, Perkins, Caruso, & Salovey, 2001; Mayer, Salovey, & Caruso, 2002; Mayer et al., 2003). Its predictive validity is discussed in the following.

■ Correlates and Consequences

Among the three intelligences examined here—social, personal, and emotional—the most is known about what emotional intelligence predicts, and that is not saying much. Research on social intelligence remains focused on demonstrating its independence from cognitive intelligence. Thus, the most recent studies in the area by Wong and colleagues have mostly employed multitrait, multimethod approaches in an attempt to determine whether social intelligence can be separated from general cognitive intelligence (J.-E. Lee et al., 2000). Now that these demonstrations have established the existence of a separate social intelligence, future research can turn to examining the relations between social intelligence and various outcomes of importance.

If personal intelligence is taken as the ability to understand one's performance more accurately (i.e., a correspondence between one's actual ability and the degree to which one understands that ability), then there are relevant findings as well. Research consistently indicates that those people who have relatively realistic appraisals of their ability in a given area perform better at their chosen occupations than those who do not (Bandura, 1997).

Although emotional intelligence was the most recent of the hot intelligences to be introduced, it has also surpassed the others in the number of published research studies examining it. Since the development of the MEIS and more recent MSCEIT, there has been a gradually increasing emphasis on discovering what these tests might predict. We examine two areas: test-to-test correlations, and test-to-external-life-criteria correlations. Test-to-test correlations using tests measuring similar or related constructs are generally expected to be fairly high, for example, above $r = .50$. Emotional intelligence, measured as an ability, appears relatively independent of other personality and intelligence tests (Brackett & Mayer, 2003; Caruso, Mayer, & Salovey, 2002; Ciarrochi, Chan, & Caputi, 2000; Mayer, 2000). Correlations between the MSCEIT (or MEIS) and the Big Five traits and other measures are generally between zero and $r = +/-.30$, occasionally rising to $r = .35$ for measures of self-reported empathy and verbal intelligence. This is exciting because it indicates a new variable is being measured.

Test correlations with external criteria—life surveys, life behaviors, and actual observed behavior—are expected to be in the $r = .10$ to $.40$ range. This is because surveys of individuals' actual lifestyles, possessions, memberships, and the like represent the diversity and complexity of everyday life, unfiltered through a simplified self-concept. The correlations are also lower because such surveys ask detail-based questions that must be aggregated (relative to personality tests) to obtain comparable reliability (Mayer, Carlsmith, & Chabot, 1998). At the same time, these small relationships can make extremely important differences in real-life applications (Rosenthal & Rubin, 1982). Within that context, the findings for emotional intelligence are very exciting—albeit preliminary. The preliminary nature of these findings is reflected in the fact that some of the ensuing references are to unpublished senior honors, master's, and dissertation theses. With that qualification, the early evidence suggests that people high in emotional intelligence exhibit patterns of modestly better life judgment and smoother social functioning. People higher on the emotional understanding scale of emotional intelligence show more adaptive defense styles (Pelletteri, 1999). In student populations, emotional intelligence appears to predict lower levels of drug and alcohol use, particularly among men (Brackett & Mayer, 2003; Brackett, Mayer, & Warner, in press; Formica, 1998; Trinidad & Johnson, 2002) and lower levels of interpeer aggression (Formica, 1998; Mayer et al., 2001; M. M. Rubin, 1999). In business settings, people with higher emotional intelligence may provide better customer service (C. L. Rice, 1999). The findings concerning lower problem behaviors such as drug use and aggression seem to represent a pattern. The remaining findings probably are too new to elicit strong confidence, but they suggest potentially promising areas for future research.

■ Development

Little is known about the development of the hot intelligences. For the time being, it makes sense to compare them to traditional—general—intelligence. As research continues, this comparison may require some qualifications. Early on, general intelligence was recognized to reflect a rate of mental growth: a certain level of mental attainment in relation to chronological age. The first intelligence quotients were called *rate IQs* because they reflected a rate of growth, be it average, slower than average, or faster (Stern, 1914). The average person learns about the world in a regular, persistent fashion over time, gradually building up knowledge. The lower-than-average individual lags behind, whereas the higher-than-average individual pulls ahead. The original rate IQs, and the deviation IQs that came after them (and which were calculated in a different way), tend to be grossly, coarsely, stable across the life span. Put another way, extremely high scorers almost always continue to score high; extreme low scorers, regrettably, rarely do better, but there is some room for meaningful change in the broad middle.

The development of general intelligence is often divided into two parts: the raw capacity, speed, and fluidity of learning, called *fluid intelligence*, on the one hand, and the pool of accumulated knowledge acquired by an individual, called *crystallized intelligence*, on the other. Fluid intelligence refers to the capacity to learn, analyze, and understand at the moment. It is often associated with the developmental, neurological health of the individual. Crystallized intelligence, in contrast, refers to the accumulated expert knowledge a person acquires in various fields (Cattell, 1943). Crystallized intelligence is generally the more stable of the two, and recent work by Ackerman (1997) has gone some way toward understanding the sorts of crystallized knowledge structures involved. It appears possible that the fluid-crystallized division would apply to the hot intelligences as well. For example, in the case of emotional intelligence, the perception of emotion might be relatively fluid and depend on the mental activities of the moment, whereas the understanding of emotional meanings and relationships might be acquired over time and be more identified with a crystallized aspect. Fluid intelligence in the cognitive realm can be affected by such issues as fatigue and anxiety. Factors related to fluid intelligence in hot intelligences are unknown as of yet.

A good deal has been written on the psychological development involved in the hot intelligences, and it is impossible to review it all here. Saarni (1999, 2001), in particular, has summarized the early childhood development of social and emotional competencies. H. Gardner's (1983) work on the personal intelligences covers both child and adult development. Erikson's (1963) essay on the Eight Ages of human beings remains a classic in this regard. Although these authors make relatively specific age-based discriminations, our summary will address four times of life: (a) infancy and toddlerhood, (b) middle childhood, (c) adolescence, and (d) adulthood. The following summary closely follows descriptions by Saarni, Gardner, and Erikson.

Infancy and toddlerhood are periods during which the young child begins to assemble a group of mostly unintegrated but critical abilities that will serve as foundations for later development. These include, most internally, the ability to sense positive and negative mood states, the emergence of consciousness and self-awareness, and the ability to symbolize awareness and feelings and call them by their names. More socially, the individual begins to learn to play games with others, such as peekaboo; she or he learns to engage in pretend games and also to simulate distress and crying to gain attention. The young child also begins to learn some important forms of self-control, including patience, sharing, and temper management. The child also begins to empathize with others.

In middle childhood, greater and more integrated self-regulation of emotional, personal, and social qualities is present, with a particular emphasis on "fitting in" and achieving. During this time, the child may adopt a "cool" front with peers and be particularly sensitive to embarrassment and shame. Children focus on abilities and industries and attempt to distance themselves a bit from feelings. This requires increased coordination of social skills and a good understanding of social scripts and how they unfold. Children begin to understand that they may possess contradictory feelings toward the same person; they begin to use personal information as aid in the development of close friendships (Saarni, 2001).

With adolescence comes an increased focus on internal emotions, including the perception and recognition of emotional cycles, progressions, and meta-moods (e.g., feeling guilt about feeling anger). There is a further integration of mutual communication, as well as an embeddedness of feeling and emotion in that communication. More socially, there is a focus on morality, meaning, and identity. A person may fully commit himself or herself to an ideology or cause that seems particularly important (Erikson, 1963; Saarni, 2001).

Finally, in adulthood, a number of maturational changes take place. According to Saarni (2001),

> The individual views herself or himself as feeling, overall, the way she or he wants to feel. That is, one accepts one's emotional experience, whether unique and eccentric or culturally conventional, and this acceptance is in alignment with the individual's beliefs about what constitutes emotional "balance." In essence, one is living in accord with one's personal theory of emotion. (p. 77)

At the more global level of the personal intelligences, the individual becomes mature, and this maturity involves a more sophisticated sense of self. To conclude this section with another aptly put description, we quote H. Gardner (1993b), who wrote:

> The end-goal of these developing processes is a self that is highly developed and fully differentiated from others. . . . [Individuals] appear to have understood much about themselves and the frailties of the human condition, while at the same time inspiring others around them to lead more productive lives. (p. 252)

Cognitive intelligence is generally viewed as possessing a strong genetic factor. The convergent evidence for this is fairly strong. Generally speaking, intelligence-like behavior increases over animal species according to the brain-size-to-body ratio (Jerison, 2000). Continued research indicates that intelligence is related to brain size and other physiological measures of neural efficiency among human beings (e.g., Flashman, Andreasen, Flaum, & Swayze, 1998; Schretlen et al., 2000; Wickett, Vernon, & Lee, 2000). Genetic studies, including twin studies, adoption studies, and studies of familial inbreeding, all indicate significant genetic aspects of cognitive intelligence, as it is customarily measured. The exact estimate of heritability is a matter of some controversy.

On the one hand, responsible estimates seem to have settled in the range between ratios of .50 to .78 for intelligence (Grigorenko, 2000, p. 60). On the other hand, there is a dissatisfaction about heritability estimates altogether due to new understandings of how genes work and a desire to study the genetic mechanisms of intelligence themselves (Grigorenko, 2000).

Turning to the hot intelligences, there is virtually no research related to the presence or absence of a genetic component. Genetic studies are typically reserved for clearly measured psychological components. In the case of social intelligence, the inadequate discriminant validity (in plainer terms, the difficulty of distinguishing it from cognitive intelligence) has made it an unattractive candidate for inclusion in heritability studies. Personal and emotional intelligence, on the other hand, are too new for investgators to have studied their heritability. It seems reasonable to suppose there is some genetic component to them because there is one for most psychological traits. As of yet, however, the relevant empirical evidence does not exist.

■ Enabling and Inhibiting Factors

Again, the relative newness of acceptable measures of the hot intelligences means that little is known about factors that inhibit or facilitate these intelligences. For example, one might believe that being in a powerful emotional state—say, depression—might interfere with measured emotional intelligence, yet the evidence does not seem to bear that out (Caruso et al., 2002). The lack of relation between feeling positive and being emotionally intelligent is interesting. Perhaps there is a certain realism about events that occurs with sadness (e.g., Alloy & Abramson, 1979), or perhaps, often, the skills offered by those high in emotional intelligence are simply undervalued in society. Some of those high in emotional intelligence may voluntarily choose emotionally difficult and even depressing occupations that they perceive someone must do (e.g., Mayer, 2001).

■ Gender, Cross-National, and Cross-Cultural Aspects

There is now a well-documented performance advantage of women over men on scales of emotional intelligence. Women score between one quarter and one half a standard deviation above men, on average, which represents a moderate-sized group difference (Mayer & Geher, 1996; Mayer et al., 1999, 2002).

Measures of social and personal intelligence have not yet been subjected to cross-cultural or cross-national studies. Measures of emotional intelligence have been employed cross-nationally and cross-culturally, but no study examining such issues has been published.

■ Deliberate Interventions

Recall that intelligence is a combination of mental ability and the accumulated knowledge that arises from that ability. Although it appears relatively difficult to raise intelligence per se (because the ability portion is fairly recalcitrant to intervention), it is quite easy to raise a person's accumulated knowledge in areas of social interaction (for social intelligence), self-understanding (for personal intelligence), and emotion (for emotional intelligence).

Educators have long proposed that curricula in these areas are of potential benefit to students. The 1920s saw the advent of character education programs such as the Boy Scouts and Girl Scouts, which attempted to address social behavior in a moral fashion. The 1970s saw the advent of affective education programs meant to address many of the same issues in a more psychologically minded fashion. Today, there has been considerable interest in a combination of these ideas under the umbrella of Social and Emotional Learning (SEL; see http://www.casel.org; Mayer & Cobb, 2000).

A learning curriculum based solely on emotional intelligence versus one based on SEL can be expected to both overlap and diverge. The emotional ability approach would focus most specifically on teaching emotional perception, using emotions to enhance thought, emotional reasoning, and emotional management. Most contemporary social and emotional learning curricula, on the other hand, mix together emotional skills, social values and social understanding, as well as learning specific behavioral skills. Empirical research will be necessary to sort out the relative advantages of these two approaches. On its face, the social and emotional learning curriculum might seem more desirable because of its breadth. One drawback might be that an overemphasis on students getting along with one another could stifle creativity, healthy skepticism, or spontaneity. Moreover, too strong an emphasis on positive psychology might disenfranchise depressed or oppositional students. Such concerns argue for a more focused education of emotions or, alternatively, a balance between social learning and more personally oriented learning (Cobb & Mayer, 2000).

Both the Fetzer Institute and the Collaborative for Academic, Social, and Emotional Learning (CASEL) have promoted the need for such curricula, along with calls for outcome studies of such work. Most recently, a number of outcome studies are under way, and answers concerning the efficacy of such programs will be known soon. A meta-analytic study of 177 outcome studies of curricula designed to improve social behavior and problem solving found promising results (Durlak & Wells, 1997). In general, programs designed to improve school environment, to directly address individuals' mental health, or to assist students in making life transitions, all had positive effects in student outcome relative to control groups. Although this speaks to personal knowledge in a general way, rather than more specifically to hot intelligences, it is important information germane to the importance of knowledge of the self and others.

■ What Is Not Known?

More is unknown than known about the hot intelligences. At a level of basic measurement, although ability measures of emotional intelligence are now fairly well developed, better measures of personal and social intelligence are still needed. Once all such measures are developed, understanding their intercorrelations will, no doubt, become a major enterprise.

At a more basic level, there is considerable interest in the neuroscience of emotional intelligence (Bechara, Tranel, & Damasio, 2000) and in the cognitive processes related to it (Mayer, 2000). Research in these areas can help us understand which areas of the brain are involved, individual differences in neurological activity, and cognitive processes that make up the components of emotional intelligence.

As measurement issues are addressed, attention needs to focus on what these measures predict. There is tantalizing evidence that emotional intelligence predicts reduced problem behavior (Brackett & Mayer, 2003; Brackett et al., in press; Cobb & Mayer, 2000; Trinidad & Johnson, 2002). If that result continues to replicate, the relation between emotional intelligence and problem behavior would demand further attention. Beyond problem behavior, the hot intelligences might have other important predictive areas not yet imagined.

Finally, research on teaching emotional, personal, and social knowledge has just begun. Research is needed to determine what sorts of training programs are best in these regards, and whether they can reduce problem behaviors and enhance interpersonal relationships.

■ Must-Read Articles and Books

Brody, N. (2000). History of theories and measurements of intelligence. In R. J. Sternberg (Ed.), *Handbook of intelligence* (pp. 16–33). Cambridge, England: Cambridge University Press.

Durlak, J. A., & Wells, A. M. (1997). Primary prevention mental health programs for children and adolescents: A meta-analytic review. *American Journal of Community Psychology, 25*, 115–152.

Gardner, H. (1983). *Frames of mind: The theory of multiple intelligences.* New York: Basic Books.

Mayer, J. D., Salovey, P., & Caruso, D. R. (2000). Models of emotional intelligence. In R. J. Sternberg (Ed.), *Handbook of intelligence* (pp. 396–420). Cambridge, England: Cambridge University Press.

Plucker, J. A., Callahan, C. M., & Tomchin, E. M. (1996). Wherefore art thou, multiple intelligences? Alternative assessments for identifying talent in ethnically diverse and economically disadvantaged students. *Gifted Child Quarterly, 40*, 81–92.

Saarni, C. (2001). Emotional competence: A developmental perspective. In R. Bar-On & J. D. A. Parker (Eds.), *The handbook of emotional intelligence* (pp. 68–91). San Francisco: Jossey-Bass.

Salovey, P., & Mayer, J. D. (1990.). Emotional intelligence. *Imagination, Cognition, and Personality, 9,* 185–211.

INTRODUCTION:
STRENGTHS OF JUSTICE

CRITERIA FOR *Strengths of Justice*

	Fulfilling	Morally valued	Does not diminish others	Nonfelicitous opposite	Traitlike	Distinctiveness	Paragons	Prodigies	Selective absence	Institutions and rituals	
	1	2	3	4	5	6	7	8	9	10	TALLY
Citizenship	X	X	X	X	~X		X	X	X	X	9/10
Fairness	X	X	X	X	~X	X	X		X	X	9/10
Leadership	X	X	X	X	X		X	X	X	X	9/10

~ Somewhat satisfies criterion.

We regard strengths of justice as broadly interpersonal, relevant to the optimal interaction between the individual and the group or the community. As the group shrinks in size and becomes more personalized, the strengths of justice begin to converge with the one-on-one strengths of humanity discussed in the previous section. We maintain the distinction by proposing that strengths of justice are strengths *among*, whereas those of humanity are strengths *between*, but the difference is perhaps one of degree more than kind. Regardless, three of the positive traits included in our classification fit well under the virtue class of justice, and we discuss them in terms of how they satisfy our criteria (see Criteria Table).

- Citizenship [Social Responsibility, Loyalty, Teamwork]

This strength of character entails an identification with and sense of obligation to a common good that includes oneself but stretches beyond one's personal interests to include the groups of which one is a member—any and all family members, fellow workers on the night shift, current residents of one's dormitory or apartment building, fellow parishioners, other Hoosiers, those with whom one shares an ethnic heritage, or even the entire human race. People with this strength have a sense of duty to the group in question and pull their own weight as group members, not because external circumstances force them but because they regard it as what a group member should do.

CRITERION 1 *Fulfilling* We are on firm ground when we conclude that citizenship and teamwork are fulfilling. Family pride, school spirit, esprit de corps, and patriotism all feel good to the individual, sometimes overwhelmingly so, which alerts us to the moral downside of this individual difference. As social psychologists have well documented, loyalty to one's own group can be accompanied by the disparaging of other groups and thereby contribute to all manner of isms (Sherif, 1966). We believe that the character strength of "good" citizenship need not produce prejudice as long as the focus is on behavior within the in-group and not on behavior directed toward the out-group. Furthermore, keeping the focus on actual behavior—doing one's share in group activities—highlights the fulfilling nature of this strength. When an Amish farmer helps his neighbor raise a barn or when his wife helps a neighbor raise a child, their satisfaction does not result from thinking about "English" communities that lack such teamwork but simply from knowing that they are contributing to local welfare.

CRITERION 2 *Morally Valued* Teamwork is morally valued, especially when it involves setting aside one's own glory to help the group. The sports cliché "There is no 'I' in team" reminds us that individuals are admired when they meld their energy with that of others for a common goal. To continue the sports theme, a role player is a team member who accepts a modest role so that the team can do its best. Role players may not earn astronomical salaries or endorsement deals, but they are just as valued as the stars who do.

Studies of workers who are able to craft their jobs into callings reveal one common strategy to be seeing oneself as part of a larger team devoted to a larger good (Wrzesniewski, McCauley, Rozin, & Schwartz, 1997). Emptying bedpans in a hospital is not a glamorous job at the level of its constituent actions, but if these actions are seen as a critical aspect of health care—and of course they are—then the orderly is a valued member of a health care team.

Dependability per se is not included in our classification because it cuts across several basic strengths that are included—for example, perseverance, integrity, love—but it is especially salient in the strength of citizenship and teamwork. We are grateful to people who occasionally help out, but we elevate them to a higher moral plane when they consistently do so, when we can count on them to show up rain or shine, not just when the boss is looking or free coffee is being served. Calling a teammate dependable may be redundant, because if she is not dependable, she is not a teammate but a mere team member.

Along these lines, we value people who are loyal to their groups, who do not jump ship at the first rough weather. Our contemporary society allows many of us great mobility and can even reward us handsomely when we change schools, jobs, residences, or spouses. However, those who seek greener grass are more likely to be envied than admired.

Obedience has earned itself a bad reputation in many quarters of the modern world—witness Milgram's (1963) infamous studies of destructive obedience and the even more infamous events of the Nazi Holocaust that inspired his research—so much so that we have not included this term among the synonyms we piled on to capture the character strength of citizenship. Nonetheless, this reputation is inadvertent and unfortunate, because there are many acts of obedience that are good and necessary for a group to survive and for the individual to thrive. Knee-jerk disobedience and anticonformity are no more praiseworthy than the most mindless loyalty to a group. Indeed, a common hero in books and movies is the rebel who disobeys orders and breaks rules in order to accomplish good things (e.g., any of the interchangeable protagonists in Robin Cook's medical thrillers or in the coming-of-age movies featured on the Disney Channel), but we suspect that in real life, such individuals do much more harm than good. Regardless, obedience per se is neither good nor bad; what matters is the moral integrity and purpose of the group to which one is loyal, and that judgment lies outside our designation of teamwork as a strength of character.

CRITERION 3 *Does Not Diminish Others* Good teamwork elevates others in the vicinity. We may be rewriting our personal histories here, but we seem to remember being thrilled and thinking at the moment they were introduced that the New England Patriots would win Super Bowl XXXVI. Why? Because they chose to be introduced to the worldwide television audience as a team, with no mention of individual names. Regardless of our memory, there is something exhilarating about watching good teamwork in action, whether it is a marching band, a line of Irish river dancers, or an efficient lunch crew at a fast-food restaurant. In our own groups, we want to emulate the synchrony and solidarity we have observed. As teachers, we love a "good" classroom discussion, by which we mean not insightful comments on the part of a few students sitting in the corners of the room but exchanges among all students that build on and enhance previous comments. We are most elevated as teachers when we feel no need to talk, and further when our students direct their comments to one another and not to us. Teamwork is a dance—engrossing to perform and exciting to watch.

CRITERION 4 *Nonfelicitous Opposite* The obvious antonyms of *citizenship* and *teamwork* are negative: *selfishness, self-centeredness,* and *egotism.* One need not play basketball to be a ball hog.

CRITERION 5 *Traitlike* Are citizenship and teamwork a trait? The range of groups to which one belongs is vast, and it is obvious that any given person will evidence a range of duty and loyalty across these groups. The prototype of this strength is someone who is broadly loyal and responsible—an across-the-board good teammate regardless of the team—but it is unclear how common this prototype might be. Existing research usually examines this strength with respect to a given group, and we do not know if the person who diligently votes in school board elections is the same person who volunteers for loathsome tasks at work or makes sure that distant cousins feel included at family get-togethers.

We are reminded of the comment by Linus in the comic strip *Peanuts:* "I love humanity—it's people I can't stand." However, counting toward the argument that good citizenship is traitlike is recent research into social responsibility, which shows this individual difference to be general and stable (chapter 16). We tentatively conclude that citizenship and teamwork, at least construed as social responsibility, reflect a trait, although further work is needed to show that social responsibility as an endorsed value translates into social responsibility as an overt action.

CRITERION 6 *Distinctiveness*   Citizenship and teamwork are facilitated by other strengths in our classification—kindness, persistence, self-regulation, humility, and gratitude, to name some of the obvious contributors—but they do not reduce to any given one of them. Whether some specifiable combination of these strengths necessarily leads to teamwork is an unknown but empirical question, so we must be open to the possibility that teamwork is what we term a blended strength.

CRITERION 7 *Paragons*   Teamwork paragons are widely recognized and celebrated. Willie Stargell of the 1979 Pittsburgh Pirates was named the National League's Most Valuable Player because he was the most valuable teammate, despite modest individual statistics. "We Are Family" was the team's theme song, and Stargell its revered patriarch. Politicians like Lyndon Johnson, Tip O'Neill, and Bob Dole got things done because they could work productively with the "other side" to pass legislation. We have no special insight into such individuals, but perhaps their gift was seeing that there is no "other side" when it comes to the well-being of the nation. And from our interviews of award-winning firefighters, we learned that the fire-fighting team was always what made the valorous act possible. The firefighter who saves a child from a smoke-filled building is simply the most obvious member of a team that includes others who make the decision to rescue or not, who keep lines of communication open, who resuscitate the victim, and who stand ready to rescue the rescuer if needed.

CRITERION 8 *Prodigies*   Teamwork prodigies also exist. Children who happily play right field, who voluntarily make the scenery for class plays, or who sit third trombone are common, and they deserve further study so that we can learn what makes good teamwork possible at an early age. Available research, described in chapter 16, identifies family experiences as crucial along with the consolidation in adolescence of social responsibility as part of personal identity.

CRITERION 9 *Selective Absence*   In their most notorious form, those devoid of citizenship and teamwork would seem to be the traitors and turncoats of history, although in some cases their sin, as it were, was loyalty to what we see as the wrong side in a dispute. The so-called American Taliban fighter John Walker

Lindh was disloyal to his nation of birth but perhaps not to the political group that he joined as an adult. Better examples therefore include people who are loyal to nothing but their own selfish interest, and we all know folks who undercut the group by their inaction, who can be counted on only to be uncounted.

CRITERION 10 *Institutions and Rituals*   The larger society tries to encourage good citizenship and teamwork—a society is, after all, a team. Even in an individualist culture like the mainstream United States, we urge all citizens to vote and all children to play together nicely. At least in the abstract, we believe that all drivers should share the road and that all of those summoned should serve on juries. In primary schools, students are thrown together in team sports, bands and choruses, plays and musicals, with the hope that teamwork is somehow cultivated. The lessons may not be fully learned, to be sure, and we are always bothered when voter turnout for national elections fails to exceed the estimated prevalence rates for serious mental disorders. We the people are increasingly more likely to "bowl alone" (cf. Putnam, 2000), and we think individuals in the contemporary United States have much to learn from groups in collectivist cultures in which duty and loyalty to the group are a given and societal practices are in place from birth to death to instantiate these.

■ Fairness

The character strength of fairness refers to an individual's treatment of other people in similar or identical ways—not letting one's personal feelings or issues bias decisions about others. We are reminded of an exchange between Los Angeles Dodgers baseball manager Tommy Lasorda and a reporter who charged, "You made Mike Piazza your starting catcher because he's Italian." "Not at all," said Lasorda, adding, "I named him the starting catcher because *I'm* Italian." Whatever the frame, this exchange is not about fairness. Fairness involves giving everyone a fair chance and being committed to the idea that the same rules apply to everyone. There has been a spirited debate over the millennia among philosophers concerned with justice whether it is achieved by radical equality of treatment or a more nuanced equity of treatment, a debate alive and well today in such forms as the merits of graduated versus flat income tax structures. But we need not take a position to deem fairness, however interpreted, a character strength and its absence—inequality and/or inequity of treatment—a vice.

Unlike most of the other strengths in our classification, the strength of fairness has a sustained history of study within psychology, under the rubric of moral development as pioneered by Jean Piaget, elaborated by Lawrence Kohlberg, and expanded by Carol Gilligan (chapter 3). Moral development has been regarded as a special case of cognitive development, and as they mature, children show an increasing trend toward abstractness and away from egocentrism in thinking about what is right. Very young children judge moral good solely in terms of selfish interest—what avoids punishment and/or earns reward. A more abstract style of moral reasoning entails judging whether a course of action conforms to societal laws, rules, and conventions. And the most abstract style of moral reasoning finds the individual using abstract principles of fairness—those of justice and/or care—to decide what is right. A large research literature has resulted, which we review in chapter 17. This work is developmental, which means that the focus is on differences across the life course of an individual. All children are thought to pass through the stages identified by moral reasoning theorists. There is disagreement whether these are discrete stages of thinking or simply signposts along a more continuous process of change, but the fact and thrust of overall development are incontestable.

Relatively little work has examined this individual difference across individuals at the same point in the life course. Indeed, because these stages and trends in moral development are regarded as universal, differences at a given point are either not expected or regarded as developmental lags on the part of some. Thus, we need to offer some qualifications about this body of work vis-à-vis our interest in this character strength as a positive trait.

This work is aligned strongly with a theory about cognitive development. Remember that our intent in creating this classification was to approach character in terms of a description of its components and not in terms of a priori theory. In the case of fairness, the theory is limiting in the sense that it has directed research attention to developmental differences early in life and not to variations across adults, which certainly exist. Perhaps only 20% of adults in the United States achieve the stage that Kohlberg regarded as the most advanced (Colby, Kohlberg, Gibbs, & Lieberman, 1983), so it is possible to use these data to conclude that fairness constitutes a positive trait—an individual difference. Let us turn to how well the character strength of fairness satisfies our criteria for a character strength.

CRITERION 1 *Fulfilling*   Fairness is fulfilling if not always fun. Fairness is the bedrock of any system of justice, and all societies have such systems (chapter 2). People want to do the right thing, and doing the right thing often entails setting aside one's own prejudices in deciding how to regard and treat others. In some cases where principles of fairness are codified and consensually accepted, it is easy to be fair because everyone buys the principle. Most of us in the United States accept that all citizens should have one and only one vote, and we are satisfied when this is what happens and outraged when it does not.

In other cases, fairness falls by the wayside because it has too high a cost. Nepotism rules in the workplace used to exist because it is unreasonable to expect a supervisor to treat her spouse or children the same as other employees, even though this is the fair thing to do. Our own forays into the assessment of character strengths suggest that fairness is not a common signature strength and furthermore that asking people if they treat strangers the same as friends rarely resulted in an affirmative response.

The most interesting case to us is when fairness is shown despite cost, which can include hurt feelings and resentment on the part of loved ones who have been treated "only" fairly and criticism or worse on the part of vested societal groups offended by a particular take on what is fair. The story of the Civil Rights movement in the United States has many themes, but one of the most striking is the commitment of its members, black and white, to the ideal of fair treatment for all. Ditto for those who helped to end apartheid in South Africa. These individuals did something difficult and dangerous, and we think that the character strength of fairness made it possible.

CRITERION 2 *Morally Valued* Perhaps because it is uncommon in the extreme, fairness is highly valued when it is shown. As parents, we treat our own children fairly and are respected when we do so, if not immediately then eventually. As teachers, we treat other people's children fairly and again are respected when we do so, at least in the long run. Political leaders who set aside their own political agenda in the spirit of fairness are respected for their action; we think here of Lyndon Johnson supporting civil rights and Richard Nixon going to China.

CRITERION 3 *Does Not Diminish Others* The observation of fairness can elevate others in the vicinity or at least not diminish them. We like to see justice done, whether it is carried out by a grocery checkout clerk in the express line who enforces the "10-item limit" or by a judge who treats white-collar criminals the same as their blue-collar counterparts. We feel good when a coach lets all players take the field. "Fair" elections give us closure, regardless of how we may have voted.

CRITERION 4 *Nonfelicitous Opposite* The obvious opposite of fairness is unfairness, whether we call it *bias* or *prejudice* or *caprice* (we doubt, though, that it is ever random). There is a huge social psychological literature dealing with the various isms, which give us a rich vocabulary for describing particular manifestations of unfair ways of thinking, feeling, and acting.

CRITERION 5 *Traitlike* Fairness is traitlike inasmuch as individuals vary in terms of their commitment to it as a guiding principle, and at least among adults, this variation appears stable and general. As noted, though, studies of fairness have usually not been conducted in the spirit of trait psychology—looking at the causes, correlates, and consequences of this characteristic as an individual difference among individuals otherwise comparable—so we know less about fairness in these terms than we do about many of the other strengths in the present classification.

CRITERION 6 *Distinctiveness*   Fairness is not decomposable into other classified strengths, although such characteristics as kindness may lay its foundation and such characteristics as self-regulation may facilitate its implementation.

CRITERION 7 *Paragons*   Paragons of fairness include the Freedom Riders like James Farmer, and the American Civil Liberties Union lawyers, some of them Jewish, who argued for the right of Nazi sympathizers to march in Skokie, Illinois. King Solomon's offering to cut the contested baby in two is a provocative paragon because he achieved justice by showing that fairness (as equality) was not desirable.

CRITERION 8 *Prodigies*   As the research literature on moral development shows, prodigies of fairness cannot exist until youngsters are capable of abstract thinking that allows them to entertain abstractions, not only in terms of principles of justice and care but also in terms of a generalized other to whom these principles apply. However, once abstract thinking becomes possible, so too does a recognizable form of fairness on the part of some youth. Indeed, adolescents may embrace a social cause or issue embodying a no-holds-barred principle of fairness simply because their newly acquired psychological repertoire allows them to do so. We wonder what happens to most of them along the way to adulthood.

CRITERION 9 *Selective Absence*   People conspicuously devoid of fairness include inside traders of all sorts, not just CEOs led away in handcuffs but all those who take a perk not available to others—whether reserved parking spaces, free upgrades to first-class airline seats, spots at the front of any line, excused absences at work, extensions on a term paper, useless military bases in their hometown, or Johnny Cochran as their defense attorney—and of course those who offer these perks. Indeed, those on both sides of the special deal represent failures of fairness. They may have sincere motives for suspending the rules of justice or care, but fairness is not among them.

CRITERION 10 *Institutions and Rituals*   As a value found in all societies, fairness is encouraged and sustained by too many rituals and institutions to enumerate. However, many of these emphasize the rules to be followed—whether playing baseball, sharing toys, running meetings, taking turns at the Xerox machine in the office or the elliptical training machine in the gym—and not the internal character strength that results in fairness even in the absence of explicit rules. Still, there is enough research evidence to conclude that fairness as we construe it can be encouraged by early familial emphasis on justice and equality as important values and the consolidation of these values into a personal identity in adolescence. This process can be encouraged by training in perspective taking or seeing the issue at hand from multiple points of view. So, children should be told to share toys not just by edict ("because I said so") but by an invitation to consider what it feels like when others do or do not share with them.

■ Leadership

People belong to countless social groups, and many of these groups are hierarchically structured with a leader—formal or informal—who dictates and directs the activities of the followers. Theorists concerned with leadership usually distinguish two tasks of any leader: getting the group members to do what they are supposed to do, and creating and preserving good relationships and morale among these members. One can readily think of examples in which one of these tasks overshadows the other—for example, a pit crew at an auto race needs to change tires as quickly as possible without "sharing feelings," and a group of teenagers hanging out at a mall needs to enjoy spending time with one another without any performance goal to distract them—but for many other groups, the leader must attend to both tasks because each facilitates the other. A leader is anyone who directs group activities, and a good leader of course is someone who sets the course well by inspiring group members. When we talk about leadership as a character strength, we refer in particular to the latter type of leader, what organizational scholars term a *transformational leader* (Tichy & Devanna, 1986).

CRITERION 1 *Fulfilling*   Leadership is fulfilling when done well. Setting goals and accomplishing them, enlisting effective help, building coalitions, smoothing ruffled feathers—all these are heady activities, which is why many leaders hold firmly to such roles. People want to have a lasting impact on the world, and effective leadership is one of the guaranteed ways to accomplish this goal. History is much more the story of leaders than of followers, and all leaders want to have their place in history, whether it is recorded in textbooks or merely recounted around the water cooler.

CRITERION 2 *Morally Valued*   Likewise, effective leadership is highly valued. We praise leaders who rise to the occasion, seize the moment, take the lead, show the way, take charge, get the job done, do what is needed, say what has to be said, get everyone on the same page, build morale, inspire followers, instill pride, restore order, make changes, voice common concerns, and serve as moral compasses or consciences. For decades, the Gallup Organization has surveyed Americans about the people they most admire. Anyone near the top of the list must have considerable celebrity, but what is striking about the poll results is the relative absence of mere celebrities (actors, singers, and athletes) and the fact that the top spot is invariably held by the current U.S. president.

CRITERION 3 *Does Not Diminish Others*   The observation of good leadership is elevating, so much so that we even have a term—*charismatic leadership*—that captures both the features of such leaders and the emotional reaction of awe and elevation that they produce in others. Indeed, an inherent part of being a transformational leader is the ability to elevate followers, by rhetoric ("Ask not what your country can do for you") or by moral example ("The buck stops here").

CRITERION 4 *Nonfelicitous Opposite*   The absence of effective leadership refers either to the person who never takes charge or to the person who guides his or her group poorly, neglecting one or both of the crucial tasks of leadership. Regardless, both can be negative, the latter unambiguously so. We usually excuse the lack of leadership on the part of those who are temperamentally or situationally unable to fill this role, so long as there are alternative leaders. After all, the ability to be a good follower (a teammate) is no less valued than the ability to be a good leader. But if someone who is the "logical" choice to lead demurs for reasons that do not compel us, we are not amused.

CRITERION 5 *Traitlike*   So, is leadership a trait? The history of psychological thinking on this matter is worth reviewing. Once upon a time, the notion that there were "great men" and "great women" who were leaders because of their personalities went unquestioned. It was obvious that military leaders like Alexander the Great, Caesar, and Napoleon made their mark on history because of who they were and that in other eras and other circumstances they would have been effective football coaches, CEOs, college deans, head nurses, or directors of nonprofit organizations. When situationalism swept psychology in the 1960s and 1970s and trait theory became dormant (chapter 3), the great man/woman view of leadership fell into disrepute. Instead, so-called contingency theories of leadership were emphasized that regarded good leadership as contingent on the features of the group to be led. Personality traits, if they existed at all, did not form a generic leadership constellation. What mattered was a coming together of very specific characteristics of a leader and very specific characteristics of the group he or she was leading. A good match resulted in effective leadership, and a poor match, not.

We doubt that the general public ever accepted this view of leadership,[1] which is just as well, because the current view within psychology has since

---

[1]At least in the United States, there has been a pervasive assumption that a good leader of one sort of group will necessarily be a good leader of another sort of group. Consider the military leaders who were elected president—for example, Washington, Grant, and Eisenhower—and the current manifestations of this assumption in the form of sports figures (Tom Osborne, Steve Largent, Jesse Ventura) and entertainers (Sonny Bono, Fred Grandy) elected to political office. The assumption is self-fulfilling, of course, which means that we cannot point to such examples as proof that leadership is a general trait.

come back to the view that effective leaders indeed have personality characteristics that set them apart from ineffective leaders or nonleaders: for example,
intelligence, dominance, and flexibility. Supporting this current view are laboratory studies showing that the same individuals emerge as leaders across
different groups, and that those who emerge bring distinct characteristics to
the group.

Leadership is therefore a trait, although we can never overlook the importance of other factors in determining who is allowed to lead or to lead well. The
same qualification holds for all character strengths (chapter 1) but is patently
obvious in the case of leadership. That the United States has never had a female
president says nothing about the leadership traits of women but speaks instead
to the social filters in place along the route to the Oval Office.

CRITERION 6 *Distinctiveness*   Like teamwork, leadership is facilitated by other
strengths in the classification—for example, social intelligence, perspective,
persistence, and hope—but does not reduce to any given one of them. Also like
teamwork, whether there is a constellation of other strengths that is equivalent
to leadership is an unknown but ultimately answerable question. Leadership
may therefore be a blended strength, although further research is needed to
identify the possible components.

CRITERION 7 *Paragons*   As noted, history is so replete with leadership paragons that we need not list them here to argue that they exist.

CRITERION 8 *Prodigies*   Prodigies of leadership also exist, as soon as youngsters gather into groups that can be led. Someone decides that a bunch of kids
should play ball, tag, or make-believe. Someone becomes captain of the debat-
ing team or president of the high school student body. Some prodigious adolescent leaders—like William Pitt the Younger and Bill Clinton—grow up to
lead on a larger scale, although we do not know how common this trajectory
might be.

CRITERION 9 *Selective Absence*   Think of people who run their businesses into
the ground, who steer their nations into disaster, and who alienate or demoral-
ize their followers, in ways small and large. Nero's fiddling while Rome burned
has become a paragon of leadership ineptitude, and Pontius Pilate's refusing
to get involved is another well-known instance of the absence of leadership.
Charlie Manson led his followers to prison.

CRITERION 10 *Institutions and Rituals*   Many societal rituals and institutions
cultivate leadership by making such roles available to the young and helping
them to find their legs. We remember extracurricular activity groups from our
school days in which everyone was an officer—that is, a leader. This did not

strike us as silly at the time, nor does it now. For adults at work or in the community, leadership roles are often rotated explicitly so that everyone can take a turn, and new leaders are usually cut some slack as they learn how to lead. Along these lines, many new leaders are assigned mentors and advisers or seek them out for second-order guidance.

16. CITIZENSHIP

[Social Responsibility, Loyalty, Teamwork]

■ *Sam Nzima may not be a name with which most readers are familiar. But many know the moment in South Africa's struggle for democracy that he captured on film. It was Sam Nzima's photograph of Hector Pieterson, the child martyred in the 1976 Soweto youth uprising against Afrikaans education, that revealed the depths of the apartheid system. But it is Nzima's life after that incident that makes him a paragon of citizenship, generativity, and social responsibility.*

The publication of that photograph in the newspaper World *was a turning point in Nzima's life. Warned by a police informant that his life was in danger if he remained in Soweto, Nzima returned to the rural community of Lillydale in the Northern Province, where he had grown up and where, to this day, he has, as he puts it, "chipped in." "I got support from this community and I decided to chip in, to help my community change with the times. If you don't serve your community, then you don't plow anything back." For nearly 30 years now, Nzima has been plowing back into the community that harbored him.*

Toward that end, he has taken advantage of the international connections made during his years as a photojournalist and helped to build infrastructure and capacity in Lillydale. While the media focused on urban townships like Soweto, Nzima was aware of the challenges that Black people in rural areas were facing. He leveraged funding from international nongovernmental organizations (NGOs) matched with contributions from the community for projects such as building health clinics and expanding local schools. His plowing back has included educating and organizing local people to raise funds and to lobby the government for services such as electrification. In recognition of his contributions, an English-medium preschool in Lillydale has been named after him.

Mr. Nzima's "plowing back"' activities have regularly raised political issues. For example, when Mozambican refugees were fleeing into South Africa from the civil war in their own country in the 1980s, he organized the Operation Hunger relief committee. "Our camp was different from those overseas. We had no fences. People in the camp were free to mix with others in the community. They were like us—Shangaan-speaking people." But when the United Nations High Commission on Refugees tried to intervene, the apartheid regime repudiated the refugee status of the Mozambicans. Again Nzima's civic activism put him at odds with the police. And again people in the community, including the traditional leaders and chief minister of the former Gazankulu Homeland, were supportive. Ultimately they succeeded in getting the central government to stop sending refugees back across the border and set a model for other communities along the eastern border of South Africa to follow. Now refugees in Lillydale are one with local residents.

Mr. Nzima contends that the Soweto uprising opened his eyes to the power of youth leadership. "In 1976 the youth resisted Afrikaans education. They said 'enough is enough.' Soweto was the cutoff line. Then their parents followed suit. Democracy came from there."

The phrase Batho Pele *(People First) represents a principle of the transition to democracy in South Africa. Sam Nzima's life illustrates this commitment. He has followed a generative path and now reflects that "as an older member of the community I have to part with what I've learned—giving it to the younger generation. If one in 10 gets it, my time's well spent."* ▪

▪ Consensual Definition

Citizenship, social responsibility, loyalty, and teamwork represent a feeling of identification with and sense of obligation to a common good that includes the self but that stretches beyond one's own self-interest. The individual with these strengths has a strong sense of duty, works for the good of the group rather than for personal gain, is loyal to friends, and can be trusted to pull his or her weight. He or she is a good teammate. A generative spirit and sense of responsibility for the community are further indicators of this strength. Individuals with this strength would be likely to be active in the civic affairs of their communities— by voting, joining voluntary associations, or contributing time and money to social or environmental causes. Political protest also signals this cluster of strengths. National surveys of Americans indicate that those who engage in protest overwhelmingly do so out of a sense of duty to the larger community (Verba, Schlozman, & Brady, 1995). The common thread for people exhibiting these values is that they endorse public interest over self-interest goals as values by which to live. They identify with the common good and want to make the world a better place for future generations.

They would endorse such statements as the following:

- I have a responsibility to improve the world in which I live.
- Everybody should give some of their time for the good of their town or country.
- It is important to me personally that I work to correct social and economic inequalities.
- It is important to me personally that I help others who are in difficulty.
- It is important to me personally to be involved in programs to clean up the environment.

Citizenship, social responsibility, loyalty, and *teamwork* are not exact synonyms, and distinctions are important. Besides its reference to civic commitment and engagement, citizenship implies a legal status. It refers to membership in a polity or political community and the rights and obligations that are integral to that membership. Walzer (1989) described a citizen as "a member of a political community, entitled to whatever prerogatives and encumbered with whatever responsibilities are attached to membership" (p. 211). It is by virtue of his or her membership in a group, community, or polity that an individual enjoys rights. But loyalty, allegiance, and a sense of duty to the group and its principles ensure those rights. Likewise, as William James (1967) maintained, the virtues of a good citizen—a sense of duty and responsibility to the common good—are the "rock upon which states are built" (p. 668). In other words, civic responsibility to the polity and its principles ensures political stability. However, it does not follow that the good citizen is blindly obedient. Rather he or she exercises informed judgment in the interests of the whole. At times this can even involve a challenge to unjust laws. Indeed, acts of civil disobedience were marks of committed citizens in the struggle against apartheid in South Africa and against segregation in the United States.

Social responsibility, defined as an orientation to help others even when there is nothing to be gained from them, has a more altruistic tone than its semantic cousins (L. Berkowitz & Lutterman, 1968). *Loyalty* connotes an unwavering commitment, a bond of trust—whether in friendship or in fidelity to a group, its principles, and cause. *Patriotism* is a sign of loyalty to one's homeland or nation without the corresponding hostility to citizens of other nations implied in the concept of nationalism. These strengths share aspects of generativity, particularly as the latter is expressed in a public way, that is, an orientation to make an enduring contribution to future generations beyond one's own kin. *Teamwork* is perhaps the most behavioral of the synonyms we have piled on this character strength; it refers to one's ability to work with others in a group for a common purpose—to collaborate and cooperate.

■ Theoretical Traditions

Although we consider this set of strengths within an individual difference framework, they are essentially relational, describing individual behavior within the context of interpersonal relationships but, more important, within group relationships—that is, loyalty to friends, kin, or country; social responsibility to groups of which one is a member; and civic responsibility to polities and the principles that bind their members together.

Citizenship, in particular, has been the domain of political science, and the focus has been on the social and political ties that bind citizens in pursuit of a common good. The ideology of citizenship can be traced to the Roman and Greek republics, where the virtuous person was the citizen who acted on behalf of the polity. Because the polity was composed of a homogeneous, almost familial, group (which excluded slaves and women), citizens knew and could trust one another. Aristotle (1948) described the polity as a network of friends bound together by the pursuit of a common good and an isolate as either a beast or a god who is unable or has no need to share in the benefits of political association.

Later, in Rousseau's (1762/1950) *Social Contract*, citizenship was grounded in notions of autonomy, consent, and reciprocity. Because the citizen had a voice in shaping the principles that bound fellow citizens together, it followed that she or he would be committed to those principles and realize happiness in public or civic activity. However, with industrialization and the rise of the market, private life and self-interest eclipsed public life as a source of happiness. The obligations of citizenship took a backseat to a personal rights framing of the concept in modern liberalism. But even in this tradition the protection of rights and the common liberty is assured only by active civic participation (Walzer, 1989). Citizenship is not a passive concept, particularly within a democratic framework where the members of a polity rule themselves. The notion of a social contract, a responsibility that citizens have for the public welfare, also figures prominently in Rawls's (1971) theory of justice.

In this view altruism is not the basis for citizenship because the interests of each person are realized in the pursuit of a common good. The concept of citizenship or public responsibility is better captured by de Tocqueville's (1848/1966) phrase "self interest properly understood," that is, a commitment to preserving public goods that are held in common. In principle, the common good is not achieved by individuals' setting aside their own interests.

In practice, however, individuals with this set of strengths are likely to sacrifice their own immediate gratification in the longer term interests of the group. Of course, by curbing short-term gains they are likely to be sustaining public goods and thus realizing "self-interest properly understood." Psychologists describe these strengths as having elements of empathy (Eisenberg, 1986) and as indicative of a high stage of moral reasoning that reflects loyalty and trustworthiness (Higgins, Power, & Kohlberg, 1984). Individuals with these strengths can be quite resolute in their refusal to act in their own interests at the expense of others. Experimental studies suggest that, even under conditions of anonymity, between a quarter and a third of participants refuse self-gain at group expense (Dawes, van de Kragt, & Orbell, 1990). Thus, there are individual differences in the disposition to act in the interests of the group, which, in principle, should generalize across contexts. We know of no studies that assess whether this strength is manifest across different venues, but both longitudinal studies and test–retest evidence for the measurement of this capacity indicate that it is stable over time and in different contexts.

Although rational choice and the cost–benefit calculations of civic engagement are dominant theories in political science, there is weak empirical support for these models of civic behavior. Rational choice predicts that few people will be active when in fact many are. When Americans are asked in national surveys why they are involved in civic and political affairs, they indicate that it is not to further their own self-interest but out of concern for the common good (Verba et al., 1995). Regardless of discipline, most formulations imply that those who exhibit these strengths feel connected or identified in some way to the persons or group whose welfare concerns them. Thus, the notion of membership laid out in Walzer's (1989) description of a citizen, the feeling of inclusion and mattering to other members of the group, is the foundation on which this cluster of strengths is built.

In summary, the essence of these strengths inheres in valuing one's social bond to others and to groups and in working to sustain and build those relationships. Within S. H. Schwartz's (1996) typology of human values, these strengths reflect a self-transcendent as opposed to a self-enhancing orientation. Thus, individuals would be less likely to consider personal achievement and social dominance high on their hierarchy of values and more likely to place benevolence and concern for the welfare of others high on their list. Such commitment to the broader community is considered a characteristic of self-actualizing people (Maslow, 1970).

Three interrelated phenomena are emphasized in Walzer's (1989) definition of a citizen—membership, prerogatives, and obligations. The latter two (rights and responsibilities) are rooted in the historical traditions of liberalism and civic republicanism that have waxed and waned in U.S. history. In the liberal tradition, an individual's rights are emphasized and responsibilities are given somewhat short shrift. But the republican tradition emphasizes the virtue of social responsibility and concern for others and links self-interest to the public interest.

In their book, *Habits of the Heart*, Bellah, Madsen, Sullivan, Swidler, and Tipton (1985) made the case that the character of a democratic society is intimately related to the values and character of its people. One study of American teens' views of democracy bears this out insofar as those aspects of democracy that were most salient to individual adolescents were significantly related to their personal goals and family values. Those for whom material achievements were a high priority and whose families emphasized vigilance toward and mistrust of "others" were more likely to emphasize the rights and freedoms of individuals. In contrast, youth with more altruistic values and whose families emphasized compassion were more likely to say that democracy is a form of government in which principles of tolerance and civil liberties should prevail (C. A. Flanagan & Faison, 2001).

The goal of socializing younger generations into responsible citizenship cannot be accomplished without attending to issues of membership or inclusion, the third element in Walzer's (1989) definition. The ties that bind younger generations to the broader community are reciprocal, that is, when young people feel that the community cares about them and that they have a say in community affairs, they are more likely to identify with the community's goals and to want to commit to its service. The evidence from prevention and community youth development studies is clear: When youths feel connected to others in the institutions of their communities, they are less likely to violate the norms and more likely to serve the common good of those communities (Eccles & Gootman, 2002; C. A. Flanagan, in press).

The choices of adult authority figures matter in this process. When schools are inclusive environments and when teachers practice a civic ethic (holding the same high standards for and respecting the ideas of all students, insisting that students listen to and respect one another, and actively intervening to stop acts of bullying or exclusion), they play a critical role in promoting the younger generation's support for the polity. When students feel that their teachers practice this ethic, they are more committed to the kinds of public interest goals that would sustain a democratic polity (i.e., contributing to their communities, serving their country, working to improve race relations, and helping the disenfranchised; C. A. Flanagan & Faison, 2001).

Evidence from a host of experimental studies suggests that individuals are more likely to manifest these strengths toward others with whom they share a social bond or with whom they feel a sense of solidarity (Dawes et al., 1990). To the extent that individuals identify with a group, they are more willing to forgo individual gain to enhance the collective good (Brewer & Gardner, 1996). Although identification with a group and its goals plays a key role in the development of this set of strengths, it is the particular groups and their values that determine whether social responsibility or loyalty will maintain tradition or motivate change. Within the Big Five, these strengths reflect the personality structure of conscientiousness, including dependability. If one is loyal to traditional values and groups, these qualities would imply conservatism.

But group solidarity and loyalty to a cause also are strengths of activists working for social change. A sense of racial or ethnic solidarity is a motivational factor in the political activism of many African Americans who mix civic action that maintains the system with protest activities that challenge it in what F. C. Harris (1999) has referred to as an *oppositional civic culture*. Solidarity with a group and identification with a cause may be particularly important when the odds of achieving change seem overwhelming. Such strengths seem to help individuals cope with the uncertainty of their situation in the face of a bulwark of opposition (Keniston, 1968). But blind obedience and conformity are not even definitive features of a patriot. Although its meaning is contested, there is consensus among Americans that marks of patriotism include civic participation and a critical assessment of government that holds it accountable to the nation's ideals (J. L. Sullivan, Fried, & Dietz, 1992).

Although typically considered strengths, there are downsides to group solidarity and loyalty that should be mentioned. The very processes that bring benefits to members of groups (strong ties, trust, loyalty) may restrict access to the organization for those on the outside (Portes, 1998). If group solidarity is exclusionary of newcomers or favors an in-group at the expense of outsiders, if bonding precludes the abilities of members to bridge to others, then those very loyalties can undermine diverse democratic polities. Within-group loyalties that are exclusionary would directly contrast with the descriptions of persons with democratic dispositions, that is, those with

> a preparedness to work with others different from oneself toward shared ends; a combination of strong convictions with a readiness to compromise in the recognition that one can't always get everything one wants; and a sense of individuality and a commitment to civic goods that are not the possession of one person or one small group alone. (Elshtain, 1995, p. 2)

Affiliation is considered a basic human motivation, even by scholars who focused on hostility toward out-groups (Allport, 1979). And connections to groups and institutions are fundamental in the consolidation of identity. Erikson (1968) worried that without meaningful institutional affiliations and connections to the community, young people would experience "identity-vacua," a lack of direction and purpose in their own lives, and disaffection from their society. Continuity of personal character is a goal of identity work, but so are loyalty to and solidarity with a group and its ideals integral to the process (Erikson, 1956). And individuals are more likely to be loyal to a group and its values if they feel a sense of solidarity with other members. Affiliation and social bonding also are reasons that some people engage in volunteer work. Among adults who do not have particularly close relationships with their parents, social bonding and cohesion with fellow volunteers are important aspects that sustain their commitment to organizational work (Clary & Snyder, 1999).

■ Measures

Self-report measures of citizenship in studies of Americans often focus on behaviors such as voting, campaign work, getting together with others in the community to address an issue, contacting public officials, or engaging in or making financial contributions to political causes (Verba et al., 1995). More activist indicators include such things as signing petitions or joining a protest. Perhaps the most common behavioral measure, especially in national studies of youth, is engagement in volunteer work. However, over the past decade, the integration of service learning into the curricular requirements of high schools has made community service a more normative part of schooling in the United States. Furthermore, as Clary and Snyder (1999) showed, volunteering serves different functions in people's lives. Besides being motivated because they value helping others, people volunteer to fulfill social or career goals, to learn new skills, or to protect or enhance the self.

Several derivations of self-report scales to measure social responsibility were developed in the 1950s and 1960s, and there are several contemporary measures as well (Table 16.1). Gough, McClosky, and Meehl (1952) developed a scale for use with high school and college students, with most of the items drawn from the MMPI. Clusters of items in the scale point to the following tendencies associated with social responsibility: greater concern for social and moral issues; disapproval of privilege and favor; emphasis on duties and self-discipline; greater conventionality; less rebelliousness; greater sense of trust and confidence in the world; greater poise, assurance, and personal security. Scores on this scale were positively and significantly related to peer group nominations of most responsible peers but not significantly related to the subject's self-assessment of responsibility. The more responsible subjects were less cynical, hostile, ethnocentric, anxious, and rebellious. They were more compliant, tolerant, sociable, and secure in relations with the outer world. They also appeared to be better adjusted at school, motivated and successful in academics, and engaged in extracurricular activities. Politically, they tended to be open-minded on social issues.

L. Berkowitz and Lutterman (1968) adapted D. B. Harris's (1957) scale that measured social responsibility in children and administered the resultant eight-item scale to a statewide probability sample of Wisconsin adults. Items in the Social Responsibility Scale (SRS) tap attitudes about the proper duties of individuals to their friends and their communities ("Letting your friends down is not so bad because you can't do good all the time for everybody") (reversed) and of self-reflections ("I feel very bad when I have failed to finish a job I promised I would do"). SRS scores are positively related to subjective social class and education and inversely related to age. Women tend to have higher SRS scores than do men. Individuals with high SRS scores are more likely to be involved in faith-based and community organizations and are more interested in politics.

TABLE 16.1   *Measures of Social Responsibility*

Social Responsibility Scale

    Gough, McClosky, & Meehl (1952)

    56-item scale for use with high school and college students

    ▪ split-half reliability $r = .73$

Social Responsibility Scale

    L. Berkowitz & Lutterman (1968)

    8-item scale for use with adults

    ▪ "Good" internal consistency

Youth Social Responsibility Scale (YSRS)

    Pancer, Pratt, & Hunsberger (2000)

    29-item scale for use with high school students

    ▪ Internal consistency alpha = .87

    ▪ Test–retest (over 2 years) reliability $r = .62$

Youth Inventory of Involvement (YII)

    Pancer, Pratt, & Hunsberger (2000)

    30-item scale for use with high school students

    ▪ Internal consistency alpha = .90

    ▪ Test–retest (over 2 years) reliability $r = .62$

Global Social Responsibility

    Starrett (1996)

    16-item scale for use with adults

    ▪ Internal consistency alpha > .70

Responsibility of People

    Starrett (1996)

    12-item scale for use with adults

    ▪ Internal consistency alpha > .70

Loyola Generativity Scale (LGS)

    McAdams & de St. Aubin (1992)

    20-item scale for use with adults

    ▪ Internal consistency alpha = .84

    ▪ Test–retest (over 3 weeks) reliability $r = .73$

Visions of Morality Scale (VMS)

    Shelton & McAdams (1990)

    45-item scale for use with adolescents

Pancer, Pratt, and Hunsberger (2000) developed the 29-item Youth Social Responsibility Scale (YSRS), as well as a short (10-item) form, which correlates .89 with the longer form. Items tap youths' views about normative responsibilities people should have for one another ("Young people have an important role to play in making the world a better place") and ("In hard times people have to look out for themselves") (reversed). In addition to the YSRS, Pancer and colleagues developed the Youth Inventory of Involvement (YII), a measure with subscales tapping the frequency with which one is involved in various political, community, and social service activities. Both the YSRS and the YII correlate with measures of social support, optimism, self-esteem, authoritative parenting, identity achievement, and discussions of social issues with parents and peers.

Starrett (1996) argued that, because we inhabit a global community, our civic responsibilities transcend the borders of nation-states. To measure individual differences in global social responsibility, he tested an inventory of items with a sample of 219 adults who differed in their levels of social activism. Three subscales emerged. The first, Global Social Responsibility, is a scale that taps attitudes about individual and government responsibility for global issues ("Even to work on the problems of global ecology such as deforestation, we cannot afford to risk giving more power to the UN") (reverse coded). The second scale, Responsibility for People, taps what the author referred to as a "community or intranational perspective of responsibility" (p. 543) ("Every person should give some of his time for the good of his town or country"). The third is a Social Conservatism scale, which taps attitudes at odds with a global perspective ("The American way of life is superior to that of any other country"), although some of the items in this scale do measure social responsibility ("I would like to devote my life to the service of others"). Global Social Responsibility was positively correlated with Responsibility for People and negatively correlated with Social Conservatism. Global Social Responsibility was also positively correlated with measures of international harmony and equality values.

The Loyola Generativity Scale (LGS) is a self-report scale that assesses individual differences in generative concern, including concern for passing on skills and knowledge to others, for making contributions to better one's community, to doing things that will leave an enduring legacy, and for nurturance of and assuming responsibility for others (McAdams & de St. Aubin, 1992). The scale is positively associated with reports of generative behaviors and narrative themes of generativity. Among men, being a parent is positively associated with scores on the LGS. McAdams, Diamond, de St. Aubin, and Mansfield (1997) also developed a coding system to assess the use of generative themes (creating, maintaining, offering help to younger generations or to a legacy beyond oneself) in life stories. Individuals who score high on the LGS tend to tell life stories that focus on themes of caring for the young, use a commitment script in their stories, and are more resolute in their pledge to a personal ideology.

They tell stories in which initial negative experiences were often "redeemed" by transformative positive affect. Women score higher than men on both measures, especially the LGS. Scores on the LGS are positively related to political participation and commitment to the community at midlife among African American and White women who were activists in their youth (Cole & Stewart, 1996). LGS scores also are positively correlated with mothers' authoritative parenting style and with positive views of adolescent development (Pratt, Danso, Arnold, Norris, & Filyer, 2001).

The Visions of Morality Scale (VMS; Shelton & McAdams, 1990) was developed to tap moral choices in everyday life. The scale, developed for and tested with adolescents, measures subjects' responses to 45 everyday occurrences in adolescents' lives. Scores reflect the respondent's own assessment on a 7-point Likert scale of how likely she or he would be to make the moral choice for each of the 45 scenarios, that is, the behavior that would benefit others. The VMS has three subscales: private, interpersonal, and social. Social morality emphasizes the subject's responses to social and humanitarian issues and is akin to the civic dimension discussed in this chapter. Female adolescents scored higher than males on all three dimensions, and the three subscales were highly correlated for both males and females, suggesting that the scale taps an overall prosocial orientation. Scores on the VMS were positively related to measures of empathy and liberal political attitudes.

Other self-report measures tap the personal importance individuals attach to a set of public-interest goals such as helping to promote racial understanding, participating in a community action program, working to correct social and economic inequalities, or helping others who are in difficulty. Over the past 30 years, two nationally representative studies have tracked trends in these public-interest goals as well as in a set of self-interest goals among high school seniors (Monitoring the Future; L. D. Johnston, Bachman, & O'Malley, 1999) and college freshmen (the Cooperative Institutional Research Program; CIRP; Astin, Green, & Korn, 1987). From the early 1970s to the early 1990s, there was a decline in public-interest and an increase in self-interest goals among American youth. Respondents who say that they want to find purpose and meaning in life also rate public-interest goals high in importance. Self-interest and materialist goals are unrelated to public-interest goals or to the desire to find purpose and meaning in life (Easterlin & Crimmins, 1991).

A similar community feeling index was developed by Kasser and Ryan (1993). This seven-item scale asks respondents to rate the importance they attach to such things as making the world a better place, helping people in need, or working for the betterment of society. In studies with college students and other adults, this index was negatively correlated with aspirations for financial success and positively correlated with the importance attached to self-acceptance and affiliation. Community feeling also was positively and significantly related to standard measures of self-actualization and physical and mental vitality. Women rated the importance of community feeling higher than did their male peers.

J. L. Sullivan et al. (1992) used a Q-methodology to collect data on patriotism perspectives and then used the results to conduct an R-methodology survey on a representative sample of adults. They found a wide range of perspectives on the definition of patriotism, including an iconoclastic view of an individual who worked for economic and political change; an emotional attachment to symbols; a commitment to capitalist values blending economic growth with love of country; and a nationalist perspective dedicated to preserving the status quo. This conceptualization of patriotism differs fundamentally from those scales that tap affective regard for one's country (Kosterman & Feshbach, 1989).

Kosterman and Feshbach (1989) distinguished patriotism (attachment to one's country) from nationalism (belief in the superiority of one's country). They administered a 120-item survey to 239 subjects (college undergraduates, high school students, and adults) and found that patriotic and nationalistic attitudes loaded on separate factors. Whereas the former taps a love for and pride in one's nation, the latter reflects national chauvinism, a belief that one's country and its traditions and symbols are superior to others. The two factors are positively correlated at .28, although they also are distinct. For example, nationalism is strongly correlated with a positive attitude toward nuclear preparedness, but patriotism is not. Foreign-born respondents had higher scores on nationalism but not on patriotism when compared with respondents who were born in the United States.

Loyalty and responsibility to an organization are known to be promoted by the organizational practices of a workplace. To measure the climates of workplaces, Vaicys, Barnett, and Brown (1996) developed the Ethical Climate Questionnaire. This 36-item measure, which is based on the perceptions of members of an organization or workplace, factors into six dimensions of an ethical work climate: team spirit, rules and codes, social responsibility, self-interest, efficiency, and personal maturity.

In a similar vein, Bryk and his colleagues developed a set of constructs to measure the organizational climates of schools, including measures of trust and collective responsibility. Alphas for all constructs are above .78 (Bryk & Schneider, 2002). In a series of studies, these aspects of the social climates of schools and of the shared commitment of those concerned with students' education are strong predictors of how well schools function and how well students learn and develop.

■ Correlates and Consequences

By definition, individuals who are socially responsible or "good citizens" are involved in the affairs of their communities. It is therefore not surprising that they have higher levels of social trust and a more positive view of human nature (Staub, 1978), and that they score low on measures of alienation and ethnocentrism. Compared with social isolates, adolescents who are engaged in at least one extracurricular activity at school or community-based organization have more positive views of fellow community members, including the police (C. A. Flanagan, Gill, & Gallay, in press). Although the direction of effects is debated, data from several studies point to what has been called a *virtuous circle* between social trust and civic engagement (Brehm & Rahn, 1997; Putnam, 2000; Rahn & Transue, 1998; Sullivan & Transue, 1999; Verba et al., 1995). People who are more trusting of others in general are more likely to join community organizations and get involved in civic issues. What is less clear is whether there is a boost to social trust (and ultimately to civic engagement) from being involved in any community organization. It does appear that involvement in organizations with a diverse membership and in groups that engage in acts of charity or community service boosts social trust (Stolle, 1998; Uslaner, 2002). However, there is less consistent evidence that spending time in interest-based groups with others who are like oneself increases social trust or a positive view of humanity, a factor that is related to civic engagement.

Youth from better educated families are more positive about civic participation (C. Chapman, Nolin, & Kline, 1997), and youth who get involved in political or quasi-political activities tend to be more tolerant (Avery, 1992). People who are engaged in civic affairs are more knowledgeable about politics and the political process (Delli Carpini & Keeter, 1996; Verba et al., 1995). Socioeconomic inequalities in political participation are higher in the United States than in other democracies (Verba, Nie, & Kim, 1978), and education plays a multifaceted role in those participatory inequities (Verba et al., 1995). Formal education also is associated with the likelihood of working in professional jobs in which recruitment into community associations tends to occur. As Verba et al. (1995) showed, recruitment into community associations is mainly a matter of being asked to join, and the likelihood of being asked is higher for the better educated and for those with jobs, especially professional jobs. Their model of the participatory process—dubbed the Civic Voluntarism Model—proposes that factors fostering political and civic activity (e.g., education, jobs, and professional connections) are stockpiled over a lifetime, frequently conferring more advantage on those who are already privileged.

■ Development

The civic identities, political views, and values of young people are rooted in their social relations and in the opportunities they have for civic practice. The early years of childhood are formative, and family values play a key role in the socialization of social responsibility. In a study of youth from seven nations, to the extent that families emphasized attending to others and their needs, not just to the self, youth incorporated in their own identities the values of social responsibility and citizenship as standards to live by (C. A. Flanagan, Bowes, Jonsson, Csapo, & Sheblanova, 1998). American adolescents' theories about inequality also are concordant with their personal and familial values: Those who contend that poverty, unemployment, and homelessness are the fault of individuals (e.g., for failing to work hard) are more committed to materialist values, whereas those who give individuals the benefit of the doubt and focus instead on the systemic roots of inequality tend to be more altruistic and report that social responsibility is a value emphasized in their families (C. A. Flanagan & Tucker, 1999).

Although empathy is biased toward others who are similar to the self, that bias can be reduced by teaching children to look beyond their own needs and to consider how their actions may affect others. Hoffman (2000) theorized that when empathy for others is part of an individual's early socialization, by early adolescence he or she is likely to be moved by the plight of disenfranchised groups. As such, empathy can be a foundation for a political ideology and a motive base for activism.

Empirical tests of this thesis are limited. However, research with activists in the Civil Rights and antiwar movements of the 1950s and 1960s (Dunham & Bengston, 1992) and of those who sheltered Holocaust survivors during World War II (Oliner & Oliner, 1988) confirm that compassion, empathy, and social responsibility were core family values that motivated their actions. Once exercised in action, values of social responsibility and service to others may become integral to identity. And it is the integration of these values with the self-concept that mediates the connection between political awareness and commitment to sustained action (Colby & Damon, 1992; Youniss, McLellan, & Yates, 1997). Once engendered, a commitment to citizenship or social responsibility is natural because it is an integral part of the self.

Identity consolidation is a core developmental task of the adolescent and young adult years, and personality psychologists have argued that the way an individual grapples with and resolves the salient political and social issues during the period in which they come of age becomes an integral part of personality thereafter (Stewart & Healy, 1989). Despite some mellowing with age, social activism in early adulthood influences political attitudes and involvement through midlife (M. K. Jennings, 1991). Longitudinal studies of 1960s activists show that at mid-life not only were they more altruistic and rebellious than former nonactivists but, as a group, they had taught their children the importance of understanding others and of serving the common good (Franz & McClelland, 1994). After more than two decades of following 1960s activists, Fendrich and Lovoy (1988) observed that youth activists were ideal citizens as adults, more active in their communities than others in their generation, including those who had been active in student government. Similarly, M. K. Jennings (2002) found that adults at mid-life who had participated in political protest as youth were more likely than their uninvolved peers to be engaged in conventional politics and to encourage a civic ethic, including volunteer work, in their children. Twenty-five years after Mississippi Freedom Summer, participants in that movement for civil rights were more likely than nonparticipants to be active in politics in their local communities and in movements for women's rights, peace, and the environment (McAdams, 1989). According to McAdams, participants in such movements are likely to experience a radical resocialization of identity, a personal transformation that results from the combination of intense social action and membership in an organizational network that shares a dedication to a cause.

Generativity is considered normative in the middle and late adult years—so much so that people are considered "off time" or at odds with the "social clock" if, by their 40s, they are not assuming such responsibility through family or work (Helson, Mitchell, & Moane, 1984). Generativity is not limited to family or kin. Nor does generativity seek necessarily to maintain the status quo. As Erikson made clear in drawing attention to the generative themes in the lives of Martin Luther and Mohandas Gandhi, a concern for future generations can be manifest by political actions that challenge the way things are. Engaging in community volunteer work, especially for religious causes, confers particular benefits on the elderly. Panel data reveal that such community involvement lowers levels of depression in the elderly (Musick & Wilson, 2003).

■ Enabling and Inhibiting Factors

When Alexis de Tocqueville wrote *Democracy in America*, he observed that local community associations were the schools of democracy, where citizens from all backgrounds and walks of life worked through the issues and made decisions for their communities. For young people, extracurricular activities and voluntary community organizations serve a similar function by offering opportunities for hands-on training in citizenship. With the possible exception of sports, involvement in extracurricular activities in high school and participation in courses that include discussions of current events predict civic and political participation in adulthood (Verba et al., 1995). Although young people are less likely to be involved in political organizations, longitudinal studies also have shown that participation in such activities in high school predicts political activity in the college years (C. A. Flanagan, Bowes, et al., 1998) and later in adulthood (DeMartini, 1983).

Historically, youth groups have shared a common mission in fostering the character of the next generation of citizens by integrating young people into the norms and mores of the social order. These groups provide structure for free time, a prosocial peer reference group, and adult mentors who typically are volunteering their own time. The nonformal learning atmosphere and egalitarian structure and the fact that young people themselves are often in charge offer unique advantages for civic practice. Together, young people can shape the character of the organization, collectively decide on group goals, and hold one another accountable for the realization of those goals. Features of successful programs include an emphasis on the collective rather than the individual nature of youth agency and a leadership style that keeps the group, not the individual, at the forefront of attention; opportunities for all members to practice a range of roles; a balance between freedom and structure and adults who mentor and coach but do not lead; and a serious role for youth in decision making and in providing things of worth to their communities (Flanagan, in press).

■ Gender, Cross-National, and Cross-Cultural Aspects

Gender differences have been documented in several studies of social responsibility as well as its behavioral and attitudinal correlates. The picture is fairly consistent: Females are more likely than males to exhibit qualities of altruism and empathy and to feel guilty for failures to attend to the needs of others (Beutel & Marini, 1995). Likewise, females in the United States and in several other countries are more likely than their male peers to be engaged in voluntary service in their communities (C. A. Flanagan, Jonsson, et al., 1998; Niemi, Hepburn, & Chapman, 2000). Whereas studies of traditional politics typically have reported a male bias in interest and engagement, research in Europe and the United States on what has been dubbed *new politics* (i.e., concerns for the health and welfare of others and for public goods like water, air, and environmental quality) show that women are equally or more invested when compared with men.

Cross-national comparisons of the civic culture of five countries suggest that cultural expectations in the United States and England of social trust and of expectations for participation in community affairs fostered social responsibility in these countries, whereas such cultural expectations were less likely to be found in Germany, Italy, and Mexico (Almond & Verba, 1965).

According to one large comparative study of 14-year-olds, voluntary community service is a more normative expectation for adolescents in the United States than for their peers in 27 other nations (Torney-Purta, Lehmann, Oswald, & Schulz, 2001). Comparisons of adolescents in four fledgling democracies in Eastern Europe with those in three stable Western democracies revealed consistent roles of family values and school climates in the development of civic values and behaviors. In all seven nations, a family's emphasis on compassion for others distinguished youth who were engaged in volunteer work from their compatriots who were not (C. A. Flanagan, Bowes, et al., 1998).

An inclusive school climate, in which students felt a sense of solidarity with fellow students that cut across the borders of cliques, and a sense of pride in being part of the institution were related to youths' commitment to public interest goals such as serving their communities and country and sustaining the environment for future generations (C. A. Flanagan, Jonsson, et al., 1998). Finally, youth who are involved in extracurricular activities or community groups have higher levels than their uninvolved peers of social trust, altruism, commitments to the common good, and endorsements of the rights of immigrants to full inclusion in their society. In contrast, the uninvolved are more likely to endorse materialist values and self-interest (Buhl, 2001).

■ Deliberate Interventions

Over the past decade, service learning has been becoming institutionalized in public education in the United States. These programs vary considerably in several aspects: in terms of content, duration, and intensity; whether a reflective component is part of the learning; whether the program is done by individuals or groups; and whether it involves young people and/or community members in the design and decision making. However, the evidence is building that participation in service learning programs is associated with such positive outcomes as increased tolerance, trust, commitments to equal opportunity, and cultural diversity (Billig, 2000). Based on their research on service learning, Youniss and Yates (1999) recommend several principles that organizations can apply when planning service learning programs. These include meaningful (rather than busywork) activities, performed by and reflected on by groups rather than individuals. The collective nature of the reflection raises the work and the community issue it addresses to a level of public discussion. Thus, what could be a private act of charity can become an issue for public or political action. Youniss and Yates also emphasize the importance of connecting the service with the history of the organization providing it. The decision to engage in particular types of service reflects the organization's ideology. By making that connection salient for young people, they can see that they are members of an organization with a history and that, by participating in the organization's actions, they are also making history. Mandated service to the community also has been used as an alternative to detention for juvenile offenders, and the results of at least one longitudinal study suggest that engagement in such programs in late adolescence reduces the likelihood of arrest in early adulthood (Uggen & Janikula, 1999).

Besides community service, several new directions in community youth development deserve mention as innovative directions in providing young people with opportunities to exercise civic muscle (see C. A. Flanagan, in press, for summary of new models of grassroots community-based youth activist organizations). YouthBuild (see http://www.youthbuild.org) combines skills training in the construction trades with the provision of affordable housing in local communities in a program where the youth are in charge. Trainees learn leadership and decision-making skills, which they exercise by governing the organization and by speaking out in the public arena. In contrast to many service learning programs in which young people serve others outside of their own communities, young people in YouthBuild exercise civic muscle in their own backyard.

Citizen Schools (see http://www.citizenschools.org) is an NGO in Boston that apprentices 9- to 14-year-olds to professionals in the greater Boston area. This after-school and summer program is based on guided, hands-on learning in groups that results in a tangible product that benefits the community (whether upgrading computers or providing information about health services). In addition, communication skills are emphasized. The program also connects citizens in Boston across the borders of neighborhood and social class, potentially exposing them to a broader view of the common good.

Balanced and restorative justice is a new approach to juvenile crime that conceives of crime as an act that not only harms people but also violates relationships in a community (Bazemore & Walgrave, 1999). Thus, rather than a retributive approach, in which the state punishes an offender, restorative justice practices emphasize healing of the victim, the offender, and the community. Offenders are held accountable for their actions in concrete ways such as community service, where they learn to repair the harm to the community of which they are a member. And service done in the company of law-abiding adults is a means of strengthening cross-generation relationships and reintegrating the young offender into the community.

The Positive Coaching Alliance (PCA) is a national effort to change the culture of youth sports and coaching (J. Thompson, 2000). Concerned that the potential of sports to teach teamwork, cooperation, and fair play was being eroded by a "win at all costs" mentality, the PCA has returned teamwork to the game. The importance of the adult who coaches young people is at the core of the program, and the PCA believes that coaches have historically played an authoritarian role, one which the PCA contests. Because coaches typically lack training in understanding children's needs and their own roles as mentors, training coaches is high on the priority list. The "positive coach" is one who redefines the meaning of winner, fills players' emotional tanks, and honors the game.

Civics and social studies texts have been criticized for emphasizing a rights-based approach to citizenship, with comparatively little attention given to a citizen's responsibilities (Avery & Simmons, 2000–2001). And national assessments of civics learning suggest that a factual approach to history and politics may not rouse students to the importance of taking a stand on issues (Niemi & Junn, 1998). In contrast, programs such as Facing History and Ourselves (http://www.facinghistory.org) and the Southern Poverty Law Center's Teaching Tolerance (http://www.teachingtolerance.org) help children understand that they are actors in a democracy with choices to make and that their collective decisions shape the character and ultimately the history of their society. Finally, Public Adventures is a citizenship curriculum developed in cooperation with the 4-H Cooperative Curriculum System, a national collaboration of state extension services. The curriculum available from the University of Minnesota's Extension System (copyright@extension.umn.edu) is group and action oriented, with modules exploring such areas as what it means to be a member of the "public" and how to identify stakeholder issues, find information and develop action plans to address issues, and then participate in the public adventure (for a recent summary of best practices in civic education, see http://www.civicmissionofschools.org).

Character education is a deliberate intervention with the goal of teaching young people a core set of values; in many programs, "citizenship" figures in these virtues (see http://www.character.org). Other common virtues promoted in these programs include caring, respect, trustworthiness, fairness, and responsibility. The programs vary considerably in their message and pedagogical methods. Some programs are didactic and narrowly conceived, ignoring, for example, the unequal contexts such as poverty and discrimination which the young people experience. In some programs, the civic competencies such as the capacity to understand issues from multiple perspectives, to make an informed judgment, and to take a stand are missing. Obedience is not the primary virtue of a good citizen, and as the Civil Rights movement in the United States and the struggle against apartheid in South Africa showed, a good citizen is not someone who merely stays out of trouble. Other less didactic programs inspire children by sharing stories of exemplary citizens. The Giraffe Project (see http://www.giraffe.org) is a good example and is based on stories of real-life people who take a stand on behalf of the common good. These giraffes show that they are willing to stick their necks out.

■ **What Is Not Known?**

There are three directions in which future research could fill in what is not known about this set of strengths. The first concerns developmental issues. For example, do these strengths manifest in different ways during different periods in the life course? Are there stages of life that are too early to feel a sense of social responsibility, or are such natural inclinations as empathy a good starting point even early in life? Are there particularly sensitive periods of heightened awareness, and what is the potential for developing these strengths throughout the life course? Are there some sine qua nons, some basic physical and psychological needs that have to be fulfilled, before one can develop these values? Are the gender differences often noted in the manifestation of these values an artifact of measurement, norms and socialization influences, or something else?

A second set of unanswered questions concerns the characteristics of environments and relationships in which one develops these values and the radius of groups and communities to which these virtues generalize. More specifically, do feelings of loyalty and responsibility to "others," which would typically be learned in familiar and somewhat homogeneous groups, generalize to heterogeneous groups of "others"? What are the practices and conditions that facilitate the generalization and extension of these strengths? Given a highly mobile society, are a "sense of place" and the responsibilities it entails transportable? How do opportunities, norms, and expectations for social connectedness and participation at different stages of life influence the development of these strengths over time? Although social responsibility is typically measured in the context of human relationships, is this virtue also manifest toward other forms of life?

A final set of questions concerns why the same set of strengths might manifest in different behaviors depending on the political persuasion or social background of the person. Put succinctly, why do some people manifest virtues of loyalty and social responsibility by conserving the status quo, whereas others act out these same virtues by activism that challenges the way things are?

■ Must-Read Articles and Books

Bellah, R. N., Madsen, R., Sullivan, W. M., Swidler, A., & Tipton, S. M. (1985). *Habits of the heart: Individualism and commitment in American life.* Berkeley: University of California Press.

Bryk, A. S., & Schneider, B. (2002). *Trust in schools: A core resource for improvement.* New York: Sage.

Flanagan, C. A. (in press). Volunteerism, leadership, political socialization, and civic engagement. In R. M. Lerner & L. Steinberg (Eds.), *Handbook of adolescent psychology.* New York: Wiley.

Flanagan, C. A., & Tucker, C. J. (1999). Adolescents' explanations for political issues: Concordance with their views of self and society. *Developmental Psychology, 35,* 1198–1209.

Kasser, T. (2002). *The high price of materialism.* Cambridge, MA: MIT Press.

Schwartz, S. H. (1996). Value priorities and behavior: Applying a theory of integrated value systems. In C. Seligman, J. M. Olson, & M. P. Zanna (Eds.), *The psychology of values: The Ontario symposium* (Vol. 8, pp. 1–24). Mahwah, NJ: Erlbaum.

Sullivan, J. L., & Transue, J. E. (1999). The psychological underpinnings of democracy: A selective review of research on political tolerance, interpersonal trust, and social capital. *Annual Review of Psychology, 50,* 625–650.

Uslaner, E. M. (2002). *The moral foundations of trust.* Cambridge, England: Cambridge University Press.

Verba, S., Schlozman, K. L., & Brady, H. E. (1995). *Voice and equality: Civic voluntarism in American politics.* Cambridge, MA: Harvard University Press.

Walzer, M. (1989). Citizenship. In T. Ball, J. Farr, & R. Hanson (Eds.), *Political innovation and conceptual change* (pp. 211–219). Cambridge, England: Cambridge University Press.

Youniss, J., & Yates, M. (1999). Promoting identity development: Ten ideals for school-based service learning programs. In J. Claus & C. Ogden (Eds.), *Service learning for youth empowerment and social change* (pp. 43–68). New York: Peter Lang.

17. FAIRNESS

■ *Mohandas Gandhi (the Mahatma) is a good example of someone who successfully developed his moral reasoning, in both the justice and the care senses of that term. As most readers know well, Gandhi (1869–1948) played a pivotal role in India's struggle to free itself from British colonial rule, and he was influential in helping shape modern India, especially regarding issues of cultural and religious tolerance.*

Gandhi evolved a sophisticated understanding of justice, emphasizing the universality of justice claims in a cultural and political context that denied equal rights to all. He argued that the same moral standard must apply to colonizer (the British) and colonized (the Indians) alike and to all Indians regardless of their position in the traditional Indian caste system. He articulated a universal moral point of view beyond the contentious parochial positions articulated and defended by those to whom he preached. Gandhi argued that the way to realize this moral stance was through dialogue and consensus, though he reserved the right to follow his own inner sense of moral being and argued for the importance of developing individual moral autonomy.

In response to governmental policies that Gandhi considered abusive to the Indian people, and which he decried as unjust because they were imposed by an indifferent colonial ruler, he advocated nonviolent resistance. In this way, he hoped to avoid the violence and bloodshed that usually results from the overthrow of a colonial power. In addition, Gandhi maintained that each Indian involved in resisting colonial rule be free of doing harm to any living being in the process. Beyond refraining from harming other living things, Gandhi argued that we should all try to live in a positive state of love and doing good for others. Toward this end, he was a tireless champion of the rights and well-being of the poor and powerless, not only in his own country but around the world. On a personal level, he put himself at the service of others, often tending the sick and nursing the injured. While living in South Africa he organized a "stretcher corps" to assist in the medical treatment of "enemy" wounded. When his father was ill, he devoted himself to nursing him for months before his death. And when his wife became pregnant, Gandhi took it upon himself to study midwifery to be able to assist in the delivery of their children. Gandhi's insistence on nonviolence almost cost him his life many times as he would fast until his countrymen ceased their violence against the British or against each other.

Gandhi's life is a story of compassion for those in need, a defense of universal justice, and a passionate articulation of the effectiveness of dialogue and nonviolent resistance. Each of these aspects of his moral reasoning demonstrates the depth and breadth of Gandhi's fairness. A close reading of how he addressed the major moral crises of his life also illustrates the typical integration of justice and care considerations in the resolution of real-life moral problems. ▪

■ Consensual Definition

Fairness is the product of moral judgment—the process by which people determine what is morally right, what is morally wrong, and what is morally proscribed. Although there are other aspects to moral development and moral understanding beyond judgment, we follow the lead of previous psychologists and regard reasoning to be critical to moral development and to enabling moral behavior. Moral reasoning has been explored and explicated in two main traditions: the justice reasoning approach and the care reasoning approach. Accompanying the development of moral judgment is a broader set of values that come to be embodied psychologically and socially through the development of psychosocial skills and ways of being. Being committed to fairness in all of one's social relations, developing skill in the abstract logic of equitable arrangements, becoming sensitized to issues of social injustice, coming to embody compassion and caring for others, and developing the perceptiveness necessary for relational understanding are desirable developmental outcomes. These terms name psychological strengths and virtues that allow us to be responsible citizens, trustworthy friends, and generally moral people.

Individuals who have developed the psychological strengths associated with fairness would strongly endorse such statements as the following:

- Everyone should get her fair share.
- It's wrong to *use* people.
- I wouldn't want to cheat anyone, any more than I would want to be cheated.

- I try to be kind to everyone.
- Everyone deserves respect.
- We're all in this together.
- People are ends in themselves.
- No one deserves to be discriminated against because of the color of his skin.
- We are responsible for our own behavior.
- Even if society says it's all right to do something, if it doesn't match my personal sense of what's right, I wouldn't do it.

■ Theoretical Traditions

Moral judgment refers to the development of the cognitive capacity to ascertain what is ethically right and what is ethically wrong through deliberation of the moral context, the relationships of the people involved, and the relevant values and principles. It is the capacity to reason about moral issues and make judgments about which course(s) of action can be ethically justified and which are morally proscribed. Moral deliberation does, of course, involve more than abstract cognition. Moral judgment is part of a more complex constellation of moral psychological competencies that include affective, cognitive, behavioral, and personality dimensions (M. W. Berkowitz, 1997; Sherblom, 1997).

It has been firmly established in psychological research that the various ways in which people deliberate about the moral aspects of their experience and choices, deciding what is right, and what they ought to do, usually consist of a mix of moral judgment approaches and concerns (Blum, 1988; O. J. Flanagan & Jackson, 1987; Gilligan, 1987; Higgins, 1980; Nucci, 2001; L. J. Walker, de Vries, & Trevethan, 1987). Extensive research in moral psychology has documented that when faced with moral conflicts, people spontaneously resolve moral quandries by using a range of moral language and patterns that reflect both care and justice (Gilligan & Attanucci, 1987; Jaffee & Hyde, 2000; L. J. Walker, 1991). Although there is evidence that some people use one or the other approach predominantly in their everyday lives, the consensus is that most individuals are familiar with and believe in values reflecting each approach, and the commonsense notion of moral includes both (Clopton & Sorell, 1993; Galotti, 1989).

Care reasoning is differentiated from justice reasoning in two ways. First, care has different criteria for determining which aspects of human experience are to be included in the moral domain and moral deliberation. The ethic of care expands the justice perspective on morality by including caring and compassion, and it complements the justice emphasis on logic with other forms of knowing such as empathy and other types of relational understanding. Second, the end goal of care is somewhat different. Whereas justice is primarily an objective weighing of principles for a determination of moral rights and responsibilities (cf. chapter 6), care is intended to provide a compassionate determination of how people's needs might best be met (cf. chapter 11). Still, people operating in the ethic of care engage in judgment as a central activity. People deliberating in both care and justice frameworks must reason about the moral context, interpreting the issues to be considered and the tensions and consequences associated with each choice and action.

The conceptual and theoretical distinctions between justice and care as ways of operating psychologically in the moral domain should not obscure the fact that the moral aspects of our experience do not break down neatly along philosophical lines, and our psychological capacities are not segmented, but elements of a whole person. We will begin by exploring the justice approach.

Justice Tradition

There are two lines of work in psychology that address how people relate to others in terms of justice. One approach—equity theory—was developed in social and cognitive psychology. It describes the conditions under which people act more or less fairly and is intended to be descriptive of human behavior. It tends to focus heavily on external conditions that lead to variations in human behavior, for example, under which circumstances a person will tend to share resources equally, act altruistically, or take a disproportionate share of resources for himself or herself. Because it is an economic theory rather than a psychological one, we do not focus on equity theory here. Rather, we will focus on the second line of work, which comes from developmental psychology and attempts to be both descriptive and prescriptive (Kohlberg, 1971). This approach—justice reasoning theory—prescribes more and less desirable ways of determining what is fair and equitable and describes the developmental trajectories that humans take as they develop such a psychological strength.

Historically, psychology has relegated issues of morality either to other disciplines (e.g., philosophy, theology, literature) or to noncognitive areas of psychology (e.g., psychoanalytic explanations of moral affect such as guilt and shame). However, in the early 20th century, the Swiss biologist and philosopher Jean Piaget began his explorations of child cognitive development with a study titled *The Moral Judgment of the Child*, published in French in 1932. In this work, he carved out the study of (a) moral cognition and (b) the development of such capacities. This work was grounded in the structuralist tradition that Piaget adapted for psychology. The basic tenets are that cognitive capacities develop as an interaction between the organism and the environment through the tension created by inadequate cognitive capacities (stages) confronting problems beyond its ability to solve. Each newly developed stage (in a universal sequence of general structures or ways of knowing the world) subsumes the prior stage and improves upon it, being both more logical and functional.

Piaget's work on moral judgment was clearly an unfinished project, which he put aside for a focus on more scientific content (such as causality, time, space). Because this work was not translated into English until 1965, it remained obscure in English-speaking countries. This work was re-invigorated in the late 1950s, by Lawrence Kohlberg, then a psychology graduate student at the University of Chicago. Kohlberg took Piaget's unfinished project and expanded it to elaborate a full structural model of the development of moral judgment that encompasses childhood through late adulthood. Kohlberg (1969, 1976) identified six stages of justice reasoning development, ranging from an egocentric focus on the physical consequences of one's actions to a balanced consideration of the legitimate moral claims of all stakeholders in a given moral issue, based on universal ethical principles of justice.

These stages are grouped into three pairs or levels. The preconventional level (Stages 1 and 2) defines morality or justice as that which produces the greatest benefit for an individual. Focus is on concrete consequences for the individual. Stage 1 is egocentric and considers right to be directly related to the inevitable consequences of an action (it is wrong because you *will* get punished) or the labeling of the action as right or wrong by an authority or power figure. Stage 2 is a morality of exchange (it is right to help others because they might do something nice for you in return) and probability (it is wrong because you *might* get punished).

The conventional level (Stages 3 and 4) approaches right and wrong at the social (interpersonal) level. What is right serves the social unit and is what others say is right. Stage 3 focuses on the dyadic relationship, for example, maintenance of friendships. What is right (or wrong) is what will nurture (or harm) a relationship. Stage 4 focuses on larger social units, such as the family or society. What is right is what serves the social system or what adheres to system-defined role obligations.

The postconventional level (Stages 5 and 6) shifts to universal criteria for right and wrong, that is, to principles of justice. Stage 5 embraces the social contract: Right is determined by the fulfillment of obligations we have agreed to follow as members of a society, but it allows for conscientious objection and revision of the system. Stage 6 entails pure adherence to abstract universal principles of justice.

Kohlberg's (1984) resulting stage model attracted numerous challenges, including theoretical and empirical critiques. Some were friendly critiques that attempted to expand the model. Turiel (1980), suggesting that Kohlberg had identified only one domain of social reasoning (moral), identified alternative domains (social conventional, personal, prudential). Gilligan (1979) argued that Kohlberg had missed an alternative track of moral reasoning development. She suggested that he had focused solely on issues of justice and independent rationality, but that many individuals instead or in conjunction rely on moral issues of care and interpersonal responsibility to determine what is right or wrong. We discuss this care approach shortly.

Others offered more fundamental challenges to the basic assumptions of the Kohlberg model. Snarey (1985) and Shweder, Mahapatra, and Miller (1987) questioned whether Kohlberg's model was universal, suggesting that it was culturally specific. J. C. Gibbs (1977) suggested that the final two stages in Kohlberg's developmental scheme were not universal structures.

Despite these challenges, a massive amount of data was collected that supported most of Kohlberg's structuralist claims (Colby & Kohlberg, 1987). It is clear that the stages exist, that they develop in an invariant sequence, that they are related to cognitive and social cognitive development, and that they are related to other aspects of moral psychology such as behavioral outcomes, personality, and values. Due to the relative rarity of the highest two stages, these claims can be made more strongly for the first four stages than for the last two.

Care Tradition

The extension of moral reasoning to include care reasoning was part of a broader feminist critique of social science and an exploration of the moral and psychological significance of aspects of human behavior traditionally ascribed to females (Gilligan, 1979, 1982; Noddings, 1984; Tronto, 1987). There are many ways in which activities of caring and personality traits associated with caring have been "gendered" in Western culture, that is, heavily associated with femininity and regarded as women's work. Being caring, compassionate, and nurturant (as a personological disposition) is stereotypically labeled feminine and indeed expected of women. Although not wholly absent from Western philosophy, the perspectives, values, and behaviors delineated by the care approach have largely been marginalized in favor of more masculine approaches that emphasize reasoning, logic, and so-called objective deliberation (Blum, 1980; Connell, 1995; O. J. Flanagan & Adler, 1983; Kittay & Meyers, 1987).

As Kohlberg's cognitive-developmental theory ascended, critics argued that the justice concerns at its heart did not capture all of what is commonly considered moral, and that the cognitive focus precluded recognizing or finding other psychosocial aspects of moral deliberation (Larrabee, 1993; J. R. Martin, 1989). Care theorists argued that an ethic of care is both legitimate and coherent as a philosophical perspective (an ethic) and that it could be shown that people use this ethic in their spontaneous moral deliberation (L. M. Brown, Debold, Tappan, & Gilligan, 1991; Gilligan & Attanucci, 1987; Noddings, 1984). There has been much debate about both the philosophical and the empirical basis of their claims, and some claims have not been supported, but it is fair to say that most everyone now recognizes the ethic of care, and care reasoning has become an important part of the moral domain and moral reasoning as it is generally understood.

The questions asked by each approach reflect the aspects of the moral context each believes most vital to understanding its moral dynamic and nature, the things that one must understand in order to engage in adequate moral deliberation. In contrast to the objectivity of blind justice and the abstract logic of principled reasoning, care reasoning requires understanding particularity—the needs, interests, and well-being of another person—and understanding the relationship between oneself and that other person (Blum, 1994). This requires a moral stance "informed by care, love, empathy, compassion, and emotional sensitivity" (Blum, 1988, p. 474).

■ Measures

The original means of assessing an individual's stage of justice reasoning development came from Kohlberg's dissertation work. It was a clinical interview method based directly on Piaget's *methode clinique*. Kohlberg devised a set of moral dilemma vignettes that were presented verbally to an individual. A trained interviewer then used standard probe questions to elicit the interviewee's moral judgment (action choice for the protagonist in the dilemma) and moral reasoning (ethical justification for that action choice). Other probes elicited the individual's ethical justification for basic values such as life, property, and respect for law. For example, the best known moral dilemma from the most commonly used of the three parallel forms of the Kohlberg measure is the Heinz dilemma. This entails the choice of a man whose wife is dying of a rare form of cancer. He cannot afford the exorbitant price the sole producer charges for the only drug that can save her, so he must choose between letting her die or stealing the drug.

This assessment approach evolved through different incarnations until it became the Standard Moral Judgment Interview (SMJI; Colby & Kohlberg, 1987; Table 17.1). This semiclinical interview method relies on a detailed clinical scoring manual for the coding of open-ended responses of individuals, in either written or oral form. One of three parallel sets of dilemma stories are used, each with standard probes. In the Heinz dilemma, for example, interviewees are asked for their action choice (steal or not steal) and are probed for their justification for that choice. Interviewers follow up the responses to a series of set probes (e.g., What if Heinz did not love his wife? Why is it important to save a life?). Psychometric properties of the SMJI are well established (Colby & Kohlberg, 1987).

James R. Rest (1979) developed an alternative, objective assessment method entitled the Defining Issues Test (DIT), which has become the most widely used assessment method. It is based on a series of dilemmas and uses objective questions to elicit an individual's preference for and ranking of prototypical moral arguments that represent different structures according to the Kohlberg framework. It can be individually or group administered and can be hand or computer scored. The DIT presents dilemmas (including the Heinz dilemma) and

---

TABLE 17.1   *Measures of Fairness*

Justice reasoning measures

Standard Moral Judgment Interview (SMJI)
> Colby & Kohlberg (1987)
> Clinical interview format with clinical scoring guide

Defining Issues Test (DIT)
> Rest (1979)
> Written, group-administered, objectively scored version of the SMJI

Sociomoral Reflection Measure (SRM)
> Gibbs, Basinger, & Fuller (1992); Gibbs, Widaman, & Colby (1982)
> Written, group-administered, clinically scored version of the SMJI

Sociomoral Reflection Objective Measure (SROM)
> Gibbs et al. (1984)
> Written, group-administered, objectively scored version of the SMJI

Care reasoning measures

Scheme for Coding Considerations of Response and Considerations of Rights
> Lyons (1983)
> Clinical interview with coding scheme

Responsive Readers' Guide
> Brown et al. (1988); Brown, Debold, Tappan, & Gilligan (1991)
> Clinical interview format with interpretive guide

Measure of Moral Orientation
> Liddell, Halpin, & Halpin (1992)
> Written, group-administered test of preference for moral orientation (justice or care)

---

arguments for both action choices that represent each of the stages in the developmental model. Respondents rate and rank the arguments. Psychometric properties for the DIT are also well established.

John Gibbs and his colleagues created a set of instruments. The first two instruments (Sociomoral Reflection Measure; SRM) were shorter (J. C. Gibbs, Basinger, & Fuller, 1992) and longer (J. C. Gibbs, Widaman, & Colby, 1982) versions, respectively, of a written, group-administered version of the SMJI. The goal was to collect data more effectively in a written, group format. Respondents read the dilemmas and questions and write open-ended responses, which are individually scored with a coding manual. The next two instruments (Sociomoral Reflection Objective Measure [SROM], again in a shorter and a longer form) were intended to parallel the DIT by offering objective items for group written administration and objective scoring (J. C. Gibbs et al., 1984). In this format, the dilemmas are not included. Rather, research participants merely respond to prepared moral arguments.

Other scoring systems, although less centrally focused on the specific Kohlberg moral reasoning scheme, nonetheless assess the development of moral reasoning. William Damon (1977, 1988) devised methods for assessing the moral reasoning of younger children (preschool and elementary school age), developmental levels for which the SMJI and related assessment methods are inappropriate. Nancy Eisenberg (1986) presented a model of specifically prosocial moral reasoning and has a method for assessing its development.

Gilligan (1977) offered a three-level developmental progression for care reasoning with transition periods between levels. At the first level (orientation to individual survival), the self is the sole object of concern. This level is transcended when one learns to be responsible for another, and the previous position is then seen as selfish. This move from selfishness to responsibility is a move into social participation, though this second level (goodness as self-sacrifice) is also a move away from the self to an overemphasis on the well-being of others. "Here the conventional feminine voice emerges with great clarity, defining the self and proclaiming its worth on the basis of the ability to care for and protect others" (p. 496). This level is transcended with "the reconsideration of the relationship between self and other, as the woman starts to scrutinize the logic of self-sacrifice in the service of a morality of care" (p. 498). At this phase women start to ask if it is not possible to care for themselves while maintaining care for others, recognizing that there is a fundamental imbalance when moral questions are decided solely for the benefit of others. Gilligan called this the transition from goodness to truth, where a woman's dedication to being "good" and being seen as good is replaced with a greater desire to know what is true and to act truly according to one's own beliefs. The third, and last, level is called the morality of nonviolence. Gilligan argued, "By elevating nonviolence—the injunction against hurting—to a principle governing all moral judgment and action, she [the moral agent] is able to assert a moral equality between self and other" (p. 504).

Research on care reasoning has not yielded a stage-type developmental model of the kind Kohlberg created for justice reasoning. This domain of research is more preliminary and has focused more on articulating care concerns and the underlying epistemology associated. Much of the research involving care reasoning has focused on sex differences in moral orientation, on whether males and females both use care and justice (Jaffee & Hyde, 2000; Page & Tyrer, 1995). However, several other interesting topics and intervening variables have been investigated, including whether certain personality traits predispose one to a particular moral orientation (R. J. Glover, 2001), and the role of "critical experiences" in development of orientation (Barnett, Quackenbush, & Sinisi, 1995; Conley, Jadack, & Hyde, 1997). Additionally, research suggests that the standard dilemmas used to measure moral orientation and development can themselves be shown to emphasize attachment or inequality or some other conception that has a philosophical bias attached to its formulation. Dilemmas that emphasize attachment pull for care solutions; and dilemmas that emphasize inequality pull for justice solutions (Gilligan & Wiggins, 1987; D. K. Johnston, 1988; L. J. Walker, 1984).

Care reasoning has been assessed in three ways: two by Gilligan and her colleagues, with the second method superseding the first; and a more recent paper-and-pencil version by another researcher (Liddell, Halpin, & Halpin, 1992). Gilligan and her research team initially used a relatively simple approach that assessed moral orientation, involving identifying all the moral concerns expressed in an interview, and classifying them as either justice based or care based (Lyons, 1983). They then simply tallied each and designated the interview as being oriented toward justice or care if a predominance of the concerns fell into one category or the other. Although this method generated "hard numbers," and therefore had a certain empirical appeal, the method came to be seen as needing refinement. A more "voice-sensitive" method was developed that attempted to render more of the texture and substance of people's care reasoning as embodied in their interview transcripts.

Gilligan and her research team developed the Responsive Reader's Guide (L. M. Brown et al., 1988, 1991). The Reader's Guide is a method for reading interview texts (or other narratives) for various "voicings" in the text—initially for care and justice voices, as well as the speaker's sense of self. It has been argued that how one defines oneself in relation to others in a global sense is related to one's moral orientation, with a connected sense of self correlating with a care voice, and a separate sense of self correlating with a justice voice (Lyons, 1983). The process of reading illustrated in the Reader's Guide involves working through the text a number of times, as a form of qualitative/interpretive research, each time listening for specific things. This technique is premised on the finding that attuning your ear to a specific voicing (self or care or justice) allows you to be more sensitive to the nuance of that voice than you would be if you just worked your way through the text once, assigning labels to everything as you go. Another important and practical feature of this method is the worksheet where each reading and the reader's interpretation are documented. The reader is asked to highlight passages deemed to represent the self, care, and justice concerns and to articulate his or her interpretation of each segment.

For example, when reading for self, one would highlight how the self is represented in the text: "I thought . . . felt . . . decided . . . I'm not sure . . . I believe . . . I felt responsible." Focusing on the self allows inquiry into how active or passive the self is regarding the moral perceptions, deliberation, and actions discussed. It can give a sense of the depth of commitment one feels for the values one is espousing and the centrality of these values and actions to one's sense of moral identity. When reading for justice, one focuses on moral justifications involving the concepts of rights and responsibilities, moral principles, fairness, and reciprocity. In addressing Kohlberg's Heinz dilemma, if someone argues that "Heinz should steal the drug because life is more important than property," the reader would quote the justification on the worksheet and then in his or her own words explain how this statement is an example of justice reasoning. The reader might characterize this justification as arranging a hierarchy of relevant principles, after weighing each side's moral claim. When reading for care, the reader focuses on moral reasoning involving compassion, concern, being emotionally moved, recognizing oneself as socially related to others, and being concerned with how people's needs might best be met. It is not enough to look for particular phrases, such as "I did it because I care about her" or "because she needed some help." This interpretive method requires listening beyond the individual words and phrases to understand the underlying logic of the justification. Recording not just the myriad quotes that exemplify care or justice, but one's reading of each passage—one's interpretation of the reasoning offered, and ultimately the ways that reasoning functions in the interview—facilitates other people following the logic of your interpretation, making possible the group discourse necessary for a productive interpretive community (L. M. Brown et al., 1988).

This method, by graphically highlighting the different voices in the text, allows the reader to hear and see how specific voicings of justice and care interact in the participant's moral reasoning. Many moral development researchers have noted that justice and care are not as dichotomous and nonoverlapping as it may sometimes sound when care and justice are defined in opposition to one another. Additionally, two studies of moral voicings found integrated responses containing both justice and care concerns interwoven so tightly that they could not be meaningfully separated (Sherblom, Shipps, & Sherblom, 1993; Ward, 1991).

It should also be noted that part of the strength of the Reader's Guide actually lies in the rich texts that result from the kind of interviewing style used to elicit people's real-life moral experiences. Research methodologists have written extensively on the differences in the data collected when using methods that elicit people's own meaning-making schemes versus those that evaluate people on a researcher-designed scale.

The Measure of Moral Orientation (Liddell et al., 1992) is a paper-and-pencil, Likert-scale, self-report measure designed to rate people regarding their preference for either care or justice reasoning. This measure has become popular with those engaged in sex-difference research regarding usage of care and justice by women and men, respectively, because it is very easy to administer and score.

■ Correlates and Consequences

A number of psychological strengths are common outcomes of development in justice and care moral reasoning. In fact, optimal developmental outcomes (including Kohlberg's highest stage and Gilligan's conceptions of mature caring) require facility with a wide range of moral capacities (Gilligan, 1987; Kohlberg, 1984). We mention five domains of healthy psychological development that are commonly strengthened by the development of moral reasoning.

Moral Identity Formation

The self-chosen nature of moral commitments, along with their affective strength, ensures that as children develop strong personal moral beliefs, adherence to those beliefs comes to figure prominently in the child's sense of self (Blasi, 1993; Colby & Damon, 1992). Not only will they name themselves morally, and wish to think of themselves as a "good girl," a "nice person," and a "true friend," but they will use the standards of their understanding of these roles to judge their own moral character.

One's moral identity and one's understanding of morality (justice and care) support each other. The more you identify with a moral standard, whether as an act of will (such as committing oneself to a religious tradition) or as an act of insight (such as seeing someone suffer a social injustice and being deeply "moved" by the experience), the more that standard (and the identity that is the internalization of that standard) will direct your attention and flavor and filter your perception and interpretation. At the same time, the more able one becomes with moral understanding and judging, and the more moral evaluation becomes a part of one's general evaluative abilities, the more likely it is that moral evaluation itself will figure in self-evaluations and become tied to self-esteem. Identity, then, contributes to development by its demand for identity-related focus and practice, and the focus and practice contribute to your sense of mastery in your developing moral identity. As Aristotle noted, in some sense you are what you repeatedly do.

The sensitivity to fairness that comes with a commitment to justice, the exposure to alternative interpretations of reality that one gets in negotiating equitable solutions, and the insights and emotional responsiveness that develop with each act of compassion are elements of moral experience that constantly change who you are and how you perceive and engage morally. This dynamic makes moral identity formation an ongoing, ever-changing part of one's larger identity and sense of self. This is deep identity, not simply a claim to be a caring person or a professed devotion to fairness, but identity as integral, even foundational, to who one is and how one defines oneself to oneself. Identity, in this sense, is not only definitional but motivational (Colby & Damon, 1992).

Self-Esteem Based in (Self-Perceived) Moral Behavior

Adherence to self-expectations, that is, living up to your own ideal, is important for your self-esteem. Moral identity (as one locus of self-expectations) and the self-esteem that comes from successful adherence to that identity help create a positive cycle in which people engage in fairness and caring and are rewarded with positive feedback, both verbal and relational, for doing so. Their identity and self-esteem are reinforced together, making it more likely that they will engage others in these ways in the future. The important people in your life, your family, models, and mentors (and the proverbial village), together must set up and maintain this positive cycle.

Perspective Taking

Perspective taking, the ability to imaginatively place yourself in the proverbial shoes of another, is a psychological ability that provides a foundational source of knowledge for moral deliberation. Justice and care frame perspective taking somewhat differently, as the ethic of care conceptualizes perspective taking to include affective elements of an empathic kind, and the ethic of justice does not. For justice adherents, perspective taking is a cognitive endeavor, emphasizing and evaluating the universal role components of a person's position—the generalizable obligations people have in this situation. In contrast, care adherents tend to emphasize the particularity of the person's perspective and experience and legitimate more affectively based knowing, such as empathy. For care theorists, taking another's perspective requires a melding of cognitive and affective sources of knowledge, and there is the added implication that this more emotional knowing brings with it motivation in the form of being moved by the other's situation, not simply being aware of that situation. Being able to conceive moral contexts from multiple sides and being able to more deeply understand each person involved are major achievements in moral development.

For both justice and care, perspective taking is a source of knowledge about others and about the possible consequences of one's own actions as they have impact on the lives of others. Developing this ability, in either its strictly cognitive form or its cognitive and affective mix, constitutes an epistemological advantage. That is to say, it deepens and broadens one's knowledge and the forms of one's knowledge regarding moral contexts, deliberation, action, and likely consequences.

Self-Reflection

Another psychological strength developed as an integral component of moral development is self-reflection and its product, self-knowledge/awareness (cf. chapter 15). Taking the perspective of others, in whichever form, inevitably casts one's own position and understanding in a new light, providing contrast and exposure to alternate if not contradictory views, beliefs, assumptions, and values. Self-reflection is also a component of moral identity formation, coming to see oneself as this or that kind of person; as a person who is committed to this standard and that cause; as a person who is or is not likely to do certain things. Part of moral identity is the network of self-chosen commitments one comes to embody. Reflection upon these commitments and the ways in which they are woven into the fabric of one's life and psychic being helps refine that identity and strengthen one's adherence to those values and that aspect of oneself. The experience of being "moved" by another's plight, of witnessing yourself being morally responsive, is also part of what you come to know about yourself as a moral person.

Relational Problem Solving

Although justice and care tend to frame moral dilemmas differently, relational problem solving is relevant to both. In both justice and care, a person must (a) be sensitive to the fact that a relational problem exists; (b) assemble relevant facts about the case; (c) make some kind of determination of what morality demands in this situation; and (d) decide what to do about it. Relational problem solving is a psychological strength that contributes broadly to understanding and getting along with other people (cf. chapter 15).

Other Correlates

Over the past four decades, justice reasoning has been correlated with a vast array of variables. Most of these relationships have been established in studies using the SMJI or DIT. For example, lower stage justice reasoning is related to greater delinquency (Blasi, 1980; Marston, cited in Thoma, Rest, & Barnett, 1986); cheating and academic dishonesty (Leming, 1978); risky sexual behavior (J. Hernandez & DiClemente, 1992); drug and alcohol use (M. W. Berkowitz, Kahn, Mulry, & Piette, 1995); bystander apathy (McNamee, 1978); aggression (Bredemeier & Shields, 1984); and lower conscientious objection (Hay, 1983). Higher state justice reasoning is linked to cooperation (Jacobs, cited in Thoma et al., 1986); whistle-blowing (Brabeck, 1984); leadership (Lupfer et al., cited in Thoma et al., 1986); professional medical performance (Candee, Sheehan, Cook, Husted, & Bargen, 1982; Cook, cited in Thoma et al., 1986; Sheehan, Candee, Willms, Donnelly, & Husted, 1985; Sheehan, Husted, Candee, Cook, & Bargen, 1980); civil disobedience (Candee & Kohlberg, 1987); and altruism (Eisenberg et al., 1987). Additionally, moral reasoning is related to a wide variety of attitudes. For example, lower stages are associated with more supportive attitudes toward and evaluations of capital punishment (DeWolfe & Jackson, 1984; Kohlberg & Elfenbein, 1975); more acceptance of aggression (M. W. Berkowitz,

Mueller, Schnell, & Padberg, 1986); greater conservatism (Fincham & Barling, 1979); and less support of women's rights (Letchworth & McGee, cited in Thoma et al., 1986) and human rights (Getz, cited in Thoma et al., 1986).

The pattern of correlations suggests that justice reasoning maturity is related to increased prosocial and decreased antisocial behavior, reduced immoral behavior, and more liberal attitudes. Reviews of the research on the relation of moral reasoning to behavior and attitudes include Blasi (1980), Kohlberg and Candee (1984), Eisenberg (1986), and Thoma et al. (1986).

Due to the fact that moral reasoning development is understood to be based on a slow natural developmental process of increasing cognitive sophistication, evidence about the effects of justice reasoning is limited. When reasoning development occurs naturally, it is by necessity confounded with the development of many other psychological characteristics. In such cases, we are limited to correlational evidence as reviewed earlier. To directly assess the impact of justice reasoning development on behavior and other psychological characteristics, intervention studies must be examined. In fact, there are many intervention studies in the field of moral development. However, they tend to focus on how to intervene to foster the development of justice reasoning, rather than on the impact of such gains on other psychological variables. In other words, the outcome variable in most such studies is justice reasoning.

Another window on this question is provided by studies that engage in naturalistic longitudinal research, including the justice reasoning stage. The classic study is Kohlberg's own original dissertation sample, followed for 25 years (Colby, Kohlberg, Gibbs, & Lieberman, 1983). Candee, Graham, and Kohlberg (1978) followed subjects from this study and the Oakland Growth Study into adulthood to "deepen our understanding of the mechanisms by which moral reasoning is translated into daily behavior and . . . gain some picture of the individuals that sustained programs in moral education are likely to produce" (p. 60). The authors reported the following:

- Persons at higher stages of justice reasoning hold higher status jobs (more prestigious and responsible jobs).
- Attainment of at least Stage 4 reasoning is necessary for holding high-status jobs, likely due to the conceptual complexity required for social decisions in such jobs.
- Higher stage subjects are no more satisfied with their jobs or marriages than are lower stage subjects.
- Higher stage parents do not use love withdrawal as a parenting technique and prefer discussion-based parenting (e.g., induction).
- Higher stage parents are less likely to endorse "conventional" values (e.g., obedience, manners, respect for rules and law) and are more likely to endorse values that promote autonomy and commitment to and respect for others.

- Higher stage adults are more politically active.
- Work and family values of higher stage adults center around social ideals and justice, whereas lower stage adults tend to focus on issues of pay, hours, promotion, and providing material and emotional benefits for their families.
- Higher stage individuals resolve family conflicts through taking the other's point of view and seriously considering his or her claims, whereas lower stage individuals tend to resort to shouting, demands, or making concessions.

Rest, Deemer, Barnett, Spickelmier, and Volker (1986) reported that those who develop more in justice reasoning report more career fulfillment, continue their intellectual stimulation, are more involved in their community, and are more socially conscious in young adulthood.

To examine directly the outcomes of justice reasoning development, one would have to tie the outcome variables directly to changes in justice reasoning capacity. One way to do this is to engage in longitudinal follow-ups of individuals who participate in interventions designed to foster the development of justice reasoning capacity. For example, during the 1970s, Lawrence Kohlberg mentored a set of schools (Just Community Schools) that were designed to promote justice reasoning capacity (Power, Higgins, & Kohlberg, 1989). One study examined a small sample of graduates of one of those schools (Grady, 1994). More than a decade after graduation, this sample exhibited significant differences in certain social values (gender values, racial sensitivity) compared with graduates of the parent high school. However, the sample was extremely small, and the results were not directly related to justice reasoning scores.

Interventions with incarcerated youth have provided longitudinal follow-up data on recidivism. Leeman, Gibbs, and Fuller (1993) reported a significant relation between moral reasoning gains and postrelease recidivism. These findings are paralleled by similar results reported by Arbuthnot and Gordon (1986).

There is little research on outcomes associated with the development of care reasoning. This may be because the ethic of care is a more recent addition to mainstream psychology, and long-term research programs may not yet be reported. Second, researchers may believe that it is intuitively obvious that developing one's ability to care, in whatever form, is supportive of prosocial and empathic behavior, but because no definitive detailed developmental progression of care reasoning has been articulated, this kind of comparison is difficult.

We suggest, however, that outcomes associated with the psychological strengths highlighted by care are being taken up in other forms and by other names. For example, the care perspective, more so than justice, emphasizes the importance of the interpersonal relationships involved in the moral context—thereby highlighting a need for understanding and sensitivity on both ends of the relational bond: self-awareness on one end and relational understanding on the other. In addition, the care perspective legitimates emotional responsiveness, in the form of empathy or being moved by the plight of another, as a source of knowledge and appropriate motivation. The strong emotional sense that one must prevent harm or right an interpersonal or social injustice is seen as a moral voice as undeniable as our justice-based codes and laws regarding moral conduct.

These aspects of moral knowledge championed by the care perspective—self-awareness, relational understanding, and emotional responsiveness—have all been identified as important developmental accomplishments elsewhere (Cohen, 2001; Dasho, Lewis, & Watson, 2001). H. Gardner's (1993b) personal and interpersonal intelligences highlight self-awareness and relational understanding, respectively, and emotional intelligence (Goleman, 1995) highlights both of those and emotional responsiveness. Many of these skills also fall under the currently popular rubric of social-emotional learning. As Cohen (1999) argued, social and emotional competencies, self-reflective capacities on the one hand and the ability to recognize what others are thinking and feeling on the other,

> provide the foundation for children to understand, manage, and express the social and emotional aspects of life. . . . These competencies allow us to modulate emotions, to solve social problems creatively, to be effective leaders or collaborators, to be assertive and responsible, or to be able to ask evocative emotional and/or social questions that lead to new learning. (p. 11)

Shriver, Schwab-Stone, and DeFalco (1999) proposed that there is a "social-emotional health crisis" in the United States, with estimates ranging from 25% to 50% of high school students engaging in some type of high-risk behavior. They attribute this directly to a breakdown in the caring aspects of students' lives: to the dissolution of stable families, to neglect and abuse in their important relationships, and to emotional distance in school relationships with teachers and the school community. The caring environment and relationships that support the development of care in children also seem to be psychologically protective.

Character education programs are another site for future research on care-related outcomes, as well as justice-related outcomes. Common virtues promoted by character education programs range from those generally associated with a justice approach (honesty, honor, tolerance, freedom of speech, equal opportunity) to those clearly articulated in care terms (love, generosity, helpfulness, empathy). Still others are shared by both approaches (responsibility, respect, loyalty, courage, conviction, freedom of choice, cooperation), and still others might be thought of as practical skills, arguably falling outside the boundaries of either justice or care and perhaps the moral domain altogether (optimism, sound use of time and talents, assertion, self-control; Goble & Brooks, 1983; Wood, 1994).

■ Development

The development of justice reasoning is conceptualized as a process of natural cognitive growth. Following a cognitive-structuralist framework, it is assumed that the competencies represented by stages of moral reasoning are a product of the interaction of biological maturation and the experience of encountering the world. At any given point in development, one's existing competency (stage) is applied to managing one's experiences. Some experiences are readily managed with the current competency, but others are not. In such circumstances, the individual experiences a sense of disequilibrium or lack of fit. This experience is part of a natural process of adaptation in which the individual both alters the current competency to better fit and manage the circumstances and cognitively distorts the circumstances to make them more compatible with one's existing way of knowing the world (one's current stage of moral reasoning development). The balance between these two responses determines whether a qualitatively new, higher level, and more adequate way of making meaning of the moral world will result.

For such development to occur, typically an accumulation of such experiences of disequilibrium must amass. Also, a state of readiness is necessary; that is, prerequisite conditions must be in place. For instance, certain levels of logical competency (Kuhn, Langer, Kohlberg, & Haan, 1977; L. J. Walker & Richards, 1979) and social perspective taking (L. J. Walker, 1980) are necessary (but not sufficient) for the development of certain levels of justice reasoning capacity.

■ Enabling and Inhibiting Factors

Certain factors can be leveraged in interventions to accelerate or remediate the development of justice reasoning. Parenting is important in the development of a child's moral reasoning. Most specifically, parental stage of justice reasoning, the use of induction, democratic family decision-making processes, and authoritative parenting style are related to higher stages of children's justice reasoning development (M. W. Berkowitz & Grych, 1998). Most of these data are correlational, however. One study found that parental training in moral discussion raised adolescent justice reasoning development only if parent training occurred with their children (Stanley, 1980). Such parents also demonstrated a decrease in authoritarian parenting as a result of the training. Grimes (cited in Higgins, 1980) also reported greater increases in adolescent justice reasoning when parents were involved in their moral discussion intervention program. It also appears that parent-to-child moral discussion should be more emotionally supportive and less conflictual than peer moral discussion in order to effectively promote moral reasoning development (Kruger, 1992; S. I. Powers, 1982).

Rest et al. (1986), in a qualitative study of the life experiences and developmental pathways related to moral reasoning development, concluded that

> the people who develop in moral judgment are those who love to learn, who seek new challenges, who enjoy intellectually stimulating environments, who are reflective, who make plans and set goals, who take risks, who see themselves in the large social contexts of history and institutions and broad cultural trends, who take responsibility for themselves and their environs. (p. 57)

Furthermore, they receive encouragement from others to further their education, they experience stimulating environments, and they have broad social support for their work and accomplishments.

■ Gender, Cross-National, and Cross-Cultural Aspects

Research suggests five main findings regarding sex differences and moral reasoning. First, virtually all men and women are familiar with both the justice and the care ways of framing moral issues. Second, most people actually use both justice and care reasoning when discussing their moral concerns (Gilligan, 1987; L. J. Walker et al., 1987). Third, most recent studies of justice reasoning (MJI and DIT) find that men and women achieve equivalent developmental levels of justice reasoning (L. J. Walker, 1984). Fourth, the nature of the dilemma used in assessment may bias the orientation chosen to deal with it—with rights-oriented dilemmas pulling more strongly for justice, and relationship-based dilemmas pulling for care (Clopton & Sorell, 1993). And fifth, the only sex difference found is in the type of dilemma chosen and language used when participants are asked to generate moral dilemmas from their own experience (L. J. Walker et al., 1987). Under those conditions, women as a group tend to relate more care-oriented dilemmas and produce more care reasoning, and men as a group tend to relate more justice-oriented dilemmas and produce more justice reasoning. This would appear to be a difference of experience and preference of relational style more than a difference in ability.

It is theoretically claimed that cognitive structures such as justice reasoning stages are universal; that is, they apply equally in different nationalities, for different races and cultures, across religious differences, and to both males and females. Much research has addressed the different parts of this question. In a comprehensive review of 45 studies of justice reasoning development in 27 countries, Snarey (1985) concluded that the Kohlberg stage model is "reasonably culture fair" (p. 226). The claim of invariant sequence was strongly supported. The claim of universality was clearly supported for the first four stages in the five-stage scheme. The only problematic finding was that Stage 5 (postconventional, principled) justice reasoning was found only in urban or middle-class cultures and never in folk cultural groups. Snarey concluded that this finding is likely the result of the ethnocentrism of the scoring manual section on Stage 5, the relative rarity of its empirical manifestation, and the reliance on Western philosophy for operationalization.

■ Deliberate Interventions

Most intervention research has been done in school settings. It is clear that there are two major processes of school-based stimulation of moral reasoning development: direct social-cognitive stimulation and social climate engineering. The direct social-cognitive stimulation takes the form of both curricular emphasis on moral problems and adult-facilitated peer discussion of moral issues and dilemmas. Most typical are programs of structured classroom discussions of moral issues and dilemmas (M. W. Berkowitz, 1985; Montford, 1999; Rest & Thoma, 1986). Research has revealed that the characteristics of developmentally stimulating moral discussion programs are peer interaction, peer moral reasoning heterogeneity, focus on moral issues, and an orientation to consensus or resolution of disagreement. A particular form of peer discourse called *transactive discussion* has been directly related to increased development (M. W. Berkowitz & Gibbs, 1983). Transactive discussion is cognitively interpenetrating discussion in which participants reason about each other's moral reasoning and actively attempt to operate on that reasoning.

The social climate approach stems largely from Kohlberg's Just Community Schools project (Power et al., 1989). Such schools were experiments in school democracy designed specifically to promote moral reasoning development by focusing such democratic processes on increasing the level of justice and the level of community in the school. It is clear that such schools promote moral reasoning of students, increase their belief in prosocial attitudes, and reduce their antisocial behavior. One follow-up study suggested that increases in moral reasoning are maintained into adulthood and some prosocial attitudes remain (Grady, 1994). Interestingly, the current character education movement is finding that promoting a positive social atmosphere (caring community) in schools is a central element in the effectiveness of such interventions (Schaps, 2001). There is also evidence that the moral atmosphere of institutions in which individuals function can serve to enhance or thwart the development of moral reasoning capacities. Such institutions include families (Speicher, 1994), schools (Power et al., 1989), prisons (Hickey & Scharf, 1980), workplaces (Higgins & Gordon, 1985), and even entire cultures (Snarey, 1985).

Clearly, then, the central factors that promote the development of justice reasoning are cognitive development generally (as a prerequisite condition); parenting style (characterized by nurturance and support, and a democratic and participatory interactional style); peer discourse about conflictual moral issues; and caring, participatory institutions, especially schools.

While experience with justice dilemmas is said to engage children's reasoning, care deliberation also involves reasoning but validates much more of the emotional and empathic parts of moral experience—both as a source of legitimate knowledge and as moral motivation. Care reasoning, like justice reasoning, is facilitated by experience and the development of cognitive sophistication. Any number of deliberative processes are required to generate plausible interpretations, evaluate contradictory information, and synthesize the wide array of facts and feelings commonly present in moral conflicts. Exposure to people who openly reflect on relational issues in their lives may provide valuable models. Additionally, discussion with children of common relational problems, moral considerations, and possible options for resolution is likely to facilitate their own thinking in this regard, just as it does for justice reasoning. Other activities and modeling supportive of their knowing their own preferences, values, reasons for doing things, and limitations will encourage self-awareness. Plentiful social experience with a variety of people will expose children to various cultural and familial patterns. Teaching open-mindedness and modeling tolerance of difference and appreciation for the cultures of others can assist children in developing their relational understanding.

■ What Is Not Known?

Although we know quite a bit about the development and functioning of moral reasoning, we do not fully understand its relative role in the more complex mix of the diverse psychological strengths that constitute moral character; that is, how does moral reasoning interface with values, moral emotion, or moral identity? Other issues in need of further exploration include the following:

- Recent research and theory regarding the characteristics of moral reasoning development and functioning in individuals who manifest symptoms of mental illness or dysfunctional behavior open the question of how moral reasoning might be influenced by psychological dysfunction.
- More needs to be known about the etiology or developmental history of moral reasoning capacities and tendencies. Certain parental characteristics and peer interaction experiences have been identified, but many other factors have not been studied adequately. Historically, peers have been identified as supplying the primary influence, but it is their egalitarian interactions that have been emphasized. A more differentiated understanding of diverse influences is needed.
- We do not yet know how to map the complexities involved in the relationship between an individual's achieved moral capacity and his or

her faithful enactment of behavior consistent with that level of moral understanding, that is, the correspondence between thought and action, intent and behavior, expressed values and enacted values.

- We do not adequately understand the relationship between the justice and care reasoning in a person's response to a moral context—when the two ethics will have contrasting and competing ways of illustrating the dilemma, and when the two will have supplementary views enhancing the depth and breadth of our understanding of the moral context.

■ Must-Read Articles and Books

Blasi, A. (1980). Bridging moral cognition and moral action: A critical review of the literature. *Psychological Bulletin, 88,* 1–45.

Brown, L. M., Debold, E., Tappan, M., & Gilligan, C. (1991). Reading narratives of conflict and choice for self and moral voices: A relational method. In W. M. Kurtines & J. L. Gewirtz (Eds.), *Handbook of moral behavior and development: Vol. 2. Research* (pp. 25–61). Hillsdale, NJ: Erlbaum.

Cohen, J. (2001). *Caring classrooms/intelligent schools: The social emotional education of young children.* New York: Teachers College Press.

Colby, A., & Kohlberg, L. (1987). *The measurement of moral judgment (Vols. 1 & 2).* New York: Cambridge University Press.

Colby, A., Kohlberg, L., Gibbs, J. C., & Lieberman, M. (1983). A longitudinal study of moral judgment. *Monographs of the Society for Research in Child Development, 48,* 1–124.

Gilligan, C. (1982). *In a different voice.* Cambridge, MA: Harvard University Press.

Jaffee, S., & Hyde, J. S. (2000). Gender differences in moral orientation: A meta-analysis. *Psychological Bulletin, 126,* 703–726.

Kohlberg, L. (1984). *Essays on moral development: Vol. 2. The psychology of moral development.* San Francisco: Harper & Row.

Piaget, J. (1932/1965). *The moral judgment of the child.* New York: Free Press.

Power, F. C., Higgins, A., & Kohlberg, L. (1989). *Lawrence Kohlberg's approach to moral education.* New York: Columbia University Press.

Rest, J. R., & Thoma, S. (1986). Educational programs and interventions. In J. R. Rest (Ed.), *Moral development: Advances in research and theory* (pp. 59–88). New York: Praeger.

Thoma, S. J., Rest, J. R., & Barnett, M. (1986). Moral judgment, behavior, decision-making, and attitudes. In J. R. Rest (Ed.), *Moral development: Advances in research and theory* (pp. 133–175). New York: Praeger.

18. LEADERSHIP

■ *John is the pastor of a small parish. Before he arrived, parish membership
had dwindled to a small number. The church building was very old, in need of
repair and modernization. Community outreach activities were minimal, and
church finances were often precarious. John came from a nearby parish and had
a reputation as a charismatic and transformational leader. When he arrived,
several of his old parishioners followed. John infused services at his new church
with a dynamic quality, encouraged parishioners to contribute their different
talents in worship, added community-building elements to each service, and
even changed the physical setting of the service to emphasize a new sense of
community and inclusion. He established a series of Bible reading groups for
different ages, organized trips to Mexico and Appalachia to build homes for the
poor, and planned retreats for different groups of parishioners. He created a
building committee that organized community resources and sought
contributions to build a new church. He organized youth activities and made
himself available to all parishioners, who came to him with the usual
assortment of needs that greet most ministers. The parish improved on all
indicators of organizational success, including numbers of parish members,
attendance at services, contributions to the church and to the building fund, and
involvement of parishioners in community service. The church exhibited a new
morale and climate, exemplified by the numbers of potential members coming
to services on the word of their friends who were already regular members.
Perhaps John's most important leadership quality was that he insisted that the
new spirit and climate was not to be attributed primarily to his efforts but
instead to the contributions, spirit, and vitality of the community in the church.
Indeed, he asked many of the parishioners to take on leadership roles, including
running various key committees, conducting Bible classes, organizing and
running food banks and other community outreach efforts, even conducting*

services and reaching out to parishioners who needed spiritual help and guidance. John is an example of what leadership means as a positive human quality. ▨

■ Consensual Definition

Leadership as a personal quality refers to an integrated constellation of cognitive and temperament attributes that foster an orientation toward influencing and helping others, directing and motivating their actions toward collective success. Individuals with this predisposition aspire to dominant roles in relationships and social situations. They comfortably manage their own activities and the activities of others in an integrated system.

Leadership is inherently a social phenomenon. Many theorists treat leadership as residing in the interaction or relationship between an individual who occupies, by virtue of appointment or election, a leadership role and individuals who are in follower roles. According to this perspective, the quality of leadership depends on the separate and joint influences of leader attributes, follower attributes, and contextual or situational constraints. However, the practice of leadership can be distinguished from leadership as a personal quality. Leadership as practice includes (a) defining, establishing, identifying, or translating a direction for collective action by one's followers; and (b) facilitating or enabling the collective processes that lead to achieving this purpose (Zaccaro & Klimoski, 2001). Leadership as a personal quality reflects the motivation and capacity to seek out, attain, and successfully carry out leader roles in social systems.

Personality attributes that correspond to leadership, and have often been treated as synonymous, include socialized power, authority, dominance, charisma, ascendancy, and social assertiveness. Leadership as a personal quality reflecting an ability and desire to influence and motivate collective action has a long history in psychology (e.g., Bernard, 1926; Bowden, 1926). More recently, theorists have begun to emphasize leadership as charismatic or transformational influence, in which leaders use vision and force of personality to inspire and empower others to extraordinary action (Bass, 1985, 1996; House, 1977; Tichy & Devanna, 1986). Examples of influential individuals in the 20th century who possessed this quality include Franklin Roosevelt, Winston Churchill, Mohandas Gandhi, Martin Luther King, Jr., John F. Kennedy, and Ronald Reagan.

Individuals with this strength are likely to strongly endorse such statements about themselves as the following:

- I prefer to take on the leadership role in a group.
- I am often able to plan a course of action for my group.
- I am often able to motivate others to act in a certain way.
- I am often able to help others do a task better.

- I am often able to organize others so that they can work together more effectively.
- People generally look to me to help solve complex problems.
- People generally look to me to resolve conflicts and keep a group together.
- I am often the spokesperson for my group.
- I generally take the initiative in social situations.
- I usually take charge in emergencies.

■ Theoretical Traditions

The study of leadership dates back to antiquity. Egyptian hieroglyphics included symbols for leader, leadership, and follower (Bass, 1990). Most mythological accounts center around the leader as a heroic figure. For example, Homer's *Iliad* used the attributes of its major characters to explore and teach such leadership qualities as wisdom, cunning, intelligence, courage, audacity, and virtue (Saracheck, 1968). Historical study and early oral tradition also focused on the actions and exploits of famous leaders. The Bible, particularly the Old Testament, explains ancient Jewish history in terms of the consequences of moral and immoral leadership, morality defined in terms of the leaders' adherence to a code handed from God to humankind. In these treatments, leadership referred to an orientation and capability to direct the lives of others. Intelligence, morality, and a predisposition toward action reflected the core of this leadership quality.

Eastern and Western philosophies have sought to understand the quality of leadership and advise individuals on principles of effective leadership. Lao-tzu's *Tao Te Ching* described the attributes of wise and effective leaders, emphasizing the selfless aspects of leadership service (J. Heider, 1985). The leader exists to help others in an unbiased and unassuming way, nourishing any and all followers ("The wise leader is like water"). Plato's (1968) *Republic* emphasized the inherent qualities of leadership among certain individuals (i.e., "philosopher-kings") and even proposed a sort of lifelong "assessment plan" to identify and select these individuals. Plato discussed the nature of the ideal state and its governance. Leaders were to use the faculties of reason and intelligence, eschewing emotion, to govern wisely. Aristotle (1900) also described the ideal state and the virtues of effective leaders in *Politics*. He emphasized that people should seek virtue and goodness for themselves. Aristotle implied, then, that leaders need to model this search for goodness by being virtuous themselves. He goes on to prescribe the means of developing young leaders through education. The major Greek philosophers, then, continued the early emphasis on reason and virtue as the core of a leadership disposition. Plutarch (1932) contributed to this tradition by showing that Greek and Roman leaders possessed common attributes—that leadership was an immutable quality and not driven by situational contingencies.

One of the most famous, and still widely read, early philosophical treatises on leadership is Machiavelli's (1513/1813/1954) *The Prince*, in which he described the qualities and practice of effective state leadership. He explained the various means leaders have of gaining power to create and sustain social order. Machiavelli added power, or rather skill in attaining and using power for common action, to the leadership personality cluster. He also suggested that the leaders have skills in social acuity or the ability to understand social situations and manipulate them in the practice of leadership. However, contrary to Aristotle's teachings, Machiavelli prescribed less than virtuous means of gaining power and social legitimacy if more virtual means were inadequate.

These early treatments of leadership emphasized the inherent qualities of individuals that predisposed them to be effective leaders. The work of Francis Galton in the 19th century represents perhaps the earliest statistical treatment of leadership as a personal quality. Following the contributions of his cousin Charles Darwin, Galton (1869) argued in *Hereditary Genius* that the qualities of leadership were inherited, not acquired through environmental exposure. He emphasized extraordinary intelligence or genius as a key leadership quality. He extended his notions to propose eugenics, a highly controversial plan relying on selective mating to produce individuals with the best combination of leadership qualities.

The scientific study of leadership dates back about 100 years (Terman, 1904). Since that time, several conceptual frameworks and theoretical paradigms have taken their turn onstage. The social exchange perspective perhaps represents the most dominant approach in the extant literature. This approach focuses on the relationship between leader and follower. Models that adopt this perspective emphasize one or more elements—characteristics of the leader, characteristics of the followers, and characteristics of their relationship. Models of leader attributes that dominated in the early part of the 20th century emphasized leader traits. Several surveys and reviews of this literature identified a number of dispositional qualities that distinguished leaders from nonleaders, including intelligence, originality, dependability, initiative, desire to excel, sociability, adaptability, extroversion, and dominance (C. Bird, 1940; Jenkins, 1947; Stogdill, 1948). However, no single personal quality was strongly and consistently correlated with leadership (Mann, 1959).

A general dissatisfaction with the yield of this research tradition led to an emphasis on the dominant behavioral styles of leaders. Leadership research turned toward identifying the behaviors of effective leaders. Such leaders adopted either a structuring task-oriented style toward their subordinates or a considerate, socioemotional style. For example, Fleishman and his colleagues defined initiating structure and consideration as key leadership behaviors (Fleishman, 1953, 1973; Fleishman & Harris, 1962; Stogdill & Coons, 1957). Likert

(1961) argued for task-oriented and relationship-oriented behaviors as differentiating effective from ineffective managers.

This research tradition moved leadership away from its consideration as a personal quality to its depiction as a set of behavioral activities. It was short leap from this perspective to the argument that leadership was purely situational, in which leader behavior and effectiveness were contingent mostly on the demands of the situation and/or the needs of the followers. Thus, who successfully adopts the leadership role would shift according to a variety of situational contingencies. Early proponents of this viewpoint existed even in the heyday of leader trait research (e.g., Bogardus, 1918; E. Mumford, 1909; A. J. Murphy, 1941). Even Stogdill's (1948) review of the leader trait research concluded that the characteristics and skills required in a leader are determined to a large extent by situational demands. Subsequent models of leadership such as those of Fiedler (1964, 1971), Hersey and Blanchard (1969, 1984), and Kerr and Jermier (1978) described the situational contingencies that constrained leadership. This extensive research tradition, which continues to the present in many forms, minimizes the perspective of leadership and leader effectiveness as a personal quality or individual disposition.

Four alternate perspectives that emerged in the 1970s and 1980s returned personal qualities to the forefront of thinking about leadership. The first, paradoxically, placed its central focus on followers as influences on the practice of leadership. For example, Hollander (1964; Hollander & Julian, 1970) examined the role of followers in granting legitimacy to the leader to be innovative. In essence, followers conferred the status and power of leadership on individuals who have earned the role. Lord and his colleagues (R. G. Lord, Foti, & DeVader, 1984; R. G. Lord & Maher, 1993; Rush, Thomas, & Lord, 1982) took these notions further to describe what cognitive representations followers used to determine and bestow leadership status. The crux of this approach is that certain personal qualities of the leader formed the core of leadership schemas retained by followers and used to evaluate leader candidates. Leadership schemas generally encode such attributes as intelligence, dominance, sociability, honesty, and determination (R. G. Lord, DeVader, & Alliger, 1986; Lord et al., 1984). Individuals perceived as possessing these qualities in abundance were likely to be judged as leaders.

The second research tradition accepted the situational variability of leadership but argued that leaders differed from nonleaders in their ability to respond effectively across a variety of social situations. Kenny and Zaccaro (1983) found that leader emergence was attributable to a stable quality of the individual and argued that it reflected an "ability to perceive needs and goals of a constituency and to adjust one's personal approach to group action accordingly" (p. 678). Zaccaro, Gilbert, Thor, and Mumford (1991) specified this quality a social intelligence (see also Zaccaro, 2002). Several empirical studies have linked social intelligence and its components to indices of leadership (Connelly et al.,

2000; J. A. Gilbert, 1995; Hooijberg, 1996; Ritchie, 1994; Zaccaro, Foti, & Kenny, 1991). Thus, leadership as a personal quality reflects a high level of social acuity and skill that promotes leader effectiveness across different situations presenting different leadership demands. Although these ideas are relatively recent in leadership research, their roots go back to some of the leadership qualities exemplied in Machiavelli's *The Prince.*

The third tradition that emphasized leader qualities was the research on charismatic or inspirational leadership that became prominent in the 1980s (Bass, 1985, 1996; Burns, 1978; Conger & Kanungo, 1987, 1988; House, 1977; Tichy & Devanna, 1986). This research, influenced by Max Weber (1924/1949), focused on a dynamic established between leader and follower that reflected an intense reverence for and loyalty to the leader and a strong sense of empowerment in the follower. This dynamic followed from exceptional qualities possessed by the leader who provides to followers a vision for change leading to a better future. These leader qualities included need for power (for helping others, though, not for self-aggrandizement), self-confidence, propensity for risk taking, creative thinking skills, reasoning skills, social skills, and an orientation toward nurturing others and being concerned for their progress, either collectively or individually (Bass, 1985; Conger & Kanungo, 1987; House, 1977; House & Howell, 1992; Sashkin, 1988; Tichy & Devanna, 1986; Zaccaro, 2001). This last attribute typically leads to charismatic leaders displaying great personal sacrifice and disregard for personal welfare.

A socialized power motive is an important attribute that deserves greater scrutiny. The history of humankind contains numerous examples of destructive charismatic leaders. From Adolf Hitler to Jim Jones, certain leaders have established a corrosive vision and path for their followers that ultimately destroyed their community. These examples have prompted many theorists to examine the "dark side" of charismatic leadership (Conger, 1990; R. Hogan, Raskin, & Fazzini, 1990; Howell, 1988). A major difference between constructive and destructive charismatic leaders resides in their motive for power and their orientation toward followers. Destructive charismatics gather power for personal aggrandizement and use their social skills and extraordinary persuasiveness to gain follower submissiveness. Constructive charismatics are oriented to serving, empowering, and transforming their followers. They seek power to help others. McClelland (1985) termed this *activity inhibition.* House and Howell (1992) defined this quality as "an unconscious motive to use social influence, or to satisfy the power need, in socially desirable ways, for the betterment of the collective rather than for personal self-interest" (p. 95). Constructive charismatics promote the welfare of others, whereas destructive charismatics form warped perceptions of what others need or dismiss such considerations out of hand.

The existence of a crisis represents an important facilitating condition for charismatic leadership (Conger & Kanungo, 1987, 1992). Charismatic leaders offer a vision that portends a better future for followers. For such a vision to be appealing, followers need to be dissatisfied with existing conditions to the point where they will consider even drastic change. Thus, Franklin Roosevelt emerged as a leader during the Great Depression and led the United States through a second crisis in World War II. His colleague in arms Winston Churchill also vividly emerged during the crisis of World War II. Interestingly, he was ineffective as a leader before the war and was removed from office after its cessation.

The performance effectiveness approach from organizational psychology represents the fourth tradition in leadership research that reintroduced an emphasis on leader qualities. Several leadership theorists have argued for the centrality of leader personality and other leader attributes in explaining organizational performance (Barrick, Day, Lord, & Alexander, 1991; D. V. Day & Lord, 1988; Hambrick & Mason, 1984; House, 1988; Zaccaro, 2001). This assumption has been reflected in a strong emphasis in organizational research on leader assessment and development. For example, the longitudinal assessment center research conducted at American Telephone & Telegraph (AT&T; Bray, 1982; Bray, Campbell, & Grant, 1974; A. Howard & Bray, 1988) developed a number of managerial assessment tasks targeting characteristics that purportedly predicted career advancement. In a longitudinal research program, researchers found that such characteristics as need for power, interpersonal and cognitive skills, and motivational orientations predicted subsequent rank.

These research traditions, and even the musings about leadership from antiquity, converge on several characteristics that distinguish the personal quality of leadership. Leadership reflects an orientation to promote, direct, and manage social action. This orientation is grounded in a need for dominance and constructive power. The effective engagement of leadership processes follows from high self-confidence and from significant cognitive and social capabilities.

■ Measures

When considering the measurement of leadership, it is necessary to distinguish among measures of leader attributes, leader processes, and leadership outcomes. Measures of leader attributes focus on the assessment of personal qualities that predict leader effectiveness, including cognitive capabilities, social capabilities, need for dominance, need for power, and self-confidence. However, these are not measures of leadership per se, but of the qualities that foster its display. Measures of leadership outcomes center on consequences of leadership for individual subordinates, teams, and organizations. These include attitudinal and motivational measures, such as satisfaction, climate, cohesion, and commitment, as well as performance measures, such as work quantity, quality, and profitability. These do not actually reflect leadership but rather the results garnered from its display.

The measurement of leadership should then focus primarily on the behaviors and activities that denote the effective management of social action. Fleishman et al. (1991) classified these activities into 4 superordinate and 13 subordinate categories. They validated this taxonomy against 65 other leadership classifications. Most measures of leadership processes contain assessment of one or more of these activities, which are as follows:

- Information search and structuring
  - Acquiring information
  - Organizing information
  - Feedback and control
- Information Use in Problem Solving
  - Identifying needs and requirements
  - Planning and coordinating
  - Communicating information
- Managing Personnel Resources
  - Obtaining and allocating personnel resources
  - Developing personnel resources
  - Motivating personnel resources
  - Utilizing and monitoring personnel resources
- Managing Material Resources
  - Obtaining and allocating material resources
  - Maintaining material resources
  - Utilizing and monitoring material resources

Researchers have developed many measures of leadership processes. Most of these are surveys that are usually completed by a leader's subordinates. One exception is the Leadership Opinion Questionnaire (Fleishman, 1953), a self-report instrument that focuses on what leaders believe is appropriate leadership or supervisory behavior. More recently, researchers have adopted a "360-degree" methodology, in which measures are completed not only by a leader's subordinates but also by himself or herself, as well as by his or her own supervisors and peers. This format examines potential variability in leadership perceptions. Commonality in the perceptions of subordinates, superiors, and peers suggests a strongly consistent pattern of leadership. However, some models of leadership argue for variability in leadership practice, where leader effectiveness requires different responses to different constituencies (Zaccaro, 1999, 2002; Zaccaro, Gilbert, et al., 1991). This suggests that responses on 360-degree leadership instruments ought not to be consistent across respondents. Results of research on this question have been mixed, however, with variability often attributed more to differing perceptions and frames of references possessed by different constituencies than to differing activities displayed by the leader across these constituencies.

Although many leader assessment instruments exist in the literature, Zaccaro, Klimoski, Boyce, Chandler, and Banks (1999) identified four measures of leadership processes as being the strongest psychometrically. We have added a fifth, the Leader Behavior Description Questionnaire (LBDQ- XII), also because of its psychometric strength and because of its ubiquity in the leadership literature. Table 18.1 summarizes these instruments.

The LBDQ-VII is one of the earliest and most widely used instruments of leadership behavior. It emerged from the Ohio State leadership research teams (Fleishman, 1953; Stogdill, 1963; Stogdill & Coons, 1957) and evolved to its present form to cover 12 aspects of leadership behavior. These were representation, demand reconciliation, tolerance of uncertainty, persuasiveness, initiating structure, tolerance of freedom, role assumption, consideration, production empha-

---

TABLE 18.1 *Measures of Leadership*

Leader Behavior Description Questionnaire (LBDQ-XII; Stogdill, 1963)

This survey is completed by a leader's subordinates. The measure is composed of 100 items measuring 12 leadership behaviors.
- Internal reliabilities of the subscales are generally acceptable.

Leader–Member Exchange Measure (LMX-7; Schriesheim, Neider, Scandura, & Tepper, 1992)

This is a seven-item measure that assesses the quality of interaction and exchange that managers form with each of their subordinates.
- Internal reliability: .86

Managerial Practices Survey (MPS; Yukl, Wall, & Lepsinger, 1990)

This survey is completed by a manager's self-reports and is designed to help managers identify and expand their repertoire of leadership skills. The instrument measures 14 leadership behaviors.
- Internal reliabilities for subscales: .84–.91
- Test–retest reliabilities for the subscales: .48–.94

Benchmarks (McCauley & Lombardo, 1990)

This 360-degree instrument is completed by a manager's peers and supervisor. It is also completed by the manager. The primary purpose of the survey is developmental.
- Average internal consistencies: .88
- Test–retest reliability: .72 for self-ratings, .85 for ratings by others
- Average interrater agreement: .58

Multifactor Leadership Questionnaire (MLQ; Bass & Avolio, 1990)

This is another 360-degree instrument that assesses transformational or charismatic leadership and transactional leadership. The measure contains five transformational leadership scales and three transactional leadership scales.
- Average internal consistencies for the scales: .72–.92
- Test–retest reliabilities: .44–.74.

sis, predictive accuracy, integration, and superior orientation. Note, however, that these categories represent a mix of behaviors (e.g., initiating structure, consideration), personality attributes (e.g., tolerance for uncertainty), social skills (e.g., persuasiveness, integration), and cognitive skills (e.g., predictive accuracy).

The Leader–Member Exchange measure (LMX-7) grew out of a concern that most leadership instruments, particularly the LBDQ-XII, assessed average leadership style and minimized the degree of variation leaders could display across different followers (Dansereau, Graen, & Haga, 1975). The LMX-7 assesses the quality of exchange between the leader and each of his or her followers. Leader–follower interactions can be characterized as close and trusting (i.e., "in-group") or more distant and less trusting (i.e., "out-group").

The Managerial Practices Survey (MPS) assesses 14 categories of leadership behavior, namely, informing, clarifying, monitoring, planning, problem solving, consulting, delegating, inspiring, recognizing, rewarding, supporting, mentoring, networking, and team building (Yukl, Wall, & Lepsinger, 1990). This assessment tool focuses more specifically than other tools on leadership activities and has a wider range than most other instruments. Research has demonstrated both the content and the criterion-related validity of this instrument (Yukl et al., 1990; Yukl & Van Fleet, 1992).

The instrument known as Benchmarks was prepared by researchers at the Center for Creative Leadership to assist in their managerial development programs. Like the MPS, it covers a range of managerial practices, with 22 subscales. However, its scores are used to help identify personal factors that may derail the progress of rising managers and also to offer ways of building on managerial strengths (McCauley & Lombardo, 1990). Thus, unlike other leadership instruments, this one contains both positive leader attributes (e.g., being a quick study, setting a developmental climate) and negative attributes (e.g., problems with interpersonal relationships, difficulty in molding a staff).

The remaining assessment tool, the Multifactor Leadership Questionnaire (MLQ), differs from the other instruments described here in that it seeks to capture the transforming or charismatic quality of leadership (Bass, 1996; Bass & Avolio, 1990). Thus, its scales assess charisma, inspiration, intellectual stimulation, and individualized consideration. The MLQ also contains assessment of nontransformational leadership, including the leader's use of contingent reward, active management by exception, and passive management by exception.

These five measures are all widely used and are very good assessments of leadership processes. They measure the activities of leadership—there are few measures in the literature that focus on leadership as a fundamental dispositional quality. Gough (1990) described use of the California Psychological Inventory to identify a leadership prototype that appears to reflect a motivation and capability to directive interpersonal engagement. The interpersonal attributes that form this prototype include dominance, capacity for status, sociability, social presence, self-acceptance, independence, and empathy. This interpersonal engagement prototype demonstrated significant correlations with several indices of leadership rankings and nominations.

Morrow and Stern (1990) offered an alternate approach to assessing the leadership personality. Using data from an assessment center, they derived a leadership profile that included attributes such as mental ability, mental versatility and flexibility, ascendancy, sociability, vigor, and original thinking. Participants in the assessment center who were rated as superior in leadership potential scored higher on these measures than those rated as average or poor. This approach, related conceptually to the pioneering AT&T assessment center research (Bray, 1982; Bray et al., 1974; A. Howard & Bray, 1988), is more extensive than the paper-and-pencil tests described thus far. Its utility as an assessment of leadership personality is limited by its time-consuming scope. Also, assessment centers have been criticized on several grounds for their discriminant validity (Klimoski & Strickland, 1977).

■ Correlates and Consequences

The outcomes of leadership can be examined at multiple levels—organizational, team, and individual. D. V. Day and Lord (1988) reviewed a number of executive succession studies to assess the effects of new leaders on organizational effectiveness. They reported that the ascent of a new leader explained between 5.6% and 24.2% of the variance in organizational performance indices across multiple studies. N. Weiner and Mahoney (1981) examined such succession effects in 193 companies across a 19-year time span. They found that leadership accounted for 44% to 47% of the variance in organizational performance indices. Hitt and Tyler (1991) found that after controlling for industry characteristics and environmental influences, executive leader characteristics such as cognitive complexity and risk propensity explained significant variance in simulated acquisition decisions.

Shipper and Wilson (1992) reported significant correlations between 10 of 11 managerial behaviors and organizational subunit performance. Quast and Hazucha (1992) reported that leader initiating structure and consideration behaviors, respectively, were significantly correlated with multiple indices of team success. Avolio and Howell (1992) examined the link between leader personality and unit performance. They found that leader locus of control (Rotter, 1966), and risk taking and innovation (Jackson, 1976) predicted the percentage of financial goals achieved by a manager's business unit.

Several meta-analyses have been conducted to examine the influence of leadership on individual attitudes and performance. Gerstner and Day (1997) found that indices of leader member exchange quality were significantly associated with measures of job satisfaction, organizational commitment, job performance, and job turnover intentions. Lowe, Kroeck, and Sivasubramaniam (1996) reported mean corrected correlations of .81 between leader charisma and subordinate ratings of effectiveness. However, this correlation is inflated because of same-source method bias. The mean corrected correlation between leadership and performance measures not gathered from the subordinates who rated the leader was .35.

Taken together, these studies demonstrate support for the powerful effect of leadership and leader personality on organizational, team, and individual performance and attitudes. Several studies of leader promotion rates have found that individuals who possess leadership quality are more likely to be promoted (Bray et al., 1974; A. Howard & Bray, 1988; McCauley & Lombardo, 1990; Ritchie, 1994; Stamp, 1988).

Correlates of leadership have been grouped into four categories: cognitive skills, social skills, technical skills, and disposition variables (Yukl, 2002; Zaccaro, 2001). Table 18.2 summarizes findings from five reviews of leadership correlates. An important point is that the relationship of certain attributes to leadership varies according to the rank or level of the leader within the organization (T. O. Jacobs & Jaques, 1987, 1990, 1991; M. D. Mumford, Marks, Connelly, Zaccaro, & Reiter-Palmon, 2000; M. D. Mumford, Zaccaro, Harding, Jacobs, & Fleishman, 2000; Zaccaro, 2001). For example, technical skills and interpersonal skills are more important than conceptual skills for lower level leadership; the reverse is true for more senior leaders (R. L. Katz, 1955; Yukl, 2002; Zaccaro, 2001).

■ Development

Although there have been relatively few systematic investigations of early developmental influences on leadership, several interesting findings have been reported that document such influence. A number of studies have demonstrated consistency in attainment of leadership roles from early childhood through adolescence to adulthood (Courtenay, 1938; C. M. Cox, 1926; Levi, 1930; D. P. Page, 1935; F. J. Williams & Harrell, 1964; Yammarino & Bass, 1990). Other studies have found that children who became leaders later in life displayed attributes of leadership early in life (C. M. Cox, 1926). Specific early parental interactions that appear to promote leadership later in life include modeling sociability and reliability (H. H. Jennings, 1943), displaying leadership behaviors themselves (W. A. Anderson, 1943), and setting high performance standards (Avolio & Gibbons, 1988).

■ Deliberate Interventions

Many leadership interventions have been developed to foster leader attributes (Saari, Johnson, McLaughlin, & Zimmerle, 1988). These interventions occur in

TABLE 18.2   *Summaries of Leader Correlates*

Stogdill (1974)

Ability to enlist cooperation	Energy	Resourcefulness
Adaptability	Independence	Self-confidence
Adjustment	Intelligence	Sociability, interpersonal skills
Administrative ability	Judgment, decisiveness	Social participation
Alertness	Knowledge	Social status
Ascendance	Mobility	Strength of conviction
Assertiveness	Nurturance	Tact, diplomacy
Attractiveness	Originality, creativity	Tolerance of stress
Cooperativeness	Personal integrity	Tough-mindedness
Dominance	Popularity	Verbal fluency
Education level		

Center for Creative Leadership (McCall & Lombardo, 1983)

Cognitive Skills	Emotional stability	Interpersonal Skills
Defensiveness (derailing factor)	Integrity	Technical Skills

Locke et al. (1991)

Cognitive ability	Knowledge of the business	Leadership motivation
Drive		Self-confidence
Honesty and integrity		

Zaccaro (2001)

Adaptability	Intelligence	Need for socialized power
Analytical reasoning	Knowledge of environmental elements	Risk propensity
Behavioral flexibility		Self-discipline
Creativity	Locus of control	Self-efficacy
Curiosity	Metacognitive skill	Social expertise
Flexible integrative complexity	Need for achievement	Verbal/writing skill
Functional expertise		

Yukl (2002)

Emotional stability	Moderately high achievement orientation	Socialized power motivation
High energy		Stress tolerance
Internal locus of control	Personal integrity	
Low need for affiliation		

three general formats—formal instruction, developmental work experiences, and self-help programs (Yukl, 2002; Zaccaro, 2001). Many of these programs have sprung from specific theoretical models (Avolio, 1999; Fiedler & Chemers, 1982; Hersey & Blanchard, 1984; Vroom & Jago, 1978). Others involve more systems-oriented interventions that blend formal instruction with developmental assignments (McCauley, Moxley, & Van Velsor, 1998; M. D. Mumford, Marks, et al.,

2000). The primary, indeed almost exclusive, focus of these programs is on growing leadership skills, and they generally are successful (Bass, 1990; M. J. Burke & Day, 1986; Tetrault, Schriesheim, & Neider, 1988; Yukl, 2002).

Few, if any, interventions focus on developing the dispositional quality of leadership. This quality is grounded in motivational and personality attributes that are relatively immutable to the kinds of short-term interventions typically offered by companies. Few companies are willing to invest in the long-term interventions required to grow such attributes as self-confidence, sociability, socialized power needs, and conceptual capacities. Some programs do target the "personal growth" of the leader and focus on developing self-awareness and self-understanding (Conger, 1993; Yukl, 2002). Such programs are intense and intensive, but their effectiveness in developing leadership quality remains in question (Yukl, 2002).

■ Gender, Cross-National, and Cross-Cultural Aspects

Much research has been completed on leadership and gender to explore possible male–female differences in leadership style and effectiveness. Meta-analyses of this research completed by Eagly and her colleagues (Eagly & Johnson, 1990; Eagly & Karau, 1991; Eagly, Karau, & Makhijani, 1995) found that female managers were comparable to male managers in effectiveness and in the use of most leadership styles; they differed only in their use of more participative styles. Eagly et al. (1995) and Eagly and Karau (1991) also reported some differentiation based on position requirements—more task-oriented positions favored male leaders, whereas more interpersonally oriented positions favored female managers. Taken as a whole, however, the broad swath of research conducted on the question of leadership and gender suggests that, stereotypes aside, the differences between male and female managers are much smaller than the range of behaviors and effectiveness residing among leaders within the same gender.

Recently, leadership researchers have begun to tackle the question of cross-cultural differences and similarities in leadership. One project, the Global Leadership and Organizational Behavior Effectiveness (GLOBE) study, was undertaken to determine if leader attributes and behaviors are consistently related to effectiveness across 62 countries from different world regions (House et al., 1999). This research has so far found that attributes related to leader effectiveness across all cultures include integrity, visioning, transformational or inspirational ability, decisiveness, ability to manage conflict effectively to the gain of all participants, and administrative or organizational strengths. Some leader attributes that vary significantly in their link to effectiveness across cultures include preference for autonomy, risk-taking propensity, dominance, consideration behaviors, and formality.

Cultural dimensions play an important role in determining how leadership attributes will be related to effectiveness. Hofstede (1980, 1993) noted that cultures could be distinguished along four dimensions: power distance, individualism, uncertainty avoidance, and masculinity/femininity. Power distance refers to the amount of authority, status, and power sharing (or lack thereof) expected of leaders. Individualism means the degree to which an emphasis is placed on individual versus collective achievement and accomplishments. Uncertainty avoidance reflects the degree of tolerance a culture has for ambiguity, uncertainty, and unpredictability. The masculinity/femininity dimension refers to the extent both men and women are accorded comparable status, with low or nonexistent degrees of gender differentiation in leadership positions. Each of these dimensions has implications, indeed parallels, in leader attributes. Thus, cultures that vary widely along these dimensions would be expected to vary as well on the attributes they perceive as important for leader effectiveness. The GLOBE project has reported evidence for this assertion, finding, for example, that team-building skills are more valued in collectivistic cultures than in those high in individualism.

■ What Is Not Known?

Much of the literature on leadership has emphasized a position-based perspective of leader, considering leadership as residing in a position established within an organizational or other collective structure. Indeed, the notions of power and legitimacy, so integral to many conceptions of leadership, are grounded in such hierarchical definitions of leadership. Nevertheless, there exists the phenomenon of "impromptu or informal leadership" whereby individuals step forward in situations requiring collective direction and action. The stories of September 11, 2001, abound with such examples of people without official leadership status who led others out of the World Trade Center or through the Pentagon. We learn of such leadership when tragedies occur and become part of the national focus, but many unheard examples occur daily when collections of people need impromptu guidance. Someone emerges at the moment, displays leadership, and the collective, or its individuals, move on as the need of the moment dissipates. Such acts in large events that grab national attention are considered heroism, yet their occurrence in lesser degrees as part of "everyday" life may be no less instrumental for collective success. Studies have not explored such instances of impromptu leadership. Nonetheless, this form of leadership is perhaps most emblematic of psychological strength and human positivism.

■ Must-Read Articles and Books

Bass, B. M. (1990). *Bass & Stogdill's handbook of leadership: Theory, research and managerial applications* (3rd ed.). New York: Free Press.

Eagly, A. H., & Johnson, B. T. (1990). Gender and leadership style: A meta-analysis. *Psychological Bulletin, 108,* 233–256.

Fiedler, F. E. (1971). Validation and extension of the contingency model of leadership effectiveness: A review of the empirical findings. *Psychological Bulletin, 76,* 128–148.

Fleishman, E. A., Mumford, M. D., Zaccaro, S. J., Levin, K. Y, Korotkin, A. L., & Hein, M. B. (1991). Taxonomic efforts in the description of leader behavior: A synthesis and functional interpretation. *Leadership Quarterly, 2,* 245–287.

Lord, R. G., & Maher, K. J. (1993). *Leadership and information processing.* London: Routledge.

Yukl, G. (2002). *Leadership in organizations* (4th ed.). Englewood Cliffs, NJ: Prentice Hall.

Zaccaro, S. J. (2001). *The nature of executive leadership: A conceptual and empirical analysis of success.* Washington, DC: APA Books.

INTRODUCTION:
STRENGTHS OF TEMPERANCE

CRITERIA FOR   *Strengths of Temperance*

	Fulfilling	Morally valued	Does not diminish others	Nonfelicitous opposite	Traitlike	Distinctiveness	Paragons	Prodigies	Selective absence	Institutions and rituals	
	1	2	3	4	5	6	7	8	9	10	TALLY
Forgiveness and mercy	X	X	X	X	X	X	X		X	X	9/10
Humility and modesty	X	X	X	X	~X	X	X		X	X	9/10
Prudence	X	X	~X	X	X		X	~X	X	X	9/10
Self-regulation	X	X	X	X	X	X	X	X	X	X	10/10

~ Somewhat satisfies criterion.

We classify the positive traits that protect us from excess as strengths of temperance. What are the types of excess of special concern? Hatred—against which forgiveness and mercy protect us. Arrogance—against which humility and modesty protect us. Short-term pleasure with long-term costs—against which prudence protects us. And destabilizing emotional extremes of all sorts—against which self-regulation protects us. It is worth emphasizing that the strengths of temperance temper our activities rather than bringing them to a complete halt. We may be highly forgiving, but we can still defend ourselves while being pummeled. Modesty does not require falsehood—just authentic acknowledgment of who we are and what we do. A prudent course of action is still a course of action. Optimal self-regulation of emotions does not mean suspending our feelings, good or bad, but only taking charge of them.

We could have included some or all of the strengths of courage under this rubric but have not done so because the strengths of courage lead us to behave in positive ways regardless of temptations to the contrary (e.g., fear, sloth, inauthenticity, fatigue), whereas the defining feature of temperance lies in tackling the temptation head-on. Strengths of temperance may therefore predispose strengths of courage, but they are distinct.

Temperance strengths are defined in part by what a person refrains from doing, and they may be more apparent to observers in their intemperate absence than in their temperate presence. Indeed, in our attempts to measure this class of strengths, we have found that among people in the mainstream United States, strengths of temperance are infrequently endorsed and seldom praised. Perhaps in cultures in which the middle path of Buddhism or other teachings about balance and harmony are influential, these particular strengths are more frequently celebrated. Regardless, the strengths of temperance are important. They are included in virtually all philosophical and religious discussions of virtue (chapter 2), and they have a rich array of consequences for the psychological good life, as the chapters in this section document. So, let us turn our attention to how well these four temperance traits satisfy our criteria for a character strength (see Criteria Table).

■ Forgiveness and Mercy

Fortunate is the person who has never been wronged by others. She has no need to forgive because there has been no offense. Fortunate, too, is the person who has never been put in the position of being able to exact revenge on those who have done wrong. He has no need to be merciful because there is no punishment to minimize, suspend, or cancel. But these people are rare, if they exist at all, and most of us find ourselves in the position where forgiveness and mercy can be enacted—or not. Those who consistently let bygones be bygones—not because of negative states and traits like fear, shame, guilt, or permissiveness and not because of external incentives (bribes or damages awarded in civil suits) or threats (restraining orders) but from a positive strength of character—display forgiveness and mercy.

CRITERION 1 *Fulfilling*   Forgiveness and mercy are fulfilling for the individual, although not necessarily fun. Indeed, it is precisely when forgiveness is difficult and produces no immediate hedonic payoff that it is most fulfilling in the sense of allowing individuals to know they have done the right thing. Revenge can be very sweet, and grudges can have considerable staying power, but these are negative actions that often satisfy only deficiency motives—even when sated, they leave us empty. Turning the other cheek, loving our enemies, giving people a second chance, starting over—these satisfy us even if they effect no permanent change in the world in which we live. One need not be cynical to observe that forgiveness and mercy do not always prevent future transgressions against us. That is why a general trait needs to exist to handle the repeat business.

CRITERION 2 *Morally Valued*   Forgiveness and mercy are highly valued when we are on the receiving end. But we value this positive trait in other cases as well. Because this character strength undoes hatred, it removes palpable evil from the world, and that is good. We want our children to make up after squabbles with their friends. We admire a woman who stands by her man even if he may not "deserve" someone as steadfast as she. We celebrate employers and leaders who give their people a second chance.

Can there be too much forgiveness or too much mercy? Of course, just as there can be too much curiosity, kindness, or playfulness. But even when forgiveness and mercy exceed what we regard as acceptable limits, it is not the displayed character strength per se that we criticize but how its consequences work against other values dear to us. So, forgiveness to an extreme can wreak havoc with notions of fairness. Mercy to an extreme can undercut accountability. There is always a balancing act involved in judging the value of a behavior, even one born of virtuous motives. But even if we exact punishment for a misdeed, we can be forgiving by regarding the punishment as wiping the slate clean. We can be merciful by making sure the magnitude of the punishment does not exceed the magnitude of the crime.

CRITERION 3 *Does Not Diminish Others*   The display of forgiveness and mercy can elevate others in the vicinity. We are moved when we hear the victim of a crime ask the court to treat the perpetrator with mercy. We thrill when we hear about those who make the most of a second or third chance, but it is forgiveness after all that allowed them to be in this position in the first place. Forgiveness is a dance that always starts with someone hurting someone else. In some cases, the next step is an apology or the making of amends (cf. Step Nine of Alcoholics Anonymous), and in other cases, the next step is unsolicited forgiveness: "No hard feelings, friend."

Forgiveness and mercy are a social strength, and we might decide eventually to classify this trait with other strengths of love like kindness. We recently read about Kermit Washington and Rudy Tomjanovich, professional basketball players 25 years ago on opposite sides of a haymaker that almost cost Tomjanovich his life. The punch and its aftermath for both men have been complex, but looking back, Tomjanovich said of Washington, "I hope he does really well . . . because we are brothers."

CRITERION 4 *Nonfelicitous Opposite*   The opposites of this character strength include *unforgiving*, *spiteful*, *punitive*, *vengeful*, *merciless*, and *hard-hearted*. These are all negative characterizations, and when we refrain from forgiveness or mercy, we do not embrace these as our rationale but instead point to the magnitude of the transgression, to the irredeemable character of the transgressor, and/or to inviolate rules governing punishment: "Certain acts are unforgivable"; "That is a capital offense"; "Three strikes, and you are out" (in baseball and in California); "You leave me no option"; "Look what you made me do"; "I warned you!"

CRITERION 5 *Traitlike*   Is this a general trait? One tradition of psychological research has studied only transgression-specific forgiveness, which does not allow this question to be answered. However, a second tradition looks at forgiveness writ large, and from this work we are able to conclude that forgiveness is a trait both general and stable, as long as we offer the qualification that forgiveness is a phasic strength. A transgression needs to take place to create the occasion to which the strength of forgiveness and mercy allows one to rise. At almost any moment, we can walk up to a friend or a family member and say, "I love you," and be acknowledged with a smile and nod of the head. But if we say to the same people, "I forgive you," they are apt to be puzzled and ask, "What did I do?"

CRITERION 6 *Distinctiveness*   Forgiveness and mercy cannot be reduced to other strengths in our classification. Strengths like social intelligence and kindness may facilitate this strength, though, as may hope and spirituality.

CRITERION 7 *Paragons*   Paragons of forgiveness and mercy exist. One of our favorite examples is Abraham Lincoln and his second inaugural address, which was a call for mercy on the part of the North to its brethren in the South:

> With malice toward none, with charity for all, with firmness in the right as God gives us to see the right, let us strive on to finish the work we are in, to bind up the nation's wounds, to care for him who shall have borne the battle and for his widow and his orphan, to do all which may achieve and cherish a just and lasting peace among ourselves and with all nations.

And remember that the last words of Jesus on the cross were "Forgive them father, for they know not what they do." An example from the contemporary world of tabloids is Mary Jo Buttafuoco, who forgave not only her straying husband but also the teenager who shot her, even petitioning a judge to let Amy Fisher be released early from prison. We can point to spouses who take back their husbands and wives who have strayed, or simply to our friends who do not dwell on our failure to stay in touch for months or even years, and instead just welcome our tardy phone call by saying, "I have missed you."

CRITERION 8 *Prodigies*   Chapter 19 describes the developmental trajectory of forgiveness, which seems to require certain degrees of cognitive and emotional sophistication to be displayed. Forgiveness is facilitated by the ability to take the point of view of the transgressor and to empathize with him or her. Children are necessarily more unforgiving than adults, and we do not know if prodigies of forgiveness exist. If they do, they are rare.

CRITERION 9 *Selective Absence*   Those who cannot forgive can be found anywhere that sustained hatred simmers. The lack of forgiveness may permeate entire families (e.g., the storied Hatfields and McCoys of 19th-century West Virginia) or even entire cultures that harbor resentment against other cultures for misdeeds committed centuries ago (e.g., the Battle of Kosovo Polje in 1389). It is worth emphasizing that despite the aphorism "forgive and forget," forgiveness does not require forgetting and indeed is probably not really forgiveness if occasioned only by the failure of recall.

The merciless deserve their own mention. "Hanging judges" like the English judge George Jeffreys of Wem (1645–1689), the Arkansas federal judge Isaac Parker (1838–1896), and the Pecos County (Texas) judge and saloon keeper Roy Bean (1825–1903), whose motto was "Hang 'em first, try 'em later," mixed cruelty and unfairness in equal and excessive measure. One of the "games that people play" described by transactional analyst Eric Berne (1964) was "Now I've Got You, You Son of a Bitch," which takes the form of a person patiently waiting for a minor transgression on the part of an unsuspecting other and then unleashing the interpersonal equivalent of nuclear weapons in retaliation. Road rage murders qualify as well as examples of black holes of mercy.

CRITERION 10 *Institutions and Rituals*   Society provides us with institutions and rituals for encouraging the dance of forgiveness. Children are told to shake hands after a fight. Lovers are told to send flowers and accept them after a misunderstanding. Public figures are expected to offer a mea culpa after some outrage. Convicted criminals are allowed to throw themselves on the mercy of the court prior to sentencing. All of us have our own strategies for dealing with hurt feelings. In our own cases, these include counting to 10 when angered; saying to a flip critic of our work, "That is a good question; further research is needed"; never responding the same day to an e-mail message that makes our blood boil; and never ever responding to an entire e-mail list.

There are some qualifications here about the cultivation of forgiveness and mercy. Although we value this character strength, we seem to regard it as so extraordinary and potentially in conflict with other virtues and values that we are loath to demand it of others. Provided rituals are thus treated as optional, which only contributes to the scarcity of the strength. Added to this state of affairs is an apparent reluctance on the part of many transgressors to take responsibility for misdeeds and offer an apology, which is one obvious route to forgiveness. Sportswriter Steve Rushin (2002) coined the acronym BOOP (blown out of proportion) to describe the lack of contrition on the part of celebrity athletes apprehended in some terrible act: "Well, sure, I was driving drunk at 120 mph on a side street where children were playing, but that incident has been blown out of proportion."

■ Humility and Modesty

This character strength is a quiet one. Those who are modest let their accomplishments speak for themselves. They do not seek the spotlight. They do not toot their own horns. They acknowledge mistakes and imperfections. They do not take undue credit for their accomplishments, instead regarding themselves as fortunate to be in a position where something good has happened to them.

Although we introduce this character strength with the roughly synonymous labels of *modesty* and *humility*, it is possible and indeed important to distinguish the two. Modesty is more external; it refers not just to a style of behaving but also to how one dresses, the car one drives, the house one owns—more generally to the absence of what we term "look at me" affectations from waxed moustaches to garish tattoos to T-shirts sporting four-letter words to anything worn (or not) by pop idol Christina Aguilera. Humility, in contrast, is more internal; it refers to the person's own sense that he or she is not the center of the universe. Ostensible modesty can exist without true humility—for example, football players like Deion Sanders, who conspicuously praised God after scoring a touchdown, or the occasional academic we meet who adopts a "good old boy" demeanor and says "I'm not all that smart" but clearly believes otherwise. But true humility necessarily leads to modesty. When we discuss this trait as a strength of character, it is humility that we highlight, not modesty as a self-conscious style of drawing attention to the self.

Humility and modesty are easily misunderstood in the contemporary United States, where we are encouraged to be full of pride and brimming with self-esteem and self-importance. To be humble and modest does not entail self-derogation or self-humiliation. These traits do not mark a person as a loser, a shrinking violet, or a depressive. In these cases, the focus remains on the self, often painfully so: "Look how inept/shy/sad I am." Rather, the traits of humility and modesty lead to a presentation of the self in an accurate way but, more important, in a way that deflects attention from the self and onto other people or circumstances. This latter characterization distinguishes humility and modesty from honesty and authenticity. The humble or modest person is necessarily honest and authentic, but the honest or authentic person may or may not be humble and modest. In any event, humility and modesty satisfy our criteria for a character strength.

CRITERION 1 *Fulfilling*   Humility and modesty are fulfilling; they are associated with acceptance of oneself and an appreciation of one's place in the larger world. There is a reason why "pride" has been considered one of the deadly sins. If nothing else, it is exhausting to promote constantly one's own accomplishments. In chapter 20, we link humility to a lack of defensiveness, and here we have some insight about the route to fulfillment that this trait provides.

CRITERION 2 *Morally Valued*   This trait is highly valued, if not always in ourselves then certainly in others. We admire people who are down-to-earth and without pretense—the regular guys who carry a lunch pail to work and never ask for special treatment.

CRITERION 3 *Does Not Diminish Others*   Humility by definition can never diminish people in the vicinity. Indeed, this character strength elevates others. It leads one to spread the credit, to acknowledge the importance of everyone else.

CRITERION 4 *Nonfelicitous Opposite* The opposites of this character strength include *arrogance, pride, pomposity, grandiosity,* and *self-centeredness.* Clinicians have introduced the term *special person misconception* to describe the mistaken notion of adolescents that their experiences of puberty are somehow unique and impossible for others (especially parents) to understand, when of course the physical, emotional, and cognitive changes of adolescence are simply part of human nature. For our purposes, the special person misconception is an apt psychological antonym of humility or modesty.

CRITERION 5 *Traitlike* This positive trait appears to be an individual difference that is both stable and general. However, as chapter 20 explains, attempts to measure humility and modesty have not advanced nearly as far as attempts to measure their absence, in the form of pride, arrogance, footless self-esteem, self-centeredness, narcissism, and the like. Perhaps researchers have shied away from attempts to assess modesty with a self-report questionnaire because it seems contradictory to ask people if they are modest. Would we be willing to believe anyone who makes this self-attribution? In chapter 28, we describe our own solution to the apparent dilemma, which entails asking people about the behavioral manifestations of this trait ("I prefer to let others speak about themselves") rather than about the trait per se. Humility and modesty so measured fare well by our strategy of verifying self-reports of character strengths against nominations by others.

CRITERION 6 *Distinctiveness* Modesty and especially humility are not decomposable into the other strengths in the classification except that they may qualify as special cases of the strength we identify as self-regulation; there the excessive emotion that is controlled or regulated is pride. It will be interesting to explore the empirical association between these two strengths of temperance.

CRITERION 7 *Paragons* Paragons of humility and modesty exist, but they rarely become famous. There are some exceptions. Abraham Lincoln and Harry Truman strike us as humble men—we cannot imagine them playing the saxophone on the *Arsenio Hall Show.* Years ago in Boulder, Colorado, one of us (CP) happened to stumble—literally—into the living room of Frank Shorter, 1972 Olympic gold medallist in the marathon. As CP entered Shorter's home to meet a mutual friend who was staying there, he tripped over the dozens of pairs of running shoes piled in the hallway. Shorter apologized profusely for the clutter, adding only "I do some running" and then proceeding to ask CP about his graduate studies in psychology. Munich was never mentioned. Three decades later, the memory remains vivid of an extraordinary man acting in an ordinary way.

CRITERION 8 *Prodigies* If they exist, modesty prodigies are apt to be found among securely attached children who have been encouraged to base their sense of self on internal assets rather than on good looks and expensive clothes (chapter 13). At the same time, it is very difficult for youngsters to pride themselves, as it were, on being ordinary, especially when they are bombarded with messages about the importance of individuality, self-esteem, and loving the self. Furthermore, because humility and modesty require a degree of cognitive sophistication to move beyond normative egocentrism, we posit that humility or modesty prodigies may not emerge until adolescence.

CRITERION 9 *Selective Absence*   The immodest are rampant in the modern world, where so many try to secure their 15 minutes of fame. Shameless self-promoters can be found in all walks of life, from students to athletes to scientists to politicians to entertainers. We will not sadden the reader by providing specific examples.

CRITERION 10 *Institutions and Rituals*   Rituals and institutions exist that may encourage modesty, but sometimes their goal seems more to beat someone down and build group solidarity than to foster a positive trait in its own right. Consider boot camp, fraternity hazing, the first year of law school, and the practice in Mao's Cultural Revolution of sending intellectuals to rural farms to pull weeds. These experiences are perhaps humbling and certainly humiliating, but it is unclear whether they make someone truly humble. Indeed, as rites of passage, most have explicit endings, which may signal to participants that they need no longer act in a humble or modest way. More lasting in their effects, we suspect, are rituals that become lifestyles, like those in Alcoholics Anonymous or various religious orders. And the Japanese geisha is taught quite explicitly to be humble and modest.

■ Prudence

Like the other strengths of temperance in this section, prudence has an occasional bad reputation. To label someone a prude is hardly to praise him or her. Prudes are timid, uptight, overly cautious, and boring. Indeed, we tell people to go for it, to live with gusto, to throw caution to the winds, to seize the day, to take chances—nothing ventured, nothing gained. So why do we consider prudence a strength of character? The answer comes from a nuanced view. As we detail in chapter 21, prudence is an orientation to one's personal future, a form of practical reasoning and self-management that helps one to achieve long-term goals effectively by considering carefully along the way the consequences of actions taken and not taken. The prudent person does not sacrifice long-term goals for short-term pleasures but instead keeps in mind what will eventually produce the most satisfaction. The prudent person makes "smart" choices as opposed to no choices at all. Prudence is akin to the strength we have described as critical thinking and active open-mindedness, but it is a special case in which the evidence to be weighed pertains to future courses of action and their personal costs and benefits. As already implied, prudence is not paralysis. It is a strength of character when it leads us to do things in a judicious way.

CRITERION 1 *Fulfilling*   As we have said about the other strengths of temperance, prudence is fulfilling but not necessarily fun. It leads us to refrain from actions that are unduly dangerous or otherwise threatening, because they might produce regret, guilt, or shame. It leads us to engage in actions with long-term intended consequences. The prudent individual charts his or her own course as opposed to bobbing along on local currents, and how can this not be fulfilling?

CRITERION 2 *Morally Valued*   Prudence is morally valued. In particular, it is a trait that we want to cultivate in our children. A friend of ours just had a baby girl several years after a little boy entered her life. "What am I going to do with a girl?" she asked. "The same thing you have been doing with your son," we replied, "worry!" "Yes," she said, "but I'm going to worry about different things." In both cases, though, the antidote entails encouraging prudence. If children can be taught to think before acting, to look before leaping, to make smart choices, and to ask "Why?" as well as "Why not?" then they will become prudent adolescents and prudent adults, worthy of praise for forethought and practical intelligence.

CRITERION 3 *Does Not Diminish Others*   The display of prudence does not diminish others except insofar as its example can slow people down as they themselves embark on imprudent courses of action. Here we have an example of dreaded peer pressure that cuts both ways. The prudent person may be derogated by friends and acquaintances as a stick-in-the-mud, but we can be inspired to our own smart choices by seeing others do their homework, save their allowance, and eat their brussels sprouts. In Aesop's fable, we admire the ant more than the grasshopper.

CRITERION 4 *Nonfelicitous Opposite*   The absence of prudence is marked not by spontaneity or zest but by *recklessness, foolishness, thoughtlessness*, and *irresponsibility*. Consider the difference between thrill seeking per se and the senseless courting of disaster. A prudent person might relish unusual foods and atonal music—there is no contradiction here because these experiences provide interesting sensations without danger. But a prudent person will not Rollerblade down the middle of an interstate highway.

CRITERION 5 *Traitlike*   Prudence is traitlike. As we describe in chapter 21, prudence has rarely been operationalized as an individual difference carrying this exact label, but it is approximated by the notion of conscientiousness and—in its absence—by impulsivity and sensation seeking. These are well-established and extensively investigated traits with considerable generality and stability.

CRITERION 6 *Distinctiveness*   It may be possible to render prudence as a blend of other strengths like open-mindedness (chapter 6) and self-regulation (chapter 22), so we will refrain from concluding at present that this is a nondecomposable positive trait.

CRITERION 7 *Paragons*   Paragons of prudence exist at the mundane level—those who wear a seat belt, change batteries in smoke detectors, heed storm warnings, and arrange for a designated driver when out carousing. They also exist at the heroic level. Remember our discussion of especially courageous people and our distinction between valor and foolhardiness (chapter 9). Good firefighters, no matter how brave, never rush into a burning building unless retreat is possible. They need to be prudent, even as they take what seem to us to be large risks. More generally, truly brave people choose their moments carefully, and their thoughtfulness is a sign of prudence.

Another example of a paragon of prudence is unusual but apt: rock parody singer Al Yankovic. We recently heard an interview with him in which he wondered whether he was "really" a pop star because he had never been in a motorcycle accident or drug rehabilitation. But then he reminded himself and listeners that he must be doing something right because he had an ongoing career that had spanned decades and earned him several Grammy awards. Despite cultivating the public persona of a fool, Weird Al is no buffoon.

CRITERION 8 *Prodigies*   Prodigies of prudence cannot exist until children have the cognitive capacity to engage in counterfactual thinking that weighs pros and cons of hypothetical courses of actions. It is obvious that some children are more able than others to delay gratification and curb impulses, but missing in research to date is compelling evidence that such children are displaying a character strength of prudence as opposed to more task-specific strategies for minimizing distraction and maximizing perseverance. We are more confident in concluding that prodigies of prudence can be found among adolescents. They may sometimes be teased by their peers as goody-two-shoes, but they are precisely the good kids we trust as baby-sitters or simply able to stay home alone.

CRITERION 9 *Selective Absence*   The imprudent can be found in all walks of life, but they seem especially visible in the emergency rooms of hospitals. A trauma surgeon of our acquaintance tells us that victims of bizarre "accidents" so frequently account for their mishaps with the same preface that it has earned its own acronym in hospital notes: STMMOB (sitting there minding my own business). One must probe a bit further to discover that such patients may have had balloons filled with heroin in their stomach or a loaded gun in their waistband. They may have been pouring gasoline onto a charcoal fire or running with a fountain pen in their mouths. The Mutter Medical Museum in Philadelphia displays thousands of needles, buttons, and razor blades surgically removed from patients who had inadvertently swallowed them. "What were they thinking?" is the only reaction one can have to this exhibit, and the answer in most cases is probably nothing.

Or consider these finalists for the 2002 Darwin awards (cf. chapter 1):

- a San Francisco stockbroker, apparently in the zone while running, who jogged off a 100-foot-high cliff
- a 20-year-old ROTC cadet stabbed to death by a fellow cadet after arguing that his flak jacket was impenetrable by knife
- two snowmobilers in Windsor, Ontario, who died in a head-on collision while playing a game of chicken
- an Oklahoma man killed by a ricocheting bullet from the rifle of a friend who was trying to shoot a millipede
- an Ohio man who died in a fire he set himself while cleaning cobwebs away in his basement with a propane torch
- a German zookeeper who died after giving a constipated elephant 22 doses of laxative and—impatient for results—proceeding to administer an olive oil enema; he suffocated under an explosion of more than 200 pounds of elephant dung

Do not be distracted by how bizarre these examples seem. They are striking only because they resulted in deaths, but they would be imprudent in any event.

CRITERION 10 *Institutions and Rituals*   Institutions and rituals certainly attempt to cultivate and encourage prudence, but again we are critical of what many actually teach. Consider practices taking the form of admonitions only: "You are going to put your eye out!" The media help worried parents by providing countless stories of the dangers and disasters that can lurk around every corner. But what do these cautionary tales really teach? They may tell us simply that the world is a scary place. Or consider practices that backfire altogether because they overstate dangers. Most adolescents who drink or smoke marijuana do not end up in the morgue or on a locked psychiatric ward. There are all sorts of reasons for them to refrain from alcohol and drugs, but guaranteed disaster in each and every case is contradicted by their everyday experience and thus unlikely to be a compelling rationale for prudence.

More useful strategies for cultivating this character strength are those that provide instruction in prudent action (as opposed to inaction) and, even more important, in the practical reasoning that marks prudence: "What are the pros and cons of this college major, of this job choice, of this vacation plan?" Accordingly, we do not regard strictly behavioral strategies for curbing impulses—"Take a cold shower"—as prudence rituals because they neglect the cognitive frame that defines prudence. A better example is one we have seen promoted in a Philadelphia bank that encourages youngsters to save money for long-term goals. A bank representative visits a grade school and explains savings accounts, passbooks, and compound interest. The emphasis is not on hoarding money for no purpose but on what one can eventually do with the money.

■ Self-Regulation [Self-Control]

In exercising the character strength of self-regulation, the individual exerts control over his or her own responses so as to pursue goals and live up to standards. These responses importantly include those that might be occasioned by extreme impulses and emotions. *Self-control* is sometimes used as a synonym for self-regulation and sometimes used more narrowly to refer specifically to controlling one's impulses so as to behave in a moral fashion. The term *self-discipline* is related to self-control and usually is used in an even more narrow sense to refer to making oneself do things that one does not want to do in the face of temptation to the contrary. Here we discuss this positive trait in broad terms to refer to the individual's ability to regulate or control excesses of all types. Paradigm cases include folks who can stay on a diet, who can quit smoking, or who can refrain from lashing out at others who have hurt them. In these broad terms, self-regulation seems to be the most generic of the temperance strengths and no doubt contributes to the others so far discussed. The distinction is that regulation of oneself need not involve the undoing of hatred (cf. forgiveness), arrogance (cf. humility), or short-term hedonic impulses (cf. prudence)—simply their control. The self-regulated individual may on occasion give in to each or all of these feelings, but it is deliberate choice. In any event, self-regulation satisfies our criteria for a strength of character.

CRITERION 1 *Fulfilling*   Self-regulation is fulfilling so long as we remember that as a strength of character it is used in the service of goals and the meeting of standards. Self-control for its own sake is silly, if not bizarre, and may be at the root of such psychopathologies as anorexia. The self-regulated person is neither austere nor ascetic. To use modern psychological language, this person instead has an internal locus of control and experiences all the fulfillment and positive outcomes that such an orientation can produce. He or she is efficacious, an origin rather than a pawn, in control rather than helpless.

CRITERION 2 *Morally Valued*   Self-regulation is highly valued. Even if we find them a bit tedious, we admire people who stick to an exercise regimen. We certainly value people who do not express every negative emotion they experience, those who are "low maintenance" because they can control their reactions to disappointment and insecurity. We can count on the self-controlled person to keep her promises because she will not be distracted in the course of so doing.

CRITERION 3 *Does Not Diminish Others*   Especially when self-regulation takes the form of moral discipline, we are elevated by its observation. The plight of Job is an inspiring example of a man able to keep his faith despite constant challenges to which others would have reacted with anger and dismay. In chapter 22, we note that the seven deadly sins can be construed as failures of self-regulation, which means that self-regulation keeps us on the path to virtue, elevating those who observe our journey. If we recast the self-disciplined person as one who models for others a self-efficacy, what we have is not only elevation but also contagion, because we learn about our own ability to control outcomes by observing others who can do so (Bandura, 1986). Conversely, we are shocked and saddened by lapses in self-regulation. Intoxication per se does not bother us, but we are equally embarrassed by angry drunks and by happy drunks.

CRITERION 4 *Nonfelicitous Opposite*   The antonyms of self-regulation—*out of control, impulsive, explosive, undisciplined, wild, raging*—are clearly negative. If we turn to the field of psychopathology for psychological antonyms, we find *borderline personality disorder, substance abuse,* and *obsessive-compulsive disorder,* as well as impulse control disorders like *kleptomania, pyromania,* and *explosive rage disorder.* Indeed, lack of self-control may be at the root of all emotional disorders, so named because the person is controlled by anxiety and depression rather than vice versa. Everyone experiences negative emotions; what determines whether they escalate to full-blown disorders may simply be whether the person has the ability to circumscribe them (cf. Nolen-Hoeksema, 1991).

CRITERION 5 *Traitlike*   Recent evidence shows this positive trait to be general and stable. Early research tended to be very narrow and behavioral in focus, looking at the delay of gratification in specific situations. Current studies have approached self-regulation and self-control as a more pervasive trait, which proves to have an array of important correlates across the life span (chapter 22).

CRITERION 6. *Distinctiveness*   Self-regulation does not reduce to the other positive traits included in the classification, although our future work may result in some of these other traits being reduced to self-regulation.

CRITERION 7 *Paragons*   Paragons of self-regulation include monks and nuns who have taken vows of silence, athletes who put in long hours on the practice field (e.g., Jackie Joiner Kersey and Jerry Rice), students who go to the library every day and actually study, or lifelong practitioners of yoga or the martial arts. From Greek lore, we have the example of Demosthenes, who perfected his oratory ability by practicing with stones in his mouth while heavy winds from the Aegean Sea blew in his face. More contemporary examples come from the military: pilots taught to fly planes in dizzying free fall and snipers taught to shoot after 72 hours without sleep. Less dramatic but still familiar examples include friends and colleagues who never lose their cool. We never know from which side of the bed they arose that morning.

CRITERION 8 *Prodigies*   Psychologists interested in delay of gratification have long studied children—is this because adult research participants would not cooperate?—and thus we know that children as young as 4 years of age can say no to a short-term reward in favor of a larger but delayed reward.

CRITERION 9 *Selective Absence*   Those with no self-control include all those folks who warrant the *DSM* diagnoses just mentioned, as well as celebrities like Mike Tyson, who apparently did not build the self-regulation muscle while he was doing roadwork and hitting the heavy bag. Indeed, we the people seem fascinated by celebrities who are out of control—in and out of drug rehabilitation, legal scrapes, and marriages—and the source of this fascination needs an explanation. We doubt that positive psychology will provide it.

CRITERION 10 *Institutions and Rituals*   Societal rituals for encouraging self-regulation include such familiar parental admonitions as sit up straight, stop fidgeting, and finish your dinner. Recent research suggests that these apparently mundane exercises actually build the generic character strength of self-control, which can then be used in more important domains, leading theorists to liken self-regulation to a muscle that grows with use. Psychology's contribution to the understanding of discipline is its articulation of the cognitive and behavioral pathways to self-control, and knowledge of these can be used to craft deliberate interventions. Do you remember the scene in Skinner's (1948) utopian novel *Walden Two* in which children are required to be in the presence of savory deserts without sampling them?

19. FORGIVENESS AND MERCY

■ *Anyone who has seen the image did not soon forget it. In 1972, at the height of the Vietnam War, the village of Trang Bang was pummeled by an American air raid. An Associated Press photographer captured the image of a 9-year-old Vietnamese girl named Phan Thi Kim Phuc, moments after she and several other children fled the village. The Pulitzer Prize–winning photograph shows Kim Phuc running from her devastated village, naked, screaming in agony, her arms held up and away from her body. During the raid, Kim Phuc and her family sought shelter in a pagoda, but after it became unsafe to stay there, Kim ran into the street, where she encountered the falling napalm, which covered most of her body. She tore off her clothes seeking relief. Kim Phuc's napalm burns were so extensive that few people expected her to survive.*

An American soldier named John Plummer had set up the air strike on Trang Bang after being assured twice that there were no civilians in the area. Plummer did not realize the full extent of the civilian casualties that ensued in the bombing until seeing the now-famous photograph of Kim Phuc. Plummer said that the photo, which went on to become a famous symbol for the horrors of war, and his own guilt haunted him unrelentingly for years. Although he wanted desperately to tell Kim Phuc how sorry he was for the devastation that his actions had created, including the scars on her body and in her memory, he had no way of doing so. He could not bring himself to return to Vietnam and seriously doubted that she had even survived the attack.

But nearly 25 years later, after extensive plastic surgery, marriage, and a successful relocation to Canada, Kim Phuc was alive and raising a family. In 1996, Plummer—himself now a minister in the United Methodist Church—learned that Kim Phuc would be speaking at the Vietnam Veterans Memorial in Washington, D.C. He was sure to be there on the day she spoke.

In Kim Phuc's address to the several thousand people who had assembled, she said that if she could ever meet the pilot of the plane responsible for dropping the napalm on her village, she would tell him that she forgives him and that she hoped they could work together in the future. Plummer managed to get word to Kim Phuc that he was indeed there and that he wanted to meet her. Over the course of two meetings that very day, Plummer tearfully related his profound guilt and remorse for the bombing. Kim Phuc assured him that she had forgiven him, that she was ready to move on, and that she hoped they could become friends and even partners in working together for peace.

They now have become friends. To one reporter who followed the story, Plummer said of Kim Phuc, "She is the closest thing to a saint I have ever met."

■ Consensual Definition

Forgiveness represents a suite of prosocial changes that occur within an individual who has been offended or damaged by a relationship partner (McCullough, Pargament, & Thoresen, 2000a). When people forgive, their basic motivations or action tendencies regarding the transgressor become more positive (e.g., benevolent, kind, generous) and less negative (e.g., vengeful, avoidant). It is useful to distinguish between forgivingness, which is a readiness or proneness to forgive (R. C. Roberts, 1995), and forgiveness, which can be thought of as psychological changes vis-à-vis a specific transgressor and a specific transgression. Forgiveness can be considered a specialized form of mercy, which is a more general concept reflecting kindness, compassion, or leniency toward (a) a transgressor, (b) someone over whom one has power or authority, or (c) someone in great distress (see Gove et al., 1966).

Individuals with a strong disposition to forgive would endorse statements such as the following:

- When someone hurts my feelings, I manage to get over it fairly quickly.
- I don't hold a grudge for very long.
- When people make me angry, I am usually able to get over my bad feelings toward them.
- Seeking revenge doesn't help people to solve their problems.
- I think it is important to do what I can to mend my relationships with people who have hurt or betrayed me in the past.
- I am not the type of person to harm someone simply because he or she harmed me.
- I am not the type of person who spends hours thinking of how to get even with people who have done bad things to me.

■ Theoretical Traditions

Although forgiveness is by no means a strictly religious virtue, its strongest historical and philosophical roots are within religious soil. As is the case with many traditional Western virtues, forgiveness has figured prominently in both Jewish and Christian understandings of what it means to live a life in harmony with others. However, most of the world's major religions advocate for a worldview that affirms the value of forgiveness, although these religious conceptions of forgiveness differ in many of the particulars. In describing the stances of five of the world's major religions (Judaism, Christianity, Islam, Hinduism, and Buddhism), we draw heavily on several recent reviews (McCullough & Worthington, 1999; Rye et al., 2000; Tsang, McCullough, & Hoyt, in press).

Judaism

The notion that God is capable of forgiving people of their sins was one of the features that distinguished Hebrew religion from the other religions among which Judaism first arose (Klassen, 1966). Correspondingly, followers of Judaism forgive because they believe that God has forgiven them and because God commands them to forgive their transgressors in turn. Forgiveness can be defined as the removal or cancellation of a transgression or debt so that a transgressor becomes a candidate for a restored relationship with the offended party or parties (Rye et al., 2000). Yet forgiveness is not an obligatory action in all circumstances. In Jewish thought, forgiveness is frequently paired with repentance, or *teshuvah* (which means "return"), on the part of the transgressor. Through *teshuvah*, the transgressor expresses sincere remorse, offers compensation to the victim, and resolves to behave differently in the future. When a transgressor does repent, the victim is morally required to forgive.

Christianity

Christianity, like Judaism, elevated the notion of forgiveness to a foundational point of doctrine. Unlike Judaism, however, Christianity has embraced the idea that forgiveness is not necessarily conditional upon the transgressor's repentance. Christian theology typically distinguishes forgiveness from reconciliation, which is the restoration of the broken relationship. In this tradition, complete reconciliation between victim and transgressor is not possible unless the victim forgives.

Islam

God's ability to forgive all sins is a foundational belief in Islam also. One of Allah's appellations is Al-Ghafoor, or the Forgiving One (Rye et al., 2000). Islam emphasizes that people should forgive so that they might receive forgiveness from Allah for their own sins, and also so that they might achieve happiness. Nonetheless, Islam permits revenge if it is equal to the harm done by the transgressor. However, because it is often difficult to tell when the scales have been balanced through revenge, forgiveness is frequently seen as a superior alternative that does not lead to the lingering animosities between individuals and clans that characterized the world in which Islam was founded. When one is seeking revenge, one might overstep the boundaries and thus offend Allah. As in Christianity, Islam does not hold that forgiveness is contingent upon the repentance of the transgressor (Rye et al., 2000).

Buddhism

Although there is no Buddhist concept that corresponds directly to the Western notion of forgiveness, two virtues that may approximate forgiveness—forbearance and compassion—do receive high praise within Buddhist thought and are central to Buddhist practice (Rye et al., 2000). Within Buddhism, these traits emerge from an emphasis on easing the suffering of others—even the suffering of people who deserve punishment because of their wrong actions. Forbearance comprises tolerating a transgression and relinquishing one's resentment toward the transgressor. Compassion motivates people to ease the suffering of others and can, of course, even be directed toward a transgressor so that he or she is viewed with tenderness rather than with anger. Although Buddhism is a nontheistic religion, it presumes that the universe is governed by karma—"the law of moral cause-and-effect" (Rye et al., 2000, p. 28) dictating that good actions produce good outcomes and evil actions produce evil outcomes. Because of karma, holding on to one's resentment and lack of compassion may cause one to be viewed resentfully and with a lack of compassion by others in the future; thus, it is in one's best interests to be forbearing and compassionate. The exercise of forbearance and compassion is not predicated on any remorse or repentance on the part of the transgressor.

Hinduism

Hindu treatises on righteousness (the *dharma sastras*) discuss forgiveness along with other virtues such as duty, forbearance, compassion, and patience (Rye et al., 2000). As in Buddhism, the law of karma is relevant to the Hindu concept of forgiveness. Though some Hindu traditions are nontheistic, versions of Hinduism that do incorporate belief in a supreme being or beings also provide examples of divine forgiveness for believers to follow. Prayers to Varuna in the *Rig Veda*, for instance, demonstrate this deity's eagerness to forgive people who humbly admit their sins. Other sacred writings teach that the goddess Sri or Lakshmi is inclined to forgive even in the absence of repentance. Regarding human-to-human relations, however, Hindu teaching is fairly realistic, expecting that people would only forgive a transgressor who was contrite and repentant. Although there is no definitive teaching in Hinduism regarding the relationship between forgiveness and reconciliation, Hindu teachings acknowledge that repentance and forgiveness are both important precursors to the complete restoration of relationships that have been damaged by a transgression.

Modern Traditions

Most modern scholars and scientists agree on several points about forgiveness. First, they concur with Enright and Coyle (1998) that forgiveness should be distinguished from pardon, condonation, excusing, forgetting, and denial. Moreover, most scholars stress that the term *forgiveness* should be kept distinct from *reconciliation*, the former being reserved for "the restoration of trust in an interpersonal relationship through mutual trustworthy behaviors" (Worthington & Drinkard, 2000, p. 93).

Still, scholars continue to disagree somewhat regarding the essence of what forgiveness is (Kaminer, Stein, Mbanga, & Zungu-Dirwayi, 2000; Scobie & Scobie, 1998), although these differences are perhaps smaller than often portrayed. What unites the many definitions of forgiveness is intraindividual, prosocial change toward a perceived transgressor that is set within a specific interpersonal context (McCullough, Pargament, & Thoresen, 2000b). In other words, forgiveness involves positive social psychological changes within an individual vis-à-vis an interpersonal transgression and the transgressor who committed it. When people forgive, then, psychological responses whose referent is the transgression or transgressor become more positive (i.e., benevolent) and less negative (i.e., malevolent). Nonetheless, scholars have worked out the specifics in slightly different ways.

Enright and colleagues (e.g., Enright & Coyle, 1998; Enright, Gassin, & Wu, 1992) defined "genuine forgiveness" following philosopher J. North (1987), who proposed that forgiveness occurs when an individual who has incurred an interpersonal transgression is able to "view the wrongdoer with compassion, benevolence, and love while recognizing that he [*sic*] has willfully abandoned his right to them" (p. 502). Three general points regarding Enright's approach are worth noting. First, Enright's developmental theorizing emphasizes that reasoning about the use of forgiveness appears to mature as people age, with the lowest levels of maturity reflecting the idea that forgiveness is appropriate only after revenge has been obtained or after restitution has been made (Enright, 1994; Enright, Santos, & Al-Mabuk, 1989). As people's moral reasoning develops, their reasoning about forgiveness becomes oriented toward viewing forgiveness as an unconditional gift given to transgressors based on the belief in the innate value of all persons.

Second, Enright has emphasized that forgiveness is a process that takes place within multiple psychological systems. Forgiveness can be said to have occurred, in this view, when a person has improved his or her feelings, thoughts, and behaviors regarding an interpersonal transgressor. What is implied here is that emotional or even cognitive change on the part of a victim does not reflect complete forgiveness in the absence of improved behaviors regarding the transgressor. Third, Enright has advocated the use of stage-sequential thinking for understanding how an individual comes to forgive a transgressor. In one of the more recent iterations of this process model, Enright and Coyle (1998) identified 20 "units" that, they hypothesize, must occur for a person to forgive. This model has been used largely in the context of psychotherapy research.

McCullough and colleagues have worked with a more circumscribed definition of forgiveness. They have defined forgiveness as motivational changes whereby a person becomes less motivated toward revenge and avoidance of a transgressor, and simultaneously more benevolent toward the transgressor (McCullough, 2001; McCullough, Bellah, Kilpatrick, & Johnson, 2001; McCullough, Worthington, & Rachal, 1997; McCullough et al., 1998). Obviously, transgression recipients who experience these motivational changes would probably be more likely to behave toward their transgressors with more benevolence and less malevolence, but not in all cases (McCullough, 2001).

McCullough and colleagues have demonstrated the importance of empathy as a determinant of forgiveness (McCullough et al., 1997, 1998) and have developed conceptual tools for modeling forgiveness mathematically on the basis of time-series data (McCullough, Fincham, & Tsang, 2003). However, McCullough et al.'s main contribution to a scientific understanding of the disposition to forgive is found in the work of McCullough and Hoyt (McCullough & Hoyt, 2002; McCullough, Hoyt, & Rachal, 2000; Tsang et al., in press). These researchers have conceptualized the capacity to forgive as the product of stable individual differences among persons that are reflected consistently (but weakly) in their forgiveness responses to individual transgressions. They have shown that measures of the disposition to forgive are improved considerably when based on people's reactions to multiple transgressions. Aggregating responses to multiple transgressions causes transgression-specific and relationship-specific determinants of people's responses to individual transgressions to cancel out, leaving essentially "pure" estimates of their personality-based propensity to forgive.

Worthington and his colleagues have conceptualized forgiveness as a largely affective phenomenon (Berry, Worthington, Parrott, O'Connor, & Wade, 2001). For instance, Worthington, Berry, and Parrott (2001) defined forgiveness as "the contamination or prevention of unforgiving emotions by experiencing strong, positive, love-based emotions as one recalls a transgression" (p. 109). The distinctive element to this definition is the notion that unforgiving emotions are undone or negated through experiencing love-based emotions (e.g., empathy, sympathy, or even romantic love). Importantly, forgiveness and unforgiveness are not envisioned as poles on a single continuum but as relatively independent adaptive systems. Like McCullough and colleagues, Worthington and colleagues assume that these changes will frequently lead to behavioral changes (e.g., reconciliation), but the link between forgiveness and changed behavior is by no means a perfect one.

Because forgiveness and unforgiveness are viewed as distinct constructs with only a modest degree of overlap, Worthington et al. (2001) speculated that these constructs will possess distinct patterns of psychological and physiological correlates.

■ Measures

Researchers have developed many measures for assessing various aspects of forgiveness, including measures of transgression-specific forgiveness and the general disposition toward forgiveness. Here we focus on this latter set of measures. Space does not permit an exhaustive survey, so attention is limited to several measures that have been published in peer-reviewed journals and for which there is a growing body of evidence to support claims of construct validity (Table 19.1). However, many investigators are developing similar instruments that might eventually complement the existing measures in important ways.

It is important to note that measuring forgiveness at the dispositional level is no substitute for assessing the degree to which people forgive for specific transgressions (McCullough, Hoyt, et al., 2000). Many published measures that are not reviewed herein exist for assessing transgression-specific forgiveness (e.g., S. W. Brown, Gorsuch, Rosik, & Ridley, 2001; McCullough et al., 1998; Rye et al., 2001; Subkoviak et al., 1995).

Researchers will continue to develop measures of the disposition to forgive over the next several years, but even today there are published scenario measures (e.g., Berry et al., 2001; Rye et al., 2001); measures that employ self-descriptions that people endorse to describe their own personalities (e.g., Mauger et al., 1992; Mullet, Houdbine, Laumonier, & Girard, 1998); and even a measure for assessing reasoning about forgiveness (Enright et al., 1989). Peer-report measures (see Berry et al., 2001) have also been developed and should be included in future research because of their usefulness in concluding that forgiveness-related phenomena that are obtained using self-report measures are not due exclusively to mono-method bias. Other measures involving less obtrusive methods (e.g., perhaps, measurements involving the assessment of reaction times or other behavioral measures) would be most welcome additions to the existing suite of pencil-and-paper measures.

■ Correlates and Consequences

Forgiveness is associated with a variety of traits that are of value for personal and societal well-being. Forgiving people appear to be slightly lower in a vari-

---

TABLE 19.1   *Measures of Forgiveness*

Forgiveness Likelihood Scale

> Rye et al. (2001)
>
> This is a scenario-based instrument with 10 transgression scenarios. Participants read each scenario and picture themselves as the victim in each of them, and they then indicate their hypothetical likelihood of forgiving the transgression on a 5-point scale.
>
> - Internal reliability: Cronbach's alpha = .85
> - Test–retest reliability: 15-day test–retest r = .81
> - Construct validity: Correlates positively with intrinsic religious motivation and religious well-being; correlates negatively with trait anger but is virtually uncorrelated with state anger; correlates weakly but positively with social desirability; correlates positively with people's self-reports of the extent to which they have forgiven a specific transgressor for a specific transgression

Forgiveness of Others Scale

> Mauger et al. (1992)
>
> This 15-item self-report scale assesses people's perceptions of themselves as forgiving (vs. vengeful). Items are rated in a true-false format. High scores indicate a high proneness to forgive, and low scores indicate proneness toward revenge.
>
> - Internal reliability: Cronbach's alpha = .79
> - Test–retest reliability: 2-week test–retest r = .94
> - Construct validity: People who score at the "forgiving" end of the scale tend to have low scores on all of the MMPI clinical scales; they also tend to be low in neuroticism, depressive symptoms, and anxiety symptoms (Maltby, Macaskill, & Day, 2001)

---

ety of negative affects, including anger, anxiety, depression, and hostility (Berry et al., 2001; Maltby, Macaskill, & Day, 2001). Forgivers also tend to endorse socially desirable attitudes and behavior (Mauger et al., 1992; Rye et al., 2001), and self-ratings of the disposition to forgive correlate negatively with clinicians' ratings of hostility and passive-aggressive behavior.

People who score high on a dispositional measure of the tendency toward forgiveness or nonretaliation report themselves as willing to allocate more money in a joint allocation task to someone who had previously been rude, nasty, or inconsiderate toward them than do people who score lower on this measure (Ashton, Paunonen, Helmes, & Jackson, 1998). Interestingly, high scorers were not willing to allocate more money to a close friend than were people who scored lower on this measure, suggesting that self-reports of forgiveness tap specifically the tendency to respond to offenses with benevolence instead of malice.

Forgivingness Scale

> Mullet, Houdbine, Laumonier, & Girard (1998)
> This is a 38-item, 4-factor scale that assesses people's perceptions of their
> abilities to forgive across a variety of situations and circumstances. Items are
> rated on 7-point scales (ranging from disagree completely to agree com-
> pletely). The four factors are (a) "Revenge vs. Forgiveness," (b) "Personal
> and Social Circumstances," (c) "Forgiveness Block," and (d) "Obstacles to
> Forgiveness."
> - Internal reliability: not reported
> - Test–retest reliability: not reported
> - Construct validity: Factor 1 (Revenge vs. Forgiveness) was associated with
>   age and gender (i.e., older adults and women are more inclined to forgive-
>   ness instead of revenge than are younger adults and men); people who
>   frequently attend religious services and who believe in God score more
>   forgiving on several subscales than do people who do not frequently attend
>   religious services and who do not believe in God

Transgression Narrative Test of Forgiveness (TNTF)

> Berry, Worthington, Parrott, O'Connor, & Wade (2001)
> This is a scenario-based instrument with five transgression scenarios. Partici-
> pants read each scenario and picture themselves as the victim in each of them,
> and then indicate their hypothetical likelihood of forgiving the transgression on
> a 5-point scale.
> - Internal reliability: alphas = approx. .79; Rasch Person R = approx. .82;
>   Rasch Item R = approx. .99
> - Test–retest reliability: 8-week test–retest r = .69
> - Construct validity: correlates negatively with self-report measures of angry
>   temperament, angry reactivity, hostility, angry rumination, and neuroti-
>   cism; correlates positively with agreeableness, conscientiousness, and
>   extroversion; virtually uncorrelated with social desirability; correlation of
>   self-ratings and ratings by romantic partner were r = .60

Within the Big Five taxonomy, the disposition to forgive appears to be most
strongly related to agreeableness and neuroticism (Ashton et al., 1998; Berry
et al., 2001; McCullough & Hoyt, 2002). For example, Ashton et al. (1998) found
that a global self-report measure of the disposition to forgive was positively
correlated with agreeableness and positively correlated with emotional stability (which is, essentially, a mirror image of neuroticism).

Currently, there is great theoretical interest in the possibility that the disposition to forgive (or, importantly, forgiveness for specific interpersonal transgressions) is causally involved in promoting mental and physical health or
preventing mental and physical health problems (McCullough & Witvliet,
2001). Although the forgiveness–health hypothesis is appealing, the claims in
support of this hypothesis are typically based on weak data (such as cross-
sectional correlational evidence regarding the relations of measures of forgive-

ness with self-report measures of affect or well-being). No prospective or experimental evidence demonstrates that people who are highly prone to forgive (or less prone to revenge; see McCullough, Bellah, et al., 2001) are differentially prone to good health or well-being.

In support of the forgiveness–health hypothesis, people also frequently cite intervention research in which treatments designed to promote forgiveness have been compared with no-treatment control groups (see later section, "Deliberate Interventions"). The finding that psychosocial treatments work better than nothing at all is one of the most robust and well-accepted findings in all of psychology (Lipsey & Wilson, 1993), so studies that demonstrate that forgiveness treatments work in comparison with no-treatment controls give us very little reason to believe that forgiveness per se causes health and well-being. The field sorely needs high-quality prospective studies or experiments in which the unique effects of forgiveness (above and beyond the robust effects of psychosocial interventions in general) on health can be detected. In conducting these studies, it is important that researchers control for other likely personality traits (e.g., the Big Five) that may be responsible for the apparent relationship between measures of forgiveness and measures of well-being. Witvliet, Ludwig, and Vander Laan's (2001) intriguing study showed that forgiveness can influence short-term markers for sympathetic nervous system arousal. This finding may give some important clues regarding possible long-term effects of forgiveness on health.

■ Development

Enright et al. (1989) specifically situated their theory of how people reason about forgiveness within a developmental framework. Specifically, they posited that reasoning about forgiveness would develop along the same trajectory as did Kolhbergian justice reasoning. Their preliminary work confirmed that individuals' level of Kohlbergian reasoning concerning justice was highly correlated with their level of reasoning about forgiveness according to Enright et al.'s developmental model. Enright (1994) also elaborated a Piagetian account of how reasoning concerning forgiveness develops as a function of general cognitive development.

Empirical research has confirmed that willingness to forgive varies as a function of age, with young children generally being least willing to forgive and older adults being most willing (Darby & Schlenker, 1982; Enright et al., 1989; Girard & Mullet, 1997; Mullet et al., 1998; for a review, see Mullet & Girard, 2000). However, longitudinal studies are needed to confirm that these cross-sectional age differences truly reflect a developmental process rather than simply cohort effects.

■ Enabling and Inhibiting Factors

People who experience empathic affect for their transgressors and who adopt the cognitive perspective of their transgressors tend to forgive specific transgressors more readily than do people who do not experience empathy or engage in perspective taking (McCullough et al., 1997, 1998, 2003). The personality-based capacities for empathy and perspective taking seem to be derivatives of agreeableness; thus, highly agreeable people (see earlier section on "Correlates and Consequences") might obtain their "advantage" because of the relative ease with which they experience empathy for others. Conversely, ruminating about the offense appears to put people at a considerable disadvantage in forgiving (McCullough, Bellah, et al., 2001). Because the tendency to ruminate is identified most closely with the neuroticism dimension of the Big Five, people low in neuroticism might be prone to forgive because of their tendency not to ruminate about negative events they encounter.

Attributions and appraisals regarding the transgression and transgressor also influence the extent to which people forgive particular transgressions. People tend not to forgive transgressions that they perceived to be intentionally committed and that have severe consequences (Boon & Sulsky, 1997; Girard & Mullet, 1997; Takaku, Weiner, & Ohbuchi, 2001). The effects of attributions of intentionality on forgiveness may be mediated partially by the effects of intentionality attributions on empathy (i.e., when transgressions are viewed as unintentional, it is easier to empathize with the transgressor; McCullough et al., 2003), but these social-cognitive variables probably have a variety of reciprocal influences on one another.

Apologies also promote forgiveness (Darby & Schlenker, 1982; McCullough et al., 1997, 1998). By and large, the effects of apology appear to be indirect. Victims develop greater empathy for apologetic transgressors (McCullough et al., 1997, 1998) and apologies appear to cause reductions in offenders' negative affect regarding their transgressors (Ohbuchi, Kameda, & Agarie, 1989). Also, victims form more generous impressions of apologetic transgressions (Ohbuchi et al., 1989).

Finally, forgiveness may be influenced by characteristics of the relationship in which the transgression occurs. Studies have shown that partners are more willing to forgive one another for transgressions if their relationship is characterized by high satisfaction, commitment, and closeness (E. J. Finkel, Rusbult, Kumashiro, & Hannon, 2002; McCullough et al., 1998). The fact that forgiveness is associated with relationship factors like satisfaction, commitment, and closeness suggests that the dynamics of forgiveness may be different for different types of relationships. We would not expect people to forgive perfect strangers in the same way that they forgive the most intimate of relationship partners.

However, we know very little about how the dynamics of forgiveness vary within different types of relationships (Fincham, 2000).

■ Gender, Cross-National, and Cross-Cultural Aspects

The best research to date suggests that men and women are not substantially different in their propensity to forgive (Berry et al., 2001).

Although cross-cultural research on forgiveness is limited, the available evidence indicates that cultural factors clearly influence how forgiveness is understood to operate and the factors that motivate it. People from non-Western cultures construe forgiveness according to different cultural considerations than do people from Western cultures (Sandage, Hill, & Vang, 2001; Temoshok & Chandra, 2000). Using examples from Hmong culture, Sandage et al. (2001) illustrated how a culture based on collectivism, hierarchical social relations, a spirituality involving animism and ancestor worship, and third-party mediation leads to very different understandings of how transgressions create harm, the circumstances under which people should be forgiven, and who has the moral authority to forgive (see also Temoshok & Chandra, 2000).

Relatedly, people from individualist cultures may be motivated to forgive by different factors than are people from collectivist cultures. People from collectivist cultures are motivated to forgive by concern about maintaining positive relationships with others and about maintaining social norms regarding how a victim should respond, whereas people from individualist cultures are more motivated by the desire to maintain a favorable self-identity or to fulfill abstract moral principles (e.g., justice; Takaku et al., 2001).

Takaku et al. (2001) found a slight tendency for Japanese students to be less forgiving in response to a hypothetical transgression than were American students. Berry et al. (2001) also found, using Rasch scaling methods, that European Americans scored significantly higher on their Transgression Narrative Test of Forgiveness (TNTF) than did Asian Americans and Hispanic Americans, with African Americans scoring no higher or lower than did any of the other groups. Ironically, despite possible ethnic differences in the disposition to forgive, differences in willingness to forgive as a function of religious differences may be slight. In a study of Lebanese people from six religious groups (Shiite, Sunni, Druze, Catholic, Maronite, and Orthodox), Azar and Mullet (2001) found no group differences in willingness to forgive across a variety of transgression situations. Similarly, Heim and Rye (2001) found that Jews and Christians from the American Midwest did not have significantly different propensities to forgive across a variety of situations (although Jews tended to believe more strongly that forgiveness does not obviate the need for criminal prosecution and that forgiveness should be predicated on contrition from the transgressor). These initial findings notwithstanding, more research is needed on how culture shapes people's understandings of what forgiveness is and when it is appropriate.

■ Deliberate Interventions

Psychologists have developed methods for encouraging forgiveness in individual psychotherapy (for reviews see Enright & Coyle, 1998; Kaminer et al., 2000; Malcom & Greenberg, 2000; McCullough & Worthington, 1994); marital therapy (Gordon, Baucom, & Snyder, 2000); and psychoeducational groups (see Worthington et al., 2000; Worthington, Sandage, & Berry, 2000). Research has begun to accumulate on many of these intervention methods.

Interventions for encouraging forgiveness based on Enright's 20-unit process model are more effective than waiting list control conditions in encouraging forgiveness with several client populations (Enright & Coyle, 1998). Enright's intervention program is also typically superior to no-treatment control conditions at reducing negative affective states such as anger and anxiety, and at increasing positive states like hope. However, Malcom and Greenberg (2000) explain that we should be cautious in concluding that the efficacy of such interventions constitutes evidence for the clinical potency of forgiveness per se because these intervention effects have yet to be unbundled completely from the general effects of psychotherapy.

Enright's process model has also been applied with success to psychoeducational interventions administered to college students (e.g., Al-Mabuk, Enright, & Cardis, 1995). Other approaches to encouraging forgiveness through psychoeducational groups have been based, for example, on the promotion of empathy (McCullough et al., 1997). Yet other brief psychoeducational interventions for encouraging forgiveness in group interventions appear to be effective as well (see Worthington, Kurusu, et al., 2000; Worthington, Sandage, et al., 2000).

One of the key factors that accounts for these various interventions' potency is simply the length of the treatment (Worthington, Sandage, et al., 2000). Interventions involving 6 or more hours of client contact are considerably more efficacious than are interventions involving only 1 or 2 hours of client contact. On the basis of this fact, Worthington, Sandage, et al. argued convincingly that intervention researchers should plan on interventions of at least 6 hours (and perhaps more) to facilitate clinically significant changes in forgiveness. In addition, they recommended that the interventions be conducted across several weeks, rather than in one or two long sessions, to obtain maximum effects.

Does forgiveness per se make a substantial and unique contribution to the promotion of mental and/or physical health? The current intervention studies do not yield convincing answers, and more studies that compare forgiveness treatments to no-treatment control groups are unlikely to improve matters because the general effects of psychosocial interventions irrespective of content are already known to be quite strong. Questions regarding the unique contributions of forgiveness to intervention efforts could be addressed through one or more large, multicomponent intervention trials. Ideally, such an intervention study would examine whether a sample of individuals with a serious forgiveness-related problem (and concomitant mental and/or physical health problems) who completed a forgiveness-based intervention actually improved more than did people who completed an empirically verified treatment (e.g., a fully manualized form of cognitive-behavioral therapy) and an active (*not* waiting-list) control group. Ideally, investigators would assess not only participants' forgiveness and the relevant indices of mental or physical health but also the psychological mediators through which such interventions are purported to exert their effects. Assuming that the forgiveness interventions were found to be more efficacious at (a) encouraging forgiveness and (b) promoting health, investigators could proceed to conduct mediational analyses to determine whether forgiveness accounted for the differential efficacy of the forgiveness interventions.

■ What Is Not Known?

Several important issues merit sustained empirical attention:

- We lack a good understanding of how basic personality processes produce a propensity to forgive, and how people who possess this personality-based proneness to forgive differ from less forgiving people in how they think about and respond to specific transgressions (McCullough, 2001).
- Given the strong links of measures of the disposition to forgive with the agreeableness and neuroticism constructs within the Big Five taxonomy, it is important to investigate whether the propensity to forgive correlates with other psychological variables in a nontrivial fashion when the Big Five are controlled statistically.
- What are the relative strengths and shortcomings of the existing measures of the disposition to forgive? Some of these tools are probably superior to others in some applications.
- Because forgiveness, by definition, is a change process, it necessarily unfolds across some amount of time (even presumably rare cases of forgiveness that seem to occur instantaneously unfold over some amount of time, even if it is relatively quick). However, the temporal dynamics of forgiveness have not been adequately explored (see McCullough et al., 2003).
- It would be good to know whether isolated instances of forgiveness are causally linked to health and well-being, and if so, through which psychosocial and physiological pathways these effects occur.

- More work is needed on how the disposition to forgive may influence the strength and quality of ongoing family and community relations.
- Finally, many forgiveness theorists have proposed elaborate and dynamic psychological processes as the substrates for forgiveness. Almost without exception, such propositions about these dynamic processes languish as untested assumptions, which probably allows some models to remain unnecessarily elaborate and, in some cases, just plain wrong. Theoretical diversity is good for a new research area, but articulating the most important of these basic assumptions and then testing them rigorously would bring more coherence to a field that is already off to an ambitious start.

■ Must-Read Articles and Books

Berry, J. W., Worthington, E. L., Parrott, L., O'Connor, L. E., & Wade, N. G. (2001). Dispositional forgivingness: Development and construct validity of the Transgression Narrative Test of Forgiveness (TNTF). *Personality and Social Psychology Bulletin, 27,* 1277–1290.

Enright, R. D. (1994). Piaget on the moral development of forgiveness: Identity or reciprocity? *Human Development, 37,* 63–80.

Enright, R. D., & Coyle, C. T. (1998). Researching the process model of forgiveness within psychological interventions. In E. L. Worthington (Ed.), *Dimensions of forgiveness: Psychological research and theological perspectives* (pp. 139–161). Philadelphia: Templeton Foundation Press.

Enright, R. D., Gassin, L. A., & Wu, C. (1992). Forgiveness: A developmental view. *Journal of Moral Education, 21,* 99–114.

McCullough, M. E., Pargament, K. I., & Thoresen, C. T. (Eds.). (2000). *Forgiveness: Theory, research, and practice.* New York: Guilford Press.

Witvliet, C. V., Ludwig, T. E., & Vander Laan, K. L. (2001). Granting forgiveness or harboring grudges: Implications for emotion, physiology, and health. *Psychological Science, 12,* 117–123.

20. HUMILITY AND MODESTY

Humility is the most difficult of all virtues to achieve; nothing
dies harder than the desire to think well of oneself.
—T. S. ELIOT (1927, p. 8)

Who might be cited as a paragon of humility? We turned first to the early Christian monastic writers such as Saint Benedict and Bernard of Clairvaux. Their writings centered on humility, but they also communicated self-abasement and asceticism that did not resonate fully with our thinking about the construct. Other religious figures (Christ, Buddha, Moses, Saint Paul) often showed deep humility along with other virtues, with humility not standing out above the others. And because a truly humble person would presumably not seek fame for fame's sake, we had great difficulty pulling recognizable examples from current popular culture. Yet our search was not in vain, for it revealed another category of exemplars: those who knew the value of humility and struggled to become more humble.

■ *One such example is Bill Wilson ("Bill W."), the cofounder of Alcoholics Anonymous (Hartigan, 2000; Raphael, 2000). After an unsuccessful battle with alcoholism, Wilson had a religious conversion that caused him to reorder his priorities and opened the doorway to abstinence. He then used his life lessons to promote a "12-step" approach to the treatment of alcoholism. Humility-related themes played a central role within Wilson's 12-step framework (e.g., admitting personal and moral limitations; making amends; relying on a higher power). Yet throughout his life Bill often wavered between low self-esteem and arrogance, struggling to come to terms with his own personal demons while managing near-celebrity status in what was supposed to be an anonymous self-help organization. Bill Wilson was clearly someone who understood the central value of humility. However, he also understood firsthand the difficulty of attaining this virtue, and he wrestled throughout his lifetime in his attempts to cultivate it.* ■

■ Consensual Definition

In the time of Thomas Aquinas, pride was considered sufficiently evil to be included among the deadly sins (Schimmel, 1992). Some even considered pride the ultimate sin, the root of all others (Murray, 2001). Yet—in the guise of self-esteem—modern Western culture encourages the pursuit of pride. When seeking to place blame for social ills such as drug abuse and violence, the modern world often points the finger at low self-esteem. The crusade to raise self-esteem has spawned countless self-help books (e.g., Branden, 1994) and even state-funded task forces (Mecca, Smelser, & Vasconcellos, 1989). If people can only feel better about themselves, the logic goes, they will be happy and behave well—and society will benefit. Individuals now view pride as not only acceptable but worthy, whether it takes the form of overestimating one's good qualities and traits, viewing the self as better than average, or basking in unconditional praise despite lukewarm performance.

Feeling good about the self can yield benefits, such as positive emotions and the confidence to pursue goals. But society's eagerness to facilitate positive views of the self at all costs has created a dangerous imbalance. By focusing attention on the benefits of positive views of the self, we can easily overlook the dangers. We can certainly overlook the benefits of some rather unassuming virtues: humility and modesty.

What does it mean to be humble or modest, and why do we consider these qualities desirable? Although the present chapter addresses these questions from a psychological perspective, we acknowledge our debt to virtue ethicists, who have long debated the definitions and merits of humility and modesty (e.g., Ben-Ze'ev, 1993; N. Richards, 1988, 1992). Many theologians, devotional writers, and scholars of religious history have also written on these strengths of character (Casey, 2001; Murray, 2001). The past decade has also witnessed a surge of interest in the link between humility and science (Herrmann, 2000; Templeton, 1998) and in the role that humility might play within organizational and business settings (J. Collins, 2001).

In her review and critique of the existing theoretical literature, Tangney (2000, 2002) identified a number of humility's key features:

- an accurate (not underestimated) sense of one's abilities and achievements
- the ability to acknowledge one's mistakes, imperfections, gaps in knowledge, and limitations (often with reference to a "higher power")
- openness to new ideas, contradictory information, and advice
- keeping one's abilities and accomplishments in perspective
- relatively low focus on the self or an ability to "forget the self"
- appreciation of the value of all things, as well as the many different ways that people and things can contribute to our world

In contrast, the term *modesty* refers primarily to the moderate estimation of one's merits or achievements and also extends into other issues relating to propriety in dress and social behavior. Social psychological studies have often approached modesty in behavioral terms—for example, not taking full credit for success (Hareli & Weiner, 2000) or lowering estimates for one's future success when in the presence of another (Heatherington, Burns, & Gustafson, 1998).

■ Theoretical Traditions

We would like to take the analysis of humility and modesty a step further by trying to identify the crucial elements associated with these virtues. Our aim is not to make fine distinctions between modesty and humility but to emphasize common elements. Discussion will focus on humility, which we regard to be a private stance toward the evaluation of the self. We view modesty as a more socially oriented virtue, a style of presentation that can be consistent with an inner sense of humility but can also arise for other reasons, such as situational pressures and demands. Even those who are highly egotistical can behave modestly if they believe that modesty is appropriate in a particular situation. So, part of the script for being named MVP of a professional sports championship is to acknowledge the great effort of the loser, to thank God, and to mention one's team (all ostensible acts of modesty) and then to say, "I'm going to Disneyland" and to collect endorsement deals—certainly not acts of modesty.

The term *humility* has negative associations (Tangney, 2000). One might think of a humble person as weak and passive, with eyes downcast and lacking self-respect and confidence. Others might associate humility with humiliation, prompting images of shame, embarrassment, or disgust with the self. However, humility need not imply such negative views of the self. In fact, some humble individuals can have quite positive opinions of themselves (Exline & Geyer, in press) if they base their sense of worth on their intrinsic value (J. D. Brown, 1993), their good qualities (James, 1890), a sense of compassion toward the self (Neff, 2003, in press), their connections with other people (Leary & Baumeister, 2000), or their alignment with a higher power (Crocker & Wolfe, 2001).

What, then, is the essence of humility? We believe that humility involves a nondefensive willingness to see the self accurately, including both strengths and limitations. Humble individuals will not willfully distort information in order to defend, repair, or verify their own image (cf. Swann, 1997). For humble people, there should be no press toward self-importance and no burning need to see—or present—themselves as being better than they actually are (cf. chapter 11). They should also not be particularly interested in dominating others in order to receive entitlements or to elevate their own status. On the other hand, humility should not lead people to take harsh or condemning approaches toward themselves, magnifying weaknesses and severely punishing failures while overlooking strengths and successes.

Our perspective on humility implies a willingness to see the self accurately rather than the absolute attainment of accuracy. Nonetheless, from our perspective, accuracy is secondary to whether a person is willing and able to weigh information in a nondefensive way (cf. chapter 6). Granted, a person who is willing to take an objective look at the self should acquire a more accurate view than a person who defensively distorts. Thus, the accuracy of a person's appraisals could serve as a useful marker for humility. Whether or not complete accuracy is attained, the crucial point is that humble people welcome accurate information about themselves and thus should be teachable.

Some scholars have argued that humility implies people's ability to transcend a focus on the self or to view themselves from a broader perspective (Morgan, 2001; Murray, 2001; Statman, 1992; Tangney, 2000). People are humble to the extent that they consider their own small role in the universe, their weakness in comparison to an omnipotent God, or their indebtedness to other people. Some theorists have gone further, arguing that assumptions about a transcendent (and usually religious) reality are so fundamental to humility that the construct cannot truly be understood from a secular perspective. We take a less extreme view and propose that self-transcendent beliefs and experiences are not essential components of humility—we know humble people who are not religious—but that these beliefs can nonetheless facilitate humility (cf. chapters 23 and 27). For example, when students were asked to identify situations in which they felt humble, a number of them identified situations involving contemplation of natural wonders (Exline, Bushman, Faber, & Phillips, 2000; Exline & Geyer, in press).

In our view, humility and modesty do not require self-disparagement, negativity, or a contemptuous attitude toward the self. We would even argue for the theoretically interesting possibility that some self-deprecating individuals might exercise humility by overriding impulses to verify a negative view of the self (Swann, 1997). But research suggests that, by and large, people tend to distort in a self-enhancing rather than self-deprecating direction (D. G. Myers, 2000; S. E. Taylor & Brown, 1988), which means that humility usually takes the form of lowering rather than lifting one's evaluation of the self. Similarly, attempts at modesty should more frequently involve resisting the temptation to boast rather than the temptation to self-deprecate. The preponderance of self-enhancement bias may help to explain why lay and dictionary conceptions of humility so often involve low self-evaluations or feelings of smallness.

■ Measures

Attempts to assess modesty have been more straightforward than attempts to assess humility. Because modesty is a social virtue, self-presentational behaviors provide a way to tap the construct. For example, modesty can be operationalized as the tendency to give public credit to others for success (R. S. Miller & Schlenker, 1985) or to downplay predictions of one's future performance (Heatherington et al., 1998). Granted, purely behavioral measures are problematic. They do not allow researchers to detect whether a modest self-presentation stems from a genuinely modest or humble attitude or from other goals, such as a desire to follow social norms or to manipulate the perceptions of others. Nonetheless, these behavioral measures provide a good starting point for studying modesty.

Attempts to assess humility have proved more difficult (but see Table 20.1). Efforts to create simple self-report inventories have often yielded measures with low internal consistency (Tangney, 2000, 2002). Diverging opinions about the essential features of humility have no doubt contributed to low reliability. Given the continued efforts to refine the constructs of humility and modesty, we hope that an internally consistent measure might exist in the near future (see chapter 28). We nonetheless need to be open to the possibility that humility is not unidimensional, in part because it is often defined by what a person does *not* do. Humility, rather than involving the presence of certain thoughts or behaviors, might better be construed as the absence of narcissism, self-enhancement, or defensiveness. We shortly review studies using such proxy measures for low humility. Another alternative is to assess specific attitudes or behaviors related to humility without claiming to measure the whole construct.

Another problem with self-report measures involves social desirability. To what extent can we trust a person who reports that he or she is modest or humble? On the flip side, would an authentically humble person recognize that he or she is humble, or would such a person readily admit to any small sign of pride, thus appearing less humble on paper than he or she actually is? Some

TABLE 20.1   *Measures of Humility and Modesty*

Strategy (see text)

Self-report questionnaires (chapter 28)

Scenario methods

Proxy measures for *low* humility, e.g., narcissism, entitlement, self-enhancement, or defensiveness (e.g., Exline, Bushman, Campbell, & Baumeister, 2002)

Physiological responses to ego threat

"Think-aloud" paradigms in which people describe their goals and thought processes in situations involving ego threat

Comparing evaluations of the self to evaluations by others (e.g., Robins & John, 1997)

Comparing private vs. public self-evaluations (e.g., Shultz & Veschio, 2001)

data suggest that social desirability correlates positively with self-reported humility (Landrum, 2002). The waters are further muddied by the fact that people are even more likely to self-enhance in moral domains than in intellectual domains (Allison, Messick, & Goethals, 1989).

Given the inherent difficulty in the use of self-report to study humility and modesty, it seems wise to consider alternative measurement strategies. One worth exploring is the development of a scenario-based measure of humility that would contain humble and nonhumble items that are roughly equivalent in terms of social desirability. Similar approaches have been effective in assessing constructs such as shame and guilt (Tangney, 1995). Laboratory-based approaches to tap humility might also be considered, including physiological responses to ego threat, "think-aloud" paradigms in which people describe their goals and thought processes, or behavioral choices in situations involving ego threat.

Another avenue deserving further exploration is the use of experimental manipulations to put people in humble or nonhumble states of mind. The utility of such priming studies might depend partly on whether a state-based measure of humility can first be developed to serve as a manipulation check. Modest self-presentations might also serve as behavioral markers of humility.

In still another approach, people's evaluations of their personal attributes can be compared with reports made by others who know them well (D. L. Paulus, 1998; see Robins & John, 1997, for a review). Even without outside observers, other measurable criteria could be used as a basis for comparison, such as grade point averages or task performance (Krueger & Mueller, 2002). Using these discrepancy-based paradigms, a humble person would be someone whose self-report aligned quite closely with the self-reports of others (Tangney, 2000), rather than someone whose self-reports were much higher or lower than the reports of others.

A final option is to compare ratings of the self given in a private condition (i.e., when participants do not believe that others will be rating them) with those given in a public condition (i.e., when participants believe that friends or peers will also be rating them). A person whose self-ratings were very similar in both private and public conditions might be considered high in humility or modesty. A study using this method was reported by Shultz and Veschio (2001) and suggested that a low discrepancy between private and public scores was associated with higher humility as measured by self-report.

■ Correlates and Consequences

Given the problems surrounding measurement of humility and modesty, hard-headed empiricists might conclude that nothing is known about the correlates or consequences of these virtues. But such a conclusion is not warranted. Studies of related constructs have yielded some interesting results pertinent to humility. Because much of this research involves narcissism and its absence, we briefly turn our attention to narcissism before proceeding.

Although narcissistic personality disorder is a clinical condition, narcissism also appears more generally as a personality trait normally distributed in the general population. One hallmark of narcissism is a highly positive self-conception, including a belief that one is better than other people. In particular, narcissists' inflated beliefs reflect agentic concerns (e.g., intelligence, social extroversion). Narcissists do not necessarily see themselves as better than others on communal traits such as agreeableness or morality (W. K. Campbell, Rudich, & Sedikides, 2002).

The narcissist's highly positive view of the self is maintained in several ways. On an intrapersonal level, narcissists fantasize about fame and success and attribute failures to external factors. Interpersonally, narcissists are competitive and seek esteem by strategies like publicly outperforming others and winning admiration (Wallace & Baumeister, 2002). From a social point of view, feelings of entitlement are an especially important part of narcissism. Narcissists believe that they deserve special treatment and other benefits, and they are focused on collecting all that they deserve.

Narcissists derive some benefits from their lofty self-views, such as low social anxiety (Emmons, 1984; P. J. Watson & Biderman, 1993) and high self-esteem (R. N. Raskin, Novacek, & Hogan, 1991). They enjoy a belief in their own superior intelligence and physical attractiveness, although these flattering views of self do not have much basis in reality (Gabriel, Critelli, & Ee, 1994). Despite these benefits, the weight of evidence paints narcissism in unattractive colors. In particular, the benefits just cited all pertain to good feelings about the self and are probably the main reasons that people are drawn to become narcissistic. Yet when we look at the interpersonal sphere, we find major drawbacks of narcissism. Here, humility seems a better option.

If people are not preoccupied with maintaining highly positive self-views, they will not lash out at others who threaten or challenge their self-views. Narcissists score high on questionnaire measures of competitiveness (P. J. Watson, Morris, & Miller, 1997–1998), dominance (Emmons, 1984), hostility (P. L. Hart & Joubert, 1996), and anger (McCann & Biaggo, 1989). Laboratory work confirms that narcissists show high levels of aggression, particularly when their sense of superiority is questioned (Bushman & Baumeister, 1998; Rhodewalt & Morf, 1998). They appear hypersensitive to threats to their esteem and willing to react with anger at any sign of disrespect. In the worst case, defensively high self-esteem sets the stage for violence (Baumeister, Smart, & Boden, 1996).

A sense of psychological entitlement—in which people are preoccupied with their own rights and overestimate the amount that is owed to them—is also associated with aggressive and unforgiving behavior. For example, studies using the Prisoner's Dilemma Game suggest a negative interpersonal role of entitlement (cf. R. Axelrod, 1980a, 1980b). This game gives people a series of chances either to cooperate with another player or to defect. Although long-term outcomes are best if both players cooperate, cooperating can also leave a player vulnerable to exploitation. The game creates the temptation to defect in order to take advantage of the other player, assuming that he or she cooperates. Entitled people are more likely than others to defect on the very first turn, to defect frequently during the game, and to respond with aggressive messages when provoked by the other player (Exline et al., 2000). Narcissistic entitlement also predicts antisocial responses in the wake of transgression. Bushman and Baumeister (2002) found that violent criminals scored significantly higher on personal entitlement than did college students. This finding is ironic because incarceration removes rather than bestows entitlements. Narcissistic entitlement has also been associated with less forgiveness (Exline et al., 2000).

In sharp contrast with entitled feelings, humble self-views may curb conflict escalation. In a Prisoner's Dilemma study, participants began by writing about a time when they felt humble, a time when they felt important, or no essay (Exline et al., 2000). They then played the game against an opponent (actually a computer program) who defected on the first turn. Males who had written humble essays waited longer to defect than males who had written important essays or no essay. Content coding suggested that individual interpretations of the word *humility* were critical. The players who waited the longest to defect were those who wrote about a time when they saw themselves from a larger perspective—not an incident in which they felt ashamed, guilty, or foolish.

In the wake of transgression, a willingness to look at one's flaws prompts people to seek and offer forgiveness (Means, Wilson, Sturm, Biron, & Bach, 1990; Sandage, 1999; Sandage, Worthington, Hight, & Berry, 2000). As demonstrated in one study, people induced to feel morally similar (rather than superior) to a perpetrator rated the perpetrator's offense as more forgivable (Exline, Baumeister, Faber, & Holland, 2002). Parallel results have been found in autobiographical recall studies: People are more forgiving to the extent that they can see their own capability for committing an act like the one done to them (Exline, Bushman, Campbell, & Baumeister, 2002). Narcissism, in contrast, is negatively associated with the seeking of forgiveness (Sandage et al., 2000).

To what extent are modest or humble people liked? Despite a stereotype that high self-esteem makes a person more likable, the evidence is more complicated. Positive self-views lead people to think they are more likable, just as they lead them to think they are more attractive and intelligent. And narcissists may initially be viewed as charming (Masterson, 1988). They surround themselves with admirers and try to associate with popular and attractive others (W. K. Campbell, 1999). However, the charms of a narcissist soon wear thin, leaving others with impressions of superficiality, hostility, and arrogance (D. L. Paulus, 1998). Narcissists are also more willing to behave in ways likely to provoke interpersonal conflict, such as cheating on dating partners (W. K. Campbell & Foster, 2002) and taking credit from close others on interdependent tasks (W. K. Campbell, Sedikides, Reeder, & Elliot, 2000).

In terms of self-enhancement more generally, Colvin, Block, and Funder (1995) studied people who overvalued themselves (relative to how others saw them) and found that other people reacted negatively to them even in a first meeting. Individuals who evidenced inflated self-views were self-centered. They interrupted others and showed little interest in what others had to say. These findings also hold in clinical settings: Among youthful psychiatric inpatients, Perez, Pettit, David, Kistner, and Joiner (2001) found that those with very high self-esteem reported the fewest interpersonal problems, but they were the least liked by their fellow patients.

Why is it so easy to dislike those who think too highly of themselves? For one thing, an intense self-focus works against close relationships by precluding empathy, caring, and commitment. Not surprisingly, each of these prosocial qualities is negatively associated with narcissism (W. K. Campbell, 1999; W. K. Campbell & Foster, 2002). A person who overvalues the self may brag, and braggarts are universally disliked (Godfrey, Jones, & Lord, 1986; Leary, Bednarski, Hammon, & Duncan, 1997). An inflated self-view—particularly if it involves feelings of entitlement—will also preclude equitable division of tasks and rewards (Ross & Sicoly, 1979). Narcissists also have difficulty acknowledging or expressing gratitude (McCullough, Kilpatrick, Emmons, & Larson, 2001), another tendency likely to lead to social resentment and rifts.

Humble individuals, in contrast, have fewer needs to impress and dominate others, and they should also be less preoccupied with collecting special benefits for themselves. This may also help explain why in communal cultures, where social networks are quite stable and getting along with a fixed, unchangeable group of people is an important challenge throughout life, egotism is held in disregard, whereas humility is strongly encouraged (Heine, Lehman, Markus, & Kitayama, 1999; Markus & Kitayama, 1991). Even in American culture, self-promotion is most common among new acquaintances; in established friendships, modesty becomes more the norm (Tice, Butler, Muraven, & Stillwell, 1995).

Is it possible that the benefits of humility and modesty are entirely interpersonal? Do modest and humble people maintain good relationships by sacrificing their own interests entirely? To the contrary, we believe that a humble approach is likely to carry some potent benefits for the individual, both in terms of emotional well-being and self-regulation. Although some evidence suggests that positive distortions may promote mental health (S. E. Taylor & Brown, 1988) and physical health (S. E. Taylor, Kemeny, Reed, Bower & Gruenewald, 2000), other studies find that positive distortions are indicative of personality pathology, particularly of the narcissistic and antisocial types (cf. Asendorpf & Ostendorf, 1998; Colvin et al., 1995). Individuals who frequently enhance themselves may base their self-evaluations on grounds that are fragile (see also Kernis, Cornell, Sun, Berry, & Harlow, 1993). Threats to self-esteem should therefore be common, and frequent negative affect ensues.

A humble self-view may aid in self-regulation attempts (H. M. Weiss & Knight, 1980). Under conditions of ego threat, for example, humility may protect people from taking foolish risks and making poor decisions. When facing threats to self-image, proud people can become preoccupied with maximizing their esteem at any cost. In laboratory settings, for example, people with high self-esteem facing ego threat often set inappropriately risky goals far beyond their capabilities (Baumeister, Heatherton, & Tice, 1993). A humble person, having less reason to defend self-esteem, should thus take a more cautious approach and be less likely to fail.

Humble people should benefit in other ways by being free of self-preoccupation. When individuals strive to maintain a certain image of self, they may find that doing so creates a psychological burden. The load may become so heavy that it prompts a need to escape, sometimes through destructive means such as substance abuse, masochism, eating disorders, or even suicide (Baumeister, 1991). A more humble approach, particularly if accompanied by the ability for self-transcendence, should preclude this need to escape. On a related note, narcissism has been linked with unstable self-esteem (Rhodewalt, Madrian, & Cheney, 1998), suggesting that narcissists are likely to spend considerable energy working to maintain their inflated self-images. The humble person, in contrast, should be able to conserve emotional and psychological energy by not having to constantly defend the self-image from threat.

Finally, cross-cultural research suggests that willingness to self-criticize, if moderated, may ultimately help people move toward self-improvement goals (Heine et al., 2001). Personal deficits will be addressed only if we are willing to see that they exist.

■ Development

We propose that factors that promote secure attachment also lay the foundation for humility (cf. Bowlby, 1973; chapter 13). Secure attachment provides a sense of security that can serve as a buffer against the effects of negative feedback. A sense of security by itself should be insufficient to foster humility, however, because a highly secure person might become arrogant if not given realistic feedback. In order to become humble, it seems crucial that a child learn that both positive feedback and negative feedback are worth considering. Such lessons could come from parental modeling of humility, or they might come from humbling feedback. Reality-based feedback from a parent or teacher about one's strengths and weaknesses would probably be especially useful, particularly if conveyed in an atmosphere of caring and respect. Other sources of humbling feedback might include awe-inspiring experiences, educational approaches that emphasize the limits of human knowledge, or situations in which a person encounters failure or disappointment.

On the flip side, it is easy to think of factors that would work against the development of humility. To give just a few examples, we propose that humility would be unlikely to stem from parenting or educational styles that involve (a) an extreme emphasis on performance, appearance, popularity, or other external sources of self-evaluation, particularly if combined with perfectionist performance standards; (b) inaccurate, excessive praise or criticism; (c) frequent comparison of the child against siblings or peers, especially if this comparison is accompanied by competitive messages; and (d) communicating to the child that he or she is superior or inferior to other people. Such practices would predispose a child to turn to external sources of validation for a sense of security, and they would also encourage the child to make competitive, invidious comparisons.

■ Enabling and Inhibiting Factors

Because identity development is a necessary condition for the presence of humility or modesty, factors that facilitate this process will undoubtedly foster the development of these two virtues, namely, "appearance of attachment, the development of a sense of self, the emergence of independence in infancy, openness to new experiences, experience with decision making, and life review and integration in old age" (Santrock, 1996, pp. 332–333). Democratic parenting facilitates adolescents' identity development; autocratic and permissive parenting does not. Cooper, Baker, Polichar, and Welsh (1992; see also Cooper & Grotevant, 1989) showed that connectedness in family relations facilitates identity formation, whereas Hauser and colleagues (1984) found that enabling behaviors (such as explaining, giving empathy, and accepting) promote identity development more than constraining behaviors (such as judging and devaluing). These factors and other disciplinary and family interaction styles only indirectly foster the development of modesty and humility. Direct influences (both positive and negative) on these virtues remain unexplored to date.

■ Gender, Cross-National, and Cross-Cultural Aspects

A number of studies suggest more modest self-presentation in women than in men (Berg, Stephan, & Dodson, 1981; Heatherington et al., 1998; see Exline & Lobel, 1999, for a discussion). Because of the measurement problems surrounding humility, we are not aware of any data that directly address gender differences in humility. However, women in general have slightly lower self-esteem than men (Kling, Hyde, Showers, & Buswell, 1999), and narcissism also tends to be higher in males than in females (L. Carroll, 1989).

It seems reasonable to predict that both modesty and humility would be more highly valued in communal or collectivist cultures than in those in which independence and individualism are prized. For example, a substantial body of research suggests that modesty is assigned higher value in Japanese culture, which is collectivist, than in American culture, which is individualist (Heine et al., 1999, 2001; Markus & Kitayama, 1991).

Finally, cross-cultural research suggests that willingness to self-criticize, if moderated, may ultimately help people move toward self-improvement goals (e.g., Heine et al., 2001). Personal deficits will be addressed only if we are willing to see that they exist. For example, empirical data suggest that success in "12-step" recovery programs for addictions may be especially difficult for narcissists, as narcissists find it difficult to acknowledge their own limitations (K. E. Hart & Huggett, 2003; Kurtz & Ketcham, 1992).

■ Deliberate Interventions

Given the potential benefits of humility and modesty, we must ask whether individuals can cultivate these attributes. In order for individuals to become more humble or modest, they need to override tendencies to inflate their self-images. A large body of work in social cognition suggests the existence of a pervasive drive to be better and to feel better than average (S. E. Taylor & Brown, 1988). The research focus on biases, illusions, and inaccuracies creates a rather pessimistic outlook (despite the claim that cognitive illusions are healthy). However, some evidence suggests that self-serving distortions may not be quite as common as some psychologists propose. The ostensibly high prevalence of egocentric distortions reported in the literature is partly a consequence of how these distortions are measured (Krueger, 1998a; Krueger & Funder, in press). A significant difference between self-related and other-related judgments, however small it might be, is usually taken to support the view that people, in general, are biased. Yet, by definition, many people are better than average on the dimensions of interest in these studies, meaning that not everyone with a positive self-image is engaging in self-enhancement. Once we can distinguish those who are distorting the facts from those who are seeing themselves clearly, the story of self-enhancement will become a more accurate (and more humble) one (Krueger & Mueller, 2002).

If self-enhancement is understood as a motivated and partially controllable strategy, and not as a cognitive illusion, humility seems to be within reach for most. In one study, self-enhancement was assessed by two independent measures (Krueger, 1998b). The first measure was the traditional difference between self-descriptions and descriptions of most other people. The second measure was the partial correlation (computed for each participant) between ratings of trait descriptiveness and ratings of perceived trait desirability while the group averages of these desirability ratings (i.e., social desirability) were controlled. On both measures, most participants self-enhanced. However, there was little evidence for self-enhancement among participants in a second group that was asked to estimate the social desirability of each trait (i.e., the average desirability rating obtained from the group). These participants were able to ignore their idiosyncratic definitions of trait desirability. These findings suggest that self-enhancement can be viewed as a controllable bias rather than a cognitive illusion. A simple request for a change in perspective may help to reduce such distortions. If this is true, then there is some hope that people can learn to override their tendencies to self-enhance. Another set of findings from J. Katz and Joiner (2002) is also encouraging. Across three studies, the authors found that when people received feedback about themselves from others (dating partners and roommates), they preferred accurate feedback—even when this information was relatively negative. Thus, in the service of accuracy, people do seem willing to accept some negative feedback.

Religiousness similarly fosters humility by encouraging self-transcendence. Eastern traditions such as Zen Buddhism and Taoism associate humility with a process of letting go of the self while simultaneously connecting with a greater reality (Watts, 1960). In monotheistic traditions such as Judaism, Islam, and Christianity, humility is often associated with submission before God (Fromm, 1941; Morgan, 2001; Murray, 2001). Yet simply feeling small or dependent might not be sufficient to lead to the nondefensive stance that we associate with humility. In fact, a constant sense of being lowered might lead some individuals to a sense of shame or insignificance. In order for religions to promote humility as we have defined it, they need to encourage people to see themselves not only as small but also as valuable and safe.

The basic research just cited offers some hope for the cultivation of humility and modesty. Nonetheless, we are not aware of formal interventions specifically designed to increase these strengths. As mentioned earlier, self-help groups that follow a 12-step model, such as Alcoholics Anonymous or Narcotics Anonymous, might be effective in fostering humility (Kurtz & Ketcham, 1992). Similarly, character development programs, spiritual disciplines, and psychotherapeutic interventions could also be effective in increasing humility. However, empirical tests in any of these areas are lacking.

Although empirical data are sparse, existing theory and research do suggest some strategies that might facilitate humility-related goals such as accuracy, self-transcendence, and a willingness to lower one's self-evaluation in a specific area. To foster accurate self-evaluation, for example, it would seem crucial to provide people with accurate feedback about both their strengths and their limitations, preferably from an early age. Techniques from the literature on awe (chapter 23) could be used to foster self-transcendent ability. Christian devotional literature suggests a number of behavioral techniques that could work against self-enhancement, ranging from doing menial chores to washing another person's feet (done ceremonially in some churches). Seeking forgiveness or keeping a gratitude journal might also be humbling, as each of these behaviors might make people more aware of their indebtedness to others. The development of close relationships might also facilitate greater humility and modesty. For example, some research suggests that the self-serving bias is reduced or eliminated in the context of friendships (W. K. Campbell et al., 2000). Modest self-presentations are also more likely between friends than between strangers (Tice et al., 1995).

Any or all of these interventions might increase modesty or humility, although direct empirical tests are needed. Yet we strongly suspect that these techniques, by themselves, will be insufficient to induce humble states of mind—much less increases in humility as a trait—unless they lead to a lifestyle change. We hasten to add that this conclusion probably holds for attempts to encourage any character strength, although it is particularly obvious in the case of humility.

Another potential problem is that if people receive feedback that is self-discrepant or emotionally painful to accept, they might simply not internalize it. Such problems could occur even when feedback is positive, if such information is discrepant with a negative or depressive self-view (Swann, 1997).

Any of the preceding approaches could backfire if they cause a person to feel helpless, shamed, or insignificant—feelings that could, in turn, cause negative emotion or reactance. People often defend against threat by self-enhancing or behaving aggressively. It is easy to imagine that something similar might occur with behavioral "lowering" techniques. To use the examples just cited, if someone were induced to clean toilets or to wash another person's feet in the service of humility, he or she might resist. Worse, such exercises might lead to a sense of degradation or shame that would work against the ultimate goal of increased humility. In short, successful humility inductions might require a delicate balance: They need to prompt a person to reduce self-focus or gain a new perspective on the self without feeling that the self has been obliterated or damaged.

As noted, we believe that people will be more willing and able to cultivate humility if they have a sense of security or value not entirely dependent on self-evaluative assessments. We therefore propose that any technique, resource, or relationship that would provide a person with alternate means of feeling safe—besides their own self-evaluation—would facilitate humility. A sense of safety could come from religion, from secure attachments to parents or close others, or from significant others who communicate unconditional positive regard (C. R. Rogers, 1961). It might also prove helpful for people to observe role models who are able and willing to accept both positive and negative information about themselves without overreacting. Regardless of the means used, the goal would be to enable the individual to feel safe enough to nondefensively acknowledge both strengths and limitations.

What Is Not Known?

Here are some of the important questions about modesty and humility not yet answered by research:

- Is it possible to create a measure that effectively differentiates between humility and modesty?
- Do modesty and humility have more positive manifestations than the simple absence of arrogance, boasting, and entitlement?
- How do modesty and humility vary across the life span? Because very young children are necessarily egocentric, at what age can we expect these strengths to appear, and relatedly, at what age would deliberate interventions to encourage modesty and humility have any effect?
- How do modesty and humility manifest themselves across sociodemographic contrasts in the United States and other countries: for example, gender, cohort, ethnicity, and religion?
- Does everyone have a potential to develop these strengths? Do actions motivated by these virtues come more easily for some individuals than for others?
- What types of intervention programs might be developed to foster the development of modesty and humility? Can we ensure that these programs are truly fostering the development of the internal conception of the world held by those who are truly humble, or would they only serve to minimize negative self-presentation (false modesty)?

Must-Read Articles and Books

Baumeister, R. F., Smart, L., & Boden, J. M. (1996). Relation of threatened egotism to violence and aggression: The dark side of high self-esteem. *Psychological Review, 103,* 5–33.

Casey, M. (2001). *A guide to living in the truth: Saint Benedict's teaching on humility.* Liguori, MO: Liguori/Triumph.

Murray, A. (2001). *Humility: The journey toward holiness.* Bloomington, MN: Bethany House.

Richards, N. (1992). *Humility.* Philadelphia: Temple University Press.

Tangney, J. (2000). Humility: Theoretical perspectives, empirical findings and directions for future research. *Journal of Social and Clinical Psychology, 19,* 70–82.

Tangney, J. P. (2002). Humility. In C. R. Snyder & S. J. Lopez (Eds.), *Handbook of positive psychology* (pp. 411–419). New York: Oxford University Press.

21. PRUDENCE

■   *Fred Soper (1893–1975) was a key figure in international public health who led efforts to control and eradicate malaria. In this leadership role, he displayed many of the characteristic strengths that make up prudence. He was strongly oriented to a future in which malaria was no longer a major source of death and suffering in the developing world, and in designing and implementing interventions that would take years to bear fruit, given the scale of the undertaking. He was notable for the self-discipline he demanded of himself and his public health workers, and the carefulness of his planning of eradication campaigns, in which every activity was orchestrated with a strategic and almost military precision that was largely new to the field.*

Soper's planning seems to have been eminently practical, as he distrusted purely technical malaria control proposals that recommended drug treatment of infected individuals, favoring a pragmatic approach based on fieldwork dedicated to preventing infection by killing mosquitoes. His eradication plans were cleverly tailored to the diverse physical and cultural conditions in which he worked—for example, differing modesty conventions affecting methods of applying pesticides to the body—and the distinct ecologies of the many species of mosquito involved, revealing the characteristic flexibility of prudent conduct. Finally, all these plans were developed and enacted with a consequentialist and deliberative frame of mind, one focused on efficacy and based on careful calculation of the intensity of the needed interventions and their likely benefits in preventing morbidity and mortality. The campaigns that Soper led were, in general, highly successful; it has been estimated that they saved 10 million lives worldwide (Gladwell, 2001).

It is not clear to what extent Soper exemplified prudence in his personal life, and he seems not to have exemplified some other virtues, being described as somewhat cold and domineering. However, in his life's work he clearly demonstrated prudent reasoning and conduct, and the social benefits that they can yield when harnessed to a valued goal. ■

■ Consensual Definition

Prudence is a cognitive orientation to the personal future, a form of practical reasoning and self-management that helps to achieve the individual's long-term goals effectively. Prudent individuals show a farsighted and deliberative concern for the consequences of their actions and decisions, successfully resist impulses and other choices that satisfy shorter term goals at the expense of longer term ones, have a flexible and moderate approach to life, and strive for balance among their goals and ends.

In everyday life, good examples of prudence include saving for the future; planning for unexpected as well as expected contingencies; avoiding situations known to have led in the past to impulsive choices; making life decisions by considering distant as well as immediate benefits and costs, and by paying heed to their probable consistency or conflict with one's other plans; and deliberating about one's personal goals in a pragmatic manner.

Individuals with this strength have the following attributes:

- They take a foresighted stance toward their personal future, thinking and caring about it, planning for it, and holding long-term goals and aspirations.
- They are skilled at resisting self-defeating impulses and at persisting in beneficial activities that lack immediate appeal.
- They show a style of thinking about everyday life choices that is reflective, deliberate, and practical.
- They harmonize the multiple goals and interests that motivate them, forming these into a stable, coherent, and unconflicted form of life.

Some popular misconceptions about prudence must also be dispelled:

- It does not imply excessive caution, thrift, compulsive self-restraint, timid conformity, or lack of spontaneity; it involves flexible and moderate self-management, not self-denying inhibition or compliance with rigid rules.
- It is not selfish or coldly calculative; despite being primarily about personal goals and interests rather than moral rules and societal conventions, many of these goals and interests are likely to refer to positive relationships and the well-being of others.
- It applies to the whole of life, not just to the spheres of money, work, and narrowly conceived achievement.

■ Theoretical Traditions

The history of prudence is usually traced back to Aristotle's (1984) writings on *phronesis*, a concept that held a central role in his virtue-based ethical system and is usually translated as "practical reason" or "practical wisdom." In his influential exegeses of Aristotle, Aquinas referred to this virtue as *prudentia*, a term derived by contraction from the Latin *provideo*, meaning "foresight" or "farsightedness" (Zagzebski, 1996). It is to Aquinas that we owe the modern term.

For Aristotle, *phronesis* occupied a central place among the virtues. Although he rather sharply distinguished intellectual and moral virtues, one governing reason and the other the appetites, he installed *phronesis* as a bridging virtue. Although it was in essence an intellectual virtue, it had a clear moral dimension, and in its absence moral virtue was considered impossible. As a result, the prudent person should also be more morally virtuous than the imprudent; more conscientious, dependable, just, trustworthy, and so on. In addition to enabling moral virtue, as Zagzebski (1996) noted, *phronesis* allows us to see the big picture of our conduct and thereby to mediate among the other virtues in particular contexts.

The general end of *phronesis* was to govern the appetites in the service of self-management, but to think of it simply as impulse control or inhibition is to simplify and misconstrue Aristotle's sophisticated psychology. Although long and textured philosophical commentaries on this psychology are available (e.g., Charles, 1984; D. N. Robinson, 1989; N. Sherman, 1989), here it is sufficient to point to a few of the fundamental ways in which, for Aristotle and his tradition, *phronesis* is not in any straightforward sense equivalent to self-restraint. First, it involves not simply suppression of impulse in the here and now but farsighted concern and planning for the more distant future; in short, it is a proactive and goal-directed orientation more than steely self-denial. Second, it does not counsel constant self-restraint, but rather a moderate and flexible approach to self-management. This theme of moderation and balance also includes the harmonizing of multiple goals or ends. Third, it is not simply a capacity to control impulse but a form of reasoning or wisdom. Each of these components of prudence as conceptualized by Aristotle and his followers is discussed briefly in this chapter. An extended discussion is presented in Haslam (1991) and in Haslam and Baron (1994).

As we have seen, *phronesis* or prudence is linked to foresight, which ought to be associated with better impulse control. However, it is much more to Aristotle than just a self-control tactic—thinking about a future outcome that might be endangered by an impulsive choice—that is adopted at the time an impulse arises. Instead, it is a general concern for the future and for life as a temporally extended and integrated whole. Zagzebski (1996) made use of this extended sense of the prudential future by quoting Aquinas: "Prudence is of good counsel about matters regarding man's entire life, and the end [i.e., purpose] of human life" (p. 230). The prudent person does not simply weigh the foreseen benefits of self-control against the immediate benefit of impulse expression but takes a broadly planful approach to life.

For Aristotle, moreover, this planfulness does not extend only to the means of accomplishing one's ends but also to the choice of ends themselves. That is, *phronesis* is directed to pursuing farsighted goals and pursuing them in an organized and effective fashion. Indeed, Aristotle presents the ideally prudent person as someone who, being motivated by right appetite, is not prey to impulse in the first place, desiring only what is good. In short, *phronesis* or prudence involves a much richer sense of foresight and concern for the future than any simple analysis of self-control implies. It also provides a distinctive account of impulse control, seeing this as enabled by a particular kind of organized, proactive, and goal-oriented stance toward longer term ends and interests.

A fundamental feature of Aristotelian thinking about *phronesis*, like other virtues, is that it strives for the mean, in the sense of a degree of optimal moderation between extremes. In the case of prudence, the more familiar extreme is impulsiveness or rashness, behavior or choice that is ill considered, neglectful of future consequences, impetuous, fickle, and self-defeating. Less familiar is the other pole, marked by rigidity, brittleness, or stubbornness, behavior or choice that is too inflexibly rule-governed to respond adequately to the situation as the person finds it. Such an approach to one's action—which today we might call compulsiveness—is just as imprudent as impulsiveness as it equally fails to heed and promote the person's long-term best interest. Aristotle does not, therefore, equate *phronesis* with self-restraint or impulse control but with a point on a continuum that implies flexibility and moderation.

This theme of moderation arises in two other places with *phronesis*. In the first case, the virtue is seen to play a role in coordinating and mediating among the other virtues, deciding how and when each is to be applied in the course of action. Second, several authors have noted how Aristotle argues that part of *phronesis* is the cultivation of multiple goals or ends that do not conflict but are co-satisfiable (Charles, 1984), forming a coherent set. As N. Sherman (1989) wrote, choice making for Aristotle is not simply "a process of promoting the means to single ends, but a process of promoting ends in the light of other ends, where overall fit and mutual adjustment of ends will be as important as efficiency" (p. 6). Prudence therefore implies a balance and harmony among the person's aims, aspirations, and plans. It should therefore play a mediating role in other strengths, for example, ensuring that hope is tempered by realism, that purpose is not too single-minded and blind to the person's other goals, and that self-regulation is not pursued in an overly harsh or constricting way.

The common translation of *phronesis* as practical reason or practical wisdom conveys the important point that prudence is primarily a cognitive or intellective virtue, not simply a capacity for restraining impulse. Aristotle distinguished *phronesis* both from a speculative form of intellect and from skill, its focus being not on abstract knowing or concrete making but on doing or practical action. Rather than being a specific skill in self-control or a generic intelligence, that is, prudence is a deliberative form of thinking that is oriented to action in the context of the practical affairs that bear on the person.

Summing up this account of Aristotelian prudence is difficult, but the definition presented at the beginning of this chapter is a reasonable approximation. The important observation for our present purposes is that *phronesis* or prudence is a rather complex concept that has multiple elements and is conceptually distinct from, and irreducible to, more familiar related concepts such as self-control, constraint, practical intelligence, and so on.

Skipping from ancient Greece to the present day, prudence has acquired a somewhat narrower and different sense. It is now most commonly employed in the domain of financial management, where it typically refers to the soundness of decisions about investment and spending, or in relation to high-level policy decisions. In popular usage, prudent decisions are those that indicate a sound consideration and weighing of the person's long-term interests and of the risks that the future may bring. Imprudence is usually ascribed to rash decisions that are metaphorically myopic, failing to consider outcomes beyond a nearby time horizon and taking excessive risks. Much less commonly, imprudence is attributed to someone whose decisions depart from economic rationality in the opposite direction, shying away from all risk and overweighing the future with respect to the present.

This prevailing image of prudence as something primarily economic or governmental arguably reflects a degree of cultural ambivalence toward the concept; it is held at arm's length and seen as the province of men in suits. Prudence has come to have a Victorian connotation. This seems to derive in large measure from an image of the prudent person as someone who is constricted, nonspontaneous, frightened of risk, and thrifty with money and emotion—someone, in short, who violates the values of self-expression, personal growth, free-spiritedness, and consumerism. Our contention is that such an image is a caricature. On the present understanding, prudence is neither confined to the financial domain nor equivalent to constriction or grayness of the soul. Indeed, prudence needs to be rescued from its confining connotations and understood as a strength or virtue that has broad relevance and implies harmony and balance at least as much as constraint, caution, and conformity.

Contemporary psychology rarely entertains prudence by that name. The term is lightly scattered across several areas of study, where it has subtly different connotations. Despite the term's disuse, the meanings that emerge from the discussions of prudence in Aristotle and his interpreters resonate with many traditions of psychological research and theory. Four domains in which the fundamental components of prudence resonate most deeply will be discussed here. One of the foremost is trait psychology, an obvious place to seek a modern rendering of prudence conceptualized as an individual difference.

Many trait psychologists have converged on a factor-analytically derived model of personality that proposes five broad dimensions underlying and organizing the myriad of described traits. This five-factor model is of interest because of its well-replicated structure (chapter 3) and because one of its dimensions seems to correspond quite closely to the domain of attributes described by theorists of prudence through the ages. This dimension is most often labeled *conscientiousness*, although other authors have identified the same or closely related factors as will, constraint, orderliness, superego strength, (lack of) impulsivity, compulsiveness, and work orientation. R. Hogan and Hogan (1992) explicitly designated it prudence.

Whatever the merits of particular factor labels, prototypical descriptive markers of the dimension developed by John (e.g., John & Srivastava, 1999) reveal its distinctive flavor, which closely resembles the qualities attributed to the prudent person by Aristotelians. Among the highest loading of these are *organized, thorough, planful, efficient, responsible, conscientious, practical,* and *deliberate. Foresighted* also loads on this factor (Costa, McCrae, & Dye, 1991). Strong negative loadings convey the opposites of these characteristics: *careless, disorderly, frivolous,* and *irresponsible*. In the most influential formulation of the five-factor model (Costa & McCrae, 1992), *conscientiousness* is counterposed to lack of direction and is proposed to have *competence, order, dutifulness, achievement striving, self-discipline,* and *deliberation* as facets. Although no collections of trait terms such as these can fully capture the concept of prudence, most of these terms are clearly in its orbit. They point to behavioral, cognitive, and volitional tendencies that promote the pursuit of longer term ends, implying an orientation to and concern for the future, a practically intelligent and reflective process of deliberative thinking, and a capacity to pursue goals successfully through well-coordinated action that avoids derailment by impulsive choices.

Despite its broad-brush correspondence with the conscientiousness factor, this trait psychological approach to prudence has several limitations. First, it supplies an inductively generated summary description of a personality domain rather than a theoretical formulation of the processes that underlie it, the concept of prudence being one such formulation. Prudence frames this trait domain in terms of a theory of practical rationality and future-oriented self-management. Other theoretical framings, including those implied by some alternative labels for the factor, represent the factor in terms of social conformity, willpower, superego strength, achievement motivation, or serotonin levels, although we would argue that the prudential account is richer and more accurate.

Second, and as a result of the atheoretical nature of the conscientiousness factor, it does not and cannot incorporate fundamental elements of prudence. In particular, it neglects the cognitive aspects of prudence that have to do with practical reasoning and consideration of the future, and the volitional aspects that have to do with the moderation and the balancing of goals. Neither of these aspects is easily captured by personality trait descriptors, referring more to dynamic processes rather than static attributes, to intellective rather than personality variables, and to complex conceptual analyses rather than simple descriptive terms. As a result, the conscientiousness factor cannot do full justice to the depth of the concept of prudence, even if it captures rather well the traits of the prudent individual.

Third, the factor is arguably somewhat broader in scope than the concept of prudence typically has been. Traditional understandings of prudence would seem, for example, to refer to facets of conscientiousness such as deliberation, self-discipline, and competence more than to dutifulness, order, and achievement striving. Similarly, trait terms such as *organized, thorough,* and *responsible* seem less central to prudence as described here than do planful, deliberate, or, in contrast, careless and unimpulsive. Prudence-related traits might therefore be conceptualized as composing a subdomain within the broader factor or as elements within this factor that the concept of prudence brings to the foreground, treating the other elements as attributes that covary with or derive from prudence without being at its conceptual core. In the former case, components of the conscientiousness factor would be excluded from prudence, whereas in the latter they would simply be treated as incidental but correlated aspects of it.

Whether excluded or de-emphasized, these less central components of prudence can be approximately distinguished by their focus on compliance with moral or societal norms, on the rule-governedness of behavior, or on narrowly work-related values. These components are elevated to factor-defining status by proposed factor labels such as superego strength and norm-favoring, compulsiveness and constraint, and will to achievement and work orientation, respectively. Each of these deviates from the theoretical core of prudence in different ways: the first because prudence is normally understood to refer primarily to the pursuit of personal goals and ends rather than shared moral or societal ones, the second because prudence is not conceptualized simply as restraint and suppression but as flexible self-management, and the third because prudence is, in theory, germane to the whole of life, not just the modern school or office.

Our favored analysis is to incorporate but de-emphasize the traits that fall under these three headings in an operational trait psychology definition of prudence. These traits are, we would argue, incidentally but truly related to the more fundamental aspects of prudence. For example, prudent people are less apt to disregard and violate moral or social rules (e.g., irresponsibility) because doing so often involves impulsive choices that are unwise and contrary to their interests, either directly or indirectly by harming their valued relationships and social reputations. As Aristotle argued, prudence enables moral virtue. Prudent people are more apt to appear constrained and to abide by rules of conduct because they are able—not compelled—to practice self-discipline and hold themselves to personal rules and standards when required. In addition, because impulsive myopia is more of an ever-present motivational challenge for people than is excessively farsighted delay of gratification, more prudent people may appear to be more constrained. Finally, work-related achievement striving is only incidentally related to prudence because prudent people have the self-management capacities and planfulness that promote achievement in work as well as other settings. In a later section it will be shown that prudence is associated with a variety of positive outcomes and qualities that extend far beyond the workplace. In short, these conscientiousness-related traits are indeed associated with prudence, but they are at the same time conceptually secondary to it.

Despite the limitations discussed in the foregoing, trait psychology represents a useful approach to the study of prudence. It helps to locate it within a well-mapped landscape of individual differences and implies by its relatively close correspondence with one of the primary personality factors that it represents a coherent psychological domain rather than a hodgepodge of empirically unrelated attributes. In addition, the trait psychological approach allows researchers to assess prudence by proxy using measures of conscientiousness, thereby enabling investigations of its causes, effects, and correlates. Some of the other components of prudence are more subtle and complex, and therefore more difficult to measure.

In sum, trait psychology affords a valuable approach to the study of prudence by mapping and measuring the conscientiousness factor. This factor can be taken provisionally as an operational definition of the concept so long as investigators remember several things: (a) that the factor may be somewhat broader in scope than prudence; (b) that although it may descriptively capture the static attributes of the prudent personality, it does not incorporate the theoretically formulated cognitive and motivational processes underpinning prudence; and (c) that it may be partly tied to a simplified view of prudence as control and constraint rather than as balance and harmony. More succinctly, the conscientiousness factor can be viewed as a useful but theoretically agnostic model of the attributes associated with prudence, which can be framed in terms of a theory of that concept.

Quite distinct from the tradition of trait psychological research on prudence is a line of work that addresses the more intellectual side of the concept. A move to recognize a broader sense of intelligent conduct than the primarily school-related problem-solving capacities that constitute IQ has been pioneered by Sternberg and his colleagues (e.g., Sternberg & Wagner, 1986). They promote a concept of practical intelligence whose substantial overlap with prudence is attested by Wagner and Sternberg's (1986) claim that a crucial aspect of it is the extent to which the future is planfully and purposively anticipated. Sternberg's group has found that laypeople typically hold an intuitive understanding of intelligence that includes the sorts of cognitive attributes and strengths that figure in discussions of prudence, such as practical know-how and wisdom.

Consistent with this work, Räty, Snellman, and Vainikainen (1999) found evidence of a factorially distinct ability-related dimension, which they labeled prudence and contrasted with a narrow-intelligence factor, in Finnish parents' ratings of their preadolescent children's school-relevant abilities. Central attributes of this factor included perceived thoroughness, diligence, deliberate planfulness, and reflectiveness. Children's position on this dimension was strongly associated with their success in both theoretical and practical school subjects as rated by their parents, who attributed significantly more of it to girls than to boys. Much of what is being captured by this factor is likely to be closely related to the concept of reflective (as distinct from impulsive) cognitive style (e.g., Kagan, 1966), a construct that has long attracted attention from researchers and that is deliberately conceptualized, like prudence, as bridging the personality and cognitive ability domains. Reflective cognitive style refers to a way of thinking and problem solving that is deliberate and considered rather than swift and impetuous, characteristics that are again strongly reminiscent of classical discussions of prudence and practical wisdom.

A related line of research that embodies a more intellective approach to prudence focuses on children's understanding of prudential rules of conduct, defined as rules governing behavior that is associated with self-harm. These rules are distinguishable from moral rules, which are understood to involve harmful consequences to people other than the actor, and from social conventions. Nucci (1981) initiated this work by finding evidence of a distinct personal domain understood by children and adolescents to be outside the realm of societal regulation and moral concern, a domain whose reach may tend to expand as they mature. Tisak and Turiel (1984) studied and characterized the prudential reasoning endemic to this domain as based primarily on perceived consequences to the individual and on the individual's rights to autonomous choice rather than on the social-relational thinking involved in moral reasoning. Children understand prudential thinking in this sense to be less generalizable to other people than moral thinking, as well as being less externally authorized and unalterable.

In addition to defining prudence as a distinct cognitive domain, and laying out its features in a way that both conforms to and updates traditional understandings of prudence as practical reason, this approach has given rise to some research on how children and adolescents think about drug use (e.g., M. W. Berkowitz, Kahn, Mulry, & Piette, 1995; Nucci, Guerra, & Lee, 1991). Among a number of interesting findings, this work reveals that young people differ widely among themselves in whether they define drug use as primarily a moral or a prudential issue, with further variations according to age and drug type. Defining drug use as a prudential issue is not in itself associated with less use, because use is relatively strong among those who think of it in terms of personal autonomy. Drug use is typically less prevalent among those who think of it as a moral issue—as young people tend to do for harder drugs—and among those who consider it prudential and are concerned about its future personal consequences, the truly prudent.

The components of prudence having to do with balance, harmony, and coherence—components that fall under Aristotle's concept of moderation—are difficult to encompass in the trait psychology and practical intelligence approaches. Rather than focusing on traits, abilities, or cognitive styles, this work has to do with how people negotiate and coordinate the goals and ends that drive them. Some relatively recent traditions of research and theory in personality psychology afford ways to study the properties and organization of people's goals, employing a variety of goal concepts that clothe Aristotle's ends and right appetite in more modern garb. In this approach, people are held to be animated by concerns that can be described using units such as personal projects, personal strivings, or life tasks. These units capture the temporally extended and consciously accessible goals or aims that guide behavior in Aristotelian psychology. By bringing goal concepts into personality research and theory, concepts such as these offer a complementary analysis of prudence to the one offered by trait psychology and allow its volitional aspects to be brought to the fore. In addition, they enable the person's goals, projects, or tasks to be systematically investigated on such prudence-related characteristics as farsightedness, likelihood of achievement, and degree of coordination and harmony.

Two particularly useful approaches in this regard are the personal projects account of Little and his colleagues (e.g., B. R. Little, Lecci, & Watkinson, 1991) and the personal strivings account of Emmons and King (1988). Both of these approaches allow systematic elicitation of a person's salient goals or aims, which are then assessed on a variety of dimensions. In the personal projects system, for example, projects can be rated on dimensions such as their level of personal meaning and importance, their degree of structure or organization, and the efficacy with which they are pursued. In theory, all these dimensions fall under prudence's umbrella; prudent individuals should be personally invested in or concerned about their personal futures, they should have a planfully organized approach to them, and they should be efficiently pursuing them with good means–end reasoning. More directly relevant to the issue of harmony, assessment of personal strivings allows the determination of how much coherence and congruence, or how much conflict, exists among these guiding concerns. Once again, these assessments directly operationalize a fundamental component of *phronesis* or prudence as described by Aristotle, namely, the degree of balance and co-satisfiability of ends. In short, personal projects and strivings represent approaches to the study of personality that are particularly promising as contemporary ways of conceptualizing and studying prudence, although they have not previously been framed in this way.

A third promising way of capturing the moderation-related component of prudence in contemporary psychology is through Cantor and colleagues' social intelligence approach (e.g., Cantor & Harlow, 1994). This approach shares with the previous ones an emphasis on goal concepts but favors the term *life tasks*, a concept equally congenial to Aristotelian psychology. One particularly congenial feature of this approach has been its focus on the flexibility of life task pursuit and its theoretical analysis and empirical demonstration that such flexibility is indeed a desirable quality, as its place in the conceptualization of prudence would suggest. A further appealing property of this social intelligence account is its deliberate attempt to bridge the personality and intelligence domains and to offer a prescriptive account of personality in terms of competent everyday cognition. The consistency of these stances with the account of prudence presented here is self-evident.

A good deal of contemporary research and theory on self-control fits under the umbrella of prudence, although much of it is more directly discussed in this volume in the chapter on self-regulation (chapter 22). To avoid redundancy, this work will be discussed only where the mechanism theorized to underlie self-control corresponds approximately to the sort proposed in conceptual analyses of prudence, that is, some sort of farsighted cognitive process that implies moderation rather than outright self-restraint and involves a harmonizing or balancing of goals. Several recent approaches to the study of self-control deserve special mention in this connection.

Most notable perhaps is Ainslie's (2001) analysis, which sees impulsivity as an ever-present challenge to human behavior that is built into the motivational tooling of people and other animals. Ainslie argues that people do not simply discount the future in an irrationally steep way that produces shortsighted decisions. Instead, or in addition, we discount it according to a hyperbolic function that leads us to switch preference from longer term (prudent) rewards to more short-term (impulsive or specious) rewards as the latter become available. This basic motivational fact, equally observable in people's hypothetical choices in questionnaire studies and in pigeons' pecking behavior in Skinner boxes, implies that our preferences are chronically unstable and forever veering toward suboptimal and imprudent choices. This constant conflict between our longer and shorter term interests in turn implies that if we are to act prudently, we must find ways to bind ourselves to farsighted choices in advance and overcome the inevitable impulses when they arise. Acting prudently becomes in this analysis a fundamental challenge that runs against motivational gravity, something that can be achieved only with skill and effort.

Ainslie provides a useful taxonomy of self-control tactics, involving manipulations of our social and physical environment and of our attention and emotional states. His most novel contribution from the point of view of classical accounts of prudence is his analysis of a tactic that he calls *will*, which is, we should recall, one of the alternative labels for the conscientiousness factor. The mechanism underlying will, he argues, is the formation of personal rules for self-government (cf. Tisak & Turiel's, 1984, prudential rules) and the perception that any violation of such rules sets a precedent for future violations and thus predicts wholesale defection from the person's long-term interests. The expected loss of future reward that this precedent implies serves to bind strong-willed people to their rules.

This briefly sketched account of self-control resonates in interesting ways with the concept of prudence. First, it implies that the crafting of personal rules is vital to the successful pursuit of one's long-term best interests, so that prudent conduct relies on good judgment of an almost legislative sort. Rules that are unrealistically demanding or that afford too many loopholes are likely to be sabotaged by short-term interests, phenomena readily observed in people making resolutions. Ideally, rules should be firm enough to allow the person little discretion in when or how to follow them but flexible enough that trivial violations do not collapse the people's resolve or deny them any satisfaction. Second, the efficacy of the will depends upon envisaging and caring about a temporally extended series of future choices, implying again that self-control relies on a concernful orientation to the future, as described by classical writers on prudence. This idea that prudent conduct is promoted by considering choices not simply as present-centered instances but as elements within longer term units is also found in some behavioral formulations of self-control (e.g., Rachlin, 1989) and in social psychological work on action identification (Vallacher & Wegner, 1989). Third, Ainslie does not contend that strengthening will is an unmitigated benefit, recognizing that when people become too bound by rules, a legalistic, joyless, irrationally postponing, and compulsive way of life can result. Will in Ainslie's sense is good in moderation, just as personal rules are ideally somewhat flexible.

It is also important to take note of Ainslie's explicit recognition that specious rewards—those shorter term choices that are suboptimal and interfere with our pursuit of longer term interests—extend beyond fleeting impulses to include self-control challenges that play out over longer periods. Beyond the familiar domains of impulse and addiction, people are also prone to selling out, choosing actions attractive in the medium term over more durable but initially less appealing or more demanding alternatives. Taking easy options in life, or devoting oneself too single-mindedly to a goal that impairs or forecloses more richly rewarding alternatives, is just as much a matter of imprudence as is giving in to heat-of-the-moment impulses. The opposite of prudence is therefore not precisely impulsivity, as is often stated, but is better stated as the tendency to make specious choices of all sorts, both short-term impulses and lastingly suboptimal ways of being. In summary, Ainslie's analysis of self-control is highly consonant with classical formulations of prudence and brings them up-to-date with contemporary psychology.

■ Measures

Most of the measures of prudence that have been developed derive from the trait psychological approach and are therefore primarily measures of the five-factor model's conscientiousness factor. Many scales assess this dimension by this or other names and with varying degrees of comprehensiveness and facto-rial purity. Only those that assess it relatively comprehensively are presented in Table 21.1. The many scales that are heavily saturated with the factor but have a broader or narrower scope or are admixed with other factors (e.g., scales mea-suring impulsivity, future time perspective, sensation seeking, constraint) are therefore not included. Those that are included are parts of comprehensive five-factor inventories, so the measures assess at least four additional dimensions besides the conscientiousness factor.

There are few psychometric grounds for elevating any one of these five measures above the others, and all are entirely adequate. They appear to corre-late quite highly, although they have somewhat distinctive content emphases. If brevity is paramount, the BFI, TDA, and NEO-FFI should be favored. If in-ternal consistency is paramount—for example, if statistical power is particu-larly crucial or if individuals are being clinically assessed—the NEO-PI-R is probably best, as it is if a differentiated facet analysis is desired. The HPI has

---

TABLE 21.1   *Measures of Prudence*

NEO-PI-R Conscientiousness Subscale
   Costa & McCrae (1992)
   240 items in total questionnaire
   Comments: measures facets of conscientiousness; has strong psychometrics

NEO-FFI Conscientiousness Subscale
   Costa & McCrae (1992)
   60 items in total questionnaire

Trait Descriptions Conscientiousness Subscale
   L. R. Goldberg (1992)
   100 items in total questionnaire
   Comments: 50-item instrument with bipolar adjective pairs also available

Big Five Inventory (BFI) Conscientiousness Subscale
   John & Srivastava (1999)
   44 items in total questionnaire

Hogan Personality Inventory (HPI) Conscientiousness Subscale
   R. Hogan & Hogan (1992)
   310 items in total questionnaire
   Comments: measures components of conscientiousness; internal consisten-cies weaker than NEO-PI-R

several all-around strengths and the advantage of being explicitly formulated as a measure of prudence, although Trapnell and Wiggins (1990) found that its prudence scale was composed of two rather distinct item clusters and the scale may not correspond to the NEO scales' factorially pure assessment of conscientiousness. Despite the temptation, the conscientiousness and prudence items from all these scales generally should not be administered apart from their full instruments.

Numerous self-report measures of narrower band traits related to prudence—such as impulsivity and sensation seeking—are also available. Some of these, as well as other somewhat broader conscientiousness-related scales, are well reviewed by J. Hogan and Ones (1997). However, most of the scales are questionable as measures of prudence because of their relatively narrow focus; their factorial impurity with respect to conscientiousness (e.g., contamination by items loading strongly on neuroticism, disagreeableness, and extroversion); and, possibly, their focus on the opposite, imprudent pole of the dimension. In a related fashion, measures of psychoticism or constraint, drawn from three-factor models of personality, are questionable because of their overly broad scope and their conflation of prudential traits with those involving interpersonal agreeableness. None of these measures is addressed here, and none is recommended as measures of prudence.

For those interested in assessing the goal coherence and balance aspects of prudence, the trait measures presented here are inadequate. The assessment methodologies developed by Emmons and King (1988) and by Sheldon and Kasser (1995) for eliciting personal strivings and assessing their degrees of conflict versus congruence are recommended, as are those of B. R. Little et al.'s (1991) personal projects analysis.

■ Correlates and Consequences

As is commonly the case in the study of individual differences, it is difficult to assess whether variables found to covary with measures of prudence are simply correlates of the construct or whether they are instead influenced by it. One set of correlates can be found in the personality domain. If prudence is operationalized as the latent variable normally labeled conscientiousness in the five-factor model, as argued previously, it shows interesting links to several other factors. Although the five factors are sometimes conceptualized as entirely independent, John and Srivastava (1999) found in a confirmatory factor analysis of three five-factor scales that conscientiousness is modestly associated with all four of the other factors. More conscientious (i.e., prudent) people tend to be higher than average on agreeableness, extroversion, and, perhaps, intellect (one of a few alternative renderings of the fifth factor) and lower than average on neuroticism. These findings imply that prudence is modestly associated with

interpersonal warmth and cooperativeness; sociability, assertiveness and positive emotionality; imaginativeness, curiosity, and insightfulness; and low levels of negative emotionality. Many of these associations suggest a link between
prudence and psychological well-being, and this link has been supported in
several studies. For example, Digman (1989) found conscientiousness to be
associated with positive affect in children; and Marshall, Wortman, Vickers,
Kusulas, and Hervig (1994) found it to be associated with optimism and the
absence of hopelessness.

All these associated dispositions may simply reflect descriptive associations,
but it is not implausible to suppose that some of them might represent causal
relations. Almost by definition, prudent thinking and conduct might tend, for
example, to promote positive life outcomes and minimize negative ones, with
obvious consequences for positive and negative emotionality. Similarly, it is
generally prudent to value and nurture one's relationships with others, so the
exercise of prudence might be expected to have greater cooperativeness as a
consequence. Equally, however, the causal arrow could be reversed so that, for
instance, people less troubled by negative emotions or more blessed with imagination and insight are able to show superior self-discipline and more planful
concern for their futures. Determining whether these personality correlates of
prudence influence or are influenced by it, or both, awaits further research.
However, the mere fact that they exist gives the lie to a widespread caricature
of the prudent person as constricted, joyless, self-seeking, and coldly calculative. This caricature probably stems from a romantic valuation of spontaneity
and freedom from rigidly binding rules, neither of which need be antithetical
to prudence as it is understood here.

A few studies have investigated associations between prudence or conscientiousness and psychopathology. John, Caspi, Robins, Moffitt, and Stouthamer-
Loeber (1994) found that more conscientious adolescent boys had lower levels
of both internalizing and externalizing psychopathology, as well as less delinquency; conscientiousness was the most powerful predictor of these outcomes
among the five factors. The delinquency finding is consistent with Gottfredson
and Hirschi's (1990) work, which supported a link between impulsiveness and
criminality. Wiggins and Pincus (1989) and Costa and McCrae (1990) examined associations between the five factors and personality disorder scales and
found that conscientiousness was negatively associated with antisocial personality disorder and positively associated with compulsive personality disorder.
Whether any of these associations reflect causal influences on psychopathology, with prudence serving as a protective factor, or as a diathesis in the case of
compulsiveness, is unknown.

Some research has addressed the links between prudence-related characteristics and physical well-being. Most strikingly, perhaps, conscientiousness
measured in middle childhood, alone among the five factors and measured
in part by a rating of prudence, has been found to predict longer life (H. S.

Friedman et al., 1993, 1995). This association is partially mediated by causal links between prudence and the taking of self-protective or precautionary health measures, avoiding health risk behaviors, and coping better with stress. The reduced mortality for more conscientious people was due in part to lower rates of cardiovascular disease, cancer, and violent injury.

In a related vein, Booth-Kewley and Vickers (1994) noted, this trait psychological approach to prudence has several limitations. First, it supplies an inductively generated summary description of a personality domain rather than a theoretical formulation of the processes that underlie it, the concept of prudence being one such formulation. Prudence frames this trait domain in terms of a theory of practical rationality and future-oriented self-management. Marshall et al. (1994) found that conscientiousness was associated with a variety of traits that have shown promise as predictors of health along other causal pathways, including optimism, internal locus of control, and low levels of anger expression. Importantly, conscientiousness was not associated with potentially health-damaging forms of inhibition, such as bottling up anger. It is also reasonable to suppose that more conscientious or prudent people would be more apt to follow prescribed medication and exercise regimens, with the attendant health benefits. Finally, J. Hogan (1989) found that the prudence scale on the Hogan Personality Inventory was associated with better physical fitness, especially with respect to endurance.

Research employing prudence-related measures other than those based on the conscientiousness factor has also demonstrated correlations with physical and psychological well-being. If prudence is understood in one of the more Aristotelian senses discussed earlier—as the harmonious balancing of personal desires—two studies of conflict among personal strivings are clearly relevant. Emmons and King (1988) found that such conflict is associated with self-reported health problems, and Sheldon and Kasser (1995) found that congruence among strivings is correlated with health and well-being. B. R. Little et al. (1991), finally, showed a link between striving-like phenomena, conscientiousness, and well-being, demonstrating that conscientiousness was the best predictor among the five factors of "overall positivity in individuals' personal project systems" (p. 520). More conscientious undergraduates had personal goals or projects that were more in keeping with their sense of self, more organized, and more efficacious (i.e., more likely to be achieved and showing more successful progress to date) than those of others. Besides revealing an association between prudence and a form of positivity, this study shows a clear link between our proposed operational trait measure of prudence and a more differentiated measure of prudence based on the organized, coherent, and effective pursuit of personal ends, thereby supporting the validity of the prudence construct as presented here.

Some of the strongest correlates of prudence, as assessed by measures of conscientiousness, are found in the workplace, and here a causal interpretation seems especially plausible. In a meta-analysis of personality predictors of job performance, Barrick and Mount (1991) showed that measures of conscientiousness consistently yielded stronger effect sizes than measures of the other four factors. These effect sizes were consistent across different occupational levels and types and across multiple performance criteria including productivity, success in training, duration of tenure, and salary. The greater effects for subjective performance ratings than for objective measures suggested to the authors that some of the workplace benefits of conscientiousness might be mediated by its effect on the individual's social reputation for probity. The integrity tests now used in personnel selection seem strongly associated with conscientiousness (J. Hogan & Ones, 1997; see chapter 11). In addition, a theoretical analysis which proposes that prudence offers a useful paradigm for assessing political leadership (Moskop, 1996) was vindicated in a recent study (Lall, Holmes, Brinkmeyer, Johnson, & Yapko, 1999), which found prudence to predict the performance of future military leaders.

Research extends these associations between prudence and job performance into the educational realm, with more prudent (or conscientious) students tending to display superior school achievement (e.g., Digman, 1989; John et al., 1994). This variable is perhaps the most robust personality correlate of educational attainment, adding significantly to the prediction afforded by narrowly conceived intelligence or other aptitudes. John et al. (1994) interestingly found that it was also weakly correlated with higher IQ.

There is limited evidence with regard to demographic correlates of prudence, and what there is relies on using measures of conscientiousness as a proxy. However, self-report measures of this dimension tend to show moderate positive correlations with age across several cultures (McCrae et al., 1999), suggesting that it has a gradually increasing maturational trajectory.

In summary, the personally and socially positive correlates of prudence are many and varied. These correlates are frequently more robust for the conscientiousness/prudence factor than for the other dimensions of the five-factor model, despite the fact that it has often been neglected by researchers and theorists in favor of neuroticism or extroversion-based analyses. The great variety of domains in which prudence appears to be associated with positive life outcomes belies any conceptualization that ties the concept exclusively to the domain of work and personal achievement. To sum up, prudence seems to be associated with several positively valued personality dispositions, psychological and physical well-being, the absence of certain forms of psychopathology and antisocial conduct, and superior attainment at work and school.

■ Development

Very little research has explored the development of prudence under that name. What research has been done is generally framed in terms of self-control or impulse control. The extensive research on the development of more specific strengths associated with prudence—such as impulse control and delay of gratification—is provided in the chapter on self-regulation. Very briefly, research indicates that delay of gratification improves from the preschool years into middle childhood, and that as children mature they develop more effective tactics for forestalling impulsive choices (e.g., Mischel & Metzner, 1962).

A recent study (C. Thompson, Barresi, & Moore, 1997), explicitly framed as an investigation of prudence, points to an important shift in the capacity to delay gratification at around 4 years of age that accompanies and may share a common mechanism with the propensity to make altruistic choices. The authors propose that decisions in favor of future selves and of other selves both involve an ability to represent in imagination mental states such as desires that are not immediately experienced. By implication, prudence may fundamentally involve the capacity or propensity to imaginatively identify with or project oneself into a future self. In addition, the study suggests an interesting link between prudence and a moral virtue and raises the possibility that prudence and altruism might be associated in adulthood. However, it must be remembered that the experimental paradigm in delay of gratification studies assesses impulse control over relatively short durations, and its relevance to prudence over the longer term is unclear.

Much less research has been conducted on the development of foresight, moderation, the self-management of goals and life tasks, and other such components of prudence, although the work on adolescents' thinking about prudential rules described earlier (e.g., M. W. Berkowitz et al., 1995) comes closest. Trait psychology research at least indicates that a broad dimension more or less equivalent to conscientiousness can be found even in middle childhood (Digman, 1989), that mean levels of conscientiousness increase somewhat in early adulthood (McCrae et al., 1999), and that individual differences in this dimension are quite stable from early adolescence to late adulthood (Haan, Millsap, & Hartka, 1986). Both of these findings imply a considerable degree of developmental continuity for prudence, although its manifestations are sure to differ importantly as a function of age.

■ Enabling and Inhibiting Factors

Little, if any, research has been conducted on factors that develop or interfere with prudence, although relevant work might be found under different rubrics. Behavioral genetic research (e.g., Riemann, Angleitner, & Strelau, 1997) suggests that influences filed under shared environment are probably not strong candidates, given the negligible contributions made to measures of conscientiousness by such influences. We are therefore unlikely to locate powerful developmental influences on prudence that are shared within families, such as parenting style, social class, religious background, and so on. However, the fact that these studies indicate that slightly less than half of the variance in conscientiousness measures is heritable implies that environmental influences of a nonshared kind must be important and that prudence should, in principle, be somewhat malleable by them.

Because of the dearth of research on this topic, it is necessary to draw out a few speculations to guide research. For example, prudence would in theory be thwarted in people who live (or have grown up) under chaotic and unpredictable conditions in which the future seems so uncertain and remote that long-term planning is pointless. It should be thwarted in circumstances where people do not enjoy sufficient autonomy and personal control to define a personal domain of goals and ends to be striven for. It should be thwarted when people are required to devote themselves too single-mindedly to any one goal or end so that no balancing or harmonizing of multiple goals or ends is possible. Although these speculations are somewhat abstract at this point, they may provide a guide for future work and for assimilating existing research on the consequences of psychological and social adversity into a prudential framework.

■ Gender, Cross-National, and Cross-Cultural Aspects

There is no systematic research on the relationship between prudence and gender. If prudence is understood in terms of conscientiousness, test norms suggest that there is no mean difference between men and women (Costa & McCrae, 1992). The more inhibitory and restrained aspects of prudence are perhaps stereotypically feminine. After all, Prudence is a girl's name, and one famous but reserved—remember that Prudence had to be coaxed out to play in the sun by the Beatles. However, the more agentic aspects of prudence, such as achievement motivation, have if anything a masculine connotation. Whether these stereotypes have any scientific basis remains to be seen, but there are unlikely to be any substantial gender differences in prudence per se.

Very little cross-cultural research on prudence has been conducted to date. Research on the five-factor model indicates that the model as a whole, including the conscientiousness factor, replicates quite well in diverse national and linguistic contexts, especially in European countries and when translations of English five-factor inventories are used, rather than culturally salient personality descriptors (e.g., Church & Lonner, 1998). This evidence points to at least some cross-cultural generality to prudence as a coherent individual difference. There is little systematic research on whether cultures differ in levels of prudence—always an immensely difficult comparison to make—or in its many correlates. It has been argued that traits are less relevant to and less strongly associated with everyday behavior in more collectivist non-Western cultures (Church & Lonner, 1998; Triandis, 1995), where individualist strivings and values of self-expression are weaker and societal constraints on conduct arguably stronger. If this is so, the many correlations between measures of prudence and measures of its many positive life outcomes would be attenuated in collectivist cultures, but this remains an empirical question.

■ Deliberate Interventions

No interventions known to us explicitly strive to bolster prudence, with the possible exceptions of certain programs and policies aimed at improving financial self-discipline and others aimed at encouraging "safer" sexual practices. However, certain interventions that fall under different rubrics can be reconceptualized as attempts to foster prudence. Certain forms of cognitive psychotherapy, for instance, focus on improving practical reasoning skills to strengthen emotional well-being and correct cognitive distortions and inflexibilities that deflect decision making toward myopic and impulsive choices. Many behavioral forms of treatment focus more directly on overcoming impulses—to drink, to yield to compulsions, to binge eat, and so on—that clearly and effectively address the self-control component of prudence despite having a technical rather than reasoning-based character, as a strict understanding of prudence would entail. Whether the concept of prudence offers a helpful way to frame interventions for the many demonstrated life outcomes that are associated with its absence has yet to be determined.

■ What Is Not Known?

What is not known about prudence is extensive, largely because the concept has not been fashionable and because it carves out a somewhat distinctive domain for itself. In view of this, only some of the broadest and most glaring gaps in our knowledge will be laid out here:

- To what extent does prudence play a causal role in relation to its many and diverse positive correlates?
- How do the conceptually distinct components of prudence—concern for the long-term future; harmonization and organization of goals, tasks, and strivings; self-control; practical reasoning—interrelate empirically in adulthood and over the course of development?
- Is prudence associated with life outcomes in non-Western cultures?
- What conditions promote or thwart prudence, and how malleable is it when it has been impaired?

■ Must-Read Articles and Books

Ainslie, G. (2001). *Breakdown of will.* Cambridge, England: Cambridge University Press.

Emmons, R. A., & King, L. A. (1988). Conflict among personal strivings: Immediate and long-term implications for psychological and physical well-being. *Journal of Personality and Social Psychology, 54,* 1040–1048.

Friedman, H. S., Tucker, J. S., Schwartz, J. E., Tomlinson-Keasey, C., Martin, L. R., Wingard, D. L., et al. (1995). Psychosocial and behavioral predictors of longevity: The aging and death of the "Termites." *American Psychologist, 50,* 69–78.

Haslam, N. (1991). Prudence: Aristotelian perspective on practical reason and self-control. *Journal for the Theory of Social Behaviour, 21,* 151–169.

Haslam, N., & Baron, J. (1994). Intelligence, personality, and prudence. In R. J. Sternberg & P. Ruzgis (Eds.), *Personality and intelligence* (pp. 32–58). New York: Cambridge University Press.

Little, B. R., Lecci, L., & Watkinson, B. (1991). Personality and personal projects: Linking Big Five and PAC units of analysis. *Journal of Personality, 60,* 501–525.

Sherman, N. (1989). *The fabric of character: Aristotle's theory of virtue.* Oxford, England: Oxford University Press.

Sternberg, R. J., & Wagner, R. K. (Eds.) (1986). *Practical intelligence: Nature and origins of competence in the everyday world.* Cambridge, England: Cambridge University Press.

22. SELF-REGULATION

[Self-Control]

◼ *Consider the bodybuilding practices of Arnold Schwarzenegger. According to his autobiography, Schwarzenegger set almost unattainable high standards that forced him to confront many so-called inadequacies in his body shape, size, and overall personal appearance. When confronted with a perceived flaw in his appearance, he engaged in many concentrated exercises to correct it (Schwarzenegger & Hall, 1977). At one point in his bodybuilding career, Schwarzenegger began to focus on his calves, because he had been told they were "too skinny" to win major bodybuilding competitions. His response to this discrepancy between his current and ideal states was to take all his pants and cut them off just below the knees so that his attention would always be drawn to this problem area. This allowed Schwarzenegger to focus on his calves, which encouraged him to practice vigorous exercise techniques to make them bigger. Not incidentally, Schwarzenegger's intense self-regulatory efforts brought him much success and many accomplishments, including being named Mr. Olympia seven times.*

Arnold Schwarzenegger embodies many of the characteristics of a person with strong self-regulatory abilities. His story illustrates the establishment of personal goals, recognizing discrepancies between current and ideal states, monitoring his progress, and having sufficient self-regulatory strength to reach his goals, the latter of which is especially relevant to our model of self-regulatory resources (Baumeister, Heatherton, & Tice, 1994; Baumeister & Vohs, 2003; Vohs & Heatherton, 2000). In sum, Arnold Schwarzenegger exemplifies several self-control processes, all of which helped him achieve successes in bodybuilding and most other domains of his life. ◼

■ Consensual Definition

Self-regulation refers to how a person exerts control over his or her own responses so as to pursue goals and live up to standards. These responses include thoughts, emotions, impulses, performances, and other behaviors. The standards include ideals, moral injunctions, norms, performance targets, and the expectations of other people. The term *self-control* is sometimes used as a synonym for self-regulation, but other writers use it more narrowly to refer specifically to controlling one's impulses so as to behave in a moral fashion. The term *self-discipline* is also related to self-regulation and usually is used in a somewhat narrower sense, such as to refer to making oneself do things that one does not want to do and resisting temptation.

Overriding or altering one's responses is especially important in self-regulation. Living organisms, especially complex ones such as human beings, are constantly responding to both internal and external stimuli, but to act on all these responses would not be optimal or adaptive. Hence, people often find it useful to override their initial responses. They may direct their thought processes in directions other than where their minds naturally wander, they may attempt to change their emotional responses away from how they initially feel, and they may restrain themselves from carrying out impulses and desires. They may try to perform better than they would normally do, such as by making themselves persist on a difficult task. Most acts of self-regulation involve stopping the self from having a response, such as when a dieter refrains from eating a tempting but fattening food. There are, however, some instances of self-regulation that entail initiating a response, such as when a sleepy man drags himself out of bed on a cold morning.

■ Theoretical Traditions

The term *self-regulation* was used quite early by Bandura (1977) in his efforts to adapt behaviorist theory to the complexities of human behavior. Bandura (1982) proposed that people administer rewards and punishments to themselves, thereby exerting control over their own behavior in ways that less complex species do not, insofar as their behavior is mainly controlled by externally administered rewards and punishments.

The most influential roots of contemporary research on self-regulation probably lie in studies of delay of gratification by Mischel and his colleagues (e.g., Mischel & Ebbesen, 1970; for reviews, see Mischel, 1974, 1996). In these studies, children were offered the choice between an immediate, small reward and a larger, delayed reward, and so it was necessary to resist the temptation to take the immediate reward in order to secure the larger, optimal benefit. Delay of gratification is of considerable interest in its own right, but in recent years interest in that research has been renewed as the field began to appreciate the broader importance of self-regulation. Resisting the temptation to take the immediate, salient, small reward required the child to override his or her initial response, and thus delay of gratification constitutes an important paradigm of self-regulation.

A major advance in self-regulation theory occurred in the early 1980s when Carver and Scheier (1981, 1982) began to apply cybernetic theory to the understanding of self-awareness. In their view, focusing attention on the self was more than a mere source of discomfort or cognitive orientation—it was a crucial means by which the self appraised its current status in relation to various standards. Self-awareness thus constituted a kind of test in a feedback loop. Feedback loops were borrowed from cybernetic theory (e.g., W. T. Powers, 1973), according to the acronym TOTE: test, operate, test, exit. That is, the self compares itself against the relevant standard (T), and if the current status falls short of the standard, it begins an operation (O) designed to remedy the deficit. Further tests (T) are conducted periodically. When the standard is finally met, the loop is exited (E).

Recent work has begun to focus on the operate phase of the feedback loop, which is to say the processes by which the self alters itself to bring itself into line with the standards. Research has begun to suggest that the capacity for altering the self is a form of strength. Specifically, altering the self requires a mental or psychological exertion. Just as a muscle grows tired from exertion, the capacity for self-regulation becomes depleted after it is used (e.g., Baumeister, Bratslavsky, Muraven, & Tice, 1998; Muraven & Baumeister, 2000; Vohs & Heatherton, 2000). Also like a muscle, the capacity for self-regulation appears to grow stronger through regular exercise (after it recovers from the initial fatigue; Muraven, Baumeister, & Tice, 1999).

Two primary areas in which self-regulatory efforts are directed are to obtain or maintain control over thoughts and emotions. With regard to the former, a theory of mental control by Wegner and colleagues (e.g., Wegner, 1989, 1994; Wegner & Pennebaker, 1993; Wegner, Schneider, Carter, & White, 1987) has led to investigations of the various strategies involved in thought control, the success of these strategies, and their unanticipated consequences. Wegner's ironic process model proposes that when a person tries to suppress an unwanted thought, a psychological system is established that serves two purposes: One component, the monitoring process, automatically searches the environment for indications of the unwanted thought; the other component, the operating process, is activated when the monitoring system finds a sign of the unwanted thought. The operating process uses controlled responses to override the responses that follow from detection of the unwanted thought. A classic example of the ironic process is the dieter who is trying to suppress the knowledge that there are tempting foods in the kitchen. If the dieter watches television to distract himself, the monitoring system will scan the televised images for tempting foods. And if a commercial for cookies appears, the operating process will actively override the man's desire to get up and eat the chocolate chip cookies on the kitchen counter.

Although at first glance the process appears to have been successful, there are two important caveats regarding the effectiveness of thought suppression. The first is the resurgence of the unwanted thought after the thought restrictions have been lifted. In our example, when the dieter decides that he has lost enough weight to warrant abandoning his diet, he may find himself frequently thinking of food even more so than if he had not attempted to suppress food thoughts at all. This phenomenon is called the *rebound effect*, and, counterproductively, it can render the unwanted thought more accessible than if it had not been placed off-limits. In support of this effect, Wegner, Shortt, Blake, and Page (1990) demonstrated that suppression of thrilling sexual thoughts consumed more physical energy (as indicated by heightened skin conductance) than did purposeful thinking about sex.

The second unintended effect of the thought control process involves the automaticity of the monitoring function. When one is tired, fatigued, or burdened, there may not be enough effort available to engage the operating function, but the automatic monitoring system will continue to alert the person to the signs of the unwanted thought. Consequently, a person who is taxed will have greater sensitivity to environmental cues of the undesired thought (e.g., will be more aware of the cookies in the kitchen) and will be less able to overcome any resulting responses (e.g., the desire to eat the cookies). Thus, the ironic monitoring system can be useful in keeping out unwanted thoughts (especially with the use of a purposeful distraction technique, like a red Volkswagen), but it can also lead to states that are detrimental to the person's ultimate goals.

With respect to the control of emotions, J. J. Gross (1999) proposed a theory that groups strategies according to whether they are antecedent focused or response focused. Antecedent-focused emotion regulation strategies are used early in—or before, if possible—the occurrence of the emotional response, whereas response-focused strategies are used following the emotion-invoking episode. Antecedent-focused strategies are anticipatory strategies that are aimed at managing or even preventing an upcoming emotional state. There are four basic antecedent strategies: situation selection, situation modification, attentional deployment, and cognitive change.

Situation selection involves selecting aspects of the environment (e.g., people, settings) best suited for obtaining the desired emotional state. *Situation modification* refers to actions aimed at altering the environment to modify an emotional response. *Attentional deployment* is a strategy in which attention and effort are directed at aspects of the environment that help achieve the desired emotional state. The method of *cognitive change*, which is sometimes called *reappraisal*, involves reinterpreting the situation to modify its emotional effects. Cognitive change is used mainly when the first three methods are unavailable or have failed.

Conversely, attempts to control an emotional response after it has occurred fall mainly under the method of response modulation. Response modulation involves actively changing an existing emotional response, such as when a person tries to conceal her amusement with a look of concern after another's clumsy fall.

Research on emotion control strategies has shown that the methods vary in their effectiveness. For example, work by Blascovich, Tomaka, and colleagues (e.g., Tomaka, Blascovich, Kibler, & Ernst, 1997) demonstrates that interpreting an environmental demand as challenging, as opposed to threatening, results in more positive and less negative emotional reactions, greater persistence, more productive cognitions, and better (i.e., more efficient) physiological responses. Controlling emotions using the reappraisal technique does not result in memory loss, which is a consequence of simply suppressing emotional reactions (J. M. Richards & Gross, 2000). Thus, there are immediate and meaningful consequences to selecting different strategies for emotion regulation.

In sum, these theoretical advances have occurred amid a gradually burgeoning interest in self-regulation that has seen a broad variety of approaches and methods. An enormous amount of research has been devoted to how people regulate their behavior (or fail to regulate it) in many specific spheres, such as eating and dieting, attempts to quit smoking, battles with alcohol and drug abuse, overcoming prejudice, persisting in the face of failure, achieving optimal performance, maintaining positive interpersonal relationships, restraining violence and criminal behavior, and practicing safe sex.

■ Measures

Most research on self-regulation has featured behavioral measures. In the study of the control of eating, for example, most research has measured how much people eat. Consuming large amounts of fattening food is taken as an indication of some breakdown in self-regulation, whereas restrained eating indicates effective self-control. In laboratory studies, actual behavior is carefully measured, whereas field studies may rely on self-reports of behavior (such as to ascertain whether someone has relapsed into drug or alcohol abuse).

Some trait scales have been constructed to assess individual differences in the self's ability to control and regulate its responses (see Table 22.1). These have generally failed to gain wide usage, either because they were narrowly focused or had various drawbacks. For example, Fagen, Long, and Stevens (1975) created the Self-Control Behavior Inventory, a checklist that requires systematic observation of behavior. Brandon, Oescher, and Loftin (1990) developed the Self-Control Questionnaire, which focuses mainly on health behaviors; in fact, a quarter of the items refer specifically to eating. There are indeed measures that exclusively assess regulation of eating behavior such as dieting, most notably the Restraint Scale developed by C. P. Herman and Polivy (1975). Rosenbaum

---

TABLE 22.1   *Measures of Self-Control*

Self-Control (Sc) Subscale of California Psychological Inventory
    Gough, McClosky, & Meehl (1952)
    Measures "joyful, ebullient" disinhibition

Self-Control Behavior Inventory
    Fagen, Long, & Stevens (1975)
    Requires systematic observation of behavior

Restraint Scale
    C. P. Herman & Polivy (1975)
    Specifically measures eating behaviors

Self-Control Schedule
    Rosenbaum (1980)
    Assessment of coping methods in clinical populations

Self-Control Questionnaire
    Brandon, Oescher, & Loftin (1990)
    Focuses on health, eating behaviors

Low Self-Control Scale
    Grasmick, Tittle, Bursik, & Arneklev (1993)
    Measures self-control behaviors related to criminality

Self-Control Scale
    Tangney, Baumeister, & Boone (in press)
    General self-control scale containing five subscales

(1980) developed the Self-Control Schedule, which is intended for use with clinical samples and assesses coping methods such as self-distraction and cognitive reframing and thus does not measure self-control generally.

Some researchers have employed a Self-Control (Sc) subscale from the California Psychological Inventory (CPI). Many of its items lack face validity, and so the scale may not be appropriately named. The heterogeneity of items on the CPI Self-Control (Sc) scale may well reflect the complex process by which the scale evolved. Following the development of the CPI Socialization (So) and Responsibility (Re) subscales, Gough, McClosky, & Meehl (1952) concluded that So and Re did not really capture "the kind of joyful, ebullient abandonment of restraint that one sees at certain times such as attendance at a carnival" (Gough, 1987, p. 45). Thus, they set about developing a scale to assess "impetuosity, high spirits, caprice, and a taste for deviltry" (Gough, 1987, p. 45)—clearly one pattern of behavior that may be atypical of self-control in general. The conceptual heterogeneity, along with the seeming lack of face validity of many items, may be one reason that this scale has not been popular among laboratory researchers in recent decades, despite the rapid expansion of research on self-regulation. Certainly self-control is a distinct construct that should be largely independent of high spirits and a taste for deviltry. In any case, the CPI ante-dates most of the modern research on self-control, and so on an a priori basis it would be desirable to construct a new scale based on recent developments.

Dissatisfaction with existing scales has led to the introduction of two new scales in recent years, and these both seem quite promising. One was developed by criminologists in the wake of Gottfredson and Hirschi's (1990) book *A General Theory of Crime*, which proposed that deficient self-control was the central concept needed for understanding criminality. The Low Self-Control Scale (Grasmick, Tittle, Bursik, & Arneklev, 1993) is a direct attempt to measure Gottfredson and Hirschi's (1990) theory of self-control from a criminological perspective. This scale has been used by multiple researchers, usually in connection with measures of crime or delinquency, and quite a few studies have shown that people who score high in self-control on that scale are less likely to run afoul of the law than are people who score low in it.

Working from a different research tradition, Tangney, Baumeister, and colleagues (Tangney, Baumeister, & Boone, in press) have developed the Self-Control Scale, which is a broad, general measure of trait self-control. It samples the major domains of self-control (controlling thoughts, feelings, impulses, and performances, as well as breaking bad habits). It has both a long and a short form and also has enjoyed repeated success in predicting a broad range of self-regulatory outcomes in multiple studies.

Both the Grasmick et al. (1993) scale and the Tangney et al. (in press) scale appear to have good psychometric properties, face validity, and a demonstrated capacity to produce significant results. Hence we recommend that researchers use either of them rather than the older scales.

As mentioned, it is desirable that questionnaire items from self-control scales have high face validity and assess self-regulatory abilities in a variety of domains. Both the Grasmick et al. (1993) Low Self-Control Scale and the Tangney et al. (in press) Self-Control Scale have the former property, and the latter measures self-regulatory capacity in more diverse behavioral spheres.

The Grasmick et al. (1993) Low Self-Control Scale consists of 24 items, which include statements such as the following:

- I will try to get things I want even when I know it's causing problems for other people.
- When things get complicated, I tend to quit or withdraw.
- I frequently try to avoid projects that I know will be difficult.
- I'm more concerned with what happens to me in the short run than in the long run.

Participants are asked to indicate the extent to which these statements "describe the type of person you are," such that higher numbers indicate greater agreement with the statement's description. The Grasmick et al. scale is generally considered a unidimensional construct.

The Tangney et al. (in press) Self-Control Scale scale contains 36 items, to which participants are asked to assign a numeric value (where 1 = not at all like me, and 5 = very much like me) that "best represents what you believe to be true about yourself for each question." Representative items include the following:

- I have a hard time breaking bad habits.
- I am lazy.
- I say inappropriate things.
- I never allow myself to lose control.
- I do certain things that are bad for me, if they are fun.
- People can count on me to keep on schedule.

The items on the full scale can be grouped into five subscales that assess self-control in the domains of work ethic, self-discipline, nonimpulsivity, health habits, and reliability. A short form of the measure exists for researchers who desire a briefer version.

Although researchers have access to several self-control scales, the two scales reviewed here are currently the most commonly used. As mentioned, the Grasmick et al. (1993) scale has been used largely in connection with criminal and antisocial behaviors. Personality and social psychologists, on the other hand, have begun to adopt the Tangney et al. (in press) scale as the preferred measure to assess self-control for theoretical and applied studies of a broad range of social behaviors.

■ Correlates and Consequences

According to a review by Baumeister et al. (1994), self-regulation failure is central to nearly all the personal and social problems that currently plague citizens of the modern, developed world. These problems include drug addiction and abuse, alcoholism, smoking, crime and violence, unwanted pregnancy, sexually transmitted disease, underachievement in schools, gambling, personal debt and credit card abuse, lack of financial savings, anger and hostility, failure to exercise regularly, and overeating. Clearly, part of the rising interest in self-regulation is linked to the many problems that attend failed or deficient self-regulation.

Self-Control Predicts the Presence of Positive Outcomes

With respect to the presence of positive outcomes, Mischel and colleagues have demonstrated dramatic benefits of self-control. Using longitudinal follow-ups of people who had visited their laboratory as young children, Mischel, Shoda, and Peake (1988) found that the children who had been most successful at delaying gratification at age 4 were more successful both academically and socially, as rated by teachers and peers, in young adulthood more than a decade later.

Students with high self-control appear to get better grades, which is of particular importance. Wolfe and Johnson (1995) used 32 different personality trait measures in a large study of academic performance, and self-control was the only one that predicted grade point average. Tangney et al. (in press) likewise found that high self-control predicted higher self-reported grades, and S. M. Smith (2001) replicated this with objective measures of grades (from student transcripts).

High self-control is linked to better personal adjustment. People with high self-control report fewer pathological symptoms, including somatization, obsessive-compulsive patterns, depression, anxiety, hostile anger, phobic anxiety, paranoid ideation, and psychoticism (Tangney et al., in press), as well as higher self-acceptance and self-esteem. Children with good self-control are better than others at controlling anger (Kochanska, Murray, & Harlan, 2000).

People with high self-control make better relationship partners and get along better with other people generally. They exhibit better accommodation, in the sense of adjusting their behavior to get along with their partners, and they also report more satisfying relationships and better adjustment in their relationships (E. J. Finkel & Campbell, 2000; Vohs, Ciarocco, & Baumeister, 2003). They report better family cohesion, less interpersonal conflict, better empathy, and more secure interpersonal attachments (Tangney et al., in press). S. P. Cox (2000) found that leaders who scored high in self-control were rated by their subordinates as more trustworthy, fairer, and more consistent than other leaders. Children with better self-control have fewer behavior problems and fewer angry conflicts with other children (B. C. Murphy & Eisenberg, 1997), and in fact they exhibit better social functioning overall (Eisenberg et al., 1997). Children rated by teachers as high in self-control go on to become more popular with other children, which is an important sign of their interpersonal appeal (Maszk, Eisenberg, & Guthrie, 1999).

Self-Control Predicts the Absence of Negative Outcomes

High self-control is associated with the absence of a variety of impulse control problems. For instance, people with good self-control are less likely to abuse alcohol and illegal drugs (e.g., Peluso, Ricciardelli, & Williams, 1999; Wills, DuHamel, & Vaccaro, 1995; Wills, Sandy, & Shinar, 1999). They are also less likely to exhibit pathological eating patterns (Peluso et al., 1999; Tangney et al., in press). They manage their money well, spending less and saving more (Romal & Kaplan, 1995).

Research has used multiple methods, especially including the new self-regulation trait scales, to confirm that strong self-regulation is related to the absence of deleterious outcomes. As noted, people who score high in self-control on the Grasmick et al. (1993) scale have been shown to be less likely to engage in juvenile delinquency, crime, and other antisocial behaviors (e.g., J. J.

Gibbs, Giever, & Martin, 1998; Kochanska et al., 2000; Longshore & Turner, 1998; McGuire & Broomfield, 1994).

Possible Drawbacks?

Is there a downside to self-regulation? Thus far, we are unaware of any undesirable consequences or correlates of high self-control. In particular, Tangney et al. (in press) tested for curvilinearity to see if excessive self-control ("overcontrol") might produce negative consequences, but no such patterns were found. To be sure, self-control can be employed in the service of dastardly or antisocial aims, but by and large it appears to produce mainly positive effects. It seems appropriate to regard self-control as a strength in the same way that intelligence is a strength: It brings mainly benefits and helps people achieve their goals, although it can enable bad people to be more effective at doing bad things. Although in our society there may exist a stereotype of an "overcontrolled" person—one who is overly restrained, cautious, uptight, and not spontaneous—we do not believe that too much self-control is to blame. However, we acknowledge that the emphasis on consumption in modern American society undermines the value of self-control, despite the fact that hard work and self-reliance are the cornerstones of the American dream.

■ Development

Relatively little is known about how self-control is acquired and strengthened, and this topic must be regarded as a high priority for further research (especially in view of the many benefits that self-control confers). There are some tantalizing hints and speculations.

As already noted, self-control appears to show substantial consistency across development, as indicated by the finding that effective self-control at age 4 predicts positive outcomes in adulthood (Mischel et al., 1988). What this means is not fully clear, however. It could be that the capacity for self-control is already in place by age 4 and remains largely stable throughout life, as suggested by Freudian theories about the emergence of the superego in childhood. Then again, it could be that the parents who have begun instilling superior self-control in their young children continue to exert a similar, beneficial effect throughout development, and so the adult virtues reflect a long series of influences. At the other extreme, it could even be taken to indicate that self-control is genetically prepared and therefore has a stability that has little or nothing to do with learning.

The nature–nurture debate regarding self-control will be further complicated by the fact that behavioral outcomes will likely reflect the interplay of two opposing forces, which may well have different roots. That is, the practice of self-control involves overcoming impulses, and so good behavior could reflect either highly effective self-control or relatively weak impulses. Our best guess is that impulse strength has a strong innate component, whereas the capacity for self-regulation is learned to a substantial extent.

Gottfredson and Hirschi (1990) cited the substantially higher rate of criminality among the children of single parents in their theory of self-control and crime. There is in fact some evidence that lack of adult supervision leads to greater delinquency and criminal behavior subsequently (McCord, 1979), which may well indicate some degree of learning and internalization of self-control. Research suggests that the link between low parental supervision and delinquency is mediated by the child's feelings of attachment and efficacy (Wadsworth, 2000). Jang and Smith (1997) extended previous findings by showing that parental supervision and delinquency are reciprocally related, such that each is a predictor and consequence of the other. However, it should be noted that there is some evidence that peer influence plays a larger role than parental supervision or attachment in determining delinquency (Aseltine, 1995). And strictly speaking, it is plausible that the higher rate of criminality among offspring of single parents is entirely genetic (i.e., if the same genes cause the parents to end up alone and the children to commit crimes). Nonetheless, there does appear to be a direct link between parental attentiveness and child delinquency, a finding that should be further investigated. Perhaps the presence of parents helps teach the child the situations in which self-control is particularly important and also establishes and enforces repercussions if the child does not engage in appropriate self-control. In those cases, if the child feels attached to the parent and wants to gain his or her approval, the child will learn to exert self-control.

One longitudinal study sought to improve self-control through exercising it. Based on the view of self-control as a strength, Muraven et al. (1999) hypothesized that it would become stronger from regular exercise, and they assigned participants to engage in various exercises (such as improving their posture) for 2 weeks. There was considerable noise in their data, but the results did suggest improvement in self-control. Further efforts to study how to improve self-control seem warranted.

For individuals who wish to achieve better self-control in some specific domain, the most effective short-term gains are likely to come from improved monitoring. It seems well established that people cannot control behaviors that they do not monitor. Moreover, breakdowns in self-regulation are often associated with ceasing to monitor one's own behavior, such as in eating or alcohol binges (e.g., Polivy, Herman, Hackett, & Kuleshnyk, 1986). Monitoring can be improved in the short run by keeping written records or securing the cooperation of other people to actively remind the person of his or her goals.

■ Enabling and Inhibiting Factors

Effective self-regulation depends on multiple factors, and the failure of any of these can substantially impair self-control. Recent evidence suggests that changing the self's responses involves a limited resource, akin to strength or energy, and when this resource is depleted, the self is less able to exert control. Baumeister et al. (1998; also Muraven, Tice, & Baumeister, 1998) showed that after an act of self-control or volition (even including making choices), the self's capabilities were subsequently impaired, a condition they termed *ego depletion*. Vohs and Heatherton (2000) showed that individual differences, such as being a chronic dieter, can produce ego depletion as the result of having to engage in self-regulation under conditions that would not otherwise be depleting (e.g., in the presence of chocolate). Hence, regulating the self or making a decision temporarily depletes some crucial resource of the self, so that the self is less able to perform another act of self-regulation or volition.

It is important to recognize that the same, limited resource is used for a broad variety of psychological functions, and any of these can deplete the resource, thereby impairing all the other functions. It is therefore no accident that when people are coping with deadlines or stresses, they may cease to regulate their eating, smoking, or personal hygiene; that when people make multiple New Year's resolutions (all of which require changing the self), these all fail together; that when people are trying to diet or quit smoking, they indulge other appetites or fail at affect regulation (indicated by becoming irritable and crabby); that people drink too much after they have made difficult decisions; that work stress interferes with family relationships, and vice versa; and so forth. To live a balanced, well-regulated life, it may be necessary to recognize that the capacity for controlling oneself depends on a limited resource that needs to be managed effectively and conserved for the most pressing or important demands. In practice, this entails that much of life must be guided by habit, routine, and other automatic processes, so that the demands for conscious control over oneself are kept down to the level that the self's limited resources can meet.

Attention is crucial to the success of self-regulation, and indeed attentional processes often constitute the first step toward either success or failure at self-regulation. As mentioned, reduced self-monitoring is often a precipitating factor in self-regulation failure because it is quite easy to lose track of one's status or quit regulating oneself when one cannot evaluate the distance between the current state and the goal state (e.g., Kirschenbaum, 1987). Attending to oneself is also crucial because the self has to focus on its own behaviors in order to exert conscious control over them. When people cease to attend to their own behavior, self-regulation typically deteriorates (see Carver & Scheier, 1981).

Most acts of self-control involve overcoming some incipient response to the immediate situation in order to pursue some greater, long-term benefit. Hence the ability to transcend the immediate situation is crucial. People who live only in the present moment are unlikely to exhibit good self-control, whereas future-mindedness will facilitate self-regulation. Factors that shift attention to the immediate present and the salient stimulus environment (such as emotional distress or intoxication) will undermine self-control.

Undoubtedly the environment can teach people whether self-regulation and resisting temptation are worth the effort. It has long been suggested that some environments actively teach certain children not to delay gratification, especially if the promised but delayed rewards turn out not to be forthcoming. That is, if a child forgoes an immediate reward for the sake of a promise of a larger, delayed one, and then the delayed one never materializes, the child may learn that it is generally best to take what is offered in the short run.

Conflicting or unclear standards undermine self-regulation (Emmons & King, 1988). Conflicting standards are frequently a problem because people are focused on achieving a variety of goals. Consequently, some of these goals will come into conflict with each other. The man who wants to please his wife by washing the car may find that this goal clashes with his goal of having an enjoyable Saturday at the golf course with friends. Emmons and King (1988) have demonstrated that when multiple, distinct goals are in conflict, people tend to ruminate and, as a result, not advance toward any goal. Likewise, regulating oneself involves trying to conform one's behavior and responses to standards, and if the standards are not clear and consistent, it is difficult to move one's behavior toward them.

Self-awareness is crucial for monitoring one's behavior. The human capacity for self-awareness far surpasses that of other species, and this capacity is probably vital for the emergence of effective self-regulation (Carver & Scheier, 1981, 1982). Factors that undermine self-awareness will therefore detract from self-control. For example, Hull (1981) showed that alcohol reduces self-awareness, and many studies have indicated that alcohol intoxication contributes to failure of self-control in many different spheres (see Baumeister et al., 1994, for review).

■ Gender, Cross-National, and Cross-Cultural Aspects

In nearly all cultures males exhibit more aggressive and sexual misbehavior than females, and this seems more likely due to a gender difference in impulse strength than to a difference in self-control. Trait measures of self-control generally yield no gender differences (Tangney et al., in press) unless the items within a given scale are weighted toward measuring gender-specific domains in which men and women are known to differ in self-control efforts. For instance, items tapping self-control abilities regarding binge eating would yield a gender difference because women have more problems controlling binge eating than do men (e.g., Herman & Polivy, 1975; Vohs, Bardone, Joiner,

Abramson, & Heatherton, 1999), whereas items tapping self-control abilities regarding sexual impulses—which are known to be much stronger and more robust in men (Baumeister, Catanese, & Vohs, 2001)—would yield a higher mean for men than for women. Hence, general self-control abilities appear to be similar between the two genders, but the domains in which they are applied may differ.

At present, relatively little is known about national and cultural variations in self-regulation. To the extent that self-control is learned, it seems likely that the culture can have a substantial influence. A culture sets rules about what behaviors people are supposed to regulate and when it is appropriate to lose control.

Examples of cultural differences in self-control can be enumerated, although empirical confirmation of many of them awaits further, systematic work. According to Peele (1989), Jews have low rates of alcoholism despite high rates of drinking because Jewish culture holds that people remain responsible for their actions even when they have been drinking, in contrast to Christian cultures that accept intoxication as an excuse for irresponsible behavior. American culture may be especially prone to viewing alcohol as an excuse for irresponsible behavior, perhaps because of the "just say no" (i.e., zero tolerance/abstinence) mentality of the late 20th century. Europeans, conversely, are less prone to embrace zero tolerance beliefs about alcohol, and they also have fewer alcoholics (e.g., Peele, 1989). Indeed, violating a zero tolerance rule can paradoxically lead to greater disinhibition (see Baumeister et al., 1994), a phenomenon sometimes referred to as the "what the hell" effect. (Indeed, the phrase "what the hell" itself conveys a certain cultural endorsement of unleashing restraints!)

Carr and Tan (1976) reported that the practice of running amok was accepted in the Malay culture for many centuries, according to which young men who experienced a certain kind of setback or provocation lost control of their actions and embarked on violent, destructive rampages. When the British colonialists gained power and began punishing the violent acts committed during amok phases, the practice soon died out, indicating that it had been controllable all along. Thus, cultural change brought about abrupt shifts in patterns of how people regulated their behavior. In a very different context, Barber (2000) reported that teen pregnancy rates in the 20th century covaried with latitude, consistent with the stereotype that cultures close to the equator are more prone to indulge their sexual impulses than cultures that live closer to the poles.

The Protestant ethic has long been recognized as a stimulus to self-discipline, in contrast to the presumably greater self-indulgence of Catholic cultures (Weber, 1904). Many scholars attribute Protestant self-discipline to the increased sense of personal responsibility that Protestant religion introduced, according to which people are judged (and then consigned to heaven or hell) on the basis of their actions during their lifetimes, and, moreover, earthly virtue and prosperity can be interpreted as indications of one's eternal, predestined fate. More generally, most religions have supported moral systems that encourage and promote self-control. Indeed, the seven deadly sins of medieval Christian theology were mostly various forms of self-control failure, whereas the principal virtues extolled by the same theologians reflected various positive forms of self-control (Baumeister & Exline, 1999). During the 20th century, American culture shifted away from its traditional emphasis on self-denial toward active promotion of self-indulgence and immediate gratification, stimulated in part by advertising and economic realities, and it is plausible that such shifts have reduced the overall level of self-control in American culture.

■ Deliberate Interventions

Can self-regulation be improved? A brief longitudinal study by Muraven et al. (1999) found that people who worked on their self-regulatory capacities by daily exercises such as improving their posture ended up performing better than other people on laboratory tests of self-control. Although this finding demands replication and further study, it is consistent with the advice of wise men and women throughout history who have counseled cultivating personal self-discipline as a way of building character and thereby strengthening the self for times of stress. It does suggest that it may be possible for parents, teachers, coaches, and therapists to prescribe exercises that can build a young person's self-control.

The possibility of building self-control may be especially important for parenting. Psychology has moved across radically different views on the importance of parental influence during early childhood. At one extreme, Freud's theories (e.g., 1933) suggested that how the parent treated the child during the first half dozen years of life laid a powerful foundation for adult personality that subsequent events could only build on or alter in very slight ways. At the other extreme, J. R. Harris (1995) has suggested that direct parental influence may be minimal, and adult personality is largely a result of the combination of genetic foundations and the socializing effect of peer influence. Undoubtedly both genetic factors and peer influences play some role in shaping personality, but a person with strong self-regulation is (by definition) able to alter his or her behavior and responses and hence overcome many of these influences. If parents can instill self-control in their children, they can achieve a powerful and important effect that will benefit their offspring for years to come. Indulgent parenting and an excessive concern with maximizing children's self-esteem may, however, be detrimental to self-control, producing instead a personality that is weak, narcissistic, and self-indulgent. We consider the question of how much parents can instill self-control to be one of the most pressing theoretical and practical issues for developmental research.

One promising route to increasing self-regulatory abilities involves cognitive strategies and behavioral intentions. Gollwitzer's (1993, 1999) implementation intentions theory considers the attainment of goals to be a function of action intentions—thoughts that enable people to cope with obstacles or initiate behaviors. The focus of implementation intentions is the way in which the person will achieve the goal, and intentions are often stated conditionally, such as when certain conditions are present, specific behaviors will be enacted. An example of an implementation intention is when a dieter thinks, "When I am at a restaurant for dinner, I will order only a salad." Thus, when a person dislikes a habit or behavior in which he or she engages and is seeking methods to use to stop the behavior, implementation intentions are useful tools. One interesting application of the implementation strategy would be, for example, if parents taught their children conditional statements regarding the potential for drug use. Hence, a parent could say to his or her child, "If a person offers you drugs, just tell them, 'I do not want any and I have to go home right now.'"

Empirical studies confirm the effectiveness of implementation intentions in helping people achieve goals. For example, being induced to think about when and where to write an essay, as opposed to simply being asked to write an essay, dramatically increased the number of students who subsequently completed the essay, relative to students who were simply asked to write it (75% versus 33%; Gollwitzer & Brandstaetter, 1997). Gollwitzer (1993) proposed that implementation intentions render the response to be enacted more automatic and, thus, engaging in the response requires less effort and energy. If the actions do become more automatic, then people will be less likely to experience self-regulation failure under demanding situations. Hence, one method of fostering effective self-regulation is to encourage people to create and maintain implementation intentions.

■ What Is Not Known?

There are many exciting issues to be addressed in future research on self-regulation. In this section we highlight some of the most pressing questions, with the hopes that self-regulation research will be able to answer many of them in the upcoming years:

- How wide is the range of psychological processes and outcomes related to trait self-control? What does self-control not predict? In this line of research, it will be important to use objective measures of outcomes.
- What are the antecedents of trait self-control, in terms of family background or structure, ethnicity, race, religion, or other distal factors?
- How does self-regulation develop within a person (e.g., through interactions with parents or peers, through judicious practice, through positive or negative feedback)?

- What is the trajectory in self-control abilities through the life span?
- Is there a genetic component to self-regulation behaviors? In this line of research, it will be important to separate the strength of the urge (e.g., impulsivity) from restraints on the urge (e.g., self-control abilities).
- What are the key environmental factors that contribute to or detract from building self-control?
- What is the nature of the self-regulatory ("ego") resource? Can it be replenished, and if so, by what? What keeps the resource from becoming completely depleted throughout the course of the day or one's lifetime?
- What are the cross-cultural differences in self-regulation, especially in terms of conditions under which cultures encourage or discourage self-control? For example, when it is appropriate to show anger? Is disinhibition with drugs or alcohol allowed? How are celebratory losses of self-control treated?

In sum, self-regulation and self-control are uniquely human strengths. Every organism can respond to changing environmental contingencies, but only humans intentionally and willfully modify, alter, or otherwise change their responses. Many of the most important aspects of life, such as attaining a college degree, quitting smoking, or raising a healthy child, involve self-regulation. Thus, for the betterment of mental and physical well-being, researchers and practioners should attempt to understand and promote self-control.

We have focused on the positive aspects of self-regulation and self-control and have not discussed the possible drawbacks of self-control. This omission arises from our belief that there is no true disadvantage of having too much self-control. The extant psychological findings, as well as direct empirical tests (Tangney et al., in press), give no indication that problems can arise from having high self-control. Rather, when difficulties arise during self-regulatory attempts, the problem usually involves the use of inappropriate self-regulatory strategies (see Baumeister et al., 1994).

There have been major advances in understanding self-regulation and self-control. Theoretical and empirical work established the basic components of self-regulation, and recent research has set about to study how people tailor different self-regulatory processes and strategies for different situations (e.g., J. J. Gross, 1999). Moreover, there have been advances in conceptualizing and measuring trait self-control, which can now be thought of as an individual difference or perhaps a personality trait on which people differ by degree of baseline self-control abilities. Last, this review has emphasized the wide set of influences that determine self-regulation and self-control. Variables that predict degree of self-control and the success of self-regulatory attempts include the method used to control thoughts and emotions (e.g., Wegner, 1994); the relative depletion of self-regulatory resources after previous acts of self-control (e.g., Baumeister et al., 1998; Vohs & Heatherton, 2000); parental supervision and acts of delinquency; and the vast cultural and societal influences that determine, for example, which situations require self-control and which do not.

Self-control allows people to override responses that hinder happiness or health and, further, to substitute or develop more adaptive responses. Self-control is a vital psychological strength that is crucial to personal well-being and, accordingly, should be amply cultivated and fostered.

■ Must-Read Articles and Books

Bandura, A. (1977). Self-efficacy: Toward a unifying theory of behavior change. *Psychological Review, 84,* 191–215.

Bargh, J. A. (1990). Goal≠intent: Goal-directed thought and behavior are often unintentional. *Psychological Inquiry, 1,* 248–251.

Baumeister, R. F., Heatherton, T. F., & Tice, D. M. (1994). *Losing control: How and why people fail at self-regulation.* San Diego, CA: Academic Press.

Baumeister, R. F., & Vohs, K. D. (2003). Self-regulation and the executive function of the self. In M. R. Leary & J. P. Tangney (Eds.), *Handbook of self and identity* (pp. 197–217). New York: Guilford Press.

Carver, C. S., & Scheier, M. F. (1982). Control theory: A useful conceptual framework for personality-social, clinical and health psychology. *Psychological Bulletin, 92,* 111–135.

Gollwitzer, P. M. (1999). Implementation intentions: Strong effects of simple plans. *American Psychologist, 54,* 493–503.

Gross, J. J. (1999). Emotion and emotion regulation. In L. A. Pervin & O. P. John (Eds.), *Handbook of personality: Theory and research* (2nd ed., pp. 525–552). New York: Guilford Press.

Herman, C. P., & Polivy, J. (1975). Anxiety, restraint, and eating behavior. *Journal of Abnormal Psychology, 84,* 666–672.

Hull, J. G. (1981). A self-awareness model of the causes and effects of alcohol consumption. *Journal of Abnormal Psychology, 90,* 586–600.

Mischel, W., Shoda, Y., & Peake, P. K. (1988). The nature of adolescent competencies predicted by preschool delay of gratification. *Journal of Personality and Social Psychology, 54,* 687–696.

Wegner, D. M., Shortt, J. W., Blake, A. W., & Page, M. S. (1990). The suppression of exciting thoughts. *Journal of Personality and Social Psychology, 58,* 409–418.

INTRODUCTION:
STRENGTHS OF
TRANSCENDENCE

CRITERIA FOR *Strengths of Transcendence*

	Fulfilling	Morally valued	Does not diminish others	Nonfelicitous opposite	Traitlike	Distinctiveness	Paragons	Prodigies	Selective absence	Institutions and rituals	TALLY
	1	2	3	4	5	6	7	8	9	10	
Appreciation of beauty	X	X	X	X	X		X	X	X	X	9/10
Gratitude	X	X	X	X	X	X	X	~X	X	X	10/10
Hope	X	X	X	X	X	~X	X	X	X	X	10/10
Humor	X	X	X	X	X	X	X	X	X	X	10/10
Spirituality	X	X	X	X	X	X	X	X	X	X	10/10

~ Somewhat satisfies criterion.

At first glance, our final grouping of character strengths seems mixed, but the common theme running through these strengths of transcendence is that each allows individuals to forge connections to the larger universe and thereby provide meaning to their lives. Almost all of the positive traits in our classification reach outside the individual—character, after all, is social in nature—but in the case of the transcendence strengths, the reaching goes beyond other people per se to embrace part or all of the larger universe. The prototype of this strength category is spirituality, variously defined but always referring to a belief in and commitment to the transcendent (nonmaterial) aspects of life—whether they be called universal, ideal, sacred, or divine. How do the other strengths classified approach this prototype? Appreciation of beauty is a strength that connects someone directly to excellence. Gratitude connects someone directly to goodness. Hope connects someone directly to the dreamed-of future. Humor—admittedly the most controversially placed entry—connects someone directly to troubles and contradictions in a way that produces not terror or anger but pleasure.

As noted in chapter 1, the overall usefulness of this classification does not depend on exactly under which virtue we classify each of its 24 strengths, and we would not be surprised if this final grouping is revised—collapsed or combined, expanded or contracted—in subsequent editions. So, if appreciation of beauty is discovered to be the province mainly of the expert or fan who has studied a given domain for years, then it probably belongs with other strengths of wisdom and knowledge. If gratitude and humor as character strengths play themselves out mainly between two people (and not between a person and larger world), they probably belong with the other strengths of humanity. Or maybe humor will seek the company of vitality, among the strengths of courage. We think that hope and spirituality will stay allied, given the strong historical link between them (Tiger, 1979). In any event, let us turn to a discussion of how each of the positive traits classified here for the time being satisfies our 10 criteria for a strength of character (see Criteria Table).

■ Appreciation of Beauty and Excellence
[Awe, Wonder, Elevation]

The person who notices and appreciates beauty and excellence in different domains of life has the character strength we identify as awe. This is a virtue of transcendence because it connects those who possess it to something larger than themselves, whether it is beautiful art or music; skilled athletic performance; the majesty of nature; or the moral brilliance of other people. People with this strength notice excellence and appreciate it profoundly. They may be able to talk at length about the object of their appreciation, but this strength is not to be confused with one's vocabulary. Nor is it to be confined to the pursuits of the wealthy or the effete. Someone can appreciate good wine without mastering the jargon affected by connoisseurs. Someone can deeply appreciate good chocolate milk shakes. The defining feature of this character strength is the emotional experience of awe or wonder when in the presence of beauty or excellence. How well does awe satisfy our criteria for a strength of character?

CRITERION 1 *Fulfilling* By definition, appreciation of beauty is fulfilling, an emotional reaction akin to what William James (1902/1999) described more than a century ago as the mystical experience. Here the person feels oneness with the universe, a sense of truth, an inability to express experience in mere words, and a vividness and clarity of sensations and perceptions.

CRITERION 2 *Morally Valued* Appreciation of beauty and excellence is of course highly valued, although again we need to strip away layers of snobbery and be sure just what it is that we are valuing: someone's appreciation of life's finer things and moments or merely his or her ability to afford them. In any event, when our focus is on the appreciation of moral excellence, there is no price tag to distract us. To notice and applaud and revel in someone else doing the right thing costs nothing but is priceless. Those of us less skilled at such appreciation can be guided by those who are, and we can be grateful for their help.

   Haidt (2000) provided the following example of awe occasioned by the witnessing of a good deed:

> [We] were going home from volunteering our services at the salvation army that morning. It had been snowing since the night before and the snow was a thick blanket on the ground. As we were driving through a

neighborhood near where I lived I saw an elderly woman with a shovel in her driveway. I did not think much of it, when one of the guys in the back asked the driver to let him off here. The driver had not been paying much attention so he ended up circling back around towards the lady's home. I had assumed that this guy just wanted to save the driver some effort and walk the short distance to his home. . . . But when I saw him jump out of the back seat and approach the lady, my mouth dropped in shock as I realized that he was offering to shovel her walk for her. I felt like jumping out of the car and hugging this guy. I felt like singing and running, or skipping and laughing. Just being active. I felt like saying nice things about people. Writing a beautiful poem or love song. Playing in the snow like a child.

CRITERION 3 *Does Not Diminish Others*   As this example shows, the experience of awe is uplifting, especially when it involves the witnessing of heroic deeds by others, and awe itself can be elevating to witness. This second-order appreciation of excellence requires no special skills or dispositions. We all enjoy seeing people who are in wonder of the world around them: children chasing fireflies, baseball fans cheering a squeeze bunt, and concertgoers shouting "brava!"

CRITERION 4 *Nonfelicitous Opposite*   The opposite of appreciation of beauty includes of course the lack of appreciation, what we term being *oblivious, unmoved, unmindful, philistine, ignorant,* or *insensible.* A more subtle antonym is being drawn to the mundane or the trite, what we term being *coarse, crude, hackneyed, prosaic, clichéd, shallow, uncultured,* or *trivial.* In either case, the antonyms are negative. Again, though, we need to be careful not to let our own biases intrude to determine what we designate as banal and what we designate as sublime. We think that the Grand Canyon is more awe-inspiring than a Wal-Mart parking lot, and further that someone who prefers spending his leisure time at the latter is lower with respect to this strength than someone who prefers the former. But who knows in any given case? What defines this strength of character is the emotional experience of awe, and maybe Sam Walton's parking lots can produce awe in some folks. Regardless, not to experience such awe in any setting marks someone as deficient in this strength.

CRITERION 5 *Traitlike*   We suspect that the appreciation of beauty and excellence is a traitlike individual difference, although the relevant research is more indirect than we would like. The personality trait dubbed openness to experience, allied with this character strength but more general in its scope, is certainly a disposition of demonstrable generality and stability. Future research is needed that focuses on openness to experience as the underpinning of appreciation of excellence or beauty.

CRITERION 6 *Distinctiveness*   Appreciation of beauty is distinct from most of the other character strengths in the classification, with two possible exceptions. We have already alluded to the possibility that appreciation of at least some forms of beauty and excellence requires expertise in a given domain, in which case there is overlap with such wisdom strengths as curiosity and love of learning. We have also alluded to the possibility that awe—because it is a transcendent strength—may lead a person to have a spiritual experience, in which case it becomes an example of this character strength.

CRITERION 7 *Paragons*   Paragons of awe are readily found in religious accounts, where people experience a profound reaction to the beauty or goodness of the world or God, as recounted in Paul's conversion on the road to Damascus. More secular examples include sports fans who can cheer excellent plays by the opponents of their favorite team, or music buffs who may not especially like a given genre of music but can still appreciate a rap or bluegrass performer at the top of his or her craft.

Or consider Nobel Prizes. We usually attend to the winners, but remember that Alfred Nobel established these awards in the first place out of a profound appreciation of excellence in different domains that benefited humanity. According to his 1895 will, which established Nobel Prizes,

> The whole of my remaining realizable estate shall be dealt with in the following way: the capital, invested in safe securities by my executors, shall constitute a fund, the interest on which shall be annually distributed in the form of prizes to those who, during the preceding year, shall have conferred the greatest benefit to mankind. The said interest shall be divided into five equal parts, which shall be apportioned as follows: one part to the person who shall have made the most important discovery or invention within the field of physics; one part to the person who shall have made the most important chemical discovery or improvement; one part to the person who shall have made the most important discovery within the domain of physiology or medicine; one part to the person who shall have produced in the field of literature the most outstanding work in an ideal direction; and one part to the person who shall have done the most or the best work for fraternity between nations, for the abolition or reduction of standing armies and for the holding and promotion of peace congresses.

The members of the Nobel award committees are chosen because of their ability to recognize and appreciate excellence. They are given no special instructions, although they apparently deliberate in a conference room containing pictures of past winners. Nobel guidelines forbid discussion of the deliberations, but we speculate that the committee members are paragons of the strength we describe as appreciation of excellence.

CRITERION 8 *Prodigies*   Prodigies of awe exist. Consider children who are irresistibly attracted to *Swan Lake* or to a sunset or to a neatly turned double play. These early experiences of awe may establish the foundation for lifelong passions, a topic about which psychology seems to know too little. In chapter 23, we speculate that adolescence should be the time of peak awe because that is when we establish our identity, and part of this identity includes our passions. Meng Wu, a 17-year-old essayist, wrote about her appreciation of the beauty of life:

> You can have extensive farming and intensive farming. . . . I am going to have intensive living . . . not to be forever regretting the past, or anticipating the future . . . [but to] enjoy every second . . . and know I'm enjoying it when I'm enjoying it. (Veljkovic & Schwartz, 2001)

CRITERION 9 *Selective Absence*   People devoid of awe include—to us—those who put ketchup on filet mignon, those who zip around a wintry wilderness on snowmobiles with broken mufflers, and those who "do" the Louvre in 2 hours. These are judgment calls, but few could disagree with our more abstract characterization of experiential cynics and skeptics—who never see what is good or beautiful—as failures with respect to this strength. In chapter 23, we speculate that *schadenfreude* (joy in the misfortune of others) is the opposite of the characteristic strength of awe, so perhaps the underawed include those who gleefully collect accounts of failure.

CRITERION 10 *Institutions and Rituals*   The larger society tries to cultivate this character strength, although we think its success in so doing is spotty at best. The same mistake is made here that we mentioned with respect to the character strength of curiosity (chapter 5), putting the emphasis on the activity as opposed to the psychological experience of the activity. That is, we try to cultivate appreciation of beauty among young people by emphasizing beauty and not by emphasizing appreciation. Forcing children to experience classical music or Renaissance art can turn these activities into onerous ones. Indeed, why are museum gift shops usually more crowded than actual exhibits? We suspect the best way to nurture this strength of character is to expose children (and adults) to as many examples of excellence as possible, provide some guidance in understanding the local terrain, and then standing back and letting beauty takes its own course. We should avoid a "one-size-fits-all" approach to what we regard as beautiful or excellent. Indeed, the premise of the present endeavor is that there are at least 24 ways to exemplify good character, and people can be inspired by some yet unmoved by others.

■ Gratitude

Gratitude is the sense of thankfulness in response to a gift. The gift can be tangible, and it can be deliberately provided by a specific other person—like a Father's Day necktie from our youngest child. Or the gift can be more accidental—like the notes from a beautiful symphony we overhear while passing an outdoor concert. What marks gratitude is the psychological response to the gift, whatever its nature, and the experience, however briefly, of the transcendent emotion of grace—the sense that we have benefited from the actions of another. Gratitude has long been included among the important human strengths, although only recently has it attracted the attention of research psychologists. However, as we explain in chapter 24, there has been a recent boom in gratitude research, and we have learned a fair amount about this positive trait (cf. Emmons & Hill, 2001). We know that it fits well our criteria for a strength of character.

CRITERION 1 *Fulfilling*   Gratitude is fulfilling, not just in the obvious way because it is occasioned by a gift (which can be satisfying for reasons that have nothing to do with gratitude) but because it means that someone else has taken the time to be good to us. Paychecks are not gifts, and although we may be grateful to have a decent job, we do not feel grateful for receiving our contract-mandated salary. Instead, we feel grateful when the boss singles us out for praise, tells us to take the afternoon off to be with our family, or solicits our opinion. All of this is fulfilling, and as we are filled with gratitude, we experience a variety of positive emotions and may even be inspired to act in more virtuous ways—being more humble, for example, or more persistent, or kinder ourselves. It may be more blessed to give than to receive, but it is still pretty good to receive and then to feel grateful.

CRITERION 2 *Morally Valued*   The grateful person is morally valued, just as the ungrateful person is reviled. When we talk about manners, sometimes we mean which fork to use at a French restaurant, but just as often we mean that someone says please and thank you. And we will excuse an incorrect fork if the person at our dinner table takes the time to thank us for our company. We admire people who are grateful, who notice that others have been kind to them, and who share the glory. As we have done so for other strengths, we can invoke the metaphor of a dance, and in this case it involves unlike partners—kindness leads, and gratitude follows.

CRITERION 3 *Does Not Diminish Others*   Gratitude can never diminish others. Even the most awkward Academy Award acceptance speech or muttered "thank you" by a manly man initiates an episode that elevates participants and onlookers. Philadelphia bus drivers are among the gruffest men and women we have ever encountered, but when we say something appreciative as we get off the bus, they always respond with a smile or a nod.

CRITERION 4 *Nonfelicitous Opposite*   The opposites of gratitude are glaringly negative—*ungrateful, unappreciative, entitled, unthankful,* and *rude.*

CRITERION 5 *Traitlike*   Gratitude is an individual difference of demonstrable generality and stability. It has been successfully measured with self-report surveys and proves to have an impressive array of correlates and consequences.

CRITERION 6 *Distinctiveness*   Gratitude is not decomposable into other character strengths, although as noted, it often requires kindness to set its occasion. Gratitude is not a necessary component of social intelligence, but it no doubt represents value added to this positive trait.

CRITERION 7 *Paragons*   Paragons of gratitude include Lou Gehrig and his famous retirement speech at Yankee Stadium on July 4, 1939, just 2 years before his death from ALS:

> Fans, for the past two weeks you have been reading about the bad break I got. Yet today I consider myself the luckiest man on the face of this earth. I have been in ballparks for seventeen years and have never received anything but kindness and encouragement from you fans. Look at these grand men. Which of you wouldn't consider it the highlight of his career just to associate with them for even one day? Sure I'm lucky. . . . When you have a wonderful mother-in-law who takes sides with you in squabbles with her own daughter—that's something. When you have a father and a mother who work all their lives so you can have an education and build your body—it's a blessing. When you have a wife who has been a tower of strength and shown more courage than you dreamed existed—that's the finest I know. So I close in saying that I may have had a tough break, but I have an awful lot to live for.

Babe Ruth, who had not spoken to Gehrig for 5 years following a squabble, was so moved by this speech that he put his arm around Gehrig and whispered in his ear.

CRITERION 8 *Prodigies*   Prodigies of gratitude may be hard to find. Children are egocentric and may take good things for granted. But there are exceptions— children who appreciate good times and thoughtful gifts, and even their family members. In the words of 12-year-old William Barrie, "Fortunately, I have two good parents and an adult brother and sister who all share their good values with me by their example and by giving advice" (Veljkovic & Schwartz, 2001).

CRITERION 9 *Selective Absence*   The absence of gratitude marks those people who are belligerently entitled, who proclaim themselves self-made men and rugged individualists, who see no need to say please or thank you because— after all—they deserve everything they have. Such people may believe that they live in a gift-free zone, but it is gratitude that is missing more than kindness, at least in the short run. The tragedy is that the lack of gratitude may be self-fulfilling, and kindness may cease when it persistently fails to elicit any acknowledgment. An aha experienced decades ago by one of us is relevant to this point. Halfway through a grueling clinical internship, CP complained to his supervisor, "No one [meaning the patients] ever says thank you for anything I try to do." The response from the experienced psychiatrist stopped CP mid-whine: "If they [the patients] could say thank you, how many of them do you think would be in a psychiatric hospital?"

CRITERION 10 *Institutions and Rituals*   Gratitude institutions and rituals include Thanksgiving, practiced not just as a secular United States holiday but also in virtually all religions. Hallmark provides preprinted thank-you notes for baby showers, engagement parties, and weddings, although in our own experience, it is more gratifying to buy a blank card and include a personalized note of gratitude.

Gratitude that is pro forma or overly ritualized is empty, cheating both parties of what is transcendent about the sincere expression of thanks. Years ago, we smiled at the "acknowledgment" included in a published article by Anthony Greenwald (1980), who was making a wry point: "The reader of this article should appreciate that the author is prepared to take full responsibility only for the good ideas that are to be found in it" (p. 615). We think that all acknowledgments should equally jar us.

In our own teaching, we have had the opportunity to collect gratitude rituals from our students. For example, in South Korea, a newly elected president makes a point to visit the home of his favorite grade school teacher, where he bows and expresses his gratitude. Gratitude rituals are often institutionalized within one's family. So, at Thanksgiving dinner, each family member may publicly expresses gratitude for something good that has happened during the past year. Or a long-married husband may give his wife a flower every week for no particular reason except that he is grateful.

■ Hope [Optimism, Future-Mindedness, Future Orientation]

Hope and optimism represent a stance toward the future and the goodness that it might hold. Thinking about the future, expecting that desired events and outcomes will happen, acting in ways believed to make them more likely, and feeling confident that these might well ensue given appropriate efforts sustain good cheer in the here and now and galvanize goal-directed action. Anthropologist Lionel Tiger (1979) distinguished between what he calls little optimism and big optimism (cf. Peterson, 2000). *Little optimism* subsumes specific expectations about positive outcomes: "I will find a convenient parking space this evening." *Big optimism* refers to—obviously—larger and less specific expectations: "Our nation is on the verge of something great." Big optimism in particular is easy to see as a transcendent positive trait. Big or little, this character strength fits all of our criteria.

CRITERION 1 *Fulfilling* This positive trait is fulfilling. Although rendered nowadays by psychologists as a cognitive characteristic—a belief or an expectation—it should not be forgotten that these cognitions are about occurrences in the future that are valued and desired. Optimism and hope are not dispassionate forecasts; they are also positive feelings, inherently satisfying. *Cheerful* is one of the connotations of optimism—literally full of cheer and good feelings. Hope and optimism are incompatible with anxiety or depression. They energize us. They direct us. They give us something to which to look forward. Indeed, Tiger (1979) argued that hope is what makes the human condition possible. Because our intellectual ability allows us to foresee our own mortality, hope arose to keep us in motion despite existential dread.

CRITERION 2 *Morally Valued* Hope and optimism are highly valued characteristics. We admire those who can see the bright side; who can reach for the stars; who can keep their chins up, their backs straight, and their heads high; who can find the silver lining; who run out ground balls; who can see how it might all work out in the end—even if they are wrong. But often they are not wrong, because hope and optimism can be self-fulfilling. "Happy endings" are sometimes called Hollywood endings, but we doubt they are unique to Tinsel Town or even to the contemporary United States. We sometimes hear optimists dismissed as foolish—Pollyannaish or Panglossian—but there is little empirical support for this characterization. Optimistic people are popular and successful. We certainly want our children to have hopes and dreams, our friends to be positive, our mates to believe in us, and our leaders to have a plan and a vision.

CRITERION 3 *Does Not Diminish Others* Hope and optimism do not diminish others. Especially in the case of the bigger forms of optimism, others are elevated by its expression. Possibilities are legitimized. People are inspired. In our own research, we have found that presidential candidates who express optimism in their nomination speeches are more likely to win an election than their pessimistic counterparts (Zullow, Oettingen, Peterson, & Seligman, 1988); these data have apparently been heeded by contemporary presidential candidates, who have become indistinguishable in terms of their optimistic statements (Peterson & Lee, 2000). Within psychology, attention has been paid to a personality style dubbed *defensive pessimism*, a coping strategy that keeps expectations and therefore disappointments in check (Norem, 2001). We do not deny that defensive pessimism can prove useful in some circumstances, but the relevant research also shows that defensive pessimists can annoy others. A straight-A student can only say so many times that she failed an exam before her classmates decide she is not worthy of commiseration. In any event, optimistic individuals are attractive to others, and part of this attractiveness might lie in the contagion of hope.

CRITERION 4 *Nonfelicitous Opposite*   The opposites of hope and optimism include *pessimism, hopelessness, gloom,* and *helplessness*, none of them remotely desirable. We occasionally encounter someone who tells us, "I am not a pessimist—I am a realist." We applaud realism and regard it as a close cousin to the character strength of judgment (chapter 6), but remember that we regard "good" judgment as evenhanded and open-minded, admitting to positive possibilities as well as negative ones. Too often, the self-proclaimed realist privileges only what is ugly as real. If optimism as a character strength needs to be qualified, it is by highlighting its flexibility (Seligman, 1990). Optimism should be informed by the facts of the matter, to be sure, but the facts often afford enough ambiguity to view them in a good light.

CRITERION 5 *Traitlike*   Psychologists have approached hope and optimism in different ways, but all the incarnations of this strength are traitlike. Hope and optimism are individual differences that are stable across decades and general in their consequences for the individual.

CRITERION 6 *Distinctiveness*   Hope as a character strength does not reduce to any other character strength in our classification entry, although perhaps a blend of perseverance and zest would produce a close facsimile. Further research is needed.

CRITERION 7 *Paragons*   Paragons of hope include people like the following:

- Douglas MacArthur ("I shall return")
- Robert F. Kennedy ("Some men see things as they are and say why; I dream things that never were and say why not")
- Martin Luther King, Jr. ("I have a dream")
- Jimmy Valvano ("Never give up")
- Casey Kasem ("Keep your feet on the ground and your head in the sky")

We have previously mentioned paragons of persistence like entertainers who labored for years to make a career possible; most serve double duty here as paragons of hope, because it is difficult to imagine perseverance without a dream to keep alive. And how about fans of the Chicago Cubs, who for more than half a century have known that "next year will be different"? How about Nobel Peace Prize winners like Lech Wałesa (1983), Desmond Tutu (1984), Elie Wiesel (1986), the 14th Dalai Lama (1989), Aung San Suu Kyi (1991), Nelson Mandela and Frederik de Klerk (1993), John Hume and David Trimble (1998), Kim Dae Jung (2000), and Jimmy Carter (2002), who defied the lessons of history to hope that peace indeed was possible; the fact that their own creations were not always lasting hardly detracts from what they did and certainly not from their optimism.

CRITERION 8 *Prodigies*   Prodigies of hope include all of us who as children dreamed of an impossible birthday gift or chanted to keep Tinker Bell alive in *Peter Pan*. And you must have heard the somewhat funny joke about the irrepressibly optimistic child whose father decided to teach him a lesson by placing a ton of horse manure under the family Christmas tree. His son only beamed and exclaimed, "I know there must be a pony around here somewhere!" Less cute but better documented are the children studied by Dweck (1975) who were able to sustain positive expectations despite experimenter-arranged failure at laboratory tasks.

CRITERION 9 *Selective Absence*   Consider the doomsayers and naysayers among us, the people with the word *no* in their heart, the cynics and the skeptics and the self-labeled realists who triage all of life yet place nothing in the group that can be saved or healed. We have more sympathy for the hopeless and the helpless, those who are demoralized, dispirited, and burned out—they may have reasons for being pessimistic, but we can also point to people in identically terrible circumstances who still sustain hope (S. E. Taylor, 1985).

CRITERION 10 *Institutions and Rituals*   Institutions and rituals for cultivating hope include religious teachings and practices that nurture expectations for a better life, in this world or the next. On a more mundane level, we have such rituals as Christmas wish lists and New Year's resolutions. The psychology of goal setting is uniform in documenting the benefits of setting "hard specific" goals—those infused with hope—and therefore any practice that institutionalizes the setting of such goals ends up cultivating optimism. As we review in chapter 25, researchers at the University of Pennsylvania and elsewhere have developed strategies for encouraging optimism among schoolchildren. These programs pay dividends in terms of preventing depression and physical illness and boosting positive outcomes like academic achievement.

■ Humor [Playfulness]

A late addition to our classification, the character strength of humor was added in part because of its universality and in part because our classification was too grim without it. "Too much seriousness, even about virtue, is somehow sus-pect and disturbing. . . . Humorless virtue thinks much of itself and is thereby deficient in virtue" (Comte-Sponville, 2001, p. 211). Among character strengths enumerated by philosophers and theologians, humor is rarely mentioned ex-plicitly (chapter 2), although it lurks beneath the surface of many classical treat-ments of virtue. Lao-tzu does not tell anyone to be humorous (an impossible edict in any event) but is nonetheless humorous in what he does convey. Ditto for Benjamin Franklin. We hope that this book "shows its sense" in this respect.

We may eventually classify humor and playfulness as a value-added strength, most praiseworthy when coupled with one or another strength—consider how much we admire a humorous leader or a playful teammate—but for the time being, we discuss this character strength in its own right.

We define the humorous individual as one who is skilled at laughing and gentle teasing, at bringing smiles to the faces of others, at seeing the light side, and at making (not necessarily telling) jokes. Humorous people may well tell jokes, or pass them on via e-mail, but jokes are but one part of humor. Indeed, a highly playful person may never tell a single joke but still inject humor into a situation by choosing the right moment to raise an eyebrow or make a wry comment.

The domain of humor is vast and varied, and there exists a huge terminol-ogy for describing its types. Some forms are clearly mean (e.g., mockery, ridi-cule, sarcasm), and others on the border (e.g., parody, practical jokes). We exercise our prerogative by mentioning those forms of humor that serve some moral good—by making the human condition more bearable by drawing at-tention to its contradictions, by sustaining good cheer in the face of despair, by building social bonds, and by lubricating social interaction. *This* is what we mean by playfulness as a strength of character. We acknowledge that humor can be harnessed to wrong purposes, just as can the other strengths of character; the difference between humor and the other strengths may simply be the rich vo-cabulary available for labeling its evil variants. In any event, a serious look at humor shows that it satisfies our criteria for a character strength.

CRITERION 1 *Fulfilling*   Humor and playfulness are fulfilling. Part of their very definition is that they produce amusement and other positive emotions, not just among onlookers but among those who initiate it. It feels good to play and to make others laugh.

CRITERION 2 *Morally Valued*   This is a highly valued trait. Cross-national stud-ies of the characteristics that people find most attractive in a mate or a friend al-ways reveal a sense of humor to be near the top of the list (chapter 3), edging out looks and a whole lot of money. Even youngsters nominate humor as a highly desirable characteristic among their friends. When asked to rate their own sense of humor, 85% of people believe they are above average in this characteristic!

CRITERION 3 *Does Not Diminish Others*   "Good" humor does not diminish others, although of course "evil" humor is defined precisely by the fact that it derogates someone else. Even in this latter case, though, humor can have the effect of elevating all of us by bringing some of us down to earth where we belong. Derogatory humor is most amusing when it calls attention to pomposity and pretentiousness. A wealthy businessman slipping on a banana peel as he hurries off to close a million-dollar deal is a lot funnier than a homeless mother taking the same fall on the way to a shelter. Shifting back to good humor, sharing a joke or a laugh is one of the best ways to feel close to someone else, even a stranger, because it is a sign that we have something in common. The USO does not send Shakespearean actors overseas to entertain troops by reciting lines from *Hamlet*; it sends comedians.

CRITERION 4 *Nonfelicitous Opposite*   Despite the complexities introduced by evil humor, the opposite of humor per se is hardly complex—just undesirable. Who would want to be labeled *humorless, grim, sour, dour, tedious,* or *boring*?

CRITERION 5 *Traitlike*   Humor and playfulness are traitlike, although the complexity of this characteristic and associated problems with measuring it as a unidimensional trait make this conclusion more tentative than we would like. In recent years, researchers have made some progress in devising measures of humor as an individual difference, and resulting studies reveal pervasive correlates, usually highly desirable ones.

CRITERION 6 *Distinctiveness*   Humor and playfulness cannot be broken down into other entries in our classification, although we suspect that this strength often co-occurs with zest and vitality. The distinction remains clear.

CRITERION 7 *Paragons*   Paragons of humor of course include comedians, from Charlie Chaplin to Lucille Ball to Bob Newhart to George Carlin to Bill Cosby to Margaret Cho, but perhaps even better examples are humorists like Will Rogers or Garrison Keillor or wits like Oscar Wilde or Chris Berman of *Sportscenter*. If part of being playful is not taking oneself too seriously, then how about popular singers like Ray Stevens or Shaggy, baseball players like John Kruk,[1] or—if we can believe what has been said about him by his friends, former senator Bob Dole (cf. Yarwood, 2001). But the best examples of human paragons are those who inhabit our own lives, and we have discovered that every-

---

[1] Here is one of our favorite John Kruk stories, which may or may not have happened. Kruk had just returned to the Philadelphia Phillies after undergoing surgery for testicular cancer. The pitcher delivered the first pitch, and the umpire loudly proclaimed, "Ball one!" Kruk looked over and muttered, "Don't make fun of me."

one can readily name the funniest person they happen to know, and they always smile when they think about him or her.

CRITERION 8 *Prodigies*   The more sophisticated forms of humor do not admit to prodigious display, but even infants vary in how playful they are, and it would be a fascinating longitudinal study to see if peekaboo prodigies grow up to be the most playful adults. Some children revel in puns and word play more than others, and they qualify as humor prodigies. Even more interesting are those children who can deliberately make others laugh. Consider 8-year-old Darryl Seligman, a humor prodigy in this sense and the son of you-know-who. As the story goes, he was whooping and hollering while supposedly helping his father rake leaves. His father chastised him, "We're never going to get done." "That's not an optimistic thing to say," retorted Darryl. Darryl's mother then chimed in, "Now Darryl, you know your father has written books on optimism." "Maybe," said Darryl, "but they must not be very good."

CRITERION 9 *Selective Absence*   We all know people who are too literal, too earnest, too serious, too stuffy, and too stiff. Do you remember the foil to the Robin Williams character in *Good Morning Vietnam?* More generally, the loss of a sense of humor seems to cut across virtually all forms of psychopathology, which implies to us that a good sense of humor might well be one of the defining features of so-called positive mental health.

CRITERION 10 *Institutions and Rituals*   All cultures have institutions and rituals that center around humor and playfulness. Our own social world provides musical comedies, television shows like *Seinfeld* and *Frasier,* comedy clubs, *New Yorker* cartoons, and silly bumper stickers. At least in the contemporary United States, there seems to be more emphasis on enjoying humor produced by others than on making it ourselves. Accordingly, it is difficult to specify contemporary institutions that encourage people to be funnier than they might otherwise be (although some might argue that televised congressional debates on C-SPAN have this unintended effect).

In an earlier version of this volume, we tried to be funny ourselves by asking why there were so many basketball camps for kids but no clown camps; we would much prefer our own children to have senses of humor rather than crossover dribbles. Some of our readers pointed out that clown camps do exist, as well as laughing clubs. There also exist training circuits for would-be stand-up comedians and workshops for businesspeople who wish to become funnier. Nonetheless, these are poorly publicized and poorly attended, and our point remains that society does not do enough to encourage deliberately this important positive trait. As chapter 26 describes, some researchers have investigated how to encourage humor as a strength, and the results are promising. The other point of view here is that we do not need explicit interventions to encourage humor because ongoing interaction with others does precisely this in the form of the immediate rewards it provides. Consider the childhood rituals of sharing knock-knock jokes or trading insults about mothers, so exaggerated that none can take offense.

■ Spirituality [Religiousness, Faith, Purpose]

The final entry in the classification has been included in our list from the very beginning. It is the most human of the character strengths as well as the most sublime. We define the strength of spirituality and religiousness as having coherent beliefs about the higher purpose and meaning of the universe and one's place within it. People with this strength have a theory about the ultimate meaning of life that shapes their conduct and provides comfort to them. Furthermore, spirituality and religiousness are linked to an interest in moral values and the pursuit of goodness. Extreme interest in college football and devotion to hip-hop music may seem religious in their fervor but are not explicitly moral, which is why such examples are not subsumed here. In contrast, vegetarianism, secular humanism, and laissez-faire economics fit when their rationales are moral in nature and make some reference to the transcendent.

America's first great psychologist, William James (1902/1999), wrote provocatively about religious experience from the perspective of psychology, and for many decades his work stood virtually alone in the field. We assume that many psychologists hesitated to venture into an area that was so value laden, so potentially controversial, and so apparently nonscientific (chapter 3). However, matters have changed in recent years, and psychologists as well as other social scientists have realized that it is folly to ignore such an important aspect of the human condition and further that one need not endorse (or deny) religious experiences in order to study them.

As chapter 27 elaborates, psychologists today commonly distinguish between religiousness, which refers to conventional religious practices like church attendance or tithing, and spirituality, which refers to the psychological experience and significance of ultimate beliefs (cf. the distinction between extrinsic and intrinsic religiousness; Allport & Ross, 1967). The distinction is important but should not obscure the fact that for the vast majority of people, religiousness and spirituality comfortably coexist. For other people, though, we need to allow for the possibility that they can have a coherent belief system about the transcendent aspects of life that is forged and followed outside traditional religions. This is why we tack on the supplement "sense of purpose" in labeling this character strength, and we refer the reader to Antonovsky's (1985) discussion of "sense of coherence" as a nonreligious yet spiritual individual difference. These distinctions made, let us turn our attention to how well spirituality and religiousness satisfy our criteria for a strength of character.

CRITERION 1 *Fulfilling*   That spirituality is fulfilling is obvious.[2] People secure in their faith are fulfilled, whether this fulfillment shows itself as quiet contentment or ecstasy. Even those of us who are but occasionally religious will say a brief prayer when unsettled, and comfort follows. Spirituality is the ultimate answer to the "deathbed test" we proposed in chapter 1. Indeed, most if not all faiths have celebrated martyrs who sacrificed their lives instead of their beliefs.

CRITERION 2 *Morally Valued*   Spirituality and religiousness are morally valued, even by those who hold different beliefs or none at all. We respect people who are sincerely devout. We need to acknowledge the existence of religious intolerance and the centuries-old battles and outrages that play out across religious distinctions: the Crusades, the Inquisition, the Salem witch trials, and the various jihads of the modern world.

CRITERION 3 *Does Not Diminish Others*   The observation of spirituality in practice does not diminish others. It can only elevate. One of Norman Rockwell's most famous *Saturday Evening Post* covers from the 1950s—*Saying Grace*—depicts a mother and her young son saying a prayer at a restaurant table they share with strangers, who themselves stop eating and seem to be on the verge of bowing their own heads. Here we are provided some insight into the sustained appeal of organized religion, the practices of which allow communion among all and thus a sharing in the transcendent. One need not be a Roman Catholic to be moved by a Latin mass or a Latter-day Saint to thrill at the Mormon Tabernacle Choir. The Ba'Hai Temple in suburban Chicago is an elevating sight even if we know nothing about the Ba'Hai faith.

CRITERION 4 *Nonfelicitous Opposite*   The opposites of this character strength include *spiritually empty, godless,* and *profane* and more broadly *alienation, anomie, purposelessness, living a life of quiet desperation,* and *fidgeting until death.* Atheism and agnosticism, if they are coherent beliefs, are *not* psychological opposites.

CRITERION 5 *Traitlike*   Although researchers are divided as to whether spirituality can be ascertained with single questions or demands a multidimensional approach, there is little disagreement that this is a trait with robust stability and

---

[2]For those readers who do not find this assertion so obvious, consider some survey data we recently gathered showing that an orientation toward "meaning" (seeking connections outside the self, e.g., spirituality specifically and transcendence generally) is a robust correlate of subjective well-being. An orientation toward sensory "pleasure" is dramatically less associated with well-being, despite the arguments of the hedonists, the behaviorists, Hugh Hefner, or the producers of MTV.

generality. Our own attempts to measure spirituality, with items like "My life has a strong purpose" and "My faith makes me who I am," reveal this trait to be a coherent individual difference even for pre-teens (chapter 28).

CRITERION 6 *Distinctiveness* Spirituality does not reduce to any of the other strengths in our classification, although as we have noted, the other strengths of transcendence described here can be seen as special cases of spirituality.

CRITERION 7 *Paragons* Paragons of spirituality include religious martyrs but just as strikingly those individuals who live out their beliefs through good deeds and moral example: Albert Schweitzer, Mother Teresa, and the Dalai Lama.

CRITERION 8 *Prodigies* Prodigies of spirituality exist, once we recognize that the faith of children takes a different form than that of adults. Indeed, the innocence and simplicity of children can make their spirituality blindingly pure. In the words of 16-year-old Genevieve Owusu Ansah, "My faith . . . has helped me look to God alone and at things squarely, hopefully, and with honesty, laughing at impossibilities and crying it out in the midst of all difficulties" (Veljkovic & Schwartz, 2001).

CRITERION 9 *Selective Absence* There are those who never ask the question, Is this all there is? They may simply be stones or automatons—stimulus-response machines—or they may be in a state of despair as they seek their soul without success (cf. Jung, 1934). Regardless, by their own reckoning, they are alone in the universe.

CRITERION 10 *Institutions and Rituals* Institutions and rituals that cultivate and maintain this strength exist in abundance for the religious, and even non-religious yet spiritual people have their own practices for nurturing their own version of this strength, whether it be volunteer work at a hospice or a quiet walk through Muir Woods.

23. APPRECIATION OF BEAUTY AND EXCELLENCE

[Awe, Wonder, Elevation]

■ *A paragon of appreciation of beauty and excellence is the poet Walt Whitman. William James (1902/1999, p. 82) cited Whitman as his own exemplar of healthy-mindedness, and his description makes it clear that Whitman took great pleasure in both the sights and the people that surrounded him. According to a description of Whitman written by Dr. R. M. Bucke (cited by James on p. 82), Whitman's favorite activity was to stroll outdoors by himself, admiring trees, flowers, the sky, and the shifting light of day, and listening to birds, crickets, and other natural sounds: "It was evident that these things gave him a pleasure far beyond what they give to ordinary people. Until I knew the man, it had not occurred to me that any one could derive so much absolute happiness from these things as he did. . . . Perhaps, indeed, no man who ever lived liked so many things and disliked so few as Walt Whitman. All natural objects seemed to have a charm for him. All sights and sounds seemed to please him. He appeared to like (and I believe he did like) all the men, women, and children he saw."* ■

■ Consensual Definition

Appreciation of beauty and excellence (or simply *appreciation*) refers to the ability to find, recognize, and take pleasure in the existence of goodness in the physical and social worlds. A person high on this strength frequently feels awe and related emotions (including admiration, wonder, and elevation) while, for example, walking in the woods or in a city, while reading novels or newspapers, while learning about people's lives or while watching sports or movies. A person low on this strength goes about daily life as if wearing blinders to that which is beautiful and moving, taking little pleasure in the scenes that pass by or in the strengths, talents, virtues, and accomplishments of others. We presume that people whose minds and hearts are open to beauty and excellence find more joy in daily life, more ways to find meaning in their own lives, and more ways to connect deeply with other people. The evidence we review in this chapter, although preliminary, is consistent with these claims.

We propose that there are three principal types of goodness for which it is beneficial to be responsive: (a) physical beauty (primarily the beauty of the visual environment but also auditory beauty such as music); (b) skill or talent (displays of virtuosity or superhuman ability by other people); and (c) virtue or moral goodness (displays of kindness, compassion, forgiveness, or many of the other virtues in this book). Each of these three kinds of goodness can produce awe-related emotions in observers. In the strongest cases beauty produces awe, skill produces admiration, and virtue produces the emotion of moral elevation (Haidt, 2003). All three of these emotional reactions are related as members of the family of self-transcendent emotions, of which awe appears to be the central member (Haidt, 2002; Keltner & Haidt, 2003). For linguistic simplicity we will refer to the trait of being emotionally responsive to all forms of excellence, including beauty, as appreciation.

There are currently several theories and measures of aesthetic sensitivity, but there appear to be no theories or measures about individual differences in emotional responsiveness to skills or virtues. At present, we group the three kinds of appreciation together, but empirical research will be needed to determine if these sensitivities do in fact cluster together in individuals. Even if they do not, it may still make conceptual sense to group them together. There may be multiple channels by which people can connect to excellence around themselves and create enriched and awe-filled lives. Broadening the scope of stimuli beyond classical conceptions of beauty and the arts has the added benefit of making this strength less a product of education, class, and political ideology, and more accessible to people who have had little exposure to poetry and art museums, and little encouragement to develop an appreciation of high culture.

Because of the almost complete lack of empirical research on individual differences in responsiveness to nonaesthetic excellence, this chapter takes the following form. Empirical findings are described when available about responsiveness to beauty, but many statements about responsiveness to other kinds of goodness will be speculative. The later sections of this chapter are therefore quite short. It is our hope that future versions of our classification will be able to fill in the many holes that we identify in this review.

Appreciation should be compared to the psychological trait *openness to experience* (McCrae, 1996) and to the everyday term *aesthetic sensitivity*. Appreciation is narrower than openness to experience (which includes elements of sensation seeking, intellectual broad-mindedness, and curiosity, as discussed in chapter 5) but broader than the subscale of openness labeled openness to aesthetics. Openness to aesthetics is similar to the everyday term aesthetic sensitivity, both of which can be used to describe individuals who seek out and revel in poetry, painting, and other arts. We assume here that appreciation correlates highly and overlaps substantially with openness to aesthetics, but we think it differs in two ways: (a) It is broader in that it includes responsiveness to nonaesthetic forms of excellence such as might be demonstrated by athletes, jugglers, and saints; and (b) it refers to more than just the degree of pleasure afforded by the contemplation of beauty and excellence. We think of appreciation as a specific *emotional* responsiveness, the tendency to experience at least subtle self-transcendent emotions such as awe, admiration, and elevation, triggered by the frequent perception of beauty and excellence in one's surroundings.

Appreciation is probably related to several other strengths in this classification, especially curiosity and love of learning (because high appreciation people are likely to seek out new ideas and experiences that can trigger awe), gratitude (because gratitude involves being emotionally moved by the moral excellence of another person's generosity), and spirituality (because spiritual people are likely to experience frequent and powerful awe).

One way to think about appreciation is as the opposite of *schadenfreude* (joy in another's failure or misfortune). We might even coin the term *tugendfreude* (joy in another's virtue) to refer to the taking of pleasure in the skills, virtues, and successes of others. Appreciation might then be thought of as encompassing both aesthetic sensitivity and *tugendfreude*.

The behavioral manifestations of appreciation are subtle, for awe, wonder, and responses to beauty and excellence often involve passive receptivity and stillness, as opposed to other emotions that often are marked by clear action tendencies (Frijda, 1986). Appreciation is likely to be associated with certain expressive markers, such as wide-open eyes and open mouth (Darwin, 1872/1965); physiological symptoms such as piloerection (goose bumps), tears, and the proverbial lump in the throat; and certain delayed actions that are motivated by a desire to improve the self and the greater good (Keltner & Haidt, 2003).

■ Theoretical Traditions

The human tendency to feel powerful self-transcendent emotions has been studied since ancient times in two contexts: aesthetics and religion. In both of these traditions theorists focused primarily on the characteristics of objects that produced awe rather than on characteristics (traits) of observers, but several ideas are still helpful for understanding appreciation. In more modern times appreciation and its related emotions have been discussed in some form by humanistic psychologists and by emotion researchers.

Aesthetics

As the ancient Greeks refined their skills in sculpture, architecture, drama, and music, their philosophers began to ask what makes a work excellent, and why people respond so strongly to excellent art. Plato had mixed feelings about the arts because they often portrayed bad behavior that he feared would lead the young astray. But others saw in art an important pathway for moral and spiritual advancement. One of the most important ancient treatises on the emotional response to the arts, entitled "On the Sublime," was written by the Greek Longinus in the 1st century A.D. Longinus sought to understand the power of good writing and oratory to move people emotionally and fill them with awe:

> The effect of elevated language upon an audience is not persuasion but transport. At every time and in every way imposing speech, with the spell it throws over us, prevails over that which aims at persuasion and gratification. Our persuasions we can usually control, but the influences of the sublime bring power and irresistible might to bear, and reign supreme over every hearer. . . . Sublimity flashing forth at the right moment scatters everything before it like a thunderbolt. (Longinus, 1907, I:4)

Longinus addressed the issue of individual differences among audience members by describing the sort of person who is not open to the sublime. He quoted a passage from Plato's *Republic* in which Socrates distinguished among those who pursue higher (intellectual) versus lower (corporeal) pleasures. This 2,300-year-old passage still serves well as a description of a person low on appreciation:

> Those . . . who have no experience of wisdom and goodness, and do nothing but have a good time, spend their life straying between the bottom and middle in our illustration, and never rise higher to see or reach the true top, nor achieve any real fulfillment or sure and unadulterated pleasure. They bend over their tables, like sheep with heads bent over their pasture and eyes on the ground, they stuff themselves and copulate, and in their greed for more they kick and butt each other with hooves and horns of steel. . . . (*Republic*, Book IX, 586a)

Plato's and Longinus's concern to distinguish higher from lower pleasures raises the question for us as to whether all forms of excellence are equally important. Is it as much a strength to be emotionally responsive to beauty in a sexual object as in a landscape? Is it as good to be as emotionally responsive to a baseball game as to a symphony?

A second important treatise on aesthetic responsiveness was written by Plotinus (205–270 A.D.), the founder of Neoplatonism. Plotinus argued that the soul finds joy in contemplating beauty, for it sees in works of art a hint of the divinity that it (the soul) shares. Plotinus linked all the forms of excellence that this chapter is concerned with, suggesting that people go through a developmental progression in their ability to respond to excellence. People begin with the contemplation of sensuous beauty and then move on to delight in beautiful deeds, in moral beauty, and in the beauty of institutions, getting ever closer to the more abstract Platonic form of beauty (Beardsley, 1967).

In 18th- and 19th-century Europe, philosophers took the interest in aesthetic responsiveness, or the sublime, in a new direction. Struck by the aesthetic power of landscapes, mountains, and other natural objects, theorists and artists alike advanced more secular ideas about beauty and awe, shifting the focus from divine to material causes of awe. The most focused analysis was that of the Irish philosopher Edmund Burke (1757/1990). Burke's goal was to explain the experience of the sublime, the feeling of expanded thought and greatness of mind that is produced by literature, poetry, painting, and viewing landscapes (a fascination of his day; Phillips, 1990). Burke reasoned that two properties or themes endow stimuli with the capacity to produce the sublime experience: power and obscurity. But Burke had little to say about individual differences in receptivity to the sublime.

More modern treatments of aesthetics also focused on the qualities of an object that make it beautiful (e.g., variety within unity), independent of any features of the observer (Bell, 1913; Berlyne, 1971). However, an important idea common to many modern approaches, and going back to the 18th century, is that an aesthetic attitude is disinterested; that is, one contemplates an object or listens to music without concern for its utility, or for how it furthers one's goals (E. Burke, 1757/1990; Fry, 1920; Shaftesbury, 1714/1977). This idea can help resolve the question raised earlier, about higher versus lower pleasures. If appreciation is a strength because it enables self-transcendence (and its associated loss of ego, and openness to others), then the higher forms of excellence are those that lead to self-transcendence. A person admiring a perfect body in a pornographic magazine is not disinterested, whereas a person admiring a landscape is disinterested (unless she is a real estate developer). A person who is emotionally responsive to a triple play in baseball because of an intense desire to beat the other team is not disinterested, but a person who is equally thrilled to see a great play by either team has a disinterested love of baseball that may enable self-transcendent awe or admiration.

Whatever the elicitors of aesthetic pleasure, the history of aesthetics suggests that one of the keys to understanding appreciation is to understand that works of art and drama have the capacity to create a state of deep absorption, which is experienced as a kind of self-transcendent journey into another world. This idea of self-transcendence is at the heart of an ancient Hindu theory of aesthetics contained in the *Natyashastra*, an 11th-century elaboration of a much older treatise on drama (Shweder & Haidt, 2000). The key idea of the *Natyashastra* is that the presentation of emotions onstage, or in a poem, elicits in the most sensitive members of the audience an emotional state that is parallel to the emotion portrayed, without being the emotion portrayed. An actor weeping onstage elicits in the viewer not real sadness but a meta-emotion (*rasa*) of sadness, in which observers can taste or savor an emotional experience that floods through them, taking them away from their everyday world of goals, fears, and petty concerns. Because the goal of much Eastern religious practice is precisely the forgetting of one's concerns and attachments, this state of aesthetic rapture is recognized to be a valuable spiritual state, akin to other forms of mystical experience. Even in the West, loss of self may be an important emotional and cognitive response to art and drama. Greene and Brock (2000) have recently created the Transportation Scale to measure the degree to which individuals find themselves transported into the world of a narrative; this scale should be useful in the study of appreciation. (See also Tellegen's, 1982, construct and measure of absorption.)

Religion

The importance of awe has been even more salient in the history of religion. Awe is the normal response to contact with divinity, appearing clearly in the holy scriptures of Judaism (e.g., God's appearance on Mount Sinai), Christianity (e.g., Paul's conversion), Hinduism (e.g., Arjuna's encounter with Krishna), and most other religions. In these classic cases, religious awe generally involves a mixture of fear and submissiveness with joy, ecstasy, and a malleability or openness to the teachings and commandments of the divine will. Awe seems to reprogram people, making them more pious and more prosocial, with little concern for material wealth, reputation, or other petty concerns of daily life (Keltner & Haidt, 2003).

Scholars of religion have long noted that awe is triggered not just by the presence of God but by a variety of experiences that help one to transcend the self and become absorbed in something else. Otto Grundler (1922, cited in Wulff, 1991) discussed four classes of objects that often facilitate religious transcendence: (a) the world of nature; (b) inspired works of art that have a certain loftiness and grandeur; (c) historical and personal events that suggest an insight and will that is more than human; and (d) the testimony of people, particularly saintly people, who may themselves be thought to be divine. Many other scholars have noted the power of natural and artistic beauty to facilitate mystical states and religious devotion. However, it is Grundler's third and fourth classes that are most relevant for the present discussion, for they suggest that awe is not just a response to God or to visual beauty but also to exemplary, exceptional, and virtuous people.

The preceding analyses could be taken to show that awe is the proper response to seeing any manifestation of God, God's power, or God's goodness, revealed in any aspect of creation, be it a landscape, a thunderstorm, a cathedral, or a virtuous person. However, the reverse causal path is just as plausible: People have an innate tendency to be moved by beauty and excellence, and whenever these profound and ineffable feelings are triggered, people attribute the cause to the presence of God. This analysis would suggest that it is the very existence of the human capacity for appreciation that generates religions across human societies. Many of the accoutrements of religion (music, architecture, ritual, stories about saints) can then be seen as attempts to amplify these feelings of awe-filled appreciation.

Many scholars of religion have addressed the question of individual differences in liability to awe and religious experience, and two dimensions seem to emerge most frequently: rationality versus intuition/emotion, and optimism versus pessimism. William James (1902/1999) contrasted existential judgments, which are analytical statements about what a thing is, to spiritual judgments, which are addressed to a thing's value. Throughout his Gifford Lectures on religion he tried to inspire his highly rationalistic academic audience to go against their normal analytical habits and make spiritual or intuitive judgments. Many others have noted a correlation between emotional or intuitive modes of thought and spirituality or a liability to powerful religious experiences (Maslow, 1964; Otto, 1917/1923; Schleiermacher, 1806/1967). If this correlation is real, then people high on appreciation may be expected to score high on Epstein's faith in intuition scale, and lower on need for cognition (Epstein, Pacini, Denes-Raj, & Heier, 1996).

But perhaps the most famous trait distinction in the psychology of religion is William James's (1902/1999) contrast of the healthy-minded versus the sick soul. The healthy-minded are models of appreciation. They see everything in life as beautiful or good, they look out on the world with grateful admiration, and they are wide open to the world because the world itself is a manifestation of divinity. Those with sick souls, in contrast, see evil and decay everywhere and view the world as an illusion whose temptations should be shunned. Divinity and salvation lie elsewhere, so such people are not emotionally responsive to beauty and excellence in their worlds. James's description of these two types of people clearly overlaps heavily with modern discussions of optimism and pessimism, suggesting that optimists should in general be higher on appreciation.

Humanistic Psychology

The idea that there is an innate and powerful emotional response to beauty and excellence was an important axiom of humanistic psychology. Carl Rogers (1961, cited in McCrae, 1996) thought that openness was the natural human condition, which often gets suppressed by acquired defenses. But it was Abraham Maslow who had the most to say about awe (as peak experience) and about individual differences in awe-proneness (depending on one's location on the hierarchy of needs).

Maslow himself appears to have been extraordinarily high on appreciation. He was frequently and powerfully moved by music, art, and nature, and even by reading scientific journals (Lowry, 1973). He had a deep appreciation for human virtue, and one of his major life projects was the search to find and understand good human beings (Maslow, 1970). In an earlier age, Maslow's appreciation might have made him devoutly religious, but as a psychologist in postwar America, he chose instead to interpret his awe experiences as an important kind of psychological experience that is open to all people, whether religious or secular. Maslow (1964, pp. 59–68) listed 25 aspects of these peak experiences. A few of these aspects relevant to appreciation are as follows:

- Perception is relatively ego transcending, self-forgetful, unselfish, and more object centered than ego centered.
- The world is seen as beautiful, good, desirable, and worthwhile, even as evil and suffering are recognized and accepted as part of the world.
- Cognition is much more passive, receptive, and humble. People are more ready to listen and much more able to hear.
- Emotions such as wonder, awe, reverence, humility, surrender, and even worship before the greatness of the experience are reported.
- People become more loving and more accepting.

Note that each of these aspects of a peak experience has already been discussed as an aspect of an aesthetic or religious experience.

Maslow's research suggested to him that there were large individual differences in the degree to which people were open to peak experiences. He even went so far as to label the two religions of mankind to be the peakers and the nonpeakers. That is, within any religion or any culture one finds individuals who "have private, personal, transcendent, core-religious experiences easily and often and who accept them and make use of them, and, on the other hand, those who never had them or who repress or suppress them and who, therefore, cannot make use of them for their personal therapy, personal growth, or personal fulfillment" (1964, p. 29). One personality factor said to correlate with being a nonpeaker (low on awe) is a highly rationalist or materialist approach to understanding life. Maslow had harsh words for the psychologists of his day "whose ratio of knowledge to mystery must be the smallest of all the scientists" (p. 46).

A second individual difference that correlates with being a peaker is one's location on Maslow's (1970) well-known hierarchy of needs. The lower four levels of the hierarchy (physiological, safety, belongingness, and esteem needs) involve motivations to overcome deficiencies. But if a person is both fortunate enough and wise enough to have satisfied or transcended these needs, he or she reaches the highest stage of self-actualization, where cognition changes from D-cognition (overcoming deficits) to B-cognition (a more receptive and holistic mode of thinking about Being). It is interesting to note that the penultimate level of the hierarchy is about esteem needs, which could make a person competitive or envious when faced with excellence or success in others. It therefore stands to reason that a person who is personally secure, who is no longer concerned with esteem needs, should be more able to take joy and pleasure in the skills, talents, and virtues of others (*tugendfreude*).

Emotion Research

Emotion researchers have had an abiding interest in how people respond emotionally to objects of beauty, most notably in the visual arts (Oatley, 2002) and music (Gabrielsson & Juslin, 2003). Other emotion researchers have asked whether there is a specific emotion related to the perception of beauty. Darwin (1872/1965) considered astonishment a close relative of awe and a potential response to beauty, but he largely focused on how terror can produce astonishment (e.g., when native Australians first encountered Europeans). More recent emotion theorists have suggested that there is indeed a distinct awelike state, with a unique expression, physiology, and experience (e.g., Ekman, 1992; Lazarus, 1991). The most substantive observations on this state were made by Frijda (1986), who discussed the sense of wonder. He noted that the sense of wonder is defined by the action tendency to be open and to receive passively stimuli in the environment.

More recently, Keltner and Haidt (2003) have offered a theoretical account of awe and related states such as admiration and elevation. They took a prototype approach to the family of awe-related states, positing that two features are central to awe: the perceived vastness of the stimulus, and some difficulty accommodating the stimulus into the individual's knowledge structures. They speculated that awe evolved as an adaptive response to leaders in social hierarchies (e.g., awe toward charismatic leaders, as discussed by Durkheim and Weber) and has generalized to other events and objects that are vast and difficult to accommodate, such as human actions (extraordinarily skillful or noble deeds), art (e.g., cathedrals), and nature.

Emotion researchers have not, however, created any measures of individual differences in the experience of awe or related states. In fact, widely used measures of positive experience, such as the PANAS (Positive and Negative Affect Scales; D. Watson, Clark, & Tellegen, 1988), make no mention of any state even remotely related to awe. Promising measures are on the horizon, however. McCullough, Emmons, and Tsang (2002) have created a six-item measure of individual differences in the frequency and intensity of the experience of gratitude, which is one kind of responsiveness to moral beauty. Based on recent evidence suggesting that there are many highly differentiated positive emotions, Shiota and Keltner (2003) are developing an individual difference measure of the tendency to experience different positive states. One of these states is awe, and in the scale they assess the tendency to respond to beauty, to see pattern and design, to feel interconnected with others, and to frequently experience awe.

Perhaps the most relevant scale is one being developed by Walling and Keltner (2003) on individual differences in epiphany. Their interest is in the sudden feeling of insight people have during otherwise ordinary experiences. Much like the ability to feel awe and be responsive to beauty and excellence, epiphanies are associated with elevated perceptions of pattern, design, interconnectedness, and new relations between previously separated objects. Their scale assesses the frequency of these epiphanic themes across several domains, including art, nature, spirituality, interpersonal interactions, politics, and self-reflection.

■ Measures

There is at present no self-report measure of individual differences in appreciation of beauty and excellence (but see Table 23.1). The closest currently measurable construct is the Big Five factor openness to experience (for a history of this trait and related constructs, see McCrae, 1996). This trait is defined by interests in ideas, fantasy, and aesthetics, having unconventional values, and the predilection to excitable feelings and actions motivated by broad interests and curiosities (Costa & McCrae, 1992). But only one subscale of openness to experience seems truly relevant for the measurement of appreciation: openness to aesthetics. High scorers on openness to aesthetics are described as "[appreciating] art and poetry; they may or may not have talent and good taste, but they use art to expand their knowledge. They are likely to be described as inventive and idealistic. Low scorers are relatively insensitive to and uninterested in art" (Costa & McCrae, 1992). The subscale focuses on interest, fascination, and enjoyment of the arts, with only a single question about nature, and none about human excellence or virtue.

There are also two existing scales that measure susceptibility to or frequency of self-transcendent experience. The Cloninger Temperament and Character Inventory (TCI) has seven components, one of which is self-transcendence. High scorers on this scale resemble Maslow's self-actualizing peakers: They are described as wise and patient; creative and self-forgetful; united with the universe. Low scorers are described as impatient; unimaginative and self-conscious; proud and lacking humility.

Piedmont (1999) developed the Spiritual Transcendence Scale, which he claimed represents a sixth factor, beyond the five factors of the Big Five. Piedmont defined spiritual transcendence as "the capacity of individuals to stand outside of their immediate sense of time and place to view life from a larger, more objective perspective" (p. 988). Because one third of the questions concern prayer and meditation, this scale is less useful than the Cloninger scale for work in a nonreligious population.

Moving beyond self-report measures, the field gets even thinner. Many tests and measures of aesthetic sensitivity once were used by art schools and art teachers, but most of these fared poorly when subjected to psychometric examina-

TABLE 23.1   *Measures of Appreciation of Beauty*

NEO-PI Big Five Openness to Experience

Openness to aesthetics subscale

> Costa & McCrae (1992)
>
> This scale measures interests in ideas, fantasy, and aesthetics, having unconventional values, and the predilection to excitable feelings and actions motivated by broad interests and curiosities; the most relevant facet is openness to aesthetics.

Cloninger Temperament and Character Inventory (TCI)

Self-transcendence subscale

> Cloninger, Przybeck, Svrakic, & Wetzel (1994)
>
> High scorers on this subscale are described as wise and patient; creative and self-forgetful; united with the universe, whereas low scorers are described as impatient; unimaginative and self-conscious; proud and lacking humility.

Spiritual Transcendence Scale

> Piedmont (1999)
>
> This scale measures the capacity of individuals to stand outside of their immediate sense of time and place to view life from a larger, more objective perspective.

Visual Aesthetic Sensitivity Test (VAST)

> Eysenck (1988)
>
> Participants are given dozens of pairs of similar figures and asked to select the one that is better and more harmonious; a person's score on the test is the percentage of times he or she selects the figure that was created by an artist, and validated by other artists, as being the more harmonious.

tion or construct validation (Eysenck, 1988). One test that has garnered some empirical support is Eysenck's Visual Aesthetic Sensitivity Test (VAST), in which participants are given dozens of pairs of similar figures and asked to select the one that is better and more harmonious. A person's score on the test is the percentage of times he or she selects the figure that was created by an artist and validated by other artists as being the most harmonious (see review in Eysenck, 1988).

A bolder and less conventional measure was devised by researchers in the 1970s who sought to understand individual differences in responses to psychedelic drugs. Houston and Masters (1972) created a device called the Audio-Visual Environment (AVE). The AVE was essentially a sound and light show projected onto an 8-foot semicircular rear-projection screen, designed to completely fill the subject's visual and auditory fields with beautiful images and rhythmic sounds for 30 to 45 minutes. It was then possible to measure individual differences in the degree to which subjects experienced relaxation, euphoria, distortions in perceptions of space and time, and even trance states. An approach such as this could be used to measure at least the beauty component in appreciation of beauty and excellence.

■ Correlates and Consequences

The lack of a scale assessing individual differences in appreciation makes it difficult to list its likely correlates. However, the patterns of correlations of some related constructs allow us to predict that appreciation should be correlated with the following:

- Part of openness to experience is openness to aesthetics (McCrae, 1996). Walling and Keltner (2003) found in a sample of 100 participants that their measure of epiphany correlated with a measure of the openness to experience ($r = .41$). This correlation suggests a strong relationship to openness to experience, but it also suggests that appreciation and openness are not the same construct.
- We would expect appreciation to correlate modestly with extroversion, given that this trait consistently correlates with the disposition to experience positive emotion (e.g., D. Watson & Clark, 1992).
- The Big Five trait of agreeableness correlates with several scales that may be related to appreciation, including gratitude (McCullough et al., 2002) and transcendence (Piedmont, 1999).
- Recent studies have documented negative correlations between materialism and gratitude (McCullough et al., 2002) and between materialism and epiphany (Walling & Keltner, 2003). A person whose appraisals of the world are focused on the advancement of his or her own material fortunes seems more like Plato's portrayal of a greedy boor than like Walt Whitman.
- McCrae (1996) reviewed several studies linking openness to experience to political liberalism. Liberals are also more likely to support the arts and to value the environment. This finding may, however, reflect a slight bias in the items used on the openness scale, which focus more on highbrow sources of aesthetic experience (e.g., poetry).

The evidence relating appreciation to life outcomes is almost nonexistent. What little indirect evidence there is points to a potential paradox. On the one hand, empirical studies of the experience of awe and responses to beauty and excellence (e.g., Haidt, 2003; Keltner & Haidt, 2003) point to clear ways in which proneness to appreciation should have positive life outcomes. People consistently report that experiences of awe and elevation have profound outcomes, motivating self-improvement, personal change, altruistic intentions and actions, and the devotion to others and the larger community. Given these findings, one would expect appreciation to correlate with a variety of prosocial outcomes, such as relationship commitment, altruism, warmth and connection felt toward others, enhanced social relationships, and greater meaning and purpose in life. Once appreciation scales are available, researchers will be in a position to pursue these ideas.

Yet researchers may be in for a surprise. Openness to experience, the construct closest to appreciation, has yet to relate to many life outcomes. Thus, measures of openness to experience do not significantly relate to job performance, relationship satisfaction, or personal well-being. We suspect that more specific measures of appreciation and more well-honed measures of theoretically relevant life outcomes (e.g., commitment to community as opposed to relationship satisfaction) will help uncover benefits of appreciation. Because appreciation is a more affectively based construct than is openness to experience, we believe that people high on appreciation are likely to reap the many benefits associated with positive emotions (Fredrickson, 2001).

■ Development

The developmental course of appreciation is entirely unknown. Like most personality traits, appreciation is likely to have a substantial heritable component. In fact, openness to experience appears to be the most heritable of the Big Five traits (Loehlin, 1992). But even if variance in appreciation were mostly explained by genes, it would still be of interest to map out its developmental emergence. The literature on religious development and religious conversion may be relevant here: It appears that the emotional component of religious life becomes much more complex and powerful in adolescence, compared with childhood. Studies of religious conversions and epiphanies repeatedly show that such experiences are most common among adolescents and young adults (Spilka, Hood, & Gorsuch, 1985). It makes sense that adolescence and young adulthood should be times of maximal appreciation, for these are times when young people are forming their own identities and values. An active search for excellence in potential role models and a heightened receptivity and malleability of the self would be much more effective ways to grow than, for example, simply copying one's own parents.

■ Enabling and Inhibiting Factors

Until the developmental course of appreciation is known, there is little that can be said about the factors that enable and inhibit it. We can only speculate that being raised in a family, school, or local environment in which people openly express their appreciation of beauty and excellence should enable the trait. Conversely, a cultural milieu in which admiration is equated with naïveté and cynicism is regarded as cool might inhibit it.

■ Gender, Cross-National, and Cross-Cultural Aspects

Women score higher on the connectedness subscale of Piedmont's (1999) self-transcendence scale, and on Greene and Brock's (2000) measure of transportation. Also, Haidt and Algoe (2003) found that women were much more prone to elevation—more easily moved by displays of virtuous actions.

Every culture has standards of beauty and excellence, and people in every culture want their children to internalize and live up to these standards. Appreciation should therefore be a strength in all cultures. It is, however, a major empirical challenge to establish the degree to which these standards, and the most important domains of excellence, vary across cultures. There is at present a growing body of work on cultural variation in moral intuitions, virtues, and values (S. H. Schwartz & Bilsky, 1990; Shweder, Much, Mahapatra, & Park, 1997). This work suggests that there are large cultural differences in the importance placed on particular virtues (e.g., chastity and respect for authority in hierarchical cultures vs. self-expression and autonomy in individualist cultures), but there are relatively few cases of reversals (i.e., a virtue in one culture is considered a vice in another). The general argument made in the present book—that there is a list of approximately 24 universal virtues—may well be true, as long as it is acknowledged that the relative ranking of these virtues across cultures may vary dramatically.

■ Deliberate Interventions

Beauty and excellence can be found everywhere—in nature, in the actions of ordinary people, on television, and in school textbooks. In this sense appreciation should be a profoundly democratic virtue, accessible to all. Furthermore, even if appreciation is partially determined by genetic heredity, it seems likely that each person has a range of potential levels, and it should be possible to design interventions that move people toward the top of their ranges. Many such programs already exist: There are nature-based programs (e.g., Outward Bound), art-based programs, admiration-based programs (role models; Big Sister/Big Brother), and various programs that encourage epiphanic experience (e.g., religious retreats). We would expect these sorts of programs to foster appreciation. As the empirical measurement of appreciation advances, we will be able to ascertain whether or not this is true.

One intervention particularly germane to our discussion of appreciation is the work of Kuo and colleagues on the outcomes related to being exposed to green spaces in inner-city settings (Kuo, Sullivan, Coley, & Brunson, 1998). These colleagues and others (e.g., Kweon, Sullivan, & Wiley, 1998) have found that exposure to green outdoor spaces, developed in barren inner-city settings, enhances neighborhood social ties and the individual's sense of community.

These findings fit squarely with our analysis in that experience with nature facilitates connections in the community and offers hope for other like-minded interventions.

■ What Is Not Known?

Much and perhaps most of the story about appreciation remains unknown. Among the most pressing questions are the following:

- Is there any empirical support for positing a strength called appreciation of beauty and excellence that is distinct from simple positive affectivity, from openness to experience, and from the other strengths in this classification?
- What is the factor structure of appreciation? Are people who are high on appreciation of beauty also high on appreciation of virtue or other kinds of excellence?
- What is the developmental course of appreciation? When do children begin to derive pleasure from the various forms of beauty and excellence?
- Are there any mental or physical health benefits from being highly appreciative? Does appreciation broaden and build (Fredrickson, 2001)?

■ Must-Read Articles and Books

Haidt, J. (2003). Elevation and the positive psychology of morality. In C. L. M. Keyes & J. Haidt (Eds.), *Flourishing: Positive psychology and the life well-lived* (pp. 275–289). Washington, DC: American Psychological Association.

James, W. (1999). *Varieties of religious experience: A study in human nature.* New York: Modern Library. (Original work published 1902)

Keltner, D., & Haidt, J. (2003). Approaching awe, a moral, spiritual, and aesthetic emotion. *Cognition and Emotion, 17,* 297–314.

McCrae, R. R. (1996). Social consequences of experiential openness. *Psychological Bulletin, 120,* 323–337.

24. GRATITUDE

At first blush, exemplars of the virtue of gratitude do not readily come to mind. As a private response, gratefulness does not call out for attention. Nevertheless, of the possible individuals throughout history who might stake claim to gratitude as a cardinal trait, the British writer G. K. Chesterton might be the prototype. Chesterton was one of the major literary figures in the first third of the 20th century, producing nearly 100 books in the genres of faith and philosophy, mystery, biography, poetry, and social and political commentary. He has been hailed as one of the most influential writers of the 20th century. Those who knew him well described him as exuberant and exhilarated by life. To what were these characteristics attributed?

To think of Chesterton, one recent commentator wrote, is to think of gratitude (Schall, 2000). Gratitude and a sense of wonder and appreciation for life were consistently and constantly being expressed in his life and in his writings. He delighted in the ordinary, was surprised and awed by his own existence and the existence of all else. He set for himself the conscious goal of remaining childlike in his sense of wonder and vowed not to succumb to the monotony and boredom that sap so many lives of joy and purpose. This sense of wonder at the ordinary is best illustrated in this letter to his fiancée, Frances, in which he is apologizing for an ink stain on the letter: "I like the Cyclostyle ink, it is so inky. I do not think there is anyone who takes quite such fierce pleasure in things being themselves as I do. The startling wetness of water excites and intoxicates me: the fieriness of fire, the steeliness of steel, the unutterable muddiness of mud. It is just the same with people. When we call a man 'manly' or a woman 'womanly' we touch the deepest philosophy" (cited in Fagerberg, 1998, p. 23).

In his best known book, Orthodoxy, Chesterton (1908) wrote that "the test of all happiness is gratitude. Children are grateful when Santa Claus puts

553

in their stockings gifts of toys or sweets. Could I not be grateful to Santa Claus when he puts in my stockings the gift of two miraculous legs? We thank people for birthday presents. . . . Can I thank no one for the birthday present of birth?" (p. 98)

In his autobiography, published the year of his death, he summarized his life's writings in saying that gratitude "if not the doctrine I have always taught, is the doctrine I should have always liked to teach" (1936, p. 242). One is never lacking in opportunities to be happy, according to Chesterton, because around every corner is another gift waiting to surprise us, and it will surprise us, if we can achieve control over our natural tendencies to make comparisons, to take things for granted, and to feel entitled. Chesterton was raised without religious faith, yet he was filled with gratitude for his own life, for love, for beauty, for all that is. How can one be thankful, he wondered, unless there is someone to thank? This mystery became the fundamental philosophical riddle of his life. ■

■ Consensual Definition

Gratitude is a sense of thankfulness and joy in response to receiving a gift, whether the gift be a tangible benefit from a specific other or a moment of peaceful bliss evoked by natural beauty. The word *gratitude* is derived from the Latin *gratia*, meaning "grace," "graciousness," or "gratefulness." All derivatives from this Latin root "have to do with kindness, generousness, gifts, the beauty of giving and receiving, or getting something for nothing" (Pruyser, 1976, p. 69). Prototypically, gratitude stems from the perception that one has benefited due to the actions of another person. There is an acknowledgment that one has received a gift and an appreciation of and recognition of the value of that gift. It would be unusual to say that one is grateful to oneself.

Individuals with this strength would strongly endorse such statements as the following:

- It is important to appreciate each day that you are alive.
- I often reflect on how much easier my life is because of the efforts of others.
- For me, life is much more of a gift than it is a burden.
- One of my favorite times of the year is Thanksgiving.
- I am basically very thankful for the parenting that was provided to me.
- I could not have gotten where I am today without the help of many people.
- It seems like I can even find reasons to feel thankful for bad things that happen.
- I have been so struck by the beauty or awe of something that I felt grateful in return.

A distinction can be made between personal and transpersonal gratitude. Personal gratitude is thankfulness toward a specific other person for the benefit that the person has provided (or just for their being). Transpersonal gratitude is a gratefulness to God, to a higher power, or to the cosmos. The prototype of transpersonal gratitude is seen in the peak experience (Maslow, 1964), a moment of overwhelming gratefulness. Maslow (1964) wrote:

> People during and after peak-experiences characteristically feel lucky, fortunate, graced. A common reaction is "I don't deserve this." A common consequence is a feeling of gratitude, in the religious persons, to their God, in others, to fate or to nature or to just good fortune. This can go over into worship, giving thanks, adoring, giving praise, oblation, and other reactions which fit very easily into orthodox religious frameworks. (pp. 67–68)

As a trait, gratitude is expressed as an enduring thankfulness that is sustained across situations and over time. Fitzgerald (1998) identified three components of gratitude: (a) a warm sense of appreciation for somebody or something, (b) a sense of goodwill toward that person or thing, and (c) a disposition to act that flows from appreciation and goodwill. A grateful person recognizes the receipt of someone else's generosity. Although gratitude has largely been ignored in academic psychology, it has a long history in moral philosophy and theology. We contend that gratitude is a human strength (Emmons & Crumpler, 2000) in that it enhances one's personal and relational well-being and is quite likely beneficial for society as a whole (Simmel, 1950).

■ Theoretical Traditions

Gratitude can be thought of as a virtue that contributes to living well. Classical writers focused on the good life emphasized the cultivation and expression of gratitude for the health and vitality of both citizenery and society. Across cultures and time spans, experiences and expressions of gratitude have been treated as both basic and desirable aspects of human personality and social life. For example, gratitude is a highly prized human disposition in Jewish, Christian, Muslim, Buddhist, and Hindu thought. Cicero held that "gratitude is not only the greatest of virtues, but the parent of all the others." The Buddha suggested, "A noble person is thankful and mindful of the favors he receives from others." Christian devotional writers such as Thomas à Kempis, Thomas Aquinas, and Bernard of Clairvaux expounded on the virtues of gratitude and the sinfulness of ingratitude. Indeed, the consensus among the world's religious and ethical writers is that people are obligated to feel and express gratitude in response to received benefits. Moreover, on the basis of the preceding quotations, one can infer that the responses of grateful people benefit not only themselves but the wider community as well. One dissenting voice, however, was that of Aristotle (2000), who found gratitude incompatible with magnanimity and therefore did not include it in his list of virtues. Magnanimous people, according to Aristotle, insist on their self-sufficiency and therefore find it demeaning to be indebted to others. Feeling grateful, however, does not require the perception of indebtedness as much as it requires the awareness of the beneficence of others.

Throughout history, gratitude has been portrayed as a vital civic virtue. The first influential theoretical treatment of gratitude from a broad communal perspective arose from the political economist Adam Smith (1790/1976) in his volume *The Theory of Moral Sentiments*. Smith proposed gratitude as an essential social emotion—on a par with emotions such as resentment and affection. Gratitude is, according to Smith, one of the primary motivators of benevolent behavior toward a benefactor. To this point, he wrote, "The sentiment which most immediately and directly prompts us to reward, is gratitude" (p. 68). Smith observed that society can function purely on utilitarian grounds or on the basis of gratitude, but he clearly believed that societies of gratitude were more attractive in large part because they provide an important emotional resource for promoting social stability. Following the line of thought initiated by Smith, the sociologist Simmel (1950) argued that gratitude was a cognitive-emotional supplement to sustain one's reciprocal obligations. Because formal social structures such as the law and social contracts are insufficient to regulate and ensure reciprocity in human interaction, people are socialized to have gratitude, which then serves to remind them of their need to reciprocate. Thus, during exchange of benefits, gratitude prompts one person (a beneficiary) to be bound to another (a benefactor) during exchange of benefits, thereby reminding beneficiaries of their reciprocity obligations. He referred to gratitude as "the moral memory of mankind. . . . if every grateful action . . . were suddenly eliminated, society (at least as we know it) would break apart" (1950, p. 388).

Building on the work of Smith, Simmel, Westermarck, and others, McCullough, Kilpatrick, Emmons, and Larson (2001) theorized that gratitude is a moral affect—that is, one with moral precursors and consequences. They hypothesized that by experiencing gratitude, a person is motivated to carry out prosocial behavior, energized to sustain moral behaviors, and inhibited from committing destructive interpersonal behaviors. Because of its specialized functions in the moral domain, they liken gratitude to empathy, sympathy, guilt, and shame. Like empathy, sympathy, guilt, and shame, gratitude has a special place in the grammar of moral life. Whereas empathy and sympathy operate when people have the opportunity to respond to the plight of another person, and guilt and shame operate when people have failed to meet moral standards or obligations, gratitude operates typically when people acknowledge that they are the recipients of prosocial behavior. Specifically, they posited that gratitude serves as a moral barometer, providing individuals with an affective readout that accompanies the perception that another person has treated them prosocially. Second, they posited that gratitude serves as a moral motive, stimulating people to behave prosocially after they have been the beneficiaries of other people's prosocial behavior. Third, they posited that gratitude serves as a moral reinforcer, encouraging prosocial behavior by reinforcing people for their previous prosocial behavior. McCullough, Kilpatrick, et al. (2001) adduced evidence from a wide variety of studies in personality, social, developmental, and evolutionary psychology to support this conceptualization. For example, Trivers (1971) viewed gratitude as an evolutionary adaptation that regulates people's responses to altruistic acts. In this sense, gratitude could be a key element in the emotional system underlying reciprocal altruism. Recent research indicates that gratitude may be a psychological mechanism underlying reciprocal exchange in human and nonhuman primates (de Waal & Berger, 2000). As early as 1932, the anthropologist Edward Westermarck (1932) antedated the discussion of gratitude as underlying reciprocal altruism. He depicted gratitude as a kindly retributive emotion, in a class of emotions characterized by "a desire to give pleasure in return for pleasure received" (p. 86).

Given that gratitude has potentially important consequences for individuals and society, it is remarkable that psychologists specializing in the study of emotion have, by and large, failed to explore its contours. Only a handful of emotion theorists have addressed the roots of gratitude or its position within the affective lexicon. Lazarus and Lazarus (1994) suggested that gratitude is an empathic emotion that results when people recognize that they have encountered a favorable circumstance and can empathize with the expenditure of effort that the benefactor has extended on their behalf. B. Weiner (1985) conceptualized gratitude as an attribution-dependent emotion resulting when people attribute their happiness to an external cause—most notably, the effort of another person. Similarly, Ortony, Clore, and Collins (1987) hypothesized that gratitude results from a blend of joy (one is happy for having encountered a favorable life circumstance) and admiration (the person judges the actions of his or her benefactor as praiseworthy). Initial research suggests that gratitude is a moderately pleasant and activating emotion. Mayer, Salovey, Gomberg-Kaufman, and Blainey (1991) found that gratitude is .49 standard deviations above the mean of the pleasantness dimension of affect and .42 standard deviations above the mean in terms of the activation dimension.

■ Measures

Existing gratitude theory and research demonstrate a high degree of consensus on a variety of points. First, the existing treatments imply that gratitude is part of a highly functional psychological apparatus that helps people to maintain their obligations to one another and is therefore beneficial for society. Second, most existing theoretical treatments propose that gratitude is most beneficial under a specific set of attributions: (a) when a benefit is evaluated positively, (b) when the benefit that one has encountered is not attributed to one's own effort, and (c) when the effort that led to the benefit was perceived to be caused by the intrinsic motivation of the benefactor. Finally, existing research suggests that gratitude is a typically pleasant experience that is linked to contentment, happiness, and hope.

However, the social-scientific conceptualizations of gratitude that have arisen in the last 50 years have been based on the assumption that gratitude is a monolithic, unidimensional construct. Implicitly, the existing conceptualizations of gratitude would suggest that individual experiences of gratitude differ along a single dimension that might best be referred to as intensity; that is to say, people are only more grateful or less grateful; no other distinctions need be made to understand the gratitude experience. Yet upon closer examination, there appear to be several other meaningful distinctions that might be made concerning various dimensions or facets of gratitude.

The first facet of the grateful disposition might be called *gratitude intensity*. A person with a strong grateful disposition who experienced a positive event would be expected to feel more intensely grateful than would someone less disposed toward gratitude who experienced the same positive event.

A second facet of the grateful disposition might be called *gratitude frequency*. Someone with a strong grateful disposition might report feeling grateful several times per day, and gratitude might be elicited by even the simplest favor or act of politeness. Conversely, for someone less disposed toward gratitude, such a favor or act of politeness might be insufficient to elicit gratitude. As a result, the person with a weaker grateful disposition might experience less gratitude within a specified time period (e.g., hours, days, or weeks).

A third facet of the grateful disposition might be called *gratitude span*. Gratitude span refers to the number of life circumstances for which a person feels grateful at a given time. Someone with a strong grateful disposition might be expected to feel grateful for his or her family, job, health, and life itself, along with a wide variety of other benefits. Someone less disposed toward gratitude might be aware of experiencing gratitude for fewer aspects of his or her life.

A fourth facet of the grateful disposition might be called *gratitude density*, which refers to the number of persons to whom one feels grateful for a single positive outcome or life circumstance. When asked to whom one feels grateful for a certain outcome, say, obtaining a good job, someone with a strong grateful disposition density might list a large number of others, including parents, elementary school teachers, tutors, mentors, fellow students, and God. Someone less disposed toward gratitude might feel grateful to fewer people for such a benefit. These considerations have informed our development of an individual difference measure of gratitude.

To investigate the nature and effect of gratitude, it becomes necessary to procure an accurate and reliable measurement of grateful emotion. Until recently, there has been no standardized, agreed-upon method of measuring gratitude—gratitude has been measured in a multitude of ways and forms. These different measurements of gratitude can be subsumed under four categories: free-response, ratings, attributions, and behavioral measures. Emmons, McCullough, and Tsang (2003) presented a systematic review of research that has employed these four response categories.

By far the most frequently used self-report measure of gratitude is the rating scale. Some studies employing ratings scales explore the grateful disposition. For example, Saucier and Goldberg (1998) had participants and their peers rate the participant on thankfulness, as well as other possible traits that might be independent of the Big Five Inventory. Additionally, the 1998 Gallup poll asked individuals if they knew many people who seemed grateful for no clear reason. Regarding an aspect of gratitude density, individuals have rated their gratitude toward God ("Gallup survey results," 1998; Samuels & Lester, 1986); friends (Parker & de Vries, 1993); their examination teacher (Overwalle, Mervielde, & De Schuyter, 1995); and simply "others" (i.e., "Gallup survey results," 1998).

Some studies look at gratitude frequency. For example, a 1998 Gallup poll asked individuals how often they gave thanks to God and to other people. B. Weiner, Russell, and Lerman (1979) asked students to remember a successful test and write down three emotions they felt after learning of their success. A response of gratitude could indicate a higher gratitude frequency. Other studies have asked participants to rate the intensity of their felt gratitude, along with other emotions (e.g., Overwalle et al., 1995). In many of these gratitude studies, participants read scenarios and were asked to rate the gratitude they would feel if those events happened to them, or to rate how the protagonist of the vignette would feel.

Researchers have also looked at grateful behavior. J. A. Becker and Smenner (1986) observed whether young children said thank you during trick-or-treating without being prompted by their parents. Other research on college students looked at people's reactions after having the door held open for them. Saying thank you or smiling was taken as a grateful response (Okamoto & Robinson, 1997; Ventimiglia, 1982). Taking a more sociological slant, Goldsmith and Fitch (1997) used field notes and ethnographic interviews to study advice giving and receiving. They found that individuals often accepted the advice of someone they respected as a sign of gratitude for help received by the advice giver. Stein (1989) observed grateful and ungrateful responses while working in soup kitchens and pantries. Behavioral observations such as these have an advantage over self-report measures in that they lessen social desirability concerns. However, it is often difficult for researchers to know whether they are actually measuring gratitude or instead a form of politeness or some other construct. Therefore, a combination of behavioral and self-report measures of gratitude might be the most useful for researchers studying gratitude.

Although gratitude conceivably could be conceptualized as either an enduring attitude or a short-term emotional state, advances have recently been made at the level of gratitude as an affective trait. McCullough, Emmons, et al. (2002) define the grateful disposition as a generalized tendency to recognize and respond with positive emotions to the role of other moral agents' benevolence in the positive experiences and outcomes that one obtains. These positive emotions include thankfulness, appreciation, and, of course, gratefulness. Two self-report measures of gratitude as a personality disposition have been constructed: the Gratitude, Resentment, Appreciation Test (GRAT) (Watkins, Grimm, & Hailu, 1998) and the Gratitude Questionnaire (GQ; McCullough et al., 2002; see Table 24.1).

Watkins et al. (1998) report three factors in their 44-item GRAT scale: resentment, simple appreciation, and social appreciation. The following are some sample items:

- I basically feel like life has ripped me off.
- Sometimes I find myself overwhelmed by the beauty of a musical piece.
- I feel deeply appreciative for the things that others have done for me in my life.

TABLE 24.1   *Measures of Gratitude*

The Gratitude Questionnaire (GQ-6)
   McCullough, Emmons, & Tsang (2002)
   6 items, unidimensional
   - Alpha = .82

The GRAT (Gratitude, Resentment, Appreciation Test)
   Watkins et al. (1998)
   44 items, three factors: resentment, simple appreciation, social appreciation
   - Alpha = .91

The Gratitude Adjective Checklist
   McCullough, Emmons, & Tsang (2002)
   Sum of three adjectives: grateful, thankful, and appreciative, varying time frames
   - Alpha = .87

The Gratitude Questionnaire, Observer Version
   McCullough et al. (2002)
   Same as GQ-6, except raters are asked to answer the items according to how they think the target person would respond

---

Scores on the GRAT correlate positively and moderately with positive states and traits such as internal locus of control, intrinsic religiosity, and life satisfaction; moreover, scores correlate negatively and moderately with negative states and traits such as depression, extrinsic religiosity, narcissism, and hostility (Watkins et al., 1998). In one experiment, grateful individuals showed a positive memory bias: They recalled a greater number of positive memories when instructed to do so and even rated their memories of unpleasant experiences more positively over time relative to the initial emotional impact of these negative events.

The GQ-6 (McCullough et al., 2002) contains these items:

- I have so much in life to be thankful for.
- If I had to list everything that I felt grateful for, it would be a very long list.
- When I look at the world, I don't see much to be grateful for.
- I am grateful to a wide variety of people.
- As I get older I find myself more able to appreciate the people, events, and situations that have been part of my life history.
- Long amounts of time can go by before I feel grateful to something or someone.

The GQ-6 has an alpha of .82 and is unidimensional. McCullough et al. (2002) examined the validity of a one-factor solution for the six items via structural equation models with maximum likelihood estimation. Using three different fit indices, the one-factor model provided an adequate fit to the data.

■ Correlates and Consequences

Knowledge of the correlates and consequences of gratitude comes from both experimental and correlational studies. In an experimental manipulation, those who kept gratitude journals on a weekly basis exercised more regularly, reported fewer physical symptoms, felt better about their lives as a whole, and were more optimistic about the upcoming week compared with those who recorded hassles or neutral life events (Emmons & Crumpler, 2000). A daily gratitude journal-keeping exercise (Emmons & McCullough, 2003) with young adults resulted in higher reported levels of the positive states of alertness, enthusiasm, determination, attentiveness, and energy compared with a focus on hassles or a downward social comparison (ways in which participants thought they were better off than others). Participants in the daily gratitude condition were more likely to report having helped someone with a personal problem or having offered emotional support to another, relative to the hassles or social comparison condition. This indicates that, relative to a focus on complaints, an effective strategy for producing reliably higher levels of pleasant affect is to lead people to reflect, on a daily basis, on those aspects of their lives for which they are grateful. We do not know how long these effects last and whether they can be sustained over time. Future studies will need to be designed to examine long-term consequences of counting blessings.

At the dispositional level, grateful people report higher levelsof positive emotions, life satisfaction, vitality, and optimism and lower levels of depression and stress (McCullough et al., 2002). The disposition toward gratitude appears to enhance pleasant feeling states more than it diminishes unpleasant emotions. In our intervention studies, we have not found significant differences in unpleasant emotions across the experimental groups. Grateful people do not deny or ignore the negative aspects of life.

Gratitude also correlates with religiousness and spirituality. Those who regularly attend religious services and engage in religious activities such as prayer or reading religious material are more likely to be grateful. Grateful people are more likely to acknowledge a belief in the interconnectedness of all life and a commitment to and responsibility to others. Grateful individuals place less importance on material goods; they are less likely to judge their own and others' success in terms of possessions accumulated; they are less envious of wealthy persons; and they are more likely to share their possessions with others relative to less grateful persons. In terms of basic personality dispositions, grateful people are more open to experience, more conscientious, more extroverted, more agreeable, and less neurotic than are their less grateful counterparts.

Non-self-report data indicate positive correlates and consequences of gratitude. The informants of people with strong dispositions toward gratitude reported that their grateful friends engaged in more prosocial behaviors (e.g., lending money, providing compassion, sympathy, and emotional support) in the previous month than did less grateful individuals. Grateful individuals were also rated by their informants as engaging in such supportive behaviors more frequently in general than did less grateful individuals (McCullough et al., 2002). There is also some evidence that gratitude serves to inhibit destructive interpersonal behavior (R. A. Baron, 1984). Data on the interpersonal consequences of gratefulness are scarce. All in all, however, it is reasonable to hypothesize that expressions of gratitude and appreciation are vital to successful, thriving, long-term relationships.

Further, gratefulness is an attitude that underlies successful functioning over the life course. In his longitudinal study of male adult development, Vaillant (1993) theorized that a key to mature adaptation to life is the ability to replace bitterness and resentment toward those who have perpetrated harm with gratitude and acceptance. Gratitude is part and parcel of a creative process whereby self-destructive emotions are transformed into ones that permit healing and restoration. According to Vaillant, "Mature defenses grow out of our brain's evolving capacity to master, assimilate, and feel grateful for life, living, and experience" (p. 337).

In addition to the psychological and interpersonal benefits of gratitude, there appears to be growing evidence that gratitude and related states can affect physiological functioning and physical health. Studies of the physiological effects of positive emotions closely related to gratitude—namely, appreciation and compassion—suggest that reliable changes in cardiovascular and immune functioning may underlie these findings (McCraty, Atkinson, Tiller, Rein, & Watkins, 1995). Subjects were instructed to experience consciously appreciation or anger for 5 minutes. Appreciation increased parasympathetic activity and also produced entrainment or coherence across various autonomic measures (e.g., heart rate variability, pulse transit time, and respiration rate).

Grateful people might actually live longer than the nongrateful. Danner, Snowdon, and Friesen (2001) found a strong inverse association between positive emotional content in handwritten autobiographies from 180 Catholic sisters (at mean age 22) and risk of mortality in late life (ages 75–95). Cox regression analyses revealed a 2.5-fold difference in mortality between the lowest and highest quartiles of positive emotional expression. Positive emotional content (contentment, gratitude, happiness, hope, love) in early-life autobiographies was strongly associated with longevity six decades later. There was a mean difference of 6.9 years between the highest and lowest quartiles of positive emotion content.

■ Development

From a developmental perspective, psychological research has shown that children's comprehension of gratitude is a process played out over several years. More specifically, gratitude does not appear to occur regularly in response to receiving benefits until middle childhood. Gleason and Weintraub (1976), for example, found that few children (i.e., 21%) younger than 6 years of age expressed thanks to adults who gave them candy, whereas most children (i.e., more than 80%) of 10 years of age or older expressed gratitude in the same situation. Based on these data, it appears that the link between attributions of responsibility for positive outcomes, the experience of gratitude, and the desire to do good to one's benefactor probably is solidified between ages 7 and 10 (see also S. Graham & Weiner, 1986, and B. Weiner & Graham, 1988, for reviews). Despite these studies, relatively little research has been conducted on the emergence of gratitude in children. A sustained research commitment that revealed the most effective strategies for increasing thanksgiving literacy would enable parents and educators to guide more effectively their child's passage into responsible and grateful adulthood. In these efforts, psychologists would be wise to enlist the assistance of schools, religious organizations, and parenting groups to develop climates that educate for gratitude. Some schools, for example, use gratitude journals in which students reflect on what they are thankful for and how they show gratitude. The Thanksgiving Leadership Forum of Dallas, composed of business and civic leaders, has sponsored essay-writing contests for high school students in which they write 1,000-word essays on gratitude and thanksgiving as a way of life. College scholarships are awarded for the best essays. Given that gratitude is highly encouraged by all major world religions, faith-based institutions should take the lead in cultivating experiences and expressions of gratitude in their members.

■ Enabling and Inhibiting Factors

Empirical research on gratitude is still in its infancy; therefore, it is difficult to state with precision what might be the personal and situational factors that encourage or thwart gratefulness. Given the pattern of correlates of the grateful disposition, it would appear that an optimistic, generous outlook on life would foster gratitude, as would spiritual awareness and intrinsic religiousness, along with empathy, humility, and perspective taking. To feel grateful, one needs a broad perspective on life, without which it is difficult to sense the contributions that others make to one's well-being. Finally, the ability to perceive the elements in one's life and life itself as gifts would appear essential.

Obstacles to gratitude include the perception that one is a passive victim, a sense of entitlement, a preoccupation with materialism, and a lack of self-reflection. Gratitude would also appear to require some sort of awareness of or sensitivity to prior deprivation (in order to fully appreciate one's blessings). One greatly appreciates a mild spring after a harsh winter, a gourmet meal following a fast, and sexual intimacy after a period of abstinence. There is an old saying that blessings are not known until they are lost (cf. Joni Mitchell's "Big Yellow Taxi"). The capacity for reflection and contemplation, the ability to savor one's positive experiences, and the ability to relinquish some self-sufficiency in order to recognize that others may be responsible for one's successes are additional factors that might encourage gratitude.

One of the major personality variables likely to thwart gratitude (as well as thwarting other virtues) is narcissism. People with narcissistic tendencies erroneously believe they are deserving of special rights and privileges. Along with being demanding and selfish, they exhibit an exaggerated sense of self-importance that leads them to expect special favors without assuming reciprocal responsibilities. The sense of entitlement combined with their insensitivity to the needs of others engenders, whether consciously or unconsciously intended, interpersonal exploitation. In short, if one is entitled to everything, then one is thankful for nothing. Gifts are transformed into rights, eliminating the need for grateful reciprocation. Expressions of gratitude are acknowledgments that one is dependent on other people for one's well-being, and therefore not self-sufficient. Given this reality, such individuals find expressions of gratitude to be highly unpleasant. Furthermore, because narcissistic individuals possess a distorted sense of their own superiority, they might be reluctant to express gratitude in response to benefactors whose generosity or kindness they summarily dismiss as little more than attempts to curry favor. Farwell and Wohlwend-Lloyd (1998) found that in the context of a laboratory-based interdependence game, narcissism was inversely related to the extent to which participants experienced liking and gratitude for their partners.

From a macro-level perspective, certain organizational factors might facilitate gratitude. Grateful families and workplaces can be constructed that encourage and foster gratitude in their members. Expressed appreciation between marital partners is one of the cornerstones of thriving marriages (Gottman, 1999). At the organizational level, gratitude modules might be incorporated into existing leadership and management training programs (Cherniss & Goleman, 2001), thereby enabling organizations to foster more appreciative climates, with expected organizational benefits (Emmons, 2003). The individual benefits of gratitude might extend to organizational outcomes, including subjective indicators (job satisfaction, morale, loyalty, citizenship behavior) and objective performance (employee turnover, profitability, customer retention).

■ Gender, Cross-National, and Cross-Cultural Aspects

There are few data that speak directly to gender differences in gratitude. Speculations about such differences raise an interesting question. Can gratitude as a strategy for increasing well-being be equally effective in men and women? Those designing gratitude interventions may have to be sensitive to different meanings that males and females might associate with gratitude. Perhaps some emotional reeducation might be needed to convince men that attributing their success to others need not undermine their own sense of self-accomplishment and autonomy.

Although around the world people experience and express gratitude in diverse ways (Streng, 1989), they typically feel grateful emotions (i.e., thankful, appreciative) and have developed linguistic and cultural conventions for expressing such gratitude (e.g., *gracias, grazie, merci, dankbarkeit*). In Japanese culture, the conventional expression of apology—*sumimasen*—is also used to express the feeling of thanks. R. C. Solomon (1995) notes how relatively infrequently Americans talk about gratitude, but how this emotion forms the foundation of interaction in many other cultures. In R. Levy's (1973) terms, gratitude is a hypocognized emotion in America, whereas anger, resentment, happiness, and romantic love tend to be hypercognized. He noted, "Gratitude presupposes so many judgments about debt and dependency that it is easy to see why supposedly self-reliant American males would feel queasy about even discussing it" (p. 282). It has been argued that conventional males may be averse to experiences and expressions of gratefulness inasmuch as they imply dependency and indebtedness (R. C. Solomon, 1995). Sommers and Kosmitzki (1988) found that American men were less likely to evaluate gratitude positively than were German men, and to view it as less constructive and useful than their German counterparts. Beyond this work, though, little systematic research has explored the contours of gratitude cross-culturally.

■ Deliberate Interventions

Can gratefulness be nurtured? The personal commitment to invest effort in developing a personal schema, outlook, or worldview of one's life as a gift or one's very self as being gifted holds considerable sway from the standpoint of achieving optimal psychological functioning. Indeed, numerous groups have absorbed this insight. For example, many religiously oriented events such as reflection days or scheduled weeklong retreats have as a recurring theme the idea of a gift (e.g., those influenced by Jesuit spirituality), as do many self-help groups and organizations (e.g., Alcoholics Anonymous). The regular practice of grateful thinking, then, should lead to enhanced psychological and social functioning. Setting aside time on a daily basis to recall moments of gratitude associated with even mundane or ordinary events, one's personal attributes, or valued people one encounters has the potential to interweave and thread together a sustainable life theme of highly cherished personal meaning just as it nourishes a fundamental life stance whose thrust is decidedly positive. On this point, a grateful outlook does not require a life full of material comforts but rather an interior attitude of thankfulness regardless of life circumstances.

A number of techniques have been offered for nurturing skills that allow for a greater awareness of gratitude in one's life. T. Miller (1995) offers a simple, four-step, behavioral-cognitive approach for learning gratitude: (a) identify nongrateful thoughts; (b) formulate gratitude-supporting thoughts; (c) substitute the gratitude-supporting thoughts for the nongrateful thoughts; and (d) translate the inner feeling into outward action. By following these four steps, people supposedly are able to "want what they have." Shelton (2000) framed gratitude as one of four key ingredients that make up a daily moral inventory that individuals can use to foster moral growth. An effective way to make one aware of benefits received is to conduct a daily examination of conscience in which one takes time to reflect on benefits and blessings in his or her life and contemplates ways to give back to others as an appropriate response for the gratitude felt. Naikan therapy (Reynolds, 1989) requires that practitioners reflect on what others have provided to them and what they have given back; in so doing, it creates feelings of gratitude, indebtedness, and the motivation to reciprocate.

The authors of children's books (Hallinan, 1981; Swamp, 1997) and articles in parenting magazines (Fisher, 1999; Kirkpatrick, 1999; Taffel, 1999) regularly encourage the cultivation of gratitude and thankfulness in children and offer strategies for parental inculcation. For example, Baumgartner-Tramer (1938) suggested that parents emphasize the sense of community created or strengthened through gratefulness and diminished or destroyed through ingratitude, rather than appeal to its politeness function or its obligatory nature. Gratitude and thankfulness make occasional appearances in character education materials (Elias, 1997; Klee, 2000), though with considerably less frequency than the broader "good citizen" virtues of honesty, integrity, trustworthiness, and responsibility. These programs have developed curricula and gratitude activities for use in schools and in parenting. In the Core Virtues Program (Klee, 2000), gratitude, defined as thankfulness for the gift of life and the gifts in life, is cultivated and practiced primarily using storytelling. A recent article examined gratitude as a civic virtue in citizenship education and advocated that teachers and educators be skillful and imaginative as they develop and implement the practice of gratitude and other social virtues in schools (P. White, 1999).

■ What Is Not Known?

Over the years, mainstream social science has been somewhat neglectful of the concept of gratitude. Negative psychological states such as anger, depression, and anxiety have generated literally thousands of scientific research projects. Research that has specifically focused on gratitude or thankfulness, on the other hand, is limited to fewer than a score of high-quality rigorous scientific studies. Much of what we have learned about gratitude reflects research conducted within the very recent past. Therefore, much is not known. We are only beginning to understand the basic personality structure of gratitude; the consequences of its experience and expression for emotional, physical, and relational well-being; and the cognitive mechanisms that sustain gratitude over time. The following questions constitute a partial agenda for the developing science of gratitude and for our understanding of the role it plays in human flourishing:

- What is the longitudinal stability of gratitude over extended periods of time? Do people become generally more grateful—or less grateful—as they age?
- How much daily, weekly, or monthly variability do people demonstrate in their experiences of gratitude?
- Is gratitude a unique route to happiness or merely a moderately positive and active emotion that happy people frequently experience?
- What are the mechanisms (cognitive, interpersonal, motivational) by which gratitude might increase long-term subjective well-being?

- What institutional factors encourage or, conversely, thwart gratitude?
- Does gratitude undermine self-determination and autonomous striving?
- Given the sex differences in dispositional gratitude, can the state of gratitude be cultivated equally well in men and women?
- Might gratitude serve as a buffer for people at risk for depression? Similarly, by experiencing gratitude, could a person perhaps control anger or other interpersonally destructive emotions?
- Does gratitude speak to a core experience that can serve as a bridge between the increasingly polarized concepts of spirituality and religion?
- How might gratitude interventions encourage less emphasis on consumerism as the royal road to happiness?

■ Must-Read Articles and Books

Baumgartner-Tramer, F. (1938). "Gratefulness" in children and young people. *Journal of Genetic Psychology, 53,* 53–66.

Danner, D. D., Snowdon, D. A., & Friesen, W. V. (2001). Positive emotions in early life and longevity: Findings from the nun study. *Journal of Personality and Social Psychology, 80,* 804–813.

Emmons, R. A., & Hill, J. (2001). *Words of gratitude for the mind, body, and soul.* Radnor, PA: Templeton Foundation Press.

McCullough, M. E., Emmons, R. A., & Tsang, J. (2002). The grateful disposition: A conceptual and empirical topography. *Journal of Personality and Social Psychology, 82,* 112–127.

McCullough, M. E., Kilpatrick, S., Emmons, R. A., & Larson, D. (2001). Gratitude as moral affect. *Psychological Bulletin, 127,* 249–266.

Simmel, G. (1950). *The sociology of Georg Simmel.* Glencoe, IL: Free Press.

Smith, A. (1976). *The theory of moral sentiments* (6th ed.). Oxford, England: Clarendon Press. (Original work published 1790)

Steindl-Rast, D. (1984). *Gratefulness, the heart of prayer.* New York: Paulist Press.

White, P. (1999). Gratitude, citizenship, and education. *Studies in Philosophy and Education, 18,* 43–52.

25. HOPE

[Optimism, Future-Mindedness, Future Orientation]

■ *Optimist International sponsors clubs throughout the United States and other parts of the world (see http://www.optimist.org/index.html). It adopted the following creed in 1912:*

Promise yourself—

- *To be so strong that nothing can disturb your peace of mind.*
- *To talk health, happiness and prosperity to every person you meet.*
- *To make all your friends feel that there is something in them.*
- *To look at the sunny side of everything and make your optimism come true.*
- *To think only of the best, to work only for the best and to expect only the best.*
- *To be just as enthusiastic about the success of others as you are about your own.*
- *To forget the mistakes of the past and press on to the greater achievements of the future.*
- *To wear a cheerful countenance at all times and give every living creature you meet a smile.*
- *To give so much time to the improvement of yourself that you have no time to criticize others.*
- *To be too large for worry, too noble for anger, too strong for fear, and too happy to permit the presence of trouble.*

Optimist Clubs put this creed into practice through good deeds that embody the essence of optimism: expecting good events to happen in the future and working to make them so. For example, members of the Optimist Club of Treynor, Iowa, instituted a recycling program when they noticed that their town's residents continued to throw cans and bottles along the road, despite a *redeemable deposit. The Treynor Optimist Club created a central recycling location and spread the word to the town through newspaper advertisements. Local youth organizations like 4-H and Girl Scouts were recruited to take turns helping the Optimist Club sort through the cans and bottles, and they are given the proceeds to support their various activities and charities of their choice. According to Treynor Optimist Club organizers, the program is only incidentally about money—less than $500 per month is recouped—and really about showing young people that they can make a difference in the world through their own efforts.* ■

■ Consensual Definition

Hope, optimism, future-mindedness, and future orientation represent a cognitive, emotional, and motivational stance toward the future. Thinking about the future, expecting that desired events and outcomes will occur, acting in ways believed to make them more likely, and feeling confident that these will ensue given appropriate efforts sustain good cheer in the here and now and galvanize goal-directed actions.

Individuals with this strength would strongly endorse such statements as the following:

- Despite challenges, I always remain hopeful about the future.
- I always look on the bright side.
- I am confident that my way of doing things will work out for the best.
- I believe that good will always triumph over evil.
- I expect the best.
- I have a clear picture in my mind about what I want to happen in the future.
- I have a plan for what I want to be doing 5 years from now.
- I know that I will succeed with the goals I set for myself.
- I never go into a game or competition expecting to lose.
- If I get a bad grade or evaluation, I focus on the next opportunity and plan to do better.

Distinctions within this family of synonyms exist, although the overlap is considerable. *Hope* seems more emotional than its cousins and *optimism* more purely expectational. *Future-mindedness* and *future orientation* imply an articulate theory about what the individual needs to do to get from here to there (from the present to the desired future). In practice, we suspect that all co-occur. As we describe, different research traditions exist that focus respectively on different members of this family. Despite differences in operationalization, correlates are strikingly similar. Hope, optimism, future-mindedness, and future orientation have been equally linked with all manner of desirable outcomes. Our strategy here is to emphasize common themes and threads in the research literatures addressing these related constructs.

■ Theoretical Traditions

The term *hope* has a long history, figuring prominently in Judeo-Christian discourse and naming one of the chief theological virtues (along with faith and charity). Throughout the history of hope, it has referred to positive expectations about matters that have a reasonable likelihood of coming to pass. In principle, there is a darker side of hope, to be sure, but it usually is a qualified version (blind hope, false hope, foolish hope, and so on). Whether this darker side of hope actually exists is debatable (Snyder, Rand, King, Feldman, & Taylor, 2002).

In contrast, the term *optimism* is a relatively recent arrival on the historical scene, as is its ostensible cousin *pessimism* (Sicinski, 1972). In the 1700s, Leibniz characterized optimism as a mode of thinking, and Voltaire popularized the term in his novel *Candide* (1759), which was highly critical of the shallowness of an optimistic perspective. Interestingly, pessimism appeared fully a century later, when it was independently introduced by Schopenhauer and Coleridge.

At least in their original forms, optimism and pessimism were not symmetrical. Optimism as discussed by Leibniz was cognitive in its emphasis, reflecting a reasoned judgment that good would predominate over evil, even if goodness were sometimes associated with suffering. In contrast, pessimism as discussed by Schopenhauer had an emotional referent: The pessimistic individual was one for whom suffering would outweigh happiness. Note, therefore, that someone can be optimistic in the cognitive Leibniz sense yet pessimistic in the emotional Schopenhauer sense.

Future-mindedness is a more contemporary term that rolls comfortably off the tongues of social scientists. The term apparently became popular around the time of World War I in discussions of mental retardation: The retarded were characterized as not future-minded because they presumably did not engage in means–ends thinking (e.g., Mateer, 1917; Mulford, 1918). The narrowly intellectual connotations have since been stripped from future-mindedness, and it refers today simply to the individual who thinks ahead to what the future may hold and how it might come to pass (cf. Zimbardo & Boyd, 1999).

In his controversial discussion of social class in the city, Banfield (1990) argued that future orientation is the major psychological dimension distinguishing among the classes. Upper-class people (the haves) think about the future, invest their resources in its possibilities, and expect to be able to influence what happens. Lower-class people (the have-nots) are oriented only toward the present. Whether future orientation is a defining property of social class is irrelevant for our purposes, and we ask the reader not to be distracted by Banfield's hypothesis. The point to emphasize is that Banfield's observations about the reality basis of future orientation are pertinent to our eventual discussion of enabling conditions. So, Banfield observed that we find a future orientation mainly among those who expect a long life and have material resources at their disposal to make this a good life.

As these notions have evolved in the language, optimism and pessimism became juxtaposed, and the connotations of all their synonyms spilled over into one another. The resulting composite is what we mean by this strength; as already noted, it is a cognitive, emotional, and motivational stance toward the future. Optimism and hope refer to a belief—perhaps *wish* would be a better term or even *motive*—that in the future good events and associated positive feelings will outweigh or be more likely than bad events and associated negative feelings.

As we discuss shortly, contemporary approaches to this strength return, explicitly or implicitly, to the original meaning of hope as somewhat grounded in reality—illusory perhaps but not delusional (cf. S. E. Taylor, 1989). Contemporary approaches also assume that this strength entails a belief about agency: the notion that good events can be made more likely and bad events less by appropriate actions on the part of the individual. Contemporary approaches to this strength at first glance seem purely cognitive, phrased in the language of expectancy theory, but they also are implicitly emotional and thus motivational because the events about which expectations are entertained are matters about which people feel strongly.

Contemporary writers approach this family of strengths in two ways. Some (usually social philosophers) treat these as features of general human nature to be praised or decried depending on the writer's own biases, whereas others (usually research-minded psychologists in the personality or clinical tradition) regard optimism and pessimism as individual differences, characteristics that people possess to varying degrees (Peterson, 2000).

At present, there are three well-known approaches within psychology to this strength as an individual difference. Each line of work has an associated self-report measure; each has focused extensively on the consequences of the individual difference; and each has spawned a large empirical literature demonstrating that hope and optimism (or at least the absence of their opposites) are associated with all manner of desirable outcomes: positive mood and good morale; perseverance and effective problem solving; academic, athletic, military, occupational, and political success; popularity; good health; and even long life and freedom from trauma.

First, Carver and Scheier (1981, 1990) have studied a personality variable they identify as dispositional optimism: the global expectation that good things will be plentiful in the future and bad things scarce. Scheier and Carver's overriding perspective is in terms of how people pursue goals, defined as desirable values. To them, virtually all realms of human activity can be cast in goal terms, and people's behavior entails the identification and adoption of goals and the regulation of actions vis-à-vis these goals. They therefore refer to their approach as a self-regulatory model. Optimism enters into self-regulation when people ask themselves about impediments to the achievement of the goals they have adopted. In the face of difficulties, do people nonetheless believe that goals will be achieved? If so, they are optimistic—if not, pessimistic. Optimism leads to continued efforts to attain the goal, whereas pessimism leads to giving up.

Second, Seligman and his colleagues have approached optimism in terms of an individual's characteristic explanatory style—how he or she explains the causes of bad events (Buchanan & Seligman, 1995; Gillham, 2000; Peterson, Maier, & Seligman, 1993). Those who explain bad events in a circumscribed way, with external, unstable, and specific causes, are described as optimistic, whereas those who favor internal, stable, and global causes are described as pessimistic. The notion of explanatory style emerged from the attributional reformulation of the learned helplessness model (Abramson, Seligman, & Teasdale, 1978). Briefly, the original helplessness model proposed that following experience with uncontrollable aversive events, animals and people become helpless—passive and unresponsive—presumably because they have "learned" that there is no contingency between actions and outcomes (Maier & Seligman, 1976; Seligman, 1975). This learning is represented as a generalized expectation that future outcomes will be unrelated to actions. It is this generalized expectation of response–outcome independence that produces later helplessness. However, the helplessness/explanatory style research tradition has infrequently looked at expectations. Rather, researchers measure explanatory style and correlate it with outcomes thought to revolve around helplessness: depression, illness, and failure in academic, athletic, and vocational realms. In contrast to dispositional optimism, explanatory style is a construct concerning agency (Peterson & Seligman, 1984).

Third, Snyder's (1994, 2000b, 2000c) studies of hope in effect combine these two visions of optimism—expectation and agency. Snyder traced the origins of his thinking to earlier work by Averill, Catlin, and Chon (1990) and Stotland (1969), in which hope was cast in terms of people's expectations that goals could be achieved. According to Snyder's view, goal-directed expectations are composed of two separable components. The first is agency, and it reflects someone's determination that goals can be achieved. The second is identified as pathways: the individual's beliefs that successful plans can be generated to reach goals.

One of the ideas we have discussed with respect to our classification of strengths and their measurement is whether a given characteristic is tonic (constant) or phasic (waxing and waning according to its use; chapter 1). Said another way, are there settings or situations in which one can rise to the occasion (or not) vis-à-vis the characteristic? Hope and optimism are usually measured as if they were tonic, but we suspect they are especially pertinent at times of potential transition, when personally relevant outcomes loom on the horizon.

This idea is explicit in theorizing about explanatory style, where explanatory style is deemed most relevant in the wake of a setback or failure. The idea is more implicit in the dispositional optimism and hope traditions, but note that each line of theorizing points to goal setting as the occasion in which the individual difference ends up predicting outcomes. By implication, the individual who sets no goals—someone who is *not* future-minded—cannot be optimistic or hopeful. It will behoove us in some if not all cases to mention the relevant settings in our assessment of this strength, specifying critical incidents where this strength is most apt to be used, for example, "At school, when I receive a poor grade on a test, I always expect that I will do better the next time."

■ Measures

Let us move more fully to measurement. Optimism (and/or pessimism) and hope (and/or hopelessness) have over the years inspired several dozen measures (Kenneth Pope, personal communication, March 2, 2000). Most have been face-valid self-report questionnaires, and some have used interviews, observer reports, or content analyses of written or spoken material. We also note in passing the development of an optimism subscale composed of MMPI or MMPI-2 items, which allows the hundreds of thousands of archived MMPI protocols to be rescored after the fact for this individual difference (Malinchoe, Offord, & Colligan, 1995).

Measures of hope and optimism are usually based on what an individual says on a questionnaire about what he or she usually believes. This strategy follows from the central role accorded expectations in the various definitions of these constructs; expectations are sensibly measured by self-report of beliefs. Nonetheless, we think it worth exploring additional ways to assess hope and optimism, for example, by observation of hopeful behaviors in simulations, by measuring hopeful emotions in the various ways that emotions can be measured, or by behaviorally anchored questions about hopeful actions in the past week or month (cf. Buss & Craik's, 1983, act-frequency approach).

In the meantime, what we have are questionnaires. As noted, each of the well-known contemporary research traditions has been facilitated by the existence of reliable and valid measures, such as the Life Orientation Test (LOT) and its revised version (LOT-R) to measure dispositional optimism (Scheier & Carver, 1985; Scheier, Carver, & Bridges, 1994); the Attributional Style Questionnaire (ASQ) to measure explanatory style (Peterson et al., 1982; Peterson & Villanova, 1988); and the dispositional and state Hope Scales to measure agency and pathways (Snyder et al., 1991, 1996). Each of these measures has been refined and revised several times to improve reliability and validity, and they are respected tools in the arsenal of research psychologists (see Table 25.1).

In the case of explanatory style and hope, there are separate self-report measures available for children and adults, as well as content analysis strategies

---

TABLE 25.1 *Measures of Optimism and Hope*

Revised Life Orientation Test (LOT-R)
Scheier, Carver, & Bridges (1994)
This is a self-report questionnaire composed of eight items (two fillers)
reflecting optimism or pessimism, which respondent rates in terms of
endorsement on a scale of 0 to 4.
- Internal reliability (alpha coefficients): ~.80
- Test–retest reliability: ~.60–.80
- Construct validity: correlates .30 with active coping and .50 with coping by
  positive reframing, even when controlling for neuroticism and self-esteem

Attributional Style Questionnaire (ASQ)
Peterson et al. (1982)
This self-report questionnaire is composed of six good events and six bad
events for which respondent writes "one major cause" and then rates each
cause on a scale of 1 to 7 according to its internality, stability, and globality.
- Internal reliability (alpha coefficients): .40–.60 for individual dimensions;
  .70 for composites
- Test–rerest reliability: .50–.60 for individual dimensions; .70 for composites
- Construct validity: correlates ~.25 with various indices of helpless behavior: depressive symptoms, academic failure, morbidity, and so on

Dispositional Hope Scale
Snyder et al. (1991)
This self-report questionnaire is composed of 12 items (4 fillers) reflecting
agency or pathways, which respondent rates in terms of endorsement on a
scale of 1 to 4.
- Internal reliability (alpha coefficients): ~.80
- Test–retest reliability: ~.80
- Construct validity: correlates –.50 with hopelessness scale and –.40 with
  depressive symptoms

---

for scoring these characteristics from written or spoken material (see reviews
by Reivich, 1995, and by Lopez, Ciarlelli, Coffman, Stone, & Wyatt, 2000). Ways
to assess hope by observer report and from interviews also exist. Hope measures and to some degree explanatory style measures have spawned various
domain-specific versions (e.g., hope concerning family life; explanatory style
for academics). Dispositional optimism and pessimism have apparently *not* been
assessed among children and youth (Michael Scheier, personal communication,
October 2, 2000), although we suspect the straightforwardness of the LOT
would allow its use with early teens or even younger individuals.

A troubling fact with respect to explanatory style is that questionnaire and
content-analysis measures do not impressively converge, although their correlates are usually identical. More generally, convergence among the different

measures of hope and optimism has not been the subject of much research, although the typical study finds a modicum of agreement.

It matters whether measured expectations are about good events or bad events. Thus, the LOT and LOT-R have separate optimism and pessimism items, and these are somewhat independent and occasionally have different correlates. Explanatory style for good events is strikingly independent of explanatory style for bad events; the correlates are usually opposite for "good" versus "bad" explanatory styles, and more robust for the "bad" style. This latter finding may be an artifact of the tendency in the explanatory-style tradition to study negative outcomes (depression, disease, and failure). Regardless, studies of hope and optimism from the perspective of positive psychology will need to measure both positive and negative expectations.

A fruitful assessment strategy is suggested by Stipek, Lamb, and Zigler's (1981) Optimism-Pessimism Test Instrument, a measure of children's optimism. Respondents are presented with a picture and accompanying scenario like the following:

> Oh dear! Spot has just moved to a new home, and he is taking a walk around the block. Then he meets three other dogs from the neighborhood. You can see that two of them don't look very friendly. Do you think they'll be mean to Spot, or do you think they will see that Spot wants to make friends? (p. 136)

The second alternative is an optimistic expectation, the first a pessimistic one. We like this questionnaire format because the scenario is relatively well developed yet still terse. Additional questions could be asked that tap other aspects of hope and optimism (agency, pathways, reality basis, positive vs. negative outcomes, whatever). We think that scenarios need to be recast to make the respondent the primary actor in them and perhaps to ask about personally relevant goals, but the approach seems richer and less likely to demand top-of-the head answers than the very terse questions asked in the LOT/LOT-R, the children's ASQ, and the Hope Scale.

■ Correlates and Consequences

We have noted that hope and optimism predict many desirable outcomes: achievement in all sorts of domains (academic, athletic, military, political, and vocational); freedom from anxiety and depression; good social relationships; and physical well-being (see representative reviews in Buchanan & Seligman, 1995; Seligman, 1990; Snyder, 2000b, 2002). More specific correlates of hope and optimism include active problem solving and attention to problem-relevant sources of information (e.g., Aspinwall & Brunhart, 1996; Scheier, Weintraub, & Carver, 1986). Future-mindedness and future orientation are associated with conscientiousness, diligence, and the ability to delay gratification (e.g., Agarwal, Tripathi, & Srivastava, 1983; Davids & Sidman, 1962; Griffith & Hom, 1988; Mischel, Shoda, & Rodriguez, 1989). People high in this character strength make "to do" lists, use day planners, and wear wristwatches; they also balance their checkbooks (Zimbardo & Boyd, 1999)—all these activities imply an orientation to the future.

Sometimes we dub hope and optimism "Velcro constructs" because everything seems to stick to them for reasons that are not always apparent. No one has mounted a study in which the full range of correlates and consequences has been assessed and linked to hope or optimism measures. Perhaps some outcomes of this strength are primary and end up producing the others; perhaps different outcomes ensue for different subsamples of research participants; perhaps the psychologically rich simply diversify and get still richer; we do not know. Said another way, mediators of hope/optimism–outcome links have been relatively neglected by researchers. Our suspicion—perhaps simply a bias—is that mundane behavior is the most typical and robust mediator (as opposed to biology, mood, or social relations), but this possibility is very difficult to test definitively because given constructs may shift from outcome to mediator and even to predisposing factor or moderator, depending on the time perspective embodied in the research design.

The only well-documented downside of this strength is its link with what has been dubbed an optimistic bias in risk perception (Weinstein, 1989). People with an optimistic explanatory style exaggerate the widespread tendency of individuals to see themselves as below average for such dire occurrences as cancer and heart disease, failure and heartbreak, and so on (Peterson & de Avila, 1995; Peterson & Vaidya, 2001). This bias can be a problem when reality matters and hope leads one to neglect preventive or remedial actions. The good news is that if people acknowledge the possibility of risk, the more optimistic among them take the most appropriate coping steps.

So, the reality basis of hope and optimism is underscored, which helps to make sense of findings described by Isaacowitz and Seligman (2001) that fly in the face of the research so far summarized: Among the elderly, "optimistic" explanatory style predicts depression in the wake of stressful events. Perhaps extreme optimism among the elderly is unrealistic, and the occurrence of something terrible can devastate the optimistic older individual, who may realize that his or her optimism is clearly wrong, a realization much more infrequent for younger individuals, whose future—to use a sports cliché—is in front of them.

Something else we do not know except in the most approximate way is whether desirable outcomes are produced by optimism and hope or whether they result simply from the absence of hopelessness and pessimism, what some have called the power of nonnegative thinking (Robinson-Whelen, Kim, MacCallum, & Kiecolt-Glaser, 1997). Research designs typically treat optimism and pessimism (hope and hopelessness) as polar opposites and then correlate scores with outcomes but do not check whether statistically significant correlations are strictly linear. Because of measurement error, doing so would require very large sample sizes.

We have done a few very tentative analyses of several explanatory style data sets which imply that for some outcomes (depression), the degree of pessimism matters but not—after a certain point—the degree of optimism; for other outcomes (vigor), just the opposite nonlinear pattern is obtained (Peterson & Vaidya, 2003). We do not yet have a handle on what these data mean—it would be beyond elegant if negative outcomes were predicted only by degrees of pessimism and if positive outcomes were predicted only by degrees of optimism—but these results do imply that the goal of interventions may vary depending on the outcome on focus. So, to achieve some outcomes (freedom from depression), we may simply want to encourage individuals not to be pessimistic, whereas for other outcomes (emotional vibrancy), no benefit will be evident until individuals become quite optimistic.

■ Development

This discussion is limited to optimistic explanatory style and hope because research on dispositional optimism has not taken a life span tack. Explanatory style as an individual difference seems to solidify around age 8, and it stays relatively stable unless external events impinge upon it, for better or for worse (Seligman, Reivich, Jaycox, & Gillham, 1995). There is not a lot of evidence that children are more optimistic than adults (or vice versa), although some research hints that the correlates of optimism may change across the life span. Males and females do not seem to differ in explanatory style (although there is the interesting fact that correlates of explanatory style, like depression and traumatic accidents, often show striking sex differences). There are some hints that ethnic minorities within the United States are more pessimistic than their majority counterparts, but this research has not taken into account the myriad of possible contrasts among these groups that would account for this difference.

Snyder (2000a, 2003) provided a thorough discussion of how hope might develop across childhood, arguing that its components are acquired sequentially: first pathways and then agency. Snyder seemed to state that hope develops among children as a default unless something derails the process, like the absence of an emotional attachment with a caregiver. He also discussed conditions that allow hope to appear even under conditions of adversity. These are all reasonable ideas but apparently not yet supported with fine-grained research (C. R. Snyder, personal communication, October 5, 2000).

Both dispositional optimism and explanatory style are heritable, about to the same degree that most personality traits are influenced by genetic variation

(Plomin, Scheier, Bergeman, & Pedersen, 1992; Schulman, Keith, & Seligman, 1993). These findings are probably less interesting than they at first seem. Even if the Human Genome Project isolates a gene with a big smiley face signature, it will not be one that codes directly for optimism. Rather, optimism is probably influenced by other characteristics of the individual plausibly based in genetic variation (attractiveness, intelligence, physical prowess, self-control, temperament, and so on).

We do not think these findings about heritability mean that optimism is immutable; indeed, we know that it can be changed by life events or deliberate interventions (see later discussion). Nonetheless, these data do imply that individuals might begin life predisposed to different baselines of hope and optimism, and interventions may therefore need to be tailored differently depending on the baseline.

■ Enabling and Inhibiting Factors

Most of the relevant research has looked at the environmental influences on explanatory style, and here we have a good idea of what makes explanatory style more pessimistic: trauma and failure of all sorts. We know less about what fosters an optimistic style, although an inconsistent literature finds that the explanatory styles of children and parents sometimes converge. Perhaps modeling is implicated, but so, too, might be shared family environment or even indirect genetic influence as already discussed. If explanatory style is modeled, we need to consider not just parents but also teachers, coaches, peers, and the media (Peterson & Steen, 2002). Along these lines, a neglected but likely important influence on the development of hope and optimism is adherence to orthodox religion (Sethi & Seligman, 1993). Seligman et al. (1995) speculated that singular events can be transforming, suddenly making someone more optimistic or pessimistic, but they also acknowledged that such a hypothesis is all but impossible to test.

■ Gender, Cross-National, and Cross-Cultural Aspects

There is little evidence that males and females differ in hope and optimism, a fact implying the need for sophistication in making sense of the correlates of this strength, some of which—like depression or traumatic accidents—show dramatic sex differences (e.g., Peterson et al., 2001). Hope and optimism in their own right cannot account for these differences, and there is a need to look further at how this trait may become entwined with sex roles or social settings to lead to different outcomes for men and women.

Researchers have begun translating the LOT, the ASQ, and the Hope Scale and administering it around the world. Findings with respect to explanatory style are representative (e.g., Y.-T. Lee & Seligman, 1997). Two conclusions sum up most of the research: (a) people in different cultures (sometimes) show mean differences that are easily interpretable along cultural dimensions (e.g., people in collectivist Asian cultures have a more even-handed [less optimistic] explanatory style than their individualistic Western counterparts; residents of communist countries are more pessimistic than those who live in democracies; and so on); and (b) the correlates of explanatory style are nonetheless similar across cultures. There are subtleties here that we are ignoring, but we are encouraged that the constructs of hope and pessimism appear sensible cross-nationally and cross-culturally (Peterson & Chang, 2003).

■ Deliberate Interventions

McDermott and Hastings (2000) discussed school-based hope interventions that rely on the exposure of children to hopeful narratives: essays written by other children, children's books, and the like. This strategy is exciting not just because it increases hope but because it is cost-efficient and able to be deployed within an already-existing institutional structure. Perhaps narrative-based interventions can be developed for most or all of the strengths and virtues that concern us, giving new meaning to a great books curriculum.

Irving et al. (in press) showed that a five-session pretherapy motivational intervention targeting the components of hope—agency and pathways—resulted in more satisfactory outcomes following conventional therapy of a variety of types: psychodynamic, cognitive-behavioral, and family systems. The pretherapy intervention consisted of instruction in setting goals and planning how to achieve them. Initial levels of hope predicted good outcome, as did changes toward more hopeful ways of thinking.

A different approach to intervention, in this case targeting explanatory style, is provided by the Penn Prevention Program (aka the Penn Resiliency Project). Schoolchildren are taught basic cognitive-behavioral strategies, especially disputation and decatastrophizing, for thinking about the causes of events in a more optimistic fashion (Seligman et al., 1995). This intervention makes explanatory style more optimistic and prevents the later development of depression and anxiety.

We know that both hope and explanatory style change in the course of individual psychotherapy with adults, especially of the cognitive ilk, which is hardly surprising. More interesting for the present purposes are attempts by the explanatory-style group to generalize intervention to nondepressed adults, in group format and in self-paced instruction (see Seligman, 2000).

Missing to date in these intervention projects is an explicit focus on the fulfillments that presumably accompany hope and optimism. So, we know that the Penn Resiliency Project makes emotional distress and even physical illness less likely; this is all good news, but as positive psychologists we also want to know whether this intervention makes youngsters happy and healthy, responsible friends and citizens, and so on.

Also missing to date with respect to these interventions is a cost–benefit analysis. The Penn Resiliency Project is labor-intensive and thus expensive to implement. The good news here is that the Penn researchers are currently exploring ways to put the intervention on-line. Start-up will be expensive, but once the program is in place, it will be available at the click of a mouse.

Is there a downside to such interventions? The Penn Resiliency Project has seen no intervention casualties (Jane Gillham, personal communication, December 14, 2000). Rather, the intervention sometimes seems to work better for some groups of children than others (e.g., boys more than girls in one study; Latinos more than African Americans in another study), but different iterations of the program reveal no consistent pattern except—hardly surprising—that conduct-disordered children do not participate well in the classroom format.

Although this effect has not been documented, we suggest that intervention leaders be alert to the possibility that the intervention, with its explicit cognitive focus, might make some participants more mindful of emotional problems they may have. In the short term, they may be more likely to label themselves as distressed. We add, however, that this is hardly a reason to abandon the intervention, just a caution that for some children, the intervention may need to entail a longer time frame to work through this process.

■ What Is Not Known?

We have already mentioned several immediate tasks for future research. Let us gather them together here:

- Is it possible to create a composite measure of hope and optimism suitable for a variety of samples?
- How do hope and optimism manifest themselves across important sociodemographic contrasts in the contemporary United States: for example, gender, cohort, ethnicity, and religion?
- Which of the documented consequences of this strength are primary, and do these primary consequences vary across groups?
- Do hope and optimism have benefits beyond those conferred by the absence of hopelessness and pessimism?
- Do intervention programs that boost hope and optimism result in positive outcomes or merely the absence of negative outcomes?

■ Must-Read Articles and Books

Buchanan, G. M., & Seligman, M. E. P. (Eds.). (1995). *Explanatory style.* Hillsdale, NJ: Erlbaum.

Carver, C. S., & Scheier, M. F. (1990). Origins and functions of positive and negative affect: A control-process view. *Psychological Review, 97,* 19–35.

Gillham, J. E. (Ed.). (2000). *The science of optimism and hope: Research essays in honor of Martin E. P. Seligman.* Radnor, PA: Templeton Foundation Press.

Peterson, C. (2000). The future of optimism. *American Psychologist, 55,* 44–55.

Peterson, C., Maier, S. F., & Seligman, M. E. P. (1993). *Learned helplessness: A theory for the age of personal control.* New York: Oxford University Press.

Seligman, M. E. P. (1975). *Helplessness: On depression, development, and death.* San Francisco: Freeman.

Seligman, M. E. P. (1990). *Learned optimism.* New York: Knopf.

Seligman, M. E. P., Reivich, K., Jaycox, L., & Gillham, J. (1995). *The optimistic child.* Boston: Houghton Mifflin.

Snyder, C. R. (1994). *The psychology of hope: You can get there from here.* New York: Free Press.

Snyder, C. R. (Ed.). (2000). *Handbook of hope: Theory, measures, and applications.* San Diego, CA: Academic Press.

Snyder, C. R. (2002). Hope theory: Rainbows of the mind. *Psychological Inquiry, 13,* 249–275.

Tiger, L. (1979). *Optimism: The biology of hope.* New York: Simon & Schuster.

26. HUMOR

[Playfulness]

On the evening of his 70th birthday, Samuel Langhorn Clemens (1835–1910) told a journalist that he had never done a day's work in his life. "No, sir, not a day's work in all my life. What I have done I have done because it has been play. If it had been work I shouldn't have done it" (Twain, 1909).

Judged from events recorded in his biographies, his life did not sound like sheer fun. He lost his father at the age of 11, and his formal education soon ended. From then on, young Samuel got into trouble and even served time in jail. Work started at the age of 12 when he became a printer's apprentice. He participated briefly in the Civil War. His wife died early, and three of his four children died before he did. His company filed for bankruptcy in 1894, leaving him in considerable debt.

Simply for fun, Samuel wrote short stories for newspapers under the pen name Mark Twain, a Mississippi River phrase meaning two fathoms deep. Using humor as his weapon, Twain attacked hypocrisy, oppression, intolerance, and injustice. "You see in me a talent for humorous writing," Mark Twain commented in a private letter at the outset of his literary career. Today, few readers of American literature have any doubts about the accuracy of this statement.

But Twain's talent was not merely a professional pose. Humor was a substantial part of his everyday life. As a boy, Clemens asked people to tell him gossip, which he printed in the paper when the owner was absent. Indeed, his own childhood was characterized by frequent pranks. His mother's own sense of humor may have exposed the boy early to a humorous outlook on life. Twain biographer Albert B. Paine (1912) recounted an episode that exemplifies the joking atmosphere in which Twain grew up: After he had played a prank on his mother, she told him that he was giving her more trouble than any of her other children. When he said, "I suppose you were afraid I wouldn't live," she looked *at him and said, "No; afraid you would" (Paine, 1912, vol. 1, p. 29). Another time, when the boy almost drowned in the waters of the Mississippi River, his mother did not seem much alarmed. "I guess there wasn't much danger. People born to be hanged are safe in water" (p. 35).*

As a newspaper writer in San Francisco, Twain sharpened his skills by ridiculing local officials for incompetence and dishonesty. This style of writing— humor alternating with serious fact—became his trademark. In 1865, his national fame was established with the publication of "The Notorious Jumping Frog of Calaveras County." He followed with the stories of Pudd'nhead Wilson, Huckleberry Finn, and Tom Sawyer that are still read today.

According to his daughters, Twain's sense of humor brightened their everyday family life as much as it did the larger world. His daughter Susy called her father "a very good man, and a very funny one. . . . He does tell perfectly delightful stories" (Neider, 1985, p. 84). In a letter written in 1886, she gave more details: "Papa can make exceedingly bright jokes and he enjoys funny things, and when he is with people he jokes and laughs" (p. 207). Years later, Clemens's oldest daughter, Clara, substantiated the impressions recorded by her younger sister: "Father was always ready to make jokes at the breakfast table. . . . I would say that my father was the only one at the table who found real joy in life so early in the morning, and of course he didn't find it; he created it" (Clemens, 1931, p. 3).

Clemens never abandoned his trademark humor, believing that it made life bearable. "Humor is the great thing," he wrote, "the saving thing after all. The minute it crops up, all our hardnesses yield, all our irritations, and resentments flit away, and a sunny spirit takes their place" (Twain, 1897). ■

■ Consensual Definition

Humor may be easier to recognize than to define, but among its current meanings are (a) the playful recognition, enjoyment, and/or creation of incongruity; (b) a composed and cheerful view on adversity that allows one to see its light side and thereby sustain a good mood; and (c) the ability to make others smile or laugh. Individuals with this strength would strongly endorse such statements as the following:

- Whenever my friends are in a gloomy mood, I try to tease them out of it.
- I welcome the opportunity to brighten someone else's day with laughter.
- Most people would say I am fun to be with.
- I try to add some humor to whatever I do.
- I never allow a gloomy situation to take away my sense of humor.
- I can usually find something to laugh or joke about even in trying situations.

A rich set of phenomena relating to humor has been accumulated in different cultures, and numerous words for their description have come into use. Different academic disciplines (e.g., anthropology, folklore) have collected the occasions for laughter (Morreall, 1983), and lexicographers have indexed funny words. However, there is still no agreed-upon terminology in research on humor and certainly no consensual definition (Ruch, 1998a).

Rather, there exist two different and conflicting terminological systems. The first comes from the field of aesthetics, where the comic—defined as that which makes someone laugh or feel amused—is distinguished from other aesthetic qualities like beauty or harmony. In this tradition, humor is but one element of the comic—along with wit, fun, nonsense, sarcasm, ridicule, satire, irony, and so on—and usually denotes a cognitive-affective style of dealing with adverse situations by finding them amusing. Humor can be distinguished from other elements of the comic domain because it reflects a sympathetic heart as opposed to a superior spirit (as is wit), haughtiness (as is ridicule), or vitality (as is fun; Schmidt-Hidding, 1963). This specific understanding of humor still prevails in some cultures, and the associated terminology is still used in some scientific literature. Although this view of humor influenced the writings of Allport, Freud, and Maslow, it was not preserved within experimental psychology, which rediscovered humor in the 1970s (Chapman & Foot, 1977; J. H. Goldstein & McGhee, 1972) and was primarily concerned with people's reactions to jokes or cartoons.

The second use of the term *humor* is as an umbrella for all funny phenomena, including the capacities to perceive, interpret, enjoy, create, and relay incongruous communications. In this usage, humor has replaced the comic as the overarching term. This understanding of humor dominates current Anglo-American psychology research, but it is problematic. Because humor now has such positive connotations, its darker side (as found in ridicule or sarcasm) is neglected. Indeed, contemporary research hypotheses rarely consider the possibility that humor might have a downside. Unlike most other topics studied by psychologists, where an examination of their positive aspects is long overdue (cf. Seligman & Csikszentmihalyi, 2000), the topic of humor would benefit from closer examination of its negative aspects.

■ Theoretical Traditions

The term *humor* has a long history, although it did not enter the field of the comic and funny until the late 16th century. For centuries prior, humors referred to bodily fluids: blood, phlegm, black bile, and yellow bile. The mixture of these four humors in given people was expressed in their physical appearance, physiognomy, and proneness to disease. Optimally, the humors were balanced, but a predominance of one over the others presumably produced a given temperament. Pathologies of all kinds were explained by imbalanced humors. As medical science progressed, humoral theory was abandoned, although it survived in folk theory. Humors were used to explain labile behavior and mood in general, and the term *humor* came to refer to one's more or less predominant mood—either positive (good humor) or negative (bad humor). *Good humored* and *bad humored* eventually became terms for dispositions, and by the beginning of the 17th century, *good humor* referred to the disposition, trait, or habit of being cheerful.

At this same time, the meaning of humor was further expanded to include behavior deviating from social norms, and the term entered the field of the comic as a way to describe the object or target of laughter. So, a humorist originally meant an odd character whose peculiarities were the appropriate subject of laughter by the person of humor. Humor and wit became seen as talents in the ability to make others laugh. Note that the talent of humor still is not the same as a sense of humor as it came to be understood later, because it may lead one to poke malicious fun at the weaknesses of specific persons and not portray human weaknesses in a general or benevolent way.

Growing humanism occasioned the next shift in the meaning of humor, with moralists arguing that people should not be laughed at because of peculiarities in temperament beyond their control. A term became necessary for the tolerant and benevolent forms of laughter, and the term that was appropriated was *good humor* and later *humor* alone (Schmidt-Hidding, 1963). During this epoch, there was also a gradual shift in the meaning of humor dispositions from sheer talent or ability at making others laugh to the virtue of having a sense of humor. While one should not poke fun at those who were simply odd, it was permissible to laugh at the pompous, the unreal, the fake, or the conceited. Of course, even a serious person could hold views that others might see as ridiculous, and one means of verifying the reasonableness of one's views was to expose oneself to a test of ridicule. Good humor was the sovereign attitude of exposing oneself to the criticism and mockery of others. Schmidt-Hidding (1963) noted this may have been the origin of the phrase "sense of humor," although this expression took many years to enter common use. Later, other elements were added to humor, for example, the ability to laugh at one's misfortunes or at one's own expense.

At the beginning of the 19th century, the conceptual distinction between wit and humor was complete. Wit referred to a cognitive ability and was hurtful. Humor came from the heart and was benevolent. According to Schmidt-Hidding (1963), in the 19th century, humor became a defining English virtue, joining others such as common sense, tolerance, and compromise. In the second half of the 19th century, a sense of humor was an explicit part of the English lifestyle, and anyone lacking it was considered incomplete. The political predominance of the British Empire spread the concept, and sense of humor as a cardinal virtue extended far beyond its borders. However, these terms and concepts did not penetrate all languages and cultures. The notion of good humor as a virtue appeared in American writings (Wickberg, 1998), but neither the term nor the concept gained much popularity among the French and certainly not among most non-Western nations.

Thus, current research has to cope with different uses and multiple meanings of the same term in one culture and with the fact that the key terms and the associated concepts may differ from culture to culture. Nonetheless, studying the interrelations of the terms—in particular when the words are used to describe people—helps uncover the dimensions that structure the domain of humor. There seems to be agreement on at least two dimensions: a cognitive dimension reflecting one's ability to put things in a funny context (wit in its traditional sense) and an affective and emotional dimension reflecting one's motivation (benevolence vs. malevolence; e.g., Ruch, 2001). On the face of it, it seems obvious that positive psychology ought to be interested in benevolent humor. At a societal level, however, cynics and satirists—like Mark Twain—play an important role. Indeed, so-called aggressive humor can have positive functions, namely, to correct and repel deviations, to make evildoing the butt of jokes, and to build group cohesion. Thus, it makes sense for psychologists to study humor in all its complexity, and not divvy it up into its presumed positive and negative aspects.

Currently humor is studied in many disciplines besides psychology, such as linguistics, sociology, philosophy, anthropology, and neuropsychology. One approach is to study humorous products; for example, linguists study jokes or humorous texts (e.g., Attardo, 2001; V. Raskin, 1985). The other major approach is to study the individual (and sometimes the group or nation) that appreciates, generates, or otherwise displays humor. The present chapter concerns itself with this second approach.

■ Measures

Throughout the 20th century there were numerous attempts to develop measures of a sense of humor and related states and traits. Typically, these were face-valid self-report questionnaires or joke or cartoon tests, but occasionally methods like humor diaries, informant questionnaires and peer reports, behavioral observations, experimental tasks, interviews, and surveys were used. Self-report measures typically are based on what an individual says on a questionnaire about how he or she typically behaves. In joke or cartoon tests, the individual does not need to reflect on how he or she typically behaves but simply responds to presented material, usually by using a rating scale. Joke and cartoon tests of humor creation—wit—are diverse, but often the individual is confronted with an incomplete joke or cartoon and is asked to write as many funny captions as possible. The frequency and quality of the captions are later evaluated.

A recent survey of humor measures uncovered more than 60 different ones (Ruch, 1998c), but many of the earlier measures were created for use in only one study. Most often, these scales were simply labeled sense of humor tests, although the contents varied greatly, and none measured sense of humor in the traditional sense (i.e., as a worldview). Although the assessment of humor is still far from being satisfactory, during the past two decades, considerable progress has been made, and several respected measures now exist (Ruch, 1996; see Table 26.1).

Rod Martin and his colleagues created several individual differences measures of humor that have been widely used (Kuiper, Martin, & Olinger, 1993; R. A. Martin, 1996; R. A. Martin & Lefcourt, 1983, 1984). The first measure is the Situational Humor Response Questionnaire (SHRQ), which defines sense of humor as the "frequency with which a person smiles, laughs, and otherwise displays mirth in a variety of life situations." This atheoretical and behavioral approach deliberately avoids theoretical debates over the processes involved in humor. Rather, Martin et al. trusted in overt mirthful behaviors sampled across both pleasant and unpleasant situations to be valid indicators of whatever processes lead to the perception, creation, and enjoyment of humor in daily life (R. A. Martin, 1996). Whereas the SHRQ is orthogonal to adversity, the Coping Humor Scale (CHS) of Martin et al. specifically assesses the degree to which respondents report using humor to cope with stress. The term *coping humor* was introduced under the assumption that people could deliberately use humor to deal with stressful situations. Both scales have been fruitful tools in research on humor as a moderator of stress. They also have led other researchers to create similar measures (for reviews, see R. A. Martin, 1998, 2001; Ruch, 1998c).

Recently, Martin revised his approach to conceptualize the interpersonal and intrapsychic functions of humor in everyday life from a functionalist perspective (R. A. Martin, Puhlik-Doris, Larsen, Gray, & Weir, 2003). According to this approach, four general functions of humor emerge from the combinations of two distinctions, namely, whether humor is used to enhance the self versus one's relationships with others, and whether humor is relatively benign versus potentially detrimental or injurious. The Humor Styles Questionnaire (HSQ) measures these four styles. Whereas the self-enhancing and affiliative humor subscales of this new measure correlate substantially with the earlier SHRQ and CHS, the aggressive and self-defeating scales seem to assess new dimensions not tapped by these other measures. In addition, the two scales of benign styles of humor are positively related to psychological health and well-being and negatively related to negative moods, whereas the two measures of detrimental humor are associated with poor psychological functioning, low self-esteem, and lack of social support. The interesting point is that psychosocial well-being may be related as much to the absence of certain (deleterious) forms of humor as to the presence of other (beneficial) forms.

style of humor. A set of 100 nonredundant statements was generated to encompass five bipolar humor styles: (a) socially warm versus cold; (b) reflective versus boorish; (c) competent versus inept; (d) earthy versus repressed; and (e) benign versus mean-spirited. Craik et al. (1996) showed that sense of humor (as judged by research participants) primarily reflected the socially warm and competent styles.

Willibald Ruch and his colleagues approached humor from a temperamental perspective, arguing that although the expression of humor may be culturally and historically bounded, its affective and intellectual foundations are more likely to be universal (1997; Ruch & Köhler, 1998, 1999; Ruch, Köhler, & van Thriel, 1996). Three traits are proposed as the temperamental basis of humor—cheerfulness, seriousness, and bad mood—and are measured with a self-report questionnaire, the State-Trait Cheerfulness Inventory (STCI-T; Ruch, Köhler, et al., 1996). For example, trait cheerfulness (or the disposition for being in good humor) is assessed by a cheerful mood, a low threshold for smiling and laughter, a composed view of adverse life circumstances, responsiveness to a broad range of elicitors of amusement and smiling/laughter, and a generally playful interaction style. As such, cheerfulness exemplifies being in good humor (and grumpiness and melancholy exemplify being in bad humor).

Wit—or humor creation—refers to the ability to perceive the incongruous and to express it in quick, sharp, spontaneous, often sarcastic remarks that delight or entertain, either in social interactions or in verbal or graphical communications. This ability to create a comical or funny effect needs to be distinguished from sheer reproduction of memorized humor, and also the talent to perform humorously. According to Feingold and Mazzella (1991), individual differences in wittiness cannot be explained just by the person's ability to create humor but also by the degree to which the person is motivated to be funny and is able to communicate the humor effectively. Hence, their model of wittiness has three dimensions: motivation, cognition, and communication. They also distinguished between two types of verbal humor ability, namely, the memory for humor (measured by tests of humor information and joke knowledge) and humor cognition (tests of humor reasoning and joke comprehension). The talent of wit has been less well investigated (O'Quin & Derks, 1997), and despite the fact that questionnaire measures exist, wit is most often acknowledged as an ability (i.e., maximal behavior) best investigated by a performance test. In tests of producing captions for caption-removed cartoons, quantity (fluency) and quality (originality) components can be reliably distinguished (Köhler & Ruch, 1996).

Finally, there is a tradition of conceptualizing humor as aesthetic appreciation. A great variety of funny material exists (jokes, cartoons, films, short stories, stage plays), as well as those who create this material (clowns, comedians, comedy writers, essayists). Being most economical to use in research, jokes and cartoons have been studied most often. An example is the work of Ruch

(1992; Ruch & Hehl, 1998), who introduced a two-mode model of individual differences in humor appreciation that combines three types of humor (incongruity-resolution, nonsensical, and sexual) with two basic responses (amusement, aversion) and operationalized it. Respondents are shown cartoons and jokes. In the 3 WD humor appreciation test, respondents rate various cartoons and jokes in terms of their funniness and aversiveness. An individual's humor is captured by the resulting profile.

What is missing altogether in the assessment of humor? Only a handful of humor tests for children have been constructed (see Ruch, 1998c). Starting with G. E. Bird (1925), they were based on appreciation of cartoons and jokes and are outdated. No questionnaire approach to the measurement of children's humor is known, impairing the life span study of humor. The construction of a scale for the measurement of children's use of humor in coping is apparently under way (Füehr, 2002).

■ Correlates and Consequences

Humor as an individual difference is apparently associated with a variety of desirable correlates and consequences, although direct comparison of findings is hampered by the use of different measures across studies. Best established are the conclusions that humor is linked to good mood and that it buffers the effects on mood of life stress and daily hassles (R. A. Martin, 1996, 2001; Ruch & Köhler, 1998). The mechanism may be cognitive, in that humor allows someone to construe threatening situations in a more benign way (Kuiper et al., 1993).

There is a widespread belief that humor improves physical health and increases longevity (cf. Cousins, 1981), but the actual data are equivocal (Martin, 2001). To be sure, we can argue that humor *should* pay health dividends. Cheerful or humorous people laugh more than their dour counterparts (Ruch, 1997; Ruch & Köhler, 1998). Habitual laughter can affect physiological changes for the better in musculoskeletal, cardiovascular, endocrine, immunological, and/ or neural systems. Therefore, humor is healthy. However, to date few empirical links have been established between trait measures of humor and immunity, pain tolerance, or symptoms of illness.

The personality correlates of humor have received much attention. The early and narrowly conceptualized humor instruments usually correlated positively with extroversion and negatively with neuroticism (Köhler & Ruch, 1996; Ruch, 1994). However, more recent instruments that distinguish different styles of humor show that almost all facets of personality are linked with humor, often in subtle ways (Ruch, 1998b). Wit, not surprisingly, is correlated with creativity and intelligence (Feingold & Mazzella, 1991; Ruch & Köhler, 1998).

As we mentioned earlier, that humor seems related only to desirable outcomes does not have much significance. Investigators have often sought such relations by framing humor as a wholly positive trait. However, it is possible to use theory to predict less desirable outcomes for certain types of humor. For example, appreciation of jokes that rely on stereotypes (e.g., the dumb blonde, the stingy Scotsman) predicts punitive attitudes and intolerance of ambiguity (Ruch, 1992; Ruch, Busse, & Hehl, 1996). Likewise, not all attempts to be funny are benevolent, and again, we call for studies that investigate the full range of humor's outcomes.

■ Development

McGhee (1999) saw playfulness as the motor underlying the sense of humor. Because humor is one form of play—play with ideas—factors that encourage or hinder play should affect humor. Without a playful frame of mind, the same event may be seen as interesting, puzzling, annoying, or frightening—but not as funny. Irony is wasted on those who take everything literally. Whereas some people might be good at spotting the incongruities, absurdities, and ironies of life, only the playful will find humor in them. McGhee assumed that most children inherit a playful temperament but that socialization can readily undo it.

If playfulness provides the foundation of humor, then societal factors and group norms relating to being playful may be crucial in the development and fostering of humor. Play behavior may be seen by some as negative (consider words like *childish, silly, ridiculous, nonsensical*). Where such attitudes prevail, the limiting of play by children may become a prime goal of the parent or teacher. However, an overemphasis on being serious might impede the development of humor.

McGhee (1979) discussed the early development of humor appreciation, and McGhee, Ruch, and Hehl (1990) provided a personality-based model of how appreciation of incongruity-resolution and nonsense humor might develop across childhood, adolescence, and adulthood. Most of the predictions were confirmed in a cross-sectional study of several thousand Germans, ranging in age from 14 through 66, who completed the 3 WD humor measure described earlier. Incongruity-resolution humor increased in funniness with age, whereas nonsense humor decreased after the late teens. Aversiveness of both forms of humor generally decreased over the ages sampled (Ruch, McGhee, & Hehl, 1990). In a study of individuals from late adolescence to old age, there were no major trends apparent in trait cheerfulness (Ruch, Köhler, et al., 1996). However, although there were no differences among individuals younger than 40, seriousness increased thereafter. A similar increase was observed for cheerful composure, a measure akin to humor in the traditional sense.

What of the heritability of the various components of humor? Correlates of humor like extroversion are known to have a genetic basis, but unfortunately, no genetic study utilizing comprehensive humor scales has been carried out to provide more direct evidence. A study of the frequency with which children use specific types of humor with their mothers, siblings, and friends showed some genetic influence on humor use (Humor Use in Multiple Ongoing Relationships [HUMOR]; Manke, 1998). In terms of cartoon humor, there is genetic influence on appreciation of aggressive humor but not of nonsense, satirical, or sexual humor (Manke, 1998; G. D. Wilson, Rust, & Kasriel, 1977). Overall, for appreciation of cartoon humor, the shared environmental influence seems to be more relevant (Cherkas, Hochberg, MacGregor, Snieder, & Spector, 2000; G. D. Wilson et al., 1977).

Joking relationships may be among the important environmental influences on the development of humor and playfulness. Peers who encourage unrestricted indulgence in all forms of humor allow people to develop skills at recognizing and creating humor. And if humor can be learned, the media are an especially rich source of models, from cartoons in daily newspapers to round-the-clock stand-up routines on Comedy Central channel. Nowadays humor is offered in such abundance that people have countless occasions to learn how to be funny, either by sheer imitation or by learning the rules for generating new humor on the spot.

There is also the view that humor develops solely from adverse circumstances. For example, Fisher and Fisher (1981) investigated the personality characteristics and familial and childhood antecedents of professional comedians and circus clowns, as well as more mundane class clowns. They found that comics described their fathers in more positive terms and their mothers in a more negative manner than did a control group of actors. Likewise, the mothers of the children identified as class clowns were seen as less kind, less sympathetic, less close, and more selfish and controlling. Consequently, Fisher and Fisher theorized that comics develop their humor skills in childhood as a means of entertaining others, gaining approval, and asserting their own goodness in the context of an uncongenial family environment characterized by limited maternal affection and warmth, a need to take on adult responsibilities at an early age, and a sense that things often are not what they appear to be on the surface. These data are of course open to alternative interpretations.

It should be emphasized that the notion of humor as a means of coping with adversity relates to humor in the traditional sense only—not to what humor has come to mean as an umbrella term. Whereas adversity may create or encourage humor, enduring or intense trauma may cause someone to lose interest in humor altogether. Hence, earlier losses and difficulties alone seem insufficient as explanations for the development of humor.

Little is known about the development of more sophisticated forms of humor, although psychoanalytic theorists from Freud (1905a) to Vaillant (1977, 1993) have regarded humor as a sign of maturity, an attitude akin to wisdom and presumably developing from experience with an imperfect world (cf. chapter 8). So far there is only anecdotal evidence that major life events have the power to transform a person's humor, perhaps by leading to the insight that nothing earthly is permanent. Here is an interesting topic for future research.

■ Enabling and Inhibiting Factors

As already menioned, Schmidt-Hidding (1963) summarized the early notions on enabling conditions; humor (in the narrow sense) stemmed from a sympathetic heart, wit from a superior spirit, and mockery and ridicule from a haughty moral sense or simply from malice. Fun was considered an expression of vitality or high-spiritedness (cf. chapter 12). Some of these intuitions have been supported by more recent empirical studies finding that the ability to create humor is correlated with intelligence or creativity (Feingold & Mazzella, 1991) and that bad moods are associated with the appreciation of satire, cynicism, and sarcasm (Ruch, 2001).

In particular, the early literature assigned cheerfulness a special role in the development of humor in the narrow sense. A humorous attitude or worldview is the product of a cheerful temperament coupled with enabling factors like negative life experiences and acquired insights into human nature and existence. A person with a humorous attitude is one who understands the insufficiencies and shortcomings of life but also tolerates them and ultimately forgives. Humor in this sense is a serious trait in that it is based on the wisdom that nothing earthly and human is perfect; accordingly, humor differs from merriment or hilarity. The former is contemplative, pensive, and profound, the latter thoughtless, superficial, and shallow (Ruch & Carrell, 1998).

Effects of mood on humor are well documented (Deckers, 1998), and the importance of a playful (as opposed to serious) frame of mind in the generation of humor has often been emphasized (McGhee, 1979). However, most humor scales have conceptualized humor as an invariant trait, and few have accommodated the waxing and waning aspect of humor dispositions. An exception is the state-trait approach of Ruch and Köhler (1998, 1999), who argued that cheerfulness, seriousness, and bad mood are not only traits based in temperament but also states that vary with situations. Traits of course predispose states; everybody is in a cheerful state now and then, but individuals high or low in trait cheerfulness differ with respect to the threshold, frequency, intensity, and duration of situationally occasioned cheerfulness. Furthermore, cheerful states are more robust—harder to disrupt—among those high in trait cheerfulness.

Humor in the traditional sense of the term is quite explicitly tied to situations; the presence of adversity gives rise to humor as a defense mechanism. Indeed, humor as a psychological strength is particularly visible when an individual or group is facing adversity, inasmuch as it helps to mitigate, suppress, interrupt, or even permanently replace negative impact. Phenomena like black humor or gallows humor have emerged in concentration camps, oppressive political systems, and during times of war (e.g., Nevo & Levine, 1994).

■ Gender, Cross-National, and Cross-Cultural Aspects

Gender differences have been reported in many studies of joke and cartoon appreciation, self-assessments, peer reports, and the like. According to a review by Lampert and Ervin-Tripp (1998), men are more likely than women to joke, tease, and kid, whereas women are more likely to act as an appreciative audience than to produce humor of their own. Also, men are more likely to enjoy humor in general and especially tendentious forms (with aggressive and sexual themes). These differences can be ascribed to gender role differences in accepted standards of behavior and status. However, as Lampert and Ervin-Tripp (1998) observed, the focus of most studies on limited forms of humor may have led to an exaggeration of actual gender differences. For example, when researchers differentiate between nonsexist and sexist humor, they find no gender differences, even for erotic humor.

Folk wisdom tells that there are national or cultural styles of humor. Some groups have earned themeselves a reputation for having a characteristic style of humor (e.g., British humor, Jewish humor), and other groups are said to have no sense of humor at all (e.g., Germans, Japanese). Most cross-national research has involved essays describing national styles of humor or comparisons of jokes in folklore archives (C. Davies, 1998; Ziv, 1988). So far, no research program has examined humor as an individual difference across several cultures simultaneously. Nevertheless, researchers are beginning to translate the humor measures described earlier. Preliminary research finds *no* evidence for folk wisdom; the questionnaires are responded to similarly by individuals from different nations (e.g., R. A. Martin, 1996; Ruch & Hehl, 1998).

■ Deliberate Interventions

Nevo, Aharonson, and Klingman (1998) articulated two views about the cultivation of humor. From a psychoanalytic perspective, an improved sense of humor is possible only as an indirect by-product of maturation or therapy. But from a cognitive-behavioral perspective, humor can be learned as any skill is learned, one component at a time through reinforcement and cognitive restructuring. Taking off from this second perspective, programs aimed at improving one's sense of humor have been created. Such programs are common in hospital, educational, and counseling settings—anywhere a sense of humor is thought to be useful—but little evaluation has been done.

A program described by McGhee (1999) is representative. It is based on the assumption that playfulness is the basis of humor and that the rediscovery of a playful attitude or outlook is essential for changing one's sense of humor for the better. The program assumes that humor skills can be taught during group meetings and practiced at home. The program involves eight steps ordered in difficulty, from simple (enjoying humor as it occurs in everyday life) to difficult (laughing at one's self, finding humor in stress). Earlier steps need to be mastered before moving to later steps. Although no published data exist on the effectiveness of the program, Simone Sassenrath (personal communication, November 1, 2001) reported that a group of 20 adults participating in the program evidenced increases in self-reported sense of humor, playfulness, and positive mood. Some of these changes were sustained 1 month after the end of the program.

Nevo et al. (1998) designed a systematic program for improving the sense of humor and tested it with 101 female high school teachers in Israel. The intervention program consisted of 14 units and was designed to train the presumed cognitive, motivational, emotional, and social components of humor. Three other groups either received only part of the program or were assigned to a no-treatment control group. Results only partly supported the hypothesis that humor could be cultivated. For example, participants in the humor improvement program were rated by their peers as higher in humor appreciation, but there were no differences in the ability to produce humor.

■ What Is Not Known?

Humor has long been neglected by psychologists. Some very basic questions therefore remain in need of answers. Furthermore, the full role of humor in people's daily lives has not been explored, so studies are still needed that document the correlates and consequences of humor as a character strength. Here are some further issues in need of study:

- What dimensions are necessary to describe humor as a habitual individual difference? Are these dimensions invariant across groups, nations, and cultures? Which can be seen as beneficial character strengths and which as detrimental?
- How can we best measure these dimensions? Is self-report valid for all aspects of humor?
- Should humor be conceptualized as an ability (i.e., maximal behavior) rather than a style (i.e., typical behavior)?
- Can the notion of humor proposed by philosophers—a smiling worldview—be operationalized by psychologists? How might this construct differ from the shallow humor typically studied? Will it have more robust and more profound correlates?
- How do different forms of humor develop over the life course, and what factors drive development?
- Do humor and cheerfulness have benefits beyond those conferred by the absence of negative emotionality?

- Which forms of humor can be learned? Does the teaching of humor skills alter a person's humor abilities and styles? Do interventions that improve components of humor result in positive outcomes or merely the absence of negative outcomes?

■ Must-Read Articles and Books

Chapman, A. J., & Foot, H. C. (Eds.). (1977). *It's a funny thing, humour.* Oxford, England: Pergamon Press.

Goldstein, J. H., & McGhee, P. E. (Eds.). (1972). *The psychology of humor: Theoretical perspectives and empirical issues.* New York: Academic Press.

Martin, R. A. (1998). Approaches to the sense of humor: A historical review. In W. Ruch (Ed.), *The sense of humor: Explorations of a personality characteristic* (pp. 15–62). New York: Mouton de Gruyter.

Martin, R. A. (2001). Humor, laughter, and physical health: Methodological issues and research findings. *Psychological Bulletin, 127,* 504–519.

McGhee, P. E. (1979). *Humor: Its origin and development.* San Francisco: Freeman.

Morreall, J. (1983). *Taking laughter seriously.* Albany: State University of New York Press.

Ruch, W. (Ed.). (1996). Measurement of the sense of humor [Double special issue]. *Humor: International Journal of Humor Research, 9*(3/4).

Ruch, W. (Ed.). (1998). *The sense of humor: Explorations of a personality characteristic.* New York: Mouton de Gruyter.

27. SPIRITUALITY

[Religiousness, Faith, Purpose]

■ *Alvira Easton Brown (Mother Brown) (1904–1984) was a deaconess and a devout Christian evangelist who lived in Trinityville, Jamaica. Mother Brown was so profoundly moved by her personal experience of God that, at times, she found herself speaking in tongues. Her enthusiastic style of worship was not acceptable in the very conservative Baptist church where she worshiped. The leaders of her church insisted that she become less vocal in her style of worship, and threatened to disfellowship her from the church unless she became less expressive. Mother Brown, noting the biblical foundations for full and joyful religious expression, continued to behave as the spirit moved her. When she was disfellowshiped from the church, more than half of the congregation followed her. She held regular prayer meetings at her home until she and the other followers joined forces with a church headed by another local minister. Soon afterward, Mother Brown had a dream in which she saw a site upon which she should build a new church. Not long after she had this dream, Mother Brown and her minister happened upon a site that was identical to the one in her dream. Following the vision that was revealed to her in her dream, she talked with the owners of the land and managed to convince them to give her both the land and time to raise the funds necessary to make a down payment. The church's followers were eventually able to raise the funds needed to purchase the land and build a church. The church, which quickly developed a strong, active outreach ministry, continues to exist on this plot of land.*

Mother Brown believed strongly in the healing powers of faith and prayer, and she was convinced that the ultimate expression of faith was found in the ministries of love and care that people developed in and through their lives. Her own deep religious faith led her to commit herself to a life of charity, sacrifice, and healing. She provided counseling and support to others. She had an encyclopedic knowledge of healing herbs and used this knowledge along with prayer and laying on of hands to heal others. In addition to her own 10 children, she raised, educated, and otherwise supported children whose parents were unable to care for them. Although poor, she used her limited resources to feed indigent families. She taught members of the community to develop cooperatives that would facilitate the sharing and bartering of food, supplies, and resources necessary for their survival. In addition, she developed numerous local charitable initiatives, including programs to teach poor men and women to read and write, to sew, and to grow subsistence crops on small plots of land. Owing to her reputation for extreme kindness and generosity, her home became a place of refuge for missionary groups and for individuals who were in need of shelter, food, clothing, healing, or other assistance. Until her death in 1984, she continued to work to support and heal others and to provide loving service through her work in the church. ■

■ Consensual Definition

Spirituality and *religiousness* refer to beliefs and practices that are grounded in the conviction that there is a transcendent (nonphysical) dimension of life. These beliefs are persuasive, pervasive, and stable. They inform the kinds of attributions that people make, the meanings they construct, and the ways they conduct relationships.

The following sorts of questions and statements distinguish between individuals who are spiritual or religious and those who are not:

- What is your current religious preference?
- Are you a member of a church or religious institution?
- How often do you attend religious or worship services?
- How religious would you say you are?
- How important is religion in your life today?
- How spiritual would you say you are?
- How often do you pray?
- How often do you meditate?
- How often do you read religious materials or watch or listen to religious programs?
- I believe there is a sacred force in all living things and that this force connects us to each other.
- I believe in life after death.
- I believe that every life has a purpose.
- I feel God's presence.
- I look to God/a Higher Power for support, guidance, and strength.
- My belief in God/a Higher Power helps me to understand my purpose in life.

- My belief in God/a Higher Power helps me to understand the meaning of the things that I experience.

Spirituality is universal. Although the specific content of spiritual beliefs varies, all cultures have a concept of an ultimate, transcendent, sacred, and divine force. Further, all religions seek to help people to grapple with core existential concerns (i.e., questions of purpose and meaning) and posit rules and values that guide individuals' relationships, as well as their efforts to cope with the travails of life.

Social science approaches to spirituality and religiousness run the gamut from a focus on the functional value of religion to a focus on the nature and content of spiritual and religious experience. Within the functionalist tradition, some scholars have explored the role of religion and religious institutions in the development and maintenance of values that promote a coherent social order (Durkheim, 1915). Others have attended to the intrapsychic functions of religiousness. For example, Freud (1912, 1927), in his effort to delineate the functional value (and the ontogeny) of religion, concluded that religion emerged as a consequence of the human need to defend against infantile impulses and fears (e.g., the fear of being destroyed). According to Freud, God and other divine figures are inventions (illusions) that fulfill the human wish for an omnipotent father whose love and protection have the kind of unconditional, enduring, salvific power that could never be achieved by human fathers. William James (1902/1999) shifted social scientific discourse about religious life by exploring both the subjective experience and the philosophical underpinnings of religiousness. In doing so, he grappled with such topics as religious conversion, religious mysticism, happiness, trance states, saintliness, optimism, repentance, and well-being.

In much of the literature in the social sciences the terms *spirituality* and *religiousness* have been treated as synonyms. However, recent studies suggest that some individuals make substantive distinctions between spirituality and religiousness (Mattis, 2000; Zinnbauer et al., 1997).[1] The importance of clearly articulating points of overlap and distinction between these two constructs has become more salient as people have become more explicit about their rejection or embrace of traditional religious life.

Social scientists have put forward a number of definitions of spirituality and religiousness. William James (1902/1999) argued that religion refers to "the feelings, acts, and experiences of individual men in their solitude, so far as they apprehend themselves to stand in relation to whatever they may consider the

---

[1]Some theorists and researchers use the term *religiosity* instead of *religiousness*, but we have tried to avoid this term because of its everyday implications of spiritual pompousness and pretense, which these scholars do not intend to convey.

divine" (pp. 31–32). George Galloway asserted that religion is "man's faith in a power beyond himself whereby he seeks to satisfy emotional needs and gain stability of life, and which he expresses in acts of worship and service" (cited in Houf, 1945, p. 7). Although subsequent definitions of religion vary (see, e.g., Batson & Ventis, 1982; Geertz, 1973), most conceptualizations share three common points of focus (Houf, 1945):

- a belief in powers that are transcendent and suprahuman
- an interest in and quest for a range of values including goodness
- a focus on behaviors, attitudes, and experiences that are consistent with these values

More recently, scholars have called for definitions of religion that highlight the notion of sacredness. Pargament's (1997) definition of religion as "a search for significance in ways related to the sacred" (p. 32) reflects a response to that call.

There are etymological, theological, and experiential grounds for distinguishing between religiousness and spirituality. The word *religiousness* (derived from the Latin word *religio*) refers both to a belief in the existence of a divine or greater-than-human force and to an individual's adherence to the beliefs and rituals that signify worship of and reverence for this divine entity (Wulff, 1991). Spirituality is derived from the Latin word *spiritus*, which means the breath of life (Berdyaev, 1939; MacQuarrie, 1972). Berdyaev (1939) noted that at different historical moments, and in different cultural contexts, the word *spiritus* has been used as a synonym for wisdom, intelligence, the capacity to reason, and the soul or any nonphysical life force. However, in the earliest passages of the Old Testament of the Christian Bible we find a concrete reference to the meaning of *spiritus*. According to the Judeo-Christian account of the genesis of human life, the physical entity that was the first human became fully alive only after God breathed "the breath of life" into him. Through that breath God accomplished two important ends. First, he achieved a profound level of intimacy with humans. Second, through that act of intimacy he imparted an essential, enlivening, divine, and sacred aspect of himself into each human being. This divine breath of life that resides in the body (Berdyaev, 1939; MacQuarrie, 1972) is believed to be the source of human strength and virtue. That is, this breath is believed to be the source of the capacity for creativity, the ability to grasp the sacred, and the capacity for love, intimacy, harmony, growth, compassion, goodness, and optimism.

Work by Zinnbauer and colleagues (1997) and by Mattis (2000) suggested that both religiousness and spirituality denote a belief in the existence of a transcendent dimension of life. However, religiousness is believed to describe an individual's degree of acceptance of the prescribed beliefs associated with the worship of a divine figure, and that individual's participation in public and private acts of worship. Spirituality, in contrast, is believed to describe both the private, intimate relationship between humans and the divine, and the range of virtues that result from that relationship. Those virtues are believed to manifest in the pursuit of a principled life and a life of goodness.

Concerns about the definitions of spirituality and religiousness raise important questions about the criteria by which we can know that an event is spiritual or religious in nature. One line of work suggests that spiritual and religious events are extraordinary happenings characterized by visions, mystical or miraculous experiences, and/or unusual encounters between individuals and God (James, 1902/1999; chapter 23). However, Nelson (1997) argued that spiritual or religious events are not distinguished by their extraordinary or transcendent nature. Instead, events are characterized as spiritual or religious because people attribute their causes or consequences to a divine or transcendent force.

■ Theoretical Traditions

Contemporary approaches to the study of religious and spiritual life tend to fall into five general domains:

- There is a body of literature that attends to measurement. These studies seek both to define various domains of religious and spiritual experience and to assess the psychometric properties of empirical measures of these domains.
- A substantial body of work is available that explores the functional significance of religiousness and spirituality. This body of work attends to the role of various dimensions of religiousness and spirituality in coping and in effecting a range of relational, psychological, and physical health outcomes.
- A third body of work examines the cognitive and emotional dimensions of religiousness and spirituality. This work is concerned with such matters as attributional styles, religious beliefs, and meaning making.
- Next is a more sociologically oriented approach to the study of religiousness and spirituality that maps patterns of involvement and delineates the impact of those forms of involvement on social cohesion.
- Finally, there is a body of work that examines the neurophysiology of religious and spiritual experience.

Contemporary studies of religiousness can also be understood in terms of what they regard as the principal unit of analysis. Most studies focus attention on the religious and spiritual lives of individuals. However, a growing number of researchers are focusing attention on churches or religious communities as the principal units of focus. These researchers are particularly attentive to the role of churches and congregation members in promoting such outcomes as volunteerism and civic involvement (Cavendish, 2000) and psychological and physical well-being (Krause, Ellison, Shaw, Marcum, & Boardman, 2001).

Researchers are beginning to pay closer attention to religious experience (e.g., Nelson, 1997). Religious and spiritual socialization (i.e., the transmission of religious and spiritual beliefs and practices within and across generations) has also begun to garner attention.

■ Measures

Researchers have actively debated the sufficiency of single-item versus multi-item, and unidimensional versus multidimensional measures of religious and spiritual life (Gorsuch, 1988; Wimberley, 1989). A number of theorists have asserted that religiousness and spirituality are best understood as a pastiche of experiences, beliefs, attitudes, values, attributions, and practices (Batson & Ventis, 1982; Dull & Skokan, 1995). They argue that researchers must use multi-item, multidimensional measures if they intend to capture the complexity of religious and spiritual life. Nevertheless, in many studies religiousness and spirituality continue to be measured in rudimentary ways. Indeed, most studies tend to use fairly parsimonious (often single-item) measures of religious affiliation, organizational religious involvement, prayer, and indices of religious salience to assess religiousness or spirituality. In addition, despite ample evidence that religiousness and spirituality are distinct constructs, many studies continue to use measures of religiousness to assess spirituality.

As interest in the empirical study of religiousness and spirituality has grown, researchers also have tended to develop their own measures of these constructs (see Table 27.1). There is some degree of overlap in the items in most novel measures of religious and spiritual life. For example, most focus on frequency of prayer and frequency of formal religious participation. However, many measures of religiousness and spirituality are atheoretical. They fail to assess the various dimensions of religious and spiritual life that have been identified in the empirical literature. Many measures are also not theologically grounded. Further, many fail to make clear conceptual distinctions between religiousness and spirituality. Finally, many researchers neglect to effectively establish the psychometric validity of their measures. The tendency of researchers to use novel measures of religious and spiritual life complicates efforts to compare the findings of studies that link religion and spirituality to other outcomes.

The concerns raised about the measurement of religious and spiritual life are serious. However, it is important to note that even rudimentary measures of these constructs tend to produce robust findings. No doubt, this is a testament to the importance that individuals attach to matters of religious and spiritual life.

TABLE 27.1   *Measures of Spirituality and Religiousness*

Spirituality

Spiritual Well-Being (SWB)

> Ellison (1983)
>
> 20 items
>
> This measures SWB as a composite of religious well-being (RWG; relationship with God) and existential well-being (EWB; sense of purpose); positively correlated with self-esteem, family togetherness, quality of parent-child relationships, psychological well-being; negatively related to individualism, success orientation, personal freedom.
>
> ▪ Reliability (alphas): RWB = .87; EWB = .78; SWB = .89

Religious coping

Religious Problem-Solving Scale

> Pargament et al. (1988)
>
> 36 items
>
> This scale measures three dimensions of coping: collaborative, self-directing, and deferring; associated with lower levels of depression, anxiety, guilt, and physical symptoms and greater psychosocial competence.
>
> ▪ Reliability (alphas): collaborative = .94; self-directing = .94; deferring = .91

Brief RCOPE (*Religious Coping*)

> Pargament, Smith, Koenig, & Perez (1998)
>
> 21 items
>
> This measures two dimensions of coping: search for significance (positive coping) and religious struggle (negative coping); positive coping associated with lower levels of psychological distress, greater spiritual growth, cooperativeness; negative coping associated with depression, poorer quality of life, psychological symptoms, callousness.
>
> ▪ Reliability (alphas): positive coping = .87; negative coping = .78

Religious/Church Support

> Krause, Ellison, Shaw, Marcum, & Boardman (2001)
>
> 11 items
>
> This measure assesses (a) emotional support from ministers; (b) emotional and spiritual support received from church members; (c) negative interactions with church members; and (d) expectations of support; associated with psychological and physical well-being (health status, reported symptoms, distress).

Religious beliefs/values

Religious Orthodoxy Scale

> Batson & Ventis (1982)
>
> This scale assesses the extent to which individuals endorse liberal versus more conservative and literal beliefs.

(*continued*)

TABLE 27.1   *Measures of Spirituality and Religiousness* (*continued*)

Religious Values Scale
> S. H. Schwartz (1992); S. H. Schwartz & Bilsky (1987)
>
> 56 items
>
> This scale measures a range of values including prosociality; negatively related to measures of individualism.

God as Causal Agent Scale
> Ritzema & Young (1983)
>
> 14 items
>
> This scale measures extent to which events are attributed to natural versus supernatural causes; associated with coping, psychological distress, psychological adjustment.
>
> - Reliability (alpha) = .74

Religious orientation

Intrinsic-Extrinsic Motivation Scale
> Allport & Ross (1967)
>
> 20 items
>
> This scale assesses intrinsic (internalized acceptance and pursuit of religiousness in everyday life) and extrinsic (utilitarian approach to religious life) religious motivation

Intrinsic Religious Motivation Scale
> Hoge (1972)
>
> This scale measures internalized acceptance and pursuit of religiousness in everyday life.
>
> - Reliability (alpha) = .85

Extrinsic Religious Motivation Scale
> Feagin (1964)
>
> This scale measures utilitarian approach to religious life.
>
> - Reliability (alpha) = .66

Religious involvement/commitment/history

Organizational Involvement
> Levin, Taylor, & Chatters (1995)
>
> 4 items

This measure assesses participation in organized religious activities, including religious affiliation and attendance; associated with positive psychological well-being, physical well-being, physical symptoms, happiness, self-esteem, and purpose.

Non-Organizational Involvement

Levin, Taylor, & Chatters (1995)

4 items

This measure assesses participation in private devotional activities, including prayer, reading religious materials, listening to religious programming; associated with psychological well-being, physical well-being, physical symptoms, happiness, self-esteem, and purpose.

Subjective Religious Involvement

Levin, Taylor, & Chatters (1995)

3 items

This measure assesses level of religious commitment and salience; associated with positive psychological well-being, physical well-being, physical symptoms, happiness, self-esteem, and purpose.

Religious History

Fetzer Institute (1999)

100 items

This measures religious commitment and participation at ages 5–12, 13–18, 20–29, 30–39, 40–49, 50–64; significant religious life events; and faith development.

RELTRAD

Steensland et al. (2000)

This measure provides a detailed system of classification for religious traditions, including Black Protestants, evangelical Protestants, mainline Protestants, and nontraditional denominational groups.

Comprehensive measure

Brief Multidimensional Measure of Religiousness/Spirituality

Fetzer Institute (1999)

40 items

This measure assesses a range of domains of religious life, including religious coping, commitment, church support, and history.

Steensland et al. (2000) developed a comprehensive tool for classifying Christian denominations. This tool builds on prior classification systems by providing a detailed way of categorizing nontraditional groups.

A number of commonly used multi-item measures are available to assess various dimensions of religious and spiritual life. Following Mindel and Vaughn (1978), Levin and his colleagues developed a three-factor scale that measures the participatory aspects of religious life. This measure assesses organizational religious involvement (e.g., church attendance), private nonorganizational religious involvement (e.g., prayer), and subjective religiousness—the extent to which individuals identify religion as important in their lives (see Levin, Taylor, & Chatters, 1995). The three dimensions of religious involvement identified by Levin et al. measure what Wimberley (1989) described as religious commitment and religious salience. Krause et al. (2001) identified a number of items that are useful for assessing people's experience of church support. Ellison (1983) developed a measure of spiritual well-being (SWB) that assesses the quality of one's relationship with God (religious well-being) and one's sense of purpose, meaning, and life direction (existential well-being). Other scholars have focused empirical attention on the measurement of specific religious values (Gorsuch & McFarland, 1972). Further, Ritzema and Young (1983) advanced a measure that assesses the religious attributions that people make about the causes of mundane as well as extraordinary life events (God as Causal Agent Scale; GCAS).

One of the most frequently used scales in the study of religious life is Allport and Ross's (1967) measure of intrinsic and extrinsic (I/E) religious motivation. *Intrinsic religiousness* refers to the private aspects of religious life and individuals' efforts to behave in ways that are consistent with their creed. *Extrinsic religiousness* refers to the individual's involvement in the public rituals of worship. Gorsuch and McPherson (1989) have offered a revised version the I/E scale. Another frequently used measure is the Religious Problem-Solving Scale developed by Pargament and colleagues (Pargament et al., 1988). This scale assesses three religious problem-solving styles: collaborative, self-directing, and deferring (to God) coping.

Elkins and his colleagues developed a measure of spirituality that comprises nine dimensions: a transcendent dimension; meaning and purpose in life; mission in life; sacredness of life; material values; altruism; idealism; awareness of the tragic; and the beneficial manifestations (fruits) of spirituality (Elkins, Hedstrom, Hughes, Leaf, & Saunders, 1988).

The Fetzer Institute (1999) has compiled a comprehensive list of measures that have proved to be useful in empirical studies of the link between religion, spirituality, and health. These measures assess an array of dimensions of religiousness and spirituality, including religious history, religious involvement, religious and spiritual beliefs, religious coping, and forgiveness.

■ Correlates and Consequences

Among youth, religiousness is associated with a tendency to avoid a range of antisocial activities, including drug use, drug selling, and other illicit activities (B. Johnson, Larson, Li, & Jang, 2000). Children and adolescents who score higher on indices of religiousness (i.e., church attendance) also tend to demonstrate greater emotional self-regulation, engage in fewer acts of aggression, are less likely to engage in illicit drug and alcohol use, have better records of academic performance, and tend to delay sexual involvement (Donahue & Benson, 1995; Maton & Wells, 1995; Stevenson, 1997). Bjarnason (1998) found that Icelandic adolescents who reported greater levels of religious participation also tended to perceive the world as a more coherent place. Importantly, Jagers (1997) found that the spirituality of one's peers can also have important implications. More specifically, urban-residing, African American children who rated their friends as spiritual, affective, and communal tended to be more empathic and less antagonistic toward others. In adult samples there is also evidence that religiousness and spirituality mitigate antisocial and risky behaviors. Work conducted with adults has provided some evidence that indices of private or nonorganizational religiousness may function differently from indices of public or organizational religiousness. In particular, Richard, Bell, and Carlson (2000) found that although church attendance was associated with reduced use of cocaine and alcohol among substance abusers, indices of private religiousness (e.g., prayer) were not associated with these outcomes.

Religiousness has significant positive consequences in relational life—particularly the quality of family life. Religiousness (measured as religious participation and religious salience) is associated with lower levels of marital conflict, greater perceived spousal support, more consistent parenting, and less conflictual and more supportive relationships between adolescents and their parents (G. Brody, Stoneman, Flor, & McCrary, 1994). Mahoney et al. (1999) found that marital quality (e.g., marital adjustment, lower levels of verbal aggression, and spousal collaboration) was positively associated with mutual participation in religious activities, the perception of marriage as sacred, and the belief that one's marriage reflects God's will and one's faith.

Religiousness, broadly speaking, also has been empirically linked to a range of human virtues, including forgiveness (Rye et al., 2000), kindness (Ellison, 1992), and compassion (Wuthnow, 1991). Religiousness, particularly church involvement, also has been identified as a robust predictor of altruism, volunteerism, and philanthropy (Hodgkinson, Weitzman, & Kirsch, 1990; Mattis et al., 2000; Regnerus, Smith, & Sikkink, 1998; Schervish, 1990; H. Smith, Fabricatore, & Peyrot, 1999). Early religious and spiritual involvement appears to play a particularly crucial role in promoting prosocial values (Mattis et al., 2000). Although empirical evidence regarding the link between religiousness and optimism is sparse, Sethi and Seligman (1993) found a link between religious fundamentalism and optimism. French and Joseph (1999) also established links among religiousness, happiness, and life purpose. Levin and Taylor (1998) found a link between religious involvement and happiness in a national probability sample of African Americans. Recent work also establishes a link between religiousness and an awareness of the sacredness of life (Pargament, 1997).

A sizable body of research has demonstrated a positive link between religiousness (particularly religious involvement) and psychological and physical well-being (see Krause, 1997; Levin, 1997, for reviews). Ellison, Gay, and Glass (1989) also have demonstrated a link between higher levels of religiousness and greater life satisfaction. Religion plays a crucial role in individuals' efforts to cope with illness and psychosocial stress (Handal, Black-Lopez, & Moergen, 1989; Pargament, 1997; D. Williams, Larson, Buckler, Heckmann, & Pyle, 1991). Prayer plays a particularly important role in coping and in promoting well-being (McCullough, 2000; Neighbors, Jackson, Bowman, & Gurin, 1983). There is evidence, however, that other dimensions of religious life, including church support and ministerial support, also play crucial roles in people's efforts to cope with adversity (Ellison, 1992; Neighbors, Musick, & Williams, 1998). Chamberlain and Zika (1992) suggested that religiousness also influences well-being through its association with meaning making.

Finally, a number of scholars have attended to the role of religion in promoting community well-being (see Maton & Pargament, 1987; Maton & Wells, 1995). Churches, particularly those that have strong social justice and service orientations, play important roles in providing a range of resources that benefit communities. These churches often instill in their congregations a sense of civic responsibility that manifests in volunteerism and other forms of prosocial civic involvement. African American churches play particularly important roles in promoting the well-being of their communities by providing a range of services, including education, psychological counseling, financial support, housing, clothing, and food to those who are in need (Billingsley, 1999; Billingsley & Caldwell, 1991; Lincoln & Mamiya, 1990).

The putative effects of religiousness and spirituality may not be entirely positive. James (1902/1999) noted that religiousness is linked to severe psychopathology in some individuals. W. Wilson (1998) noted that religion and spirituality do not cause affective or psychotic disorders, but they may play a role in the manifestation of symptoms as well as in the progression of these psychological disorders.

Allport and Ross (1967) identified a link between religious orientation and prejudice. In particular, they found that individuals who were indiscriminately pro-religious and those who scored higher on extrinsic religiousness (i.e., those who tended to use religion or religious affiliation for particular ends as opposed to internalizing and living out religious beliefs) tended to be particularly prejudiced toward African Americans and Jews. These individuals also tended to be more suspicious and were more likely to perceive the world and those in it as threatening. Allport and Ross's findings were consistent with earlier findings regarding the positive links among church attendance, ethnocentrism, and authoritarian personality styles (Adorno, Frenkel-Brunswik, Levinson, & Sanford, 1950). Recent work by Leiber and Woodrick (1997) has demonstrated associations among biblical literalness, a tendency to attribute criminal behavior to dispositional rather than societal factors, and correctional punitiveness (as measured by a tendency to support the death penalty and stricter juvenile court rules). Finally, sociological and social psychological studies have documented a link between religiousness and spirituality and escapist orientations toward social problems and to a failure to challenge social injustice (G. Marx, 1969; K. Marx, 1990; Mattis, 2001). Negative interactions in church settings also appear to have a deleterious effect on the well-being of religious individuals (Krause, Chatters, Meltzer, & Morgan, 2000). Importantly, the studies cited here suggest that the nature of the link between religiousness and negative outcomes depends, in part, on the specific index of religiousness that is employed.

■ Development

Tiger (1999) argued that the importance attached to religiousness across cultures and religion's perseverance across historical moments are indicators that religiousness is biological and is genetically heritable. However, Geertz (1973) asserted that religiousness is a cultural construct and that socialization is key in the transmission of religious beliefs and practices. Whether religiousness and spirituality are biologically heritable or transmitted through socialization (or both) remains a matter for debate. However, most scholars agree that socialization plays a central role in the transmission of religious behaviors and values within and across generations.

Over the past decade scholars have turned their attention to the role of parents in the religious socialization of their children. This body of work has raised questions about the extent to which religious affiliation, religious beliefs, and religious commitment may be influenced by parents (S. Myers, 1996; Stolzenberg, Blair-Loy, & Waite, 1995). There is some evidence that fathers and mothers play distinct roles in the religious socialization of their children. Mothers appear to play a central role in shaping their children's religious affiliation and their patterns of religious involvement (S. Myers, 1996; R. Taylor & Chatters, 1991). There is also evidence that the gender of children may be important in influencing the role that fathers and mothers play in the process of religious socialization (Clark, Worthington, & Danser, 1988). For example, Clark and colleagues found that fathers played a significant role in structuring their sons' religious beliefs and patterns of religious involvement (fathers who attended church tended to have sons who also attended church). Mothers played a central role in the ways that their sons applied the principles of religion in everyday life. The composition of the household in which children are raised and the quality of parental interaction also appear to inform the religious development of adolescents. S. Myers (1996) suggested that children raised in nuclear families, children whose mothers are not a part of the full-time labor market, and those whose parents share similar religious beliefs, values, and patterns of religious involvement tend to have children who are religiously involved.

More recently, scholars have returned to a pursuit discussed by William James in his 1902 lectures on religious experience—the quest to map the neurological or psychophysiological substrates of religious and spiritual experience (e.g., Newberg & D'Aquili, 1998). James (1902/1999) stated:

> Medical materialism finishes up Saint Paul by calling his vision on the road to Damascus a discharging lesion of the occipital cortex, he being an epileptic. . . . All such mental tensions, it says, are, when you come to the bottom of the matter, mere affairs of diathesis (auto-intoxications most probably), due to the perverted action of various glands which physiology will yet discover. (p. 16)

We must be mindful that many of the studies of the neurophysiology of religiousness and spirituality focus on samples of mystics and religious and spiritual masters. It is crucial to consider that the states of consciousness that are induced in mystics, religious leaders, and spiritual masters in laboratory settings may bear only limited resemblance to the states experienced by ordinary believers in other contexts.

Psychologists have long been interested in the role of religion in human development. Indeed, G. Stanley Hall (1904) insisted that efforts to map child and adolescent psychology are necessarily incomplete unless one has a firm understanding of religion and religious transformation in the life of youth. Despite Hall's conviction, few scholars have examined the role of religion in the psychological development in the lives of young people. Although it is clear that religious and spiritual development begin early in life, empirical data on childhood religiousness and spirituality and on the development of these phenomena across the life span are limited (Stolzenberg et al., 1995). Our understanding of religious and spiritual development is based largely on cross-sectional data gathered from samples of various ages.

Within psychology, efforts to study religious and spiritual life in the context of development have taken two distinct routes. Some studies have sought to examine the process of religious and spiritual development (e.g., changes in patterns of belief and affiliation in response to adverse life events); others have endeavored to explore the manifestations of religiousness and spirituality across the life span (e.g., age-related differences in patterns of religious involvement).

Terms such as *spiritual growth* and *spiritual maturity* are employed to describe religious and spiritual development. There is some consensus that encounters with the challenges of life inspire people to think more deeply and more clearly about their religious and spiritual beliefs (i.e., challenges can lead to spiritual growth). However, the notion of spiritual maturity remains fairly controversial, in part because of the value judgment implicit in the concept of maturity. Further, it is not clear what might be appropriate benchmarks of a mature religiousness or spirituality.

There is some debate about the process by which religiousness and spirituality develop across the life span. Borrowing from stage models of cognitive and emotional development, some scholars argue that religious development proceeds according in stages (e.g., J. Fowler, 1981). These stage-based notions of religious development are subject to the same critiques that are often levied against other stage models. In particular, it is unclear whether individuals proceed in linear fashion from one stage to the next, if they can skip stages, or if they can move fluidly backward and forward between stages. Importantly, stage models of religious and spiritual life are also problematic in that they tend to represent religiousness and spirituality as purely cognitive phenomena.

Markstrom-Adams, Hofstra, and Dougher (1994) observed that religion can play a central role in the identity formation of adolescents. There is compelling evidence that females are more religious and more spiritual than males, and that this gender-related pattern maintains across the developmental span (see Donahue & Benson, 1995, for a discussion). There is also strong empirical evidence that older adults score higher on conventional measures of religiousness than do younger people (Ainlay & Smith, 1984), and that people who are married tend to be more religiously involved than their unmarried counterparts (R. Taylor & Chatters, 1991). Gerontology literature seems consistent in its assumption that the heightened religiousness of older adults is at least partially responsive to the existential dilemmas raised by this stage of life. That is, concerns about loss, finitude, meaning, and purpose are believed to structure patterns of belief, participation, and commitment among older people. Religion may be particularly important to adolescents for similar reasons. At that critical stage of life, adolescents may turn to religion in search of concrete rules that will guide them as they make decisions.

■ Enabling and Inhibiting Factors

There is some empirical evidence that social network factors play crucial roles in promoting religious and spiritual development. J. Jacobs (2000) suggested that empathic connections among children, parents, and caretakers provide the emotional context needed for the effective transmission of religious values (e.g., a sense of connection to God) and religious commitment (e.g., religious affiliation) across generations. Individuals who are emotionally attached to caretakers tend to attach powerful emotions to their memories of the religious beliefs and practices of those caretakers. Jacobs asserted that these emotionally rich memories serve as anchor points for the religious and spiritual lives of individuals. Family cohesion appears to play an important role in setting the stage for the intergenerational transmission of religious values and commitment. Bjarnason (1998), for example, found that perceived parental support promotes religious participation and religious orthodoxy among adolescents.

Little is known about the factors that discourage spirituality and religiousness. Pargament (1997) noted that individuals who find that they cannot make meaning of profound experiences of pain and loss, and those who are unable to reconcile their encounters of adversity with the notion of a loving and just God, may turn away from religion. Other factors (e.g., stress, poor health, negative church experiences) may play a role in people's decision not to participate in formal religious activities. However, disengagement from formal religious practice must be distinguished from ideological rejection of religion.

Popular lore holds that when faced with extreme adversity even the most ardent of atheists will turn to God for support and solace. However compelling this notion may be, there is no empirical evidence that it is necessarily or universally true. There is some evidence that people who are faced with negative events, particularly events that they experience as threatening, unresolvable (by personal or general human means), and incomprehensible, turn to religion (Mattis, 2002; Pargament, 1997). However, there is reason to believe that adversity leads to religious coping and conversion only in circumstances in which religion provides a more compelling source of meaning making and comfort than do nonreligious alternatives (Pargament, 1997).

■ Gender, Cross-National, and Cross-Cultural Aspects

The assertion that women are more religious than men is ubiquitous in empirical research on religion. This assertion generally is bolstered by evidence that women and girls outscore their male counterparts on a wide array of indices of organizational and nonorganizational religious involvement (e.g., frequency of service attendance, frequency of prayer), as well as on indices of subjective religiousness.

A number of theories have been offered to explain these gender differences. Using Freud's writings on Oedipal conflicts as a foundation, psychoanalytic theorists have asserted that representations of an omnipotent male god are inherently appealing to women but are experienced as threatening by men. Women's greater religiousness (i.e., their greater attachment to a loving, powerful, and protective male god) and men's apparent rejection of religion are seen as expected resolutions to the Oedipal conflict.

Socialization theorists have asserted that women more strongly endorse religious beliefs and practices because gender role socialization and religious socialization promote a common set of beliefs and values (e.g., submissiveness, gentleness, conformity, and nurturance) among women. Men's lower levels of religiousness are seen as the consequence of incompatibility of religious values and the values associated with male gender socialization (e.g., aggressiveness and competitiveness). Structural location theories suggest that women are bearers and transmitters of culture, and, as such, they tend to assume responsibility for reinforcing the importance of cultural systems such as religion. Religion and religious institutions provide women (particularly wives and mothers) with authoritative sources for reinforcing key values, beliefs, and practices in their children and spouses. A subset of structural location theories assert that levels of participation in the paid labor force (i.e., unemployed, part-time employment, and full-time employment) may explain men's and women's relative degrees of organizational religious involvement. Empirical research has provided mixed support for this latter thesis. More recent theoretical and empirical work suggests that it is not sex but gender orientation that accounts for apparent differences in men's and women's patterns of religious involvement (Francis, 1997). That is, men as well as women who score higher on indices of feminine gender role orientation tend to score higher on measures of religiousness (Francis & Wilcox, 1996; E. Thompson, 1991).

Despite the robustness of the finding that women outscore men on religiousness, there is also evidence that this gender pattern may not be universal. Indeed, Lowenthal, MacLeod, and Cinnirella (2002) note that if we use service attendance, frequency of prayer, and the study of religious texts as indices of religiousness, then Jewish and Muslim men would appear to be more religious than the women of these faith communities. Lowenthal et al. noted that Judaism and Islam require men to participate in organized religious life, but these religions do not place the same demands on women. We must remain mindful, therefore, that gender differences in patterns of religious involvement may reflect less about men's and women's relative levels of piety and more about social and cultural rules that govern the devotional lives of each gender.

It is generally accepted that spirituality and religiousness are cultural-level phenomena. However, many studies that endeavor to explore the relationship between religiousness and culture do so by examining race rather than cultural differences in patterns of religious and spiritual experience. Few studies endeavor to explore the role of religion and spirituality in constructing, transmitting, and sustaining meaning within given cultural and national communities across time. Further, few studies endeavor to explore the ways in which people symbolize their religious beliefs and experiences in language, or the ways in which culturally informed worldviews shape and are shaped by religious and spiritual life. Recent work by J. Jacobs (2000) on the religious and spiritual development of Spanish Crypto-Jews provides something of an exception to these generalizations. Jacobs documented the process by which certain modes of intimacy and relationship that are patterned by culture (e.g., extended family networks) help to shape adult religious and spiritual beliefs and practices.

Cross-cultural and cross-ethnic studies conducted within the United States suggest that among those Americans who describe themselves as religious, most classify themselves as Christians or Jews. However, an increasing number of Americans, including native-born Americans and new Americans or members of immigrant communities, self-describe as Muslim, Buddhist, or Hindu or as followers of other non-Judeo-Christian religious traditions (J. Smith, 2002). We have fairly little empirical data about the religious lives and experiences of members of these religious communities, and we know little about the factors that influence the maintenance of or change in their religious identities over time. We also have fairly little data on the religious lives and experiences of Native American communities that practice traditional religions.

To date, the majority of U.S.-based cross-cultural and cross-ethnic research on religion has focused on Latinos, African Americans, and Whites. In general, these studies continue uncritically to use Whites as the norm for the religious lives and experiences of other groups. This body of research has demonstrated that Latino and African American youth score particularly high on conventional, paper-and-pencil measures of religiousness and spirituality (Donahue & Benson, 1995). Similarly, research involving adult samples demonstrates that African Americans tend to outscore White Americans on measures of religiousness and spirituality (Conway, 1985–1986; R. Taylor, Mattis, & Chatters, 1999). The practical significance of these differences remains underexamined.

Cross-national studies of religiousness suggest that there may be a certain degree of consistency in the way that some religious beliefs and identities shape people's social attitudes. For example, Wall et al. (1999) noted that Catholics in the United States, Croatia, Slovenia, and the Czech Republic were more likely than non-Catholics to disapprove of abortion. This finding suggests that some religious beliefs translate across lines of nationality. Cross-national research does, however, emphasize the need for scholars to attend more closely to the ways in which macro-level forces may influence the religious and spiritual lives of individuals. For example, Jelen and Wilcox (1998) demonstrated that the extent to which individuals endorse attitudes associated with their given denomination depends, in part, on whether that denomination is part of a religious minority or part of a more religiously heterogeneous national culture. They found that in countries in which Catholicism was in the minority, Catholics were particularly likely to endorse the church's attitudes toward a range of subjects including abortion. This work suggests the need for attention to the ways in which national-level, community-level, and individual-level factors intersect to inform religious attitudes, beliefs, and behaviors. Cross-national studies also suggest the need for critical attention to the ways in which macro- and meso-level sociopolitical factors (e.g., colonization, secularization, political stability, war, economic prosperity or despair, and state control of worship) may influence public and private religious beliefs and devotional practices (e.g., religious attendance, prayer), as well as outcomes known to be associated with religion and spirituality (e.g., compassion). Asian and Asian American (Matsuoka, 2001; Phan, 2001) and Latino/a and Latino/a American (Isasi-Diaz, 2001) theologians have also examined the links among religion, theology, identity, and the sociopolitical condition of particular cultural groups.

International research on religion and spirituality highlights a number of important points. First, much of the work on religiousness conducted by Western researchers assumes that people's religious beliefs and practices are individually determined and freely chosen. However, Moghadam's (1999) work on the link between religion (Islam), political revolutions, and gender politics in Afghanistan and Iran highlights the point that for many people across the world religion is deeply intertwined with historical and political forces. The emergence and decline of secular, religiously fundamentalist, or religiously liberal political regimes can determine the content of people's religious beliefs, the nature and frequency of their public and private religious practices, their relationship to sacred texts, and the structure and fate of their institutions of worship. Indices of religiousness and spirituality that are commonly used in North American and Western social sciences will not adequately or accurately capture the complexities of religious life across the globe.

Second, existing research tacitly assumes a certain degree of stability in the religious profiles of communities and nations. However, research in countries such as the Netherlands has demonstrated that even in politically stable settings, we can see rapid and dramatic shifts in the ideological stances, religious identities, and religious practices of large portions of a community. Indeed, Houtman and Mascini (2002) note that over the past four decades the Netherlands has seen a wave of disaffiliation from Christian churches (60% of the Dutch population is not affiliated with a Christian church—up from 24% in 1958) and a dramatic increase in the number of people who self-describe either as nonreligious or as members of a New Age religious community. Efforts to explain the shift in the religious profile of the Netherlands have spawned discussions about the worldwide impact of secularization (Te Grotenhuis & Scheepers, 2001).

Third, international research highlights the point that religious identity, religious beliefs, and religious practices are not always clearly linked. Research conducted with Israeli Jews demonstrates, for example, that religious and secular Jews may participate in the same religious rituals, but that their experience of those rituals, and the factors that motivate their involvement in these rituals are often quite distinct. Lazar, Kravetz, and Frederich-Kedem (2002) noted that whereas rituals are important in the worship experience of religious Jews, for secular Jews, participation in these extrinsic aspects of religious life provides a context for constructing and maintaining a coherent ethnic identity and a coherent family experience.

■ Deliberate Interventions

History demonstrates that interfaith and intrafaith conflicts have been at the heart of outrageous campaigns of repression, alienation, and displacement and have resulted in the deaths of millions of people. Indeed, many of the greatest travesties committed in human history—slavery, the Crusades, the Inquisition—have been conducted under the rubric of religious conversion or at least have had the sanction of religious leaders and institutions. Although many contemporary groups rely on reasoned ideological suasion to achieve religious conversion, in many contexts—particularly those in which there is conflict among political, economic, social, and religious concerns—religious conflicts continue to be resolved through campaigns of bloody coercion.

Traditionally, religious education has been achieved through the formal efforts of families, religious institutions (e.g., through worship services, Sunday or Saturday schools, doctrinal study groups), and religious and parochial schools. The content of religious education often is reinforced in relationships with significant others, including family and peers, as well as through involvement in altruistic activities. Importantly, many religious communities have taken advantage of technological advances by providing educational and counseling resources through electronic media. For example, some individuals are involved in Web-based prayer circles, and some religious leaders use electronic mail as a means of maintaining relationships with individuals who are either unable or unwilling to participate in church-based activities.

Religion and spirituality have played central roles in a wide spectrum of intervention and prevention programs. In many communities churches have launched programs that address a wide range of needs, including substance (ab)use, delinquency, sexual abstinence, parenting, and health education. In poor communities, churches often play central roles in intervening in cycles of poverty by providing job skills training, economic development efforts, housing, and emergency relief programs (Caldwell, Chatters, Billingsley, & Taylor, 1995). Programs such as 12–step programs (e.g., Alcoholics Anonymous) ground their interventions in spiritual and religious ideology. It has been argued that religion and spirituality are effective in intervening on negative outcomes because they provide people with a clear moral frame, they help people to construct meaning, they provide a sense of purpose, and they offer optimism and emotional support (Dull & Skokan, 1995; Maton & Pargament, 1987). More recent work suggests that religious and spiritually grounded interventions may be particularly effective, especially among people of color, because they provide ideological frames that are culturally meaningful and consistent (Neighbors et al., 1998).

Although it generally is believed that faith-based intervention efforts are more effective than secular ones, empirical evidence on the efficacy of these programs is uneven. One of the factors that complicates our ability to assess the effectiveness of faith-based programs is the fundamental question of what defines a program as faith based. V. Myers (2001) asserts that it is critical to distinguish between programs that are church based and those that are faith based. According to Myers, programs can be evaluated along three domains: (a) their location (sacred or secular); (b) their choice of laborers (religious, secular, or mixed); and (c) the philosophical foundation for their intervention (theological, secular, or values based). A program may use a church as a meeting space and may have a clear religious mission (i.e., to provide care to those who are in need), and yet that program's intervention may not be grounded in theology and may not mention religion as a part of the intervention. Programs such as these are church-based social service programs. Faith-based interventions (whether they are located in sacred or secular contexts) tend to rely on laborers from a particular faith tradition, are theologically grounded (i.e., they provide a doctrinal frame for the intervention), and seek to convey or reinforce specific religious beliefs in the targets of the intervention (V. Myers, 2001).

Although questions remain about the relative effectiveness of secular, faith-based, and church-based initiatives, there is reason to believe that interventions that involve churches, religious figures, or religious content may provide advantages that do not obtain from secular programs. For example, research on the use of ministerial (and church) supports suggests that relative to their secular counterparts, ministers may be particularly effective because they are more accessible than secular professional service providers (i.e., they are available day and night); they ground their work in a value system that their constituents find familiar and useful; they address issues that are often ignored by secular service providers (e.g., forgiveness); they often provide a wider range of supports (e.g., psychological, educational, economic); and their services are free. In addition, the fact that they are located within the community makes ministers and churches accountable to the people to whom they provide assistance (Neighbors et al., 1998).

■ What Is Not Known?

A number of areas in need of further work can be identified:

- Spirituality and religiousness: Although a significant amount of attention has been given to mapping the conceptual distinctions between religiousness and spirituality, at present the field continues to behave as if religiousness and spirituality are conceptually distinct but functionally identical. We have yet to determine whether each of these experiences is associated with distinct outcomes. Attention must be paid to potential functional differences between these constructs.

- Gender: Studies have identified gender differences in patterns of religious participation. However, studies that focus on gender have yet to clarify how the various domains of gender help to shape male and female spirituality and religiousness. In addition, much remains to be learned about the ways in which gender socialization and religious socialization intersect. Finally, although a number of studies have attended to the religious and spiritual lives of women, we know little about the religious and spiritual lives of men.
- Development: Cross-sectional studies have revealed important age-related differences in patterns of religiousness and spirituality. However, the field is in dire need of longitudinal studies that will provide meaningful data about religious and spiritual development across the life span.
- Images of God: Scholars often tacitly assume that religiousness and spirituality are positive forces in the lives of individuals. However, there is evidence that people hold positive as well as negative images of God, and that negative images may have deleterious effects on health. Little is known, however, about the conditions under which negative or positive images of God emerge. In addition, we know little about the pathways by which these images influence negative or positive outcomes. Further, there is a need for greater attention to the ways that culture informs images of God as well as images of other sacred entities (e.g., saints, spirits). The role of these sacred entities in shaping behavioral and health outcomes is a worthwhile area of study.
- Context: Much of the work on religiousness and spirituality examines these phenomena during moments of adversity. At present, we do not know whether religiousness and spirituality operate in the same way in mundane moments as in extraordinary moments of crisis.
- Strengths: Although religious doctrines and archival data suggest a link between religiousness, spirituality, and such outcomes as guilt, forgiveness, wisdom, hope, purpose, compassion, and love, there is a need for greater attention to the empirical linkages between these constructs— particularly among adult and non-White samples.
- Religious identity: At present, much of the research on the psychology and sociology of religion and spirituality focuses on Christian communities. The overwhelming attention to Christianity in research has colored the way that we understand and measure religiousness and spirituality. A great deal more attention must be paid to the meaning, manifestations, and functional significance of religion and spirituality in the lives of non-Christians. Further, it is imperative that we recognize and account for the complex ways in which culture and ethnicity shape religious and spiritual identity. For example, in examining the experiences of Catho-

lics, we must be critically attentive to the reality that there are substantive differences in the beliefs and practices of Catholics in New Orleans, those in Alabama, and those of Peruvian or Haitian descent. The failure to unpack broad categories of religious identity will limit our ability to gain complex and more accurate views of religious and spiritual life.

- Race, ethnicity, and culture: Although some research points to race differences in patterns of spirituality and religious involvement, psychology research generally has failed to delineate the aspects of race, ethnicity, and culture that inform religious and spiritual life. Social scientists often have ignored the psychological consequences of culturally determined beliefs about such topics as the nature of the divine and the existence and role of spirits or ancestors in the world of the living. We must pay closer attention to the ways in which specific culturally grounded religious and spiritual beliefs affect diet, language, patterns of intimacy, attributions, optimism, guilt, and altruism.

- Ideology: Although archival and empirical data suggest a link between religiousness, spirituality, and a range of prosocial outcomes, there is a need for greater attention to the specific theological (i.e., doctrinal) beliefs that are central in producing these outcomes. In particular, the field will benefit from more substantive attention to the role of theology in shaping the core beliefs, attitudes, behaviors, and psychological as well as physical health outcomes experienced by religious individuals.

- Religious and spiritual socialization: There is a need for greater attention to the process by which religious and spiritual values and beliefs are transmitted intergenerationally and intragenerationally. At present, virtually nothing is known about the role of friends, siblings, and proximal others (e.g., neighbors and coworkers) in the transmission of religiousness and spirituality. Further, little is known about the ways in which people of different cultural and religious backgrounds may shape each other's beliefs and practices. This line of work will be particularly important for understanding the religious and spiritual development of children and adults who reside in fairly heterogeneous urban contexts and who may affect each other's ideas about God, prayer, transcendence, and other aspects of religio-spiritual existence. Further, this line of work will help to shape our understanding of the way that religious beliefs and practices are being shaped by globalizing trends (i.e., by the use of technology and the media to gain access to or challenge new ideas and people).

■ Must-Read Articles and Books

Allport, G., & Ross, J. (1967). Personal religious orientation and prejudice. *Journal of Personality and Social Psychology, 5,* 432–443.

Batson, C. D., & Ventis, W. (1982). *The religious experience: A social-psychological perspective.* New York: Oxford University Press.

Durkheim, É. (1915). *The elementary forms of religious life.* New York: Free Press.

Freud, S. (1927). *The future of an illusion.* New York: Norton.

James, W. (1999). *Varieties of religious experience: A study in human nature.* New York: Modern Library. (Original work published 1902)

Levin, J. (1997). Religious research in gerontology, 1980–1994: A systematic review. *Journal of Religious Gerontology, 10,* 3–31.

Lincoln, C., & Mamiya, L. (1990). *The Black church in the African-American experience.* Durham, NC: Duke University Press.

Maton, K., & Wells, E. (1995). Religion as a community resource for well-being: Prevention, healing, and empowerment pathways. *Journal of Social Issues, 51*(2), 177–193.

Pargament, K. (1997). *The psychology of religion and coping: Theory, research, practice.* New York: Guilford Press.

Wulff, D. (1991). *The psychology of religion: Classic and contemporary views.* New York: Wiley.

SECTION III

CONCLUSIONS

28. ASSESSMENT AND APPLICATIONS

What distinguishes the present classification from many previous attempts to articulate good character is its simultaneous concern with assessment. In this concluding chapter, we provide an overview of the assessment work we have done to date, which has relied on surveys and structured interviews. We also discuss some of the ways in which our measures, once perfected, might be used in basic and applied research. Because our classification is a work in progress, then even more so is our assessment work. We have made what we regard as a good start in measuring strengths of character, but much of the journey remains. Accordingly, we do not present our survey and interview items in their entirety—we will do so in a subsequent publication—but instead sketch the intended directions of future work.

■ Assessment of Character Strengths

Sophisticated social scientists sometimes respond with suspicion when they hear our goal of assessing good character with surveys or interviews, reminding us of the pitfalls of self-report and the validity threat posed by social desirability (Crowne & Marlowe, 1964). We do not dismiss these considerations out of hand, but their premise is worth examining from the vantage of positive psychology. We seem to be quite willing, as researchers and practitioners, to trust what individuals say about their problems. With notable exceptions like substance abuse and eating disorders, the preferred way to measure psychological disorder relies on self-report, in the form of either symptom questionnaires or structured interviews. So why not ascertain wellness in the same way?

Suppose that people really do possess moral virtues. Most philosophers emphasize that virtuous activity involves choosing virtue in light of a justifiable life plan (Yearley, 1990). In more psychological language, this character-ization means that people can reflect on their own virtues and talk about them to others. They may of course be misled and/or misleading, but virtues are not the sort of entities that are in principle outside the realm of self-commentary. Furthermore, character strengths are not contaminated by a response set of so-cial desirability; they *are* socially desirable, especially when reported with fidelity.

We can point to previous research that measured character strengths with self-report questionnaire batteries (e.g., Buckingham & Clifton, 2001; Cawley, Martin, & Johnson, 2000; Greenberger, Josselson, Knerr, & Knerr, 1975; Ryff & Singer, 1996). In no case did a single method factor order the data. Rather, dif-ferent clusters of strengths always emerged. External correlates were sensible. These conclusions converge with what we have learned to date from our own attempts to measure character strengths among young people and adults with self-report questionnaires. We acknowledge the possibility that some strengths of character lend themselves less readily to self-report than do others, but it is easy to understand why. Almost by definition, strengths like bravery and in-tegrity are not the sorts of traits usually attributed to oneself. But this consid-eration does not preclude the use of self-report to assess other strengths of character.

We have reviewed what is known about each of the 24 strengths currently in the classification. Of relevance to this concluding chapter, consider what is known about assessment:

- In most cases, there exist reliable and valid ways of measuring these strengths as individual differences, not a surprising conclusion given that we deliberately included strengths already of interest to psychologists.
- However, there are some exceptions. Humility and modesty have eluded reliable assessment, although nomination procedures have been used to identify humble or modest paragons. And there seem to be no extant self-report measures of bravery, although again nomination procedures have been used by previous researchers.
- In most cases, the assessment strategy of choice is a self-report question-naire, although these have different formats and lengths that would work against the creation of an inclusive battery that would be practical to use.
- However, again there are some exceptions, which make sense given the nature of the strength. In these cases, additional or alternative tech-niques of assessment are needed. For example, scenario methods are often used to assess fairness; respondents are provided with a brief story in which a moral dilemma is posed, and then they are asked to describe how they would respond. Along these lines, open-mindedness is often measured by asking people to write or speak about some complex issue and then having expert judges score their responses for the use of multiple perspectives.

- Most existing measures are intended for use with adults. When measures for younger individuals exist, they make little contact with measures of analogous strengths among adults, thus precluding longitudinal studies that span developmental stages. So, there is a need for parallel measures across the life span that are at the same time developmentally appropriate. The ways in which young people show curiosity or bravery, for example, differ from the ways of adults, and assessment devices need to reflect these differences.

With these insights as a starting point, we set about creating measures that allow the character strengths in the present classification to be assessed among English speakers in the contemporary Western world. We used a multimethod strategy, devising self-report surveys and structured interviews.

Values in Action Inventory of Strengths (VIA-IS)

The assessment strategy we have most extensively developed to date entails self-report surveys able to be completed by respondents in a single session. We have devised separate inventories for adults and for young people (aged 10–17). Although our literature reviews concluded that some small number of the character strengths have not been and perhaps cannot be measured with self-report, we nonetheless attempted to create self-report scales for each of the 24 strengths.

We start by describing our survey for adults: the Values in Action Inventory of Strengths (VIA-IS). The immediate ancestry of this survey includes a nonoverlapping questionnaire—the Wellsprings—created by Ed Diener, Derek Isaacowitz, Donald Clifton, and Martin Seligman to measure various character strengths included in a classification of character strengths predating the present project. More generally, the VIA-IS took inspiration from the Gallup Organization's StrengthsFinder measure, which measures important workplace themes (chapter 1). Although their purpose and details differ, the VIA-IS followed the StrengthsFinder example by wording items in extreme fashion ("I *always . . .*") and by providing feedback to respondents concerning their top—not bottom—strengths of character (Buckingham & Clifton, 2001).

The VIA-IS uses 5-point Likert-style items to measure the degree to which respondents endorse items reflecting the 24 strengths in the VIA classification. Scores are formed by averaging responses within scales, with higher numbers reflecting more of the strength.

Most of the VIA-IS items were written by Christopher Peterson and Martin Seligman, although they were helped by a small group of undergraduate students at the University of Pennsylvania who responded to an act-frequency nomination procedure for each of the strengths in the classification; that is, they generated examples of prototypical behaviors (acts) that reflected a character strength (Buss & Craik, 1983). Their suggestions were used to craft some items.

In the fall of 2000, a version of the VIA-IS was created and piloted with more than 250 adults. Even at the beginning, internal consistencies were satisfactory for almost all scales (alphas > .70), but items that correlated poorly with the total scale of interest were replaced. This process was repeated several times until alphas for all scales exceeded .70. Along the way, items for some of the scales were suggested by Jonathan Baron, Robert A. Emmons, Lauren V. Kachorek, Todd B. Kashdan, and Tracy A. Steen.

The earlier versions of the VIA-IS contained no reverse-scored items, in part because we were following the StrengthsFinder lead and in part because the logic of character strengths is that the absence of a weakness is not necessarily a strength—people who are *not* mean may or may not be kind. However, eventually we were able to create reasonable reverse-scored items for each of the character strengths, simply by using *not* or *never* in the stems. Alphas continued to exceed .70 for all scales, and it is our sense that the reverse-scored and non-reverse-scored measures are quite comparable in terms of psychometrics and correlates.

In its current form, the VIA-IS is intended for use with adults in the contemporary United States and other English-speaking countries. Several of our colleagues elsewhere have begun translations of the VIA-IS, but this work is quite preliminary. As described, the VIA-IS uses 5-point Likert-style items to measure the degree to which respondents endorse items reflecting the 24 strengths in the VIA classification. There are 10 items per strength (scattered throughout the survey), and in the current version, three items per scale are reverse scored. Sample items are found in Table 28.1. Paper copies are available as well, and a Web-based version provides immediate feedback about signature strengths (top five scores) directly to respondents upon completion of the inventory (www.viastrengths.org). In either case, the VIA-IS takes about 30 minutes to complete.

Consistent with comparative studies by other researchers, we found no psychometric differences between paper and Web versions of the questionnaire (Birnbaum, 2000). The Web-based questionnaire has proved enormously useful to us as we developed the VIA-IS. On any given day, at least 10 to 15 individuals complete the measure, and on some days, hundreds of individuals do so. We do not pay any of these respondents, and there is no evidence whatsoever that the same individual responded more than once to the survey. About 85% of the respondents have been from the United States; almost all others are from English-speaking nations (United Kingdom, Canada, Australia), although we have had respondents from Asia, Africa, Central and South America, the Middle East, and continental Europe—in all 175 different nations. About two thirds of the respondents are women. The ethnic makeup of the U.S. sample approximates that of the country as a whole. The typical respondent is 35 years of age, married, and employed and has completed some post–high school schooling, although there is great variation across all such sociodemographic contrasts.

TABLE 28.1   *Sample Items From the VIA-IS*

Instructions. We have developed a questionnaire to measure a person's strengths. Could you help with our project by choosing one option in response to each statement? All of the questions reflect statements that many people would find desirable, but we want you to answer only in terms of WHETHER THE STATEMENT DESCRIBES WHAT YOU ARE LIKE. Please be honest and accurate! Because the questionnaire is long, work quickly, and trust your first response. Thank you for helping.

Creativity	When someone tells me how to do something, I automatically think of alternative ways to get the same thing done. ○ very much like me ○ like me ○ neutral ○ unlike me ○ very much unlike me I do not have any special urge to do something original.
Curiosity	I am never bored. I have few interests.
Open-mindedness	I make decisions only when I have all of the facts. If I like one option, I don't think about other possibilities.
Love of learning	I always go out of my way to attend educational events. I rarely read nonfiction books for fun.
Perspective	People describe me as "wise beyond my years." Others rarely come to me for advice.
Bravery	I have taken frequent stands in the face of strong opposition. I do not always stand up for my beliefs.
Persistence	I finish things despite obstacles in the way. I do not always stick with what I decide to do.
Integrity	I always keep my promises. Sometimes I feel like an imposter.
Vitality	I want to fully participate in life, not just view it from the sidelines. I dread getting up in the morning.
Love	There are people in my life who care as much about my feelings and well-being as they do about their own. I have great difficulty accepting love from anyone.
Kindness	I am never too busy to help a friend. I rarely do favors for people.

(continued)

TABLE 28.1   *Sample Items From the VIA-IS* (*continued*)

Social intelligence	I always know what makes someone tick.
	I am often puzzled by my own thoughts and feelings.
Citizenship	I never miss group meetings or team practices.
	I work at my very best when I am alone and not in a group.
Fairness	I am strongly committed to principles of justice and equality.
	If I do not like someone, I cannot help treating him or her differently.
Leadership	In a group, I try to make sure everyone feels included.
	I am not good at planning group activities.
Forgiveness and mercy	I always allow others to leave their mistakes in the past and make a fresh start.
	I am unwilling to accept apologies.
Humility and modesty	I am proud that I am an ordinary person.
	I like to talk about myself.
Prudence	"Better safe than sorry" is one of my favorite mottoes.
	My friends believe that I am impulsive in my words and deeds.
Self-regulation	I am a highly disciplined person.
	I do not exercise on a regular basis.
Appreciation of beauty and excellence	I have often been left speechless by the beauty depicted in a movie.
	I often fail to notice beauty until others comment on it.
Gratitude	I always express my thanks to people who care about me.
	When I look at my life, I find few things to be grateful for.
Hope	I always looks on the bright side.
	I do not have a plan for what I want to be doing 5 years from now.
Humor	Whenever my friends are in a gloomy mood, I try to tease them out of it.
	Few people would say I am fun to be with.
Spirituality	In the last 24 hours, I have spent 30 minutes in prayer, meditation, or contemplation.
	I do not believe in a universal power or a god.

Note.—The second item in each pair is reverse scored.

Given the need for computer literacy and access, our respondents are not a perfect match to the U.S. or world population but arguably are much closer than convenience samples otherwise obtained by psychology researchers (e.g., college sophomores enrolled in an introductory psychology course). The efficiency and economy of Web-based research seem to offset concerns about the makeup of the samples. We can complete a given study with more than adequate power in little more than a few weeks and then begin another study.

As noted, the VIA-IS has gone through five incarnations, and it has been completed by more than 150,000 adults. Here is what we know about the reliability and validity of the VIA-IS:

- All scales have satisfactory alphas ($> .70$).
- Scores are skewed to the right but still show variation.
- One may not want to make much of these findings,[1] but the highest mean scores are consistently found for the humanity strengths of kindness and love, whereas the lowest are found for the temperance strengths of forgiveness, prudence, humility, and self-regulation.
- Test–retest correlations for all scales over a 4-month period are substantial ($> .70$) and in almost all cases approach their internal consistencies.
- Demographic correlations are modest but sensible. For example, women score higher than men on all of the humanity strengths. Younger adults score higher than older adults on the scale for playfulness. Married individuals are more forgiving than those who are divorced. And so on.
- A single-item measure of political stance (conservative vs. liberal) correlates with but one VIA strength; conservative individuals are more likely to score higher on spirituality.
- We have found few ethnic differences among the major U.S. census groupings (African American, Asian American, European American, Latino/a, Native American) on the scales except that African Americans score higher than other groups on spirituality, consistent with previous research using different measures (chapter 27).
- Self-nominations of strengths correlate substantially ($rs = .5$) with the matching scale scores for all 24 strengths.
- "Other" nomination of strengths (by friends or family members) correlates modestly with the matching scale scores for most of the 24 strengths.
- Marlow-Crowne social desirability scores do not significantly correlate with scale scores, with the exception of prudence ($r = .44$) and spirituality ($r = .30$).

[1]On the face of it, these mean differences show that some strengths are more likely to be manifest than others. Complicating this conclusion, though, is the possibility that the difference resides at the level of the items and not what they purport to measure. Some of the unpopular strengths were those for which it proved difficult to write coherent items.

- Individuals scoring high on a measure of serenity not surprisingly score high as well on the scale of spirituality but, more interestingly, even higher on our scale of forgiveness.
- In a series of three large-sample studies ($ns > 600$), we explored correlations between the scales and rewarding aspects of work, love (friendship, romance), and play (recreation, leisure). The correlates we found were modest but congruent with the meanings of the strengths. For example, individuals scoring high on the strength of kindness particularly enjoyed jobs in which they can mentor others, those high in curiosity preferred sexually experienced romantic partners, those high on love of learning appreciated gardening, and so on.
- In the immediate aftermath of the September 11 terrorist attacks, scale scores significantly increased for love, kindness, gratitude, citizenship, hope, and spirituality (Peterson & Seligman, 2003).
- Individuals recovered from serious physical or psychological difficulties score higher on several scales: appreciation of beauty, gratitude, and hope.
- Students ($n = 20$) enrolled in a positive psychology class at the University of Pennsylvania showed reliable increases in the strengths of love, prudence, gratitude, perspective, and spirituality, all strengths explicitly targeted by classroom discussions and out-of-class exercises.
- Most of the strengths correlate robustly with life satisfaction, with the exception of the strengths of wisdom and knowledge (N. Park & Peterson, 2003a). This finding is interesting because our schools typically emphasize the development of these sorts of strengths but not the others, which helps explain why schooling is not an automatic pathway to a fulfilling life (D. G. Myers, 1993).
- Exploratory factor analyses of scale scores using varimax rotation suggest five factors, which we tentatively identify as follows:
  - strengths of restraint (fairness, humility, mercy, prudence)
  - intellectual strengths (e.g., creativity, curiosity, love of learning, appreciation of beauty)
  - interpersonal strengths (e.g., kindness, love, leadership, teamwork, playfulness)
  - emotional strengths (e.g., bravery, hope, self-regulation, zest)
  - theological strengths (e.g., gratitude, spirituality)

These factors are not identical to our a priori classification (see Table 1.1), but they are similar. What we call here strengths of restraint correspond closely to virtues of temperance; intellectual strengths correspond to virtues of wisdom and knowledge; interpersonal strengths collapse the virtues of humanity and justice (cf. chapter 17); emotional strengths correspond to virtues of courage; and the theological strengths are included among our transcendence virtues.

We also note that the first three factors here correspond to the Big Five factors of conscientiousness, openness, and agreeableness; the fourth factor—emotional strengths—may correspond to the *opposite* of the Big Five factor of neuroticism (chapter 3). The fifth factor—theological strengths—has no Big Five counterpart.

Values in Action Rising to the Occasion Inventory (VIA-RTO)

The only psychometrically troubling finding is that "other" nominations did not appreciably converge with VIA-IS scores for some of the strengths (bravery, fairness, forgiveness, hope, integrity, leadership, prudence, self-control, and teamwork). The traits that did not converge with nominations all entail rising to some specifiable occasion in ways that the converging traits did not—the distinction we introduced earlier between phasic strengths versus tonic strengths (chapter 1). For example, it is easier for one to be generically kind than generically brave. The VIA-IS asks about typical responses rather than those situated in the appropriate settings for the display of given strengths. Further, no one can reasonably nominate friends or acquaintances as paragons of given strengths unless they have happened to observe them in the appropriate settings.

So, we created a new questionnaire called the Values in Action Rising to the Occasion Inventory (VIA-RTO) that asks about the contrary strengths, and again we compared responses to the judgments of informed others. Respondents are asked how frequently they found themselves in the strength-relevant setting. Then they are asked to answer an open-ended question about how they typically responded in the setting; the question spelled out the essence of the strength without explicitly labeling it. These responses are not analyzed but are intended to discourage answers off the top of one's head to the next question, which explicitly asks if these situated responses reflect the strength of character on focus. In effect, the VIA-RTO embodies a streamlined scenario method akin to those already common in the literature to measure certain strengths.

In a small-sample ($n = 60$) study, individuals who completed the VIA-RTO were instructed to give a second questionnaire to someone who knew them well, who independently answered questions about the target individual's strengths in the given situations. The results were quite clear. For most of the strengths, almost all respondents had encountered the appropriate occasion, but in a few cases (e.g., extreme fear for the display—or not—of bravery), more than a few said they almost never encountered it. For most of the strengths, informants offered ratings, but in a smattering of cases, they reported that they could not say whether the target individual had a given strength. So, in analyzing the data, we excluded cases in which the target individuals almost never encountered the occasion and/or the informants demurred from a rating. Correlations between self-report and other-report were high (all *r*s between .40 and .60), implying that an eventual questionnaire battery should include these sorts of RTO questions (see Table 28.2 for a sample item).

TABLE 28.2   *Sample Item From the VIA-RTO*

Think of actual situations in which you have experienced an extreme amount of fear.

How frequently have you been in these sorts of situations?
- ○ very frequently (once a week or more)
- ○ frequently (once a month)
- ○ sometimes (several times a year)
- ○ rarely (once in a year)
- ○ almost never (once in a lifetime)

Think of how you usually acted in these situations, and briefly describe in the space below whether you let fear get in the way of how you acted.

In terms of these situations, would you say that BRAVERY or COURAGE is one of your strengths?
- ○ definitely yes
- ○ probably yes
- ○ perhaps
- ○ probably no
- ○ definitely no

Values in Action Inventory of Strengths for Youth (VIA-Youth)

With the help of Katherine Dahlsgaard and Nansook Park, we have also devised several versions of a self-report questionnaire for youth, the Values in Action Inventory of Strengths for Youth (VIA-Youth). We experimented with different item formats and phrasings before arriving at the current form of the inventory, which, we emphasize, is still under development.

Originally, we created separate inventories for preadolescents and adolescents by adapting items from the adult survey and phrasing them in what we thought were developmentally appropriate ways. Our work was informed by the results of separate focus groups with developmental and educational psychologists and with students in 20 different high school classes in Michigan (Steen, Kachorek, & Peterson, 2002). We then decided that the preadolescent and adolescent versions were not sufficiently different, so we created a single inventory suitable for children and adolescents between the ages of 10 and 17. We also varied the response format (3-point scales versus 5-point scales) before concluding that 5-point scales were able to be used by even the youngest of our respondents and that they yielded more reliable composites.

The latest version of VIA-Youth contains 198 items (6 to 12 items for each of the 24 strengths, scattered throughout the survey). Table 28.3 includes samples. As shown, respondents use a 5-point Likert scale (5 = very much like me to 1 = not like me at all) to respond to each question. Most of the scales include one or more reverse-scored items, although we believe we should have more than we do, and our next version of the VIA-Youth will include a greater number of reverse-scored items. Another challenge we have faced is the need to keep the VIA-Youth short enough not to burden young respondents but long enough so that individual scales are still reliable. In comparison, our adult survey is one-third longer than the VIA-Youth and as a result has quite consistent scales. The VIA-Youth is probably as long as it can be.

One version or another of the VIA-Youth has been completed by more than 2,300 middle and high school students of varying ethnicities and SES levels in seven states (Alabama, California, Nebraska, New Jersey, Ohio, Pennsylvania, and Texas). These inventories were administered in group format during regular class times by the regular classroom teachers, who read the instructions aloud to the students and answered any questions by the students. The typical student had no difficulty finishing the survey in 40 to 45 minutes. Few questions were asked. Break-offs did not occur, but about 3% of respondents fell into a pattern of answering all the questions on a given page with the same option; we made the executive decision to exclude their data from our analyses. These were regular classrooms, and we have no information about how academically or emotionally challenged students would respond to the demands of the survey.

Here is what we have learned so far about the reliability and validity of the VIA-Youth from the most recent sample we have analyzed (Peterson & Park, 2003):

- All scales at present have close-to-satisfactory alphas (> .65), although the strengths of temperance have proved more difficult to measure reliably than other strengths. We found the same challenge in writing converging temperance items for adults, implying that these characteristics may be less traited (more contextualized) than other strengths in our classification.
- Scores are skewed to the right but still show variation.
- As we found for adults, youth on average score especially high on the humanity strengths and especially low on the temperance strengths.
- Girls score higher than boys on a number of the strengths (e.g., appreciation of beauty, fairness, gratitude, kindness, love, perspective, spirituality).
- On the whole, older children score higher than younger children on most of the strengths, although 10th graders show a slight decrease in the strengths of temperance and spirituality.

TABLE 28.3   *Sample Items From the VIA-Youth*

Instructions. We would like to understand how you think, feel, and act. Please read each statement carefully and then think about how much it is true about you. Mark ONE answer for each question. There are no right or wrong answers. Your individual answers will not be shared with anybody, so please answer the following questions honestly. PLEASE ANSWER ALL QUESTIONS.

Creativity	I always like to do things in different ways.
	○ very much like me
	○ mostly like me
	○ somewhat like me
	○ a little like me
	○ not at all like me
	I am not good at coming up with new ideas.
Curiosity	I always want to know more.
	I am easily bored.
Open-mindedness	I am always able to look at both sides of an issue.
	Without much thinking, I usually accept what other people suggest.
Love of learning	When I want to learn something, I try to find out everything about it.
	I learn things only when someone makes me.
Perspective	I often come up with solutions to problems that make everybody happy.
	I am not good at finding solutions to conflicts.
Bravery	I have the courage to do the right thing even when it is not popular.
	I don't stand up for myself or others.
Persistence	When I start a project, I always finish it.
	Once I fail at something, I don't try again.
Integrity	I always keep my word.
	I lie to get myself out of trouble.
Vitality	Whatever I do, I throw myself into it.
	I always feel tired.
Love	When I have a problem, I know I have someone who will be there for me.
	I don't have a best friend.
Kindness	If there are new students in my class, I try to make them feel welcome.
	I don't help others if they don't ask.

Social intelligence	I always know what to say to make people feel good.
	I often make other people upset without meaning to.
Citizenship	I am very loyal to my group no matter what.
	If I don't agree with the group decision, I don't go along with it.
Fairness	When I work in a group, I give an equal chance to everybody.
	I do favors for the people I know, even if it is not fair to others.
Leadership	When I play with other kids, they want me to be the leader.
	When people in my group do not agree, I can't get them to work together.
Forgiveness and mercy	When people say they are sorry, I give them a second chance.
	Even when someone says they are sorry, I stay mad at them.
Humility and modesty	Rather than just talking about myself, I prefer to let other kids talk about themselves.
	I think that I am smarter than anybody else.
Prudence	I avoid people or situations that might get me into trouble.
	I often make mistakes because I am not careful.
Self-regulation	Once I make an exercise or study plan, I stick to it.
	If I have money, I usually spend it all at once.
Appreciation of beauty and excellence	Seeing pretty pictures or listening to beautiful music makes me feel better.
	I am not interested in art, music, dance, or theater.
Gratitude	I often feel lucky to have my parents and family.
	I am not good at expressing my gratitude.
Hope	I can find what is good in any situation, even when others can't.
	I give up hope when things do not go well.
Humor	I am good at making people laugh.
	I don't have a good sense of humor.
Spirituality	When I am upset, I often pray to myself.
	I don't believe in God.

Note.—The second item in each pair is reverse scored.

- There are no meaningful ethnic differences on any of the scales except for spirituality, where African American students score higher than White students.
- Life satisfaction and happiness correlate with most of the strengths, but less robustly with the strengths of wisdom and knowledge, just as we find among adults.
- Strengths of temperance predict grades in English, math, and science courses, even when ability test scores are controlled.
- Exploratory factor analyses of scale scores using varimax rotation suggest a four-factor solution—a somewhat simpler structure than the one found for adults but still quite similar, differing chiefly by a collapsing of intellectual and emotional strengths into one factor. If this pattern is valid, it is an interesting one, implying that something happens in the course of education and socialization that splits apart intellectual and emotional strengths. But we stress that we need to develop the VIA-Youth further and administer it to larger samples, which will allow further exploratory and confirmatory factor analyses of both individual items and scale scores.

From studies with previous versions of the VIA-Youth, which had less reliable subscales, we tentatively conclude the following (Dahlsgaard, Davis, Peterson, & Seligman, 2002):

- Self-nominations of strengths correlate with the majority of the matching scale scores.
- Teacher nominations of strengths correlate with the matching scale scores for about half of the strengths—those manifest in everyday behavior as opposed to those requiring specific occasions (like the experience of fear or threat for the display of courage)—essentially what we found for adults.
- Teacher ratings of student popularity correlate with the humanity strengths.

Values in Action (VIA) Structured Interview

Developed with the help of Tiffany A. Sawyer, the Values in Action (VIA) Structured Interview adopts the logic and format of the VIA-RTO to an individual interview format. It takes about 30 minutes to complete and has been used to date only with adults and a handful of teenagers. The interviewer asks respondents how they usually act in a given setting vis-à-vis the character strength on focus—in the case of phasic strengths, the setting is detailed, and in the case of tonic strengths, it is presented as everyday life. If people describe displaying the strength the majority of the time, follow-up questions ask (a) how they name the strength; (b) if the strength, however named, is really who they are; and (c) whether friends and family members would agree that the strength is really who they are.

To count as an individual's signature strength, a strength must be displayed the majority of the time in relevant settings, be named as the intended strength (or a synonym) as opposed to another strength, be owned by the individual, *and* be recognized by others as highly characteristic of the individual. Our studies to date show that adults usually have between two and five signature strengths for which the corresponding survey scores are—not surprisingly—elevated.

The drawback of the structured interview, as we see it, is that it does not quantify an individual's character strengths, which is at odds with our conceptualization of strengths as existing along dimensions. The benefit is that the VIA Structured Interview allows us to say that a strength is (or is not) self-consciously owned by an individual. We have theoretical reasons for believing that owned strengths are qualitatively different in their effects than non-owned strengths. For example, both of us have some skill at what can be called transactional leadership—taking charge of a group and making sure that its trains run on time. But neither of us enjoys these tasks or considers them part of our real identity. However successfully completed, they leave us exhausted and unfulfilled. In contrast, other strengths we seem to have, which we gladly embrace, leave us exhilarated when we use them. Research is needed to test our speculation, and the VIA Structured Interview will allow this research to be done.

Conclusions

We conclude that the VIA-IS and VIA-RTO are already promising measures. We underscore the convergence of self-report with nomination by informed others. A novel contribution has been made by our successful self-report measures of humility and bravery. The VIA-Youth is also on its way to being a useful measure, and the VIA Structured Interview has at least begun the journey. In future research, we intend to simplify these measures by appropriate factor analyses of items and scales and cluster analyses of individuals. Then we plan to compare these shorter versions with existing best-practice measures of different character strengths.

■ Applications of the Classification

Although we believe that the phenomena of interest to positive social science are all around us, we have nonetheless devoted a great deal of thought to where best to find them. What are the natural homes for human excellence? These should be the domains where positive psychology notions should be applied. Our rule of thumb is to identify arenas of life where virtuosity is recognized, celebrated, and encouraged. Obvious examples that satisfy this rule are sports, the performing arts, friendships and romances, child rearing, and school. We are not convinced that the clinic is a good place to look for excellence, despite calls for strengths-based approaches to assessment and therapy (Saleebey, 1992; Seligman & Peterson, 2003).

In general, the workplace is a natural home for positive psychology, although a close look suggests that some workplaces more than others consistently celebrate virtuosity (H. Gardner, Csikszentmihalyi, & Damon, 2001). Obviously, one should avoid studying jobs where rate busting and whistleblowing are dirty words. One should avoid studying individuals in organizations in which fitting in and getting by are the watchwords. Said another way, workplaces are natural homes for positive psychology to the degree that they allow workers to craft jobs and turn them into callings (Wrzesniewski, McCauley, Rozin, & Schwartz, 1997).

As positive psychology becomes its own field, the attention of some will turn to interventions intended to cultivate and to sustain the good life (Linley & Joseph, in press; Seligman & Steen, in preparation). Skeptics might worry that the field is too new to inspire interventions, but we have a different opinion. We agree with Kurt Lewin's sentiment, expressed decades ago, that the best way to understand a psychological phenomenon is to try to change it. By this view, intervention research is not something that follows basic research at a polite distance but instead its inherent complement: Part of refining our classification is seeing how it might be applied. In any event, interventions are going to be mounted by some regardless of the caution of others, and it makes sense to us that rigorous evaluation be built into interventions from the beginning.

The example of psychotherapy is instructive. Talking cures of many stripes proliferated for almost a century before anyone could say with certainty that therapy actually works and, even more interestingly, that all forms of therapies show about the same effectiveness (M. L. Smith & Glass, 1977). Think of how much effort and energy went into developing and defending different systems of psychotherapy when the data eventually showed that the more productive strategy would have been to search for common ingredients (cf. Frank, 1974). We envision something better for positive psychology interventions and propose that the slow-to-arrive gold standard of psychotherapy—empirical validation—be adopted sooner rather than later as the criterion for positive psychology interventions (Nathan & Gorman, 2002; Patrick & Olson, 2000).

Nevertheless, requiring that interventions be empirically validated before they are used with anyone can freeze innovation and progress. Experimentation with new interventions must be legitimized at the same time that empirical validation is advanced as a goal.[2] The good news is that people enjoy participating in experi-

---

[2]Our own early experience as positive psychology practitioners has involved out-of-class happiness and gratification exercises with college students enrolled in our positive psychology courses. In the spirit of informed experimentation, they are invited to try out an exercise and then to evaluate it. No student has felt cheated or misled by an exercise that did not work as intended.

mental programs (cf. Wortman, Hendricks, & Hillis, 1976). It therefore behooves positive psychology practitioners to be honest with clients regarding what is known and not known about the effectiveness of interventions.

The most critical tools for positive psychologists interested in evaluating interventions are a vocabulary for speaking about the good life and assessment strategies for investigating its components. The present classification and the collateral measures described earlier in this chapter provide precisely these tools with respect to strengths of character.[3] What are the most important of these, and how can they be measured as individual differences?

Almost all the strengths in our classification have been the subject of empirical research using various strategies of assessment. However, despite likely links, these lines of research have been conducted in relative isolation from one another—an assertion that the reader can verify by scanning the largely nonoverlapping citations in chapters 4 through 27. Part of the reason for this lack of integration has been the absence of an efficient battery of strength measures. One could of course assemble such a battery by collating existing measures, but respondent burden would quickly become prohibitive as more and more surveys were added. Our measures, in contrast, allow 24 different strengths to be assessed in an efficient way, making research possible that looks at the joint and interactive effects of character strengths. Furthermore, our measures allow an investigator to control for one strength when ascertaining the correlates, causes, or consequences of another. Conclusions can thereby become more crisp. For example, a researcher using the VIA-IS or VIA-Youth would be able to say that spirituality has (or does not have) consequences

---

For example, our students have written and delivered *gratitude letters* to individuals who have been kind to them but never received explicit thanks. This exercise was successful in that it created lingering feelings of satisfaction for all parties. In another example, our students have written (but not delivered) *forgiveness letters* to individuals who had hurt them but never received explicit absolution. This exercise was unsuccessful because almost all the students felt that delivering the letter to an individual who had never requested forgiveness would create more bad feelings than good ones. Upon reflection, they believed that in many cases they themselves had contributed to the hurt (e.g., painful romantic breakups) and that forgiving the other party would imply that they had been but innocent victims as opposed to coconspirators. This unsuccessful exercise was nonetheless informative, and in the future, we will limit this exercise to cases in which an apology had been tendered. We also plan to experiment with *apology letters*.

[3]Positive traits are just one outcome of interest to positive psychology (chapter 1). Just as important, given the goal of an intervention, might be happiness, pleasure, gratification, life satisfaction, or serenity, for both the individual per se and the individual in an interpersonal or institutional context: friendship, marriage, family, work, and community. We note in passing that positive psychology interventions that target happiness and its cognates are challenged by the fact that most people most of the time are already quite satisfied with their lives (D. G. Myers & Diener, 1995). In other words, there may be a ceiling effect for happiness, not to mention a biologically determined set point that interventions cannot readily change. We doubt that good character is so limited.

above and beyond contributions of associated strengths like gratitude or hope, a conclusion not possible if only measures of spirituality are used in a study.

Our measures can obviously be used to evaluate interventions that target the good life. Consider character education, positive youth development, life coaching, workplace wellness promotion, and the like. Hundreds of thousands of people participate in such programs every year, with virtually no empirical checks on their effectiveness (Eccles & Gootman, 2002). In some cases, strengths of character are the explicit outcome of interest, and in other cases, one or another character strength is proposed as a mediator or moderator of the effects of the intervention on other outcomes. The availability of measures will allow such interventions to be rigorously evaluated and perhaps will lead to the discovery of unanticipated effects of interventions. At this stage in the development of positive psychology, we suspect that unanticipated effects will be common, which implies that a broad outcome net should be cast.

Our measures may have some utility—theoretical and practical—when scored ipsatively. That is, rather than using someone's kindness score in comparisons and contrasts with the kindness scores of others, it can be used to judge that individual's kindness relative to his or her other strengths. We have speculated that most individuals have signature strengths (chapter 1) and that use of these strengths at work, love, and play provides a route to the psychologically fulfilling life (Seligman, 2002). These are empirical questions that we are just beginning to answer. But we suspect that a positive psychology client is probably not interested in becoming the kindest person in the world but simply in having kindness be a more salient trait than it has been.

Such ipsative assessment—based on our self-report surveys or our structured interview—would provide part of what could be termed a full "diagnosis" from a strengths perspective. Like the *DSM*, such a diagnosis would be multidimensional, noting signature strengths of character but also—perhaps—talents and abilities, passions and interests, enabling conditions, fulfillments, and positive outcomes. A strengths diagnosis would make contact with a *DSM* diagnosis at the juncture of *DSM* Axis V—global assessment of functioning—although the frame here would be what is right with a person rather than what is wrong (H. H. Goldman, Skodol, & Lave, 1992).

If our measures are used in program evaluation, certain pitfalls need to be anticipated and avoided. We have argued that self-report is a valid way to measure character strengths, but questionnaires are not foolproof if incentives are in place for confirmatory results. Practitioners may teach to the test, and clients may shade their responses to justify the investments they have made as participants. These are not reasons to forgo use of our strengths measures, but they do imply the need for ongoing validity checks—like reports of objective informants.

Rigorous evaluation research must be adequately powered—that is, outcomes studies must have a sample size that allows effects to be reliably detected. Although exact ways of determining adequate sample sizes are readily available (cf. Cohen's, 1992, power primer), they are all too frequently ignored by both basic and applied researchers. It would be not only bad science but also a societal loss if a positive psychology intervention were deemed unsuccessful simply because it was tested with too few participants.

Although we believe that positive traits can be strengthened, there is no reason to think that this is simple or easy, for practitioners or clients. Theorists as far back as Aristotle argued that virtue is the product of habitual action. One-shot positive psychology interventions can probably jump-start the process, but only sustained practice will make changes permanent. As described, the events of September 11 increased several VIA-IS scores for people in the United States, but note that these were small in absolute magnitude and detectable only because our research used a very large sample (Peterson & Seligman, 2003). Furthermore, a year after September 11, those strengths that did change had started to return to their pre-9/11 levels.

We have concluded that the measures we have developed are efficient, but they are not as quick as exit interviews. Our surveys take about 30 to 45 minutes to complete, and some respondents require supervision to prevent break-off effects due to wandering attention. Practitioners looking for single indicators of character strengths will not adopt our measures. However, we believe strongly that most character strengths are sufficiently complex that a single-indicator approach to their assessment is doomed. We offer this conclusion without apology. Anyone interested in assessing strengths needs to appreciate that there is no shortcut to measuring good character, any more than there is a shortcut to measuring intellectual achievement or ability. As noted, self-nominations of given strengths (e.g., I am [or am not] kind) tend to converge with the corresponding scale scores. Nevertheless, we do not recommend that these brief questions be substituted for the scales themselves because it is patently more valid to ask about thoughts, feelings, and actions that reflect a given strength as opposed to abstract trait labels that might be applied idiosyncratically or capriciously. Consider that grade point averages and achievement test scores probably converge impressively with answers to the question "Are you smart—yes or no," but we would not want to substitute this single-item indicator for the SATs.

As we have mentioned, we will eventually create shorter versions of both our youth and our adult surveys, not by eliminating items from a given scale but by collapsing scales following factor analyses indicating redundancy. For example, scales measuring curiosity and love of learning do not appear distinct, so there is probably no good reason to sustain their distinction.

Although our goal all along has been to create a battery of measures, we can imagine researchers or practitioners administering only selected scales if they so desire. However, we offer the caveat that presenting respondents with 8 or 10 items measuring—for example—forgiveness and nothing else might create a demand for socially desirable responses that the full batteries seem to avoid by allowing all respondents to say something positive about themselves. Furthermore, as already noted, selective use of the scales may preclude discovery of unanticipated results, so we recommend the full inventory unless there is a strong reason to the contrary.

REFERENCES

Abramowitz, A. J., O'Leary, S. G., & Rosen, L. A. (1987). Reducing off-task behavior in the classroom: A comparison of encouragement and reprimands. *Journal of Abnormal Child Psychology, 15,* 153–163.

Abramson, L. Y., Seligman, M. E. P., & Teasdale, J. D. (1978). Learned helplessness in humans: Critique and reformulation. *Journal of Abnormal Psychology, 87,* 49–74.

Ackerman, P. L. (1997). Personality, self-concept, interests, and intelligence: Which concept doesn't fit? *Journal of Personality, 65,* 171–204.

Adams, M. J. (Coordinator). (1986). *Odyssey: A curriculum for thinking.* Watertown, MA: Mastery Education Corporation.

Adler, A. (1946). *Understanding human nature.* New York: Greenburg.

Adorno, T. W., Frenkel-Brunswik, E., Levinson, D. J., & Sanford, R. N. (1950). *The authoritarian personality.* New York: Harper & Row.

Agarwal, A., Tripathi, K. K., & Srivastava, M. (1983). Social roots and psychological implications of time perspective. *International Journal of Psychology, 18,* 367–380.

Ahrens, F. (2001, July 29). Successories: Stories for a generation. *The Plain Dealer,* sec. L, 1–2.

Ainlay, S., & Smith, D. (1984). Aging and religious participation. *Journal of Gerontology, 39,* 357–363.

Ainley, M. D. (1998). Interest in learning and the disposition of curiosity in secondary students: Investigating process and context. In L. Hoffman, A. Krapp, K. A. Renninger, & J. Baumert (Eds.), *Interest and learning: Proceedings of the Seeon Conference on Interest and Gender* (pp. 257–266). Kiel, Germany: Institute for Science Education.

Ainley, M. D., Hidi, S., & Berndorff, D. (2002). Interest, learning and the psychological processes that mediate their relationship. *Journal of Educational Psychology, 94,* 545–561.

Ainslie, G. (1987). Self-reported tactics of impulse control. *International Journal of Addictions, 22,* 167–179.

Ainslie, G. (2001). *Breakdown of will.* Cambridge, England: Cambridge University Press.

Ainsworth, M. D. S., Blehar, M. C., Waters, E., & Wall, S. (1978). *Patterns of attachment: Assessed in the strange situation and at home.* Hillsdale, NJ: Erlbaum.

Alberti, E. T., & Witryol, S. L. (1994). The relationship between curiosity and cognitive ability in third and fifth grade children. *Journal of Genetic Psychology, 155,* 129–145.

Alexander, P. A., & Murphy, P. K. (1998). Profiling the differences in students' knowledge, interest, and strategic processing. *Journal of Educational Psychology, 90,* 435–447.

Alfarabi. (1961). *Aphorisms of the statesman* (D. M. Dunlop, Trans.). Cambridge, England: Cambridge University Press.

Alfarabi. (2001). Selected aphorisms. In C. E. Butterworth (Trans.), *Alfarabi: The political writings* (pp. 11–67). Ithaca, NY: Cornell University Press.

Allen, J. P., & Land, D. (1999). Attachment in adolescence. In J. Cassidy & P. R. Shaver (Eds.), *Handbook of attachment: Theory, research, and clinical implications* (pp. 319–335). New York: Guilford Press.

Alliger, G., & Dwight, S. (2000). A meta-analytic investigation of the susceptibility of integrity tests to faking and coaching. *Educational and Psychological Measurement, 60,* 59–72.

Alliger, G., Lilienfeld, S., & Mitchell, K. (1996). Susceptibility of overt and covert integrity tests to coaching and faking. *Psychological Science, 7,* 32–39.

Allison, S. T., Messick, D. M., & Goethals, G. R. (1989). On being better but not smarter than others: The Muhammad Ali effect. *Social Cognition, 7,* 275–295.

Alloy, L. B., & Abramson, L. Y. (1979). Judgment of contingency in depressed and nondepressed college students: Sadder but wiser? *Journal of Experimental Psychology: General, 108,* 441–487.

Allport, G. W. (1921). Personality and character. *Psychological Bulletin, 18,* 441–455.

Allport, G. W. (1927). Concepts of trait and personality. *Psychological Bulletin, 24,* 284–293.

Allport, G. W. (1937). *Personality: A psychological interpretation.* New York: Holt.

Allport, G. W. (1961). *Pattern and growth in personality.* New York: Holt, Rinehart & Winston.

Allport, G. W. (1979). *The nature of prejudice.* Cambridge, MA: Addison-Wesley. (Original work published 1954)

Allport, G. W., & Odbert, H. S. (1936). Trait-names: A psycho-lexical study. *Psychological Monographs, 47* (Whole No. 211).

Allport, G. W., & Ross, J. (1967). Personal religious orientation and prejudice. *Journal of Personality and Social Psychology, 5,* 432–443.

Allport, G. W., & Vernon, P. (1930). The field of personality. *Psychological Bulletin, 27,* 677–730.

Al-Mabuk, R. H., Enright, R. D., & Cardis, P. A. (1995). Forgiveness education with parentally love-deprived late adolescents. *Journal of Moral Education, 24,* 427–444.

Almond, G., & Verba, S. (1965). *The civic culture: Political attitudes and democracy in five nations.* Boston: Little, Brown.

Aluja-Fabregat, A. (2000). Personality and curiosity about TV and film violence in adolescents. *Personality and Individual Differences, 29,* 379–392.

Amabile, T. M. (1982). Social psychology of creativity: A consensual assessment technique. *Journal of Personality and Social Psychology, 43,* 997–1013.

Amabile, T. M. (1996). *Creativity in context.* Boulder, CO: Westview Press.

Amabile, T. M., Hill, K. G., Hennessey, B. A., & Tighe, E. M. (1994). The Work Preference Inventory: Assessing intrinsic and extrinsic motivational orientations. *Journal of Personality and Social Psychology, 66,* 950–967.

American Psychiatric Association. (1952). *Diagnostic and statistical manual of mental disorders.* Washington, DC: Author.

American Psychiatric Association. (1968). *Diagnostic and statistical manual of mental disorders* (2nd ed.). Washington, DC: Author.

American Psychiatric Association. (1980). *Diagnostic and statistical manual of mental disorders* (3rd ed.). Washington, DC: Author.

American Psychiatric Association. (1987). *Diagnostic and statistical manual of mental disorders* (3rd ed., Rev.). Washington, DC: Author.

American Psychiatric Association. (1994). *Diagnostic and statistical manual of mental disorders* (4th ed.). Washington, DC: Author.

Ames, C. (1992). Classrooms: Goals, structures, and student motivation. *Journal of Educational Psychology, 84,* 261–271.

Anderson, C. A. (1982). Inoculation and counterexplanation: Debiasing techniques in the perseverance of social theories. *Social Cognition, 1,* 126–139.

Anderson, C. A., Lepper, M. R., & Ross, L. (1980). Perseverance of social theories: The role of explanation in the persistence of discredited information. *Journal of Personality and Social Psychology, 39,* 1037–1049.

Anderson, W. A. (1943). The family and individual social participation. *American Sociological Review, 8,* 420–424.

Anscombe, G. E. M. (1958). Modern moral philosophy. *Philosophy, 33,* 1–19.

Anthony, E. J., & Cohler, B. J. (Eds.). (1987). *The invulnerable child.* New York: Guilford Press.

Antonovsky, A. (1985). The sense of coherence as a determinant of health. In J. D. Matarazzo, S. M. Weiss, J. A. Herd, N. E. Miller, & S. M. Weiss (Eds.), *Behavioral health: A handbook of health enhancement and disease prevention* (pp. 114–129). New York: Wiley.

Aquinas, Saint Thomas. (1989). *Summa theologiae* (T. McDermott, Trans.). Westminster, MD: Christian Classics.

Arbuthnot, J., & Gordon, D. A. (1986). Behavioral and cognitive effects of a moral reasoning development intervention for high-risk behavior-disordered adolescents. *Journal of Consulting and Clinical Psychology, 85,* 1275–1301.

Ardelt, M. (1997). Wisdom and life satisfaction in old age. *Journal of Gerontology, 52*, 15–27.

Ardelt, M. (1998). Social crisis and individual growth: The long-term effects of the Great Depression. *Journal of Aging Studies, 12*, 291–314.

Aristotle. (1900). *A treatise in government* (W. Ellis, Trans.). London: J. M. Dent & Sons.

Aristotle. (1948). *The politics* (E. Barker, Trans.). Oxford, England: Oxford University Press.

Aristotle. (1984). *The complete works of Aristotle* (J. Barnes, Ed.). Princeton, NJ: Princeton University Press.

Aristotle. (2000). *Nicomachean ethics* (R. Crisp, Trans.). Cambridge, England: Cambridge University Press.

Arkes, H. R., Faust, D., Guilmette, T. J., & Hart, K. (1988). Eliminating the hindsight bias. *Journal of Applied Psychology, 73*, 305–307.

Armsden, G. C., & Greenberg, M. T. (1987). The Inventory of Parent and Peer Attachment: Individual differences and their relationship to psychological well-being in adolescence. *Journal of Youth and Adolescence, 16*, 427–454.

Armstrong, K. (2001). *Buddha.* New York: Penguin.

Arocho, R., & McMillan, C. A. (1998). Discriminant and criterion validation of the US-Spanish version of the SF-36 Health Survey in Cuban-American population with benign prostatic hyperplasia. *Medical Care, 36*, 766–772.

Aron, A., & Westbay, L. (1996). Dimensions of the prototype of love. *Journal of Personality and Social Psychology, 70*, 535–551.

Aronson, E., & Mills, J. (1959). The effect of severity of initiation on liking for a group. *Journal of Abnormal and Social Psychology, 59*, 177–181.

Asch, S. E. (1956). Studies of independence and conformity: A minority of one against a unanimous majority. *Psychological Monographs, 70* (Whole No. 416).

Aseltine, R. H. (1995). A reconsideration of parental and peer influences on adolescent deviance. *Journal of Health and Social Behavior, 36*, 103–121.

Asendorpf, J. B., & Ostendorf, F. (1998). Is self-enhancement healthy? Conceptual, psychometric, and empirical analysis. *Journal of Personality and Social Psychology, 74*, 955–966.

Ash, P. (1988). *Life experience inventory* (Rev. ed.). Park Ridge, IL: London House.

Ashton, M. C., Paunonen, S. V., Helmes, E., & Jackson, D. N. (1998). Kin altruism, reciprocal altruism, and the Big Five personality factors. *Evolution and Human Behavior, 19*, 243–255.

Aspinwall, L. G., & Brunhart, S. M. (1996). Distinguishing optimism from denial: Optimistic beliefs predict attention to health threats. *Personality and Social Psychology Bulletin, 22*, 993–1003.

Aspinwall, L. G., & Staudinger, U. M. (Eds.). (2003). *A psychology of human strengths: Fundamental questions and future directions for a positive psychology.* Washington, DC: American Psychological Association.

Assmann, A. (1994). Wholesome knowledge: Concepts of wisdom in a historical and cross-cultural perspective. In D. L. Featherman, R. M. Lerner, & M. Perlmutter (Eds.), *Life-span development and behavior* (Vol. 12, pp. 188–224). Hillsdale, NJ: Erlbaum.

Association of Test Publishers. (1994). *Model guidelines for preemployment integrity testing* (2nd ed.). Washington, DC: Author.

Assor, A., Kapland H., & Roth, G. (2002). Choice is good, but relevance is excellent: Autonomy enhancing and suppressing teacher behaviors predicting students' engagement in schoolwork. *British Journal of Educational Psychology, 72,* 261–278.

Astin, A. W., Green, K. C., & Korn, W. S. (1987). *The American freshman: Twenty year trends.* Los Angeles: UCLA Higher Education Research Institute.

Atkinson, J. W., & Litwin, G. H. (1960). Achievement motive and test anxiety conceived as motive to approach success and motive to avoid failure. *Journal of Abnormal and Social Psychology, 60,* 52–63.

Attardo, S. (2001). *Humorous texts: A semantic and pragmatic analysis.* New York: Mouton de Gruyter.

Audia, P. G., Locke, E. A., & Smith, K. G. (2000). The paradox of success: An archival and a laboratory study of strategic persistence following radical environmental change. *Academy of Management Journal, 43,* 837–853.

Augustine, Saint. (1943). *The confessions of St. Augustine* (J. G. Pilkington, Trans.). New York: Liveright.

Austin, A., Braeger, T., Schvaneveldt, J., Lindauer, S., Summers, M., Robinson, C., et al. (1991). A comparison of helping, sharing, comforting, honesty, and civic awareness for children in home care, day care, and preschool. *Child and Youth Care Forum, 20,* 183–194.

Averill, J. R., Catlin, G., & Chon, K. K. (1990). *Rules of hope.* New York: Springer-Verlag.

Avery, P. G. (1992). Political tolerance: How adolescents deal with dissenting groups. In H. Haste & J. Torney-Purta (Eds.), *New directions for child development: The development of political understanding: A new perspective* (pp. 39–51). San Francisco: Jossey-Bass.

Avery, P. G., & Simmons, A. M. (2000–2001). Civic life as conveyed in United States civics and history textbooks. *The International Journal of Social Education, 15,* 105–130.

Avolio, B. J. (1999). *Full leadership development: Building the vital forces in organizations.* Thousand Oaks, CA: Sage.

Avolio, B. J., & Gibbons, T. C. (1988). Developing transformational leaders: A lifespan approach. In J. A. Conger & R. N. Kanungo (Eds.), *Charismatic leadership: The elusive factor in organizational effectiveness* (pp. 276–308). San Francisco: Jossey-Bass.

Avolio, B. J., & Howell, J. M. (1992). The impact of leader behavior and leader-personality match on satisfaction and unit performance. In K. E. Clark, M. B. Clark, & D. R. Campbell (Eds.), *Impact of leadership* (pp. 225–235). Greensboro, NC: Center for Creative Leadership.

Axelrod, R. (1980a). Effective choice in the Prisoner's Dilemma. *Journal of Conflict Resolution, 24*, 3–25.

Axelrod, R. (1980b). More effective choice in the Prisoner's Dilemma. *Journal of Conflict Resolution, 24*, 379–403.

Axelrod, S. R., Widiger, T. A., Trull, T. J., & Corbitt, E. M. (1997). Relations of five-factor model antagonism facets with personality disorder symptomatology. *Journal of Personality Assessment, 69*, 297–313.

Ayres, R., Cooley, E., & Dunn, C. (1990). Self-concept, attribution, and persistence in learning disabled students. *Journal of School Psychology, 28*, 153–163.

Azar, F., & Mullet, É. (2001). Interpersonal forgiveness among Lebanese: A six-community study. *International Journal of Group Tensions, 30*, 161–181.

Bacon, F. (1960). *The new organon and related writings.* New York: Liberal Arts Press. (Original work published 1620)

Bailey, D., Simeonsson, R., Buysse, V., & Smith, T. (1993). Reliability of an index of child characteristics. *Developmental Medicine and Child Neurology, 35*, 806–815.

Bailey, K. D. (1994). *Typologies and taxonomies: An introduction to classification techniques.* Thousand Oaks, CA: Sage.

Baltes, P. B. (1993). The aging mind: Potential and limits. *Gerontologist, 33*, 580–594.

Baltes, P. B., & Smith, J. (1990). Towards a psychology of wisdom and its ontogenesis. In R. J. Sternberg (Ed.), *Wisdom: Its nature, origins, and development* (pp. 87–120). Cambridge, England: Cambridge University Press.

Baltes, P. B., Smith, J., & Staudinger, U. M. (1992). Wisdom and successful aging. In T. Sonderegger (Ed.), *Nebraska symposium on motivation* (Vol. 39, pp. 123–167). Lincoln: University of Nebraska Press.

Baltes, P. B., & Staudinger, U. M. (1993). The search for a psychology of wisdom. *Current Directions in Psychological Science, 2*, 75–80.

Baltes, P. B., & Staudinger, U. M. (2000). Wisdom: A metaheuristic (pragmatic) to orchestrate mind and virtue toward excellence. *American Psychologist, 55*, 122–136.

Baltes, P. B., Staudinger, U. M., Maercker, A., & Smith, J. (1995). People nominated as wise: A comparative study of wisdom-related knowledge. *Psychology and Aging, 10*, 155–166.

Bandura, A. (1977). Self-efficacy: Toward a unifying theory of behavioral change. *Psychological Review, 84*, 191–215.

Bandura, A. (1982). Self-efficacy mechanisms in human agency. *American Psychologist, 37*, 122–147.

Bandura, A. (1986). *Social foundations of thought and action: A social cognitive theory.* Englewood Cliffs, NJ: Prentice Hall.

Bandura, A. (1997). *Self-efficacy: The exercise of control.* New York: Freeman.

Banfield, E. C. (1990). *The unheavenly city revisited.* Prospect Heights, IL: Waveland Press.

Banks, W. C., McQuater, G. V., & Hubbard, J. L. (1977). Task-liking and intrinsic-extrinsic achievement orientations in Black adolescents. *Journal of Black Psychology, 3*, 61–71.

Barber, N. (2000). On the relationship between country sex ratios and teen pregnancy rates: A replication. *Cross-Cultural Research: The Journal of Comparative Social Science, 34,* 26–37.

Bargh, J. A. (1990). Goal≠intent: Goal-directed thought and behavior are often unintentional. *Psychological Inquiry, 1,* 248–251.

Barkley, R. A. (1997). Behavioral inhibition, sustained attention, and executive functions: Constructing a unifying theory of ADHD. *Psychological Bulletin, 121,* 65–94.

Barnett, M. A., Quackenbush, S. W., & Sinisi, C. S. (1995). The role of critical experiences in moral development: Implications for justice and care orientations. *Basic and Applied Social Psychology, 17,* 137–152.

Baron, J. (1991). Beliefs about thinking. In J. F. Voss, D. N. Perkins, & J. W. Segal (Eds.), *Informal reasoning and education* (pp. 169–186). Hillsdale, NJ: Erlbaum.

Baron, J. (1995). Myside bias in thinking about abortion. *Thinking and Reasoning, 1,* 221–235.

Baron, J. (2000). *Thinking and deciding* (3rd ed.). New York: Cambridge University Press.

Baron, J., Badgio, P., & Gaskins, I. W. (1986). Cognitive style and its improvement: A normative approach. In R. J. Sternberg (Ed.), *Advances in the psychology of human intelligence* (Vol. 3, pp. 173–220). Hillsdale, NJ: Erlbaum.

Baron, R. A. (1984). Reducing organizational conflict: An incompatible response approach. *Journal of Applied Psychology, 69,* 272–279.

Barrick, M. R., Day, D. V., Lord, R. G., & Alexander, R. A. (1991). Assessing the utility of executive leadership. *Leadership Quarterly, 2,* 9–22.

Barrick, M. R., & Mount, M. K. (1991). The Big Five personality dimensions and job performance: A meta-analysis. *Personnel Psychology, 44,* 1–26.

Barron, K. E., & Harackiewicz, J. M. (2000). Achievement goals and optimal motivation: A multiple goals approach. In C. Sansone & J. M. Harackiewicz (Eds.), *Intrinsic and extrinsic motivation: The search for optimal motivation and performance* (pp. 231–254). New York: Academic Press.

Barth, R. S. (2001). *Learning by heart.* San Francisco: Jossey-Bass.

Bartholomew, K. (1990). Avoidance of intimacy: An attachment perspective. *Journal of Social and Personal Relationships, 7,* 147–178.

Bartholomew, K., & Horowitz, L. (1991). Attachment styles among young adults: A test of a four-category model. *Journal of Personality and Social Psychology, 61,* 226–244.

Bartholomew, K., & Shaver, P. R. (1998). Methods of assessing adult attachment: Do they converge? In J. A. Simpson & W. S. Rholes (Eds.), *Attachment theory and close relationships* (pp. 25–45). New York: Guilford Press.

Bass, B. M. (1985). *Leadership and performance beyond expectations.* New York: Free Press.

Bass, B. M. (1990). *Bass & Stogdill's handbook of leadership: Theory, research and managerial applications* (3rd ed.). New York: Free Press.

Bass, B. M. (1996). *A new paradigm of leadership: An inquiry into transformational leadership*. Alexandria, VA: U.S. Army Research Institute for the Behavioral and Social Sciences.

Bass, B. M., & Avolio, B. J. (1990). The implications of transactional and transformational leadership for individual, team, and organizational development. In R. W. Woodman & W. A. Passmore (Eds.), *Research in organizational change and development* (pp. 231–272). Greenwich, CT: JAI Press.

Batson, C. D. (1990). How social an animal? The human capacity for caring. *American Psychologist, 45,* 336–346.

Batson, C. D. (1991). *The altruism question: Toward a social-psychological answer.* Hillsdale, NJ: Erlbaum.

Batson, C. D. (1997). Self-other merging and the empathy-altruism hypothesis: Reply to Neuberg et al. (1997). *Journal of Personality and Social Psychology, 73,* 517–522.

Batson, C. D. (2001). Addressing the altruism question experimentally. In S. G. Post, L. B. Underwood, J. P. Schloss, & W. B. Hurlbut (Eds.), *Altruism and altruistic love: Science, philosophy, and religion in dialogue* (pp. 89–105). New York: Oxford University Press.

Batson, C. D., Bolen, M. H., Cross, J. A., & Neuringer-Benefiel, H. E. (1986). Where is the altruism in the altruistic personality? *Journal of Personality and Social Psychology, 50,* 212–220.

Batson, C. D., Dyck, J. L., Brandt, J. R., Batson, J. G., Powell, A. L., McMaster, M. R., et al. (1988). Five studies testing two new egoistic alternatives to the empathy-altruism hypothesis. *Journal of Personality and Social Psychology, 55,* 52–77.

Batson, C. D., Klein, T. R., Highberger, L., & Shaw, L. L. (1995). Immorality from empathy-induced altruism: When compassion and justice conflict. *Journal of Personality and Social Psychology, 68,* 1042–1054.

Batson, C. D., & Ventis, W. (1982). *The religious experience: A social-psychological perspective.* New York: Oxford University Press.

Baumeister, R. F. (1987). How the self became a problem: A psychological review of historical research. *Journal of Personality and Social Psychology, 52,* 163–176.

Baumeister, R. F. (1991). *Escaping the self: Alcoholism, spirituality, masochism, and other flights from the burden of selfhood.* New York: Basic Books.

Baumeister, R. F., Bratslavsky, E., Muraven, M., & Tice, D. M. (1998). Ego depletion: Is the active self a limited resource? *Journal of Personality and Social Psychology, 74,* 1252–1265.

Baumeister, R. F., Catanese, K., & Vohs, K. D. (2001). Is there a gender difference in strength of sex drive? Theoretical views, conceptual distinctions, and a review of relevant evidence. *Personality and Social Psychology Review, 5,* 242–273.

Baumeister, R. F., & Exline, J. J. (1999). Virtue, personality, and social relations: Self-control as the moral muscle. *Journal of Personality, 67,* 1165–1194.

Baumeister, R. F., & Exline, J. J. (2000). Self-control, morality, and human strength. *Journal of Social and Clinical Psychology, 19,* 29–42.

Baumeister, R. F., Heatherton, T. F., & Tice, D. M. (1993). When ego threats lead to self-regulation failure: Negative consequences of high self-esteem. *Journal of Personality and Social Psychology, 64,* 141–156.

Baumeister, R. F., Heatherton, T. F., & Tice, D. M. (1994). *Losing control: How and why people fail at self-regulation.* San Diego, CA: Academic Press.

Baumeister, R. F., Smart, L., & Boden, J. M. (1996). Relation of threatened egotism to violence and aggression: The dark side of high self-esteem. *Psychological Review, 103,* 5–33.

Baumeister, R. F., & Vohs, K. D. (2003). Self-regulation and the executive function of the self. In M. R. Leary & J. P. Tangney (Eds.), *Handbook of self and identity* (pp. 197–217). New York: Guilford Press.

Baumgartner-Tramer, F. (1938). "Gratefulness" in children and young people. *Journal of Genetic Psychology, 53,* 53–66.

Bazemore, G., & Walgrave, L. (1999). *Restorative juvenile justice: Repairing the harm of youth crime.* New York: Criminal Justice Press.

Beardsley, M. C. (1967). Aesthetics, history of. In P. Edwards (Ed.), *The encyclopedia of philosophy* (Vols. 1 and 2, pp. 18–35). New York: Macmillan.

Bechara, A., Tranel, D., & Damasio, A. R. (2000). Poor judgment in spite of high intellect. In R. Bar-On & J. D. A. Parker (Eds.), *The handbook of emotional intelligence* (pp. 192–214). San Francisco: Jossey-Bass.

Beck, A. T. (1976). *Cognitive therapy and the emotional disorders.* New York: International University Press.

Beck, U. (1992). *Risk society: Towards a new modernity.* London: Sage.

Becker, H. S. (1986). *Writing for social scientists.* Chicago: University of Chicago Press.

Becker, J. A., & Smenner, P. C. (1986). The spontaneous use of *thank you* by preschoolers as a function of sex, socioeconomic status, and listener status. *Language in Society, 15,* 537–546.

Becker, T. (1998). Integrity in organizations: Beyond honesty and conscientiousness. *Academy of Management Review, 23,* 154–161.

Bell, C. (1913). *Art.* London: Putnam.

Bellah, R. N., Madsen, R., Sullivan, W. M., Swidler, A., & Tipton, S. M. (1985). *Habits of the heart: Individualism and commitment in American life.* Berkeley: University of California Press.

Bem, D. J., & Allen, A. (1974). On predicting some of the people some of the time: The search for cross-situational consistencies in behavior. *Psychological Review, 81,* 506–520.

Benjamin, J., Ebstein, R. P., & Belmaker, R. H. (1997). Personality genetics. *Israel Journal of Psychiatry and Related Sciences, 34,* 270–280.

Benjamin, J., Osher, Y., Lichtenberg, P., Bachner-Melman, R., Gritsenko, I., Kotler, M., et al. (2000). An interaction between the catechol O-methyltransferase and serotonin transporter promoter region polymorphisms contributes to Tridimensional Personality Questionnaire persistence scores in normal subjects. *Neuropsychobiology, 41,* 48–53.

Bennett, W. J. (1993). *The book of virtues.* New York: Simon & Schuster.

Bennett, W. J. (1997). *The children's book of heroes.* New York: Simon & Schuster.

Bennion, L. D., & Adams, G. R. (1986). A revision of the extended objective measure of ego-identity status: An identity instrument for use with late adolescents. *Journal of Adolescent Research, 1,* 183–198.

Benson, P. L., Leffert, N., Scales, P. C., & Blyth, D. A. (1998). Beyond the "village" rhetoric: Creating healthy communities for children and adolescents. *Applied Developmental Science, 2,* 138–159.

Benton, S. L., Corkill, A. J., Sharp J. M., Downey R. G., & Khramsova, I. (1995). Knowledge, interest and narrative writing. *Journal of Educational Psychology, 87,* 66–79.

Ben-Ze'ev, A. (1993). The virtue of modesty. *American Philosophical Quarterly, 30,* 235–246.

Ben-Zur, H., & Zeidner, M. (1988). Sex differences in anxiety, curiosity, and anger: A cross-cultural study. *Sex Roles, 19,* 335–347.

Berdyaev, N. (1939). *Spirit and reality.* London: Geoffrey Bles.

Berg, J. H., Stephan, W. G., & Dodson, M. (1981). Attributional modesty in women. *Psychology of Women Quarterly, 5,* 711–727.

Bergeman, C. S., Chipuer, H. M., Plomin, R., Pedersen, N. L., McClearn, G. E., Nesselroade, J. R., et al. (1993). Genetic and environmental effects on openness to experience, agreeableness, and conscientiousness: An adoption/twin study. *Journal of Personality, 61,* 159–179.

Bergin, D. A (1999). Influences on classroom interest. *Educational Psychologist, 34,* 87–92.

Berkowitz, L. (1972). Social norms, feelings, and other factors affecting helping and altruism. In L. Berkowitz (Ed.), *Advances in experimental social psychology* (Vol. 6, pp. 63–108). New York: Academic Press.

Berkowitz, L., & Lutterman, K. G. (1968). The traditional socially responsible personality. *Public Opinion Quarterly, 32,* 169–185.

Berkowitz, M. W. (1985). The role of discussion in moral education. In M. W. Berkowitz & F. Oser (Eds.), *Moral education: Theory and application* (pp. 197–218). Hillsdale, NJ: Erlbaum.

Berkowitz, M. W. (1997). The complete moral person: Anatomy and formation. In J. M. Dubois (Ed.), *Moral issues in psychology: Personalist contributions to selected problems* (pp. 11–41). Lanham, MD: University Press of America.

Berkowitz, M. W. (2000). Civics and moral education. In B. Moon, S. Brown, & M. Ben-Peretz (Eds.), *Routledge international companion to education* (pp. 897–909). New York: Routledge.

Berkowitz, M. W., & Gibbs, J. C. (1983). Measuring the developmental features of moral discussion. *Merrill-Palmer Quarterly, 29,* 399–410.

Berkowitz, M. W., & Grych, J. H. (1998). Fostering goodness: Teaching parents to facilitate children's moral development. *Journal of Moral Education, 27,* 371–391.

Berkowitz, M. W., Kahn, J. P., Mulry, G., & Piette, J. (1995). Psychological and philosophical considerations of prudence and morality. In M. Killen &

D. Hart (Eds.), *Morality in everyday life: Developmental perspectives* (pp. 201–224). New York: Cambridge University Press.

Berkowitz, M. W., Mueller, C. W., Schnell, S. V., & Padberg, M. T. (1986). Moral reasoning and judgments of aggression. *Journal of Personality and Social Psychology, 51,* 885–891.

Berlyne, D. E. (1949). "Interest" as a psychological concept. *British Journal of Psychology, 39,* 184–195.

Berlyne, D. E. (1960). *Conflict, arousal, and curiosity.* New York: McGraw-Hill.

Berlyne, D. E. (1962). Uncertainty and epistemic curiosity. *Journal of British Psychology, 53,* 27–34.

Berlyne, D. E. (1967). Arousal and reinforcement. In D. Levine (Ed.), *Nebraska symposium on motivation* (pp. 1–110). Lincoln: University of Nebraska Press.

Berlyne, D. E. (1971). *Aesthetics and psychobiology.* New York: Appleton-Century-Crofts.

Bernard, L. L. (1926). *An introduction to social psychology.* New York: Holt.

Berne, E. (1964). *Games people play: The psychology of human relationships.* New York: Grove Press.

Bernstein, J. H., & Ryan, R. M. (2001). *Nature's impact on subjective vitality: A first foray.* Unpublished manuscript, University of Rochester, NY.

Berry, J. W., Worthington, E. L., Parrott, L., O'Connor, L. E., & Wade, N. G. (2001). Dispositional forgivingness: Development and construct validity of the Transgression Narrative Test of Forgiveness (TNTF). *Personality and Social Psychology Bulletin, 27,* 1277–1290.

Berscheid, E., & Walster, E. H. (1978). *Interpersonal attraction* (2nd ed.). Reading, MA: Addison-Wesley.

Beswick, D. G. (1971). Cognitive process theory of individual differences in curiosity. In H. I. Day, D. E. Berlyne, & D. E. Hunt (Eds.), *Intrinsic motivation: A new direction in education* (pp. 156–170). New York: Holt, Rinehart & Winston.

Beswick, D. G., & Tallmadge, K. (1971). Reexamination of two learning style studies in the light of the cognitive process theory of curiosity. *Journal of Educational Psychology, 62,* 456–462.

Bettelheim, B. (1988). *A good enough parent.* New York: Vintage Books.

Beutel, A. M., & Marini, M. M. (1995). Gender and values. *American Sociological Review, 60,* 436–448.

The Bhagavadgita (N. V. Thadani, Trans.). (1990). New Delhi, India: Munshiram Manoharlal.

Bhatt, S. R. (2001). The Buddhist doctrine of universal compassion and quality of life. In R. P. Singh & G. F. McLean (Eds.), *The Buddhist world view* (pp. 111–120). Faridabad, India: Om Publications.

Bianchi, E. (1994). *Elder wisdom: Crafting your own elderhood.* New York: Crossroad.

Bierhoff, H. W., Klein, R., & Kramp, P. (1991). Evidence for the altruistic personality from data on accident research. *Journal of Personality, 59,* 263–280.

Bieri, J. (1955). Cognitive complexity-simplicity and predictive behavior. *Journal of Abnormal and Social Psychology, 51*, 263–268.

Billig, S. H. (2000, May). Research on K–12 school based service learning: The evidence builds. *Phi Delta Kappan*, 658–664.

Billingsley, A. (1999). *Mighty like a river: The Black church and social reform*. New York: Oxford University Press.

Billingsley, A., & Caldwell, C. (1991). The church, the family and the school in the African American community. *Journal of Negro Education, 60*, 427–440.

Bird, C. (1940). *Social psychology*. New York: Appleton-Century.

Bird, G. E. (1925). Objective humor test for children. *Psychological Bulletin, 22*, 137–138.

Birnbaum, M. H. (Ed.). (2000). *Psychological experiments on the Internet*. San Diego, CA: Academic Press.

Birren, J. E., & Fisher, L. M. (1990). The elements of wisdom: Overview and integration. In R. J. Sternberg (Ed.), *Wisdom: Its nature, origins, and development* (pp. 317–332). New York: Cambridge University Press.

Bjarnason, T. (1998). Parents, religion and perceived social coherence: A Durkheimian framework of adolescent anomie. *Journal for the Scientific Study of Religion, 37*, 742–754.

Bjorklund, D. F., & Kipp, K. (1996). Parental investment theory and gender differences in the evolution of inhibition mechanisms. *Psychological Bulletin, 120*, 163–188.

Blasi, A. (1980). Bridging moral cognition and moral action: A critical review of the literature. *Psychological Bulletin, 88*, 1–45.

Blasi, A. (1990). Kohlberg's theory and moral motivation. *New Directions for Child Development, 47*, 51–57.

Blasi, A. (1993). The development of identity: Some implications for moral functioning. In T. Wren & G. Noam (Eds.), *The moral self* (pp. 99–122). Cambridge, MA: MIT Press.

Blinco, P. M. (1992). A cross-cultural study of task persistence of young children in Japan and the United States. *Journal of Cross-Cultural Psychology, 23*, 407–415.

Block, J. (1978). *The Q-sort method in personality assessment and psychiatric research*. Palo Alto, CA: Consulting Psychologists Press.

Block, J. H., Gjerde, P. F., & Block, J. H. (1991). Personality antecedents of depressive tendencies in 18-year-olds: A prospective study. *Journal of Personality and Social Psychology, 60*, 726–738.

Blum, L. (1980). *Friendship, altruism, and morality*. London: Routledge and Kegan, Paul.

Blum, L. (1988). Gilligan and Kohlberg: Implications for moral theory. *Ethics, 98*, 472–491.

Blum, L. (1994). *Moral perception and particularity*. Cambridge, England: Cambridge University Press.

Bly, R. (1992). *Iron John: A book about men*. New York: Vintage Books.

Bogardus, E. S. (1918). *Essentials of social psychology*. Los Angeles: University of Southern California Press.

Bok, S. (1995). *Common values*. Columbia: University of Missouri Press.

Boon, S. D., & Sulsky, L. M. (1997). Attributions of blame and forgiveness in romantic relationships: A policy-capturing study. *Journal of Social Behavior and Personality, 12,* 19–44.

Booth-Kewley, S., & Vickers, R. R. (1994). Association between major domains of personality and health behavior. *Journal of Personality, 62,* 281–298.

Bostic, T. J., Rubio, D. M., & Hood, M. (2000). A validation of the Subjective Vitality Scale using structural equation modeling. *Social Indicators Research, 52,* 313–324.

Bowden, A. O. (1926). A study of personality of student leaders in the United States. *Journal of Abnormal and Social Psychology, 21,* 149–160.

Bowlby, J. (1951). *Maternal care and mental health*. Geneva, Switzerland: World Health Organization.

Bowlby, J. (1969). *Attachment and loss: Vol. 1. Attachment*. New York: Basic Books.

Bowlby, J. (1973). *Attachment and loss: Vol. 2. Separation: Anxiety and anger*. New York: Basic Books.

Bowlby, J. (1979). *The making and breaking of affectional bonds*. London: Tavistock.

Bowlby, J. (1980). *Attachment and loss: Vol. 3. Loss, sadness, and depression*. New York: Basic Books.

Bowlby, J. (1988). *A secure base: Clinical applications of attachment theory*. London: Routledge.

Boy Scouts of America. (1998). *Boy Scout handbook* (11th ed.). Irving, TX: Author.

Boyle, G. J. (1989). Breadth-depth or state-trait curiosity? A factor analysis of state-trait curiosity and state anxiety scales. *Personality and Individual Differences, 10,* 175–183.

Brabeck, M. (1984). Ethical characteristics of whistle blowers. *Journal of Research in Personality, 18,* 41–53.

Brackett, M. A., & Mayer, J. D. (2003). Convergent, discriminant, and incremental validity of competing measures of emotional intelligence. *Personality and Social Psychology Bulletin, 29,* 1147–1158.

Brackett, M. A., Mayer, J. D., & Warner, R. M. (in press). Emotional intelligence and the prediction of behavior. *Personality and Individual Differences*.

Branden, N. (1994). *The six pillars of self-esteem*. New York: Bantam Books.

Brandon, J. E., Oescher, J., & Loftin, J. M. (1990). The self control questionnaire: An assessment. *Health Values, 14,* 3–9.

Bransford, J. D., Brown, A. L., & Cocking, R. R. (1999). *How people learn: Brain, mind, experience, and school*. Washington, DC: National Academy Press.

Bray, D. W. (1982). The assessment center and the study of lives. *American Psychologist, 37,* 180–189.

Bray, D. W., Campbell, R. J., & Grant, D. L. (1974). *Formative years in business: A long-term AT&T study of managerial lives.* New York: Wiley.

Bredemeier, B. J., & Shields, D. L. (1984). The utility of moral stage analysis in the investigation of athletic aggression. *Sociology of Sport Journal, 1,* 138–149.

Brehm, J., & Rahn, W. M. (1997). Individual level evidence for the causes and consequences of social capital. *American Journal of Political Science, 41,* 999–1023.

Brennan, K. A., & Bosson, J. K. (1998). Attachment-style differences in attitudes toward and reactions to feedback from romantic partners: An exploration of the relational bases of self-esteem. *Personality and Social Psychology Bulletin, 24,* 699–714.

Brennan, K. A., Clark, C. L., & Shaver, P. R. (1998). Self-report measurement of adult attachment: An integrative overview. In J. A. Simpson & W. S. Rholes (Eds.), *Attachment theory and close relationships* (pp. 46–76). New York: Guilford Press.

Brennan, K. A., & Shaver, P. R. (1995). Dimensions of adult attachment, affect regulation, and romantic relationship functioning. *Personality and Social Psychology Bulletin, 23,* 23–31.

Brennan, K. A., Shaver, P. R., & Tobey, A. E. (1991). Attachment styles, gender and parental problem drinking. *Journal of Personal and Social Relationships, 8,* 451–466.

Brewer, M. B., & Gardner, W. (1996). Who is this "We"? Levels of collective identity and self representations. *Journal of Personality and Social Psychology, 71,* 83–93.

Brightman, B. K. (1990). Adolescent depression and the susceptibility to helplessness. *Journal of Youth and Adolescence, 19,* 441–449.

Brim, O. G., Glass, D. C., Lavin, D. E., & Goodman, N. (1962). *Personality and decision processes.* Stanford, CA: Stanford University Press.

Brockner, J., Rubin, J. Z., & Lang, E. (1981). Face-saving and entrapment. *Journal of Experimental Social Psychology, 17,* 68–79.

Brody, G., Stoneman, Z., Flor, D., & McCrary, C. (1994). Religion's role in organizing family relationships: Family process in rural, two-parent African American families. *Journal of Marriage and the Family, 56,* 878–888.

Brody, N. (2000). History of theories and measurements of intelligence. In R. J. Sternberg (Ed.), *Handbook of intelligence* (pp. 16–33). Cambridge, England: Cambridge University Press.

Bronfenbrenner, U. (1977). Toward an experimental ecology of human development. *American Psychologist, 32,* 513–531.

Bronfenbrenner, U. (1979). *The ecology of human development: Experiments by nature and design.* Cambridge, MA: Harvard University Press.

Bronfenbrenner, U. (1986). Ecology of the family as a context for human development: Research perspectives. *Developmental Psychology, 22,* 723–742.

Brown, J. D. (1993). Self-esteem and self-evaluation: Feeling is believing. In J. M. Suls (Ed.), *The self in social perspective* (pp. 27–58). Hillsdale, NJ: Erlbaum.

Brown, J. D. (1998). *The self.* New York: McGraw-Hill.

Brown, L. M., Argyris, D., Attanucci, J., Bardige, B., Gilligan, C., Johnston, K., et al. (1988). *A guide to reading narratives of moral conflict and choice for self and moral voice* (Monograph No. 1). Cambridge, MA: Harvard Graduate School of Education, Center for the Study of Gender, Education, and Human Development.

Brown, L. M., Debold, E., Tappan, M., & Gilligan, C. (1991). Reading narratives of conflict and choice for self and moral voices: A relational method. In W. M. Kurtines & J. L. Gewirtz (Eds.), *Handbook of moral behavior and development: Vol. 2. Research* (pp. 25–61). Hillsdale, NJ: Erlbaum.

Brown, S. W., Gorsuch, R. L., Rosik, C. H., & Ridley, C. R. (2001). Development of a scale to measure forgiveness. *Journal of Psychology and Christianity, 20,* 85–90.

Bryan, J. H., & Test, M. A. (1967). Models and helping: Naturalistic studies in aiding behavior. *Journal of Personality and Social Psychology, 6,* 400–407.

Bryk, A. S., & Schneider, B. (2002). *Trust in schools: A core resource for improvement.* New York: Sage.

Buchanan, G. M., & Seligman, M. E. P. (Eds.). (1995). *Explanatory style.* Hillsdale, NJ: Erlbaum.

Buckingham, M., & Clifton, D. O. (2001). *Now, discover your strengths.* New York: Free Press.

Buhl, M. (2001). Involvement in free time activities and thoughts about society— Correlates and gender differences in seven nations. In A. Ittel & H. P. Kuhn (Cochairs), *Political development and identity: The role of gender.* Biennial meetings of the Society for Research in Child Development, April 19–22, Minneapolis, MN.

Bullinger, M. (1995). German translation and psychometric testing of the SF-36 Health Survey: Preliminary results from the IQOLA project. *Social Science and Medicine, 41,* 1359–1366.

Burger, J. M. (1985). Desire for control and achievement-related behaviors. *Journal of Personality and Social Psychology, 48,* 1520–1533.

Burke, E. (1990). *A philosophical inquiry into the origin of our ideas of the sublime and beautiful.* Oxford, England: Oxford University Press. (Original work published 1757)

Burke, M. J., & Day, R. R. (1986). A cumulative study of the effectiveness of managerial training. *Journal of Applied Psychology, 71,* 242–245.

Burns, J. M. (1978). *Leadership.* New York: Harper & Row.

Burrell, B. (1997). *The words we live by.* New York: Free Press.

Burt, C. (1955). The evidence for the concept of intelligence. *British Journal of Educational Psychology, 25,* 158–177.

Burton, R. V. (1963). Generality of honesty reconsidered. *Psychological Review, 70,* 481–499.

Bushman, B. J., & Baumeister, R. F. (1998). Threatened egotism, narcissism, self-esteem, and direct and displaced aggression: Does self-love or self-hate lead to violence? *Journal of Personality and Social Psychology, 75,* 219–229.

Bushman, B. J., & Baumeister, R. F. (2002). Does self-love or self-hate lead to violence? *Journal of Research in Personality, 36,* 543–545.

Busman, D. (1992, April). *The myth of the teacher resister: The influence of authenticity and participation on faculty trust.* Paper presented at the annual meeting of the American Educational Research Association, San Francisco. (ERIC Document Reproduction Service No. ED349268)

Buss, D. M. (1989). Sex differences in human mate preferences: Evolutionary hypotheses tested in 37 cultures. *Behavioral and Brain Sciences, 12,* 1–14.

Buss, D. M. (1994). *The evolution of desire: Strategies of human mating.* New York: Basic Books.

Buss, D. M. (1998). The psychology of human mate selection: Exploring the complexity of the strategic response. In C. Crawford & D. L. Krebs (Eds.), *Handbook of evolutionary psychology: Ideas, issues, and applications* (pp. 405–419). Mahwah, NJ: Erlbaum.

Buss, D. M. (1999). Evolutionary psychology: A new paradigm for psychological science. In D. H. Rosen & M. C. Luebbert (Eds.), *Evolution of the psyche: Human evolution, behavior, and intelligence* (pp. 1–33). Westport, CT: Praeger.

Buss, D. M., Abbott, M., Angleitner, A., Asherian, A., Biaggio, A., Blanco-Villasenor, A., et al. (1990). International preferences in selecting mates: A study of 37 cultures. *Journal of Cross-Cultural Psychology, 21,* 5–47.

Buss, D. M., & Craik, K. H. (1983). The act frequency approach to personality. *Psychological Review, 90,* 105–126.

Buss, D. M., & Schmitt, D. P. (1993). Sexual strategies theory: An evolutionary perspective on human mating. *Psychological Review, 100,* 204–232.

Bussey, K. (1992). Lying and truthfulness: Children's definitions, standards, and evaluative reactions. *Child Development, 63,* 129–137.

Bussey, K., & Grimbeek, E. (2000). Children's conception of lying and truth-telling: Implications for child witnesses. *Legal and Criminological Psychology, 5,* 187–199.

Butler, R. (1987). Task-involving and ego-involving properties of evaluation: Effects of different feedback conditions on motivational perceptions, interest and performance. *Journal of Educational Psychology, 79,* 474–482.

Butterworth, C. E. (2001). Introduction to selected aphorisms. In C. E. Butterworth (Trans.), *Alfarabi: The political writings* (pp. 3–10). Ithaca, NY: Cornell University Press.

Cacioppo, J. T., & Petty, R. E. (1982). The need for cognition. *Journal of Personality and Social Psychology, 42,* 116–131.

Cacioppo, J. T., Petty, R. E., Feinstein, J. A., & Jarvis, W. B. G. (1996). Dispositional differences in cognitive motivation: The life and times of individuals varying in need for cognition. *Psychological Bulletin, 119,* 197–253.

Caldwell, C., Chatters, L., Billingsley, A., & Taylor, R. (1995). Church-based support programs for elderly Black adults: Congregational and clergy characteristics. In M. Kimble, S. McFadden, J. Ellor, & J. Seeber (Eds.),

Aging, spirituality, and religion (pp. 306–324). Minneapolis, MN: Fortress Press.

Camara, W., & Schneider, D. (1995). Questions of construct breadth and openness of research in integrity testing. *American Psychologist, 50,* 459–460.

Cameron, K. S., Dutton, J. E., & Quinn, R. E. (Eds.). (2003). *Positive organizational scholarship: Foundations of a new discipline.* San Francisco: Berrett-Koehler.

Campbell, J. (1949). *The hero with a thousand faces.* New York: Pantheon Books.

Campbell, W. K. (1999). Narcissism and romantic attraction. *Journal of Personality and Social Psychology, 77,* 1254–1270.

Campbell, W. K., & Foster, C. A. (2002). Narcissism and commitment in romantic relationships: An investment model analysis. *Personality and Social Psychology Bulletin, 28,* 484–495.

Campbell, W. K., Rudich, E., & Sedikides, C. (2002). Narcissism, self-esteem, and the positivity of self-views: Two portraits of self-love. *Personality and Social Psychology Bulletin, 28,* 358–368.

Campbell, W. K., Sedikides, C., Reeder, G. D., & Elliot, A. J. (2000). Among friends? An examination of friendship and the self-serving bias. *British Journal of Social Psychology, 39,* 229–239.

Candee, D., Graham, R., & Kohlberg, L. (1978). *Moral development and life outcomes* (Report to the National Institute of Education, NIE-6-74-0096). Cambridge, MA.

Candee, D., & Kohlberg, L. (1987). Moral judgment and moral action: A reanalysis of Haan, Smith, and Block's (1968) Free Speech Movement data. *Journal of Personality and Social Psychology, 52,* 554–564.

Candee, D., Sheehan, T. J., Cook, C. D., Husted, S. D. R., & Bargen, M. (1982). Moral reasoning and decisions in dilemmas of neonatal care. *Pediatric Research, 16,* 846–850.

Cantor, N., & Harlow, R. (1994). Social intelligence and personality: Flexible life-task pursuit. In R. J. Sternberg & P. Ruzgis (Eds.), *Personality and intelligence* (pp. 137–168). New York: Cambridge University Press.

Cantor, N., & Kihlstrom, J. F. (1987). *Personality and social intelligence.* Englewood Cliffs, NJ: Prentice Hall.

Caporael, L. R. (1997). The evolution of truly social cognition: The core configurations model. *Personality and Social Psychology Review, 1,* 276–298.

Capps, J. P. (1984). *Mathematics laboratory and personalized system of instruction: A workshop presentation.* Somerville, NJ: Somerset County College. (ERIC Document Reproduction Service No. 246 969)

Carlo, G., Eisenberg, N., Troyer, D., Switzer, G., & Speer, A. L. (1991). The altruistic personality: In what contexts is it apparent? *Journal of Personality and Social Psychology, 61,* 450–458.

Carlo, G., Koller, S. H., Eisenberg, N., Da Silva, M. S., & Frohlich, C. B. (1996). A cross-national study on the relations among prosocial moral reasoning, gender role orientations, and prosocial behaviors. *Developmental Psychology, 32,* 231–240.

Carlson, M., Charlin, V., & Miller, N. (1988). Positive mood and helping behavior: A test of six hypotheses. *Journal of Personality and Social Psychology, 55,* 211–229.

Carnelley, K. B., Pietromonaco, P. R., & Jaffe, K. (1994). Depression, working models of others, and relationship functioning. *Journal of Personality and Social Psychology, 66,* 127–140.

Carns, M. R., & Carns, A. W. (1998). A review of the professional literature concerning the consistency of the definition and application of Adlerian encouragement. *Journal of Individual Psychology, 54,* 72–89.

Carr, J. E., & Tan, E. K. (1976) In search of the true amok: Amok as viewed within the Malay culture. *American Journal of Psychiatry, 133,* 1295–1299.

Carroll, J. B. (1993). *Human cognitive abilities: A survey of factor analytic studies.* New York: Cambridge University Press.

Carroll, L. (1989). A comparative study of narcissism, gender, and sex-role orientation among bodybuilders, athletes, and psychology students. *Psychological Reports, 64,* 999–1006.

Carter, C. S. (1992). Oxytocin and sexual behavior. *Neuroscience and Biobehavioral Reviews, 16,* 131–144.

Caruso, D. R., Mayer, J. D., & Salovey, P. (2002). Relation of an ability measure of emotional intelligence to personality. *Journal of Personality Assessment, 79,* 306–320.

Carver, C. S., Blaney, P. H., & Scheier, M. F. (1979). Reassertion and giving up: The interactive role of self-directed attention and outcome expectancy. *Journal of Personality and Social Psychology, 10,* 1859–1870.

Carver, C. S., & Scheier, M. F. (1981). *Attention and self-regulation: A control-theory approach to human behavior.* New York: Springer-Verlag.

Carver, C. S., & Scheier, M. F. (1982). Control theory: A useful conceptual framework for personality-social, clinical and health psychology. *Psychological Bulletin, 92,* 111–135.

Carver, C. S., & Scheier, M. F. (1990). Origins and functions of positive and negative affect: A control-process view. *Psychological Review, 97,* 19–35.

Carver, C. S., & White, T. L. (1994). Behavioral inhibition, behavioral activation, and affective responses to impending reward and punishment: The BIS/BAS Scales. *Journal of Personality and Social Psychology, 67,* 319–333.

Casey, M. (2001). *A guide to living in the truth: Saint Benedict's teaching on humility.* Liguori, MO: Liguori/Triumph.

Caspi, A., & Bem, D. J. (1990). Personality continuity and change across the life course. In L. A. Pervin (Ed.), *Handbook of personality: Theory and research* (pp. 549–575). New York: Guilford Press.

Cassandro, V. J., & Simonton, D. K. (2003). Creativity and genius. In C. L. M. Keyes & J. Haidt (Eds.), *Flourishing: Positive psychology and the life well-lived* (pp. 163–183). Washington, DC: American Psychological Association.

Cassey, W., & Burton, R. (1982). Training children to be consistently honest through verbal self-instructions. *Child Development, 53,* 911–919.

Catalano, R. F., Berglund, M. L., Ryan, J. A. M., Lonczak, H. S., & Hawkins, J. D. (1999). *Positive youth development in the United States: Research findings on evaluations of positive youth development programs.* Washington, DC: U.S. Department of Health and Human Services.

Cattell, R. B. (1943). The measurement of adult intelligence. *Psychological Bulletin, 40,* 153–193.

Cavanagh, G. F., & Moberg, D. J. (1999). The virtue of courage within the organization. *Research in Ethical Issues in Organizations, 1,* 1–25.

Cavendish, J. (2000). Church-based community activism: A comparison of Black and White Catholic congregations. *Journal for the Scientific Study of Religion, 39,* 371–384.

Cawley, M. J., Martin, J. E., & Johnson, J. A. (2000). A virtues approach to personality. *Personality and Individual Differences, 28,* 997–1013.

Chaleff, I. (1996). Effective followership. *Executive Excellence, 13*(4), 16–18.

Chamberlain, K., & Zika, S. (1992). Religiosity, meaning in life, and psychological well-being. In K. Chamberlain & S. Zika (Eds.), *Religion and mental health* (pp. 138–148). New York: Oxford University Press.

Chang, E. C. (Ed.) (2001). *Optimism and pessimism: Implications for theory, research, and practice.* Washington, DC: American Psychological Association.

Chapman, A. J., & Foot, H. C. (Eds.). (1977). *It's a funny thing, humour.* Oxford, England: Pergamon.

Chapman, C., Nolin, M., & Kline, K. (1997). *Student interest in national news and its relation to school courses (NCES 97–970).* Washington, DC: U.S. Department of Education, National Center for Education Statistics.

Charles, D. (1984). *Aristotle's philosophy of action.* London: Duckworth.

Cheng, D. H. (2000). *On Lao Tzu.* Belmont, CA: Wadsworth.

Cherkas, L., Hochberg, F., MacGregor, A. J., Snieder, H., & Spector, T. D. (2000). Happy families: A twin study of humour. *Twin Research, 3,* 17–22.

Cherniss, C., & Goleman, D. (Eds.). (2001). *The emotionally intelligent workplace: How to select for, measure, and improve emotional intelligence in individuals, groups, and organizations.* San Francisco: Jossey-Bass.

Chernow, R. (1998). *Titan: The life of John D. Rockefeller, Sr.* New York: Random House.

Chessick, R. (1996). Heidegger's "authenticity" in the psychotherapy of adolescents. *American Journal of Psychotherapy, 50,* 208–216.

Chesterton, G. K. (1908). *Orthodoxy.* New York: John Lane.

Chesterton, G. K. (1936). *The autobiography of G. K. Chesterton.* New York: Sheed & Ward.

Chodron, P. (1991). *The wisdom of no escape and the path of loving-kindness.* Boston: Shambhala.

Chodron, P. (2001). *The places that scare us.* Boston: Shambhala.

Chou, K. (1996). The Rushton, Chrisjohn, and Fekken Self-Report Altruism Scale: A Chinese translation. *Personality and Individual Differences, 21,* 297–298.

Church, A. T., & Lonner, W. J. (1998). The cross-cultural perspective in the study of personality: Rationale and current research. *Journal of Cross-Cultural Psychology, 29*, 32–62.

Cialdini, R. B. (1991). Altruism or egoism? That is (still) the question. *Psychological Inquiry, 2*, 124–126.

Cialdini, R. B., Brown, S. L., Lewis, B. P., Luce, C., & Neuberg, S. L. (1997). Reinterpreting the empathy-altruism relationship: When one into one equals oneness. *Journal of Personality and Social Psychology, 73*, 481–494.

Cialdini, R. B., Schaller, M., Houlihan, D., Arps, K., Fultz, J., & Beaman, A. L. (1987). Empathy-based helping: Is it selflessly or selfishly motivated? *Journal of Personality and Social Psychology, 52*, 749–758.

Ciarrochi, J. V., Chan, A. Y., & Caputi, P. (2000). A critical evaluation of the emotional intelligence concept. *Personality and Individual Differences, 28*, 539–561.

Cicero, M. T. (1949). *De inventione: De optimo genere oratorum* (H. M. Hubbell, Trans.). Cambridge, MA: Harvard University Press.

Clark, C., Worthington, E., & Danser, D. (1988). The transmission of religious beliefs and practices from parents to firstborn early adolescent sons. *Journal of Marriage and the Family, 50*, 463–472.

Clarke, J. J. (2000). *The Tao of the West: Western transformations of Taoist thought.* New York: Routledge.

Clarke-Stewart, K. A., Friedman, S., & Koch, J. (1985). *Child development: A topical approach.* New York: Wiley.

Clary, E. G., & Snyder, M. (1999). The motivations to volunteer: Theoretical and practical considerations. *Current Directions in Psychological Science, 8*, 156–159.

Clayton, V. P. (1982). Wisdom and intelligence: The nature and function of knowledge in the later years. *International Journal of Aging and Human Development, 15*, 315–321.

Clayton, V. P., & Birren, J. E. (1980). The development of wisdom across the life span: A reexamination of an ancient topic. In P. B. Baltes & O. G. Brim (Eds.), *Life-span development and behavior* (Vol. 3, pp. 103–135). San Diego, CA: Academic Press.

Cleary, T. (Ed. & Trans.). (1991). *Vitality, energy, spirit: A taoist sourcebook.* Boston: Shambhala.

Cleary, T. (1992). Introduction. In T. Cleary (Trans.), *The essential Confucius* (pp. 1–11). New York: HarperCollins.

Clemens, C. (1931). *My father Mark Twain.* New York: Harper.

Cloninger, C. R., Przybeck, T. R., & Svrakic, D. M. (1991). The Tridimensional Personality Questionnaire: US normative data. *Psychological Reports, 69*, 1047–1057.

Cloninger, C. R., Przybeck, T. R., Svrakic, D. M., & Wetzel, R. D. (1994). *The Temperament and Character Inventory (TCI): A guide to its development and use.* St. Louis, MO: Center for Psychobiology of Personality.

Clopton, N. A., & Sorell, G. T. (1993). Gender differences in moral reasoning: Stable or situational? *Psychology of Women Quarterly, 17,* 85–101.

Cobb, C. D., & Mayer, J. D. (2000). Emotional intelligence: What the research says. *Educational Leadership, 58,* 14–18.

Cognition and Technology Group at Vanderbilt. (1990). Anchored instruction and its relationship to situated cognition. *Educational Researcher, 19,* 2–10.

Cognition and Technology Group at Vanderbilt. (1991). Technology and the design of generative learning environments. *Educational Technology, 31,* 34–40.

Cohen, J. (1992). A power primer. *Psychological Bulletin, 112,* 155–159.

Cohen, J. (1999). *Educating minds and hearts: Social emotional learning and the passage into adolescence.* New York: Teachers College Press.

Cohen, J. (2001). *Caring classrooms/intelligent schools: The social emotional education of young children.* New York: Teachers College Press.

Coie, J. D. (1974). An evaluation of the cross-situational stability of children's curiosity. *Journal of Personality, 42,* 93–117.

Coie, J. D., Watt, N. F., West, S. G., Hawkins, J. D., Asarnow, J. R., Markman, H. J., et al. (1993). The science of prevention: A conceptual framework and some directions for a national research program. *American Psychologist, 48,* 1013–1022.

Colby, A., & Damon, W. (1992). *Some do care: Contemporary lives of moral commitment.* New York: Free Press.

Colby, A., & Kohlberg, L. (1987). *The measurement of moral judgment* (Vols. 1 & 2). New York: Cambridge University Press.

Colby, A., Kohlberg, L., Gibbs, J. C., & Lieberman, M. (1983). A longitudinal study of moral judgment. *Monographs of the Society for Research in Child Development, 48,* 1–124.

Cole, E. R., & Stewart, A. J. (1996). Meanings of political participation among Black and White women: Political identity and social responsibility. *Journal of Personality and Social Psychology, 71,* 130–140.

Coles, R. (1964). *Children of crisis: A study of courage and fear.* Boston: Little, Brown.

Colin, V. L. (1996). *Human attachment.* New York: McGraw-Hill.

Collins, J. (2001). Level five leadership: The triumph of humility and fierce resolve. *Harvard Business Review, 79,* 66–76.

Collins, J. D. (1962). *The lure of wisdom.* Milwaukee, WI: Marquette University Press.

Collins, N. L., & Read, S. J. (1990). Adult attachment, working models, and relationship quality in dating couples. *Journal of Personality and Social Psychology, 58,* 644–663.

Colvin, C. R., Block, J., & Funder, D. C. (1995). Overly positive self-evaluations and personality: Negative implications for mental health. *Journal of Personality and Social Psychology, 68,* 1152–1162.

Comte-Sponville, A. (2001). *A small treatise on the great virtues* (C. Temerson, Trans.). New York: Metropolitan Books.

Confucius. (1992). *Analects* (D. Hinton, Trans.). Washington, DC: Counterpoint.

Conger, J. A. (1990). The dark side of leadership. *Organizational Dynamics, 19,* 44–55.

Conger, J. A. (1993). The brave new world of leadership training. *Organizational Dynamics, 21,* 46–58.

Conger, J. A., & Kanungo, R. N. (1987). Toward a behavioral theory of charismatic leadership in organizational settings. *Academy of Management Review, 12,* 637–647.

Conger, J. A., & Kanungo, R. N. (1988). Behavioral dimensions of charismatic leadership. In J. A. Conger & R. N. Kanungo (Eds.), *Charismatic leadership: The elusive factor in organizational effectiveness* (pp. 78–97). San Francisco: Jossey-Bass.

Conger, J. A., & Kanungo, R. N. (1992). Perceived behavioural attributes of charismatic leadership. *Canadian Journal of Behavioural Science, 24,* 86–102.

Conley, T. D., Jadack, R. A., & Hyde, J. S. (1997). Moral dilemmas, moral reasoning, and genital herpes. *Journal of Sex Research, 34,* 256–266.

Connell, R. W. (1995). *Masculinities.* Berkeley: University of California Press.

Connelly, M. S., Gilbert, J. A., Zaccaro, S. J., Threlfall, K. V., Marks, M. A., &, Mumford, M. D. (2000). Cognitive and temperament predictors of organizational leadership. *Leadership Quarterly, 11,* 65–86.

Conway, K. (1985–1986). Coping with the stress of medical problems among Black and White elderly. *International Journal of Aging and Human Development, 21,* 39–48.

Cook, M. L., & Peterson, C. (1986). Depressive irrationality. *Cognitive Therapy and Research, 10,* 293–298.

Cooper, C. R., Baker, H., Polichar, D., & Welsh, M. (1992, March). *Ethnic perspectives on individuality and connectedness in adolescents' relationships with families and peers.* Paper presented at the meeting of the Society for Research in Child Development, Kansas City, MO.

Cooper, C. R., & Grotevant, H. D. (1989, April). *Individuality and connectedness in the family and adolescents' self and relational competence.* Paper presented at the meeting of the Society for Research in Child Development, Kansas City, MO.

Costa, P. T., & McCrae, R. R. (1990). Personality disorders and the five-factor model of personality. *Journal of Personality Disorders, 4,* 362–371.

Costa, P. T., & McCrae, R. R. (1992). *The revised NEO personality inventory (NEO-PI-R) and NEO five factor inventory (NEO-FFI) professional manual.* Odessa, FL: Psychological Assessment Resources.

Costa, P. T., McCrae, R. R., & Dye, D. A. (1991). Facet scales for agreeableness and conscientiousness: A revision of the NEO personality inventory. *Personality and Individual Differences, 12,* 887–898.

Courtenay, M. E. (1938). Persistence of leadership. *School Review, 46,* 97–107.

Cousins, N. (1981). *The anatomy of an illness.* New York: Norton.

Covington, M. V. (1984). The self-worth theory of achievement motivation: Findings and implications. *Elementary School Journal, 85,* 5–20.

Covington, M. V. (1999). Caring about learning: The nature and nurturing of subject matter appreciation. *Educational Psychologist, 34,* 127–136.

Covington, M. V., Crutchfield, R. S., Davies, L., & Olton, R. M. (1974). *The productive thinking progam: A course in learning to think.* Columbus, OH: Merrill.

Cox, C. M. (1926). *Genetic studies of genius: Vol. 2: The early mental traits of three hundred geniuses.* Stanford, CA: Stanford University Press.

Cox, D., Hallam, R., O'Connor, K., & Rachman, S. (1983). An experimental analysis of fearlessness and courage. *British Journal of Psychology, 74,* 107–117.

Cox, S. P. (2000). *Leader character: A model of personality and moral development.* Unpublished doctoral dissertation, University of Tulsa, OK.

Craik, K. H., Lampert, M. D., & Nelson, A. J. (1996). Sense of humor and styles of everyday humorous conduct. *Humor, 9,* 273–302.

Craik, K. H., & Ware, A. P. (1998). Humor and personality in everyday life. In W. Ruch (Ed.), *The sense of humor: Explorations of a personality characteristic* (pp. 63–94). New York: Mouton de Gruyter.

Crammond, B. (1994). The Torrance Tests of Creative Thinking: From design through establishment of predictive validity. In R. F. Subotnik & K. D. Arnold (Eds.), *Beyond Terman: Contemporary longitudinal studies of giftedness and talent* (pp. 229–254). Norwood, NJ: Ablex.

Craske, M. L. (1985). Improving persistence through observational learning and attribution training. *British Journal of Educational Psychology, 55,* 138–147.

Crocker, J., & Wolfe, C. T. (2001). Contingencies of self-worth. *Psychological Review, 108,* 593–623.

Cronbach, L. J. (1960). *Essentials of psychological testing* (2nd ed.). New York: Harper & Row.

Cross, S. E., Kanagawa, C., Markus, H. R., & Kitayama, S. (1995). *Cultural variation in self-concept.* Unpublished manuscript, Iowa State University, Ames.

Crowell, J. A., Fraley, R. C., & Shaver, P. R. (1999). Measurement of individual differences in adolescent and adult attachment. In J. Cassidy & P. R. Shaver (Eds.), *Handbook of attachment: Theory, research, and clinical applications* (pp. 434–468). New York: Guilford Press.

Crowne, D. P., & Marlowe, D. (1960). A new scale of social desirability independent of psychopathology. *Journal of Consulting Psychology, 24,* 349–354.

Crowne, D. P., & Marlowe, D. (1964). *The approval motive: Studies in evaluative dependence.* New York: Wiley.

Csikszentmihalyi, M. (1978). Intrinsic rewards and emergent motivation. In M. R. Lepper & D. Greene (Eds.), *The hidden costs of reward* (pp. 205–216). Hillsdale, NJ: Erlbaum.

Csikszentmihalyi, M. (1990). *Flow: The psychology of optimal experience.* New York: Harper & Row.

Csikszentmihalyi, M., Rathunde, K., & Whalen, S. (1993). *Talented teenagers: The roots of success and failure.* New York: Cambridge University Press.

Cynn, V. E. (1992). Persistence and problem-solving skills in young male alcoholics. *Journal of Studies on Alcohol, 53,* 57–62.

Dahlsgaard, K., Davis, D., Peterson, C., & Seligman, M. E. P. (2002, October). *Is virtue more than its own reward?* Poster presented at the First Positive Psychology International Summit, Washington, DC.

Damasio, A. (1999). *The feeling of what happens: Body and emotion in the making of consciousness.* San Diego, CA: Harcourt.

Damon, W. (1977). *The social world of the child.* San Francisco: Jossey-Bass.

Damon, W. (1988). *The moral child: Nurturing children's natural moral growth.* New York: Free Press.

Danner, D. D., Snowdon, D. A., & Friesen, W. V. (2001). Positive emotions in early life and longevity: Findings from the nun study. *Journal of Personality and Social Psychology, 80,* 804–813.

Dansereau, F., Graen, G., & Haga, W. J. (1975). A vertical dyad linkage approach to leadership within formal organizations: A longitudinal investigation of the role making process. *Organizational Behavior and Human Performance, 13,* 46–78.

Darby, B. W., & Schlenker, B. R. (1982). Children's reactions to apologies. *Journal of Personality and Social Psychology, 43,* 742–753.

Darley, J. M., & Latané, B. (1968). Bystander intervention in emergencies: Diffusion of responsibility. *Journal of Personality and Social Psychology, 8,* 377–383.

Darwin, C. (1965). *The expression of the emotions in man and animals.* Chicago: University of Chicago Press. (Original work published 1872)

Dasho, S., Lewis, C., & Watson, M. (2001). Fostering emotional intelligence in the classroom and school: Strategies from the Child Development Project. In J. Cohen (Ed.), *Caring classrooms/intelligent schools: The social emotional education of young children* (pp. 87–107). New York: Teachers College Press.

Davids, A., & Sidman, J. (1962). A pilot study: Impulsivity, time orientation, and delayed gratification in future scientists and in under-achieving high school students. *Exceptional Children, 29,* 170–174.

Davies, C. (1998). *Jokes and their relation to society.* New York: Mouton de Gruyter.

Davies, M., Stankov, L., & Roberts, R. D. (1998). Emotional intelligence: In search of an elusive construct. *Journal of Personality and Social Psychology, 75,* 989–1015.

Davis, G. A. (1975). In frumious pursuit of the creative person. *Journal of Creative Behavior, 9,* 75–87.

Davis, M. H., Luce, C., & Kraus, S. J. (1994). The heritability of characteristics associated with dispositional empathy. *Journal of Personality, 62,* 369–391.

Dawes, R. M., van de Kragt, A. J. C., & Orbell, J. (1990). Cooperation for the benefit of us—Not me, or my conscience. In J. J. Mansbridge (Ed.), *Beyond self-interest* (pp. 97–110). Chicago: University of Chicago Press.

Dawkins, R. (1976). *The selfish gene.* New York: Oxford University Press.

Dawson, R. (1982). *Confucius.* New York: Hill and Wang.

Day, D. V., & Lord, R. G. (1988). Executive leadership and organizational performance: Suggestions for a new theory and methodology. *Journal of Management, 14,* 453–464.

Day, H. I. (1971). The measurement of specific curiosity. In H. I. Day, D. E. Berlyne, & D. E. Hunt (Eds.), *Intrinsic motivation: A new direction in education* (pp. 99–112). New York: Holt, Rinehart & Winston.

de Bono, E. (1973). *CoRT thinking.* Blanford, England: Direct Educational Services.

De Kremer, D., & Van Lange, P. A. M. (2001). Why prosocials exhibit greater cooperation than proselfs: The roles of social responsibility and reciprocity. *European Journal of Personality, 15,* S5–S18.

De Rougement, D. (1940). *Love in the Western world.* New York: Harcourt.

de Tocqueville, A. (1848/1966). *Democracy in America.* New York: Harper & Row.

de Waal, F. (2000). Primates—A natural heritage of conflict resolution. *Science, 289,* 586–590.

de Waal, F., & Berger, M. L. (2000). Payment for labour in monkeys. *Nature, 404,* 563.

Deaux, K., White, L., & Farris, E. (1975). Skill versus luck: Field and laboratory studies of male and female preferences. *Journal of Personality and Social Psychology, 32,* 629–636.

Deci, E. L. (1971). Effects of externally mediated rewards on intrinsic motivation. *Journal of Personality and Social Psychology, 18,* 105–115.

Deci, E. L. (1975). *Intrinsic motivation.* New York: Plenum Press.

Deci, E. L. (1992). The relation of interest to the motivation of behavior: A self-determination theory perspective. In K. A. Renninger, S. Hidi, & A. Krapp (Eds.), *The role of interest in learning and development* (pp. 43–70). Hillsdale, NJ: Erlbaum.

Deci, E. L., & Ryan, R. M. (1985a). The general causality orientations scale: Self-determination in personality. *Journal of Research in Personality, 19,* 109–134.

Deci, E. L., & Ryan, R. M. (1985b). *Intrinsic motivation and self-determination in human behavior.* New York: Plenum Press.

Deci, E. L., & Ryan, R. M. (1991). A motivational approach to self: Integration in personality. In R. Dienstbier (Ed.), *Nebraska symposium on motivation: Vol. 38. Perspectives on motivation* (pp. 237–288). Lincoln: University of Nebraska Press.

Deci, E. L., & Ryan, R. M. (1992). The initiation and regulation of intrinsically motivated learning and achievement. In A. K. Boggiano & T. S. Pittman (Eds.), *Achievement and motivation: A social-developmental perspective* (pp. 9–36). Cambridge, England: Cambridge University Press.

Deci, E. L., & Ryan, R. M. (2000). The "what" and "why" of goal pursuits: Human needs and the self-determination of behavior. *Psychological Inquiry, 4,* 227–268.

Deci, E. L., & Ryan, R. M. (2001). *Home page for self-determination theory.* Document available at http://www.scp.rochester.edu/SDT/index.html.

Deckers, L. (1998). Influence of mood on humor. In W. Ruch (Ed.), *The sense of humor: Explorations of a personality characteristic* (pp. 309–328). New York: Mouton de Gruyter.

Delli Carpini, M. X., & Keeter, S. (1996). *What Americans know about politics and why it matters.* New Haven, CT: Yale University Press.

DeMartini, J. R. (1983). Social movement participation: Political socialization, generational consciousness, and lasting effects. *Social Forces, 64,* 1–16.

DeMulder, E. K., & Radke-Yarrow, M. (1991). Attachment with affectively ill and well mothers: Concurrent behavioral correlates. *Development and Psychopathology, 3,* 227–242.

den Ouden, M. D., & Russell, G. W. (1997). Sympathy and altruism in response to disasters: A Dutch and Canadian comparison. *Social Behavior and Personality, 25,* 241–248.

Depue, R. A. (1996). A neurobiological framework for the structure of personality and emotion: Implications for personality disorders. In J. F. Clarkin & M. F. Lenzenweger (Ed.), *Major theories of personality disorder* (pp. 347–391). New York: Guilford Press.

Depue, R. A., & Collins, P. F. (1999). Neurobiology of the structure of personality: Dopamine, facilitation of incentive motivation, and extraversion. *Behavioral and Brain Sciences, 22,* 491–569.

Deutsch, M. (1961). Courage as a concept in social psychology. *Journal of Social Psychology, 55,* 49–58.

Dewey, J. (1913). *Interest and effort in education.* Boston: Riverside Press.

Dewey, J. (1922/1998). *Human nature and conduct.* Carbondale: Southern Illinois University Press.

Dewey, J. (1933). *How we think: A restatement of the relation of reflective thinking to the educative process.* Boston: Heath.

DeWolfe, T. E., & Jackson, L. A. (1984). Birds of a brighter feather: Level of moral reasoning and attitude similarity as determinants of interpersonal attraction. *Psychological Reports, 54,* 303–308.

The Dhammapada (J. R. Carter & M. Palihawadana, Trans.). (2000). New York: Oxford University Press.

Digman, J. M. (1989). Five robust personality dimensions: Development, stability, and utility. *Journal of Personality, 57,* 195–214.

Dion, K., Berscheid, E., & Walster, E. (1972). What is beautiful is good. *Journal of Personality and Social Psychology, 24,* 285–290.

DiPaula, A., & Campbell, J. D. (2002). Self-esteem and persistence in the face of failure. *Journal of Personality and Social Psychology, 83,* 711–724.

Do-Dinh, P. (1969). *Confucius and Chinese humanism* (C. L. Markmann, Trans.). New York: Funk and Wagnalls.

Donahue, M., & Benson, P. (1995). Religion and the well-being of adolescents. *Journal of Social Issues, 51*(2), 145–160.

Dorsel, T. N., & Salinksky, D. M. (1990). Enhancing willingness to practice golf through use of mastery approach. *Perceptual and Motor Skills, 70,* 415–418.

Draper, T. W. (1981). Praise, reproof and persistence in preadolescent girls. *Journal of Early Adolescence, 1,* 407–411.

Drucker, P. M., Drucker, D. B., Litto, T., & Stevens, R. (1998). Relation of task difficulty to persistence. *Perceptual and Motor Skills, 86,* 787–794.

Dulawa, S. C., Grandy, D. K., Low, M. J., Paulus, M. P., & Mark, A. (1999). Dopamine D4 receptor-knock-out mice exhibit reduced exploration of novel stimuli. *Journal of Neuroscience, 19,* 9550–9556.

Dull, V., & Skokan, L. (1995). A cognitive model of religion's influence on health. *Journal of Social Issues, 51*(2), 49–64.

Dunham, C., & Bengston, V. (1992). The long-term effects of political activism on intergenerational relations. *Youth and Society, 24,* 31–51.

Dunlop, D. M. (1971). *Arab civilization to A.D. 1500.* London: Longman Press.

Dunn, J., & Munn, P. (1986). Siblings and the development of prosocial behaviour. *Journal of Behavioral Development, 93,* 265–284.

Durkheim, É. (1915). *The elementary forms of religious life.* New York: Free Press.

Durlak, J. A., & Wells, A. M. (1997). Primary prevention mental health programs for children and adolescents: A meta-analytic review. *American Journal of Community Psychology, 25,* 115–152.

Dutt, R. C. (1983). *Buddhism and Buddhist civilisation in India.* Delhi, India: Seema Publications.

Dutton, D. G., Saunders, K., Starzomski, A., & Bartholomew, K. (1994). Intimacy-anger and insecure attachment as precursors of abuse in intimate relationships. *Journal of Applied Social Psychology, 24,* 1367–1386.

Duval, T. S., Duval, V. H., & Mulilis, J. P. (1992). Effects of self-focus, discrepancy between self and standard, and outcome expectancy favorability on the tendency to match self to standard or to withdraw. *Journal of Personality and Social Psychology, 62,* 340–348.

Dweck, C. S. (1975). The role of expectations and attributions in the alleviation of learned helplessness. *Journal of Personality and Social Psychology, 31,* 674–685.

Dweck, C. S. (1986). Motivational processes affecting learning. *American Psychologist, 41,* 1040–1048.

Dweck, C. S., Goetz, T. E., & Strauss, N. L. (1980). Sex differences in learned helplessness: IV. An experimental and naturalistic study of failure generalization and its mediators. *Journal of Personality and Social Psychology, 38,* 441–452.

Dweck, C. S., & Leggett, E. L. (1988). A social-cognitive approach to motivation and personality. *Psychological Review, 95,* 256–273.

Dweck, C. S., & Reppucci, N. D. (1973). Learned helplessness and reinforcement responsibility in children. *Journal of Personality and Social Psychology, 25,* 109–116.

Dwight, S., & Alliger, G. (1997). Reactions to overt integrity test items. *Educational and Psychological Measurement, 57,* 937–948.

D'Zurilla, T., & Goldfried, M. (1971). Problem solving and behavior modification. *Journal of Abnormal Psychology, 78,* 107–126.

Eagly, A. H., & Crowley, M. (1986). Gender and helping behavior: A meta-analytic review of the social psychological literature. *Psychological Bulletin, 100*, 282–308.

Eagly, A. H., & Johnson, B. T. (1990). Gender and leadership style: A meta-analysis. *Psychological Bulletin, 108*, 233–256.

Eagly, A. H., & Karau, S. J. (1991). Gender and the emergence of leaders. *Journal of Personality and Social Psychology, 60*, 685–710.

Eagly, A. H., Karau, S. J., & Makhijani, M. G. (1995). Gender and the effectiveness of leaders: A meta-analysis. *Psychological Bulletin, 117*, 125–145.

Easterbrook, G. (2001, March 5). I'm OK, you're OK. *The New Republic*, 20–23.

Easterlin, R. A., & Crimmins, E. M. (1991). Private materialism, personal self-fulfillment, family life, and public interest. *Public Opinion Quarterly, 55*, 499–533.

Eberle, R. E. (1977). *SCAMPER*. Buffalo, NY: DOK.

Ebstein, R. P., & Belmaker, R. H. (1997). Saga of an adventure gene: Novelty seeking, substance abuse and the dopamine D4 receptor exon III repeat polymorphism. *Molecular Psychiatry, 2*, 381–384.

Eccles, J. S. (1984). Sex differences in achievement patterns. In T. B. Sonderegger (Ed.), *Nebraska symposium on motivation: Psychology and gender* (Vol. 32, pp. 97–132). Lincoln: University of Nebraska Press.

Eccles, J. S. (1994). Understanding women's educational and occupational choices. *Psychology of Women Quarterly, 18*, 585–609.

Eccles, J. S., & Gootman, J. A. (Eds.). (2002). *Community programs to promote youth development*. Washington, DC: National Academy Press.

Eccles, J. S., & Jacobs, J. E. (2000). Parents, task values, and real-life achievement-related choices. In C. Sansone & J. M. Harackiewicz (Eds.), *Intrinsic and extrinsic motivation: The search for optimal motivation and performance* (pp. 408–443). New York: Academic Press.

Eibl-Eibesfeldt, I. (1975). *Ethology: The biology of behavior*. New York: Holt, Rinehart & Winston.

Eisenberg, N. (1986). *Altruistic emotion, cognition, and behavior*. Hillsdale, NJ: Erlbaum.

Eisenberg, N., Fabes, R. A., Guthrie, I. K., & Reiser, M. (2000). Dispositional emotionality and regulation: Their role in predicting quality of social functioning. *Journal of Personality and Social Psychology, 78*, 136–157.

Eisenberg, N., Fabes, R. A., Shepard, S. A., Murphy, B. C., Guthrie, I. K., Jones, S., et al. (1997). Contemporaneous and longitudinal prediction of children's social functioning from regulation and emotionality. *Child Development, 68*, 642–664.

Eisenberg, N., Guthrie, I. K., Cumberland, A., Murphy, B. C., Shepard, S. A., Zhou, Q., et al. (2002). Prosocial development in early adulthood: A longitudinal study. *Journal of Personality and Social Psychology, 82*, 993–1006.

Eisenberg, N., Miller, P. A., Schaller, M., Fabes, R. A., Fultz, J., Shell, R., et al. (1989). The role of sympathy and altruistic personality traits in helping: A reexamination. *Journal of Personality, 57*, 41–67.

Eisenberg, N., Shell, R., Paternack, J., Lennon, R., Beller, R., & Mathy, R. M. (1987). Prosocial development in middle childhood: A longitudinal study. *Developmental Psychology, 23,* 712–718.

Eisenberger, R. (1992). Learned industriousness. *Psychological Review, 99,* 248–267.

Eisenberger, R., & Adornetto, M. (1986). Generalized self-control of delay and effort. *Journal of Personality and Social Psychology, 51,* 1020–1031.

Eisenberger, R., Carlson, J., & Frank, M. (1979). Transfer of persistence to the acquisition of a new behaviour. *Quarterly Journal of Experimental Psychology, 31,* 691–700.

Eisenberger, R., Kuhlman, D. M., & Cotterell, N. (1992). Effects of social values, effort training, and goal structure on task persistence. *Journal of Research in Personality, 26,* 258–272.

Eisenberger, R., & Leonard, J. M. (1980). Effects of conceptual task difficulty on generalized persistence. *American Journal of Psychology, 93,* 285–298.

Eisenberger, R., Mitchell, M., & Masterson, F. A. (1985). Effort training increases generalized self-control. *Journal of Personality and Social Psychology, 49,* 1294–1301.

Eisenberger, R., Myers, A. K., & Kaplan, R. M. (1973). Persistent deprivation-shift effect opposite in direction to incentive contrast. *Journal of Experimental Psychology, 99,* 400–404.

Eisenberger, R., Park, D. C., & Frank, M. (1976). Learned industriousness and social reinforcement. *Journal of Personality and Social Psychology, 33,* 227–232.

Eisenberger, R., & Selbst, M. (1994). Does reward increase or decrease creativity? *Journal of Personality and Social Psychology, 66,* 1116–1127.

Eisler, R. (1999). Spiritual courage. *Tikkun, 14,* 15–18.

Ekman, P. (1992). An argument for basic emotions. *Cognition and Emotion, 6,* 169–200.

Elias, M. J. (1997). *Promoting social and emotional learning: Guidelines for educators.* Alexandria, VA: Association for Supervision and Curriculum Development.

Eliot, T. S. (1927). *Shakespeare and the stoicism of Seneca.* London: Oxford University Press.

Elkins, D., Hedstrom, L., Hughes, L., Leaf, J., & Saunders, C. (1988). Toward a humanistic-phenomenological spirituality: Definition, description and measurement. *Journal of Humanistic Psychology, 28,* 5–18.

Elliot, A. J., & Church, M. A. (1997). A hierarchical model of approach and avoidance achievement motivation. *Journal of Personality and Social Psychology, 72,* 218–232.

Elliot, A. J., & McGregor, H. M. (2001). A 2×2 achievement goal framework. *Journal of Personality and Social Psychology, 80,* 501–519.

Elliot, A. J., & Sheldon, K. M. (1998). Avoidance personal goals and personality-illness relationships. *Journal of Personality and Social Psychology, 75,* 1282–1299.

Ellis, A. (1962). *Reason and emotion in psychotherapy*. New York: Stuart.

Ellison, C. (1983). Spiritual well-being: Conceptualization and measurement. *Journal of Psychology and Theology, 11*, 330–340.

Ellison, C. (1992). Are religious people nice people? Evidence from the national survey on Black Americans. *Social Forces, 71*, 411–430.

Ellison, C., Gay, D., & Glass, T. (1989). Does religious commitment contribute to individual life satisfaction? *Social Forces, 68*, 100–123.

Elshtain, J. B. (1995). *Democracy on trial*. New York: Basic Books.

Emmons, R. A. (1984). Factor analysis and construct validity of the Narcissistic Personality Inventory. *Journal of Personality Assessment, 48*, 291–300.

Emmons, R. A. (2003). Acts of gratitude in organizations. In K. S. Cameron, J. E. Dutton, & R. E. Quinn (Eds.), *Positive organizational scholarship: Foundations of a new discipline* (pp. 81–93). San Francisco: Berrett-Koehler.

Emmons, R. A., & Crumpler, C. A. (2000). Gratitude as human strength: Appraising the evidence. *Journal of Social and Clinical Psychology, 19*, 56–69.

Emmons, R. A., & Hill, J. (2001). *Words of gratitude for the mind, body, and soul*. Radnor, PA: Templeton Foundation Press.

Emmons, R. A., & King, L. A. (1988). Conflict among personal strivings: Immediate and long-term implications for psychological and physical well-being. *Journal of Personality and Social Psychology, 54*, 1040–1048.

Emmons, R. A., & McCullough, M. E. (2003). Counting blessings versus burdens: An experimental investigation of gratitude and subjective well-being in daily life. *Journal of Personality and Social Psychology, 84*, 377–389.

Emmons, R. A., McCullough, M. E., & Tsang, J. (2003). The assessment of gratitude. In S. J. Lopez & C. R. Snyder (Eds.), *Positive psychology assessment: A handbook of models and measures* (pp. 327–341). Washington, DC: American Psychological Association.

Enright, R. D. (1994). Piaget on the moral development of forgiveness: Identity or reciprocity? *Human Development, 37*, 63–80.

Enright, R. D., & Coyle, C. T. (1998). Researching the process model of forgiveness within psychological interventions. In E. L. Worthington (Ed.), *Dimensions of forgiveness: Psychological research and theological perspectives* (pp. 139–161). Philadelphia: Templeton Foundation Press.

Enright, R. D., Gassin, L. A., & Wu, C. (1992). Forgiveness: A developmental view. *Journal of Moral Education, 21*, 99–114.

Enright, R. D., Santos, M. J. D., & Al-Mabuk, R. (1989). The adolescent as forgiver. *Journal of Adolescence, 12*, 99–110.

Epstein, S. (1973). The self-concept revisited: Or a theory of a theory. *American Psychologist, 28*, 404–416.

Epstein, S., Pacini, R., Denes-Raj, V., & Heier, H. (1996). Individual differences in intuitive-experiential and analytical-rational thinking styles. *Journal of Personality and Social Psychology, 71*, 390–405.

Erikson, E. H. (1956). The problem of ego identity. *Journal of the American Psychoanalytic Association, 4*, 56–121.

Erikson, E. H. (1963). *Childhood and society* (2nd ed.). New York: Norton.

Erikson, E. H. (1964). *Insight and responsibility.* New York: Norton.

Erikson, E. H. (1968). *Identity: Youth and crisis.* New York: Norton.

Erikson, E. H. (1982). *The life cycle completed.* New York: Norton.

Evans, P. D., & White, D. G. (1981). Towards an empirical definition of courage. *Behaviour Research and Therapy, 19,* 419–424.

Exline, J. J., Baumeister, R. F., Faber, J., & Holland, C. (2002). *Can admitting weakness be a strength? Seeing one's capability for a similar misdeed predicts forgiveness.* Unpublished manuscript, Case Western University, Cleveland, OH.

Exline, J. J., Bushman, B., Campbell, W. K., & Baumeister, R. F. (2002). *Psychological entitlement as a barrier to forgiveness.* Unpublished manuscript, Case Western University, Cleveland, OH.

Exline, J. J., Bushman, B., Faber, J., & Phillips, C. (2000, February). Pride gets in the way: Self-protection works against forgiveness. In J. J. Exline (Chair), *Ouch! Who said forgiveness was easy?* Symposium presented at the annual meeting of the Society for Personality and Social Psychology, Nashville, TN.

Exline, J. J., & Geyer, A. L. (in press). Perceptions of humility: A preliminary study. *Self and Identity.*

Exline, J. J., & Lobel, M. (1999). The perils of outperformance: Sensitivity about being the target of a threatening upward comparison. *Psychological Bulletin, 125,* 307–337.

Eysenck, H. (1988). Personality and scientific aesthetics. In F. H. Farley & R. W. Neperud (Eds.), *The foundations of aesthetics, art, and art education* (pp. 117–160). New York: Praeger.

Fagen, S. A., Long, N. J., & Stevens, D. J. (1975). *Teaching children self-control: Preventing emotional and learning problems in the elementary school.* Columbus, OH: Merrill.

Fagerberg, D. W. (1998). *The size of Chesterton's Catholicism.* South Bend, IN: University of Notre Dame Press.

Fakhry, M. (1983). *A history of Islamic philosophy* (2nd ed.). New York: Columbia University Press.

Farwell, L., & Wohlwend-Lloyd, R. (1998). Narcissistic processes: Optimistic expectations, favorable self-evaluations, and self-enhancing attributions. *Journal of Personality, 66,* 65–83.

Feagin, J. (1964). Prejudice and religious types: A focused study of southern Fundamentalists. *Journal for the Scientific Study of Religion, 4,* 3–13.

Feather, N. T. (1961). The relationship of persistence at a task to expectation of success and achievement-related motives. *Journal of Abnormal and Social Psychology, 63,* 552–561.

Feeney, J. A. (1999). Adult romantic attachment and couple relationships. In J. Cassidy & P. R. Shaver (Eds.), *Handbook of attachment: Theory, research, and clinical applications* (pp. 355–377). New York: Guilford Press.

Feeney, J. A., & Noller, P. (1990). Attachment style as a predictor of adult romantic relationships. *Journal of Personality and Social Psychology, 58,* 281–291.

Feeney, J. A., Noller, P., & Hanrahan, M. (1994). Assessing adult attachment: Developments in the conceptualization of security and insecurity. In M. B. Sperling & W. H. Berman (Eds.), *Attachment in adults: Clinical and developmental perspectives* (pp. 128–152). New York: Guilford Press.

Fehr, B., & Russell, J. A. (1991). The concept of love viewed from a prototype perspective. *Journal of Personality and Social Psychology, 60,* 425–438.

Feighner, J. P., Robins, E., Guze, S. B., Woodruff, R. A., Winokur, G., & Munoz, R. (1972). Diagnostic criteria for use in psychiatric research. *Archives of General Psychiatry, 26,* 57–63.

Feingold, A. (1992). Gender differences in mate selection preferences: A test of the parental investment model. *Psychological Bulletin, 112,* 125–139.

Feingold, A., & Mazzella, R. (1991). Psychometric intelligence and verbal humor ability. *Personality and Individual Differences, 12,* 427–435.

Feist, G. J. (1994). Personality and working style predictors of integrative complexity: A study of scientists' thinking about research and teaching. *Journal of Personality and Social Psychology, 67,* 474–484.

Feist, G. J. (1998). A meta-analysis of personality in scientific and artistic creativity. *Personality and Social Psychology Review, 2,* 290–309.

Feldman, D. H. (1993). Child prodigies: A distinctive form of giftedness. *Gifted Child Quarterly, 37,* 188–193.

Feldman-Barrett, L., & Salovey, P. (2002). *The wisdom in feeling: Psychological processes in emotional intelligence.* New York: Guilford Press.

Fendrich, J. M., & Lovoy, K. L. (1988). Back to the future: Adult political behavior of former student activists. *American Sociological Review, 53,* 780–784.

Ferrari, J. R. (1993). Procrastination and impulsivity: Two sides of a coin? In W. McCown, M. B. Shure, & J. Johnson (Eds.), *The impulsive client: Theory, research, and treatment* (pp. 265–276). Washington, DC: American Psychological Association.

Ferrari, J. R., Johnson, J. L., & McCown, W. (1995). *Procrastination and task avoidance: Theory, research, and treatment.* New York: Plenum Press.

Ferrari, J. R., & Tice, D. M. (2000). Procrastination as a self-handicap for men and women: A task-avoidance strategy in a laboratory setting. *Journal of Research in Personality, 34,* 73–83.

Festinger, L. (1957). *A theory of cognitive dissonance.* Evanston, IL: Row, Peterson.

Fetzer Institute/National Institute on Aging Workgroup. (1999). *Multidimensional measurement of religiousness/spirituality for use in health research.* Kalamazoo, MI: Fetzer Institute.

Fiedler, F. E. (1964). A contingency model of leadership effectiveness. In L. Berkowitz (Ed.), *Advances in experimental social psychology* (Vol. 1, pp. 149–190). New York: Academic Press.

Fiedler, F. E. (1971). Validation and extension of the contingency model of leadership effectiveness: A review of the empirical findings. *Psychological Bulletin, 76,* 128–148.

Fiedler, F. E., & Chemers, M. (1982). *Improving leader effectiveness: The leader match concept* (2nd ed.). New York: Wiley.

Fincham, F. D. (2000). The kiss of the porcupines: From attributing responsibility to forgiving. *Personal Relationships, 7*, 1–23.

Fincham, F. D., & Barling, J. (1979). Effects of alcohol on moral functioning in male social drinkers. *Journal of Genetic Psychology, 134*, 79–88.

Finfgeld, D. (1999). Courage as a process of pushing beyond the struggle. *Qualitative Health Research, 9*, 803–814.

Finkel, E. J., & Campbell, W. K. (2000). Self-control and accommodation in close relationships: An interdependence analysis. *Journal of Personality and Social Psychology, 81*, 263–277.

Finkel, E. J., Rusbult, C. E., Kumashiro, M., & Hannon, P. A. (2002). Dealing with betrayal in close relationships: Does commitment promote forgiveness? *Journal of Personality and Social Psychology, 82*, 956–974.

Finkel, N. J. (1995). *Commonsense justice: Jurors' notions of the law.* Cambridge, MA: Harvard University Press.

Finkel, N. J. (2000). But it's not fair! Commonsense notions of unfairness. *Psychology, Public Policy, and Law, 6*, 898–952.

Fischhoff, B. (1975). Hindsight≠foresight: The effect of outcome knowledge on judgment under uncertainty. *Journal of Experimental Psychology: Human Perception and Performance, 1*, 288–299.

Fischhoff, B., Slovic, P., & Lichtenstein, S. (1977). Knowing with certainty: The appropriateness of extreme confidence. *Journal of Experimental Psychology: Human Perception and Performance, 3*, 552–564.

Fisher, S., & Fisher, R. L. (1981). *Pretend the world is funny and forever: A psychological analysis of comedians, clowns, and actors.* Hillsdale, NJ: Erlbaum.

Fisher, S. W. (1999, January/February). Raising thankful kids: How to develop the virtue of gratefulness. *Christian Parenting Today, 12*, 19–21.

Fitzgerald, P. (1998). Gratitude and justice. *Ethics, 109*, 119–153.

Flanagan, C. A. (in press). Volunteerism, leadership, political socialization, and civic engagement. In R. M. Lerner & L. Steinberg (Eds.), *Handbook of adolescent psychology.* New York: Wiley.

Flanagan, C. A., Bowes, J., Jonsson, B., Csapo, B., & Sheblanova, E. (1998). Ties that bind: Correlates of male and female adolescents' civic commitments in seven countries. *Journal of Social Issues, 54*(3), 457–476.

Flanagan, C. A., & Faison, N. (2001). Youth civic development: Implications of research for social policy and programs. *Social Policy Report* (Vol. 15). Ann Arbor, MI: Society for Research in Child Development.

Flanagan, C. A., Gill, S., & Gallay, L. S. (in press). Social participation and social trust in adolescence: The importance of heterogeneous encounters. In A. Omoto (Ed.), *Social participation in processes of community change and social action.* Mahwah, NJ: Erlbaum.

Flanagan, C. A., Jonsson, B., Botcheva, L., Csapo, B., Bowes, J., Macek, P., et al. (1998). Adolescents and the "social contract": Developmental roots of citizenship in seven countries. In M. Yates & J. Youniss (Eds.), *Community service and civic engagement in youth: International perspectives* (pp. 135–155). New York: Cambridge University Press.

Flanagan, C. A., & Tucker, C. J. (1999). Adolescents' explanations for political issues: Concordance with their views of self and society. *Developmental Psychology, 35,* 1198–1209.

Flanagan, O. J., & Adler, J. E. (1983). Impartiality and particularity. *Social Research 50,* 576–596.

Flanagan, O. J., & Jackson, K. (1987). Justice, care, and gender: The Kohlberg-Gilligan debate revisited. *Ethics, 97,* 622–637.

Flashman, L. A., Andreasen, N. C., Flaum, M., & Swayze, V. W. (1998). Intelligence and regional brain volumes in normal controls. *Intelligence, 25,* 149–160.

Fleishman, E. A. (1953). The description of supervisory behavior. *Personnel Psychology, 37,* 1–6.

Fleishman, E. A. (1973). Twenty years of consideration and structure. In E. A. Fleishman & J. G. Hunt (Eds.), *Current developments in the study of leadership* (pp. 1–37). Carbondale: Southern Illinois University Press.

Fleishman, E. A., & Harris, E. F. (1962). Patterns of leadership behavior related to employee grievances and turnover. *Personnel Psychology, 15,* 43–56.

Fleishman, E. A., Mumford, M. D., Zaccaro, S. J., Levin, K. Y., Korotkin, A. L., & Hein, M. B. (1991). Taxonomic efforts in the description of leader behavior: A synthesis and functional interpretation. *Leadership Quarterly, 2,* 245–287.

Flowers, B., & Richardson, F. (1996). Why is multiculturalism good? *American Psychologist, 51,* 609–621.

Foa, U. G., & Foa, E. B. (1975). *Resource theory of social exchange.* Morristown, NJ: General Learning Press.

Foellings-Albers, M., & Hartinger, A. (1998). Interest of girls and boys in elementary school. In L. Hoffmann, A. Krapp, K. A. Renninger, & J. Baumert (Eds.), *Interest and learning: Proceedings of the Seeon Conference on Interest and Gender* (pp. 175–183). Kiel, Germany: Institute for Science and Education.

Forkman, B. (1996). The foraging behaviour of Mongolian gerbils: A behavioural need or a need to know? *Behaviour, 133,* 129–143.

Formica, S. (1998). *Description of the socio-emotional life space: Life qualities and activities related to emotional intelligence.* Unpublished senior honors thesis, University of New Hampshire, Durham.

Fowers, B. J. (1998). Psychology and the good marriage: Social theory as practice. *American Behavioral Scientist, 41,* 516–541.

Fowler, H. (1965). *Curiosity and exploratory behavior.* New York: Macmillan.

Fowler, J. (1981). *Stages of faith: The psychology of human development and the quest for meaning.* San Francisco: Harper & Row.

Fowler, M. (1999). *Buddhism: Beliefs and practices.* Portland, OR: Sussex Academic Press.

Fraley, R. C., & Waller, N. G. (1998). Adult attachment patterns: A test of the typological model. In J. A. Simpson & W. S. Rholes (Eds.), *Attachment theory and close relationships* (pp. 77–114). New York: Guilford Press.

Fraley, R. C., Waller, N. G., & Brennan, K. A. (2000). An item response theory analysis of self-report measures of adult attachment. *Journal of Personality and Social Psychology, 78,* 350–365.

Francis, L. (1997). The psychology of gender difference in religion: A review of empirical research. *Religion, 27,* 81–96.

Francis, L., & Wilcox, C. (1996). Religion and gender orientation. *Personality and Individual Differences, 20,* 119–121.

Frank, J. D. (1974). *Persuasion and healing* (Rev. ed.). New York: Schocken Books.

Frankel, A., & Snyder, M. L. (1978). Poor performance following unsolvable problems: Learned helplessness or egotism? *Journal of Personality and Social Psychology, 36,* 1415–1423.

Frankl, V. E. (1984). *Man's search for meaning.* New York: Washington Square Press. (Original work published 1946)

Franklin, B. (1961). The autobiography. In L. J. Lemisch (Ed.), *The autobiography and other writings* (pp. 15–180). New York: Signet Classic. (Original work published ca. 1790)

Franz, C. E., & McClelland, D. C. (1994). Lives of women and men active in the social protests of the 1960's: A longitudinal study. *Journal of Personality and Social Psychology, 66,* 196–205.

Fraser, D. (2001). *Frederick the Great: King of Prussia.* New York: Fromm.

Fredrickson, B. L. (1998). What good are positive emotions? *Review of General Psychology, 2,* 300–319.

Fredrickson, B. L. (2001). The role of positive emotions in positive psychology: The broaden-and-build theory of positive emotions. *American Psychologist, 56,* 218–226.

French, S., & Joseph, S. (1999). Religiosity and its association with happiness, purpose in life and self-actualisation. *Mental Health, Religion, and Culture, 2,* 117–120.

Freud, S. (1905a). Humor and its relation to the unconscious. *Standard edition of the complete psychological works of Sigmund Freud* (J. Strachey, Trans.) (Vol. VIII, pp. 9–236). London: Hogarth Press.

Freud, S. (1905b). Three essays on the theory of sexuality. *Standard edition of the complete psychological works of Sigmund Freud* (J. Strachey, Trans.) (Vol. VII, pp. 136–243). London: Hogarth Press.

Freud, S. (1912). Totem and taboo: *Standard edition of the complete psychological works of Sigmund Freud* (J. Strachey, Trans.) (Vol. XIII, pp. 1–164). London: Hogarth Press.

Freud, S. (1923). The ego and the id. *Standard edition of the complete psychological works of Sigmund Freud* (J. Strachey, Trans.) (Vol. XIX, pp. 12–68). London: Hogarth Press.

Freud, S. (1927). The future of an illusion. *Standard edition of the complete psychological works of Sigmund Freud* (J. Strachey, Trans.) (Vol. XXI, pp. 3–58). London: Hogarth Press.

Freud, S. (1933). New introductory lectures on psychoanalysis. *Standard edition of the complete psychological works of Sigmund Freud* (J. Strachey, Trans.) (Vol. XXII, pp. 7–184). London: Hogarth Press.

Frey, D. (1986). Recent research on selective exposure to information. In L. Berkowitz (Ed.), *Advances in experimental social psychology* (Vol. 19, pp. 41–80). New York: Academic Press.

Fried, R. L. (1996). *The passionate teacher.* Boston: Beacon Press.

Fried, R. L. (2001). *The passionate learner: How teachers and parents can help children reclaim the joy of discovery.* Boston: Beacon Press.

Friedman, D. E., & Medway, F. J. (1987). Effects of varying performance sets and outcome on the expectations, attributions, and persistence of boys with learning disabilities. *Journal of Learning Disabilities, 20,* 312–316.

Friedman, H. S., Tucker, J. S., Schwartz, J. E., Tomlinson-Keasey, C., Martin, L. R., Wingard, D. L., et al. (1995). Psychosocial and behavioral predictors of longevity: The aging and death of the "Termites." *American Psychologist, 50,* 69–78.

Friedman, H. S., Tucker, J. S., Tomlinson-Keasey, C., Schwartz, J. E., Wingard, D. L., & Criqui, M. H. (1993). Does childhood personality predict longevity? *Journal of Personality and Social Psychology, 67,* 278–286.

Frijda, N. (1986). *The emotions.* Cambridge, England: Cambridge University Press.

Fromm, E. (1941). *Escape from freedom.* New York: Farrar & Rinehart.

Fry, R. (1920). *Vision and design.* New York: Meridian Books.

Füehr, M. (2002). Coping humor in early adolescence. *Humor, 15,* 283–304.

Fuh, J. L., Wang, S. J., Lu, S. R., Juang, K. D., & Lee, S. J. (2000). Psychometric evaluation of a Chinese (Taiwanese) version of the SF-36 health survey amongst middle-aged women from a rural community. *Quality of Life Research: An International Journal of Quality of Life Aspects of Treatment, Care and Rehabilitation, 9,* 675–683.

Funder, D. C., & Ozer, D. J. (1983). Behavior as a function of the situation. *Journal of Personality and Social Psychology, 44,* 107–112.

Furnham, A., & Akande, A. (1997). Cross-cultural differences in attributions for overcoming specific psychological problems. *Journal of Social Behavior and Personality, 12,* 727–742.

Gabriel, M. T., Critelli, J. W., & Ee, J. S. (1994). Narcissistic illusions in self-evaluations of intelligence and attractiveness. *Journal of Personality, 62,* 143–155.

Gabrielsson, A., & Juslin, P. (2003). Emotional expression in music. In R. Davidson, K. Scherer, & H. Goldsmith (Eds.), *Handbook of affective sciences* (pp. 503–534). New York: Oxford University Press.

Gaines, S. O., Reis, H. T., Summers, S., Rusbult, C. E., Cox, C. L., Wexler, M. O., et al. (1997). Impact of attachment style on reactions to accommodative dilemmas in close relationships. *Personal Relationships, 4,* 93–113.

Gal, R. (1995). Personality and intelligence in the military. In D. H. Saklofske & M. Zeidner (Eds.), *International handbook of personality and intelligence* (pp. 727–735). New York: Plenum Press.

Gallup, G., & Jones, T. (2000). *The next American spirituality.* Colorado Springs, CO: Cook Communications.

Gallup News Service. (2000, August). *American teens say they get along well with their parents.* Document available at http://www.gallup.com/poll/releases/pr000811b.asp.

Gallup survey results on "gratitude," adults and teenagers. (1998). *Emerging Trends, 20,* 9.

Galotti, K. (1989). Gender differences in self-reported moral reasoning: A review and new evidence. *Journal of Youth and Adolescence, 18,* 475–488.

Galton, F. (1869). *Hereditary genius: An inquiry into its laws and consequences.* London: Macmillan.

Garcia-Coll, C., Kagan, J., & Reznick, J. S. (1984). Behavioral inhibition in young children. *Child Development, 55,* 1005–1019.

Gardner, H. (1983). *Frames of mind: The theory of multiple intelligences.* New York: Basic Books.

Gardner, H. (1993a). *Creating minds: An anatomy of creativity seen through the lives of Freud, Einstein, Picasso, Stravinsky, Eliot, Graham, and Gandhi.* New York: Basic Books.

Gardner, H. (1993b). *Frames of mind: The theory of multiple intelligences* (10th anniversary edition). New York: Basic Books.

Gardner, H. (1993c). Intelligence and intelligences: Universal principles and individual differences. *Archives de Psychologie, 61,* 169–172.

Gardner, H., Csikszentmihalyi, M., & Damon, W. (2001). *Good work: When excellence and ethics meet.* New York: Basic Books.

Gardner, P. L. (1985). Students' interest in science and technology: An international overview. In M. Lehrke, L. Hoffmann, & P. L. Gardner (Eds.), *Interests in science and technology education* (pp. 15–34). Kiel, Germany: Institute for Science Education.

Garner, R., Alexander, P. A., Gillingham, M. G., Kulikowich, J., & Brown, R. (1991). Interest and learning from text. *American Educational Research Journal, 28,* 643–659.

Garner, R., Brown, R., Sanders, S., & Menke, D. J. (1992). "Seductive details" and learning from text. In K. A. Renninger, S. Hidi, & A. Krapp (Eds.), *The role of interest in learning and development* (pp. 239–254). Hillsdale, NJ: Erlbaum.

Geen, R. G. (1981). Effects of being observed on persistence at an insoluble task. *British Journal of Social Psychology, 20,* 211–216.

Geertz, C. (1973). *The interpretation of cultures.* New York: Basic Books.

General Social Survey. (2001, March 20). *1972–1998 cumulative codebook.* Document available at http://www.icpsr.umich.edu/GSS/.

George, C., Kaplan, N., & Main, M. (1985). *The adult attachment interview.* Unpublished manuscript, Department of Psychology, University of California, Berkeley.

George, L. K., Larson, D. B., Koenig, H. G., & McCullough, M. E. (2000). Spirituality and health: What we know, what we need to know. *Journal of Social and Clinical Psychology, 19,* 102–116.

Gergen, K. (1991). *The saturated self: Dilemmas of identity in contemporary life.* New York: Basic Books.

Gerstner, C. R., & Day, D. V. (1997). Meta-analytic review of leader-member exchange theory: Correlates and construct issues. *Journal of Applied Psychology, 82,* 827–844.

Giambra, L. M., Camp, C. J., & Grodsky, A. (1992). Curiosity and stimulation seeking across the adult life span: Cross-sectional and 6–8-year longitudinal findings. *Psychology and Aging, 7,* 150–157.

Gibbs, J. C. (1977). Kohlberg's stages of moral judgment: A constructive critique. *Harvard Educational Review, 47,* 43–61.

Gibbs, J. C., Arnold, K. D., Morgan, R. L., Schwartz, E. S., Gavaghan, M. P., & Tappan, M. B. (1984). Construction and validation of a multiple choice measure of moral reasoning. *Child Development, 55,* 527–536.

Gibbs, J. C., Basinger, K. S., & Fuller, D. (1992). *Moral maturity: Measuring the development of sociomoral reflection.* Hillsdale, NJ: Erlbaum.

Gibbs, J. C., Widaman, K., & Colby, A. (1982). *Social intelligence: Measuring the development of sociomoral reflection.* Englewood Cliffs, NJ: Prentice Hall.

Gibbs, J. J., Giever, D., & Martin, J. S. (1998). Parental management and self-control: An empirical test of Gottfredson and Hirschi's general theory. *Journal of Research in Crime and Delinquency, 35,* 40–70.

Gilbert, J. A. (1995). *Leadership, social intelligence, and perceptions of environmental opportunities: A comparison across levels of leadership.* Unpublished doctoral dissertation, George Mason University, Fairfax, VA.

Gilbert, J. I. (1989). Logical consequences: A new classification for the classroom. *Individual Psychology, 45,* 425–432.

Gilleard, C. J. (1997). Education and Alzheimer's disease: A review of recent international epidemiological studies. *Aging and Mental Health, 1,* 33–46.

Gillham, J. E. (Ed.). (2000). *The science of optimism and hope: Research essays in honor of Martin E. P. Seligman.* Radnor, PA: Templeton Foundation Press.

Gilligan, C. (1977). In a different voice: Women's conceptions of self and morality. *Harvard Educational Review 47,* 481–517.

Gilligan, C. (1979). Woman's place in man's life cycle. *Harvard Educational Review, 49,* 431–446.

Gilligan, C. (1982). *In a different voice.* Cambridge, MA: Harvard University Press.

Gilligan, C. (1987). Moral orientation and moral development. In E. F. Kittay & D. T. Meyers (Eds.), *Women and moral theory* (pp. 19–36). Totowa, NJ: Rowman & Littlefield.

Gilligan, C., & Attanucci, J. (1987). Two moral orientations: Gender differences and similarities. *Merrill-Palmer Quarterly, 34,* 223–237.

Gilligan, C., & Wiggins, G. (1987). The origins of morality in early childhood relationships. In J. Kagan & S. Lamb (Eds.), *The emergence of morality in young children* (pp. 277–306). Chicago: University of Chicago Press.

Girard, M., & Mullet, É. (1997). Propensity to forgive in adolescents, young adults, older adults, and elderly people. *Journal of Adult Development, 4,* 209–220.

Gladwell, M. (2001, July 2). The mosquito killer. *The New Yorker*, 42–51.

Gleason, J. B., & Weintraub, S. (1976). The acquisition of routines in child language. *Language in Society, 5,* 129–136.

Gloria, A. M., Kurpius, S. E. R., Hamilton, K. D., & Willson, M. S. (1999). African American students' persistence at a predominantly white university: Influence of social support, university comfort, and self-beliefs. *Journal of College Student Development, 40,* 257–268.

Glover, J. A., Ronning, R. R., & Reynolds, C. R. (Eds.). (1989). *Handbook of creativity.* New York: Plenum Press.

Glover, R. J. (2001). Discriminators of moral orientation: Gender role or personality? *Journal of Adult Development, 8,* 1–7.

Goble, F. G., & Brooks, B. D. (1983). *The case for character education.* Ottawa, IL: Green Hill Publishers.

Godfrey, D. K., Jones, E. E., & Lord, C. G. (1986). Self-promotion is not ingratiating. *Journal of Personality and Social Psychology, 50,* 106–113.

Goldberg, C., & Simon, J. (1982). Toward a psychology of courage: Implications for the change (healing) process. *Journal of Contemporary Psychotherapy, 13,* 107–128.

Goldberg, L. R. (1992). The development of markers for the Big-Five factor structure. *Psychological Assessment, 4,* 26–42.

Goldberg, L. R. (1993). The structure of phenotypic personality traits. *American Psychologist, 48,* 26–34.

Goldberg, L. R., Grenier, J., Guion, R., Sechrest, L., & Wing, H. (1991). *Questionnaires used in the prediction of trustworthiness in pre-employment selection decisions: An APA Task Force Report.* Washington, DC: American Psychological Association.

Goldman, H. H., Skodol, A. E., & Lave, T. R. (1992). Revising Axis V for DSM-IV: A review of measures of social functioning. *American Journal of Psychiatry, 149,* 1148–1156.

Goldman, S. R., Mayfield-Stewart, C., Bateman, H., Pellegrino, J. W., & The Cognition and Technology Group at Vanderbilt. (1998). Environments that support meaningful learning. In L. Hoffmann, A. Krapp, K. A. Renninger, & J. Baumert (Eds.), *Interest and learning: Proceedings of the Seeon Conference on Interest and Gender* (pp. 184–196). Kiel, Germany: Institute for Science Education.

Goldsmith, D. J., & Fitch, K. (1997). The normative context of advice as social support. *Human Communication Research, 23,* 454–476.

Goldstein, J. H., & McGhee, P. E. (Eds.). (1972). *The psychology of humor: Theoretical perspectives and empirical issues.* New York: Academic Press.

Goldstein, K. M., & Blackman, S. (1978). *Cognitive style: Five approaches and relevant research.* New York: Wiley.

Goleman, D. (1995). *Emotional intelligence.* New York: Bantam Books.

Gollwitzer, P. M. (1993). Goal achievement: The role of intentions. In W. Stroebe & M. Hewstone (Eds.), *European review of social psychology* (Vol. 4, pp. 141–185). Chichester, England: Wiley.

Gollwitzer, P. M. (1999). Implementation intentions: Strong effects of simple plans. *American Psychologist, 54,* 493–503.

Gollwitzer, P. M., & Brandstaetter, V. (1997). Implementation intentions and effective goal pursuit. *Journal of Personality and Social Psychology, 73,* 186–199.

Goodwin, D. W., & Guze, S. B. (1996). *Psychiatric diagnosis* (5th ed.). New York: Oxford University Press.

Gordon, K. C., Baucom, D. H., & Snyder, D. K. (2000). The use of forgiveness in marital therapy. In M. E. McCullough, K. I. Pargament, & C. E. Thoresen (Eds.), *Forgiveness: Theory, research, and practice* (pp. 203–227). New York: Guilford Press.

Gorsuch, R. (1988). Psychology of religion. *Annual Review of Psychology, 39,* 201–221.

Gorsuch, R., & McFarland, S. (1972). Single versus multiple scales for measuring religious values. *Journal for the Scientific Study of Religion, 11,* 53–64.

Gorsuch, R., & McPherson, S. (1989). Intrinsic/extrinsic measurement: I/E revised and single-item scales. *Journal for the Scientific Study of Religion, 28,* 348–354.

Gottfredson, M. R., & Hirschi, T. (1990). *A general theory of crime.* Stanford, CA: Stanford University Press.

Gottfried, A. E. (1986). *Children's Academic Intrinsic Motivation Inventory.* Odessa, FL: Psychological Assessment Resources.

Gottman, J. M. (1999). *The marriage clinic: A scientifically-based marital therapy.* New York: Norton.

Gough, H. G. (1979). A Creative Personality Scale for the Adjective Check List. *Journal of Personality and Social Psychology, 37,* 1398–1405.

Gough, H. G. (1987). *California Psychological Inventory administrator's guide.* Palo Alto, CA: Consulting Psychologists Press.

Gough, H. G. (1990). Testing for leadership with the California Psychological Inventory. In K. E. Clark & M. B. Clark (Eds.), *Measures of leadership* (pp. 343–354). West Orange, NJ: Leadership Library of America.

Gough, H. G., & Heilbrun, A. B. (1983). *The Adjective Checklist manual.* Palo Alto, CA: Consulting Psychologists Press.

Gough, H. G., McClosky, H., & Meehl, P. E. (1952). A personality scale for social responsibility. *Journal of Abnormal and Social Psychology, 47,* 73–80.

Gould, S. J. (1981). *The mismeasure of man.* New York: Norton.

Gove, P. B., & Merriam-Webster Editorial Staff (Eds.). (1966). *Webster's third new international dictionary.* Springfield, MA: G. & C. Merriam Company.

Gräber, W. (1998). Schooling for lifelong attention to chemistry issues: The role of interest and achievement. In L. Hoffmann, A. Krapp, K. A. Renninger, & J. Baumert (Eds.), *Interest and learning: Proceedings of the Seeon Conference on Interest and Gender* (pp. 280–290). Kiel, Germany: Institute for Science Education.

Grady, E. (1994). *After Cluster School: A study of the impact in adulthood of a moral development intervention project.* Unpublished doctoral dissertation, Harvard University.

Graham, A. C. (1998). The origins of the legend of Lao Tan. In L. Kohn & M. LaFargue (Eds.), *Lao-tzu and the Tao-te-ching* (pp. 23–40). Albany: State University of New York Press.

Graham, S. (1988). Children's developing understanding of the motivational role of affect: An attributional analysis. *Cognitive Development, 3*, 71–88.

Graham, S., & Weiner, B. (1986). From an attributional theory of emotion to developmental psychology: A round trip ticket? *Social Cognition, 4*, 152–179.

Grasmick, J. F., Tittle, C. R., Bursik, R. J., & Arneklev, B. J. (1993). Testing the core empirical implications of Gottfredson and Hirschi's general theory of crime. *Journal of Research in Crime and Delinquency, 30*, 5–29.

Greenberg, J., Pyszczynski, T., & Solomon, S. (1995). Toward a dual-motive depth psychology of self and social behavior. In M. Kernis (Ed.), *Efficacy, agency, and self-esteem* (pp. 73–99). New York: Plenum Press.

Greenberg, M. T., Domitrovich, C., & Bumbarger, B. (1999). *Preventing mental disorders in school-age children.* Washington, DC: Center for Mental Health Services, U.S. Department of Health and Human Services.

Greenberg, M. T., Domitrovich, C., & Bumbarger, B. (2001). The prevention of mental disorders in school-aged children: Current state of the field. *Prevention and Treatment.* Document available at http://journals.apa.org/prevention/volume/pre0020010.html.

Greenberger, E. (1984). Defining psychosocial maturity in adolescence. *Advances in Child Behavioral Analysis and Therapy, 3*, 1–37.

Greenberger, E., Josselson, R., Knerr, C., & Knerr, B. (1975). The measurement and structure of psychosocial maturity. *Journal of Youth and Adolescence, 4*, 127–143.

Greenberger, E., & Sørenson, A. B. (1974). Toward a concept of psychosocial maturity. *Journal of Youth and Adolescence, 3*, 329–358.

Green-Demers, I., Pelletier, L. G., Stewart, D. G., & Gushue, N. R. (1998). Coping with the less interesting aspects of training: Towards a model of interest and motivation enhancement in individual sports. *Basic and Applied Social Psychology, 20*, 251–261.

Greene, M. C., & Brock, T. C. (2000). The role of transportation in the persuasiveness of public narratives. *Journal of Personality and Social Psychology, 79*, 701–722.

Greenfield, P. M. (1994). Independence and interdependence as developmental scripts: Implications for theory, research, and practice. In P. M. Greenfield & R. R. Cocking (Eds.), *Cross-cultural roots of minority child development* (pp. 1–40). Hillsdale, NJ: Erlbaum.

Greenwald, A. G. (1980). The totalitarian ego: Fabrication and revision of personal history. *American Psychologist, 35*, 603–618.

Grice, P. (1975). Logic and conversation. In P. Cole & J. L. Moran (Eds.), *Syntax and semantics III: Speech acts* (pp. 41–58). New York: Academic Press.

Griffin, D. W., & Bartholomew, K. (1994). Models of the self and other: Fundamental dimensions underlying measures of adult attachment. *Journal of Personality and Social Psychology, 67*, 430–445.

Griffith, R. W., & Hom, P. W. (1988). Locus of control and delay of gratification as moderators of employee turnover. *Journal of Applied Social Psychology, 18,* 1318–1333.

Grigorenko, E. L. (2000). Heritability and intelligence. In R. J. Sternberg (Ed.), *Handbook of intelligence* (pp. 53–91). Cambridge, England: Cambridge University Press.

Gross, J. J. (1999). Emotion and emotion regulation. In L. A. Pervin & O. P. John (Eds.), *Handbook of personality: Theory and research* (2nd ed., pp. 525–552). New York: Guilford Press.

Gross, M. (1994). Jewish rescue in Holland and France during the Second World War: Moral cognition and collective action. *Social Forces, 73,* 463–496.

Grotevant, H. D., & Adams, G. R. (1984). Development of an objective measure to assess ego identity in adolescence: Validation and replication. *Journal of Youth and Adolescence, 13,* 419–438.

Gruber, H. E., & Wallace, D. B. (1999). The case study method and evolving systems approach for understanding unique creative people at work. In R. J. Sternberg (Ed.), *Handbook of creativity* (pp. 93–115). New York: Cambridge University Press.

Grundler, O. (1922). *Elemente zu einer Religionsphilosophie auf phanomenologischer Grundlage.* Munich, Germany: Josef Kosel & Friedrich Pustet.

Guilford, J. P. (1950). Creativity. *American Psychologist, 5,* 444–454.

Guilford, J. P. (1967). *The nature of human intelligence.* New York: McGraw-Hill.

Haan, N., Millsap, R., & Hartka, E. (1986). As time goes by: Change and stability in personality over fifty years. *Psychology and Aging, 1,* 220–232.

Haberman, D. L. (1998a). Confucianism: The way of the sages. In L. Stevenson & D. L. Haberman, *Ten theories of human nature* (3rd ed., pp. 25–44). New York: Oxford University Press.

Haberman, D. L. (1998b). Upanishadic Hinduism: Quest for ultimate knowledge. In L. Stevenson & D. L. Haberman, *Ten theories of human nature* (3rd ed., pp. 45–67). New York: Oxford University Press.

Haidt, J. (2000). The positive emotion of elevation. *Prevention and Treatment, 3*(3). Document available at http://journals.apa.org/prevention/volume3/pre0030003c.html.

Haidt, J. (2002). The moral emotions. In R. J. Davidson, K. Scherer, & H. H. Goldsmith (Eds.), *Handbook of affective sciences* (pp. 852–870). Oxford, England: Oxford University Press.

Haidt, J. (2003). Elevation and the positive psychology of morality. In C. L. M. Keyes & J. Haidt (Eds.), *Flourishing: Positive psychology and the life well-lived* (pp. 275–289). Washington, DC: American Psychological Association.

Haidt, J., & Algoe, S. (2003). *The elevation-altruism hypothesis: Evidence for a new prosocial emotion.* Unpublished manuscript, University of Virginia, Charlottesville.

Haitch, R. (1995). How Tillich and Kohut both find courage in faith. *Pastoral Psychology, 44,* 83–96.

Hall, D. L., & Ames, R. T. (1987). *Thinking through Confucius.* Albany: State University of New York Press.

Hall, G. (1904). *Adolescence.* New York: Appleton Press.

Hallinan, P. K. (1981). *I'm thankful each day.* Nashville, TN: Hambleton-Hill.

Hambrick, D. C., & Mason, P. A. (1984). Upper echelons: The organization as a reflection of its top managers. *Academy of Management Review, 9,* 195–206.

Hamilton, E., & Cairns, H. (Eds.). (1961). *The collected dialogues of Plato.* New York: Pantheon Books.

Handal, P., Black-Lopez, W., & Moergen, S. (1989). Preliminary investigation of the relationship between religion and psychological distress in Black women. *Psychological Reports, 65,* 971–975.

Handelsman, M. M., Knapp, S., & Gottlieb, M. C. (2002). Positive ethics. In C. R. Snyder & S. J. Lopez (Eds.), *Handbook of positive psychology* (pp. 731–744). New York: Oxford University Press.

Hantula, D. A., & Crowell, C. R. (1994). Intermittent reinforcement and escalation processes in sequential decision making: A replication and theoretical analysis. *Journal of Organizational and Behavioral Management, 14,* 7–36.

Harackiewicz, J. M. (1979). The effects of reward contingency and performance feedback on intrinsic motivation. *Journal of Personality and Social Psychology, 37,* 1352–1363.

Harackiewicz, J. M., Barron, K. E., Carter, S. M., Lehto, A. T., & Elliot, A. J. (1997). Predictors and consequences of achievement goals in the college classroom: Maintaining interest and making the grade. *Journal of Personality and Social Psychology, 73,* 1284–1295.

Harackiewicz, J. M., Barron, K. E., Carter, S. M., Tauer, J. M., & Elliot, A. J. (2000). Short-term and long-term consequences of achievement goals: Predicting interest and performance over time. *Journal of Educational Psychology, 92,* 316–330.

Harackiewicz, J. M., Barron, K. E., & Elliot, A. J. (1998). Rethinking achievement goals: When are they adaptive for college students and why? *Educational Psychologist, 22,* 1–21.

Harackiewicz, J. M., Barron, K. E., Tauer, J. M., & Elliot, A. J. (2002). Predicting success in college: A longitudinal study of achievement goals and ability measures as predictors of interest and performance from freshman year through graduation. *Journal of Educational Psychology, 94,* 562–575.

Harackiewicz, J. M., & Elliot, A. J. (1993). Achievement goals and intrinsic motivation. *Journal of Personality and Social Psychology, 65,* 904–915.

Harackiewicz, J. M., Manderlink, G., & Sansone, C. (1984). Rewarding pinball wizardry: The effects of evaluation on intrinsic interest. *Journal of Personality and Social Psychology, 47,* 287–300.

Hareli, S., & Weiner, B. (2000). Accounts for success as determinants of perceived arrogance and modesty. *Motivation and Emotion, 24,* 215–236.

Harker, L. A., & Keltner, D. (2001). Expressions of positive emotion in women's college yearbook pictures and their relationship to personality and life outcomes across adulthood. *Journal of Personality and Social Psychology, 80,* 112–124.

Harlow, H. F. (1958). The nature of love. *American Psychologist, 13,* 673–685.

Harris, D. B. (1957). A scale for measuring attitudes of social responsibility in children. *Journal of Abnormal and Social Psychology, 55,* 322–326.

Harris, F. C. (1999). *Something within: Religion in African American political activism.* New York: Oxford University Press.

Harris, J. R. (1995). Where is the child's environment? A group socialization theory of development. *Psychological Review, 102,* 458–489.

Harris, P. L., Olthof, T., Meerum Terwogt, M., & Hardman, C. E. (1987). Children's knowledge of the situations that provoke emotion. *International Journal of Behavioral Development, 10,* 319–344.

Hart, K. E., & Huggett, C. (2003). *Lack of humility as a barrier to surrendering to the spiritual aspect of Alcoholics Anonymous.* Unpublished manuscript, University of Windsor, Windsor, Canada.

Hart, P. L., & Joubert, C. E. (1996). Narcissism and hostility. *Psychological Reports, 79,* 161–162.

Harter, S. (1981). A self-report scale of intrinsic versus extrinsic orientation in the classroom: Motivational and informational components. *Developmental Psychology, 17,* 300–312.

Harter, S. (1998). The development of self-representations. In N. Eisenberg (Vol. Ed.), *Social, emotional, and personality development* (Vol. 3, pp. 553–618). In W. Damon (Gen. Ed.), *Handbook of child psychology* (5th ed.). New York: Wiley.

Harter, S. (1999). *The construction of the self: A developmental perspective.* New York: Guilford Press.

Harter, S., & Monsour, A. (1992). Development analysis of conflict caused by opposing attributes in the adolescent self-portrait. *Developmental Psychology, 28,* 251–260.

Harter, S., Waters, P., & Whitesell, N. (1997). Lack of voice as a manifestation of false self-behavior among adolescents: The school setting as a stage upon which the drama of authenticity is enacted. *Educational Psychologist, 32,* 153–173.

Harter, S., Waters, P. L., Whitesell, N. R., & Kastelic, D. (1998). Level of voice among female and male high school students: Relational context, support, and gender orientation. *Developmental Psychology, 34,* 892–901.

Hartigan, F. (2000). *Bill W.: A biography of Alcoholics Anonymous cofounder Bill Wilson.* New York: St. Martin's Press.

Hartman, P. S. (2000). *Women developing wisdom: Antecedents and correlates in a longitudinal sample.* Unpublished doctoral dissertation, University of Michigan, Ann Arbor.

Hartmann, H. (1958). *Ego psychology and the problem of adaptation.* New York: International Universities Press. (Original work published 1939)

Hartmann, H. (1964). *Essays on ego psychology*. New York: International Universities Press.

Hartshorne, H., & May, M. A. (1928). *Studies in deceit*. New York: Macmillan.

Harvey, O. J. (1964). Some cognitive determinants of influencibility. *Sociometry, 27*, 208–221.

Harvey, O. J., Hunt, D. E., & Schroder, H. M. (1961). *Conceptual systems and personality*. New York: Wiley.

Harvey, P. (1990). *An introduction to Buddhism: Teaching, history and practices*. Cambridge, England: Cambridge University Press.

Haslam, N. (1991). Prudence: Aristotelian perspective on practical reason and self-control. *Journal for the Theory of Social Behaviour, 21*, 151–169.

Haslam, N., & Baron, J. (1994). Intelligence, personality, and prudence. In R. J. Sternberg & P. Ruzgis (Eds.), *Personality and intelligence* (pp. 32–58). New York: Cambridge University Press.

Hatfield, E. (2000). *An autobiography*. Document available at http://www2.hawaii.edu/~elaineh/.

Hauser, S. T., Powers, S. I., Noam, G. G., Jacobson, A. M., Weisse, B., & Follansbee, D. J. (1984). Familial contexts of adolescent ego development. *Child Development, 55*, 195–213.

Haussler, P. (1987). Measuring students' interests in physics: Design and results of a cross-sectional study in the Federal Republic of Germany. *International Journal of Science Education, 9*, 79–92.

Haussler P., & Hoffmann, L. (1998). Qualitative differences in students' interests in physics and the dependence on gender and age. In L. Hoffmann, A. Krapp, K. A. Renninger, & J. Baumert (Eds.), *Interest and learning: Proceedings of the Seeon Conference on Interest and Gender* (pp. 280–290). Kiel, Germany: Institute for Science Education.

Hay, J. (1983). A study of principled moral reasoning within a sample of conscientious objectors. *Moral Education Forum, 7*, 1–8.

Hayamizu, T. (1997). Between intrinsic and extrinsic motivation: Examination of reasons for academic study based on the theory of internalization. *Japanese Psychological Research, 39*, 98–108.

Hayes, J. R. (1989). *The complete problem solver* (2nd ed.). Hillsdale, NJ: Erlbaum.

Hazan, C., & Diamond, L. M. (2000). The place of attachment in human mating. *Review of General Psychology, 4*, 186–204.

Hazan, C., & Shaver, P. R. (1987). Romantic love conceptualized as an attachment process. *Journal of Personality and Social Psychology, 52*, 511–524.

Hazan, C., & Shaver, P. R. (1990). Love and work: An attachment theoretical perspective. *Journal of Personality and Social Psychology, 59*, 270–280.

Hazan, C., & Shaver, P. R. (1994). Attachment as an organizational framework for research on close relationships. *Psychological Inquiry, 5*, 1–22.

Hazan, C., & Zeifman, D. (1994). Sex and the psychological tether. *Advances in Personal Relationships, 5*, 151–177.

Hazan, C., & Zeifman, D. (1999). Pair bonds as attachments: Evaluating the evidence. In J. Cassidy & P. R. Shaver (Eds.), *Handbook of attachment theory and research* (pp. 336–354). New York: Guilford Press.

Heath, S. B. (1999). Rethinking youth transitions. *Human Development, 42,* 376–382.

Heatherington, L., Burns, A. B., & Gustafson, T. B. (1998). When another stumbles: Gender and self-presentation to vulnerable others. *Sex Roles, 38,* 889–913.

Heatherton, T. F., & Vohs, K. D. (1998). Why is it so difficult to inhibit behavior? *Psychological Inquiry, 9,* 212–216.

Hebb, D. O. (1949). *The organization of behavior.* New York: Wiley.

Heckhausen, J., Dixon, R., & Baltes, P. B. (1989). Gains and losses in development throughout adulthood as perceived by different adult age groups. *Developmental Psychology, 25,* 109–121.

Hedge, A., & Yousif, Y. H. (1992). Effects of urban size, urgency, and cost on helpfulness: A cross-cultural comparison between the United Kingdom and the Sudan. *Journal of Cross-Cultural Psychology, 23,* 107–115.

Heidegger, M. (1962). *Being and time* (J. Macquarrie & E. Robinson, Trans.). New York: Harper & Row. (Original work published 1927)

Heider, F. (1958). *The psychology of interpersonal relations.* New York: Wiley.

Heider, J. (1985). *The tao of leadership.* Atlanta, GA: Humanics Limited.

Heim, T. A., & Rye, M. S. (2001, August). *Forgiveness and mental health: A comparison between Judaism and Christianity.* Paper presented at the annual meeting of the American Psychological Association, San Francisco.

Heine, S. J., Kitayama, S., Lehman, D. R., Takata, T., Ide, E., Leung, C., et al. (2001). Divergent consequences of success and failure in Japan and North America: An investigation of self-improving motivations and malleable selves. *Journal of Personality and Social Psychology, 81,* 599–615.

Heine, S. J., Lehman, D. R., Markus, H. R., & Kitayama, S. (1999). Is there a universal need for positive self-regard? *Psychological Review, 106,* 766–794.

Helmreich, R. L., & Spence, J. T. (1978). The Work and Family Orientation Questionnaire: An objective instrument to assess components of achievement motivation and attitudes toward family and career. *JSAS Catalog of Selected Documents in Psychology, 8,* 35.

Helson, R., Mitchell, V., & Moane, G. (1984). Personality and patterns of adherence to the social clock. *Journal of Personality and Social Psychology, 46,* 1079–1096.

Helson, R., & Srivastava, S. (2001). Three paths of adult development: Conservers, seekers, and achievers. *Journal of Personality and Social Psychology, 80,* 995–1010.

Henderson, J. E., & Hoy, W. K. (1983). Leader authenticity: The development and test of an operational measure. *Educational and Psychological Research, 3,* 63–75.

Herek, G. M., Janis, I. L., & Huth, P. (1987). Decision making during international crises. Is quality of process related to outcome? *Journal of Conflict Resolution, 31,* 203–226.

Herman, C. P., & Polivy, J. (1975). Anxiety, restraint, and eating behavior. *Journal of Abnormal Psychology, 84,* 666–672.

Herman, S. (1971). Toward a more authentic manager. *Training and Development Journal, 25*(10), 8–10.

Hernandez, J., & DiClemente, R. J. (1992). Moral reasoning and unprotected sex among young men. *Journal of Health Education, 23,* 347–351.

Hernandez, M., & Iyengar, S. S. (2001). What drives whom? A cultural perspective on human agency. *Social Cognition, 19,* 269–294.

Herrmann, R. L. (Ed.). (2000). *God, science, and humility: Ten scientists consider humility theology.* Radnor, PA: Templeton Foundation Press.

Herrnstein, R. J., Nickerson, R. S., de Sanchez, M., & Swets, J. A. (1986). Teaching thinking skills. *American Psychologist, 41,* 1279–1289.

Hersey, P., & Blanchard, K. H. (1969). *Management of organizational behavior.* Englewood Cliffs, NJ: Prentice Hall.

Hersey, P., & Blanchard, K. H. (1984). *Management of organizational behavior* (4th ed.). Englewood Cliffs, NJ: Prentice-Hall.

Hertel, G., Neuhof, J., Theuer, T., & Kerr, N. L. (2000). Mood effects on cooperation in small groups: Does positive mood simply lead to more cooperation? *Cognition and Emotion, 14,* 441–472.

Hesse, E. (1999). The adult attachment interview: Historical and current perspectives. In J. Cassidy & P. R. Shaver (Eds.), *Handbook of attachment: Theory, research, and clinical applications* (pp. 395–433). New York: Guilford Press.

Hickey, J. E., & Scharf, P. L. (1980). *Toward a just correctional system.* San Francisco: Jossey-Bass.

Hickman, K. L., Stromme, C., & Lippman, L. G. (1998). Learned industriousness: Replication in principle. *Journal of General Psychology, 125,* 213–217.

Hidi, S. (1990). Interest and its contribution as a mental resource for learning. *Review of Educational Research, 60,* 549–571.

Hidi, S. (2001). Interest, reading and learning: Theoretical and practical considerations. In K. A. Renninger & S. E. Wade (Guest Eds.), Student interest and engagement. *Educational Psychology Review, 13,* 191–210.

Hidi, S., & Baird, W. (1986). Interestingness—A neglected variable in discourse processing. *Cognitive Science, 10,* 179–194.

Hidi, S., & Berndorff, D. (1998). Situational interest and learning. In L. Hoffmann, A. Krapp, K. A. Renninger, & J. Baumert (Eds.), *Interest and learning: Proceedings of the Seeon Conference on Interest and Gender* (pp. 74–90). Kiel, Germany: Institute for Science Education.

Hidi, S., & Renninger, K. A. (2003). *Four phases of interest development: A working proposal.* Unpublished manuscript, University of Toronto, Ontario, Canada.

Higgins, A. (1980). Research and measurement issues in moral education interventions. In R. L. Mosher (Ed.), *Moral education: A first generation of research* (pp. 92–107). New York: Praeger.

Higgins, A., & Gordon, F. (1985). Work climate and socio-moral development in two worker-owned companies. In M. W. Berkowitz & F. Oser (Eds.), *Moral education: Theory and application* (pp. 241–268). Hillsdale, NJ: Erlbaum.

Higgins, A., Power, C., & Kohlberg, L. (1984). The relationship of moral atmosphere to judgments of responsibility. In W. M. Kurtines & J. L. Gewirtz (Eds.), *Morality, moral behavior, and moral development* (pp. 74–106). New York: Wiley.

Hill, R. (1987). *Skywalkers: A history of Indian ironworkers.* Brantford, Ontario, Canada: Woodland Cultural Center.

Hinde, R. A. (1983). The human species. In R. A. Hinde (Ed.), *Primate social relationships* (pp. 334–349). Oxford, England: Blackwell.

Hitt, M. A., & Tyler, B. B. (1991). Strategic decision models: Integrating different perspectives. *Strategic Management Journal, 12,* 327–351.

Hitz, R., & Driscoll, A. (1989). *Praise in the classroom.* Urbana, IL: ERIC Clearinghouse on Elementary and Early Childhood Education. (ERIC Document Reproduction Service No. ED252 310)

Hoare, C. H. (2000). Ethical self, spiritual self: Wisdom and integrity in the writings of Erik H. Erikson. In M. E. Miller & S. R. Cook-Greuter (Eds.), *Creativity, spirituality, and transcendence: Paths to integrity and wisdom in the mature self* (pp. 75–98). Stamford, CT: Ablex.

Hodgins, H. S., Koestner, R., & Duncan, N. (1996). On the compatibility of autonomy and relatedness. *Personality and Social Psychology Bulletin, 22,* 227–237.

Hodgkinson, V., Weitzman, M., & Kirsch, A. (1990). From commitment to action: How religious involvement affects giving and volunteering. In R. Wuthnow, V. Hodgkinson, & Associates (Eds.), *Faith and philanthropy in America: Exploring the role of religion in America's voluntary sector* (pp. 93–114). San Francisco: Jossey-Bass.

Hoffman, M. L. (2000). *Empathy and moral development: Implications for caring and justice.* Cambridge, England: Cambridge University Press.

Hoffmann, L. (2002). Promoting girls' learning and achievement in physics classes for beginners. *Learning and Instruction, 12,* 447–465.

Hofstede, G. (1980). *Culture's consequences: International differences in work-related values.* London: Sage.

Hofstede, G. (1993). Cultural constraints in management theories. *Academy of Management Executive, 7,* 81–90.

Hogan, J. (1989). Personality correlates of physical fitness. *Journal of Personality and Social Psychology, 56,* 284–288.

Hogan, J., & Ones, D. S. (1997). Conscientiousness and integrity at work. In R. Hogan, J. Johnson, & S. Briggs (Eds.), *Handbook of personality psychology* (pp. 849–870). San Diego, CA: Academic Press.

Hogan, R., & Hogan, J. (1992). *Hogan Personality Inventory manual.* Tulsa, OK: Hogan Assessment Systems.

Hogan, R., Raskin, R., & Fazzini, D. (1990). The dark side of charisma. In K. E. Clark & M. B. Clark (Eds.), *Measures of leadership* (pp. 343–354). West Orange, NJ: Leadership Library of America.

Hoge, D. (1972). A validated intrinsic religious motivation scale. *Journal for the Scientific Study of Religion, 11,* 368–376.

Hollander, E. P. (1964). *Leaders, groups, and influence.* New York: Oxford University Press.

Hollander, E. P., & Julian, J. W. (1970). Studies in leader legitimacy, influence, and motivation. In L. Berkowitz (Ed.), *Advances in experimental social psychology* (Vol. 5, pp. 33–69). New York: Academic Press.

Holliday, S. G., & Chandler, M. J. (1986). *Wisdom: Explorations in adult competence.* Basel, Switzerland: Karger.

Holmes, R. L. (1998). *Basic moral philosophy* (2nd ed.). Belmont, CA: Wadsworth.

Hooijberg, R. (1996). A multidirectional approach toward leadership: An extension of the concept of behavioral complexity. *Human Relations, 49,* 917–946.

Horney, K. (1950). *Neurosis and human growth.* New York: Norton.

Houf, H. (1945). *What religion is and does: An introduction to the study of its problems and values.* New York: Harper and Brothers.

House, R. J. (1977). A 1976 theory of charismatic leadership. In J. G. Hunt & L. Larson (Eds.), *Leadership: The cutting edge* (pp. 189–207). Carbondale: Southern Illinois University Press.

House, R. J. (1988). Power and personality in organizations. *Research in Organizational Behavior, 10,* 305–357.

House, R. J., Hanges, P. J., Ruiz-Quintanilla, S. A., Dorfman, P. W., Javidan, M., Dickson, M., et al. (1999). Cultural influences on leadership and organizations: Project GLOBE. In W. H. Mobley, M. J. Gessner, & V. Arnold (Eds.), *Advances in global leadership* (pp. 171–233). Stamford, CT: JAI Press.

House, R. J., & Howell, J. M. (1992). Personality and charismatic leadership. *Leadership Quarterly, 3,* 81–108.

Houston, J., & Masters, R. E. L. (1972). The experimental induction of religious-type experiences. In J. White (Ed.), *The highest state of consciousness* (pp. 303–321). New York: Doubleday.

Houtman, D., & Mascini, P. (2002). Why do churches become empty, while New Age grows? Secularization and religious change in the Netherlands. *Journal for the Scientific Study of Religion, 41,* 455–473.

Howard, A., & Bray, D. W. (1988). *Managerial lives in transition: Advancing age and changing times.* New York: Guilford Press.

Howard, S. (1976). Oedipus of Thebes: The myth and its other meanings. *American Journal of Psychoanalysis, 36,* 147–154.

Howell, J. M. (1988). Two faces of charisma: Socialized and personalized leadership in organizations. In J. A. Conger & R. N. Kanungo (Eds.), *Charismatic leadership: The elusive factor in organizational effectiveness* (pp. 213–236). San Francisco: Jossey-Bass.

Hoza, B., Waschbusch, D. A., Owens, J. S., Pelham, W. E., & Kipp, H. (2001). Academic task persistence of normally achieving ADHD and control boys: Self-evaluations, and attributions. *Journal of Consulting and Clinical Psychology, 69,* 271–283.

Hsiao, E. T., & Thayer, R. E. (1998). Exercising for mood regulation: The importance of exercise. *Personality and Individual Differences, 24,* 829–836.

Huang, C. (1997). Terms. In C. Huang (Trans.), *The analects of Confucius* (pp. 14–35). New York: Oxford University Press.

Huhnke, C. (1984). *An annotated bibliography of the literature dealing with enhancing student motivation in the elementary school.* Indiana University, South Bend, IN. (ERIC Document Reproduction Service No. ED336562)

Hull, J. G. (1981). A self-awareness model of the causes and effects of alcohol consumption. *Journal of Abnormal Psychology, 90,* 586–600.

Humphries, T., Swanson, J. M., Kinsbourne, M., & Yiu, L. (1979). Stimulant effects on persistence of motor performance of hyperactive children. *Journal of Pediatric Psychology, 4,* 55–66.

Hunter, J. D. (2000). *The death of character: Moral education in an age without good or evil.* New York: Basic Books.

Hupp, S. C., & Abbeduto, L. (1991). Persistence as an indicator of mastery motivation in young children with cognitive delays. *Journal of Early Intervention, 15,* 219–225.

Hyland, M. E., Coates, D. S., Curtis, C., Hancocks, M., Mean, L., Ogden, C., et al. (1988). Experimental manipulation of the vacillating-persisting tendency. *British Journal of Social Psychology, 27,* 133–145.

Independent Sector. (1999). *Giving and volunteering in the United States: Findings from a national survey.* Document available at http://independentsector.org/GandV/s_keyf.htm.

Inglis, I. R., & Shepherd, D. S. (1994). Rats work for food they then reject: Support for the information-primacy approach to learned industriousness. *Ethology, 98,* 154–164.

Insel, T. R. (1997). A neurobiological basis of social attachment. *American Journal of Psychiatry, 154,* 726–735.

Intelligence and its measurement: A symposium. (1921). *Journal of Educational Psychology, 12,* 123–147, 195–216, 271–275.

Irving, L. M., Snyder, C. R., Cheavens, J., Gravel, L., Hanke, J., Hilberg, P., et al. (in press). The relationship between hope and optimism in the pre-treatment, beginning, and later phases of psychotherapy. *Journal of Psychotherapy Integration.*

Isaac, J., Sansone, C., & Smith, J. L. (1999). Other people as a source of interest in an activity. *Journal of Experimental Social Psychology, 35,* 239–265.

Isaacowitz, D. M., & Seligman, M. E. P. (2001). Is pessimistic explanatory style a risk factor for depressive mood among community-dwelling older adults? *Behaviour Research and Therapy, 39,* 255–273.

Isasi-Diaz, A. (2001). A new mestizaje/mulatez: Reconceptualizing difference. In E. Fernandez & F. Segovia (Eds.), *A dream unfinished: Theological reflections on America from the margins* (pp. 203–219). Maryknoll, NY: Orbis Books.

Ivanhoe, P. J. (2002). *Ethics in the Confucian tradition.* Indianapolis, IN: Hackett.

Iwao, S. (1997). Consistency orientation and models of social behavior: Is it not time for West to meet East? *Japanese Psychological Research, 39,* 323–332.

Iyengar, S. S., & Lepper, M. R. (1999). Rethinking the value of choice: A cultural perspective on intrinsic motivation. *Journal of Personality and Social Psychology, 76,* 349–366.

Izard, C. E. (1977). *Human emotions.* New York: Plenum Press.

Jackson, D. N. (1974). *Personality research form manual.* Goshen, NY: Research Psychologists Press.

Jackson, D. N. (1976). *Jackson personality inventory.* Goshen, NY: Research Psychologists Press.

Jacobs, B., Prentice-Dunn, S., & Rogers, R. W. (1984). Understanding persistence: An interface of control theory and self-efficacy theory. *Basic and Applied Social Psychology, 5,* 333–347.

Jacobs, J. (2000). The spiritual self-relation: Empathy and the construction of spirituality among modern descendants of the Spanish Crypto-Jews. *Journal for the Scientific Study of Religion, 39,* 53–63.

Jacobs, J. E., Finken, L. L., Griffin, N. L., & Wright, J. D. (1998). The career plans of science-talented rural adolescent girls. *American Educational Research Journal, 35,* 681–704.

Jacobs, T. O., & Jaques, E. (1987). Leadership in complex systems. In J. Zeidner (Ed.), *Human productivity enhancement* (pp. 7–65). New York: Praeger.

Jacobs, T. O., & Jaques, E. (1990). Military executive leadership. In K. E. Clark & M. B. Clark (Eds.), *Measures of leadership* (pp. 281–295). Greensboro, NC: Center for Creative Leadership.

Jacobs, T. O., & Jaques, E. (1991). Executive leadership. In R. Gal & A. D. Manglesdorff (Eds.), *Handbook of military psychology* (pp. 431–447). Chichester, England: Wiley.

Jaffee, S., & Hyde, J. S. (2000). Gender differences in moral orientation: A meta-analysis. *Psychological Bulletin, 126,* 703–726.

Jagacinski, C., & Duda, J. (2001). A comparative analysis of contemporary achievement goal orientation measures. *Educational and Psychological Measurement, 61,* 1013–1039.

Jagers, R. (1997). Afrocultural integrity and the social development of African American children: Some conceptual, empirical and practical considerations. *Journal of Prevention and Intervention in the Community, 16,* 7–31.

Jahoda, M. (1958). *Current concepts of positive mental health.* New York: Basic Books.

James, W. (1890). *Principles of psychology* (2 vols.). New York: Holt, 1890.

James, W. (1999). *Varieties of religious experience: A study in human nature.* New York: Modern Library. (Original work published 1902)

James, W. (1967). The moral equivalent of war. In J. J. McDermott (Ed.), *The writings of William James* (pp. 660–671). New York: Random House.

Jang, S. J., & Smith, C. A. (1997). A test of reciprocal causal relationships among parental supervision, affective ties, and delinquency. *Journal of Research in Crime and Delinquency, 34,* 307–336.

Janis, I. L. (1982). *Groupthink: Psychological studies of policy decisions and fiascos.* Boston: Houghton Mifflin.

Janis, I. L., & Mann, L. (1977). *Decision making: A psychological analysis of conflict, choice, and commitment.* New York: Free Press.

Janoff-Bulman, R., & Brickman, P. (1982). Expectations and what people learn from failure. In N. T. Feather (Ed.), *Expectations and actions* (pp. 207–237). Hillsdale, NJ: Erlbaum.

Jaynes, J. (1976). *The origin of consciousness in the breakdown of the bicameral mind.* Boston: Houghton Mifflin.

Jeffrey, F., & Lilly, J. C. (1990). *John Lilly, So far. . . .* Los Angeles: Tarcher.

Jelen, T., & Wilcox, C. (1998). Context and conscience: The Catholic Church as an agent of political socialization in Western Europe. *Journal for the Scientific Study of Religion, 37,* 28–40.

Jenkins, W. O. (1947). A review of leadership studies with particular reference to military problems. *Psychological Bulletin, 44,* 54–79.

Jennings, H. H. (1943). *Leadership and isolation.* New York: Longmans, Green.

Jennings, M. K. (1991). Thinking about social injustice. *Political Psychology, 12,* 187–204.

Jennings, M. K. (2002). Generation units and the student protest movement in the United States: An intra- and intergenerational analysis. *Political Psychology, 23,* 303–324.

Jerison, H. J. (2000). The evolution of intelligence. In R. J. Sternberg (Ed.), *Handbook of intelligence* (pp. 216–244). Cambridge: Cambridge University Press.

Jessor, R., & Jessor, S. L. (1977). *Problem behavior and psychosocial development: A longitudinal study of youth.* New York: Academic Press.

Jha, P. K., Yadav, K. P., & Kumari, U. (1997). Gender-difference and religio-cultural variation in altruistic behavior. *Indian Journal of Psychometry and Education, 28,* 105–108.

Johansen, K. F. (1998). *A history of ancient philosophy: From the beginnings to Augustine* (H. Rosenmeier, Trans.). New York: Routledge.

John, O. P., Caspi, A., Robins, R. W., Moffitt, T. E., & Stouthamer-Loeber, M. (1994). The "little five": Exploring the nomological network of the five-factor model of personality in adolescent boys. *Child Development, 65,* 160–178.

John, O. P., & Srivastava, S. (1999). The Big Five trait taxonomy: History, measurement, and theoretical perspectives. In L. A. Pervin & O. P. John (Eds.), *Handbook of personality: Theory and research* (2nd ed., pp. 102–138). New York: Guilford Press.

Johnson, B., Larson, D., Li, S., & Jang, S. (2000). Escaping from the crime of the inner cities: Church attendance and religious salience among disadvantaged youth. *Justice Quarterly, 17,* 377–391.

Johnson, R. C., Danko, G. P., Darvill, T. J., Bochner, S., Bowers, J. K., Huang, Y.-H., et al. (1989). Cross-cultural assessment of altruism and its correlates. *Personality and Individual Differences, 10,* 855–868.

Johnson, S., & Greenberg, L. (1985). Emotionally focused couples therapy: An outcome study. *Journal of Marital and Family Therapy, 11,* 313–317.

Johnson, S., Hunsley, J., Greenberg, L., & Schindler, D. (1999). Emotionally focused couples therapy: Status and challenges. *Clinical Psychology: Science and Practice, 6,* 67–79.

Johnston, D. K. (1988). Adolescents' solutions to dilemmas in fables: Two moral orientations—Two problem-solving strategies. In C. Gilligan, J. V. Ward, & J. M. Taylor (Eds.), *Mapping the moral domain* (pp. 49–72). Cambridge, MA: Harvard University Press.

Johnston, L. D., Bachman, J. G., & O'Malley, P. M. (1999). *Monitoring the future: Questionnaire responses from the nation's high school seniors.* Ann Arbor: Institute for Social Research, University of Michigan.

Jones, K., & Day, J. D. (1997). Discrimination of two aspects of cognitive-social intelligence from academic intelligence. *Journal of Educational Psychology, 89,* 486–497.

Jung, C. G. (1934). *Modern man in search of a soul.* New York: Harcourt, Brace & World.

Jung, C. G. (1939). *The integration of the personality.* New York: Farrar & Rinehart.

Kagan, J. (1966). Reflection-impulsivity: The generality and dynamics of conceptual tempo. *Journal of Abnormal Psychology, 71,* 17–27.

Kagan, J. (1972). Motives and development. *Journal of Personality and Social Psychology, 22,* 51–66.

Kagan, J. (1989). Temperamental contributions to social behavior. *American Psychologist, 44,* 668–674.

Kahneman, D., & Tversky, A. (1973). On the psychology of prediction. *Psychological Review, 80,* 237–251.

Kail, R. V. (1975). Freedom of choice, task performance, and task persistence. *Journal of Experimental Education, 44,* 32–35.

Kalish, C. (2000). Children's thinking about truth: A parallel to social domain judgments? *New Directions for Child and Adolescent Development, 89,* 3–17.

Kaminer, D., Stein, D. J., Mbanga, I., & Zungu-Dirwayi, N. (2000). Forgiveness: Toward an integration of theoretical models. *Psychiatry, 63,* 344–357.

Kant, I. (1998). *Critique of pure reason* (P. Guyer & A. W. Wood, Trans.). New York: Cambridge University Press. (Original work published 1781)

Kashdan, T. B. (2002). Social anxiety dimensions, neuroticism, and the contours of positive psychological functioning. *Cognitive Therapy and Research, 26,* 789–810.

Kashdan, T. B., & Roberts, J. E. (2002). *Individual differences in interpersonally-generated positive and negative affect.* Unpublished manuscript, University at Buffalo, State University of New York.

Kashdan, T. B., & Roberts, J. E. (in press). Trait and state curiosity in the genesis of intimacy: Differentiation from related constructs. *Journal of Social and Clinical Psychology.*

Kashdan, T. B., Rose, P., & Fincham, F. D. (2002). *Curiosity and exploration:*

Facilitating positive subjective experiences and personal growth opportunities.
Unpublished manuscript, State University of New York at Buffalo.

Kasser, T. (2002). *The psychology of materialism.* Cambridge, MA: MIT Press.

Kasser, T., & Ryan, R. M. (1993). A dark side of the American Dream: Correlates of financial success as a central life aspiration. *Journal of Personality and Social Psychology, 65,* 410–422.

Kasser, V. G., & Ryan, R. M. (1999). The relation of psychological needs for autonomy and relatedness to vitality, well-being, and mortality in a nursing home. *Journal of Applied Social Psychology, 29,* 935–954.

Kassinove, J. I., & Schare, M. L. (2001). Effects of the "near miss" and the "big win" on persistence at slot machine gambling. *Psychology of Addictive Behaviors, 15,* 155–158.

Katz, J., & Joiner, T. E. (2002). Being known, intimate, and liked: Self-verification and relationship quality. *Journal of Personality, 70,* 33–58.

Katz, R., Santman, J., & Lonero, P. (1993). Findings on the Revised Morally Debatable Behaviors Scale. *Journal of Psychology, 128,* 15–21.

Katz, R. L. (1955, January–February). Skills of an effective administrator. *Harvard Business Review,* 33–42.

Katzman, R. (1973). Education and the prevalence of dementia and Alzheimer's disease. *Neurology, 43,* 13–20.

Kavanagh, D. J. (1987). Mood, persistence, and success. *Australian Journal of Psychology, 39,* 307–318.

Keegan, J. (1993). *A history of warfare.* New York: Knopf.

Keelan, J. P. R., Dion, K. L., & Dion, K. K. (1994). Attachment style and heterosexual relationships among young adults: A short-term panel study. *Journal of Social and Personal Relationships, 11,* 201–214.

Keen, S. (1992). *Fire in the belly: On being a man.* New York: Bantam Books.

Kekes, (1995). *Moral wisdom and good lives.* Ithaca, NY: Cornell University Press.

Kelley, H. H., Berscheid, E., Christensen, A., Harvey, J. H., Huston, T. L., Levinger, G., et al. (Eds.). (1983). *Close relationships.* New York: Freeman.

Kelley, S. A., Brownell, C. A., & Campbell, S. B. (2000). Mastery motivation and self-evaluative affect in toddlers: Longitudinal relations with maternal behavior. *Child Development, 71,* 1061–1071.

Kelly, A., Kahn, J., & Coulter, R. (1996). Client self-presentations at intake. *Journal of Counseling Psychology, 43,* 300–309.

Kelly, F. D., & Chick, J. M. (1982). *Basic parent counseling skills for the occupational specialist.* Tallahassee: Florida State University Center for Studies in Vocational Education. (ERIC Document Reproduction Service No. ED236562)

Kelly, G. A. (1955). *The psychology of personal constructs: Vol. 1. A theory of personality.* New York: Norton.

Keltner, D., & Haidt, J. (2003). Approaching awe, a moral, spiritual, and aesthetic emotion. *Cognition and Emotion, 17,* 297–314.

Kendall, P. C. (1992). Healthy thinking. *Behavior Therapy, 23,* 1–11.

Keniston, K. (1968). *Young radicals: Notes on committed youth.* New York: Harcourt, Brace, & World.

Kenny, D. A., & Zaccaro, S. J. (1983). An estimate of variance due to traits in leadership. *Journal of Applied Psychology, 68,* 678–685.

Kernberg, O. (1976). *Object relations theory and clinical psychoanalysis.* New York: Jason Aronson.

Kernis, M. H., Cornell, D. P., Sun, C., Berry, A., & Harlow, T. (1993). There's more to self-esteem than whether it is high or low: The importance of stability of self-esteem. *Journal of Personality and Social Psychology, 65,* 1190–1204.

Kernis, M. H., Zuckerman, M., Cohen, A., & Spadafora, S. (1982). Persistence after failure: The interactive role of self-awareness and the attributional basis for negative expectancies. *Journal of Personality and Social Psychology, 43,* 1184–1191.

Kerr, S., & Jermier, J. M. (1978). Substitutes for leadership. *Organizational Behavior and Human Performance, 22,* 375–403.

Keyes, C. L. M., & Haidt, J. (Eds.). (2003). *Flourishing: Positive psychology and the life well-lived.* Washington, DC: American Psychological Association.

Khanna, R., Singh, P., & Rushton, J. P. (1993). Development of the Hindi version of a Self-Report Altruism Scale. *Personality and Individual Differences, 14,* 267–270.

Kihlstrom, J. F., & Cantor, N. (2000). Social intelligence. In R. J. Sternberg (Ed.), *Handbook of intelligence* (pp. 359–379). Cambridge, England: Cambridge University Press.

Kilpatrick, W., Wolfe, G., & Wolfe, S. M. (1994). *Books that build character.* New York: Simon & Schuster.

Kirkpatrick, L. (1999, November/December). Giving thanks: Thirteen creative ways to encourage gratefulness this Thanksgiving. *Christian Parenting Today, 12,* 54.

Kirkpatrick, L. A., & Davis, K. E. (1994). Attachment style, gender, and relationship stability: A longitudinal analysis. *Journal of Personality and Social Psychology, 66,* 502–512.

Kirschenbaum, D. S. (1987). Self-regulatory failure: A review with clinical implications. *Clinical Psychology Review, 7,* 77–104.

Kittay, E. F., & Meyers, D. T. (1987). *Women and moral theory.* Totowa, NJ: Roman & Littlefield.

Klassen, W. (1966). *The forgiving community.* Philadelphia: Westminster Press.

Klee, M. B. (2000). *Core virtues: A literature-based program in character education.* Redwood City, CA: Link Institue.

Klimoski, R. J., & Strickland, W. J. (1977). Assessment centers—valid or merely prescient. *Personnel Psychology, 33,* 543–555.

Kling, K. C., Hyde, J. S., Showers, C., & Buswell, B. (1999). Gender differences in self-esteem: A meta-analysis. *Psychological Bulletin, 125,* 470–500.

Klostermaier, K. K. (1999). *Buddhism: A short introduction.* Oxford, England: Oneworld Publications.

Klump, C., Reed, H., & Perman, S. (1985). The Stanton Survey. In J. V. Mitchell (Ed.), *The ninth mental measurements yearbook* (Vol. 2, pp. 1469–1473). Lincoln: University of Nebraska–Lincoln, Buros Institute of Mental Measurements.

Knight, G. P., Johnson, L. G., Carlo, G., & Eisenberg, N. (1994). A multiplicative model of the dispositional antecedents of a prosocial behavior: Predicting more of the people more of the time. *Journal of Personality and Social Psychology, 66,* 178–183.

Kobak, R. R., & Hazan, C. (1991). Attachment in marriage: The effects of security and accuracy of working models. *Journal of Personality and Social Psychology, 60,* 861–869.

Kobasa, S. C. (1979). Hardiness and health: A prospective study. *Journal of Personality and Social Psychology, 42,* 168–177.

Kobasa, S. C., Maddi, S. R., & Kahn, S. (1982). Stressful life event, personality, and health: An inquiry into hardiness. *Journal of Personality and Social Psychology, 37,* 1–11.

Kochanska, G., Murray, K. T., & Harlan, E. T. (2000). Effortful control in early childhood: Continuity and change, antecedents, and implications for social development. *Developmental Psychology, 36,* 220–232.

Koeller, O., Baumert, J., & Schnabel, K. (2001). Does interest matter? The relationship between academic interest and achievement in mathematics. *Journal for Research in Mathematics Education, 32,* 448–470.

Koestner, R., & Zuckerman, M. (1994). Causality orientations, failure, and achievement. *Journal of Personality, 62,* 321–346.

Kohlberg, L. (1969). Stage and sequence: The cognitive-developmental approach to socialization. In D. Goslin (Ed.), *Handbook of socialization theory and research* (pp. 347–480). Chicago: Rand McNally.

Kohlberg, L. (1971). From is to ought: How to commit the naturalistic fallacy and get away with it. In T. Mischel (Ed.), *Cognitive development and epistemology* (pp. 151–235). New York: Academic Press.

Kohlberg, L. (1976). Moral stages and moralization: The cognitive-developmental approach. In T. Lickona (Ed.), *Moral development and behavior: Theory, research and social issues* (pp. 31–53). New York: Holt, Rinehart & Winston.

Kohlberg, L. (1981). *Essays on moral development: Vol. 1. The philosophy of moral development.* New York: Harper & Row.

Kohlberg, L. (1984). *Essays on moral development: Vol. 2. The psychology of moral development.* San Francisco: Harper & Row.

Kohlberg, L., & Candee, D. (1984). The relation of moral judgment to moral action. In W. M. Kurtines & J. L. Gewirtz (Eds.), *Morality, moral development, and moral behavior* (pp. 52–73). New York: Wiley Interscience.

Kohlberg, L., & Elfenbein, D. (1975). The development of moral judgments concerning capital punishments. *American Journal of Orthopsychiatry, 45,* 614–640.

Köhler, G., & Ruch, W. (1996). Sources of variance in current sense of humor inventories: How much substance, how much method variance? *Humor, 9,* 363–397.

Kohn, L. (1998). The Lao-Tzu myth. In L. Kohn & M. LaFargue (Eds.), *Lao-Tzu and the Tao-te-ching* (pp. 41–62). Albany: State University of New York Press.

Kokis, J., Macpherson, R., Toplak, M., West, R. F., & Stanovich, K. E. (2002). Heuristic and analytic processing: Age trends and associations with cognitive ability and cognitive styles. *Journal of Experimental Child Psychology, 83,* 26–52.

Koole, S. L., Jager, W., van den Berg, A. E., Vlek, C. A. J., & Hofstee, W. K. B. (2001). On the social nature of personality: Effects of extraversion, agreeableness, and feedback about collective resource use on cooperation in a resource dilemma. *Personality and Social Psychology Bulletin, 27,* 289–301.

Kopp, C. B., & Wyer, N. (1994). Self-regulation in normal and atypical development. In D. Cicchetti & S. L. Toth (Eds.), *Disorders and dysfunctions of the self: Rochester Symposium on Developmental Psychopathology* (pp. 31–56). Rochester, NY: University of Rochester Press.

Koriat, A., Lichtenstein, S., & Fischhoff, B. (1980). Reasons for confidence. *Journal of Experimental Psychology: Human Learning and Memory, 6,* 107–118.

Kosterman, R., & Feshbach, S. (1989). Toward a measure of patriotic and nationalistic attitudes. *Political Psychology, 10,* 257–274.

Kozub, F. M., Porretta, D. L., & Hodge, S. R. (2000). Motor task persistence of children with and without mental retardation. *Mental Retardation, 38,* 42–49.

Kramer, D. A. (1990). Conceptualizing wisdom: The primacy of affect-cognitive relations. In R. J. Sternberg (Ed.), *Wisdom: Its nature, origins, and development* (pp. 212–229). Cambridge, England: Cambridge University Press.

Kramer, D. A. (2000). Wisdom as a classical source of human strength: Conceptualization and empirical inquiry. *Journal of Social and Clinical Psychology, 19,* 83–101.

Kramer, D. A., & Bacelar, W. T. (1994). The educated adult in today's world: Wisdom and the mature learner. In J. D. Sinnot (Ed.), *Interdisciplinary handbook of adult lifespan learning* (pp. 31–50). London: Greenwood Press.

Krapp, A. (2000). Interest and human development during adolescence: An educational-psychological approach. In J. Heckhausen (Ed.), *Motivational psychology of human development: Developing motivation and motivating development* (pp. 109–129). New York: Elsevier.

Krapp, A., & Fink, B. (1992). The development and function of interests during the critical transition from home to preschool. In K. A. Renninger, S. Hidi, & A. Krapp (Eds.), *The role of interest in learning and development* (pp. 397–429). Hillsdale, NJ: Erlbaum.

Krapp, A., & Lewalter, D. (2001). Development of interests and interest-based motivational orientations: A longitudual study in vocational school and work settings. In S. Volet & S. Järvela (Eds.), *Motivation in learning contexts: Theoretical and methodological implication* (pp. 201–32). London: Elsevier.

Krause, N. (1997). Religion, aging, and health: Current status and future prospects. *Journals of Gerontology, 52B,* S291–S293.

Krause, N., Chatters, L., Meltzer, T., & Morgan, D. (2000). Negative interactions in the church: Insights from focus groups with older adults. *Review of Religious Research, 41,* 510–533.

Krause, N., Ellison, C. G., Shaw, B., Marcum, J., & Boardman, J. (2001). Church-based social support and religious coping. *Journal for the Scientific Study of Religion, 40,* 637–656.

Krebs, J. R., & Davies, N. B. (1993). *An introduction to behavioural ecology* (3rd ed.). Boston: Blackwell Scientific.

Krechevsky, I. (1937). Brain mechanisms and variability, II. Variability where no learning is involved. *Journal of Comparative Physiological Psychology, 23,* 139–163.

Kreitler, S., Kreitler, H., & Zigler, E. (1974). Cognitive orientation and curiosity. *British Journal of Psychology, 65,* 43–52.

Krueger, J. (1998a). The bet on bias: A foregone conclusion? *Psycoloquy, 9*(46). Document available at http://www.cogsci.soton.ac.uk=/cgi/psyc/newpsy?9.46.

Krueger, J. (1998b). Enhancement bias in descriptions of self and others. *Personality and Social Psychology Bulletin, 24,* 505–516.

Krueger, J., & Funder, D. C. (in press). Towards a balanced social psychology: Causes, consequences, and cures for the problem-seeking approach to social behavior and cognition. *Behavioral and Brain Sciences.*

Krueger, J., & Mueller, R. A. (2002). Unskilled, unaware, or both? The contribution of social-perceptual skills and statistical regression to self-enhancement biases. *Journal of Personality and Social Psychology, 82,* 180–188.

Kruger, A. C. (1992). The effect of peer and adult-child transactive discussions on moral reasoning. *Merrill-Palmer Quarterly, 38,* 191–211.

Kubiszyn, T. W., & Reed, G. M. (2001). Psychological testing and psychological assessment. *American Psychologist, 56,* 128–165.

Kuhl, J., & Goschke, T. (1994). A theory of action control: Mental subsystems, modes of control, and volitional conflict-resolution strategies. In J. Kuhl & J. Beckmann (Eds.), *Volition and personality: Action versus state orientation* (pp. 93–124). Göttingen, Germany: Hogrefe.

Kuhn, D. (1991). *The skills of argument.* New York: Cambridge University Press.

Kuhn, D., Amsel, E., & O'Loughlin, M. (1988). *The development of scientific thinking skills.* New York: Academic Press.

Kuhn, D., Langer, J., Kohlberg, L., & Haan, N. (1977). The development of formal operations in logical and moral judgment. *Genetic Psychology Monographs, 95,* 97–188.

Kuiper, N. A., Martin, R. A., & Olinger, L. J. (1993). Coping humour, stress, and cognitive appraisals. *Canadian Journal of Behavioural Science, 25,* 81–96.

Kumpfer, K. L. (1999). Factors and processes contributing to resilience: The resilience framework. In M. D. Glantz & J. L. Johnson (Eds.), *Resilience and development: Positive life adaptations* (pp. 179–224). New York: Kluwer/Plenum.

Kuo, F. E., Sullivan, W. C., Coley, R. L., & Brunson, L. (1998). Fertile ground for community: Inner-city neighborhood common spaces. *American Journal of Community Psychology, 26,* 823–851.

Kurtz, E., & Ketcham, K. (1992). *The spirituality of imperfection: Storytelling and the journey to wholeness.* New York: Bantam Books.

Kweon, B. S., Sullivan, W. C., & Wiley, A. R. (1998). Green common spaces and the social integration of inner-city older adults. *Environment and Behavior, 30,* 832–858.

Kyle, P. B. (1991). Developing cooperative interaction in schools for teachers and administrators. *Individual Psychology, 47,* 261–265.

Labouvie-Vief, G. (1990). Wisdom as integrated thought: Historical and developmental perspectives. In R. J. Sternberg (Ed.), *Wisdom: Its nature, origins, and development* (pp. 52–83). New York: Cambridge University Press.

Lacayo, R., & Ripley, A. (2002, December 30). Persons of the year—the whistleblowers: Sherron Watkins of Enron; Coleen Rowley of the FBI; Cynthia Cooper of WorldCom. *Time,* 30–33.

LaFargue, M. (1998). Recovering the Tao-te-ching's original meaning: Some remarks on historical hermeneutics. In L. Kohn & M. LaFargue (Eds.), *Lao-tzu and the Tao-te-ching* (pp. 255–276). Albany: State University of New York Press.

Laing, R. D. (1960). *The divided self.* Harmondsworth, England: Penguin.

Lall, R., Holmes, E. K., Brinkmeyer, K. R., Johnson, W. B., & Yapko, B. R. (1999). Personality characteristics of future military leaders. *Military Medicine, 164,* 906–910.

Lamborn, S., Fischer, K., & Pipp, S. (1994). Constructive criticism and social lies: A developmental sequence for understanding honesty and kindness in social interactions. *Developmental Psychology, 30,* 495–508.

Lampert, M., & Ervin-Tripp, S. M. (1998). Exploring paradigms: The study of gender and sense of humor at the end of the 20th century. In W. Ruch (Ed.), *The sense of humor: Explorations of a personality characteristic* (pp. 231–270). New York: Mouton de Gruyter.

Landrum, R. E. (2002, May). *Humility: Its measurement and impact on person-perception.* Poster presented at the annual meeting of the Midwestern Psychological Association, Chicago.

Langevin, R. L. (1971). Is curiosity a unitary construct? *Canadian Journal of Psychology, 25,* 360–374.

Lansing, A. (1959). *Endurance: Shackleton's incredible voyage.* New York: Carroll & Graf.

Lanyon, R. (1993). Development of scales to assess specific deception strategies on the Psychological Screening Inventory. *Psychological Assessment, 5,* 324–329.

Lao-tzu. (1963). *Tao Te Ching* (D. C. Lau, Trans.). New York: Viking Penguin.

Larrabee, M. J. (Ed.). (1993). *An ethic of care: Feminist and interdisciplinary perspectives.* New York: Routledge.

Larsen, K. S., & Giles, H. (1976). Survival or courage as human motivation: Development of an attitude scale. *Psychological Reports, 39,* 299–302.

Larson, R. W. (2000). Toward a psychology of positive youth development. *American Psychologist, 55,* 150–183.

Lash, J. (1995). *The hero: Manhood and power.* London: Thames and Hudson.

Layton, E. (1984). *Through the looking glass: Drawings by Elizabeth Layton.* Kansas City, MO: Mid-America Arts Alliance.

Lazar, A., Kravetz, S., & Frederich-Kedem, P. (2002). The multidimensionality of motivation for Jewish religious behavior: Content, structure, and relationship to religious identity. *Journal for the Scientific Study of Religion, 41,* 509–519.

Lazarus, R. S. (1991). *Emotion and adaptation.* New York: Oxford University Press.

Lazarus, R. S., & Lazarus, B. N. (1994). *Passion and reason: Making sense of our emotions.* New York: Oxford University Press.

Leahy, R. (1986). Educating for authenticity. *Counseling and Values, 30,* 175–182.

Leaman, O. (1999). *Key concepts in Eastern philosophy.* New York: Routledge.

Leaman, O. (2002). *An introduction to classical Islamic philosophy.* New York: Cambridge University Press.

Leary, M. R., & Baumeister, R. F. (2000). The nature and function of self-esteem: Sociometer theory. In M. P. Zanna (Ed.), *Advances in experimental social psychology* (Vol. 32, pp. 1–62). San Diego, CA: Academic Press.

Leary, M. R., Bednarski, R., Hammon, D., & Duncan, T. (1997). Blowhards, snobs, and narcissists: Interpersonal reactions to excessive egotism. In R. M. Kowalski (Ed.), *Aversive interpersonal behaviors* (pp. 111–131). New York: Plenum Press.

Lee, F., & Peterson, C. (1997). Content analysis of archival data. *Journal of Consulting and Clinical Psychology, 65,* 959–969.

Lee, J.-E., Wong, C.-M. T., Day, J. D., Maxwell, S. E., & Thorpe, P. (2000). Social and academic intelligence: A multi-trait-multimethod study of their crystallized and fluid characteristics. *Personality and Individual Differences, 29,* 539–553.

Lee, Y.-T., & Seligman, M. E. P. (1997). Are Americans more optimistic than the Chinese? *Personality and Social Psychology Bulletin, 23,* 32–40.

Leeman, L. W., Gibbs, J. C., & Fuller, D. (1993). Evaluation of a multi-component group treatment program for juvenile offenders. *Aggressive Behavior, 19,* 281–292.

Leffert, N., Benson, P. L., Scales, P. C., Sharma, A. R., Drake, D. R., & Blyth, D. A. (1998). Developmental assets: Measurement and prediction of risk behaviors among adolescents. *Applied Developmental Science, 2,* 209–230.

Lehman, D. R., & Nisbett, R. E. (1990). A longitudinal study of the effects of undergraduate training on reasoning. *Developmental Psychology, 26,* 952–960.

Lehrer, K., Lum, B. J., Slichta, B. A., & Smith, N. D. (1996). *Knowledge, teaching, and wisdom.* Dordrecht, Netherlands: Kluwer.

Leiber, M., & Woodrick, A. (1997). Religious beliefs, attributional styles, and adherence to correctional orientations. *Criminal Justice and Behavior, 24,* 495–511.

Leming, J. S. (1978). Cheating behavior, situational influence and moral development. *Journal of Educational Research, 5,* 214–219.

Lent, R. W., Brown, S. D., & Hackett, G. (1994). Toward a unifying social cognitive theory of career and academic interest, choice, and performance. *Journal of Vocational Behavior, 45,* 79–122.

Lepper, M. R., & Cordova, D. L. (1992). A desire to be taught: Instructional consequences of intrinsic motivation. *Motivation and Emotion, 16,* 187–208.

Lepper, M. R., Greene, D., & Nisbett, R. E. (1973). Undermining children's intrinsic interest with extrinsic rewards: A test of the "overjustification" hypothesis. *Journal of Personality and Social Psychology, 28,* 129–137.

Lepper, M. R., & Henderlong, J. (2000). Turning "play" into "work" and "work" into "play": 25 years of research into intrinsic vs. extrinsic motivation. In C. Sansone & J. M. Harackiewicz (Eds.), *Intrinsic and extrinsic motivation: The search for optimal motivation and performance* (pp. 257–307). New York: Academic Press.

Lerner, M. J. (1980). *The belief in a just world: A fundamental delusion.* New York: Plenum Press.

Lerner, R. M., Jacobs, F., & Wertlieb, D. (Eds.). (2003). *Promoting positive child, adolescent, and family development: A handbook of program and policy innovations.* Thousand Oaks, CA: Sage.

Leuner, B. (1966). Emotional intelligence and emancipation. *Praxis der Kinderpsychologie und Kinderpsychiatrie, 15,* 193–203.

Levi, I. J. (1930). Student leadership in elementary and junior high school and its transfer into senior high school. *Journal of Educational Research, 22,* 135–139.

Levin, J. (1997). Religious research in gerontology, 1980–1994: A systematic review. *Journal of Religious Gerontology, 10,* 3–31.

Levin, J., & Taylor, R. (1998). Panel analyses of religious involvement and well-being in African Americans: Contemporaneous vs. longitudinal effects. *Journal for the Scientific Study of Religion, 37,* 695–709.

Levin, J., Taylor, R., & Chatters, L. (1995). A multidimensional measure of religious involvement for African Americans. *Sociological Quarterly, 36,* 157–173.

Levy, B. R., Slade, M. D., Kunkel, S. R., & Kasl, S. V. (2002). Longevity increased by positive self-perceptions of aging. *Journal of Personality and Social Psychology, 83,* 261–270.

Levy, M. B., & Davis, K. E. (1988). Lovestyles and attachment styles compared: Their relations to each other and to various relationship characteristics. *Journal of Social and Personal Relationships, 5,* 439–471.

Levy, R. (1973). *The Tahitians.* Chicago: University of Chicago Press.

Lewis, M., Stanger, C., & Sullivan, M. (1989). Deception in 3-year-olds. *Developmental Psychology, 25,* 439–443.

Li, J. (2002). A cultural model of learning: Chinese "heart and mind for wanting to learn." *Journal of Cross-Cultural Psychology, 33,* 246–267.

Liddell, D. L., Halpin, G., & Halpin, W. G. (1992). The measure of moral orientation: Measuring the ethics of care and justice. *Journal of College Student Development, 33,* 325–330.

Lieblich, A. (1997). The POW wife—Another perspective on heroism. *Women's Studies International Forum, 20,* 621–630.

Lightfoot, C. (1997). *The culture of adolescent risk-taking*. New York: Guilford Press.

Likert, R. (1961). *New patterns of management*. New York: McGraw-Hill.

Lilly, J. C. (1972a). *The center of the cyclone*. New York: Crown.

Lilly, J. C. (1972b). *Programming and metaprogramming the human biocomputer*. New York: Crown.

Lincoln, C., & Mamiya, L. (1990). *The Black church in the African-American experience*. Durham, NC: Duke University Press.

Linley, P. A., & Joseph, S. (Eds.). (in press). *Positive psychology in practice*. New York: Wiley.

Linnenbrink, E. A., & Pintrich, P. R. (2000). Multiple pathways to learning and achievement. In C. Sansone & J. M. Harackiewicz (Eds.), *Intrinsic and extrinsic motivation: The search for optimal motivation and performance* (pp. 196–230). New York: Academic Press.

Lipsey, M. W., & Wilson, D. B. (1993). The efficacy of psychological, educational, and behavioral treatment: Confirmation from meta-analysis. *American Psychologist, 48*, 1181–1209.

Litman, J. A., & Spielberger, C. D. (2003). Measuring epistemic curiosity and its diversive and specific components. *Journal of Personality Assessment, 80*, 75–86.

Little, B. R., Lecci, L., & Watkinson, B. (1991). Personality and personal projects: Linking Big Five and PAC units of analysis. *Journal of Personality, 60*, 501–525.

Little, T. D. (1997). Mean and covariance structures (MACS) analyses of cross-cultural data: Practical and theoretical issues. *Multivariate Behavioral Research, 32*, 53–76.

Locke, E. A. (1997). The motivation to work: What we know. In M. L. Maehr & P. R. Pintrich (Eds.), *Advances in motivation and achievement* (Vol. 10, pp. 375–412). Greenwich, CT: JAI Press.

Locke, E. A., Kirkpatrick, S. A., Wheeler, J., Schneider, J., Niles, K., Goldstein, H., et al. (1991). *The essence of leadership*. New York: Lexington Books.

Loehlin, J. C. (1992). *Genes and environment in personality development*. Newberry Park, CA: Sage.

Loewenstein, G. (1994). The psychology of curiosity: A review and reinterpretation. *Psychological Bulletin, 116*, 75–98.

Loewenstein, G., Adler, D., Behrens, D., & Gillis, J. (1992). *Why Pandora opened the box: Curiosity as a desire for missing information*. Unpublished manuscript, Department of Social and Decision Sciences, Carnegie Mellon University, Pittsburgh, PA.

Londerville, S., & Main, M. (1981). Security of attachment, compliance, and maternal training methods in the second year of life. *Developmental Psychology, 17*, 289–299.

London House, Inc. (1999a). *Personnel Selection Inventory*. Park Ridge, IL: Author.

London House, Inc. (1999b). *Station Employee Applicant Inventory.* Park Ridge, IL: Author.

Longinus. (1907). *On the sublime* (2nd ed.; W. Rhys Roberts, Ed. and Trans.). Cambridge, England: Cambridge University Press. (Original work written first century A.D.)

Longshore, D., & Turner, S. (1998). Self-control and criminal opportunity: Cross-sectional test of the general theory of crime. *Criminal Justice and Behavior, 25,* 81–98.

Lopez, S. J., Ciarlelli, R., Coffman, L., Stone, M., & Wyatt, L. (2000). Diagnosing for strength: On measuring hope building blocks. In C. R. Snyder (Ed.), *Handbook of hope: Theory, measures, and applications* (pp. 57–83). San Diego, CA: Academic Press.

Lord, C. G., Ross, L., & Lepper, M. R. (1979). Biased assimilation and attitude polarization: The effects of prior theories on subsequently considered evidence. *Journal of Personality and Social Psychology, 37,* 2098–2109.

Lord, R. G., De Vader, C. L., & Alliger, G. M. (1986). A meta-analysis of the relation between personality traits and leadership perceptions: An application of validity generalization procedures. *Journal of Applied Psychology, 71,* 402–410.

Lord, R. G., Foti, R. J., & DeVader, C. L. (1984). A test of leadership categorization theory: Internal structure, information processing, and leadership perceptions. *Organizational Behavior and Human Performance, 34,* 343–378.

Lord, R. G., & Maher, K. J. (1993). *Leadership and information processing.* London: Routledge.

Lorenz, K. Z. (1956). Comparative behaviorology. In J. M. Tanner & B. Inhelder (Eds.), *Discussions on child development* (Vol. 1). London: Tavistock.

Lorr, M., McNair, D. M., & Weinstein, G. J. (1964). Early effects of chlordiazepoxide (Librium) used with psychotherapy. *Journal of Psychiatric Research, 1,* 257–270.

Lousig-Nont, G., & Ishmael, R. (1985). Phase II profile integrity status inventory. In J. V. Mitchell (Ed.), *The ninth mental measurements yearbook* (Vol. 2, p. 1162). Lincoln: University of Nebraska–Lincoln, Buros Institute of Mental Measurements.

Lovejoy, D. S. (1985). *Religious enthusiasm in the New World: Heresy to revolution.* Cambridge, MA: Harvard University Press.

Lowe, K. B., Kroeck, K. G., & Sivasubramaniam, N. (1996). Effectiveness of correlates of transformational and transactional leadership: A meta-analytic review of the MLQ literature. *Leadership Quarterly, 7,* 385–425.

Lowenthal, K., MacLeod, A., & Cinnirella, M. (2002). Are women more religious than men? Gender differences in religious activity among different religious groups in the UK. *Personality and Individual Differences, 32,* 133–139.

Lowin, A. (1967). Approach and avoidance: Alternative modes of selective exposure to information. *Journal of Personality and Social Psychology, 6,* 1–9.

Lowry, R. J. (1973). *A. H. Maslow: An intellectual portrait.* Monterey, CA: Brooks/Cole.

Lubart, T. I. (1999). Creativity across cultures. In R. J. Sternberg (Ed.), *Handbook of creativity* (pp. 339–350). New York: Cambridge University Press.

Luchins, A. S. (1942). Mechanization in problem solving—The effect of Einstellung. *Psychological Monographs, 54* (Whole No. 95).

Ludwig, A. M. (1992). The Creative Achievement Scale. *Creativity Research Journal, 5,* 109–124.

Lufi, D., & Cohen, A. (1987). A scale for measuring persistence in children. *Journal of Personality Assessment, 51,* 178–185.

Lufi, D., & Parish-Plass, J. (1995). Personality assessment of children with attention deficit hyperactivity disorder. *Journal of Clinical Psychology, 51,* 94–99.

Lynn, R. J. (1999). Introduction. In R. J. Lynn (Trans.), *The classic of the way and virtue: A new translation of the Tao-te-Ching of Laozi as interpreted by Wang Bi* (pp. 3–29). New York: Columbia University Press.

Lyons, N. (1983). Two perspectives: On self, relationship, and morality. *Harvard Educational Review, 49,* 125–145.

Lyons-Ruth, K. (1991). Rapprochement or approchement: Mahler's theory reconsidered from the vantage point of recent research on early attachment relationships. *Psychoanalytic Psychology, 8,* 1–23.

Machiavelli, N. (1513). *The prince* (translated 1813, republished 1954). New York: Limited Editions Club.

MacQuarrie, J. (1972). *Paths in spirituality.* London: SCM Press.

Mahdi, M. S. (2001). *Alfarabi and the foundations of Islamic political philosophy.* Chicago: University of Chicago Press.

Mahoney, A., Pargament, K., Jewell, T., Swank, A., Scott, E., Emery, E., et al. (1999). Marriage and the spiritual realm: The role of proximal and distal religious constructs in marital functioning. *Journal of Family Psychology, 13,* 321–338.

Maier, S. F., & Seligman, M. E. P. (1976). Learned helplessness: Theory and evidence. *Journal of Experimental Psychology: General, 105,* 3–46.

Main, M., & Goldwyn, R. (1984). Predicting rejection of her infant from mother's representation of her own experiences: A preliminary report. *International Journal of Child Abuse and Neglect, 8,* 203–217.

Main, M., & Solomon, J. (1990). Procedures for identifying infants as disorganized/disoriented during the Ainsworth Strange Situation. In M. Greenberg, D. Cicchetti, & M. Cummings (Eds.), *Attachment in the preschool years: Theory, research, and intervention* (pp. 121–160). Chicago: University of Chicago Press.

Malcom, W. M., & Greenberg, L. S. (2000). Forgiveness as a process of change in individual psychotherapy. In M. E. McCullough, K. I. Pargament, & C. E. Thoresen (Eds.), *Forgiveness: Theory, research, and practice* (pp. 179–202). New York: Guilford Press.

Malinchoc, M., Offord, K. P., & Colligan, R. C. (1995). Revised Optimism-Pessimism Scale for the MMPI-2 and MMPI. *Journal of Clinical Psychology, 51,* 205–214.

Malinowski, B. (1926). *Myth in primitive psychology.* London: Kegan Paul, Trench, Trubner.

Maltby, J., Macaskill, A., & Day, L. (2001). Failure to forgive self and others: A replication and extension of the relationship between forgiveness, personality, social desirability and general health. *Personality and Individual Differences, 30,* 881–885.

Manke, B. (1998). Genetic and environmental contributions to children's interpersonal humor. In W. Ruch (Ed.), *The sense of humor: Explorations of a personality characteristic* (pp. 361–384). New York: Mouton de Gruyter.

Mann, R. D. (1959). A review of the relationship between personality and performance in small groups. *Psychological Bulletin, 56,* 241–270.

Marcia, J. E. (1994). The empirical study of ego identity. In H. A. Bosma & T. L. Graafsma (Eds.), *Identity and development: An interdisciplinary approach* (pp. 67–80). Thousand Oaks, CA: Sage.

Markstrom-Adams, C., Hofstra, G., & Dougher, K. (1994). The ego-virtue of fidelity: A case for the study of religion and identity formation in adolescence. *Journal of Youth and Adolescence, 23,* 453–469.

Markus, H. R., & Kitayama, S. (1991). Culture and the self: Implications for cognition, emotion, and motivation. *Psychological Review, 98,* 224–253.

Markus, H. R., Kitayama, S., & Heiman, R. (1996). Culture and basic psychological principles. In E. T. Higgins & A. W. Kruglanski (Eds.), *Social psychology: Handbook of basic principles* (pp. 857–913). New York: Guilford Press.

Markus, H. R., & Nurius, P. (1986). Possible selves. *American Psychologist, 4,* 954–969.

Marsh, H. W., Craven, R. G., & Debus, R. (1991). Self-concepts of young children 5 to 8 years of age: Measurement and multidimensional structure. *Journal of Educational Psychology, 83,* 377–392.

Marshall, G. N., Wortman, C. B., Vickers, R. R., Kusulas, J. W., & Hervig, L. K. (1994). The five-factor model of personality as a framework for personality-health research. *Journal of Personality and Social Psychology, 67,* 278–286.

Martin, J. R. (1989). Transforming moral education. In M. Brabeck (Ed.), *Who cares?* (pp. 183–196). New York: Praeger.

Martin, K. (2001). *Women of spirit: Stories of courage from the women who lived them.* Novato, CA: New World Library.

Martin, R. A. (1996). The Situational Humor Response Questionnaire (SHRQ) and Coping Humor Scale (CHS): A decade of research findings. *Humor, 9,* 251–272.

Martin, R. A. (1998). Approaches to the sense of humor: A historical review. In W. Ruch (Ed.), *The sense of humor: Explorations of a personality characteristic* (pp. 15–62). New York: Mouton de Gruyter.

Martin, R. A. (2001). Humor, laughter, and physical health: Methodological issues and research findings. *Psychological Bulletin, 127,* 504–519.

Martin, R. A., & Lefcourt, H. M. (1983). Sense of humor as a moderator of the relation between stressors and moods. *Journal of Personality and Social Psychology, 45,* 1313–1324.

Martin, R. A., & Lefcourt, H. M. (1984). Situational Humor Response Question-naire: Quantitative measure of sense of humor. *Journal of Personality and Social Psychology, 47,* 145–155.

Martin, R. A., Puhlik-Doris, P., Larsen, G., Gray, J., & Weir, K. (2003). Individual differences in interpersonal and intrapersonal functions of humor: Develop-ment of the Humor Styles Questionnaire. *Journal of Research in Personality, 37,* 1–104.

Marx, G. (1969). *Protest and prejudice.* New York: Harper & Row.

Marx, K. (1977). Critique of the Gotha program. In D. McLellan (Ed.), *Karl Marx: Selected writings* (pp. 564–570). London: Oxford University Press. (Original work published 1875)

Marx, K. (1990). Religion, the opium of the people. In J. Pelikan (Ed.), *The world treasury of modern religious thought* (pp. 79–91). Boston: Little, Brown.

Maslow, A. H. (1959). Creativity in self-actualizing people. In H. H. Anderson (Ed.), *Creativity and its cultivation* (pp. 83–95). New York: Harper & Row.

Maslow, A. H. (1964). *Religions, values, and peak experiences.* New York: Penguin.

Maslow, A. H. (1970). *Motivation and personality* (2nd ed.). New York: Harper & Row.

Masten, A. S. (2001). Ordinary magic: Resilience processes in development. *American Psychologist, 56,* 227–238.

Masters, J. C., & Santrock, J. W. (1976). Studies in the self-regulation of behavior: Effects of contingent cognitive and affective events. *Developmental Psychol-ogy, 12,* 334–348.

Masterson, J. F. (1988). *The search for the real self.* New York: Free Press.

Maszk, P., Eisenberg, N. G., & Guthrie, I. K. (1999). Relations of children's social status to their emotionality and regulation: A short-term longitudinal study. *Merrill-Palmer Quarterly, 45,* 468–492.

Matas, L., Arend, R. A., & Sroufe, L. A. (1978). Continuity of adaptation in the second year: The relationship between quality of attachment and later competence. *Child Development, 49,* 547–556.

Mateer, F. (1917). The moron as a war problem. *Journal of Applied Psychology, 1,* 317–320.

Maton, K., & Pargament, K. (1987). The roles of religion in prevention and promotion. *Prevention in Human Services, 5,* 161–205.

Maton, K., & Wells, E. (1995). Religion as a community resource for well-being: Prevention, healing, and empowerment pathways. *Journal of Social Issues, 51*(2), 177–193.

Matsuoka, F. (2001). Reformations of identities and values within Asian North American communities. In E. Fernandez & F. Segovia (Eds.), *A dream unfinished: Theological reflections on America from the margins* (pp. 119–128). Maryknoll, NY: Orbis Books.

Matthews, G., Zeidner, M., & Roberts, R. D. (2002). *Emotional intelligence: Science and myth.* Cambridge, MA: MIT Press.

Mattis, J. (2000). African American women's definitions of spirituality: A qualitative analysis. *Journal of Black Psychology, 26,* 101–122.

Mattis, J. (2001). Religiosity and African American political life. *Political Psychology, 22*, 263–278.

Mattis, J. (2002). Religion and spirituality in the meaning making and coping experiences of African American women: A qualitative analysis. *Psychology of Women Quarterly, 26*, 308–320.

Mattis, J., Jagers, R., Hatcher, C., Lawhon, G., Murphy, E., & Murray, Y. (2000). Religiosity, communalism, and volunteerism among African American men: An exploratory analysis. *Journal of Community Psychology, 28*, 391–406.

Maturana, H. R. (1999). The organization of the living: A theory of the living organization. *International Journal of Human-Computer Studies, 51*, 149–168.

Mauger, P. A., Perry, J. E., Freeman, T., Grove, D. C., McBride, A. G., & McKinney, K. E. (1992). The measurement of forgiveness: Preliminary research. *Journal of Psychology and Christianity, 11*, 170–180.

May, R. (1978). *The courage to create.* New York: Bantam Books.

Mayer, J. D. (1986). How mood influences cognition. In N. E. Sharkey (Ed.), *Advances in cognitive science* (pp. 290–314). Chichester, West Sussex, England: Ellis Horwood.

Mayer, J. D. (2000). Emotion, intelligence, emotional intelligence. In J. P. Forgas (Ed.), *The handbook of affect and social cognition* (pp. 410–431). Mahwah, NJ: Erlbaum.

Mayer, J. D. (2001). A field guide for emotional intelligence. In J. Ciarrochi, J. P. Forgas, & J. D. Mayer (Eds.), *Emotional intelligence and everday life* (pp. 3–24). New York: Psychology Press.

Mayer, J. D., Carlsmith, K. M., & Chabot, H. F. (1998). Describing the person's external environment: Conceptualizing and measuring the life space. *Journal of Research in Personality, 32*, 253–296.

Mayer, J. D., Caruso, D. R., & Salovey, P. (1999). Emotional intelligence meets traditional standards for an intelligence. *Intelligence, 27*, 267–298.

Mayer, J. D., & Cobb, C. D. (2000). Educational policy on emotional intelligence: Does it make sense? *Educational Psychology Review, 12*, 163–183.

Mayer, J. D., DiPaolo, M. T., & Salovey, P. (1990). Perceiving affective content in ambiguous visual stimuli: A component of emotional intelligence. *Journal of Personality Assessment, 54*, 772–781.

Mayer, J. D., & Geher, G. (1996). Emotional intelligence and the identification of emotion. *Intelligence, 17*, 89–113.

Mayer, J. D., & Mitchell, D. C. (1998). Intelligence as a subsystem of personality: From Spearman's g to contemporary models of hot processing. In W. Tomic & J. Kingma (Eds.), *Advances in cognition and educational practice* (Vol. 5, pp. 43–75). Greenwich, CT: JAI Press.

Mayer, J. D., Perkins, D., Caruso, D. R., & Salovey, P. (2001). Emotional intelligence and giftedness. *Roeper Review, 23*, 131–137.

Mayer, J. D., & Salovey, P. (1993). The intelligence of emotional intelligence. *Intelligence, 17*, 433–442.

Mayer, J. D., & Salovey, P. (1997). What is emotional intelligence? In P. Salovey & D. Sluyter (Eds.), *Emotional development and emotional intelligence: Implications for educators* (pp. 3–31). New York: Basic Books.

Mayer, J. D., Salovey, P., & Caruso, D. R. (2000). Models of emotional intelligence. In R. J. Sternberg (Ed.), *Handbook of intelligence* (pp. 396–420). Cambridge, England: Cambridge University Press.

Mayer, J. D., Salovey, P., & Caruso, D. R. (2002). *Mayer-Salovey-Caruso Emotional Intelligence Test (MSCEIT) users manual.* Toronto, Ontario, Canada: Multi-Health Systems.

Mayer, J. D., Salovey, P., Caruso, D. R., & Sitarenios, G. (2001). Emotional intelligence as a standard intelligence. *Emotion, 1,* 232–242.

Mayer, J. D., Salovey, P., Caruso, D. R., & Sitarenios, G. (2003). Measuring emotional intelligence with the MSCEIT V2.0. *Emotion, 3,* 97–105.

Mayer, J. D., Salovey, P., Gomberg-Kaufman, S., & Blainey, K. (1991). A broader conception of mood experience. *Journal of Personality and Social Psychology, 60,* 100–111.

McAdams, D. P. (1989). The biographical consequences of activism. *American Sociological Review, 54,* 744–760.

McAdams, D. P. (1993). *The stories we live by: Personal myths and the making of the self.* New York: Guilford Press.

McAdams, D. P. (1999). Personal narratives and the life story. In L. Pervin & O. John (Eds.), *Handbook of personality: Theory and research* (2nd ed., pp. 478–500). New York: Guilford Press.

McAdams, D. P., & de St. Aubin, E. (1992). A theory of generativity and its assessment through self-report, behavioral acts, and narrative themes in autobiography. *Journal of Personality and Social Psychology, 62,* 1003–1015.

McAdams, D. P., Diamond, A., de St. Aubin, E., & Mansfield, E. (1997). Stories of commitment: The psychological construction of generative lives. *Journal of Personality and Social Psychology, 72,* 678–694.

McCall, M. W. (1994). Identifying leadership potential in future international executives: Developing a concept. *Consulting Psychology Journal, 46,* 49–63.

McCall, M. W., & Lombardo, M. M. (1983). *Off the track: Why and how successful executives get derailed.* Greensboro, NC: Center for Creative Leadership.

McCallum, M., & Piper, W. E. (1987). *The psychological mindedness assessment procedure.* Unpublished manual and videotape. Department of Psychiatry, University of Alberta, Edmonton, Canada.

McCallum, M., & Piper, W. E. (Eds.). (1997). *Psychological mindedness: A contemporary understanding.* Mahway, NJ: Erlbaum.

McCann, J. T., & Biaggo, M. K. (1989). Narcissistic personality features and self-reported anger. *Psychological Reports, 64,* 55–58.

McCauley, C. D., & Lombardo, M. M. (1990). Benchmarks: An instrument for diagnosing managerial strengths and weaknesses. In K. E. Clark & M. B. Clark (Eds.), *Measures of leadership* (pp. 535–545). West Orange, NJ: Leadership Library of America.

McCauley, C. D., Moxley, R. S., & Van Velsor, E. (Eds.). (1998). *Handbook of leadership development*. San Francisco: Jossey-Bass.

McClelland, D. C. (1985). *Human motivation*. Glenview, IL: Scott Foresman.

McClelland, D. C. (1987). Characteristics of successful entrepreneurs. *Journal of Creative Behavior, 21,* 219–233.

McClelland, D. C., Atkinson, J. W., Clark, R. A., & Lowell, E. L. (1953). *The achievement motive*. New York: Appleton-Century-Crofts.

McCombs, B. L. (1991). Motivation and lifelong learning. *Educational Psychologist, 26,* 117–127.

McCord, J. (1979). Some child-rearing antecedents of criminal behavior in adult men. *Journal of Personality and Social Psychology, 37,* 1477–1486.

McCown, W., & Johnson, A. (1989, August). *Nonstudent evaluation of an adult inventory of procrastination*. Paper presented at the annual conference of the American Psychological Association, New Orleans, LA.

McCrae, R. R. (1993–1994). Openness to experience as a basic dimension of personality. *Imagination, Cognition, and Personality, 13,* 39–55.

McCrae, R. R. (1996). Social consequences of experiential openness. *Psychological Bulletin, 120,* 323–337.

McCrae, R. R., & Costa, P. T. (1988). Recalled parent-child relations and adult personality. *Journal of Personality, 56,* 417–434.

McCrae, R. R., & Costa, P. T. (1997a). Conceptions and correlates of openness to experience. In R. Hogan, J. Johnson, & S. Briggs (Eds.), *Handbook of personality psychology* (pp. 825–847). San Diego, CA: Academic Press.

McCrae, R. R., & Costa, P. T. (1997b). Personality trait structure as a human universal. *American Psychologist, 52,* 509–516.

McCrae, R. R., Costa, P. T., Lima, M. P., Simoues, A., Ostendorf, F., Angleitner, A., et al. (1999). Age differences in personality across the adult life span: Parallels in five cultures. *Developmental Psychology, 35,* 466–477.

McCraty, R., Atkinson, M., Tiller, W., Rein, G., & Watkins, A. D. (1995). The effects of emotions on short-term power spectrum analysis of heart rate variability. *American Journal of Cardiology, 76,* 1089–1093.

McCullough, M. E. (2000). Forgiveness as human strength: Theory, measurement, and links to well-being. *Journal of Social and Clinical Psychology, 19,* 43–55.

McCullough, M. E. (2001). Forgiveness: Who does it and how do they do it? *Current Directions in Psychological Science, 10,* 194–197.

McCullough, M. E., Bellah, C. G., Kilpatrick, S. D., & Johnson, J. L. (2001). Vengefulness: Relationships with forgiveness, rumination, well-being, and the Big Five. *Personality and Social Psychology Bulletin, 27,* 601–610.

McCullough, M. E., Emmons, R. A., & Tsang, J. A. (2002). The grateful disposition: A conceptual and empirical topography. *Journal of Personality and Social Psychology, 82,* 112–127.

McCullough, M. E., Fincham, F. D., & Tsang, J. (2003). Forgiveness, forbearance, and time: The temporal unfolding of transgression-related interpersonal motivations. *Journal of Personality and Social Psychology, 84,* 540–557.

McCullough, M. E., & Hoyt, W. T. (2002). Transgression-related motivational dispositions: Personality substrates of forgiveness and their links to the Big Five. *Personality and Social Psychology Bulletin, 28,* 1556–1573.

McCullough, M. E., Hoyt, W. T., & Rachal, K. C. (2000). What we know (and need to know) about assessing forgiveness constructs. In M. E. McCullough, K. I. Pargament, & C. E. Thoresen (Eds.), *Forgiveness: Theory, research, and practice* (pp. 65–88). New York: Guilford Press.

McCullough, M. E., Kilpatrick, S., Emmons, R. A., & Larson, D. (2001). Gratitude as moral affect. *Psychological Bulletin, 127,* 249–266.

McCullough, M. E., Pargament, K. I., & Thoresen, C. T. (Eds.). (2000a). *Forgiveness: Theory, research, and practice.* New York: Guilford Press.

McCullough, M. E., Pargament, K. I., & Thoresen, C. T. (2000b). The psychology of forgiveness: History, conceptual issues, and overview. In M. E. McCullough, K. I. Pargament, & C. E. Thoresen (Eds.), *Forgiveness: Theory, research, and practice* (pp. 1–14). New York: Guilford Press.

McCullough, M. E., Rachal, K. C., Sandage, S. J., Worthington, E. L., , Brown, S. W., & Hight, T. L. (1998). Interpersonal forgiving in close relationships. II: Theoretical elaboration and measurement. *Journal of Personality and Social Psychology, 75,* 1586–1603.

McCullough, M. E., & Snyder, C. R. (2000). Classical source of human strength: Revisiting an old home and building a new one. *Journal of Social and Clinical Psychology, 19,* 1–10.

McCullough, M. E., & Witvliet, C. V. (2001). The psychology of forgiveness. In C. R. Snyder & S. Lopez (Eds.), *Handbook of positive psychology* (pp. 446–458). New York: Oxford University Press.

McCullough, M. E., & Worthington, E. L. (1994). Models of interpersonal forgiveness and their applications to counseling: Review and critique. *Counseling and Values, 39,* 2–14.

McCullough, M. E., & Worthington, E. L. (1999). Religion and the forgiving personality. *Journal of Personality, 67,* 1141–1164.

McCullough, M. E., Worthington, E. L., & Rachal, K. C. (1997). Interpersonal forgiving in close relationships. *Journal of Personality and Social Psychology, 73,* 321–336.

McDaniel, M. A., Waddill, P. J., Finstad, K., & Bourg, T. (2000). The effects of text-based interest on attention and recall. *Journal of Educational Psychology, 92,* 492–502.

McDermott, D., & Hastings, S. (2000). Children: Raising future hopes. In C. R. Snyder (Ed.), *Handbook of hope: Theory, measures, and applications* (pp. 185–199). San Diego, CA: Academic Press.

McFarlin, D. B. (1985). Persistence in the face of failure: The impact on self-esteem and contingency information. *Personality and Social Psychology Bulletin, 11,* 153–163.

McFarlin, D. B., Baumeister, R. F., & Blascovich, J. (1984). On knowing when to quit: Task failure, self-esteem, advice, and nonproductive persistence. *Journal of Personality, 52,* 138–155.

McGhee, P. E. (1979). *Humor: Its origin and development.* San Francisco: Freeman.

McGhee, P. E. (1999). *Humor, health and the amuse system.* Dubuque, IA: Kendall/Hunt.

McGhee, P. E., Ruch, W., & Hehl, F.-J. (1990). A personality-based model of humor development during adulthood. *Humor, 3,* 119–146.

McGuire, J., & Broomfield, D. (1994). Violent offences and capacity for self-control. *Psychology Crime and Law, 1,* 117–123.

McHorney, C. A., Ware, J. E., Lu, J. F. R., & Sherbourne, C. D. (1994). The MOS 36–Item Short-Form Health Survey (SF-36): III. Tests of data quality, scaling assumptions, and reliability across diverse patient groups. *Medical Care, 32,* 40–66.

McHorney, C. A., Ware, J. E., & Raczek, A. E. (1993). The MOS 36–Item Short-Form Health Survey (SF-36): II. Psychometric and clinical tests of validity in measuring physical and mental health constructs. *Medical Care, 31,* 247–263.

McNair, D. M., Goldstein, A. P., Lorr, M., Cibelli, L. A., & Roth, I. (1965). Some effects of chlordiazepoxide and meprobamate with psychiatric outpatients. *Psychopharmacologia, 7,* 256–265.

McNair, D. M., Lorr, M., & Droppleman, L. (1971). *Profile of Mood States manual.* San Diego, CA: Educational and Industrial Testing Service.

McNamee, S. (1978). Moral behavior, moral development and motivation. *Journal of Moral Education, 7,* 27–31.

McNeely, B. L., & Meglino, B. M. (1994). The role of dispositional and situational antecedents in prosocial behavior: An examination of the intended beneficiaries of prosocial behavior. *Journal of Applied Psychology, 79,* 836–844.

McNeill, W. (1982). *The pursuit of power: Technology, armed force, and society since A.D. 1000.* Chicago: University of Chicago Press.

Meacham, J. A. (1983). Wisdom and the context of knowledge: Knowing that one doesn't know. *Contributions to Human Development, 8,* 111–134.

Meacham, J. A. (1990). The loss of wisdom. In R. J. Sternberg (Ed.), *Wisdom: Its nature, origins, and development* (pp. 181–211). Cambridge, England: Cambridge University Press.

Means, J. R., Wilson, G. L., Sturm, C., Biron, J. E., & Bach, P. J. (1990). Humility as a psychotherapeutic formulation. *Counseling Psychology Quarterly, 3,* 211–215.

Mecca, A. M., Smelser, N. J., & Vasconcellos, J. (1989). *The social importance of self-esteem.* Berkeley: University of California Press.

Mednick, S. A. (1962). The associative basis of the creative process. *Psychological Review, 69,* 220–232.

Meglino, B., Ravlin, E., & Adkins, C. (1989). A work values approach to corporate culture: A field test of the value congruence process and its relationship to individual outcomes. *Journal of Applied Psychology, 74,* 424–432.

Mellen, S. L. W. (1981). *The evolution of love.* San Francisco: Freeman.

Merlin, T. W. (2001, March 21). *The percepts of Merlin.* Document available at http://members.tripod.com/Father_Moonshyne/the.htm.

Meyer, G. J., Finn, S. E., Eyde, L., Kay, G. G., Moreland, K. L., Dies, R. R., et al. (2001). Psychological testing and psychological assessment: A review of evidence and issues. *American Psychologist, 56*, 128–165.

Meyer, W. U. (1987). Perceived ability and achievement-related behavior. In F. Halisch & J. Kuhl (Eds.), *Motivation, intention, and volition* (pp. 73–86). Berlin: Springer-Verlag.

Midgley, C., Kaplan, A., Middletown, M., Maehr, M. L., Urdan, T., Anderman, L., et al. (1998). The development and validation of scales assessing students' achievement goal orientations. *Contemporary Educational Psychology, 23*, 113–131.

Midlarsky, E., Kahana, E., Corley, R., Nemeroff, R., & Schonbar, R. A. (1999). Altruistic moral judgment among older adults. *International Journal of Aging and Human Development, 49*, 27–41.

Mikulay, S., & Goffin, R. (1998). Measuring and predicting counterproductivity in the laboratory using integrity and personality testing. *Educational and Psychological Measurement, 58*, 768–790.

Mikulincer, M. (1997). Adult attachment style and information processing: Individual differences in curiosity and cognitive closure. *Journal of Personality and Social Psychology, 72*, 1217–1230.

Mikulincer, M., Florian, V., & Weller, A. (1993). Attachment styles, coping strategies, and posttraumatic psychological distress: The impact of the Gulf War in Israel. *Journal of Personality and Social Psychology, 64*, 817–826.

Milgram, S. (1963). Behavioral study of obedience. *Journal of Abnormal and Social Psychology, 67*, 371–378.

Milich, R., & Okazaki, M. (1991). An examination of learned helplessness among attention-deficit hyperactivity disordered boys. *Journal of Abnormal Child Psychology, 19*, 607–623.

Mill, J. S. (1859). *On liberty.* London: J. W. Parker & Son.

Miller, A., & Hom, H. L. (1990). Influence of extrinsic and ego incentive value on persistence after failure and continuing motivation. *Journal of Educational Psychology, 82*, 539–545.

Miller, J. G. (1994). Cultural diversity in the morality of caring: Individually-oriented versus duty-based interpersonal moral codes. *Cross-Cultural Research: The Journal of Comparative Social Science, 28*, 3–39.

Miller, P. A., Eisenberg, H., Shell, R., & Fabes, R. A. (1996). Relations of moral reasoning and vicarious emotion to young children's prosocial behavior toward peers and adults. *Developmental Psychology, 32*, 210–219.

Miller, R. S., & Schlenker, B. R. (1985). Egotism in group members: Public and private attributions of responsibility for group performance. *Social Psychology Quarterly, 48*, 85–89.

Miller, T. (1995). *How to want what you have.* New York: Avon.

Miller, W. I. (2000). *The mystery of courage.* Cambridge, MA: Harvard University Press.

Mindel, C., & Vaughn, C. (1978). A multidimensional approach to religiosity and disengagement. *Journal of Gerontology, 33,* 103–108.

Mischel, W. (1968). *Personality and assessment.* New York: Wiley.

Mischel, W. (1973). Toward a cognitive social learning reconceptualization of personality. *Psychological Review, 80,* 252–283.

Mischel, W. (1974). Processes in delay of gratification. In L. Berkowitz (Ed.), *Advances in experimental social psychology* (Vol. 7, pp. 249–292). San Diego, CA: Academic Press.

Mischel, W. (1996). From good intentions to willpower. In P. Gollwitzer & J. Bargh (Eds.), *The psychology of action* (pp. 197–218). New York: Guilford Press.

Mischel, W., & Ebbesen, E. B. (1970). Attention in delay of gratification. *Journal of Personality and Social Psychology, 16,* 329–337.

Mischel, W., & Metzner, R. (1962). Preference for delayed reward as a function of age, intelligence, and the length of delay interval. *Journal of Abnormal and Social Psychology, 64,* 425–431.

Mischel, W., Shoda, Y., & Peake, P. K. (1988). The nature of adolescent competencies predicted by preschool delay of gratification. *Journal of Personality and Social Psychology, 34,* 687–696.

Mischel, W., Shoda, Y., & Rodriguez, M. L. (1989). Delay of gratification in children. *Science, 244,* 933–938.

Mitchell, S. A. (1992). True selves, false selves, and the ambiguity of authenticity. In N. J. Skolnick & S. C. Warshaw (Eds.), *Relational perspectives in psychoanalysis* (pp. 1–20). Hillsdale, NJ: Analytical Press.

Moghadam, V. (1999). Revolution, religion, and gender politics: Iran and Afghanistan compared. *Journal of Women's History, 10*(4), 172–195.

Montford, S. D. (1999). *Moral dilemma discussions: The role of moral judgement in their human leadership and the viability of their computer facilitation.* Unpublished doctoral dissertation, University of Birmingham, England.

Moon, S. (1970). *A magic dwells: A poetic and psychological study of the Navaho emergence myth.* Middletown, CT: Wesleyan University Press.

Morgan, V. G. (2001). Humility and the transcendent. *Faith and Philosophy, 18,* 307–322.

Morreall, J. (1983). *Taking laughter seriously.* Albany: State University of New York Press.

Morris, D. R. (1965). *The washing of the spears.* New York: Simon & Schuster.

Morrow, I. J., & Stern, M. (1990). Stars, adversaries, producers, and phantoms at work: A new leadership typology. In K. E. Clark & M. B. Clark (Eds.), *Measures of leadership* (pp. 535–545). West Orange, NJ: Leadership Library of America.

Moskop, W. W. (1996). Prudence as a paradigm for political leaders. *Political Psychology, 17,* 619–642.

Mueller, C. M., & Dweck, C. S. (1998). Praise for intelligence can undermine children's motivation and performance. *Journal of Personality and Social Psychology, 75,* 33–52.

Mulford, H. J. (1918). The human mind: A suggestion as to the constitution of the normal, subnormal and supernormal mind. *American Journal of Psychology, 29,* 272–290.

Mullet, É., & Girard, M. (2000). Developmental and cognitive points of view on forgiveness. In M. E. McCullough, K. I. Pargament, & C. E. Thoresen (Eds.), *Forgiveness: Theory, research, and practice* (pp. 111–132). New York: Guilford Press.

Mullet, É., Houdbine, A., Laumonier, S., & Girard, M. (1998). "Forgivingness": Factor structure in a sample of young, middle-aged, and elderly adults. *European Psychologist, 3,* 289–297.

Multon, K. D., Brown, S. D., & Lent, R. W. (1991). Relation of self-efficacy beliefs to academic outcomes: A meta-analytic investigation. *Journal of Counseling Psychology, 38,* 30–38.

Mumford, E. (1909). *The origins of leadership.* Chicago: University of Chicago Press.

Mumford, M. D., Marks, M. A., Connelly, M. S., Zaccaro, S. J., & Reiter-Palmon, R. (2000). Development of leadership skills: Experience, timing, and growth. *Leadership Quarterly, 11,* 87–114.

Mumford, M. D., Zaccaro, S. J., Harding, F. D., Jacobs, T. O., & Fleishman, E. A. (2000). Leadership skills for a changing world: Solving complex social problems. *Leadership Quarterly, 11,* 11–35.

Muraven, M., & Baumeister, R. F. (2000). Self-regulation and depletion of limited resources: Does self-control resemble a muscle? *Psychological Bulletin, 126,* 247–259.

Muraven, M., Baumeister, R. F., & Tice, D. M. (1999). Longitudinal improvement of self-regulation through practice: Building self-control strength through repeated exercise. *Journal of Social Psychology, 139,* 446–457.

Muraven, M., Tice, D. M., & Baumeister, R. F. (1998). Self-control as a limited resource: Regulatory depletion patterns. *Journal of Personality and Social Psychology, 74,* 774–789.

Murphy, A. J. (1941). A study of the leadership process. *American Sociological Review,* 674–687.

Murphy, B. C., & Eisenberg, N. (1997). Young children's emotionality, regulation and social functioning and their responses when they are a target of a peer's anger. *Social Development, 6,* 18–36.

Murphy, P. K., & Alexander, P. A. (1998). Using the Learning and Study Strategies Inventory–High School version with Singaporean females: Examining psychometric properties. *Educational and Psychological Measurement, 58,* 493–510.

Murphy-Berman, V., & Berman, J. J. (2002). Cross-cultural difference in perceptions of distributive justice: A comparison of Hong Kong and Indonesia. *Journal of Cross-Cultural Psychology, 33,* 157–170.

Murphy-Berman, V., Berman, J. J., Singh, P., Pachauri, A., & Kumar, P. (1984). Factors affecting allocation to needy and meritorious recipients: A cross-cultural comparison. *Journal of Personality and Social Psychology, 46,* 1267–1272.

Murray, A. (2001). *Humility: The journey toward holiness.* Bloomington, MN: Bethany House.

Musick, M. A., Herzog, A. R., & House, J. S. (1999). Volunteering and mortality among older adults: Findings from a national sample. *Journals of Gerontology: Series B: Psychological Sciences and Social Sciences, 54B,* S173–S180.

Musick, M. A., & Wilson, J. (2003). Volunteering and depression: The role of psychological and social resources in different age groups. *Social Science and Medicine, 56,* 259–269.

Myers, A. M., Malott, O. W., Gray, E., Tudor-Locke, C., Ecclestone, N. A., Cousins, S. O., et al. (1999). Measuring accumulated health-related benefits of exercise participation for older adults: The Vitality Plus Scale. *Journal of Gerontology, 54,* M456–M466.

Myers, D. G. (1993). *The pursuit of happiness.* New York: Avon Books.

Myers, D. G. (2000). The psychology of humility. In R. L. Herrmann (Ed.), *God, science, and humility: Ten scientists consider humility theology* (pp. 153–175). Radnor, PA: Templeton Foundation Press.

Myers, D. G., & Diener, E. (1995). Who is happy? *Psychological Science, 6,* 10–19.

Myers, S. (1996). An interactive model of religiosity inheritance: The importance of family context. *American Sociological Review, 61,* 858–866.

Myers, V. (2001, June). *Faith-based interventions: Closing the knowing doing gap.* Paper presented at the Annual Conference on Religion in Black and White America, University of Michigan, Ann Arbor.

Nagao, G. M. (2000). The Bodhisattva's compassion described in the *Mahayanasutralamkara.* In J. A. Silk (Ed.), *Wisdom, compassion, and the search for understanding: The Buddhist studies legacy of Gadjin M. Nagao* (pp. 1–38). Honolulu: University of Hawaii Press.

Nathan, P. E., & Gorman, J. (1998). *A guide to treatments that work.* New York: Oxford University Press.

Nathan, P. E., & Gorman, J. (2002). *A guide to treatments that work* (2nd ed.). New York: Oxford University Press.

Nathan, P. E., Zare, N. C., Ferneau, E. W., & Lowenstein, L. M. (1970). Effects of congener differences in alcoholic beverages on the behavior of alcoholics. *Quarterly Journal of Studies on Alcohol* (Suppl. 5), 87–100.

Nation, J. R., Cooney, J. B., & Gartrell, K. E. (1979). Durability and generalizability of persistence training. *Journal of Abnormal Psychology, 88,* 121–136.

Nation, J. R., & Massad, P. (1978). Persistence training: A partial reinforcement procedure for reversing learned helplessness and depression. *Journal of Experimental Psychology: General, 107,* 436–451.

Naylor, F. D. (1981). A state-trait curiosity inventory. *Australian Psychologist, 16,* 172–183.

Neff, K. (2003). Self-compassion: An alternative conceptualization of a healthy attitude toward oneself. *Self and Identity, 2,* 85–101.

Neff, K. (in press). The development and validation of a scale to measure self-compassion. *Self and Identity.*

Neher, A. (1991). Maslow's theory of motivation: A critique. *Journal of Humanistic Psychology, 31*, 89–112.

Neider, C. (1985). *Papa: An intimate biography of Mark Twain by his thirteen-year-old daughter Susy.* Garden City, NY: Doubleday.

Neighbors, H., Jackson, J., Bowman, P., & Gurin, G. (1983). *Stress, coping, and Black mental health: Preliminary findings from a national study.* Newbury Park, CA: Sage.

Neighbors, H., Musick, M., & Williams, D. (1998). The African American minister as a source of help for serious personal crises: Bridge or barrier to mental health care? *Health Education and Behavior, 25*, 759–777.

Nelson, T. (1997). He made a way out of no way: Religious experience in an African American congregation. *Review of Religious Research, 39*, 5–26.

Nemeth, C., & Chiles, C. (1988). Modeling courage: The role of dissent in fostering independence. *European Journal of Social Psychology, 18*, 275–280.

Neumann, A. (1999, April). *Passionate talk about passionate thought: The view from professors at early mid-career.* Paper presented at the 80th annual meeting of the American Educational Research Association. Montreal, Quebec, Canada.

Nevo, O., Aharonson, H., & Klingman, A. (1998). The development and evaluation of a systematic program for improving sense of humor. In W. Ruch (Ed.), *The sense of humor: Explorations of a personality characteristic* (pp. 385–404). New York: Mouton de Gruyter.

Nevo, O., & Levine, J. (1994). Jewish humor strikes again: Humor in Israel during the Gulf War. *Western Folklore, 53*, 125–146.

New Merriam Webster Dictionary. (1989). Springfield, MA: Merriam-Webster.

Newberg, A., & D'Aquili, E. (1998). The neuropsychology of spiritual experience. In H. Koenig (Ed.), *Handbook of religion and mental health* (pp. 76–94). New York: Academic Press.

Nicholls, J. G. (1984). Achievement motivation: Conceptions of ability, subjective experience, task choice and performance. *Psychological Review, 91*, 328–346.

Nicholson, I. A. M. (1998). Gordon Allport, character, and the "culture of personality": 1897–1937. *History of Psychology, 1*, 52–68.

Nickerson, R. S. (1999). Enhancing creativity. In R. J. Sternberg (Ed.), *Handbook of creativity* (pp. 392–430). New York: Cambridge University Press.

Niemi, R. G., Hepburn, M., & Chapman, C. (2000). Community service by high school students: A cure for civic ills? *Political Behavior, 21*, 45–69.

Niemi, R. G., & Junn, J. (1998). *Civic education: What makes students learn.* New Haven, CT: Yale University Press.

Nisbett, R. E., Peng, K., Choi, I., & Norenzayan, A. (2001). Culture and systems of thought: Holistic versus analytic cognition. *Psychological Review, 108*, 291–310.

Nisbett, R. E., & Wilson, T. D. (1977). Telling more than we can know: Verbal reports on mental processes. *Psychological Review, 84*, 231–259.

Nix, G. A., Ryan, R. M., Manly, J. B., & Deci, E. L. (1999). Revitalization through self-regulation: The effects of autonomous and controlled motivation on happiness and vitality. *Journal of Experimental Social Psychology, 35,* 266–284.

Noddings, N. (1984). *A feminine approach to ethics.* Berkeley: University of California Press.

Noddings, N. (1992). *The challenge to care in schools: An alternative approach to education.* New York: Teachers College Press.

Nolen-Hoeksema, S. (1991). Responses to depression and their effects on the duration of depressive episodes. *Journal of Abnormal Psychology, 100,* 569–582.

Norem, J. (2001). *The positive power of negative thinking.* New York: Basic Books.

Norman, W. T. (1963). Toward an adequate taxonomy of personality attributes: Replicated factor structure in peer nomination personality ratings. *Journal of Abnormal and Social Psychology, 66,* 574–583.

North, J. (1987). Wrongdoing and forgiveness. *Philosophy, 62,* 499–508.

Northcutt, W. (2000). *The Darwin awards: Evolution in action.* New York: Dutton Books.

Nowak, A., & Vallacher, R. R. (1998). *Dynamical social psychology.* New York: Guilford Press.

Nucci, L. (1981). Conceptions of personal issues: A domain distinct from moral or societal concepts. *Child Development, 52,* 114–121.

Nucci, L. (2001). *Education in the moral domain.* New York: Cambridge University Press.

Nucci, L., Guerra, N., & Lee, J. (1991). Adolescent judgments of the personal, prudential, and normative aspects of drug usage. *Developmental Psychology, 27,* 841–848.

Nunn, O. B., & Hazler, R. J. (1990). The affective component of early moral development: Does it deserve greater emphasis? *Journal of Human Behavior and Learning, 7,* 28–33.

Nygard, R. (1977). *Personality, situation, and persistence: A study with emphasis on achievement motivation.* Oslo, Norway: Universitetsforlaget.

Oatley, K. (2002). Creative expression and communication of emotions in the visual and narrative arts. In R. Davidson, K. Scherer, & H. Goldsmith (Eds.), *Handbook of affective sciences* (pp. 481–502). New York: Oxford University Press.

O'Connor, K., Hallam, R., & Rachman, S. (1985). Fearlessness and courage: A replication experiment. *British Journal of Psychology, 76,* 187–197.

Ohbuchi, K., Kameda, M., & Agarie, N. (1989). Apology as aggression control: Its role in mediating appraisal of and response to harm. *Journal of Personality and Social Psychology, 56,* 219–227.

Okamoto, S., & Robinson, W. P. (1997). Determinants of gratitude expressions in England. *Journal of Language and Social Psychology, 16,* 411–433.

Oliner, S., & Oliner, P. (1988). *The altruistic personality.* New York: Free Press.

Olson, L. (1998). The assessment of moral integrity among adolescents and adults. *Dissertation Abstracts International, 60*(6), 2989B.

Oman, D., Thoresen, C. E., & McMahon, K. (1999). Volunteerism and mortality among the community-dwelling elderly. *Journal of Health Psychology, 4,* 301–316.

Omoto, A. M., & Snyder, M. (1995). Sustained helping without obligation: Motivation, longevity of service, and perceived attitude change among AIDS volunteers. *Journal of Personality and Social Psychology, 68,* 671–686.

O'Neill, M. (2001, September). Virtue and beauty: The Renaissance image of the ideal woman. *Smithsonian,* 62–69.

Ones, D., Viswesvaran, C., & Schmidt, F. (1995). Integrity tests: Overlooked facts, resolved issues, and remaining questions. *American Psychologist, 50,* 456–457.

O'Quin, K., & Derks, P. (1997). Humor and creativity: A review of the empirical literature. In Marc A. Runco (Ed.), *Creativity research handbook* (Vol. 1, pp. 227–256). Cresskill, NJ: Hampton Press.

Orbach, I., Mikulincer, M., Stein, D., & Cohen, O. (1998). Self-representation of suicidal adolescents. *Journal of Abnormal Psychology, 107,* 435–439.

Ortony, A., Clore, G. L., & Collins, A. (1987). *The cognitive structure of emotions.* New York: Cambridge University Press.

Orwoll, L., & Perlmutter, M. (1990). The study of wise persons: Integrating a personality perspective. In R. J. Sternberg (Ed.), *Wisdom: Its nature, origins, and development* (pp. 160–177). New York: Cambridge University Press.

O'Sullivan, M., & Guilford, J. P. (1976). *Four factor tests of social intelligence: Manual of instructions and interpretations.* Orange, CA: Sheridan Psychological Services.

O'Sullivan, M., Guilford, J. P., & deMille, R. (1965). *Reports from the Psychological Laboratory, University of Southern California* (No. 34). Los Angeles: University of Southern California.

Oswalt, W., & Neely, S. (1999). *This land was theirs.* Mountain View, CA: Mayfield Publishing.

Otto, R. (1923). *The idea of the holy: An inquiry into the non-rational factor in the idea of the divine and its relation to the rational* (J. W. Harvey, Trans.). London: Oxford University Press. (Original work published 1917)

Overwalle, F. V., Mervielde, I., & De Schuyter, J. (1995). Structural modeling of the relationships between attributional dimensions, emotions, and performance of college freshmen. *Cognition and Emotion, 9,* 59–85.

Page, D. P. (1935). Measurement and prediction of leadership. *American Journal of Sociology, 41,* 31–43.

Page, S., & Tyrer, J. (1995). Gender and prediction of Gilligan's justice and care orientations. *Journal of College Student Psychotherapy, 10,* 43–56.

Paine, A. B. (1912). *Mark Twain: A biography* (3 vols.). New York: Harper.

Palmer, P. J. (1998). *The courage to teach: Exploring the inner landscape of a teacher's life.* New York: Wiley.

Pancer, S. M., Pratt, M., & Hunsberger, B. E. (2000, July). *The roots of community and political involvement in Canadian youth.* Paper presented at the biennial meeting of the International Society for the Study of Behavioral Development, Beijing, China.

Pantanjali. (1979). *The yoga-sutra* (G. Feuerstein, Trans.). Folkstone, England: Dawson.

Pargament, K. (1997). *The psychology of religion and coping: Theory, research, practice.* New York: Guilford Press.

Pargament, K., Kennell, J., Hathaway, W., Grevengoed, N., Newman, J., & Jones, W. (1988). Religion and the problem-solving process: Three styles of coping. *Journal for the Scientific Study of Religion, 27,* 90–104.

Pargament, K., Smith, B., Koenig, H., & Perez, L. (1998). Patterns of positive and negative religious coping with major life stressors. *Journal for the Scientific Study of Religion, 37,* 711–725.

Park, L. C., & Park, T. J. (1997). Personal intelligence. In M. McCallum & W. E. Piper (Eds.), *Psychological mindedness: A contemporary understanding* (pp. 133–167). Mahway, NJ: Erlbaum.

Park, N., & Peterson, C. (2003a, August). *Character strengths and subjective well-being.* Poster presented at the annual convention of the American Psychological Association, Toronto, Ontario, Canada.

Park, N., & Peterson, C. (2003b). Virtues and organizations. In K. S. Cameron, J. E. Dutton, & R. E. Quinn (Eds.), *Positive organizational scholarship; Foundations of a new discipline* (pp. 33–47). San Francisco: Berrett-Koehler.

Parker, S., & de Vries, B. (1993). Patterns of friendship for women and men in same and cross-sex relationships. *Journal of Social and Personal Relationships, 10,* 617–626.

Parnes, S. J. (1963). The deferment of judgment principle: Clarification of the literature. *Psychological Reports, 12,* 521–522.

Parnes, S. J., & Meadow, A. (1963). Development of individual creative talent. In C. W. Taylor & F. Barron (Eds.), *Scientific creativity: Its recognition and and development* (pp. 311–320). New York: Wiley.

Pasupathi, M., Staudinger, U. M., & Baltes, P. B. (2001). Seeds of wisdom: Adolescents' knowledge and judgment about difficult life problems. *Developmental Psychology, 37,* 351–361.

Patrick, C. L., & Olson, K. (2000). Empirically supported therapies. *Journal of Psychological Practice, 6,* 19–34.

Paulus, D. L. (1998). Interpersonal and intrapsychic adaptiveness of trait self-enhancement: A mixed blessing? *Journal of Personality and Social Psychology, 74,* 1197–1208.

Paulus, D. L., Lysy, D. C., & Yik, M. S. M. (1998). Self-report measures of intelligence: Are they useful as proxy IQ tests? *Journal of Personality Psychology, 66,* 525–554.

Paulus, P. B. (1999). Group creativity. In M. A. Runco & S. Pritzker (Eds.), *Encyclopedia of creativity* (Vol. 1, pp. 779–784). San Diego, CA: Academic Press.

Paulus, P. B., & Konicki, K. P. (1973). Effect of positive and negative evaluations on perseverance on a simple task. *Psychological Reports, 32,* 711–714.

Paulus, P. B., & Nijstad, B. A. (Eds.). (2003). *Group creativity.* New York: Oxford University Press.

Payne, W. L. (1986). A study of emotion: Developing emotional intelligence: Self-integration; relating to fear, pain and desire. *Dissertation Abstracts International, 47,* 203A. (UMI No. AAC 8605928)

Pears, D. F. (1978). Aristotle's analysis of courage. *Midwestern Studies in Philosophy, 3,* 273–285.

Pearson, C. S. (1998). *The hero within: Six archetypes we live by.* San Francisco: HarperCollins.

Peele, S. (1989). *The diseasing of America.* Boston: Houghton Mifflin.

Pelletteri, J. (1999). The relationship between emotional intelligence, cognitive reasoning, and defense mechanisms. *Dissertation Abstracts International: Section B: The Sciences & Engineering, 60,* 403. (UMI No. AAM 9917182)

Peluso, T., Ricciardelli, L. A., & Williams, R. J. (1999). Self-control in relation to problem drinking and symptoms of disordered eating. *Addictive Behaviors, 24,* 439–442.

Pennebaker, J. W., & Keough, K. A. (1999). Revealing, organizing, and reorganizing the self in response to stress and emotion. In R. J. Contrada & R. D. Ashmore (Eds.), *Self, social identity, and physical health: Interdisciplinary explorations* (pp. 101–121). New York: Oxford University Press.

Penninx, B. W. J. H., Guralnik, J. M., Bandeen-Roche, K., Kasper, J. D., Simonsick, E. M., Ferrucci, L., et al. (2000). The protective effects of emotional vitality on adverse health outcomes in disabled older women. *Journal of the American Gerontological Society, 48,* 1359–1366.

Penninx, B. W. J. H., Guralnik, J. M., Simonsick, E. M., Kasper, J. D., Ferrucci, L., & Fried, L. P. (1998). Emotional vitality among disabled older women: The women's health and aging study. *Journal of the American Gerontological Society, 46,* 807–815.

Perez, M., Pettit, J. W., David, C. F., Kistner, J. A., & Joiner, T. (2001). The interpersonal consequences of inflated self-esteem in an inpatient youth psychiatric sample. *Journal of Consulting and Clinical Psychology, 69,* 712–716.

Perkins, D. N. (1985). Postprimary education has little impact on informal reasoning. *Journal of Educational Psychology, 77,* 562–571.

Perkins, D. N., Bushey, B., & Faraday, M. (1986). *Learning to reason.* Unpublished manuscript, Harvard Graduate School of Education, Cambridge, MA.

Peters, R. A. (1978). Effects of anxiety, curiosity, and perceived instructor threat on student verbal behavior in the college classroom. *Journal of Educational Psychology, 70,* 388–395.

Peterson, C. (1992). *Personality* (2nd ed.). Fort Worth, TX: Harcourt Brace Jovanovich.

Peterson, C. (2000). The future of optimism. *American Psychologist, 55,* 44–55.

Peterson, C., Bishop, M. P., Fletcher, C. W., Kaplan, M. R., Yesko, E. S., Moon, C. H., et al. (2001). Explanatory style as a risk factor for traumatic mishaps. *Cognitive Therapy and Research, 25,* 633–649.

Peterson, C., & Chang, E. C. (2003). Optimism and flourishing. In C. L. M. Keyes

& J. Haidt (Eds.), *Flourishing: Positive psychology and the life well-lived* (pp. 55–79). Washington, DC: American Psychological Association.

Peterson, C., & de Avila, M. E. (1995). Optimistic explanatory style and the perception of health problems. *Journal of Clinical Psychology, 51,* 128–132.

Peterson, C., & Lee, F. (2000, September/October). Reading between the lines: Speech analysis. *Psychology Today,* 50–51.

Peterson, C., Maier, S. F., & Seligman, M. E. P. (1993). *Learned helplessness: A theory for the age of personal control.* New York: Oxford University Press.

Peterson, C., & Park, C. (1998). Learned helplessness and explanatory style. In D. F. Barone, V. B. Van Hasselt, & M. Hersen (Eds.), *Advanced personality* (pp. 287–310). New York: Plenum.

Peterson, C., & Park, N. (2003, March). *Assessment of character strengths among youth: Progress report on the Values in Action Inventory for Youth.* Paper presented at the Child Trends Conference on Indicators of Positive Youth Development, Washington, DC.

Peterson, C., Peterson, J., & Seeto, D. (1983). Developmental changes in ideas about lying. *Child Development, 54,* 1529–1535.

Peterson, C., & Seligman, M. E. P. (1984). Causal explanations as a risk factor for depression: Theory and evidence. *Psychological Review, 91,* 347–374.

Peterson, C., & Seligman, M. E. P. (2003). Character strengths before and after 9/11. *Psychological Science, 14,* 381–384.

Peterson, C., Semmel, A., von Baeyer, C., Abramson, L. Y., Metalsky, G. I., & Seligman, M. E. P. (1982). The Attributional Style Questionnaire. *Cognitive Therapy and Research, 6,* 287–299.

Peterson, C., & Steen, T. A. (2002). Optimistic explanatory style. In C. R. Snyder & S. Lopez (Eds.), *Handbook of positive psychology* (pp. 244–256). New York: Oxford University Press.

Peterson, C., & Vaidya, R. S. (2001). Explanatory style, expectations, and depressive symptoms. *Personality and Individual Differences, 31,* 1217–1223.

Peterson, C., & Vaidya, R. S. (2003). Optimism as virtue and vice. In E. C. Chang & L. J. Sanna (Eds.), *Virtue, vice, and personality: The complexity of behavior* (pp. 23–37). Washington, DC: American Psychological Association.

Peterson, C., & Villanova, P. (1988). An expanded attributional style question-naire. *Journal of Abnormal Psychology, 97,* 87–89.

Phan, P. (2001). A common journey, different paths, the same destination: Method in liberation theologies. In E. Fernandez & F. Segovia (Eds.), *A dream unfinished: Theological reflections on America from the margins* (pp. 129–151). Maryknoll, NY: Orbis Books.

Phillips, A. (1990). Introduction to *A philosophical inquiry into the origin of our ideas of the sublime and beautiful* (pp. ix–xxiii). Oxford, England: Oxford University Press. (Original work published 1757)

Piaget, J. (1965). *The moral judgment of the child.* New York: Free Press. (Original work published 1932)

Piaget, J. (1966). *The psychology of intelligence.* Totowa, NJ: Littlefield, Adams.

Pianta, R. C., & Walsh, D. J. (1998). Applying the concept of resilience in schools: Cautions from a developmental systems perspective. *School Psychology Review, 27,* 407–417.

Piedmont, R. L. (1999). Does spirituality represent the sixth factor of personality? Spiritual transcendence and the five-factor model. *Journal of Personality, 67,* 985–1013.

Pierrehumbert, B., Iannotti, R. J., & Cummings, E. M. (1985). Mother-infant attachment, development of social competencies and beliefs of self-responsibility. *Archives de Psychologie, 53,* 365–374.

Pierrehumbert, B., Iannotti, R. J., Cummings, E. M., & Zahn-Waxler, C. (1989). Social functioning with mother and peers at 2 and 5 years: The influence of attachment. *International Journal of Behavioral Development, 12,* 85–100.

Pintrich, P. R. (2000). The role of goal orientation in self-regulated learning. In M. Boekaerts, P. R. Pintrich, & M. Zeidner (Eds.), *Handbook of self-regulation* (pp. 451–502). San Diego, CA: Academic Press.

Piper, W. E., McCallum, M., Joyce, A. S., Azim, H. F., & Ogrodniczuk, J. S. (1999). Follow-up findings for interpretive and supportive forms of psychotherapy and patient personality variables. *Journal of Consulting and Clinical Psychology, 67,* 267–273.

Pistole, M. C. (1989). Attachment in adult romantic relationships: Style of conflict resolution and relationship satisfaction. *Journal of Social and Personal Relationships, 6,* 505–510.

Pitsounis, N. D., & Dixon, P. N. (1988). Encouragement versus praise: Improving productivity of the mentally retarded. *Individual Psychology, 44,* 507–512.

Pittman, K. J. (1991). *Promoting youth development: Strengthening the role of youth-serving and community organizations.* Washington, DC: U.S. Department of Agriculture Extension Services.

Pittman, K. J. (2000, May). *What youth need: Services, supports, and opportunities, the ingredients for youth.* Paper prepared for presentation at the White House Conference on Teenagers, Washington, DC.

Plant, R. W., & Ryan, R. M. (1985). Intrinsic motivation and the effects of self-consciousness, self-awareness, and ego-involvement: An investigation of internally controlling styles. *Journal of Personality, 53,* 435–449.

Plato. (1968). *Republic* (A. Bloom, Trans.). New York: Basic Books.

Plomin, R., & Caspi, A. (1999). Behavior genetics and personality. In L. A. Pervin & O. P. John (Eds.), *Handbook of personality* (2nd ed., pp. 251–276). New York: Guilford Press.

Plomin, R., Scheier, M. F., Bergeman, C. S., & Pedersen, N. L. (1992). Optimism, pessimism, and mental health: A twin/adoption analysis. *Personality and Individual Differences, 13,* 921–930.

Plucker, J. A., Callahan, C. M., & Tomchin, E. M. (1996). Wherefore art thou, multiple intelligences? Alternative assessments for identifying talent in ethnically diverse and economically disadvantaged students. *Gifted Child Quarterly, 40,* 81–92.

Plutarch. (1932). *The parallel lives.* New York: Modern Library.

Polivy, J. (1998). The effects of behavioral inhibition: Integrating internal cues, cognition, behavior, and affect. *Psychological Inquiry, 9,* 181–204.

Polivy, J., Herman, C. P., Hackett, R., & Kuleshnyk, I. (1986). The effects of self-attention and public attention on eating in restrained and unrestrained subjects. *Journal of Personality and Social Psychology, 50,* 1253–1260.

Portes, A. (1998). Social capital: Its origins and applications in modern sociology. *Annual Review of Sociology, 24,* 1–24.

Power, F. C., Higgins, A., & Kohlberg, L. (1989). *Lawrence Kohlberg's approach to moral education.* New York: Columbia University Press.

Powers, S. I. (1982). *Family interaction and parental moral development as a context for adolescent moral development.* Unpublished doctoral dissertation, Harvard University, Cambridge, MA.

Powers, W. T. (1973). Feedback: Beyond behaviorism. *Science, 179,* 351–356.

Pratt, M. W., Danso, H. A., Arnold, M. L., Norris, J. E., & Filyer, R. (2001). Adult generativity and the socialization of adolescents: Relations to mothers' and fathers' parenting beliefs, styles, and practices. *Journal of Personality, 69,* 89–120.

Pratt, M. W., Diessner, R., Pratt, A., Hunsberger, B., & Pancer, S. M. (1996). Moral and social reasoning and perspective taking in later life: A longitudinal study. *Psychology and Aging, 11,* 66–73.

Pratt, M. W., Pancer, M., Hunsberger, B., & Manchester, J. (1990). Reasoning about the self and relationships in maturity: An integrative complexity analysis of individual differences. *Journal of Personality and Social Psychology, 59,* 575–581.

Prenzel, M. (1992). The selective persistence of interest. In K. A Renninger, S. Hidi, & A. Krapp (Eds.), *The role of interest in learning and development* (pp. 71–98). Hillsdale, NJ: Erlbaum.

Prince, R. M. (1984). Courage and masochism in psychotherapy. *Psychoanalytic Review, 71,* 47–61.

Pruyser, P. W. (1976). *The minister as diagnostician: Personal problems in pastoral perspective.* Philadelphia: Westminster Press.

Public Agenda. (1999). *Kids these days '99: What Americans really think about the next generation.* New York: Author.

Putnam, D. (1997). Psychological courage. *Philosophy, Psychiatry and Psychology, 4,* 1–11.

Putnam, R. D. (2000). *Bowling alone: The collapse and revival of American community.* New York: Simon & Schuster.

Quast, L. N., & Hazucha, J. F. (1992). The relationships between leaders' management skills and their groups' effectiveness. In K. E. Clark, M. B. Clark, & D. R. Campbell (Eds.), *Impact of leadership* (pp. 199–213). Greensboro, NC: Center for Creative Leadership.

Quinn, E. P., Brandon, T. H., & Copeland, A. L. (1996). Is task persistence related to smoking and substance abuse? The application of learned industriousness theory to addictive behaviors. *Experimental and Clinical Psychopharmacology, 4,* 186–190.

Quinn, K. (1988). Children and deception. In R. Rogers (Ed.), *Clinical assessment of malingering and deception* (pp. 105–119). New York: Guilford Press.

Rachels, J. (1999). *The elements of moral philosophy* (3rd ed.). New York: McGraw-Hill.

Rachlin, H. (1989). *Judgment, decision, and choice: A cognitive/behavioral synthesis.* New York: Freeman.

Rachman, S. J. (1990). *Fear and courage* (2nd ed.). New York: Freeman.

Rahilly, D. (1993). A phenomenological analysis of authentic experience. *Journal of Humanistic Experience, 33,* 49–71.

Rahn, W. M., & Transue, J. E. (1998). Social trust and value change: The decline of social capital in American youth, 1976–1995. *Political Psychology, 19,* 545–565.

Raphael, M. J. (2000). *Bill W. and Mr. Wilson: The legend and life of AA's co-founder.* Amherst: University of Massachusetts Press.

Raskin, R. N., Novacek, J., & Hogan, R. (1991). Narcissistic self-esteem management. *Journal of Personality and Social Psychology, 60,* 911–918.

Raskin, V. (1985). *Semantic mechanisms of humor.* Dordrecht, Netherlands: D. Reidel.

Rathvon, N. W. (1990). The effects of encouragement on off-task behavior and academic productivity. *Elementary School Guidance and Counseling, 24,* 189–199.

Räty, H., Snellman, L., & Vainikainen, A. (1999). Parents' assessments of their children's abilities. *European Journal of Psychology of Education, 14,* 423–437.

Rawls, J. (1971). *A theory of justice.* Cambridge, MA: Belknap Press of Harvard University Press.

Rawls, J. (2001). *Justice as fairness: A restatement* (E. Kelly, Ed.). Cambridge, MA: Harvard University Press.

Redding, R. E., Harmon, R. J., & Morgan, G. A. (1990). Relationships between maternal depression and infant's mastery behaviors. *Infant Behavior and Development, 13,* 391–395.

Redding, R. E., Morgan, A., & Harmon, R. J. (1988). Mastery motivation in infants and toddlers: Is it greatest when tasks are moderately challenging? *Infant Behavior and Development, 11,* 419–430.

Redelmeier, D. A., & Singh, S. M. (2001). Survival in Academy Award–winning actors and actresses. *Annals of Internal Medicine, 134,* 955–962.

Regnerus, M., Smith, C., & Sikkink, D. (1998). Who gives to the poor? The influence of religious tradition and political location on the personal generosity of Americans toward the poor. *Journal for the Scientific Study of Religion, 37,* 481–493.

Reid, C., Udall, A., Romanoff, B., & Algozzine, B. (1999). Comparison of traditional and problem solving assessment criteria. *Gifted Child Quarterly, 43,* 252–264.

Reio, T. G., & Wiswell, A. (2000). Field investigation of the relationship among adult curiosity, workplace learning, and job performance. *Human Resource Development Quarterly, 11,* 5–30.

Reis, H. T., & Shaver, P. R. (1988). Intimacy as an interpersonal process. In S. Duck (Ed.), *Handbook of research in personal relationships* (pp. 367–389). London: Wiley.

Reis, H. T., Sheldon, K. M., Gable, S. L., Roscoe, J., & Ryan, R. M. (2000). Daily well-being: The role of autonomy, competence, and relatedness. *Personality and Social Psychology Bulletin, 26,* 419–435.

Reivich, K. (1995). The measurement of explanatory style. In G. M. Buchanan & M. E. P. Seligman (Eds.), *Explanatory style* (pp. 21–47). Hillsdale, NJ: Erlbaum.

Renninger, K. A. (1989). Individual differences in children's play interest. In L. T. Winegar (Ed.), *Social interaction and the development of children's understanding* (pp. 147–172). Norwood, NJ: Ablex.

Renninger, K. A. (1990). Children's play interests, representation, and activity. In R. Fivush & K. Hudson (Eds.), *Knowing and remembering in young children* (pp. 127–165). New York: Cambridge University Press.

Renninger, K. A. (1992). Individual interest and development: Implications for theory and practice. In K. A. Renninger, S. Hidi, & A. Krapp (Eds.), *The role of interest in learning and development* (pp. 361–376). Hillsdale, NJ: Erlbaum.

Renninger, K. A. (2000). Individual interest and its implications for understanding intrinsic motivation. In C. Sansone & J. M. Harackiewicz (Eds.), *Intrinsic and extrinsic motivation: The search for optimal motivation and performance* (pp. 375–407). New York: Academic Press.

Renninger, K. A., Ewen, L., & Lasher, A. K. (2002). Individual interest as context in expository text and mathematical problems. *Learning and Instruction, 12,* 467–491.

Renninger, K. A., & Hidi, S. (2002). Student interest and achievement: Developmental issues raised by a case study. In A. Wigfield & J. S. Eccles (Eds.), *Development of achievement motivation* (pp. 173–195). San Diego, CA: Academic Press.

Renninger, K. A., & Leckrone, T. G. (1991). Continuity in young children's actions: A consideration of interest and temperament. In L. Oppenheimer & J. Valsiner (Eds.), *The origins of action: Interdisciplinary and international perspectives* (pp. 205–238). New York: Springer-Verlag.

Renninger, K. A., & Shumar, W. (2002). Community building with and for teachers: The Math Forum as a resource for teacher professional development. In K. A. Renninger & W. Shumar (Eds.), *Building virtual communities: Learning and change in cyberspace* (pp. 60–95). New York: Cambridge University Press.

Renninger, K. A., & Wozniak, R. H. (1985). Effect of interest on attention shift, recognition, and recall in young children. *Developmental Psychology, 21,* 624–632.

Rest, J. R. (1979). *Development in judging moral issues.* Minneapolis: University of Minnesota Press.

Rest, J. R., Deemer, D., Barnett, R., Spickelmier, J., & Volker, J. (1986). Life experiences and developmental pathways. In J. R. Rest (Ed.), *Moral development: Advances in research and theory* (pp. 28–58). New York: Praeger.

Rest, J. R., & Thoma, S. (1986). Educational programs and interventions. In J. R. Rest (Ed.), *Moral development: Advances in research and theory* (pp. 59–88). New York: Praeger.

Reynolds, D. K. (1989). *Flowing bridges, quiet waters: Japanese psychotherapies, Morita and Naikan.* Albany: State University of New York Press.

Reznick, J. S., Kagan, J., Snidman, N., Gersten, M., Baak, K., & Rosenberg, A. (1986). Inhibited and uninhibited children: A follow-up study. *Child Development, 57,* 660–680.

Rhodewalt, F., Madrian, J. C., & Cheney, S. (1998). Narcissism, self-knowledge organization, and emotional reactivity: The effect of daily experiences on self-esteem and affect. *Personality and Social Psychology Bulletin, 24,* 75–87.

Rhodewalt, F., & Morf, C. C. (1998). Self-aggrandizement and anger: A temporal analysis of narcissism and affective reactions to success and failure. *Journal of Personality and Social Psychology, 74,* 672–685.

Rhodewalt, F., Saltzman, A. T., & Wittmer, J. (1984). Self-handicapping among competitive athletes: The role of practice in self-esteem protection. *Basic and Applied Social Psychology, 5,* 197–209.

Rice, C. L. (1999). *A quantitative study of emotional intelligence and its impact on team performance.* Unpublished master's thesis, Pepperdine University, Malibu, CA.

Rice, E. F. (1958). *The renaissance idea of wisdom.* Cambridge, MA: Harvard University Press.

Richard, A., Bell, D., & Carlson, J. (2000). Individual religiosity, moral community, and drug user treatment. *Journal for the Scientific Study of Religion, 39,* 240–246.

Richards, J. M., & Gross, J. J. (2000). Emotional regulation and memory: The cognitive costs of keeping one's cool. *Journal of Personality and Social Psychology, 79,* 410–424.

Richards, N. (1988). Is humility a virtue? *American Philosophical Quarterly, 25,* 253–259.

Richards, N. (1992). *Humility.* Philadelphia: Temple University Press.

Richards, R., Kinney, D. K., Lunde, I., Benet, M., & Merzel, A. P. C. (1988). Assessing everyday creativity: Characteristics of the Lifetime Creativity Scales and validation with three large samples. *Journal of Personality and Social Psychology, 54,* 476–485.

Rickards, T. (1999). Brainstorming. In M. A. Runco & S. Pritzker (Eds.), *Encyclopedia of creativity* (Vol. 1, pp. 219–227). San Diego, CA: Academic Press.

Ridley, M. (1996). *The origins of virtue: Human instincts and the evolution of cooperation.* New York: Penguin Books.

Rieke, M., & Guastello, S. (1995). Unresolved issues in honesty and integrity testing. *American Psychologist, 50,* 458–459.

Riemann, R., Angleitner, A., & Strelau, J. (1997). Genetic and environmental influences on personality: A study of twins reared together using the self- and peer-report NEO-FFI scales. *Journal of Personality, 65,* 449–476.

Riley, G. M. (1995). *Increasing self-esteem in children, 8–12 years old from dysfunctional families: A twofold solution to a twofold problem.* Nova Southeastern University, Fort Lauderdale, FL. (ERIC Document Reproduction Service No. ED387729)

Rind, B., & Gaudet, S. (1993). Judging personality traits of adolescents from photographs. *Journal of Social Psychology, 133,* 815–823.

Ritchie, R. J. (1994). Using the assessment center method to predict senior management potential. Special issue: Issues in the assessment of managerial and executive leadership. *Consulting Psychology Journal: Practice and Research, 46,* 16–23.

Ritzema, R., & Young, C. (1983). Causal schemata and the attributions of supernatural causality. *Journal of Psychology and Theology, 11,* 36–43.

Robbins, A., & CoVan, F. L. (1993). *Awaken the giant within: How to take immediate control of your mental, emotional, physical, and financial destiny.* New York: Simon & Schuster.

Roberts, K. T., & Aspy, C. B. (1993). Development of the Serenity Scale. *Journal of Nursing Measurement, 1,* 145–164.

Roberts, R. C. (1995). Forgivingness. *American Philosophical Quarterly, 32,* 289–306.

Robins, R. W., & John, O. P. (1997). The quest for self-insight: Theory and research on accuracy and bias in self-perception. In R. Hogan, J. A. Johnson, & S. R. Briggs (Eds.), *Handbook of personality psychology* (pp. 649–679). San Diego, CA: Academic Press.

Robinson, D. N. (1989). *Aristotle's psychology.* New York: Columbia University Press.

Robinson, J., Shaver, P., & Wrightsman, L. (Eds.). (1991). *Measures of personality and social psychological attitudes.* San Diego, CA: Academic Press.

Robinson, M. D., Johnson, J. T., & Shields, S. A. (1995). On the advantages of modesty: The benefits of a balanced self-presentation. *Communication Research, 22,* 575–591.

Robinson-Whelen, S., Kim, C., MacCallum, R. C., & Kiecolt-Glaser, J. K. (1997). Distinguishing optimism from pessimism in older adults: Is it important to be optimistic or not be pessimistic? *Journal of Personality and Social Psychology, 73,* 1345–1353.

Rodrigue, J. R., Olson, K. R., & Markley, R. P. (1987). Induced mood and curiosity. *Cognitive Therapy and Research, 11,* 101–106.

Rogers, A. (1993). Voice, play, and a practice of ordinary courage in girls' and women's lives. *Harvard Educational Review, 63,* 265–295.

Rogers, C. R. (1961). *On becoming a person: A therapist's view of psychotherapy.* Boston: Houghton Mifflin.

Rogers, C. R. (1971). Interview with Carl Rogers. In W. B. Frick (Ed.), *Humanistic psychology: Interviews with Maslow, Murphy and Rogers* (pp. 24–47). Columbus, OH: Merrill.

Rokeach, M. (1960). *The open and closed mind.* New York: Basic Books.

Rokeach, M. (1973). *The nature of human values.* New York: Free Press.

Romal, J. B., & Kaplan, B. J. (1995). Difference in self-control among spenders and savers. *Psychology: A Quarterly Journal of Human Behavior, 32,* 8–17.

Roney, C. J. R., Higgins, E. T., & Shah, J. (1995). Goals and framing: How outcome focus influences motivation and emotion. *Personality and Social Psychology Bulletin, 21,* 1151–1160.

Rosch, E., Mervis, C. B., Gray, W., Johnson, D., & Boyes-Braem, P. (1976). Basic objects in natural categories. *Cognitive Psychology, 8,* 382–439.

Rosenbaum, M. (1980). A schedule for assessing self-control behaviors: Preliminary findings. *Behavior Therapy, 11,* 109–121.

Rosenthal, D., Gurney, R., & Moore, S. (1981). From trust to intimacy: A new inventory for examining Erikson's stages of psychosocial development. *Journal of Youth and Adolescence, 10,* 525–537.

Rosenthal, R., Hall, J. A., DiMatteo, M. R., Rogers, P. L., & Archer, D. (1979). *The PONS Test.* Baltimore: Johns Hopkins University Press.

Rosenthal, R., & Rubin, D. B. (1982). A simple, general purpose display of magnitude of experimental effect. *Journal of Educational Psychology, 74,* 166–169.

Ross, M. (1975). Salience of reward and intrinsic motivation. *Journal of Personality and Social Psychology, 32,* 245–254.

Ross, M., & Sicoly, F. (1979). Egocentric biases in availability and attribution. *Journal of Personality and Social Psychology, 37,* 322–336.

Rothschild, J., & Miethe, T. D. (1999). Whistle-blower disclosures and management retaliation: The battle to control information about organization corruption. *Work and Occupations, 26,* 107–128.

Rotter, J. B. (1966). Generalized expectancies for internal versus external control of reinforcement. *Psychological Monographs, 80,* 609.

Rousseau (1762/1950). *The social contract and discourses* (G. D. H. Cole, Trans.). New York: Dutton.

Rubin, J. Z., & Brockner, J. (1975). Factors affecting entrapment in waiting situations: The Rosencrantz and Guildenstern effect. *Journal of Personality and Social Psychology, 31,* 1054–1063.

Rubin, M. M. (1999). *Emotional intelligence and its role in mitigating aggression: A correlational study of the relationship between emotional intelligence and aggression in urban adolescents.* Unpublished doctoral dissertation, Immaculata College, Immaculata, PA.

Rubin, Z. (1973). *Liking and loving: An invitation to social psychology.* New York: Holt, Rinehart, & Winston.

Ruch, W. (1992). Assessment of appreciation of humor: Studies with the 3 WD humor test. In C. D. Spielberger & J. N. Butcher (Eds.), *Advances in personality assessment* (Vol. 9, pp. 27–75). Hillsdale, NJ: Erlbaum.

Ruch, W. (1994). Temperament, Eysenck's PEN system, and humor-related traits. *Humor, 7,* 209–244.

Ruch, W. (Ed.). (1996). Measurement of the sense of humor [Double special issue]. *Humor: International Journal of Humor Research, 9*(3/4).

Ruch, W. (1997). State and trait cheerfulness and the induction of exhilaration: A FACS study. *European Psychologist, 2,* 328–341.

Ruch, W. (1998a). The sense of humor: A new look at an old concept. In W. Ruch (Ed.), *The sense of humor: Explorations of a personality characteristic* (pp. 3–14). Berlin: Mouton de Gruyter.

Ruch, W. (Ed.). (1998b). *The sense of humor: Explorations of a personality characteristic.* New York: Mouton de Gruyter.

Ruch, W. (1998c). Tools used for diagnosing humor states and traits. In W. Ruch (Ed.), *The sense of humor: Explorations of a personality characteristic* (pp. 405–412). Berlin, Germany: Mouton de Gruyter.

Ruch, W. (2001). The perception of humor. In A. W. Kaszniak (Ed.), *Emotion, qualia, and consciousness* (pp. 410–425). Tokyo: Word Scientific.

Ruch, W., Busse, P., & Hehl, F.-J. (1996). Relationship between humor and proposed punishment for crimes: Beware of humorous people. *Personality and Individual Differences, 20,* 1–12.

Ruch, W., & Carrell, A. (1998). Trait cheerfulness and the sense of humor. *Personality and Individual Differences, 24,* 551–558.

Ruch, W., & Hehl, F. J. (1998). A two-mode model of humor appreciation: Its relation to aesthetic appreciation and simplicity-complexity of personality. In W. Ruch (Ed.), *The sense of humor: Explorations of a personality characteristic* (pp. 109–142). New York: Mouton de Gruyter.

Ruch, W., & Köhler, G. (1998). A temperament approach to humor. In W. Ruch (Ed.), *The sense of humor: Explorations of a personality characteristic* (pp. 203–230). New York: Mouton de Gruyter.

Ruch, W., & Köhler, G. (1999). The measurement of state and trait cheerfulness. In I. Mervielde, I. Deary, F. De Fruyt, & F. Ostendorf (Eds.), *Personality psychology in Europe* (Vol. 7, pp. 67–83). Tilburg, Netherlands: Tilburg University Press.

Ruch, W., Köhler, G., & van Thriel, C. (1996). Assessing the "humorous temperament": Construction of the facet and standard trait forms of the State-Trait-Cheerfulness Inventory—STCI. *Humor, 9,* 303–340.

Ruch, W., McGhee, P. E., & Hehl, F.-J. (1990). Age differences in the enjoyment of incongruity-resolution and nonsense humor during adulthood. *Psychology and Aging, 5,* 348–355.

Runco, M. A., & Pritzker, S. (Eds.). (1999). *Encyclopedia of creativity.* San Diego, CA: Academic Press.

Rusbult, C. E. (1983). A longitudinal test of the investment model: The development (and deterioration) of satisfaction and commitment in heterosexual involvements. *Journal of Personality and Social Psychology, 45,* 101–117.

Rush, M. C., Thomas, J. C., & Lord, R. G. (1982). Implicit leadership theory: A potential threat to the internal validity of leader behavior questionnaires. *Organizational Behavior and Human Performance, 20,* 93–110.

Rushin, S. (2002, October 28). Who's sorry now? *Sports Illustrated, 23.*

Rushton, J. P., Chrisjohn, R. D., & Fekken, G. C. (1981). The altruistic personality and the self-report altruism scale. *Personality and Individual Differences, 2,* 293–302.

Rushton, J. P., Fulker, D. W., Neale, M. C., Nias, D. K. B., & Eysenck, H. J. (1986). Altruism and aggression: The heritability of individual differences. *Journal of Personality and Social Psychology, 50,* 1192–1198.

Rushton, J. P., Fulker, D. W., Neale, M. C., Nias, D. K., & Eysenck, H. J. (1989). Aging and the relation of aggression, altruism, and assertiveness scales to the Eysenck Personality Questionnaire. *Personality and Individual Differences, 10,* 261–263.

Rust, J. (1999). The validity of the Giotto Integrity Test. *Personality and Individual Differences, 27,* 755–768.

Rutter, M. (1999). Resilience concepts and findings: Implications for family therapy. *Journal of Family Therapy, 21,* 119–144.

Ryan, A. M., Pintrich, P. R., & Midgley, C. (2001). Avoiding seeking help in the classroom: Who and why? *Educational Psychology Review, 13,* 93–114.

Ryan, R. M., & Connell, J. P. (1989). Perceived locus of causality and internalization: Examining reasons for acting in two domains. *Journal of Personality and Social Psychology, 57,* 749–761.

Ryan, R. M., & Deci, E. L. (2000). Self-determination theory and the facilitation of intrinsic motivation, social development, and well-being. *American Psychologist, 55,* 68–78.

Ryan, R. M., & Deci, E. L. (2001). On happiness and human potentials: A review of research on hedonic and eudaimonic well-being. *Annual Review of Psychology, 52,* 141–166.

Ryan, R. M., & Frederick, C. (1997). On energy, personality, and health: Subjective vitality as a dynamic reflection of well-being. *Journal of Personality, 65,* 529–565.

Ryan, R. M., Plant, R. W., & O'Malley, S. (1995). Initial motivations for alcohol treatment: Relations with patient characteristics, treatment involvement and dropout. *Addictive Behaviors, 20,* 279–297.

Ryan, R. M., & Solky, J. A. (1996). What is supportive about social support? On the psychological needs for autonomy and relatedness. In G. R. Pierce & B. Sarason (Eds.), *Handbook of social support and the family* (pp. 249–267). New York: Plenum.

Ryans, D. G. (1939). The measurement of persistence: An historical review. *Psychological Bulletin, 36,* 715–739.

Rye, M. S., Loiacono, D. M., Folck, C. D., Olszewski, B. T., Heim, T. A., & Madia, B. (2001). Evaluation of the psychometric properties of two forgiveness scales. *Current Psychology: Developmental, Learning, Personality, Social, 20,* 260–277.

Rye, M. S., Pargament, K. I., Ali, M. A., Beck, G. L., Dorff, E. N., Hallisey, C., et al. (2000). Religious perspectives on forgiveness. In M. E. McCullough, K. I. Pargament, & C. E. Thoresen (Eds.), *Forgiveness: Theory, research, and practice* (pp. 17–40). New York: Guilford Press.

Ryff, C. D. (1989). Happiness is everything, or is it? Explorations of the meaning of psychological well-being. *Journal of Personality and Social Psychology, 57,* 1069–1081.

Ryff, C. D. (1995). Psychological well-being in adult life. *Current Directions in Psychological Science, 4,* 99–104.

Ryff, C. D., & Keyes, C. L. M. (1995). The structure of psychological well-being revisited. *Journal of Personality and Social Psychology, 69,* 719–727.

Ryff, C. D., & Singer, B. (1996). Psychological well-being: Meaning, measurement, and implications for psychotherapy research. *Psychotherapy and Psychosomatics, 65,* 14–23.

Ryff, C. D., & Singer, B. (1998). The contours of positive mental health. *Psychological Inquiry, 9,* 1–28.

Saari, L. M., Johnson, T. R., McLaughlin, S. D., & Zimmerle, D. M. (1988). A survey of management training and education practices in U.S. companies. *Personnel Psychology, 41,* 731–743.

Saarni, C. (1999). *The development of emotional competence.* New York: Guilford Press.

Saarni, C. (2001). Emotional competence: A developmental perspective. In R. Bar-On & J. D. A. Parker (Eds.), *The handbook of emotional intelligence* (pp. 68–91). San Francisco: Jossey-Bass.

Sackett, P., & Wanek, J. (1996). New developments in the use of measures of honesty, integrity, conscientiousness, dependability, trustworthiness, and reliability for personnel selection. *Personnel Psychology, 49,* 787–829.

Sadoski, M., & Quast, Z. (1990). Reader response and long-term recall for journalistic text: The roles of imagery, affect and importance. *Reading Research Quarterly, 25,* 256–272.

Saleebey, D. (Ed.). (1992). *The strengths perspective in social work practice.* New York: Longman.

Salovey, P., & Mayer, J. D. (1990). Emotional intelligence. *Imagination, Cognition, and Personality, 9,* 185–211.

Salovey, P., Mayer, J. D., & Caruso, D. R. (2002). The positive psychology of emotional intelligence. In C. R. Snyder & S. J. Lopez (Eds.), *The handbook of positive psychology* (pp. 159–171). New York: Oxford University Press.

Salovey, P., Mayer, J. D., Caruso, D. R., & Lopez, P. N. (2003). Measuring emotional intelligence as a set of abilities with the Mayer-Salovey-Caruso Emotional Intelligence Test. In S. J. Lopez & C. R. Snyder (Eds.), *Handbook of positive psychology assessment* (pp. 251–265). Washington, DC: American Psychological Association.

Salovey, P., Woolery, A., & Mayer, J. D. (2001). Emotional intelligence: Conceptualization and measurement. In G. J. O. Fletcher & M. S. Clark (Eds.), *Blackwell handbook of social psychology: Interpersonal processes* (pp. 279–307). Malden, MA: Blackwell.

Sampson, E. E. (1975). On justice as equality. *Journal of Social Issues, 31*(3), 45–64.

Samuels, P. A., & Lester, D. (1986). A preliminary investigation of emotions experienced toward God by Catholic nuns and priests. *Psychological Reports, 56,* 706.

Sandage, S. J. (1999). An ego-humility model of forgiveness: Theoretical foundations. *Marriage and Family: A Christian Journal, 2,* 259–276.

Sandage, S. J., Hill, P. C., & Vang, C. (2001, August). Forgiveness as a culturally embedded virtue: Examples in Hmong communities. In P. C. Hill & S. J. Sandage (Cochairs), *Forgiveness as positive science: Theory, research, and clinical applications.* Symposium conducted at the annual convention of the American Psychological Association, San Francisco.

Sandage, S. J., Worthington, E. L., Hight, T. L., & Berry, J. W. (2000). Seeking forgiveness: Theoretical context and an initial empirical study. *Journal of Psychology and Theology, 28,* 21–35.

Sandelands, L. E., Brockner, J., & Glynn, M. A. (1988). If at first you don't succeed, try, try again: Effects of persistence-performance contingencies, ego involvement, and self-esteem on task persistence. *Journal of Applied Psychology, 73,* 208–216.

Sanderson, C. A., & Cantor, N. (1999). A life task perspective on personality coherence: Stability versus change in tasks, goals, strategies, and outcomes. In D. Cervone & Y. Shoda (Eds.), *The coherence of personality: Social-cognitive bases of consistency, variability, and organization* (pp. 372–392). New York: Guilford Press.

Sansone, C., & Harackiewicz, J. M. (2000). Controversies and new directions—Is it déjà vu all over again? In C. Sansone & J. M. Harackiewicz (Eds.), *Intrinsic and extrinsic motivation: The search for optimal motivation and performance* (pp. 444–453). New York: Academic Press.

Sansone, C., & Morgan, C. (1992). Intrinsic motivation and education: Competence in context. *Motivation and Emotion, 16,* 249–270.

Sansone, C., & Smith, J. L. (2000). Interest and self-regulation: The relation between having to and wanting to. In C. Sansone & J. M. Harackiewicz (Eds.), *Intrinsic and extrinsic motivation: The search for optimal motivation and performance* (pp. 341–372). New York: Academic Press.

Sansone, C., Weir, C., Harpster, L., & Morgan, C. (1992). Once a boring task always a boring task? Interest as a self-regulatory mechanism. *Journal of Personality and Social Psychology, 63,* 379–390.

Sansone, C., Wiebe, D., & Morgan, C. (1999). Self-regulating interest: The moderating role of hardiness and conscientiousness. *Journal of Personality, 67,* 701–733.

Santrock, J. W. (1996). *Child development* (7th ed.). Dubuque, IA: Brown & Benchmark.

Saracheck, B. (1968). Greek concepts of leadership. *Academy of Management Journal, 11,* 39–48.

Sarouphim, K. M. (1998). Discovering multiple intelligences through a performance-based assessment: Consistency with independent ratings. *Exceptional Children, 65,* 151–161.

Sarouphim, K. M. (2000). Internal structure of DISCOVER: A performance-based assessment. *Journal for the Education of the Gifted, 23,* 314–327.

Sartre, J. (1956). *Being and nothingness: An essay in phenomenological ontology.* New York: Philosophical Library.

Sashkin, M. (1988). The visionary leader. In J. A. Conger & R. N. Kanungo (Eds.), *Charismatic leadership: The elusive factor in organizational effectiveness* (pp. 120–160). San Francisco: Jossey-Bass.

Saucier, G., & Goldberg, L. R. (1998). What is beyond the Big Five? *Journal of Personality, 66,* 495–524.

Saunders, C. (1999, October). *A reflection on my life.* Presentation at the conference Empathy, Altruism and Agape: Perspectives on Love in Science and Religion—A Research Symposium, Cambridge, MA.

Scales, P. C., Benson, P. L., Leffert, N., & Blyth, D. A. (2000). Contributions of developmental assets to the prediction of thriving among adolescents. *Applied Developmental Science, 4,* 27–46.

Schacht, T., & Nathan, P. E. (1977). But is it good for the psychologists? Appraisal and status of DSM-III. *American Psychologist, 32,* 1017–1025.

Schaefer, C. E., & Anastasi, A. (1968). A biographical inventory for identifying creativity in adolescent boys. *Journal of Applied Psychology, 58,* 42–48.

Schall, J. V. (2000). *Schall on Chesterton: Timely essays on timeless paradoxes.* Washington, DC: Catholic University of America Press.

Schaps, E. (2001). Community in school: The key to violence prevention and more. *Safe Learning, 1,* 20–21.

Scheier, M. F., & Carver, C. S. (1982). Self-consciousness, outcome expectancy, and persistence. *Journal of Research in Personality, 16,* 409–418.

Scheier, M. F., & Carver, C. S. (1985). Optimism, coping, and health: Assessment and implications of generalized outcome expectancies. *Health Psychology, 4,* 219–247.

Scheier, M. F., Carver, C. S., & Bridges, M. W. (1994). Distinguishing optimism from neuroticism (and trait anxiety, self-mastery, and self-esteem): A reevaluation of the Life Orientation Test. *Journal of Personality and Social Psychology, 67,* 1063–1078.

Scheier, M. F., Weintraub, J. K., & Carver, C. S. (1986). Coping with stress: Divergent strategies of optimists and pessimists. *Journal of Personality and Social Psychology, 51,* 1257–1264.

Schervish, P. (1990). Wealth and the spiritual secret of money. In R. Wuthnow, V. Hodgkinson, & Associates (Eds.), *Faith and philanthropy in America* (pp. 63–90). San Francisco: Jossey-Bass.

Schiefele, U. (1996). Topic interest, text representation and quality of experience. *Contemporary Educational Psychology, 12,* 3–18.

Schiefele, U. (1999). Interest and learning from text. *Scientific Studies of Reading, 3,* 257–280.

Schiefele, U., & Krapp, A. (1996). Topic interest and free recall of expository texts. *Learning and Individual Differences, 8,* 141–160.

Schiefele, U., Krapp, A., & Winteler, A. (1992). Interest as a predictor of academic achievement: A meta-analysis of research. In K. A. Renninger, S. Hidi, & A. Krapp (Eds.), *The role of interest in learning and development* (pp. 183–212). Hillsdale, NJ: Erlbaum.

Schimmel, S. (1992). *The seven deadly sins: Jewish, Christian, and classical reflections on human nature.* New York: Free Press.

Schleiermacher, F. (1967). *Christmas Eve: Dialogue on incarnation* (T. N. Tice, Ed. and Trans.). Richmond, VA: John Knox Press. (Original German edition published 1806)

Schmidt-Hidding, W. (Ed.). (1963). *Europäische Schlüsselwörter: Vol. 1. Humor und Witz.* Munich, Germany: Huber.

Schoenfeld, A. H. (1992). Learning to think mathematically: Problem solving, metacognition, and sense making in mathematics. In D. A. Grouws (Ed.), *Handbook of research on mathematics, teaching, and learning: A project of the National Council of Teachers of Mathematics* (pp. 334–370). New York: Macmillan.

Schraw, G., Bruning, R., & Svoboda, C. (1995). The effect of reader purpose on interest and recall. *Journal of Reading Behavior, 27,* 1–17.

Schraw, G., & Lehman, S. (2001). Situational interest: A review of the literature and directions for future research. *Educational Psychology Review, 13,* 23–52.

Schretlen, D., Pearson, G. D., Anthony, J. C., Aylward, E. H., Augustine, A. M., Davis, A., et al. (2000). Elucidating the contributions of processing speed, executive ability, and frontal lobe volume to normal age-related differences in fluid intelligence. *Journal of the International Neuropsychological Society, 6,* 52–61.

Schriesheim, C. A., Neider, L. L., Scandura, T. A., & Tepper, B. J. (1992). Development and preliminary validation of a new scale (LMX-6) to measure leader-member exchange in organizations. *Educational and Psychological Measurement, 52,* 135–147.

Schroder, H. M., Driver, M. J., & Streufert, S. (1967). *Human information processing.* New York: Holt, Rinehart & Winston.

Schulman, M. (2002). The passion to know: A developmental perspective. In C. R. Snyder & S. J. Lopez (Eds.), *The handbook of positive psychology* (pp. 313–327). New York: Oxford University Press.

Schulman, P., Keith, D., & Seligman, M. E. P. (1993). Is optimism heritable? A study of twins. *Behaviour Research and Therapy, 31,* 569–574.

Schwartz, B. (2000). Self-determination: The tyranny of freedom. *American Psychologist, 55,* 79–88.

Schwartz, S. H. (1992). Universals in the content and structure of values: Theoretical advances and empirical tests in 20 countries. In M. P. Zanna (Ed.), *Advances in experimental social psychology* (Vol. 25, pp. 1-65). New York: Academic Press.

Schwartz, S. H. (1994). Are there universal aspects in the structure and content of human values? *Journal of Social Issues, 50*(4), 19–45.

Schwartz, S. H. (1996). Value priorities and behavior: Applying a theory of integrated value systems. In C. Seligman, J. M. Olson, & M. P. Zanna (Eds.), *The psychology of values: The Ontario Symposium* (Vol. 8, pp. 1–24). Mahwah, NJ: Erlbaum.

Schwartz, S. H., & Bilsky, W. (1987). Toward a universal psychological structure of human values. *Journal of Personality and Social Psychology, 53,* 550–562.

Schwartz, S. H., & Bilsky, W. (1990). Toward a theory of the universal content and structure of values: Extensions and cross-cultural replications. *Journal of Personality and Social Psychology, 58,* 878–891.

Schwartz, S. H., & Sagiv, L. (1995). Identifying culture-specifics in the content and structure of values. *Journal of Cross-Cultural Psychology, 26,* 92–116.

Schwarzenegger, A., & Hall, D. K. (1977). *Arnold: The education of a bodybuilder.* New York: Simon & Schuster.

Scobie, E. D., & Scobie, G. E. W. (1998). Damaging events: The perceived need for forgiveness. *Journal for the Theory of Social Behaviour, 28,* 373–401.

Scott, W. A. (1958a). Research definitions of mental health and mental illness. *Psychological Bulletin, 55,* 29–45.

Scott, W. A. (1958b). Social psychological correlates of mental illness and mental health. *Psychological Bulletin, 55,* 65–87.

Search Institute. (1996). *Search Institute profiles of student life: Attitudes and behaviors.* Minneapolis, MN: Author.

Sedikides, C., & Skowronski, J. J. (1997). The symbolic self in evolutionary context. *Personality and Social Psychology Review, 1,* 80–102.

Seligman, M. E. P. (1975). *Helplessness: On depression, development, and death.* San Francisco: Freeman.

Seligman, M. E. P. (1990). *Learned optimism.* New York: Knopf.

Seligman, M. E. P. (1994). *What you can change and what you can't.* New York: Knopf.

Seligman, M. E. P. (2000). *Explanatory style webpage.* Available at http:// psych.upenn.edu/seligman/ research.htm.

Seligman, M. E. P. (2002). *Authentic happiness.* New York: Free Press.

Seligman, M. E. P., & Csikszentmihalyi, M. (2000). Positive psychology: An introduction. *American Psychologist, 55,* 5–14.

Seligman, M. E. P., & Peterson, C. (2003). Positive clinical psychology. In L. G. Aspinwall & U. M. Staudinger (Eds.), *A psychology of human strengths: Fundamental questions and future directions for a positive psychology* (pp. 305–317). Washington, DC: American Psychological Association.

Seligman, M. E. P., Reivich, K., Jaycox, L., & Gillham, J. (1995). *The optimistic child.* Boston: Houghton Mifflin.

Seligman, M. E. P., & Schulman, P. (1986). Explanatory style as a predictor of productivity and quitting among life insurance sales agents. *Journal of Personality and Social Psychology, 50,* 832–838.

Seligman, M. E. P., & Steen, T. A. (in preparation). *The authentic happiness workbook.* University of Pennsylvania, Philadelphia.

Selye, H. (1956). *The stress of life.* New York: McGraw-Hill.

Selz, O. (1935). Versuche zur Hebung des Intelligenzniveaus: Ein Beitrag zur Theorie der Intelligenz und ihrer erziehlichen Beeinflussung. *Zeitschrift fur Psychologie, 134,* 236–301.

Sethi, S., & Seligman, M. E. P. (1993). Optimism and fundamentalism. *Psychological Science, 4,* 256–259.

Shafir, E., & LeBoeuf, R. A. (2002). Rationality. *Annual Review of Psychology, 53,* 491–517.

Shaftesbury, A. A. C. (1977). *Characteristicks of men. An inquiry concerning virtue, or merit.* Manchester, England: Manchester University Press. (Original work published 1714)

Shaver, P. R., & Hazan, C. (1993). Adult romantic attachment: Theory and evidence. In D. Perlman & W. Jones (Eds.), *Advances in personal relationships* (Vol. 4, pp. 29–70). London: Jessica Kingsley.

Shaver, P. R., Hazan, C., & Bradshaw, D. (1984, July). *Infant-caretaker attachment and adult romantic love: Similarities and differences, continuities and discontinuities.* Paper presented at the Second International Conference on Personal Relationships, Madison, WI.

Sheehan, T. J., Candee, D., Willms, J., Donnelly, J. C., & Husted, S. D. R. (1985). Structural equation models of moral reasoning and physician performance. *Evaluation and the Health Professions, 8,* 379–400.

Sheehan, T. J., Husted, S. D. R., Candee, D., Cook, C. D., & Bargen, M. (1980). Moral judgment as a predictor of clinical performance. *Evaluation and the Health Professions, 3,* 393–404.

Sheldon, K. M. (2002). The self-concordance model of healthy goal-striving: When personal goals correctly represent the person. In E. L. Deci & R. M. Ryan (Eds.), *Handbook of self-determination research* (pp. 65–86). Rochester, NY: University of Rochester Press.

Sheldon, K. M., & Elliot, A. J. (1999). Goal striving, need-satisfaction, and longitudinal well-being: The self-concordance model. *Journal of Personality and Social Psychology, 76,* 482–497.

Sheldon, K. M., Elliot, A. J., Ryan, R. M., Chirkov, V., Kim, Y., Wu, C., et al. (2003). *Self-concordance and subjective well-being in five cultures.* Unpublished manuscript, University of Missouri, Columbia.

Sheldon, K. M., & Houser-Marko, L. (2001). Self-concordance, goal-attainment, and the pursuit of happiness: Can there be an upward spiral? *Journal of Personality and Social Psychology, 80,* 152–165.

Sheldon, K. M., & Kasser, T. (1995). Coherence and congruence: Two aspects of personality integration. *Journal of Personality and Social Psychology, 68,* 531–543.

Sheldon, K. M., Kasser, T., Smith, K., & Share, T. (2002). Personal goals and psychological growth: Testing an intervention to enhance goal-attainment and personality integration. *Journal of Personality, 70,* 5–31.

Sheldon, K. M., Ryan, R. M., Rawsthorne, L., & Ilardi, B. (1997). "True" self and "trait" self: Cross-role variation in the Big Five traits and its relations with authenticity and well-being. *Journal of Personality and Social Psychology, 73,* 1380–1393.

Sheldon, K. M., Ryan, R. M., & Reis, H. T. (1996). What makes for a good day? Competence and autonomy in the day and in the person. *Personality and Social Psychology Bulletin, 22,* 1270–1279.

Shelp, E. E. (1984). Courage: A neglected virtue in the patient-physician relationship. *Social Science and Medicine, 18,* 351–360.

Shelton, C. M. (2000). *Achieving moral health.* New York: Crossroad.

Shelton, C. M., & McAdams, D. P. (1990). In search of an everyday morality: The development of a measure. *Adolescence, 25,* 923–943.

Shepela, S. T., Cook, J., Horlitz, E., Leal, R., Luciano, S., Lutfy, E., et al. (1999). Courageous resistance: A special case of altruism. *Theory and Psychology, 9,* 787–805.

Sherblom, S. A. (1997). *Moral sensibility and experience in young children: A relational study in moral development.* Unpublished doctoral dissertation, Harvard University, Cambridge, MA.

Sherblom, S. A., Shipps, T., & Sherblom, J. C. (1993). Justice, care, and integrated concerns in the ethical decision-making of nurses. *Qualitative Health Research, 3,* 442–464.

Sherif, M. (1966). *In common predicament: Social psychology of intergroup conflict and cooperation.* Boston: Houghton Mifflin.

Sherman, N. (1989). *The fabric of character: Aristotle's theory of virtue.* Oxford, England: Oxford University Press.

Sherman, R., & Dinkmeyer, D. C. (1987). *Systems of family therapy.* New York: Brunner/Mazel.

Shiota, M., & Keltner, D. (2003). *The dispositional positive affect scale.* Unpublished manuscript, University of California, Berkeley.

Shipper, F., & Wilson, C. L. (1992). The impact of managerial behaviors on group performance, stress, and commitment. In K. E. Clark, M. B. Clark, & D. R. Campbell (Eds.), *Impact of leadership* (pp. 119–129). Greensboro, NC: Center for Creative Leadership.

Shrauger, J. S., & Sorman, P. B. (1977). Self-evaluations, initial success and failure, and improvement as determinants of persistence. *Journal of Consulting and Clinical Psychology, 45,* 784–795.

Shriver, T. P., Schwab-Stone, M., & DeFalco, K. (1999). Why SEL is the better way: The New Haven social developmental program. In J. Cohen (Ed.), *Educating minds and hearts* (pp. 43–60). New York: Teachers College Press.

Shultz, T. M., & Veschio, J. P. (2001). *Humility: A consistent self-rating across private and public conditions.* Unpublished manuscript, Grove City College, PA.

Shweder, R. A., & Haidt, J. (2000). The cultural psychology of the emotions: Ancient and new. In M. Lewis & J. M. Haviland-Jones (Eds.), *Handbook of emotions* (2nd ed., pp. 397–414). New York: Guilford Press.

Shweder, R. A., Mahapatra, M., & Miller, J. G. (1987). Culture and moral development. In J. Kagan & S. Lamb (Eds.), *The emergence of morality in young children* (pp. 1–82). Chicago: University of Chicago Press.

Shweder, R. A., Much, N. C., Mahapatra, M., & Park, L. (1997). The "big three" of morality (autonomy, community, and divinity), and the "big three" explanations of suffering. In A. Brandt & P. Rozin (Eds.), *Morality and health* (pp. 119–169). New York: Routledge.

Sicinski, A. (1972). Optimism versus pessimism (Tentative concepts and their consequences for future research). *Polish Sociological Bulletin, 25–26,* 47–62.

Silvia, P. J. (in press). *The psychology of interest.* New York: Oxford University Press.

Simmel, G. (1950). *The sociology of Georg Simmel.* Glencoe, IL: Free Press.

Simonton, D. K. (1997). Creative productivity: A predictive and explanatory model of career trajectories and landmarks. *Psychological Review, 104,* 66–89.

Simonton, D. K. (1999a). Creativity and genius. In L. Pervin & O. John (Eds.), *Handbook of personality theory and research* (2nd ed., pp. 629–652). New York: Guilford Press.

Simonton, D. K. (1999b). *Origins of genius: Darwinian perspectives on creativity.* New York: Oxford University Press.

Simonton, D. K. (1999c). Talent and its development: An emergenic and epigenetic model. *Psychological Review, 106,* 435–457.

Simonton, D. K. (2000). Creativity: Cognitive, developmental, personal, and social aspects. *American Psychologist, 55,* 151–158.

Simonton, D. K. (2002). Creativity. In C. R. Snyder & S. J. Lopez (Eds.), *The handbook of positive psychology* (pp. 189–201). New York: Oxford University Press.

Simpson, J. A. (1990). Influence of attachment styles on romantic relationships. *Journal of Personality and Social Psychology, 59,* 971–980.

Simpson, J. A., Rholes, W. S., & Nelligan, J. S. (1992). Support seeking and support giving within couples in an anxiety-provoking situation: The role of attachment styles. *Journal of Personality and Social Psychology, 62,* 434–446.

Sinnott, J. D. (1998). *The development of logic in adulthood.* New York: Plenum.

Skaalvik, E. M. (1997). Self-enhancing and self-defeating ego orientation: Relations with task and avoidance orientation, achievement, self-perceptions, and anxiety. *Journal of Educational Psychology, 89,* 71–81.

Skinner, B. F. (1948). *Walden two.* New York: Macmillan.

Slovic, P., & Fischhoff, B. (1977). On the psychology of experimental surprises. *Journal of Experimental Psychology: Human Perception and Performance, 3,* 544–551.

Smart, N. (1999). *World philosophies.* New York: Routledge.

Smith, A. (1976). *The theory of moral sentiments* (6th ed.). Oxford, England: Clarendon Press. (Original work published 1790)

Smith, C. P. (1964). Relationships between achievement-related motives and intelligence, performance level, and persistence. *Journal of Abnormal and Social Psychology, 68,* 523–532.

Smith, H., Fabricatore, A., & Peyrot, M. (1999). Religiosity and altruism among African American males: The Catholic experience. *Journal of Black Studies, 29,* 579–597.

Smith, J., Staudinger, U. M., & Baltes, P. B. (1994). Occupational settings facilitating wisdom-related knowledge: The sample case of clinical psychologists. *Journal of Consulting and Clinical Psychology, 62,* 989–999.

Smith, J. L., Morgan, C. L., & Sansone, C. (2001). Getting (inter) personal: The role of other people in the self-regulation of interest. In F. Columbus (Ed.), *Advances in psychology research* (Vol. 5, pp. 153–185). New York: Nova Science Publishers.

Smith, K. D., Keating, J. P., & Stotland, E. (1989). Altruism reconsidered: The effect of denying feedback on a victim's status to empathic witness. *Journal of Personality and Social Psychology, 57,* 641–650.

Smith, M., Duda, J., Allen, J., & Hall, H. (2002). Contemporary measures of approach and avoidance goal orientations: Similarities and differences. *British Journal of Educational Psychology, 72,* 155–190.

Smith, M. L., & Glass, G. V. (1977). The meta-analysis of psychotherapy outcome studies. *American Psychologist, 32,* 752–760.

Smith, S. M. (2001, February). *Self-control and academic performance.* Paper presented at the Society for Personality and Social Psychology, San Antonio, TX.

Smith, T. (2002). Religious diversity in America: The emergence of Muslims, Buddhists, Hindus, and others. *Journal for the Scientific Study of Religion, 41,* 577–585.

Snarey, J. (1985). Cross-cultural universality of social-moral development: A critical review of Kohlbergian research. *Psychological Bulletin, 97,* 202–232.

Snowdon, D. (2001). *Aging with grace.* New York: Bantam Books.

Snyder, C. R. (1994). *The psychology of hope: You can get there from here.* New York: Free Press.

Snyder, C. R. (2000a). Genesis: The birth and growth of hope. In C. R. Snyder (Ed.), *Handbook of hope: Theory, measures, and applications* (pp. 25–38). San Diego, CA: Academic Press.

Snyder, C. R. (Ed.). (2000b). *Handbook of hope: Theory, measures, and applications.* San Diego, CA: Academic Press.

Snyder, C. R. (2000c). *Hope webpage.* Available at http://raven.cc.ukans.edu/~crsnyder

Snyder, C. R. (2002). Hope theory: Rainbows of the mind. *Psychological Inquiry, 13,* 249–275.

Snyder, C. R. (2003, March). *Measuring hope in children.* Paper presented at the Child Trends Indicators of Positive Development Conference, Washington, DC.

Snyder, C. R., Harris, C., Anderson, J. R., Holleran, S. A., Irving, L. M., Sigmon, S. T., et al. (1991). The will and the ways: Development and validation of an individual differences measure of hope. *Journal of Personality and Social Psychology, 60,* 570–585.

Snyder, C. R., & Lopez, S. (Eds.). (2002). *Handbook of positive psychology.* New York: Oxford University Press.

Snyder, C. R., Rand, K., King, E., Feldman, D., & Taylor, J. (2002). "False" hope. *Journal of Clinical Psychology, 58,* 1003–1022.

Snyder, C. R., Sympson, S. C., Ybasco, F. C., Borders, T. F., Babyak, M. A., & Higgins, R. L. (1996). Development and validation of the State Hope Scale. *Journal of Personality and Social Psychology, 70,* 321–335.

Sober, E., & Wilson, D. S. (1998). *Unto others: The evolution and psychology of unselfish behavior.* Cambridge, MA: Harvard University Press.

Solomon, J., & George, C. (1999). The measurement of attachment security in infancy and childhood. In J. Cassidy & P. R. Shaver (Eds.), *Handbook of attachment: Theory, research, and clinical applications* (pp. 287–316). New York: Guilford Press.

Solomon, R. C. (1995). The cross-cultural comparison of emotion. In J. Marks & R. T. Ames (Eds.), *Emotions in Asian thought* (pp. 253–294). Albany: State University of New York Press.

Sommers, S., & Kosmitzki, C. (1988). Emotion and social context: An American-German comparison. *British Journal of Social Psychology, 27,* 35–49.

Speicher, B. (1994). Family patterns of moral judgment during adolescence and early adulthood. *Developmental Psychology, 30,* 624–632.

Spence, J. T., & Helmreich, R. L. (1983). Achievement-related motives and behaviors. In J. T. Spence (Ed.), *Achievement and achievement motives: Psychological and sociological approaches* (pp. 30–68). San Francisco: Freeman,

Spielberger, C. D. (1979). *Preliminary manual for the State-Trait Personality Inventory (STPI).* Unpublished manuscript, University of South Florida, Tampa.

Spielberger, C. D., & Starr, L. M. (1994). Curiosity and exploratory behavior. In H. F. O'Neil & M. Drillings (Eds.), *Motivation: Theory and research* (pp. 221–243). Hillsdale, NJ: Erlbaum.

Spilka, B., Hood, R. W. J., & Gorsuch, R. L. (1985). *The psychology of religion: An empirical approach.* Englewood Cliffs, NJ: Prentice Hall.

Spreitzer, G. M., McCall, M. W., & Mahoney, J. D. (1997). Early identification of international executive potential. *Journal of Applied Psychology, 82,* 6–29.

Sroufe, L. A. (1983). Infant-caregiver attachment and patterns of adaptation in preschool: The roots of maladaptation and competence. In M. Perlmutter (Ed.), *Minnesota Symposium in Child Psychology, 16,* 41–81.

Sroufe, L. A., Fox, N. E., & Pancake, V. R. (1983). Attachment and dependency in developmental perspective. *Child Development, 54,* 1615–1627.

Sroufe, L. A., & Waters, E. (1977). Heart rate as a convergent measure in clinical and developmental research. *Merrill-Palmer Quarterly, 23,* 3–27.

Stamp, G. P. (1988). *Longitudinal research into methods of assessing managerial potential* (ARI Tech. Rep. No. DAJA45–86–c-0009). Alexandria, VA: U.S. Army Research Institute for the Behavioral and Social Sciences.

Stanley, S. (1980). The family and moral education. In R. L. Mosher (Ed.), *Moral education: A first generation of research* (pp. 341–355). New York: Praeger.

Stanovich, K. E. (1999). *Who is rational? Studies of individual differences in reasoning.* Mahwah, NJ: Erlbaum.

Stanovich, K. E., & West, R. F. (1997). Reasoning independently of prior belief and individual differences in actively open-minded thinking. *Journal of Educational Psychology, 89,* 342–357.

Stanovich, K. E., & West, R. F. (1998). Individual differences in rational thought. *Journal of Experimental Psychology: General, 127,* 161–188.

Stanovich, K. E., & West, R. F. (2000). *Stanovich and West stimuli.* Document available at http://falcon.jmu.edu/~westrf/stimuli/Stanovich_West_stimuli. html.

Starnes, D. M., & Zinser, O. (1983). The effect of problem difficulty, locus of control, and sex on task persistence. *Journal of General Psychology, 108,* 249–255.

Starrett, R. H. (1996). Assessment of global social responsibility. *Psychological Reports, 78,* 535–554.

Statman, D. (1992). Modesty, pride, and realistic self-assessment. *Philosophical Quarterly, 42,* 420–438.

Staub, E. (1978). *Positive social behavior and morality.* New York: Academic Press.

Staudinger, U. M., & Baltes, P. B. (1996). Interactive minds: A facilitative setting for wisdom-related performance? *Journal of Personality and Social Psychology, 71,* 746–762.

Staudinger, U. M., Lopez, D. F., & Baltes, P. B. (1997). The psychometric location of wisdom-related performance: Intelligence, personality, and more? *Personality and Social Psychological Bulletin, 23,* 1200–1214.

Staudinger, U. M., Maciel, A. G., Smith, J., & Baltes, P. B. (1998). What predicts wisdom-related performance? A first look at personality, intelligence, and facilitative experiential contexts. *European Journal of Personality, 12,* 1–17.

Staudinger, U. M., Smith, J., & Baltes, P. B. (1992). Wisdom-related knowledge in a life review task: Age differences and the role of professional specialization. *Psychology and Aging, 7,* 271–281.

Staw, B. M. (1976). Knee-deep in the Big Muddy: A study of escalating commitment to a chosen course of action. *Organizational Behavior and Human Decision Processes, 16,* 27–44.

Steele, C. M. (1997). A threat in the air: How stereotypes shape intellectual identity and performance. *American Psychologist, 52,* 613–629.

Steen, T. A., Kachorek, L. V., & Peterson, C. (2003). Character strengths among youth. *Journal of Youth and Adolescence, 32,* 5–16.

Steensland, B., Park, J., Regnerus, M., Robinson, L., Wilcox, W., & Woodberry, R. (2000). The measure of American religion: Toward improving the state of the art. *Social Forces, 79,* 291–318.

Stein, M. (1989). Gratitude and attitude: A note on emotional welfare. *Social Psychology Quarterly, 52,* 242–248.

Steindl-Rast, D. (1984). *Gratefulness, the heart of prayer.* New York: Paulist Press.

Stern, W. (1914). *The psychological methods of intelligence testing* (G. M. Whipple, Trans.). Baltimore: Warwick and York.

Sternberg, R. J. (1977). *Intelligence, information processing and analogical reasoning: The componential analysis of human abilities.* Hillsdale, NJ: Erlbaum.

Sternberg, R. J. (1985). *Beyond IQ: A triarchic theory of human intelligence.* Cambridge, England: Cambridge University Press.

Sternberg, R. J. (1986a). Implicit theories of intelligence, creativity, and wisdom. *Journal of Personality and Social Psychology, 49,* 607–627.

Sternberg, R. J. (1986b). A triangular theory of love. *Psychological Review, 93,* 119–135.

Sternberg, R. J. (1990a). Wisdom and its relations to intelligence and creativity. In R. J. Sternberg (Ed.), *Wisdom: Its nature, origins, and development* (pp. 160–177). New York: Cambridge University Press.

Sternberg, R. J. (Ed.). (1990b). *Wisdom: Its nature, origins, and development.* New York: Cambridge University Press.

Sternberg, R. J. (1998). A balance theory of wisdom. *Review of General Psychology, 2,* 347–365.

Sternberg, R. J. (Ed.). (1999a). *Handbook of creativity.* New York: Cambridge University Press.

Sternberg, R. J. (1999b). Schools should nurture wisdom. In B. Z. Presseisen (Ed.), *Teaching for intelligence* (pp. 55–82). Arlington Heights, IL: Skylight Training and Publishing.

Sternberg, R. J. (2000). Intelligence and wisdom. In R. J. Sternberg (Ed.), *Handbook of intelligence* (pp. 631–649). Cambridge, England: Cambridge University Press.

Sternberg, R. J. (2001). Why schools should teach for wisdom: The balance theory of wisdom in educational settings. *Educational Psychologist, 36,* 227–245.

Sternberg, R. J., & Detterman, D. R. (1986). *What is intelligence?* Norwood, NJ: Ablex.

Sternberg, R. J., & Wagner, R. K. (Eds.). (1986). *Practical intelligence: Nature and origins of competence in the everyday world.* Cambridge, England: Cambridge University Press.

Stevenson, H. (1997). Managing anger: Protective, proactive, or adaptive racial socialization identity profiles and African American manhood development. *Journal of Prevention and Intervention in the Community, 16,* 35–61.

Stevenson-Hinde, J., & Shouldice, A. (1995). Maternal interactions and self-reports related to attachment classifications at 4.5 years. *Child Development, 66,* 583–596.

Stewart, A. J., & Healy, J. M. (1989). Linking individual development and social changes. *American Psychologist, 44,* 30–42.

Stiff, J., Corman, S., Krizek, B., & Snider, E. (1994). Individual differences and changes in nonverbal behavior. *Communication Research, 21,* 555–581.

Stipek, D. J., Lamb, M. E., & Zigler, E. F. (1981). OPTI: A measure of children's optimism. *Educational and Psychological Measurement, 41,* 131–143.

Stogdill, R. M. (1948). Personal factors associated with leadership: A survey of the literature. *Journal of Psychology, 25,* 35–71.

Stogdill, R. M. (1963). *Manual for the Leader Behavior Description Questionnaire Form XII.* Columbus: Bureau of Business Research, Ohio State University.

Stogdill, R. M. (1974). *Handbook of leadership: A survey of theory and research.* New York: Free Press.

Stogdill, R. M., & Coons, A. E. (1957). *Leader behavior: Its description and measurement.* Columbus: Bureau of Business Research, Ohio State University.

Stolle, D. (1998). Bowling together, bowling alone: The development of generalized trust in voluntary associations. *Political Psychology, 19,* 497–525.

Stolzenberg, R., Blair-Loy, M., & Waite, L. (1995). Religious participation in early adulthood: Age and family life cycle effects on church membership. *American Sociological Review, 60,* 84–103.

Stotland, E. (1969). *The psychology of hope.* San Francisco: Jossey-Bass.

Streng, F. J. (1989). Introduction: Thanksgiving as a worldwide response to life. In J. B. Carman & F. J. Streng (Eds.), *Spoken and unspoken thanks: Some comparative soundings* (pp. 1–9). Dallas, TX: Center for World Thanksgiving.

Strough, J., Berg, C., & Sansone, C. (1996). Goals for solving everyday problems across the life span: Age and gender differences in the salience of interpersonal concerns. *Developmental Psychology, 32,* 1106–1115.

Strube, M., & Boland, S. M. (1986). Postperformance attributions and task persistence among Type A and B individuals: A clarification. *Journal of Personality and Social Psychology, 50,* 413–420.

Subkoviak, M. J., Enright, R. D., Wu, C. R., Gassin, E. A., Freedman, S., Olson, L. M., et al. (1995). Measuring interpersonal forgiveness in late adolescence and middle adulthood. *Journal of Adolescence, 18,* 641–655.

Suedfeld, P. (1997). The social psychology of Invictus: Conceptual and methodological approaches to indomitability. In C. McGarty (Ed.), *The message of social psychology: Perspectives on mind in society* (pp. 328–341). Malden, MA: Blackwell.

Suedfeld, P., & Bluck, S. (1993). Changes in integrative complexity accompanying significant life events: Historical evidence. *Journal of Personality and Social Psychology, 64,* 124–130.

Suedfeld, P., & Piedrahita, L. E. (1984). Intimations of mortality: Integrative simplification as a precursor of death. *Journal of Personality and Social Psychology, 47,* 848–852.

Suedfeld, P., & Tetlock, P. E. (1977). Integrative complexity of communications in international crises. *Journal of Conflict Resolution, 21,* 169–184.

Suedfeld, P., Tetlock, P., & Streufert, S. (1992). Conceptual/integrative complexity. In C. P. Smith (Ed.), *Handbook of thematic content analysis* (pp. 393–400). New York: Cambridge University Press.

Suh, E. M. (2001). *Culture, identity consistency, and subjective well-being.* Unpublished manuscript, University of California–Riverside.

Sullivan, J. L., Fried, A., & Dietz, M. G. (1992). Patriotism, politics, and the presidential election of 1988. *American Journal of Political Science, 36,* 200–234.

Sullivan, J. L., & Transue, J. E. (1999). The psychological underpinnings of democracy: A selective review of research on political tolerance, interpersonal trust, and social capital. *Annual Review of Psychology, 50,* 625–650.

Sullivan, M., Karlsson, J., & Ware, J. E. (1995). The Swedish SF-36 Health Survey: I. Evaluation of data quality, scaling assumptions, reliability and construct validity across general populations in Sweden. *Social Science and Medicine, 41,* 1349–1358.

Sumerlin, J. R., & Norman, R. L. (1992). Self-actualization and homeless men: A known-groups examination of Maslow's hierarchy of needs. *Journal of Social Behavior and Personality, 7,* 469–481.

Summers, C. H. (2000). *The war against boys: How misguided feminism is harming our young men.* New York: Simon & Schuster.

Sumner, R. (1976). Imaginative endings. In O. G. Johnson (Ed.), *Tests and measurements in child development: Handbook II* (Vol. 1, pp. 500–501). San Francisco: Jossey-Bass.

Sunohara, G. A., Roberts, W., Malone, M., Shachar, R. J., Tannock, R., Basile, V. S., et al. (2000). Linkage of the dopamine D4 receptor gene and attention-deficit/hyperactivity disorder. *American Academy of Child and Adolescent Psychiatry, 39,* 1537–1542.

Sutton, S. K., & Davidson, R. J. (1997). Prefrontal brain asymmetry: A biological substrate of the behavioral approach and inhibition systems. *Psychological Science, 8,* 204–210.

Swamp, J. (1997). *Giving thanks: A Native American good morning message.* New York: Lee & Low.

Swan, G. E., & Carmelli, D. (1996). Curiosity and mortality in aging adults: A 5-year follow-up of the Western Collaborative Group Study. *Psychology and Aging, 11,* 449–453.

Swann, W. B. (1997). The trouble with change: Self-verification and allegiance to the self. *Psychological Science, 8,* 177–180.

Szagun, G. (1992). Age-related changes in children's understanding of courage. *Journal of Genetic Psychology, 153,* 405–420.

Szagun, G., & Schauble, M. (1997). Children's and adults' understanding of the feeling experience of courage. *Cognition and Emotion, 11,* 291–306.

Tafarodi, R. W., & Vu, C. (1997). Two-dimensional self-esteem and reactions to success and failure. *Personality and Social Psychology Bulletin, 23,* 626–635.

Taffel, R. (1999, November). Thanks, mommy: Teaching kids to be grateful. *Parents,* 138–147.

Takahashi, M., & Bordia, P. (2000). The concept of wisdom: A cross-cultural comparison. *International Journal of Psychology, 35,* 1–9.

Takaku, S., Weiner, B., & Ohbuchi, K. (2001). A cross-cultural examination of the effects of apology and perspective-taking on forgiveness. *Journal of Language and Social Psychology, 20,* 144–166.

Tan, A., Kendis, R., Fine, J., & Porac, J. (1977). A short measure of Eriksonian ego identity. *Journal of Personality Assessment, 41,* 279–284.

Tanaka, K., & Yamauchi, H. (2000). Influence of autonomy on perceived control beliefs and self-regulated learning in Japanese undergraduate students. *North American Journal of Psychology, 2,* 255–272.

Tangney, J. P. (1995). Recent advances in the empirical study of shame and guilt. *American Behavioral Scientist, 38,* 1132–1145.

Tangney, J. P. (2000). Humility: Theoretical perspectives, empirical findings and directions for future research. *Journal of Social and Clinical Psychology, 19,* 70–82.

Tangney, J. P. (2002). Humility. In C. R. Snyder & S. J. Lopez (Eds.), *Handbook of positive psychology* (pp. 411–419). New York: Oxford University Press.

Tangney, J. P., Baumeister, R. F., & Boone, A. L. (in press). Self-control predicts good adjustment, less pathology, better grades, and interpersonal success. *Journal of Personality.*

Taranto, M. A. (1989). Facets of wisdom: A theoretical synthesis. *International Journal of Aging and Human Development, 29,* 1–21.

Taylor, R., & Chatters, L. (1991). Religious life. In J. S. Jackson (Ed.), *Life in Black America* (pp. 105–123). Newbury Park, CA: Sage.

Taylor, R., Mattis, J., & Chatters, L. (1999). Subjective religiosity among African Americans: A synthesis of findings from five national samples. *Journal of Black Psychology, 25,* 524–543.

Taylor, S. E. (1985). Adjustments to threatening events: A theory of cognitive adaptation. *American Psychologist, 38,* 1161–1173.

Taylor, S. E. (1989). *Positive illusions.* New York: Basic Books.

Taylor, S. E., & Brown, J. D. (1988). Illusion and well-being: A social psychological perspective on mental health. *Psychological Bulletin, 103,* 193–210.

Taylor, S. E., Kemeny, M. E., Reed, G. M., Bower, J. E., & Gruenewald, T. L. (2000). Psychological resources, positive illusions, and health. *American Psychologist, 55,* 99–109.

Taylor, S. E., Klein, L. C., Lewis, B. P., Gruenewald, T. L., Gurung, R. A. R., & Updegraff, J. A. (2000). Biobehavioral responses to stress in females: Tend-and-befriend, not fight-or-flight. *Psychological Review, 107,* 422–429.

Te Grotenhuis, M., & Scheepers, P. (2001). Churches in Dutch: Causes of religious disaffiliation in the Netherlands, 1937–1995. *Journal for the Scientific Study of Religion, 40,* 591–606.

Tellegen, A. (1982). *Brief manual for the Differential Personality Questionnaire.* Unpublished manuscript, University of Minnesota, Minneapolis.

Temoshok, L. R., & Chandra, P. S. (2000). The meaning of forgiveness in a specific situational and cultural context: Persons living with HIV/AIDS in India. In M. E. McCullough, K. I. Pargament, & C. E. Thoresen (Eds.), *Forgiveness: Theory, research, and practice* (pp. 41–64). New York: Guilford Press.

Templeton, J. M. (1995). *Discovering the laws of life.* New York: Continuum.

Templeton, J. M. (1998). *The humble approach.* Radnor, PA: Templeton Foundation Press.

Terman, L. M. (1904). A preliminary study of the psychology and pedagogy of leadership. *Pedagogical Seminary, 11,* 413–451.

Tetlock, P. E. (1986). A value pluralism model of ideological reasoning. *Journal of Personality and Social Psychology, 50,* 819–827.

Tetlock, P. E., Armor, D., & Peterson, R. S. (1994). The slavery debate in antebellum America: Cognitive style, value conflict, and the limits of compromise. *Journal of Personality and Social Psychology, 66,* 115–126.

Tetlock, P. E., Peterson, R. S., & Berry, J. M. (1993). Flattering and unflattering personality portraits of integratively simple and complex managers. *Journal of Personality and Social Psychology, 64,* 500–511.

Tetrault, L. A., Schreisheim, C. A., & Neider, L. L. (1988). Leadership training interventions: A review. *Organizational Development Journal, 6,* 77–83.

Thayer, R. E. (1967). Measurement of activation through self-report. *Psychological Reports, 20,* 663–678.

Thayer, R. E. (1978). Factor analytic and reliability studies on the Activation-Deactivation Adjective Check List. *Psychological Reports, 42,* 747–756.

Thayer, R. E. (1986). Activation-Deactivation Adjective Check List: Current overview and structural analysis. *Psychological Reports, 58,* 607–614.

Thayer, R. E. (1987). Energy, tiredness, and tension effects of a sugar snack versus moderate exercise. *Journal of Personality and Social Psychology, 52,* 119–125.

Thayer, R. E. (1989). *The biopsychology of mood and arousal.* New York: Oxford University Press.

Thayer, R. E. (1996). *The origin of everyday moods: Managing energy, tension and stress.* New York: Oxford University Press.

Thayer, R. E. (2001). *Calm energy.* New York: Oxford University Press.

Thayer, R. E., & Moore, L. E. (1972). Reported activation and verbal learning as a function of group size and anxiety-reducing instructions. *Journal of Social Psychology, 88,* 277–287.

Thayer, R. E., Newman, J. R., & McClain, T. M. (1994). Self-regulation of mood: Strategies for changing a bad mood, raising energy, and reducing tension. *Journal of Personality and Social Psychology, 67,* 910–925.

Thibaut, J. W., & Kelley, H. H. (1959). *The social psychology of groups.* New York: Wiley.

Thoma, S. J., Rest, J. R., & Barnett, M. (1986). Moral judgment, behavior, decision-making, and attitudes. In J. R. Rest (Ed.), *Moral development: Advances in research and theory* (pp. 133–175). New York: Praeger.

Thomas, L. E. (1991). Dialogues with three religious renunciates and reflections on wisdom and maturity. *International Journal of Aging and Human Development, 32,* 211–227.

Thompson, C., Barresi, J., & Moore, C. (1997). The development of future-oriented prudence and altruism in preschoolers. *Cognitive Development, 12,* 199–212.

Thompson, E. (1991). Beneath the status characteristics: Gender variations in religiousness. *Journal for the Scientific Study of Religion, 30,* 381–394.

Thompson, J. (2000, winter). Calling all change agents. *Momentum: Positive Coaching Alliance Newsletter,* 2–3.

Thorndike, E. L. (1911). *Animal intelligence: Experimental studies.* New York: Macmillan.

Thorndike, E. L. (1920). Intelligence and its use. *Harper's Magazine, 140,* 227–235.

Thorndike, E. L. (1939). *Your city.* New York: Harcourt, Brace.

Thorndike, E. L. (1940). *Human nature and the social order.* New York: Macmillan.

Tice, D. M. (1991). Esteem protection or enhancement? Self-handicapping motives and attributions differ by trait self-esteem. *Journal of Personality and Social Psychology, 60,* 711–725.

Tice, D. M., & Baumeister, R. F. (1997). Longitudinal study of procrastination, performance, stress, and health: The costs and benefits of dawdling. *Psychological Science, 8,* 454–458.

Tice, D. M., Butler, J. L., Muraven, M. B., & Stillwell, A. M. (1995). When modesty prevails: Differential favorability of self-presentation to friends and strangers. *Journal of Personality and Social Psychology, 69,* 1120–1138.

Tice, D. M., Dale, K., & Baumeister, R. F. (2003). *Replenishing the self: Effects of positive affect on performance and persistence following ego depletion.* Unpublished manuscript, Case Western Reserve University, Cleveland, OH.

Tichy, N., & Devanna, M. A. (1986). *Transformational leadership.* New York: Wiley.

Tiger, L. (1979). *Optimism: The biology of hope.* New York: Simon & Schuster.

Tiger, L. (1999). The past of an illusion: How optimism brings us to God. *Free Inquiry, 19,* 28–29.

Tisak, M. S., & Turiel, E. (1984). Children's conceptions of moral and prudential rules. *Child Development, 55,* 1030–1039.

Tomaka, J., Blascovich, J., Kibler, J., & Ernst, J. M. (1997). Cognitive and physiological antecedents of threat and challenge appraisal. *Journal of Personality and Social Psychology, 73,* 63–72.

Torney-Purta, J., Lehmann, R., Oswald, H., & Schulz, W. (2001). *Citizenship and education in twenty-eight countries: Civic knowledge and engagement at age fourteen.* Amsterdam: International Association for the Evaluation of Educational Achievement.

Tracey, T. J. G. (2002). Development of interests and competency beliefs: A 1-year longitudinal study of fifth- to eighth-grade students using the ICA-R and structural equation modeling. *Journal of Counseling Psychology, 49,* 148–163.

Trapnell, P. D., & Wiggins, J. S. (1990). Extension of the Interpersonal Adjectives Scales to include the Big Five dimensions of personality. *Journal of Personality and Social Psychology, 59,* 781–790.

Travers, R. M. W. (1978). *Children's interests.* Kalamazoo: Western Michigan University College of Education.

Treisman, U. (1992). Studying students studying calculus: A look at the lives of minority mathematics students in college. *College Mathematics Journal, 23,* 362–372.

Triandis, H. C. (1995). *Individualism and collectivism.* Boulder, CO: Westview Press.

Trilling, L. (1972). *Sincerity and authenticity.* Cambridge, MA: Harvard University Press.

Trinidad, D. R., & Johnson, C. A. (2002). The association between emotional intelligence and early adolescent tobacco and alcohol use. *Personality and Individual Differences, 32,* 95–105.

Trivers, R L. (1971). The evolution of reciprocal altruism. *Quarterly Review of Biology, 46,* 35–57.

Tronto, J. (1987). Beyond gender difference to a theory of care. *Signs: Journal of Women in Culture and Society, 12,* 644–663.

Trope, Y. (1975). Seeking information about one's ability as a determinant of choice among tasks. *Journal of Personality and Social Psychology, 32,* 1004–1013.

Troy, M., & Sroufe, L. A. (1987). Victimization among preschoolers: Role of attachment relationship history. *Journal of American Academy of Child and Adolescent Psychiatry, 26,* 166–172.

Trungpa, C. (1978). *Shambhala: The sacred path of the warrior.* Boston: Shambhala.

Tsang, J., McCullough, M. E., & Hoyt, W. T. (in press). Psychometric and rationalization accounts for the religion-forgiveness discrepancy. *Journal of Social Issues.*

Tsui, A. S., & Ashford, S. J. (1994). Adaptive self-regulation: A process view of managerial effectiveness. *Journal of Management, 20,* 93–121.

Turiel, E. (1980). The development of social-conventional and moral concepts. In M. Windmiller, N. Lambert, & E. Turiel (Eds.), *Moral development and socialization* (pp. 69–106). Boston: Allyn and Bacon.

Turner, J. C., Midgley, C., Meyer, D. K., Gheen, M., Anderman, E. M., & Kang, Y. (2002). The classroom environment and students' reports of avoidance strategies in mathematics: A multimethod study. *Journal of Educational Psychology, 94,* 88–106.

Turner, P. J. (1991). Relations between attachment, gender, and behavior with peers in preschool. *Child Development, 62,* 1475–1488.

Turner, R. H. (1978). The role and the person. *American Journal of Sociology, 84,* 1–23.

Turner, S. E. (Trans.). (1880). *Einhard: The life of Charlemagne.* New York: Harper & Brothers.

Twain, M. (1897). What Paul Bourget thinks of us. In *How to tell a story and other essays.* New York: Harper & Brothers. Document available at http://www.boondocksnet.com/twaintexts/bourget.html/.

Twain, M. (1905, November 26). A humorist's confession. *New York Times.* Document available at http://www.twainquotes.com/.

Twenge, M., Tice, D. M., & Harter, A. C. (2001). *Measuring state self-control: Reliability, validity, and correlations with physical and psychological stress.* Unpublished manuscript, Case Western Reserve University, Cleveland, OH.

Uggen, C., & Janikula, J. (1999). Volunteerism and arrest in the transition to adulthood. *Social Forces, 78,* 331–362.

Unger, L. S., & Thumuluri, L. K. (1997). Trait empathy and continuous helping: The case of voluntarism. *Journal of Social Behavior and Personality, 12,* 785–800.

Unell, B., & Wyckoff, J. (1995). *20 teachable virtues: Practical ways to pass on lessons of virtue and character to your children.* New York: Penguin Books.

Uslaner, E. M. (2002). *The moral foundations of trust*. Cambridge, England: Cambridge University Press.

Vaicys, C., Barnett, T., & Brown, G. (1996). An analysis of the factor structure of the ethical climate questionnaire. *Psychological Reports, 79,* 115–120.

Vaillant, G. E. (1971). Theoretical hierarchy of adaptive ego mechanisms. *Archives of General Psychiatry, 24,* 107–118.

Vaillant, G. E. (1977). *Adaptation to life*. Boston: Little, Brown.

Vaillant, G. E. (1984). A debate on *DSM-III*: The disadvantages of *DSM-III* outweigh its advantages. *American Journal of Psychiatry, 141,* 542–545.

Vaillant, G. E. (1993). *The wisdom of the ego*. Cambridge, MA: Harvard University Press.

Vaillant, G. E. (2000). *Aging well*. Boston: Little, Brown.

Valera, F. J. (1999). *Ethical know-how: Action, wisdom, and cognition*. Stanford, CA: Stanford University Press.

Vallacher, R. R., & Nowak, A. (1999). The dynamics of self-regulation. In R. Wyer (Ed.), *Perspectives on behavioral self-regulation: Advances in social cognition* (pp. 241–259). Mahwah, NJ: Erlbaum.

Vallacher, R. R., & Wegner, D. M. (1989). Levels of personal agency: Individual variation in action identification. *Journal of Personality and Social Psychology, 57,* 660–671.

Vallerand, R. J., & Bissonnette, R. (1992). Intrinsic, extrinsic, and amotivational styles as predictors of behavior: A prospective study. *Journal of Personality, 60,* 599–620.

Vallerand, R. J., Fortier, M. S., & Guay, F. (1997). Self-determination and persistence in a real-life setting: Toward a motivational model of high school dropout. *Journal of Personality and Social Psychology, 72,* 1161–1176.

Vallerand, R. J., Pelletier, L. G., Blais, M. R., Brière, N. M., Senécal, C., & Vallières, E. F. (1992). The Academic Motivation Scale: A measure of intrinsic, extrinsic, and amotivation in education. *Educational and Psychological Measurement, 52,* 1003–1019.

van den Boom, D. C. (1994). The influence of temperament and mothering on attachment and exploration: An experimental manipulation of sensitive responsiveness among lower-class mothers with irritable infants. *Child Development, 65,* 1449–1469.

van den Boom, D. C. (1995). Do first-year intervention effects endure? Follow-up during toddlerhood of a sample of Dutch irritable infants. *Child Development, 66,* 1798–1816.

Van Eynde, D. F. (1998). A case for courage in organizations. *Management Review, 87,* 62.

Van Hecke, M., & Tracy, R. J. (1987). The influence of adult encouragement on children's persistence. *Child Study Journal, 17,* 251–268.

Van Ijzendoorn, M. H. (1992). Intergenerational transmission of parenting: A review of studies in non-clinical populations. *Developmental Review, 12,* 76–99.

Van Ijzendoorn, M. H., & Kroonenberg, P. M. (1988). Cross-cultural patterns of attachment: A meta-analysis of the Strange Situation. *Child Development, 59,* 147–156.

Van Ijzendoorn, M. H., & Kroonenberg, P. M. (1990). Cross-cultural consistency of coding the Strange Situation. *Infant Behavior and Development, 13,* 469–485.

Van Willigen, M. (2000). Differential benefits of volunteering over the life course. *Journals of Gerontology: Psychological Sciences and Social Sciences, 55B,* S308–S318.

Vandell, D. L., Owen, M. E., Wilson, K. S., & Henderson, V. K. (1988). Social development in infant twins: Peer and mother-child relationships. *Child Development, 59,* 168–177.

Vargas, R. (1999). Cinco de Mayo: An opportunity to inspire courage. *Hispanic, 12,* 48.

Vaughn, B. E., Lefever, G. B., Seifer, R., & Barglow, P. (1989). Attachment behavior, attachment security, and temperament during infancy. *Child Development, 60,* 728–737.

Veljkovic, P., & Schwartz, A. (Eds.). (2001). *Writing from the heart: Young people share their wisdom.* Radnor, PA: Templeton Foundation Press. Documents available at http://www.lawsoflife.org/essays/.

Ventimiglia, J. C. (1982). Sex roles and chivalry: Some conditions of gratitude to altruism. *Sex Roles, 8,* 1107–1122.

Verba, S., Nie, N., & Kim, J. (1978). *Participation and political equality.* Cambridge, England: Cambridge University Press.

Verba, S., Schlozman, K. L., & Brady, H. E. (1995). *Voice and equality: Civic voluntarism in American politics.* Cambridge, MA: Harvard University Press.

Verplanken, B. (1991). Persuasive communication of risk information: A test of cue versus message processing effects in a field experiment. *Personality and Social Psychology Bulletin, 17,* 188–193.

Vitello-Cicciu, J. M. (2001). *Leadership practices and emotional intelligence of nurse leaders.* Unpublished doctoral dissertation, Fielding Institute, Santa Barbara, CA.

Vohs, K. D., Bardone, A. M., Joiner, T. E.,, Abramson, L. Y., & Heatherton, T. F. (1999). Perfectionism, perceived weight status, and self-esteem interact to predict bulimic symptoms: A model of bulimic symptom development. *Journal of Abnormal Psychology, 108,* 695–700.

Vohs, K. D., Ciarocco, N., & Baumeister, R. F. (2003). *Interpersonal functioning requires self-regulatory resources.* Unpublished manuscript, University of Utah, Salt Lake City.

Vohs, K. D., & Heatherton, T. F. (2000). Self-regulatory failure: A resource-depletion approach. *Psychological Science, 11,* 249–254.

Voss, H., & Keller, H. (1983). *Curiosity and exploration: Theories and results.* New York: Academic Press.

Vroom, V. H., & Jago, A. G. (1978). On the validity of the Vroom-Yetton model. *Journal of Applied Psychology, 63,* 151–162.

Wade, S. E. (1992). How interest affects learning from text. In K. A Renninger, S. Hidi, & A. Krapp (Eds.), *The role of interest in learning and development* (pp. 281–296). Hillsdale, NJ: Erlbaum.

Wade, S. E. (2001). Research on importance and interest: Implications for curriculum development and future research. *Educational Psychology Review, 13,* 243–261.

Wade, S. E., Buxton, W. M., & Kelly, M. (1999). Using think-alouds to examine reader text interest. *Reading Research Quarterly, 34,* 194–216.

Wadsworth, T. (2000). Labor markets, delinquency, and social control theory: An empirical assessment of the mediating process. *Social Forces, 78,* 1041–1066.

Wagner, R. K., & Sternberg, R. J. (1986). Tacit knowledge and intelligence in the everyday world. In R. J. Sternberg & R. K. Wagner (Eds.), *Practical intelligence: Nature and origins of competence in the everyday world* (pp. 51–83). Cambridge, England: Cambridge University Press.

Waldman, J., & Dworkis, J. L. (2000). *The courage to give: Inspiring stories of people who triumphed over tragedy to make a difference in the world.* Berkeley, CA: Conari Press.

Walker, L. J. (1980). Cognitive and perspective-taking prerequisites for moral development. *Child Development, 51,* 131–139.

Walker, L. J. (1984). Sex differences in the development of moral reasoning: A critical review. *Child Development, 55,* 677–691.

Walker, L. J. (1991). Sex differences in moral reasoning. In W. Kurtines & J. L. Gewirtz (Eds.), *Handbook of moral behavior* (pp. 333–364). Hillsdale, NJ: Erlbaum.

Walker, L. J., de Vries, B., & Trevethan, S. D. (1987). Moral stages and moral orientations in real-life and hypothetical dilemmas. *Child Development, 58,* 842–858.

Walker, L. J., & Richards, B. S. (1979). Stimulating transitions in moral reasoning as function of stage of cognitive development. *Developmental Psychology, 15,* 95–103.

Walker, R. E., & Foley, J. M. (1973). Social intelligence: Its history and measurement. *Psychological Reports, 33,* 839–864.

Wall, S., Frieze, I., Ferligoj, A., Jarosova, E., Pauknerova, D., Horvat, J., et al. (1999). Gender role and religion as predictors of attitude toward abortion in Croatia, Slovenia, the Czech Republic, and the United States. *Journal of Cross-Cultural Psychology, 30,* 443–465.

Wallace, H. M., & Baumeister, R. F. (2002). The performance of narcissists rises and falls with perceived opportunity for glory. *Journal of Personality and Social Psychology, 82,* 819–834.

Walling, J., & Keltner, D. (2003). *The epiphanic person.* Unpublished manuscript, University of California–Berkeley.

Walster, E., Walster, G., & Berscheid, E. (1978). *Equity: Theory and research.* Boston: Allyn and Bacon.

Walston, S. F. (2000). *Courage: The heart and spirit of every woman.* Denver, CO: Bona Dea Publishing.

Walton, D. N. (1986). *Courage: A philosophical investigation.* Berkeley: University of California Press.

Walzer, M. (1989). Citizenship. In T. Ball, J. Farr, & R. Hanson, (Eds.), *Political innovation and conceptual change* (pp. 211–219). Cambridge, England: Cambridge University Press.

Ward, J. V. (1991). Eyes in the back of your head. *Journal of Moral Education, 20,* 267–281.

Ware, J. E., & Sherbourne, C. D. (1992). The MOS 36-Item Short-Form Health Survey (SF-36): I. Conceptual framework and item selection. *Medical Care, 30,* 473–483.

Waterman, A. S. (1993a). Finding something to do or someone to be: A eudaimonist perspective on identity formation. In J. Kroger (Ed.), *Discussions on ego identity* (pp. 147–167). Hillsdale, NJ: Erlbaum.

Waterman, A. S. (1993b). Two conceptions of happiness: Contrasts of personal expressiveness (eudaimonia) and hedonic enjoyment. *Journal of Personality and Social Psychology, 64,* 678–691.

Waterman, A. S. (1999). Identity, the identity statuses, and identity status development: A contemporary statement. *Developmental Review, 19,* 591–621.

Waters, E., Wippman, J., & Sroufe, L. A. (1979). Attachment, positive affect, and competence in the peer group: Two studies in construct validation. *Child Development, 50,* 821–829.

Watkins, P. C., Grimm, D. L, & Hailu, L. (1998, June). *Counting your blessings: Grateful individuals recall more positive memories.* Paper presented at the 11th annual convention of the American Psychological Society, Denver, CO.

Watson, D., & Clark, L. A. (1992). On traits and temperament: General and specific factors of emotional experience and their relation to the five factor model. *Journal of Personality, 60,* 441–476.

Watson, D., Clark, L. A., & Tellegen, A. (1988). Development and validation of brief measures of positive and negative affect: The PANAS scales. *Journal of Personality and Social Psychology, 54,* 1063–1070.

Watson, P. J., & Biderman, M. D. (1993). Narcissistic Personality Inventory factors, splitting, and self-consciousness. *Journal of Personality Assessment, 61,* 41–57.

Watson, P. J., Morris, R. J., & Miller, L. (1997–1998). Narcissism and the self as continuum: Correlations with assertiveness and hypercompetitiveness. *Imagination, Cognition, and Personality, 17,* 249–259.

Watts, A. (1960). *This is it and other essays on Zen and spiritual experience.* New York: Pantheon.

Way, N. (1995). "Can't you see the courage, the strength that I have?": Listening to urban adolescent girls speak about their relationships. *Psychology of Women Quarterly, 19,* 107–128.

Way, N. (1998). *Everyday courage: The lives and stories of urban teenagers.* New York: New York University Press.

Weber, M. (1904). *The Protestant ethic and the spirit of capitalism.* New York: Scribner's.

Weber, M. (1924/1947). *The theory of social and economic organization* (T. Parsons, Ed.). New York: Free Press.

Wegner, D. M. (1989). *White bears and other unwanted thoughts.* New York: Vintage.

Wegner, D. M. (1994). Ironic processes of mental control. *Psychological Review, 101,* 34–52.

Wegner, D. M., & Pennebaker, J. W. (1993). *Handbook of mental control.* Englewood Cliffs, NJ: Prentice Hall.

Wegner, D. M., Schneider, D. J., Carter, S. R., & White, T. L. (1987). Paradoxical effects of thought suppression. *Journal of Personality and Social Psychology, 53,* 5–13.

Wegner, D. M., Shortt, J. W., Blake, A. W., & Page, M. S. (1990). The suppression of exciting thoughts. *Journal of Personality and Social Psychology, 58,* 409–418.

Weiner, B. (1985). An attributional theory of achievement motivation and emotion. *Psychological Review, 92,* 548–573.

Weiner, B., & Graham, S. (1988). Understanding the motivational role of affect: Life-span research from an attributional perspective. *Cognition and Emotion, 3,* 401–419.

Weiner, B., Russell, D., & Lerman, D. (1979). The cognition-emotion process in achievement-related contexts. *Journal of Personality and Social Psychology, 37,* 1211–1220.

Weiner, N., & Mahoney, T. A. (1981). A model of corporate performance as a function of environmental, organizational, and leadership influences. *Academy of Management Journal, 24,* 453–470.

Weinstein, N. D. (1989). Optimistic biases about personal risks. *Science, 246,* 1232–1233.

Weiss, H., & Sherman, J. (1973). Internal-external control as a predictor of task effort and satisfaction subsequent to failure. *Journal of Applied Psychology, 57,* 132–136.

Weiss, H. M., & Knight, P. A. (1980). The utility of humility: Self-esteem, information search, and problem-solving efficiency. *Organizational Behavior and Human Decision Processes, 25,* 216–223.

Werner, C. M., & Makela, E. (1998). Motivations and behaviors that support recycling. *Journal of Environmental Psychology, 18,* 373–386.

West, R. F., & Stanovich, K. E. (2003). Is probability matching smart? Associations between probabilistic choices and cognitive ability. *Memory and Cognition, 31,* 243–251.

Westermarck, E. (1932). *Ethical relativity.* London: Kegan Paul.

Wheeler, J. A., Gorey, K. M., & Greenblatt, B. (1998). The beneficial effects of volunteering for older volunteers and the people they serve: A meta-analysis. *International Journal of Aging and Human Development, 47,* 69–79.

Whitbourne, S. K. (1986). *The me I know: A study of adult identity*. New York: Springer-Verlag.

Whitbourne, S. K., Zuschlag, M. K., Elliot, L. B., & Waterman, A. S. (1992). Psychosocial development in adulthood: A 22-year sequential study. *Journal of Personality and Social Psychology, 63*, 260–271.

White, P. (1999). Gratitude, citizenship, and education. *Studies in Philosophy and Education, 18*, 43–52.

White, R. W. (1959). Motivation reconsidered: The concept of competence. *Psychological Review, 66*, 297–333.

Wickberg, D. (1998). *The senses of humor: Self and laughter in modern America*. Ithaca, NY: Cornell University Press.

Wickett, J. C., Vernon, P. A., & Lee, D. H. (2000). Relationships between factors of intelligence and brain volume. *Personality and Individual Differences, 29*, 1095–1122.

Wiebe, D. J. (1991). Hardiness and stress moderation: A test of proposed mechanisms. *Journal of Personality and Social Psychology, 60*, 89–99.

Wigal, T., Swanson, J. M., Douglas, V. I., Wigal, S. B., Wippler, C. M., & Cavoto, K. F. (1998). Effect of reinforcement on facial responsivity and persistence in children with attention-deficit hyperactivity disorder. *Behavior Modification, 22*, 143–166.

Wigfield, A., & Eccles, J. S. (2000). Expectancy-value theory of achievement motivation. *Contemporary Educational Psychology, 25*, 68–81.

Wigfield, A., & Eccles, J. S. (2002). The development of competence beliefs, expectancies for success, and achievement values from childhood through adolescence. In A. Wigfield & J. S. Eccles (Eds.), *Development of achievement motivation* (pp. 91–120). San Diego, CA: Academic Press.

Wigfield, A., Eccles, J., MacIver, D., Reuman, D., & Midgley, C. (1991). Transitions at early adolescence: Changes in children's domain-specific self-perceptions and general self-esteem across the transition to junior high school. *Developmental Psychology, 27*, 552–565.

Wiggins, J. S., & Pincus, A. (1989). Conceptions of personality disorders and dimensions of personality. *Psychological Assessment: A Journal of Consulting and Clinical Psychology, 1*, 305–316.

Wilkes, J. (1981). *The gift of courage*. Philadelphia: Westminster Press.

Williams, D., Larson, D., Buckler, R., Heckmann, R., & Pyle, C. (1991). Religion and psychological distress in a community sample. *Social Science and Medicine, 32*, 1257–1262.

Williams, F. J., & Harrell, T. W. (1964). Predicting success in business. *Journal of Psychology, 48*, 164–167.

Williams, G. C., Gagne, M., Ryan, R. M., & Deci, E. L. (2002). Facilitating autonomous motivation for smoking cessation. *Health Psychology, 21*, 40–50.

Williams, M., & Paisner, D. (2001). *A dozen ways to Sunday: Stories of hope and courage*. Carlsbad, CA: Hay House.

Willis, C. (1985). The Reid Report and Reid Survey. In D. J. Keyser & R. C. Sweetland (Eds.), *Test critiques* (Vol. 2, pp. 631–636). Austin, TX: Pro-Ed.

Wills, T. A., DuHamel, K., & Vaccaro, D. (1995). Activity and mood temperament as predictors of adolescent substance use: Test of a self-regulation mediational model. *Journal of Personality and Social Psychology, 68,* 901–916.

Wills, T. A., Sandy, J. M., & Shinar, O. (1999). Cloninger's constructs related to substance use level and problems in late adolescence: A mediational model based on self-control and coping motives. *Experimental and Clinical Psychopharmacology, 7,* 122–134.

Wilson, G. D., Rust, J., & Kasriel, J. (1977). Genetic and family origins of humor preferences: A twin study. *Psychological Reports, 41,* 659–660.

Wilson, W. (1998). Religion and psychoses. In H. Koenig (Ed.), *Handbook of religion and mental health* (pp. 161–173). New York: Academic Press.

Wimberley, D. (1989). Religion and role identity: A structural symbolic interactionist conceptualization of religiosity. *Sociological Quarterly, 30,* 125–142.

Wink, P., & Helson, R. (1997). Practical and transcendent wisdom: Their nature and some longitudinal findings. *Journal of Adult Development, 4,* 1–15.

Winnicott, D. W. (1958). *Through pediatrics to psychoanalysis.* London: Hogarth Press.

Winter, D. G. (1996). *Personality: Analysis and interpretation of lives.* New York: McGraw-Hill.

Wittgenstein, L. (1953). *Philosophical investigations.* New York: Macmillan.

Witvliet, C. V., Ludwig, T. E., & Vander Laan, K. L. (2001). Granting forgiveness or harboring grudges: Implications for emotion, physiology, and health. *Psychological Science, 12,* 117–123.

Wolf, S. (1982). Moral saints. *Journal of Philosophy, 79,* 419–439.

Wolfe, R. N., & Johnson, S. D. (1995). Personality as a predictor of college performance. *Educational and Psychological Measurement, 55,* 177–185.

Wollack, S., Goodale, J. G., Wijting, J. P., & Smith, P. C. (1971). Development of the survey of work values. *Journal of Applied Psychology, 55,* 331–338.

Women in History. (1991). *Sojourner Truth biography.* Document available at http://www.lkwdpl.org/wihohio/trut-soj.htm.

Wong, E. (1997). *The Shambhala guide to Taoism.* Boston: Shambhala.

Wood, C. (1994). Responsive teaching: Creating partnerships for systematic change. *Young Children, 50,* 21–28.

World Health Organization. (1990). *International classification of diseases and related health problems* (10th rev. ed.). Geneva, Switzerland: Author.

Worline, M. C., Wrzesniewski, A., & Rafaeli, A. (2002). Courage and work: Breaking routines to improve performance. In R. Lord, R. Klimoski, & R. Kanfer (Eds.), *Emotions at work* (pp. 295–330). San Francisco: Jossey-Bass.

Worsley, F. A. (1931). *Endurance: An epic of polar adventure.* New York: Jonathan Cape and Harrison Smith.

Worthington, E. L., Berry, J. W., & Parrott, L. (2001). Unforgiveness, forgiveness, religion, and health. In T. G. Plante & A. C. Sherman (Eds.), *Faith and health* (pp. 107–138). New York: Guilford Press.

Worthington, E. L., & Drinkard, D. T. (2000). Promoting reconciliation through psychoeducational and therapeutic interventions. *Journal of Marital and Family Therapy, 26,* 93–101.

Worthington, E. L., Kurusu, T. A., Collins, W., Berry, J. W., Ripley, J. S., & Baier, S. N. (2000). Forgiveness usually takes time: A lesson learned by studying interventions to promote forgiveness. *Journal of Psychology and Theology, 28,* 3–20.

Worthington, E. L., Sandage, S. J., & Berry, J. W. (2000). Group interventions to promote forgiveness: What researchers and clinicians ought to know. In M. E. McCullough, K. I. Pargament, & C. E. Thoresen (Eds.), *Forgiveness: Theory, research, and practice* (pp. 228–253). New York: Guilford Press.

Wortman, C. B., & Brehm, J. W. (1975). Responses to uncontrollable outcomes: An integration of reactance theory and the learned helplessness model. In L. Berkowitz (Ed.), *Advances in experimental social psychology* (Vol. 8, pp. 277–336). New York: Academic Press.

Wortman, C. B., Hendricks, M., & Hillis, J. W. (1976). Factors affecting participant reactions to random assignment in ameliorative social programs. *Journal of Personality and Social Psychology, 33,* 256–266.

Wright, R. (1994). *The moral animal: The new science of evolutionary psychology.* New York: Random House.

Wright, R. (1999). *Nonzero: The logic of human destiny.* New York: Pantheon Books.

Wrzesniewski, A., McCauley, C. R., Rozin, P., & Schwartz, B. (1997). Jobs, careers, and callings: People's relations to their work. *Journal of Research in Personality, 31,* 21–33.

Wulff, D. (1991). *The psychology of religion: Classic and contemporary views.* New York: Wiley.

Wuthnow, R. (1991). *Acts of compassion: Caring for others and helping ourselves.* Princeton, NJ: Princeton University Press.

Xiaogan, L. (1998). Naturalness (tzu-jan), the core value in Taoism: Its ancient meaning and its significance today. In L. Kohn & M. LaFargue (Eds.), *Lao-tzu and the Tao-te-ching* (pp. 211–230). Albany: State University of New York Press.

Yammarino, F. J., & Bass, B. M. (1990). Long-term forecasting of transformational leadership and its effects among naval officers. In K. E. Clark & M. B. Clark (Eds.), *Measures of leadership* (pp. 151–169). West Orange, NJ: Leadership Library of America.

Yang, J., McCrae, R. R., Costa, P. T., Dai, X., Yao, S., Cai, T., et al. (1999). Cross-cultural personality assessment in psychiatric populations: The NEO-PI-R in the People's Republic of China. *Psychological Assessment, 11,* 359–368.

Yarrow, L. J., Morgan, G. A., Jennings, K. D., Harmon, R. J., & Gaiter, J. L. (1983). Infants' persistence at tasks: Relationships to cognitive functioning and early experience. In S. Chess & A. Thomas (Eds.), *Annual progress in child psychiatry and child development* (pp. 217–229). New York: Brunner/Mazel.

Yarwood, D. L. (2001). When Congress makes a joke: Congressional humor as serious and purposeful communication. *Humor: International Journal of Humor Research, 14,* 359–394.

Yearley, L. H. (1990). *Mencius and Aquinas: Theories of virtue and conceptions of courage.* Albany: State University of New York Press.

Youniss, J., McLellan, J. A., & Yates, M. (1997). What we know about engendering civic identity. *American Behavioral Scientist, 40,* 620–631.

Youniss, J., & Yates, M. (1999). Promoting identity development: Ten ideals for school-based service learning programs. In J. Claus & C. Ogden (Eds.), *Service learning for youth empowerment and social change* (pp. 43–68). New York: Peter Lang.

Yukl, G. (2002). *Leadership in organizations* (4th ed.). Englewood Cliffs, NJ: Prentice Hall.

Yukl, G., & Van Fleet, D. D. (1992). Theory and research on leadership in organizations. In M. D. Dunnette & L. M. Hough (Eds.), *Handbook of industrial and organizational psychology* (2nd ed., Vol. 3, pp. 147–197). Palo Alto, CA: Consulting Psychologists Press.

Yukl, G. A., Wall, S., & Lepsinger, R. (1990). Preliminary report on the validation of the management practices survey. In K. E. Clark & M. B. Clark (Eds.), *Measures of leadership* (pp. 223–237). West Orange, NJ: Leadership Library of America.

Zaccaro, S. J. (1999). Social complexity and the competencies required for effective military leadership. In J. G. Hunt, G. E. Dodge, & L. Wong (Eds.), *Out-of-the-box leadership: Transforming the twenty-first century army and other top performing organizations* (pp. 131–151). Stamford, CT: JAI Press.

Zaccaro, S. J. (2001). *The nature of executive leadership: A conceptual and empirical analysis of success.* Washington, DC: APA Books.

Zaccaro, S. J. (2002). Organizational leadership and social intelligence. In R. Riggio, S. Murphy, & F. J. Pirozzolo (Eds.), *Multiple intelligences and leadership* (pp. 29–54). Mahwah, NJ: Erlbaum.

Zaccaro, S. J., Foti, R. J., & Kenny, D. A. (1991). Self-monitoring and trait-based variance in leadership: An investigation of leader flexibility across multiple group situations. *Journal of Applied Psychology, 76,* 308–315.

Zaccaro, S. J., Gilbert, J. A., Thor, K. K., & Mumford, M. D. (1991). Leadership and social intelligence: Linking social perceptiveness and behavioral flexibility to leader effectiveness. *Leadership Quarterly, 2,* 317–331.

Zaccaro, S. J., & Klimoski, R. (2001). The nature of organizational leadership. In S. J. Zaccaro & R. Klimoski (Eds.), *The nature of organizational leadership: Understanding the performance imperatives confronting today's leaders* (pp. 3–41). San Francisco: Jossey-Bass.

Zaccaro, S. J., Klimoski, R. J., Boyce, L., Chandler, C., & Banks, D. (1999). *Developing a tool kit for the assessment of army leadership processes and outcomes: Version 1.0.* Alexandria, VA: U.S. Army Research Institute for the Behavioral and Social Sciences.

Zagzebski, L. (1996). *Virtues of the mind: An inquiry into the nature of virtue and the ethical foundations of knowledge.* New York: Cambridge University Press.

Zahn-Waxler, C., Radke-Yarrow, M., & King, R. (1983). Early altruism and guilt. *Academic Psychology Bulletin, 52,* 247–259.

Zaleski, Z. (1988). Close relationships and acting for self-set goals. *European Journal of Social Psychology, 18,* 191–194.

Zimbardo, P. G., & Boyd, J. N. (1999). Putting time in perspective: A valid, reliable individual-differences metric. *Journal of Personality and Social Psychology, 77,* 1271–1288.

Zimmerman, B. J. (2002). Achieving academic excellence: A self-regulatory perspective. In M. Ferrari (Ed.), *The pursuit of excellence through education* (pp. 85–110). Mahwah, NJ: Erlbaum.

Zinnbauer, B., Pargament, K., Cole, B., Rye, M., Butter, E., Belavich, T., et al. (1997). Religiousness and spirituality: Unfuzzying the fuzzy. *Journal for the Scientific Study of Religion, 36,* 549–564.

Ziv, A. (Ed.). (1988). *National styles of humor.* Westport, CT: Greenwood Press.

Zuckerman, M. (1994). *Behavioral expressions and biosocial bases of sensation seeking.* New York: Cambridge University Press.

Zuckerman, M. (1999). *Vulnerability to psychopathology: A biosocial model.* Washington, DC: American Psychological Association.

Zuckerman, M., Eysenck, S., & Eysenck, H. J. (1978). Sensation seeking in England and America: Cross-cultural, age, and sex comparisons. *Journal of Consulting and Clinical Psychology, 46,* 139–149.

Zuckerman, M., Kuhlman, D. M., Joireman, J., Teta, P., & Kraft, M. (1993). A comparison of three structural models for personality: The big three, the big five, and the alternative five. *Journal of Personality and Social Psychology, 65,* 757–768.

Zullow, H., Oettingen, G., Peterson, C., & Seligman, M. E. P. (1988). Explanatory style and pessimism in the historical record: CAVing LBJ, presidential candidates, and East versus West Berlin. *American Psychologist, 43,* 673–682.

INDEX OF NAMES

Italicized page numbers refer to tables.

SUBJECT INDEX

Italicized page numbers refer to tables.